Architecture and Design in E
and America, 1750–2000

BLACKWELL ANTHOLOGIES IN ART HISTORY ──────

The *Blackwell Anthologies in Art History* series presents an unprecedented set of canonical and critical works in art history. Each volume in the series pairs previously published, classic essays with contemporary historiographical scholarship to offer a fresh perspective on a given period, style, or genre in art history. Modeling itself on the upper-division undergraduate art history curriculum in the English-speaking world and paying careful attention to the most beneficial way to teach art history in today's classroom setting, each volume offers ample pedagogical material created by expert volume editors – from substantive introductory essays and section overviews to illustrations and bibliographies. Taken together, the *Blackwell Anthologies in Art History* will be a complete reference source devoted to the best that has been taught and written on a given subject or theme in art history.

1 *Post-Impressionism to World War II*, edited by Debbie Lewer
2 *Asian Art: An Anthology*, edited by Rebecca Brown and Deborah Hutton
3 *Sixteenth-Century Italian Art*, edited by Michael Cole
4 *Architecture and Design in Europe and America, 1750–2000*, edited by Abigail Harrison-Moore and Dorothy C. Rowe

Forthcoming

5 *Fifteenth-Century Italian Art*, edited by Robert Maniura, Gabriele Neher, and Rupert Shepherd
6 *Late Antique, Medieval, and Mediterranean Art*, edited by Eva Hoffman

Architecture and Design in Europe and America, 1750–2000

Edited by
Abigail Harrison-Moore and
Dorothy C. Rowe

Blackwell
Publishing

© 2006 by Blackwell Publishing Ltd
Editorial material and organization © 2006 by
Abigail Harrison-Moore and Dorothy C. Rowe

BLACKWELL PUBLISHING
350 Main Street, Malden, MA 02148-5020, USA
9600 Garsington Road, Oxford OX4 2DQ, UK
550 Swanston Street, Carlton, Victoria 3053, Australia

The right of Abigail Harrison-Moore and Dorothy C. Rowe to be identified as the
Authors of the Editorial Material in this Work has been asserted in accordance with
the UK Copyright, Designs, and Patents Act 1988.

First published 2006 by Blackwell Publishing Ltd

1   2006

Library of Congress Cataloging-in-Publication Data

Architecture and design in Europe and America, 1750–2000
edited by Abigail Harrison-Moore and Dorothy C. Rowe
    p.cm.—(Blackwell anthologies in art history)
Includes bibliographical references and index.
ISBN-13: 978-1-4051-1530-8 (hardback: alk. paper)
ISBN-10: 1-4051-1530-0 (hardback: alk. paper)
ISBN-13: 978-1-4051-1531-5 (pbk.: alk. paper)
ISBN-10: 1-4051-1531-9 (pbk.: alk. paper) 1. Architecture Modern—Europe. 2. Archi-
tecture, Modern—United States. 3. Design—Europe—History. 4. Design—United
States—History. I. Harrison-Moore, Abigail. II. Rowe, Dorothy, 1969- III. Series.

NA954.A73 2006
724—dc22

2006002000

A catalogue record for this title is available from the British Library.

Set in 10.5/13 pt Galliard
by SPI Publisher Services, Pondicherry, India

The publisher's policy is to use permanent paper from mills that operate a sustainable
forestry policy, and which has been manufactured from pulp processed using acid-free
and elementary chlorine-free practices. Furthermore, the publisher ensures that the text
paper and cover board used have met acceptable environmental accreditation standards.

For further information on
Blackwell Publishing, visit our website:
www.blackwellpublishing.com

For our parents with love

Contents

List of Illustrations   xii
Series Editor's Preface   xiii
Acknowledgments   xiv

Introduction: Classifying Knowledge   1
Dorothy C. Rowe and Abigail Harrison-Moore

1   The Architectural Plates from the "Encyclopédie"   13
   Denis Diderot

2   The Plates of the *Encyclopedia*   20
   Roland Barthes

3   From *The Archaeology of Knowledge*   25
   Michel Foucault

Part I   Knowledge, Taste, and Sublimity, *c.*1750–1830
Introduction   30
Abigail Harrison-Moore

4   Palladian Permeation: The Villa   49
   John Summerson

5   The Country House: Form, Function and Meaning   59
   Dana Arnold

6   Plans and Elevations for the Villa of Lord Mansfield at Kenwood   74
   Robert and James Adam

7   From *The Royal Academy Lectures on Architecture*   79
   Sir John Soane

8   From *A Description of the Villa*   85
    Horace Walpole

9   Thomas Jefferson   90
    James Ackerman

10 From *A Philosophical Enquiry into the Origin*
    of our Ideas of the Sublime and Beautiful   96
    Edmund Burke

11 On Architecture and Buildings   99
    Sir Uvedale Price

12 From *An Analytical Inquiry into the Principles of Taste*   107
    Richard Payne Knight

13 Iconography and Landscape   116
    Stephen Daniels and Denis Cosgrove

14 The Plans and Elevations of John Nash   126
    John Summerson

15 Architecture, Essay on Art   136
    Etienne-Louis Boullée

16 The Sphere: Reading a Gender Metaphor in the
    Architecture of Modern Cults of Identity   144
    Susanne von Falkenhausen

17 Karl Friedrich Schinkel   163
    David Watkin and Tilman Mellinghoff

18 Reading Architectural Herstories: The Disourses of Gender   172
    Dana Arnold

Part II   Urbanism, Reform, and Revival, *c.*1830–1910
Introduction   182
Abigail Harrison-Moore and Dorothy C. Rowe

19 An Apology for the Revival of Christian Architecture in England   209
    A. W. N. Pugin

20 Architecture in the Nineteenth Century: Importance of Method   215
    Eugène-Emmanuel Viollet-le-Duc

21 From *Science, Industry and Art*   221
    Gottfried Semper

22 The Nature of Gothic   227
    John Ruskin

23 The Revival of Architecture 233
William Morris

24 Some Recent Designs by Mr. C. F. A. Voysey 242

25 Style 249
Louis Sullivan

26 Ornament in Architecture 254
Louis Sullivan

27 The Tall Office Building Artistically Considered 258
Louis Sullivan

28 Plasticity 265
Frank Lloyd Wright

29 The Nature of Materials 267
Frank Lloyd Wright

30 Women and Architecture 270
Lynne Walker

31 The Programmes of the Architectural Section of
the École des Beaux-Arts 284
Annie Jacques

32 Adler and Sullivan at the 1893 World's Columbian
Exposition in Chicago 291
Zeynep Çelik

33 Public Parks and the Enlargement of Towns 295
Frederick Law Olmsted

34 Paris: Building a European Capital under the Second Empire 300
Anthony Sutcliffe

35 Garden Cities of Tomorrow 305
Ebenezer Howard

36 Modern Systems 309
Camillo Sitte

37 Construction 316
Otto Wagner

Part III   Architecture For Tomorrow, *c.*1910–2000

Introduction 324
Dorothy C. Rowe

38 Ornament and Crime 348
Adolf Loos

Contents

39 Architecture
    Adolf Loos   355

40 Manifesto of Futurist Architecture
    Antonio Sant'Elia   364

41 The Turbine Hall of the AEG
    Peter Behrens   368

42 The State of German Architecture
    Sigfried Giedion   370

43 Programme of the Staatliche Bauhaus in Weimar
    Walter Gropius   376

44 Letter to the Younger Generation
    Marianne Brandt   379

45 Space (Architecture)
    László Moholy-Nagy   382

46 Where Do We Stand?
    Marcel Breuer   385

47 The Problem of a New Architecture
    Eric Mendelsohn   390

48 The Creative Spirit of the World Crisis
    Eric Mendelsohn   394

49 Solved Problems: A Demand on our Building Methods
    Mies van der Rohe   397

50 Explanation of the Educational Program
    Mies van der Rohe   399

51 Report of the De Stijl Group
    Theo van Doesburg   402

52 From *Towards a New Architecture*
    Le Corbusier   403

53 Architecture in Everything, City Planning in Everything
    Le Corbusier   411

54 On Discovering Gaudí's Architecture
    Le Corbusier   418

55 The Split Wall: Domestic Voyeurism
    Beatriz Colomina   420

56 Nine Points on Monumentality   429
    José Luis Sert, Fernand Léger, and Sigfried Giedion

57 Monumentality   434
    Louis I. Kahn

58 Reaffirmation of the Aims of CIAM   441
    Congress of International Modern Architects

59 Functionalism and Technology   445
    Reyner Banham

60 The Death of Modern Architecture   455
    Charles Jencks

61 Towards a Critical Regionalism: Six Points for
    an Architecture of Resistance   465
    Kenneth Frampton

62 The Pleasure of Architecture   479
    Bernard Tschumi

63 Scale and Span in a Global Digital World   488
    Saskia Sassen

Bibliography   495
Index   508

List of Illustrations

1.1   Architectural plate from the *Encyclopédie*: marble
cutting; various marble flooring patterns   14
1.2   Architectural plate from the *Encyclopédie*: a gypsum
quarry and its tools   15
1.3   Architectural plate from the *Encyclopédie*:
masons at work and various bricklaying patterns   16
1.4   Architectural plate from the *Encyclopédie*: a tile
factory and details of tilemaking   17
1.5   Architectural plate from the *Encyclopédie*: cutting
hexagonal flooring tiles   18
1.6   Architectural plate from the *Encyclopédie*: laying floor tile;
floor-tilers' implements and patterns; plan and sections of a tile-kiln   19
6.1   Geometrical elevations of the north and south fronts
of Kenwood by Robert and James Adam   75
14.1 Streets, squares, and parks laid out by John Nash, 1811–35   128
19.1 A. W. N. Pugin, contrasted English towns, 1840 and 1440   208
29.1 Marie Mahony Griffin's design for Frank Lloyd
Wright's "Fireproof House for $5,000"   268
35.1 Ebenezer Howard's three magnets: town, country,
town–country   307
55.1 Villa Savoye, Poissy, 1929   422
55.2 Villa Savoye: view of the kitchen   422
55.3 Villa Savoye: view of the roof garden   423
55.4 Villa Savoye: still from *L'Architecture d'aujourd'hui*   424
55.5 Immeuble Clarté, Ginebra, 1930–2: view of the interior   425
55.6 Charlotte Perriand in the *chaise-longue* against the wall.
Salon d'Automne 1929   426
60.1 Pruitt-Igoe Housing, St Louis   456
60.2 Pruitt-Igoe as ruin   457

Series Editor's Preface

The *Blackwell Anthologies in Art History* series is intended to bring together writing on a given subject from a broad historical and historiographic perspective. The aim of the volumes is to present key writings in the given subject area while at the same time challenging their canonical status through the inclusion of less well known texts, including contemporary documentation and commentaries, that present alternative interpretations or understandings of the period under review.

Architecture and Design in Europe and America, 1750–2000 is a comprehensive and wide-ranging selection of texts that makes previously neglected critical views and documents available for the first time. Feminism, gender studies, and post-colonial theory are here integrated into the analysis of European and American design to offer a selection of readings that is in tune with current trends in architectural history and theory.

The volume provides a methodologically sound introduction to the architecture of the last two centuries through a synthesis of historical writings and contemporary texts which make a substantial contribution to the field. It will be invaluable to students and teachers, as well as design professionals and those with a general interest in the period. As one of the first anthologies to appear, it establishes an important benchmark for the series.

Dana Arnold
2005

Acknowledgments

The editors would like to thank the following for their assistance in bringing this book to fruition: above all, Professor Dana Arnold for her unfailing generosity, support, and foresight; Jayne Fargnoli, Ken Provencher, Janet Moth, and staff at Blackwell for their patience; the libraries, their staff, and our students and colleagues at the universities of Leeds and Roehampton, in particular Joanne Crawford and Mark Westgarth, the Brotherton Library and staff in the Special Collections, Ben Read, University of Reading Library and staff; several insightful anonymous readers along the way, and finally, our partners and each other for continued forbearance; thank you.

Text Credits

The editors and publisher gratefully acknowledge the permission granted to reproduce the copyright material in this book:

1. Architectural Plates from the "Encyclopédie," pp. 59, 77, 78, 84, 85, 87 from Denis Diderot (ed.), *The Architectural Plates from the "Encyclopédie."* London and Ontario: Dover, 1995.
2. Roland Barthes, "The Plates of the *Encyclopedia*," pp. 218–23, 229, 231–5 from Susan Sontag (ed.), *Barthes: Selected Writings*, 2nd edition. London: Fontana Press, 1983.
3. Michel Foucault, "Introduction," pp. 3–7, 10–11 from R. D. Laing, *The Archaeology of Knowledge*, trans. Alan M. Sheridan Smith. London and New York: Routledge, 1989. Reprinted by permission of Taylor & Francis.
4. John Summerson, "Palladian Permeation: The Villa," pp. 334–42, 345–8 from *Architecture in Britain 1530 to 1830*. New Haven and London: Yale University Press, 1953. Reprinted by permission of Yale University Press.

5. Dana Arnold, "The Country House: Form, Function and Meaning," pp. 1–19 from *The Georgian Country House: Architecture, Landscape and Society.* Stroud: Sutton, 1998. Reprinted by permission of Sutton Publishing Ltd.

6. Robert and James Adam, "Plans and Elevations for the Villa of Lord Mansfield at Kenwood," pp. 24–8 from Robert Oresko (ed.), *The Works in Architecture of Robert and James Adam.* London: Academy Editions, 1975.

7. Sir John Soane, "Lecture V," pp. 116–20, 122–5, 130, 132–3 from David Watkin (ed.), *Sir John Soane: The Royal Academy Lectures.* Cambridge: Cambridge University Press, 2000.

8. Horace Walpole, pp. i–iv (Preface), 1–3, 42 from *A Description of the Villa of Mr. Horace Walpole.* London, 1748.

9. James Ackerman, "Thomas Jefferson," pp. 185–6, 188–200, 295–6 from *The Villa: Form and Ideology of Country Houses.* London: Thames & Hudson, 1990. ©1990 by Princeton University Press. Reprinted by permission of Princeton University Press.

10. Edmund Burke, pp. 57, 74–7, 81 from *A Philosophical Enquiry into the Origin of our Ideas of the Sublime and Beautiful,* ed. James T. Boulton. Oxford: Basil Blackwell, 1987.

11. Sir Uvedale Price, "On Architecture and Buildings," pp. 328–33, 336–40, 343–4, 346, 350–1, 353, 408–9 from *Sir Uvedale Price on the Picturesque.* London: William. S. Orr and Co., 1797.

12. Richard Payne Knight, pp. 1–2, 153–9, 164–7, 169–72, 176–80, 216–22 from *An Analytical Enquiry into the Principles of Taste,* 2nd edition. London: Luke Hansard for T. Payne & J. White, 1805.

13. Stephen Daniels and Denis Cosgrove, "Introduction: Iconography and Landscape," pp. 1–10 from Denis Cosgrove and Stephen Daniels, *The Iconography of Landscape: Essays on the Symbolic Representation, Design and Use of Past Environments.* Cambridge: Cambridge University Press, 1988. Reproduced with permission of Cambridge University Press and Dr. S. J. Daniels and Dr. D. E. Cosgrove.

14. John Summerson, "The Plans and Elevations of John Nash," pp. 177–90 from *Georgian London,* 3rd edition. London: Barrie & Jenkins, 1978.

15. Etienne-Louis Boullée, "Architecture, Essay on Art," pp. 83–7, 145 from Helen Rosenau (ed.), *Boullée and Visionary Architecture,* trans. Sheila de Vallée. London and New York: Academy Editions, 1953.

16. Susanne von Falkenhausen, "The Sphere: Reading a Gender Metaphor in the Architecture of Modern Cults of Identity," pp. 238–67 from *Art History* 20: 2. Oxford: Blackwell, 1997. Reprinted by permission of Blackwell Publishing Ltd.

17. David Watkin and Tilman Mellinghoff, "Karl Friedrich Schinkel," pp. 85–6, 88–96, 99, 104–5, 107, 110–13, 117 from *German Architecture & the Classical Ideal, 1740–1840*. London: Thames & Hudson, 1987.

18. Dana Arnold, "Reading Architectural Herstories: The Discourses of Gender," pp. 199–204 from *Reading Architectural History*. London and New York: Routledge, 2002. Reprinted by permission of Taylor & Francis.

19. A. W. N. Pugin, pp. 1–10, 19–22 from *An Apology for the Revival of Christian Architecture in England*. Oxford: St Barnabus Press, 1968 (originally published 1843). The engraving "Contrasted English Towns, 1840 and 1440" is reproduced from Henry-Russell Hitchcock, *Early Victorian Architecture in Britain*. New York: De Capo Press, 1976.

20. Eugène-Emmanuel Viollet-le-Duc, "Lecture X: Architecture in the Nineteenth Century: Importance of Method," pp. 446–8, 467–70, 474 from *Lectures on Architecture, 1814–79*, trans. Benjamin Bucknall. London and Ontario: Dover, 1987. Reprinted by permission of Dover Publications.

21. Gottfried Semper, from *Science, Industry and Art*, pp. 331–6 from Charles Harrison, Paul Wood, and Jason Gaiger (eds.), *Art in Theory 1815–1900: An Anthology of Changing Ideas*, trans. Nicholas Walker. Oxford: Blackwell, 1998. Reprinted by permission of Blackwell Publishing Ltd. Originally published in German as Gottfried Semper, *Wissenschaft, Industrie und Kunst und andere Schriften über Architektur, Kunsthandwerk und Kunstunterricht*, ed. Hans M. Winger. Frankfurt: Florian Kupterberg Verlag, 1966, pp. 27–8, 31–2, 33, 34–8, 40, 41–2.

22. John Ruskin, "The Nature of Gothic," pp. 149–53, 156–60, 163–4, 167–8 from *The Stones of Venice*, vol. 2. London: George Allen, 1905.

23. William Morris, "The Revival of Architecture," pp. 315–24 from Nikolaus Pevsner, *Some Architectural Writers of the Nineteenth Century*. Oxford: Clarendon Press, 1972.

24. "Some Recent Designs by Mr. C. F. A. Voysey," pp. 209–18 from *The Studio* 7. London, 1897.

25. Louis Sullivan, "Style (1888)," with introduction by Robert Twombly, pp. 45–52 from Robert Twombly (ed.), *Louis Sullivan: The Public Papers*. Chicago: University of Chicago Press, 1988.

26. Louis Sullivan, "Ornament in Architecture (1892)," pp. 80–5 from Robert Twombly (ed.), *Louis Sullivan: The Public Papers*. Chicago: University of Chicago Press, 1988.

27. Louis Sullivan, "The Tall Office Building Artistically Considered (1896)," pp. 103–13 from Robert Twombly (ed.), *Louis Sullivan: The Public Papers*. Chicago: University of Chicago Press, 1988.

28. Frank Lloyd Wright, "Plasticity," pp. 132–3 from *An Autobiography.* London: Faber & Faber, 1945.

29. Frank Lloyd Wright, "The Nature of Materials," pp. 133–6 from *An Autobiography.* London: Faber & Faber, 1945.

30. Lynne Walker, "Women and Architecture," pp. 90–105 from Judy Attfield and Pat Kirkham (eds.), *A View from the Interior: Feminism, Women and Design.* London: The Women's Press, 1989.

31. Annie Jacques, "The Programmes of the Architectural Section of the École des Beaux-Arts," pp. 59–62, 65, 256 from Robin Middleton (ed.), *The Beaux-Arts and Nineteenth-Century French Architecture.* London: Thames & Hudson, 1982.

32. Zeynep Çelik, "Adler and Sullivan at the 1893 World's Columbian Exposition in Chicago," pp. 171–6, 222 from *Displaying the Orient: Architecture of Islam at Nineteenth-Century World's Fairs.* Berkeley: University of California Press, 1992. Reprinted by permission of the University of California Press.

33. Frederick Law Olmsted, "Public Parks and the Enlargement of Towns (1870)," pp. 1, 3–7, 10, 12, 14–17 from *Selected Essays,* vol. 1, ed. Richard LeGates and Frederic Stout. London and New York: Routledge, 1998.

34. Anthony Sutcliffe, "Paris as the Hub of French Industrialisation: Building a European Capital under the Second Empire," pp. 83, 85–8 from *Paris: An Architectural History.* New Haven and London: Yale University Press, 1993. Reprinted by permission of Yale University Press.

35. Ebenezer Howard, "Introduction" and "The Town and Country Magnet [Chapter 1]," pp. 2, 10–11, 13–19 from *Garden Cities of To-morrow,* 3rd edition. London: Swan Sonnenschein, 1902.

36. Camillo Sitte, "Modern Systems," pp. 229–31, 233–42 from *City Planning According to Artistic Principles,* trans. George R. Collins and Christine Crasemann Collins. New York: Rizzoli, 1986.

37. Otto Wagner, "Construction," pp. 91–101 from Harry Francis Mallgrave (ed.), *Modern Architecture,* trans. Harry Francis Mallgrave. Santa Monica: The Getty Center for the History of Art and the Humanities, 1988.

38. Adolf Loos, "Ornament and Crime (1908)," pp. 100–3 from Joanna Drew (ed.), *The Architecture of Adolf Loos.* London: Arts Council of Great Britain, 1985.

39. Adolf Loos, "Architecture (1910)," pp. 104–9 from Joanna Drew, *The Architecture of Adolf Loos.* London: Arts Council of Great Britain, 1985.

40. Antonio Sant'Elia, "Manifesto of Futurist Architecture," pp. 160–72 from Umbro Apollonio (ed.), *Futurist Manifestos,* trans. R. W. Flint. London: Thames & Hudson, 1973.

41. Peter Behrens, "The Turbine Hall of the AEG," pp. 56–7 from Charlotte Benton (ed.), *Documents: A Collection of Source Material for the Modern Movement*. Milton Keynes: Open University Press, 1975.

42. Sigfried Giedion, "The State of German Architecture," pp. 11–15 from Charlotte Benton (ed.), *Documents: A Collection of Source Material for the Modern Movement*. Milton Keynes: Open University Press, 1975.

43. Walter Gropius, "Programme of the Staatliche Bauhaus in Weimar," pp. 78–9 from Tim and Charlotte Benton et al. (eds.), *Form and Function: A Source Book for the History of Architecture and Design 1890–1939*. Milton Keynes: Open University Press, 1975.

44. Marianne Brandt, "Letter to the Younger Generation," pp. 97–100 from Eckhard Neumann, *Bauhaus and Bauhaus People*. New York: Van Nostrand Reinhold Company, 1970.

45. László Moholy-Nagy, "Space (Architecture)," pp. 59–61 from Walter Gropius, *The New Vision*, 4th edition. New York: George Wittenborn, 1947.

46. Marcel Breuer, "Where Do We Stand?," pp. 119–21 from Peter Blake (ed.), *Marcel Breuer: Architect and Designer*. New York: Museum of Modern Art, 1949. © 1949 by The Museum of Modern Art, New York. Reprinted with permission.

47. Eric Mendelsohn, "The Problem of a New Architecture," pp. 45–50 from Oskar Beyer (ed.), *Letters of an Architect*, trans. Geoffrey Strachan. London and New York: Abelard-Schuman, 1967.

48. Eric Mendelsohn, "The Creative Spirit of the World Crisis [1933]," pp. 121–3 from Oskar Beyer (ed.), *Letters of an Architect*, trans. Geoffrey Strachan. London and New York: Abelard-Schuman, 1967.

49. Mies van der Rohe, "Solved Problems: A Demand on our Building Methods," trans. Rolf Achilles, pp. 165–6 from Rolf Achilles, Kevin Harrington, and Charlotte Myhrum (eds.), *Mies van der Rohe: Architect as Educator*. Chicago: Illinois Institute of Technology, 1986.

50. Mies van der Rohe, "Explanation of the Educational Program," pp. 167–8 from Rolf Achilles, Kevin Harrington, and Charlotte Myhrum (eds.), *Mies van der Rohe: Architect as Educator*. Chicago: Illinois Institute of Technology, 1986.

51. Theo van Doesburg, "Report of the De Stijl Group at the 'International Artists Congress' in Dusseldorf," p. 59 from *Principles of Neo-Plastic Art*, trans. Janet Seligman. London: Lund Humphries, 1969.

52. Le Corbusier, "Towards a New Architecture," pp. 7–14, 15–24 from *Towards a New Architecture*, 1946 edition, trans. Frederick Etchells. London: The Architectural Press, 1965 (reprint).

53. Le Corbusier, "Architecture in Everything, City Planning in Everything," pp. 67–83 from *Precisions on the Present State of Architecture and City Planning*, trans. Edith Schreiber Aujamo. Cambridge, MA: MIT Press, 1991. Reprinted by permission of The MIT Press.

54. Le Corbusier, "On Discovering Gaudí's Architecture," pp. 20–3 from *Gaudí.* Barcelona: Ediciones Polígrafa, 1957.

55. Beatriz Colomina, "The Split Wall: Domestic Voyeurism," pp. 73–4, 98–107, 112, 124–6, 128 from *Sexuality and Space.* New York: Princeton Architectural Press, 1992.

56. José Luis Sert, Fernand Léger, and Sigfried Giedion, "Nine Points on Monumentality," with an introduction by Joan Ockman, pp. 27–30 from Joan Ockman (ed.), *Architecture Culture, 1943–1968: A Documentary Anthology.* New York: Rizzoli, 1993. Reprinted by permission of Rizzoli.

57. Louis I. Khan, "Monumentality," pp. 18–21, 24–7 from Alessandra Latour (ed.), *Louis I Khan. Writings, Lectures, Interviews.* New York: Rizzoli, 1991. Reprinted by permission of Rizzoli.

58. Congress of International Modern Architects, "Reaffirmation of the Aims of CIAM," with an introduction by Joan Ockman, pp. 100–2 from Joan Ockman (ed.), *Architecture Culture, 1943–1968: A Documentary Anthology.* New York: Rizzoli, 1993. Reprinted by permission of Rizzoli.

59. Reyner Banham, "Conclusion: Functionalism and Technology," pp. 320–30 from *Theory and Design in the First Machine Age.* London: The Architectural Press, 1960.

60. Charles Jencks, "The Death of Modern Architecture," pp. 9–10, 12–17, 19, 37, 181 (note 1) from *The Language of Post-Modern Architecture,* 5th edition. London: Academy Editions, 1977.

61. Kenneth Frampton, "Towards a Critical Regionalism: Six Points for an Architecture of Resistance," pp. 16–30 from Hal Foster (ed.), *Postmodern Culture* [first published as *The Anti-Aesthetic*]. Washington: Bay Press, 1983.

62. Bernard Tschumi, "The Pleasure of Architecture," pp. 173–83 from Andrew Ballantyne (ed.), *What is Architecture?* London and New York: Routledge, 2002. Reprinted by permission of Routledge, Taylor & Francis.

63. Saskia Sassen, "Scale and Span in a Global Digital World," pp. 44–8 from Cynthia C. Davidson (ed.), *Anything.* Cambridge, MA: MIT Press, 2001. Reprinted by permission of the MIT Press.

Every effort has been made to trace copyright holders and to obtain their permission for the use of copyright material. The publisher apologizes for any errors or omissions in the above list and would be grateful if notified of any corrections that should be incorporated in future reprints or editions of this book.

Introduction: Classifying Knowledge

Abigail Harrison-Moore and Dorothy C. Rowe

> There is no longer a tripartite division between a field of reality (the world) and a field of representation (the book) and a field of subjectivity (the author). Rather, an assemblage establishes connections between certain multiplicities drawn from each of these orders. (Deleuze and Guattari 1987: 22–3)

This reader aims to introduce students to ways of thinking about the history of architecture and design and specifically to examine how the historiography of the subject highlights key themes and questions. In each section, chronologically structured for ease of use rather than to provide a strict pattern of navigation, discursive essays preface texts that have been selected because they represent significant ways of thinking about the past. The introductions to each part aim to present the reader with ways of thinking through the selected texts, while contextualizing the particular historical moments under consideration. The anthology has been designed to support a huge range of courses in architectural and design history, from theoretically weighted programs to more standard chronological survey courses, and it can be read alongside other similar anthologies of writing on architecture and design to open up a broad field of potential inquiry for the undergraduate or beginning postgraduate student. It is inevitably conceived and located from the historical moment occupied by its editors and as such it attempts to place recent remappings of architectural and design history within a broader Western perspective that sets up the possibilities for teaching a diverse range of topics within the shifting conceptual paradigms that postmodernism has enabled. At the end of this introduction we have also included a brief, and certainly not exhaustive, selection of useful texts to encourage further research and reflection.

The three extracts in this section consider the problematic nature of any attempt to classify knowledge and the concomitant exclusions attendant upon such a selective activity. In the mid-nineteenth century, James Fergusson began his *History of Architecture in All Countries from the Earliest Times to the Present Day* (1865) with a summary of, in his opinion, the two main approaches to architecture:

1

> Like every other object of human enquiry, architecture may be studied from two distinct points of view. Either it may be regarded statically and described scientifically as a thing existing, without any reference to the manner in which it was invented; or it may be treated historically, tracing every form from its origin, and noting the influence one style has had upon another in the progress of time.

Such a choice, between a synchronic and a diachronic history, is still the challenge that faces historians today, especially those tackling a survey text like this. Should the thrust be the creation of a continuous, fluid narrative that will tie together disparate works across time, making sense of their differences and similarities? Or should greater attention be given to fewer works in order to give a fuller understanding of the complexities at a single moment? Dell Upton, in his selective history of American architecture, *Architecture in the United States* (1998), notes that all histories are constructed narratives and, by definition, selective, and these created stories attempt to make sense of complex details, facts, and visual data. As such, we must accept the premise 'that all historical narratives contain an irreducible and inexpungeable element of interpretation' (White 1985: 52). We aim to encourage the reader to examine any notion of the canon critically, asking under which set of criteria the list was constructed, what are the inherent values reflected in that choice, and what has, for practical reasons endemic to any publication of this type, been left out of the history. As cultural historian Peter Burke has commented:

> In this type of enquiry the historian is not simply concerned with the interpretation of meanings but rather with defining the ambiguities of the symbolic world, the plurality of possible interpretations of it and the struggle which takes place over symbolic as much as over material resources. (Burke 1991: 95)

The juxtaposition of the texts in this book aims to stress the provisional nature of readings – or histories – that inevitably shift and change over time. We aim to explore the nature of the discourse of architecture and design history and to question what it is that we are studying. In order to do this we must first consider what is meant by the term "history." History is an unending dialog between the present and the past. It is open to the subjectivities and preoccupations of the historian in his or her present. Structuralist and post-structuralist discourse have enabled this realization and fundamentally altered our view and understanding of knowledge and history. Michel Foucault's *Archaeology of Knowledge* (1969), extracts from the introduction to which are reproduced in this section, demonstrates the process of questioning history and knowledge that was at the forefront of philosophical writing in the 1960s. E. H. Carr (1978), in his lectures at Cambridge University in early 1961, provides us with a careful analysis of subjectivity under the powerful title *What is History?* Starting with the nineteenth-century historian's obsession with facts and the need "simply to show how it really was," Carr explores the influence of the empiricist tradition in England that presupposes a complete separation between subject and object.

The process of reception was passive, with the historian simply gathering together a corpus of ascertained facts. But, as Carr points out, facts are only the raw materials of history, rather than history itself. The historian is necessarily selective. The influence of the empiricists remained and remains strong in both American and European architectural and design history, "the belief in a hardcore of historical facts existing objectively and independently of the interpretation of the historian is a preposterous fallacy, but one which is very hard to eradicate." Carr sees such belief in the objective truth of historical facts as "having a devastating effect on the modern historian, producing in Germany, in Great Britain and in the United States, a vast and growing mass of dry-as-dust factual histories, of minutely specialised monographs of would be historians, knowing more and more about less and less, sunk without a trace in an ocean of facts" (Carr 1971: 15). In this volume we have deliberately selected a wide range of articles that both demonstrate the empiricist traditions in architectural and design history and question them. By juxtaposing texts from different periods of writing, we hope to encourage the reader to question the historian's method as well as benefiting from their research on a specific period, designer, or style.

This domination of the "facts" of history has been supported and justified by reference to the hegemony of the archive, the origins of which can be traced to the formation of historical discourse in the nineteenth century, a time of confidence and optimism, of empire-building and industrial invention, when the inclination to ask questions was limited. This becomes evident when we compare it with the moment of questioning that has dominated recent histories, that of the 1960s and the French philosophers, grouped together under the banner of post-structuralism. With student riots and unrest in Europe, writers and thinkers turned in on themselves and, borrowing from Marxist traditions, began to question the whole process of knowledge and the structure of the society in which they lived. Illustrating this shift in the introductory section of this anthology is the juxtaposition of Barthes's 1964 essay "The Plates of the *Encyclopedia*" against a selection of architectural plates from Denis Diderot's editorial *magnum opus*, the *Encylopédie*, first published in 1751 and not completed until almost a quarter of a century later. Diderot's project was initially conceived in 1745 as a business venture, but by the time the first volume was published it had far outstripped the original conception. As Daniel Brewer notes, echoing the tenor of Barthes's earlier analysis:

> judged in terms of its innovative approach to the compilation and transmission of knowledge, the financial and technical means marshalled, the size of its readership (some 4,500 subscribers), and the number of its eventual collaborators (over 150 identified), the *Encylopédie* project stands as one of the greatest exploits in the history of French culture and modern capitalism. (Brewer 1993: 13)

3

It is also a quintessential document of the Enlightenment, in which the untrammeled inquiry into all areas of human knowledge was considered a central tool in the Enlighteners' struggle to combat ignorance, superstition, and religious dogma. Brewer argues for the Enlightenment as a specific representational practice in which the *Encylopédie* is key for consolidating the form of subsequent epistemological inquiry since one of the main goals of the encyclopaedists was to change the nature of knowledge itself, "its origins and ends, its production and use" (1993: 14). Knowledge in the *Encylopédie* was codified, classified, and presented as integral to the capitalist system in which it was produced, inseparable from a process of production, discourse, and consumption while knowledge for its own sake was rejected as insufficient to abolish "unreason" and rationally restructure institutions and social values which lay at the core of the Enlightenment project. For Roland Barthes the plates of the *Encylopédie* were also precursors to that mid-nineteenth-century spectacle of capitalism, the World Exhibition, in that they included objects that covered "the entire sphere of substances shaped by man: clothes, vehicles, tools, weapons, instruments, furniture" (Barthes 1983: 219). In particular, Barthes highlights the mythological character of the *Encylopédie*'s images when he comments that "an almost naïve simplicity, a kind of Golden Legend of artisanry (for there is no sign of social distress): the *Encylopedia* identifies the simple, the elementary, the essential and the causal" (1983: 221). Further to this, his analysis of the images also highlights the disjuncture between production and consumption and how it is codified visually, "austerity of creation, luxury of commerce, such is the double régime of the Encyclopedic object: the density of the image and its ornamental charge always signifies that we are shifting from production to consumption" (1983: 222). Ultimately "the *Encylopedia* is a huge ledger of ownership" in which the classification, fragmentation, and separation of objects are the conditions under which "property is born" since, as he notes earlier and as we shall witness throughout this anthology, "we cannot separate without naming and classifying" (1983: 222) and, as Foucault reminds us a decade later, classificatory activity is predicated upon hegemonic choices and power relations between those things that are named and those that remain silenced. For Barthes, the representational splitting between the upper and lower plates is also a form of violence to the more peaceful order of the world codified in the plate above which enacts an ultimately circuitous process of signification that voids the premise on which the *Encylopédie* was constructed because, as he concludes, "in a word, the fracture of the world is impossible" (1983: 235).

Barthes's writings are symptomatic of early French post-structuralist critiques that became a dominant mode of epistemological analysis and inquiry after the 1960s and which have had a huge impact on approaches to the arts and humanities. However, in terms of architectural and design history in particular, a major moment of writing about design, especially in Britain, and which still underlines the discourse today, occurred before this period of questioning, during the immediate post-war moment, where artefacts from the past were deemed especially precious and in need of protection. Various government Acts in Britain focused attention on the objects that represented the nation.[1] Since the end of the nineteenth century, across Europe and the United States, there had been a growing interest in the landscape of the nations' pasts, but it was the devastation of World War II that acted as a catalyst for many people's attitudes to their history, or rather the historic environment and what it represented in terms of the nation's heritage (Walsh 1992: 72). The war had weakened the status of the English ruling classes, and, threatened by the welfare socialism of the post-war period, they felt an urgent need for an emphasis on the preservation of that for which they stood. This moment of recognition was powerfully endorsed by the establishment in 1946 of the National Land Fund enabling country houses to be accepted by government in lieu of tax and handed over to the National Trust, opening up many to a visiting public for the first time and, more importantly, making their archives available to scholars. The 1940s and 1950s saw history as a mode of knowledge develop a new popular appeal. Improvements in education, especially the expansion of higher education, encouraged people's interest in history and archaeology, epitomized by the success of G. M. Trevelyan's Pelican History of England series published during this era.

In the US, the early years of the twentieth century marked a significant shift in the writing of the history of architecture and design. In 1918 Fiske Kimball and George Howard Edgell published *A History of Architecture*, in which they stated that their intention was for "subjective criticism [to give] way to the impartial study of development." They continued: "the attempt has been made to present each style as a thing of growth and change, rather than as a formula based on the monuments of a supposed apogee, with respect to which the later forms have too often been treated as corrupt." At the beginning of the twentieth century, authors and publishers saw a need for a different, up-to-date, history of architecture and design that interpreted the past in light of the radical changes that had been witnessed in recent building activity. With attitudes changing towards the notion of historical precedent, the development of "modern" architecture inspired new histories of stylistic development and function. Architects such as Louis Sullivan and Peter Behrens reinterpreted the relevance and meaning of

---

[1] The Ancient Monuments Protection Act was established in 1882, but took 10 years to become law due to its perceived attack on the rights of private property. This was followed by the establishment of the Society for the Protection of Ancient Buildings in 1877, the Commons, Footpaths and Open Spaces Preservation Society (1863), and the National Trust in 1895. In France an equivalent law to the Ancient Monuments Act was passed in 1905, and in Germany the Heimatschutz was created in 1904 to protect natural areas and historical monuments. In the US the federal government, through the National Park Service, was established in 1916 and subsequently took responsibility for the Historic Sites Act of 1935. In Britain the 1943 Town and Country Planning Act began the process of listing, the National Buildings Record was set up, and the Royal Commission on Historic Monuments had its remit expanded to allow it to survey buildings dating from after 1714; see Walsh 1992: 71–2.

history in their own practice. Likewise, historians were motivated by contemporary architectural theories and practices to examine the history of the past through the lens of the present. This was equally motivated by a desire to see developments in American architecture as equal in importance to those in Europe.

As we have seen, during the twentieth century the audience for architectural history expanded. By the time of the sixteenth edition, in 1956, of *A History of Architecture in the Comparative Method* (first published in 1896), Sir Banister Fletcher would write in his preface, in light of World War II, that he hoped the book would appeal "to the wider public which influences and largely controls the architecture of to-day, so that it will demand fine buildings comparable to the great monuments of the past, yet expressive of our own times and worthy to be handed down as a national heritage to future generations." By the mid-twentieth century, the combination of the student market and a growing interest amongst the general public created a publishing opportunity. Thames & Hudson launched the World of Art series in 1957. In the 1960s and 1970s Pelican Books brought out a small number of titles as part of the series edited by John Fleming and Hugh Honour, The Architect and Society, including new studies of Inigo Jones by John Summerson (1966) and of Andrea Palladio by James Ackerman (1966), which emphasized the relationship of architecture to its political, social, and cultural context. Before World War II, surveys mainly focused on the history of style, tracing the development of form through time in order to define a pattern of visual norms. There was little sense of how meaning was formed in design, or of how this vast body of data should be interpreted (Anderson 1999: 351).

Developments in literary theory since the 1960s have highlighted the need to break down or "deconstruct" the distinction between "fact" and "fiction," in order to identify shared attributes as forms of linguistic behavior that are as much constitutive of their objects of representation as they are reflective of external reality. This "news," Hayden White (1976) claimed, "has not yet reached the historians buried in the archives"; yet in the nineteenth century the influence of contemporary culture was already being reorganized, under the banner of the philosophy of history, by theorists such as Herder, Marx, Nietzsche, and Hegel. The philosophers, however, were not themselves immune to the ideology of so-called "neutral" language, and are described by White as "anarchist, radical, liberal and conservative respectively." The very use of language itself implies or entails a specific posture before the world which is ethical, ideological, or political.

Post-structuralist theory has prompted much debate around language and specifically the role of the author (see Barthes 1977; Foucault 1981). This has illustrated the problems that occur when a history is fixed upon the person of the architect and/or designer. Yet exploring architecture and design through the life of the architect or designer remains a significant force in the discipline, particularly when the architect or designer has been identified as a major figure in the evolution of a movement. The historians of our subject have often predicated their work on the attribution, re-attribution, and provenance of objects and buildings in reference to a distinct set of designers and architects. Attribution underpins scholarship, the use and reading of historic documentation, the publication of histories, the display and curation of associated museum exhibits and – completing a self-fulfilling cycle – attribution of value by the auction house and market. The discourse avoids a Barthesian call for a recognition of the mythologies that lead to the creation of signs of cultural value. The system of assigning an "author" (architect/designer), however, is only secure if attribution seems the natural conclusion of empirical evidence. Academic research still often seems to focus on confirming or denying whether an object, interior, or building is by one of the "names" established as dominant in the discourse. It is, Barthes (1977) declares, "tyrannically centred on the author, his person, his history, his passions."

Once attribution to an architect or designer has been made, there are a number of ideas or conclusions applied to the object or building. If re-attribution occurs or misattribution is declared, what effect then does the removal of the named maker have on the object? One solution would be the acknowledgment that the name is "functional" in that it serves as a means of classification. A name can group together a number of artifacts (objects and/or buildings) and thus differentiate them from others. But Foucault's (1981) interpretation of a "name" can also highlight negative factors, especially if one name is accepted as dominating all others. A name implies relationships of homogeneity, filiation, reciprocal explanation, authentication, or common utilization which can be beneficial but may also be negative or destructive.

A historian, however, needs to order his or her facts, and for this activity to succeed categories and taxonomies, be they a name or otherwise, are necessary. Authorship is useful in this regard, but so too is the evolution of "style." Style remains a principal concern for the history of design. It has been defined as "a specific organization of form" (Arnold 2002: 83) and focuses on an aesthetic reading of design only, attempting to understand history by explaining the changes that take place in both ornamentation and in shape or plan. An aesthetic reading gives a work of art an autonomous status, and style provides a means of identifying, codifying, and interrogating this aesthetic.

Perhaps more than any other order of narrative, style invites the tracing of lines of progression and development, providing the historian with a set of observed teleological processes by which to understand how the "look" of objects changes over time. Within this, the Hegelian notion of a "spirit of the age" (*Zeitgeist*) becomes vital, where change can be understood as occurring via a dialectical process of thesis–antithesis–synthesis. Thus we can see early eighteenth-century Palladian style becoming mid-century Baroque becoming end-of-century neoclassicism or, when we combine a biographical and stylistic reading, Jones leading to Vanbrugh leading to Adam. As such, style provides a useful taxonomy for the historian, allowing him or her to structure objects into a teleological process of change. But this has inherent problems. We often only witness change via hindsight, and patterns only appear when we look from a distance. We often find the historian attempting to impose a structure upon the past which is developed from a contemporary reading and which acknowledges current concerns rather than historic ones.

Style has provided the historian with a simple and convincing taxonomic structure that allows us to break down and understand the history of design. But the author rarely acknowledges this structure, and it has assumed a dominance over our processes of understanding change which can be as dangerous as it can be illuminating. As Foucault proposed in *The Order of Things* (first published 1966 with an English translation in 1970), "in the wonderment of this taxonomy, the thing we apprehend in one great leap, the thing that is demonstrated as the exotic charm of another system of thought, is the limitation of our own." In discussing a Chinese encyclopedia, Foucault highlights the importance of understanding the "site" of classification and its effect and how unfamiliar systems can seem alien and ridiculous due to their "proximity of extremes." But this is only because of our lack of understanding of the moment in which the system was created and the fact that we are viewing it with hindsight. If we remove the "site" then we can no longer comprehend/be conscious of the system of classification being used, and thus we can be persuaded by a taxonomy that is as much a part of the contemporary writer of history as it is evidence of a system that was present at the time under consideration. The utopian world of the historian of facts is thus disturbed. By analyzing the process of the telling of history we destroy its "syntax." Style has often provided the syntax of design history, and whereas "utopias permit fables and discourse," we aim to open up the systems of classification that have allowed this in order to present an alternative, heterotopic, reading of the texts presented in this book. Foucault highlights "the profound distress" that occurs when one attempts to deconstruct language and the systems used to create a discourse, and this may be the reason why many design historians, particularly of the eighteenth and nineteenth centuries, have resisted questioning the processes by which history is created. The system of understanding historic change using a stylistic analysis alone is problematic, as it is "arbitrary in its basis, since it deliberately ignores all differences and all identities not related to the selected structure."

Why, then, has a history of design as a history of style been so dominant in the discourse? We can briefly trace its gestation by looking at the historiography of the subject. Many have located the foundation of the discipline of art history in the nineteenth-century work of German philosophical aesthetics (see Watkin 1980). Interestingly, while it has been art history that has focused our attention on the writings of Semper, Riegl, Wölfflin, and others, their work was often concerned with the analysis of architecture and design as much as with works of art. Gottfried Semper (1803–79), an architect and architectural theorist, provided the basis for a systematic treatment of art, architecture, and design history concentrated on "motifs." He explored the way architects took structural features, such as the plaited twigs of primitive buildings or the woven thread of textiles, and exploited their potential for pattern-making. He examined how such motifs are transformed using different materials, generating architectural metaphors, and adopted a method of understanding design through the piecemeal adaptation and reapplication of these motifs. Hegelian in its idea of progress, Semper's work presents design history as a synthesis of motifs. Alois Riegl (1858–1905) adapts a form of Semper's motif theory in *Stilfragen* of 1893, where he concerns himself with the transformation of one particular motif, that of the acanthus. He sees this as developing from the shape of the Egyptian lotus motif by virtue of an internal dynamic seeking richer and more integrated form, in a strictly teleological scheme. The striking feature of the account of design history in *Stilfragen* is Riegl's assumption that the generative force in the history of design and development of a design motif is man's innate sense of pattern and symmetry and the urgency to combine discrete elements in an order – producing a sense of autonomy or inner necessity in the history of ornament that remains dominant in the discourse today. Both Riegl and his contemporary Heinrich Wölfflin (1864–1945) were searching for "order" in the history of art and architecture, attempting to accommodate the art of the past within the mental life of the present. Wölfflin, in works such as *Die antiken Triumphbogen* (1893), turned to the development of architectural history as the progressive integration and elaboration of motifs from the past, grounded strongly in Hegel's dialectic. At the center of his work is the philosophical need to explain how our minds and perception lead us to see the world in certain ways. However, in attempting to do this, Wölfflin provides a cyclic view of the history of style, based in formalism, where the classical becomes the Baroque, which becomes the classical once again. Within this, Wölfflin sees art as having a teleological character of its own, linked to cultural change, but developing by an autonomous process of enriching and elaborating and then transcending. By assuming an autonomous visual tradition with its own principle of development, Wölfflin proposes that we assess the development of a group of works by the way they transform and transcend their antecedents (Podro 1982: 110). Each of these views of how design develops are problematic for a number of reasons. They are often based on the finished work; a work may invoke an earlier antecedent without presenting a variation of it, and it relies on us seeing the architect as having a sense of purpose or an aim to bring about change rather than simply to fulfill the desires of his or her client. Most crucially, it sees art in a single line of development and does not allow for variety at one point in time. And yet the German philosophers' arguments were very convincing and provided a solid basis for the twentieth-century design historian.

In Britain, Watkin (1980) links this to the influx of European scholars to the UK in the mid-twentieth century, opening up the possibility of placing British architecture in its cultural and aesthetic context and seeing it as part of a broader intellectual history of culture. In America, the Beaux Arts movement provided a similarly useful link. If the architectural history of the British Isles and the United States was to have the same academic weight at its Continental counterparts, it required recognizable formal qualities which provided distinction and allowed it to be read as signifying sets of social and cultural ideas. It would also be preferable for these formal qualities to relate to the European canon of architecture, namely the classical style. In the work of Rudolph Wittkower we can see this demonstrated. In canonical texts such as *Palladio and English Palladianism* (1945) he studies specific stylistic details, for example a window or a door frame, and provides a set of connections. "How does this motif fit into the pattern of palladian and neo-classical architecture?" he asks, and explores its genesis within the work of a distinct set of Palladian architects. In this way British architecture is linked with the architecture of Europe in formal and intellectual terms. In the work of Sir Nikolaus Pevsner, perhaps the most dominant architectural historian of twentieth-century England, we see the vital influence of a Hegelian notion of the Spirit of the Age, with a thesis–antithesis–synthesis model used for the analysis of change. "Architecture is not the product of materials and purposes, nor by the way of social condition – but of the changing spirits of changing ages" (Pevsner 1990: 23–5).

In the work of a number of historians and philosophers of design, an analysis of stylistic change often bleeds into an analysis of function, be that physical or material function, for example the move from one type of buttress to another, or metaphorical function, for example the display of nationalistic agendas. We must therefore now turn to another form of the analysis of design, which has become more prevalent in the last 30 years, specifically in Britain, as a result of the work of Mark Girouard (1978), that of the social historian. The practice of constructing and narrating the social history of the inhabitants of buildings has been extremely successful and has resulted in populist interpretations of architectural history featuring in the best-seller lists. In the 1970s Girouard made important connections between the architectural history of biography and style and the way people lived in the buildings of the past. This was seen as enlarging the picture and moving from a history that focused solely on the landowners to that of the other social groups occupying the country house, if only in a limited way.

Architecture is presented as an emblem of a set of social, economic, and political values. These, however, remain unquestioned and, as such, venerated, presented as something we might want to revere and preserve because of their intrinsic "value." The popularity of this type of writing, which frequently focuses on the eighteenth and nineteenth centuries, is intimately linked to the popularity of preservation movements such as, in England, the National Trust and English Heritage and the pastime of country house visiting. This type of social history remains acceptable and popular because it "stays within the epistemological frame of orthodox history while appearing more inclusive than previous narratives" (Arnold 2002: 128). It can be critiqued in a similar way to histories that focus on the style or biography of a building. Its historical "truth" is based on the same reconstructed experience, drawn from the same archives, which inevitably privilege the literate and property-owning classes, and on the same assumptions about the "facts" speaking for themselves. Of all the historical approaches considered in this introduction, a social reading is made to seem most relevant to our own experience and therefore is most convincing. It does not, however, question the repressed and absent voices in the archive, such as the many voices of women, servants and slaves, and tends to present stories that support rather than question the elite and the classification of the hierarchy. Any question about alternate social rituals and cultural practices remain unasked and unanswered. Throughout this book we aim to use both the texts and our brief introductions to each section to reintroduce some of these voices, or at least to question why they have remained on the peripheries of the canon of architecture and design history.

Under the influence of post-structuralism, and feminism in particular, three notions have become commonplace in recent design criticism and history: first, that the boundaries of the field are fluid and permeable, and that interdisciplinary research and analysis provide the fullest access to complex questions; second, that the critique of social relations and of ideology is inherent in the study of built form; and third, that a focus on narrowly defined sites of research – case-studies, local cultures, and specific historical monuments for example – interpreted in the framework of overlapping typological structures (patterns of everyday use, forms of language, and conventions of all kinds, including building types and design styles) in fact produces the broadest and richest interpretation of design. A corollary of this last point is that we must take account of our own position and values as observers, noting shifts that may occur over time, and differences that may exist between one individual and the next, just as we identify and assess the differences and contradictions apparent within or expressed by the historians of buildings, cultures, and artifacts under study (Friedman 1999: 407).

We encourage the reader to consider using this text in a number of ways and to divide up the readings according to a number of classificatory structures. For ease of use we have presented the text chronologically, starting with the eighteenth and early nineteenth centuries, then the nineteenth century, and concluding with the twentieth century. Within this structure, we have chosen texts written at the time under analysis, key pieces by the twentieth-century historian, and modern essays that reconsider the archive. In this introduction we have raised some questions about the ways in which the historian has approached the past and we hope that these will be taken into consideration by our readers when using any of the extracts within this anthology. Our choice has been limited by physical constraints – the size of the book, the texts available, etc. – but also by our own subjective selection process. In view of this we encourage the reader to use this text as a starting point only, a road map to begin their own journey of questioning, exploring, analyzing, and thinking about the processes and ideas of the historians of architectural and design history.

Useful Texts for Further Study

Agrest, Diana, Conway, Patricia, and Wiesman, Lesley Kanes (eds), *The Sex of Architecture*. New York: Harry N. Abrams, 1996.

Arnold, Dana, *Reading Architectural History*. London and New York: Routledge, 2002.

Ballantyne, Andrew, *Architecture: A Very Short Introduction*. Oxford: Oxford University Press, 2002.

Banham, Reyner, *Los Angeles: The Architecture of Four Ecologies*. Harmondsworth: Penguin, 1971.

Bergdoll, Barry, *European Architecture 1750–1890*. Oxford: Oxford University Press, 2000.

Bushman, Richard L., *The Refinement of America: Persons, Houses, Cities*. New York: Vintage Books, 1992.

Carr, E. H., *What Is History?* Harmondsworth: Penguin 1978.

Colomina, Beatriz (ed.), *Sexuality and Space*. New York: Princeton Architectural Press, 1992.

Friedman, Alice T., *Women and the Making of the Modern House: A Social and Architectural History*. New York: Harry N. Abrams, 1998.

Girouard, Mark, *Life in the English Country House: A Social and Architectural History*. New Haven: Yale University Press, 1978.

Hays, Michael K., *Architecture Theory Since 1968*. Cambridge, MA: MIT Press, 1998.

Leach, Neil (ed.), *Rethinking Architecture*. London and New York: Routledge, 1997.

Nesbitt, Kate, *Theorizing a New Agenda for Architecture: An Anthology of Architectural Theory, 1965–1995*. New York: Princeton Architectural Press, 1996.

Ockman, Joan (ed.), with the collaboration of Edward Eigan, *Architecture Culture, 1943–1968*. New York: Rizzoli International Publications, 1993.

Stein, Jay, and Spreckelmeyer, Ken (eds), *Classic Readings in Architecture*. Boston: WCB/McGraw-Hill, 1999.

Upton, Dell, *Architecture in the United States*. Oxford: Oxford University Press, 1998.

Venturi, Robert, Scott Brown, Denise, and Izenour, Steven, *Learning from Las Vegas: The Forgotten Symbolism of Architectural Form*. Cambridge, MA: MIT Press, 1972.

Vidler, Anthony, *The Architectural Uncanny: Essays in the Modern Unhomely*. Cambridge, MA: MIT Press, 1992.

1

The Architectural Plates from the "Encyclopédie"

Edited by Denis Diderot

Architectural Plates from the "Encyclopédie," pp. 59, 77, 78, 84, 85, 87 from Denis Diderot (ed.), *The Architectural Plates from the "Encyclopédie."* London and Ontario: Dover, 1995.

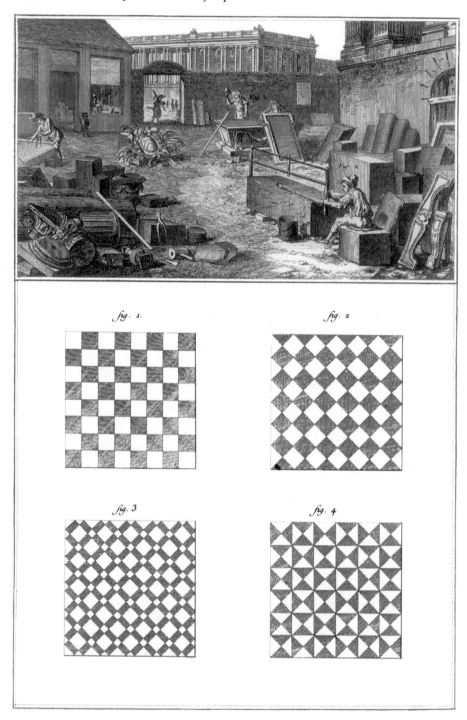

Figure 1.1 Marble cutting; various marble flooring patterns

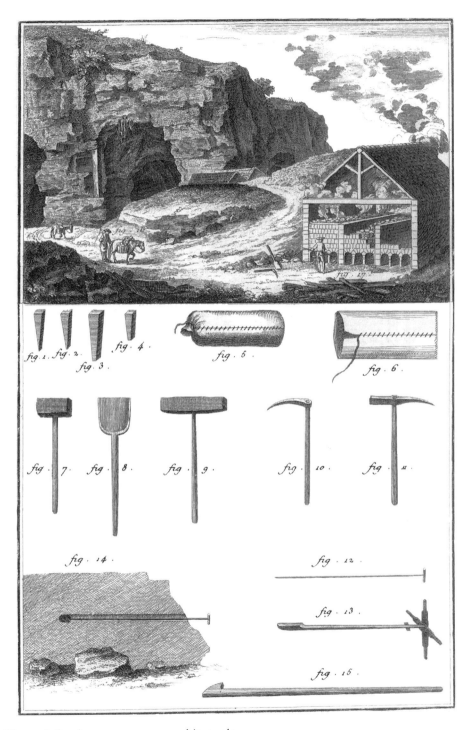

Figure 1.2   A gypsum quarry and its tools

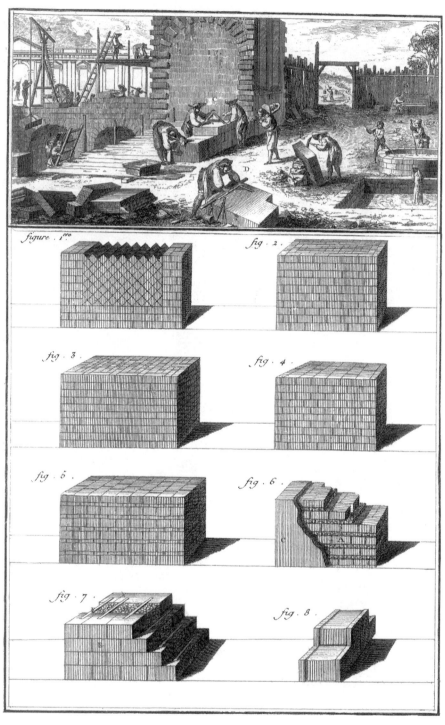

Figure 1.3 Masons at work and various bricklaying patterns

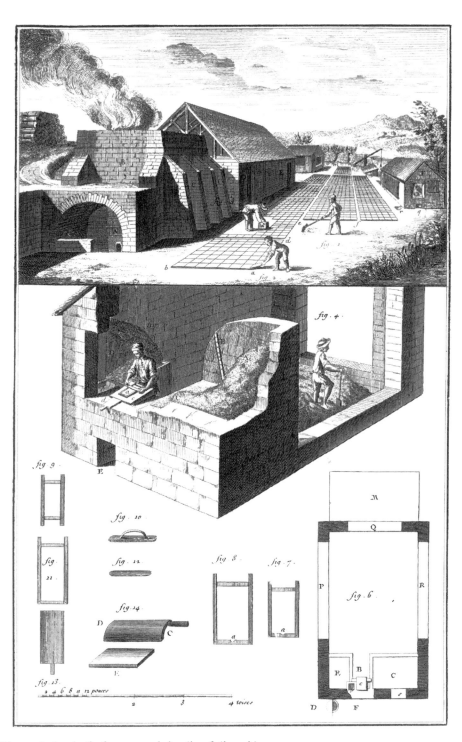

Figure 1.4   A tile factory and details of tilemaking

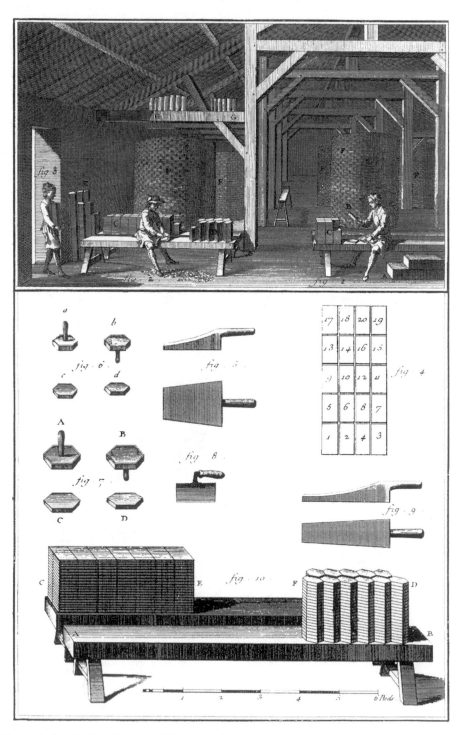

Figure 1.5 Cutting hexagonal flooring tiles

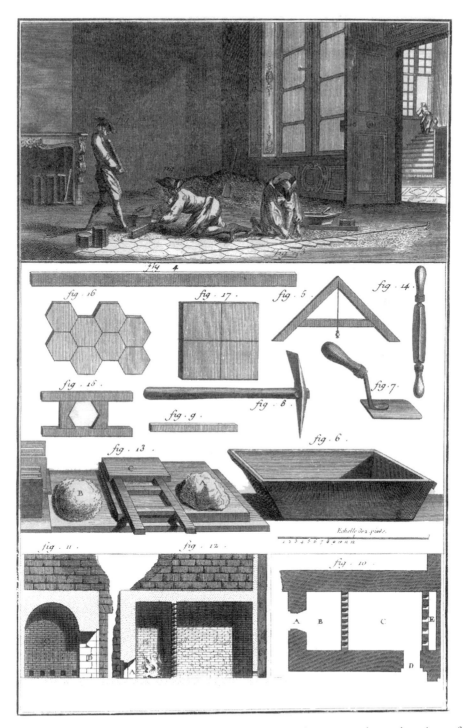

Figure 1.6   Laying floor tile; floor-tilers' implements and patterns; plan and sections of a tile-kiln

2

The Plates of the *Encyclopedia*

Roland Barthes

Long before literature, the *Encyclopedia*, particularly in its plates, practices what we might call a certain philosophy of the object, i.e., reflects on its being, produces at once an inventory and a definition; technological purpose no doubt compelled the description of objects; but by separating image from text, the *Encyclopedia* committed itself to an autonomous iconography of the object whose power we enjoy today, since we no longer look at these illustrations with mere information in mind.

The plates of the *Encyclopedia* present the object, and this presentation already adds to the illustration's didactic purpose a more gratuitous justification, of an aesthetic or oneiric order: the imagery of the *Encyclopedia* can best be compared with one of those Great Expositions held the world over in the last century or so, and of which, in its period, the Encyclopedic illustration was a kind of ancestor: in both cases, we are concerned with a census and a spectacle: we consult the plates of the *Encyclopedia* as we would visit today's World's Fair in Brussels or New York. The objects presented are literally encyclopedic, i.e., they cover the entire sphere of substances shaped by man: clothes, vehicles, tools, weapons, instruments, furniture, all that man makes out of wood, metal, glass, or fiber is catalogued here, from the chisel to the statue, from the artificial flower to the ship. This Encyclopedic object is ordinarily apprehended by the image on three levels: anthological, since the object, isolated from any context, is presented *in itself*; anecdotic, when it is "naturalized" by its insertion into a large-scale *tableau vivant* (which is what we call a vignette); genetic, when the image offers us the trajectory from raw substance to finished object: genesis, essence, praxis, the object is thus accounted for in all its categories: sometimes it *is*, sometimes it is *made*, sometimes it even *makes*. Of these three states, assigned here and there to the object-as-image, one is certainly favored by the *Encyclopedia*: that of birth: it is

Roland Barthes, "The Plates of the *Encyclopedia*," pp. 218–23, 229, 231–5 from Susan Sontag (ed.), *Barthes: Selected Writings*, 2nd edition. London: Fontana Press, 1983.

good to be able to show how we can produce things from their very nonexistence and thus to credit man with an extraordinary power of creation: here is a countryside; the plenitude of Nature (meadows, hills, trees) constitutes a kind of human void from which we cannot see what will emerge; yet the image moves, objects are born, precursors of humanity: lines are drawn on the earth, stakes are pounded in, holes dug; a cross-section shows us, beneath a desert Nature, the powerful network of galleries and lodes: a mine is born. This is a kind of symbol: Encyclopedic man *mines* all Nature with human signs; in the Encyclopedic landscape, we are never alone; however strong the elements, there is always a fraternal *product* of man: the object is the world's human signature. [...] The Encyclopedic object emerges from general substances which are still those of the artisanal era. If we visit a World's Fair today, we perceive in all the objects exhibited two or three dominant substances, glass, metal, plastic no doubt; the substance of the Encyclopedic object is of a more vegetal age: it is wood which dominates in this great catalogue; it produces a world of objects easy on the eyes, already human by their substance, resistant but not brittle, constructible but not plastic. Nothing shows wood's humanizing power better than the *Encyclopedia*'s machines; in this world of technology (which is still artisanal, for the industrial is as yet unborn), the machine is obviously a capital object; now most of the *Encyclopedia*'s machines are made out of wood; they are enormous, highly complicated scaffoldings in which metal frequently supplies only notched wheels. The wood which constitutes them keeps them subservient to a certain notion of *play*: these machines are (for us) like big toys; contrary to modern images, man, always present in some corner of the machine, does not accompany it in a simple relation of surveillance; turning a crank, pressing a pedal, spinning a thread, he participates in the machine in a manner that is both active and delicate; the engraver represents him for the most part dressed neatly as a gentleman; this is not a worker but a little lord who plays on a kind of technological organ, all of whose gears and wheels are exposed; what is striking about the Encyclopedic machine is its absence of secrecy; in it there is no hidden place (spring or housing) which would magically conceal energy, as is the case with our modern machines (it is the myth of electricity to be a self-generated, hence enclosed, power); the energy here is essentially transmission, amplification of a simple human movement; the Encyclopedic machine is never anything but an enormous relay; man is at one term, the object at the other; between the two, an architectural milieu, consisting of beams, ropes, and gears, through which, like a light, human strength is simultaneously developed, refined, focused, and enlarged: hence, in the gauze-loom, a little man in a jacket, sitting at the keyboard of a huge wooden machine, produces an extremely fine web, as if he were playing music; elsewhere, in a completely bare room, containing only a maze of wood and tarred ropes, a young woman sitting on a bench turns a crank, while her other hand rests gently on her knee. A *simpler* idea of technology is inconceivable.

An almost naïve simplicity, a kind of Golden Legend of artisanry (for there is no trace of social distress): the *Encyclopedia* identifies the simple, the elementary, the essential, and the causal. Encyclopedic technology is simple because it is reduced to a two-term space: the causal trajectory which proceeds from substance to object; hence all the plates which involve some technological operation (of transformation) mobilize an aesthetic of bareness: huge, empty, well-lighted rooms, in which man cohabits alone with his work: a space without parasites, walls bare, tables cleared; the simple, here, is nothing but the vital; this is made explicit in the bakery; as a primary element, bread implies an austere site; on the other hand, pastry, belonging to the order of the superfluous, proliferates in instruments, operations, products, whose fussy ensemble constitutes a certain *baroque*. In a general way, the object's *production* sweeps the image toward an almost sacred simplicity; its *use*, on the other hand (represented at the moment of sale, in the shop), authorizes an embellishment of the vignette, abounding in instruments, accessories, and attitudes: austerity of creation, luxury of commerce, such is the double regime of the Encyclopedic object: the density of the image and its ornamental charge always signifies that we are shifting from production to consumption.

Of course, the object's pre-eminence in this world derives from an inventorying effort, but inventory is never a neutral idea; to catalogue is not merely to ascertain, as it appears at first glance, but also to appropriate. The *Encyclopedia* is a huge ledger of ownership; [...] Formally (this is apparent in the plates), ownership depends on a certain dividing up of things: to appropriate is to fragment the world, to divide it into finite objects subject to man in proportion to their very discontinuity: for we cannot separate without finally naming and classifying, and at that moment, property is born.

[...] the plates of the *Encyclopedia* are always populated; [...] you can imagine the most naturally solitary, "savage" object; be sure that man will nonetheless appear in a corner of the image; he will be considering the object, or measuring it, or surveying it, using it at least as a spectacle; [...] what is striking in the entire *Encyclopedia* (and especially in its images) is that it proposes a *world without fear*. [...] We can even specify more clearly what the man of the Encyclopedic image is reduced to—what is, in some sense, the very essence of his humanity: his hands.

[...]

[I]f you read the plate from bottom to top, you obtain in a sense an experiential reading, you relive the object's epic trajectory, its flowering in the complex world of consumers; you proceed from Nature to sociality; but if you read the image from top to bottom, starting from the vignette, it is the progress of the analytic mind that you are reproducing; the world gives you the usual, the evident (the scene); with the Encyclopedist, you descend gradually to causes, to substances, to primary elements, you proceed from the experiential to the causal, you intellectualize the object. The privilege of the image – opposed in this to writing, which is linear – is to compel our reading to have no specific meaning: an image is always deprived of a logical vector (as certain modern experiences tend to prove); those of the *Encyclopedia* possess a precious circularity: we can read them starting from the experiential or, on the contrary, from the intelligible: the real world is not reduced, it is suspended between two great orders of reality, in truth, irreducible orders.

Such is the informative system of the Encyclopedic image. Yet the information does not end with what the image could say to the reader of its period: the modern reader also receives from this old image certain information which the Encyclopedist could not foresee: historical information, first of all: it is quite evident that the plates of the *Encyclopedia* are a mine of precious data as to the civilization of the eighteenth century [...] it is one of the *Encyclopedia*'s great gifts to *vary* the level on which one and the same object can be perceived, thereby liberating the very secrets of form: seen through the microscope, the flea becomes a horrible monster, caparisoned with plates of bronze, armed with steel spines, with the head of a wicked bird, and this monster achieves the strange sublimity of mythological dragons;

[...]

As we see, Encyclopedic poetics are always defined as a certain unrealism. It is the *Encyclopedia*'s wager (in its plates) to be both a didactic work, based consequently on a severe demand for objectivity (for "reality"), and a poetic work in which the real is constantly overcome by *some other thing* (the *other* is the sign of all mysteries). By purely graphic means, which never resort to the noble alibi of *art*, Encyclopedic drawing explodes the exact world it takes as its subject. [...] In its very order (described here in the form of the syntagm and the paradigm, the vignette and the bottom of the page), the Encyclopedic plate accomplishes this *risk* of reason. The vignette, a realistic representation of a simple, familiar world (shops, workshops, landscapes) is linked to a certain tranquil evidence of the world: the vignette is calm, reassuring; what can be more deliciously domestic than the kitchen garden with its enclosing walls, its espaliers in the sun? [...] In this Encyclopedic heaven (the upper part of the plates), evil is infrequent; scarcely a trace of discomfort over the hard labors of the glassworkers, armed with pathetic tools, poorly protected against the terrible heat; and when Nature darkens, there always remains a man somewhere to reassure us: a fisherman with a torch beside the night sea, a scientist discoursing before the black basalts of Antrim, the surgeon's light hand resting on the body he is cutting open, figures of knowledge inserted into the heart of the storm. [...] Yet as soon as we leave the vignette for the more analytic plates or images, the world's peaceful order gives way to a certain *violence*. All the forces of reason and unreason concur in this poetic disquiet; first of all metaphor itself makes an infinitely ambiguous object out of a simple, literal object: the sea urchin is *also* a sun, a monstrance: the named world is never certain, constantly fascinated by divined and inaccessible essences; and then, above all (and this is the final interrogation raised by these plates), the analytic mind itself, armed with triumphant reason, can only double the explained world by a new world *to be explained*, according to a process of infinite circularity which is that of the dictionary itself, wherein the world can be defined only by other words; [...] In a general way, the *Encyclopedia* is fascinated, at reason's instance, by the *wrong side* of things: it cross-sections, it amputates, it turns inside out, it tries to get *behind* Nature. [...] [O]nce the first nature is dissolved, another nature appears, quite as formed as the first. In a word, the fracture of the world is impossible: a glance suffices – ours – for the world to be eternally complete.

3

From *The Archaeology of Knowledge*

Michel Foucault

Introduction

For many years now historians have preferred to turn their attention to long periods, as if, beneath the shifts and changes of political events, they were trying to reveal the stable, almost indestructible system of checks and balances, the irreversible processes, the constant readjustments, the underlying tendencies that gather force, and are then suddenly reversed after centuries of continuity, the movements of accumulation and slow saturation, the great silent, motionless bases that traditional history has covered with a thick layer of events. The tools that enable historians to carry out this work of analysis are partly inherited and partly of their own making: models of economic growth, quantitative analysis of market movements, accounts of demographic expansion and contraction, the study of climate and its long-term changes, the fixing of sociological constants, the description of technological adjustments and of their spread and continuity. These tools have enabled workers in the historical field to distinguish various sedimentary strata; linear successions, which for so long had been the object of research, have given way to discoveries in depth. From the political mobility at the surface down to the slow movements of 'material civilization', ever more levels of analysis have been established: each has its own peculiar discontinuities and patterns; and as one descends to the deepest levels, the rhythms become broader. Beneath the rapidly changing history of governments, wars, and famines, there emerge other, apparently unmoving histories: the history of sea routes, the history of corn or of gold-mining, the history of drought and of irrigation, the history of crop rotation, the history of the balance achieved by the human species between hunger and abundance. The old questions of the traditional analysis (What link

Michel Foucault, "Introduction," pp. 3–7, 10–11 from R. D. Laing, *The Archaeology of Knowledge*, trans. Alan M. Sheridan Smith. London and New York: Routledge, 1989. Reprinted by permission of Taylor & Francis.

should be made between disparate events? How can a causal succession be established between them? What continuity or overall significance do they possess? Is it possible to define a totality, or must one be content with reconstituting connexions?) are now being replaced by questions of another type: which strata should be isolated from others? What types of series should be established? What criteria of periodization should be adopted for each of them? What system of relations (hierarchy, dominance, stratification, univocal determination, circular causality) may be established between them? What series of series may be established? And in what large-scale chronological table may distinct series of events be determined?

At about the same time, in the disciplines that we call the history of ideas, the history of science, the history of philosophy, the history of thought, and the history of literature (we can ignore their specificity for the moment), in those disciplines which, despite their names, evade very largely the work and methods of the historian, attention has been turned, on the contrary, away from vast unities like 'periods' or 'centuries' to the phenomena of rupture, of discontinuity. Beneath the great continuities of thought, beneath the solid, homogeneous manifestations of a single mind or of a collective mentality, beneath the stubborn development of a science striving to exist and to reach completion at the very outset, beneath the persistence of a particular genre, form, discipline, or theoretical activity, one is now trying to detect the incidence of interruptions. Interruptions whose status and nature vary considerably. There are the *epistemological acts and thresholds* described by Bachelard: they suspend the continuous accumulation of knowledge, interrupt its slow development, and force it to enter a new time, cut it off from its empirical origin and its original motivations, cleanse it of its imaginary complicities; they direct historical analysis away from the search for silent beginnings, and the never-ending tracing-back to the original precursors, towards the search for a new type of rationality and its various effects. There are the *displacements* and *transformations* of concepts: the analyses of G. Canguilhem may serve as models; they show that the history of a concept is not wholly and entirely that of its progressive refinement, its continuously increasing rationality, its abstraction gradient, but that of its various fields of constitution and validity, that of its successive rules of use, that of the many theoretical contexts in which it developed and matured. There is the distinction, which we also owe to Canguilhem, between the *microscopic* and *macroscopic scales* of the history of the sciences, in which events and their consequences are not arranged in the same way: thus a discovery, the development of a method, the achievements, and the failures, of a particular scientist, do not have the same incidence, and cannot be described in the same way at both levels; on each of the two levels, a different history is being written. *Recurrent redistributions* reveal several pasts, several forms of connexion, several hierarchies of importance, several networks of determination, several teleologies, for one and the same science, as its present undergoes change: thus historical descriptions are necessarily ordered by the present state of knowledge, they increase with every transformation and never cease, in turn, to break with themselves (in the field of mathematics, M. Serres has provided the theory of this phenomenon). There are the *architectonic unities* of systems of the kind analysed by M. Guéroult, which are concerned not with the description of cultural influences, traditions, and continuities, but with internal coherences, axioms, deductive connexions, compatibilities. Lastly, the most radical discontinuities are the breaks effected by a work of theoretical transformation 'which establishes a science by detaching it from the ideology of its past and by revealing this past as ideological'.[1] To this should be added, of course, literary analysis, which now takes as its unity, not the spirit or sensibility of a period, nor 'groups', 'schools', 'generations', or 'movements', nor even the personality of the author, in the interplay of his life and his 'creation', but the particular structure of a given *oeuvre*, book, or text.

And the great problem presented by such historical analyses is not how continuities are established, how a single pattern is formed and preserved, how for so many different, successive minds there is a single horizon, what mode of action and what substructure is implied by the interplay of transmissions, resumptions, disappearances, and repetitions, how the origin may extend its sway well beyond itself to that conclusion that is never given – the problem is no longer one of tradition, of tracing a line, but one of division, of limits; it is no longer one of lasting foundations, but one of transformations that serve as new foundations, the rebuilding of foundations. What one is seeing, then, is the emergence of a whole field of questions, some of which are already familiar, by which this new form of history is trying to develop its own theory: how is one to specify the different concepts that enable us to conceive of discontinuity (threshold, rupture, break, mutation, transformation)? By what criteria is one to isolate the unities with which one is dealing; what is *a* science? What is an *oeuvre*? What is *a* theory? What is *a* concept? What is *a* text? How is one to diversify the levels at which one may place oneself, each of which possesses its own divisions and form of analysis? What is the legitimate level of formalization? What is that of interpretation? Of structural analysis? Of attributions of causality?

In short, the history of thought, of knowledge, of philosophy, of literature seems to be seeking, and discovering, more and more discontinuities, whereas history itself appears to be abandoning the irruption of events in favour of stable structures.

But we must not be taken in by this apparent interchange. Despite appearances, we must not imagine that certain of the historical disciplines have moved from the continuous to the discontinuous, while others have moved from the tangled mass of discontinuities to the great, uninterrupted unities; we must not imagine that in the analysis of politics, institutions, or economics, we have become more and more sensitive to overall determinations, while in the analysis of ideas and of knowledge, we are paying more and more attention to the play of difference; we must not imagine that these two great forms of description have crossed without recognizing one another.

In fact, the same problems are being posed in either case, but they have provoked opposite effects on the surface. These problems may be summed up in a word: the

---

[1] L. Althusser, *For Marx*, London, Allen Lane; New York, Pantheon, 1969, p. 168.

questioning of the *document.* Of course, it is obvious enough that ever since a discipline such as history has existed, documents have been used, questioned, and have given rise to questions; scholars have asked not only what these documents meant, but also whether they were telling the truth, and by what right they could claim to be doing so, whether they were sincere or deliberately misleading, well informed or ignorant, authentic or tampered with. But each of these questions, and all this critical concern, pointed to one and the same end: the reconstitution, on the basis of what the documents say, and sometimes merely hint at, of the past from which they emanate and which has now disappeared far behind them; the document was always treated as the language of a voice since reduced to silence, its fragile, but possibly decipherable trace. Now, through a mutation that is not of very recent origin, but which has still not come to an end, history has altered its position in relation to the document: it has taken as its primary task, not the interpretation of the document, nor the attempt to decide whether it is telling the truth or what is its expressive value, but to work on it from within and to develop it: history now organizes the document, divides it up, distributes it, orders it, arranges it in levels, establishes series, distinguishes between what is relevant and what is not, discovers elements, defines unities, describes relations. [. . .] The document is not the fortunate tool of a history that is primarily and fundamentally *memory*; history is one way in which a society recognizes and develops a mass of documentation with which it is inextricably linked.

[. . .]

[T]he new history is confronted by a number of methodological problems, several of which, no doubt, existed long before the emergence of the new history, but which, taken together, characterize it. These include: the building-up of coherent and homogeneous *corpora* of documents (open or closed, exhausted or inexhaustible corpora), the establishment of a principle of choice (according to whether one wishes to treat the documentation exhaustively, or adopt a sampling method as in statistics, or try to determine in advance which are the most representative elements); the definition of the level of analysis and of the relevant elements (in the material studied, one may extract numerical indications; references – explicit or not – to events, institutions, practices; the words used, with their grammatical rules and the semantic fields that they indicate, or again the formal structure of the propositions and the types of connexion that unite them); the specification of a method of analysis (the quantitative treatment of data, the breaking-down of the material according to a number of assignable features whose correlations are then studied, interpretative decipherment, analysis of frequency and distribution); the delimitation of groups and sub-groups that articulate the material (regions, periods, unitary processes); the determination of relations that make it possible to characterize a group (these may be numerical or logical relations; functional, causal, or analogical relations; or it may be the relation of the 'signifier' (*signifiant*) to the 'signified' (*signifié*)).

All these problems are now part of the methodological field of history.

Part I

Knowledge, Taste, and Sublimity, *c*.1750–1830

Introduction

Abigail Harrison-Moore

This section aims to demonstrate, through its selection of texts and their inter-action and intersection, the methodologies by which eighteenth-century archi-tecture and design history has been understood. By drawing on key themes and key figures in this period of history I not only want to provide a historical reading of the eighteenth century, but also a historiographical one.

The architecture and design of the eighteenth century are often seen through the lens of historical thinking of the period in which it was produced. As Dana Arnold highlights in *Reading Architectural History*,

> From the later nineteenth century onwards architecture was conceived and written about in a more historicizing and self-conscious way, which either provided or facilitated the formulation of a theoretically based historical analysis. In our period, however, at the moment when history was emerging as a quasi-scientific, historical discipline, the duty of the historian was, according to key thinkers such as Ranke, writing in the 1830s, "simply to show how it really was." This has had resonance through three generations of historians and has in many ways continued to the present day in the strong empirical tradition whereby "hard" facts, "estab-lished" at the expense of interpretation, are allowed "to speak for themselves." (2002: xv–xvi)

"The Country House: Form, Function and Meaning" (1999) provides an over-view of approaches taken to eighteenth-century design history, focusing on the key themes of biography (of the architect and/or the patron), style, and society. These are useful for our purposes as they allow us to classify a number of the texts in this section. Key themes that will also be explored are the influence of gender, class, and nostalgia on the reading of architecture and design history.

Knowledge

The exploration of eighteenth-century design history has been dominated by a focus upon the archive document. While this provides us with an interesting and vital starting-point, we need to question the reliance on the archive to "speak the truth" – no document can tell us more than its author thought at the moment of its production – and this information is then processed by the historian. One should not, as Carr (1978) reminds us, make a fetish of the "facts," since by themselves they do not constitute history. In our introduction we explored this idea further, but how do the authors selected in this section reflect the dominance of the archive?

A building or an object, like a work of art, is a text that can be read. It is open to multiple and varied interpretations which can explore the interface between different discourses relevant to social and cultural theory. The late eighteenth-century proliferation of pattern-books, often core archive texts for the historian reviewing the period, and illustrated by the inclusion of selections from Robert and James Adam's three-volume *Works in Architecture* (1773, 1779, and 1882 – the last volume was published posthumously) in this anthology, betray how architecture and material culture came to be seen as self-consciously constructed artifacts with a recognized process for consumption. How was aesthetic information disseminated in the late eighteenth and early nineteenth centuries, and how were these texts received? The pattern-book can act as a guide to this process, both for its contemporary audience and for the present-day historian. According to Pierre Bourdieu (1992), taste is not merely a reflection of class distinctions but also the instrument by which these distinctions are created and maintained. It is active, not passive. In the late eighteenth century, England was increasingly a literate and visual culture which depended on texts and images for information and which placed a new value on appearances. In this new, commercial culture, where one engaged in public life through economic and intellectual exchange, sociability and refinement were valued as much as wealth. The self-conscious production of classical architectural styles such as those employed by Adam, and the amassing of collections of revivalist and historic objects, were both indications of wealth, taste, and status. The proliferation of published material and the development of a print culture made architecture and furniture available to an ever-expanding range of publics. Alexander Pope, in his *Epistle to Lord Burlington* (1730–1), tells us of the impact of the pattern-book on architecture, particularly on the design of country houses, and mocks the gentleman-designer who copies ornamental features in an attempt to create a classical power-house: "Conscious they act a true Palladian part / And if they starve, they starve by rules of art." Pattern-books can be problematic when used as an archive, as often they were produced with a clear subjective aim in mind. Right from the earliest stage of his career Robert Adam was aware of what was necessary to create and advance himself. He decided to go to Rome in 1755 with the aim of developing a practice in London, afraid of his "genius" being "thrown away upon Scotland."

31

With respect to England ... there you have rivals, and these not unformidable: you have people of real taste, and not few of them. The first will do all they can to destroy real merit and others will judge and from that condemn or approve. For this reason it is evident that unless one can appear equal if not superior to these antagonists, so as to acquire the preference from the connoisseurs, all attempts to succeed, even with good interest, won't continue for any tract of time, so that after a little blaze you are sent home with little honour and less profit. These considerations made me determine to go to the bottom of things – to outdo Chambers. (quoted in Harris 2001: 1)

Adam was competitive from the first. The *Works* therefore need to be read against the commercial background of an eighteenth-century architectural practice, as a part of

A history of the consumption of culture [that] reveal[s] to us the ways in which the mass consumption of objects of commerce and high culture meets (and perhaps might be increasingly made to meet) the specific psychological and cultural needs of dynamic social groups, providing them with a sense of individual identity, social connection and community. (Bermingham and Brewer 1997: 4)

Adam's pattern-book was vital within the patterns of social consumption as a signifier of elite taste. This is evidenced also by the chapter from John Summerson's *Architecture in Britain, 1530–1830*, part of which is published here, and its section on "Books and the Palladian Movement." Summerson surveys the vast number of English publications on classical, and particularly Palladian, design produced during the years 1714–40. These texts acted as guidebooks for the connoisseur, the patron, and the "man of taste"; but they have also acted as guides for the historian, dominating the archive, and ensuring that a body of work exists that confirms and supports the classical style. They have been used as "evidence" for a teleological history that traces design in both Britain and the US back to specifically Graeco-Roman origins; yet they not only defined popular taste but also responded. to it and were part of "this new urban and urbane commercial culture." As Bermingham and Brewer, amongst others, have observed, "wealth by itself was of no use if it could not also function in the symbolic and aesthetic realm of bourgeois sociability" (Bermingham and Brewer 1997: 12; see also Appadurai 1986; Douglas and Isherwood 1979). For example, Adam's London ambitions were greatly advanced in his mind by Piranesi, an important figure in London print culture, dedicating his plan of ancient Rome to him, "He envisaged his name sailing before him in print, giving a 'vast notion' of him to all the connoisseurs in England and Scotland whose 'preference' he sought to acquire" (Harris 2001: 1). Adam recognized the self-advertisement opportunities that this print culture offered him, following in the footsteps of successful publications such as Robert Woods's *Palmyra* (1753) and *Balbec* (1757), which, alongside Stuart and Revett's *Antiquities of Athens*, did much to advance the classical cause. Adam's first response was to produce his own archaeological investigation of the remains of the late Roman ruins of the palace of Diocletian at Spalatro in Dalmatia. On his return to England in January 1758 he brought with him an assorted collection of drawings, pictures, antique fragments, vases, figures, bas-reliefs, and other ornaments to impress those of rank and fashion in his Lower Grosvenor Street house. His *Works*, first published in 1773, have to be read in the light of this. To coincide with the publication in April 1779 of the second volume, "Roger Shanhagan, Gent" (a pseudonym for the painter Robert Smirke) issued a satirical skit entitled *The Exhibition or a Second Anticipation; being remarks on the Principle Works to be exhibited next month at the Royal Academy* containing a scathing attack on the Adam brothers, although they were not exhibitors (Harris 2001: 16). Such an attack demonstrates that the *Works* was seen as a flawed document in its own time and today should be approached, as Harris (2001: 187) reminds us, with "some caution" as an archive.

The opening up of the archives of the English country houses in the post-war period led to a renewed focus on the nation's past. Benefiting from this was the most notable architectural historian in England at this time, Sir John Summerson, whose work has been chosen to open this section. Published after the success of *Georgian London* in 1945, *Architecture in Britain, 1530–1830* (1953) offers a reading of the documents of our architectural past founded in a type of British empirical tradition which makes a clear link between the past and the present and offers a lucid, illustrated route through the development of architecture in this period. Arnold's text, "The Country House: Form, Function and Meaning," provides a critique of this book, highlighting its Hegelian tracking of architectural history with classicism and the influence of Palladianism. Summerson uses his archives to focus on a synchronic processing of historical development in architectural styles, which, although comprehensive and still vital for the student of architecture in Britain, omits as much as it includes in its need to focus on a singular, linear progression of design.

Biography

Roland Barthes (1977) reminds us that "The explanation of a work is always sought in the man/woman who produced it." Thus, the "authors" of architectural and design history, from whom these editors are seeking a historiographical thread to this anthology, in turn focus their gaze often exclusively on the "authors" of the designs produced during their period of study. It is to this latter hegemonically biographical approach to architectural and design history that we must turn in order to examine the dominance of the monograph in eighteenth-century architectural and design studies. The period has been explored using certain key names, all of whom, amongst others, feature in this section's texts, including Adam, Nash, Jefferson, Boullée, and Schinkel. Why does Adam, for example, assume such a leading role in the discourse? According to Summerson (chapter 4), "From about 1760 till about 1790, a period of thirty years, English architecture was dominated ... by two men," Adam and William Chambers. There were many more architects working at this time who were involved in a number of key country house commissions. Why does Summerson, therefore, ascribe to them such a leading role? A Hegelian discourse focuses on particular named architects who are seen as representing, often in retrospect, the apex of each architectural movement. This is clearly demonstrated by the number of texts that refer to an "Adam style," implying that architecture can be explained solely through the architect, leading to a biographical reading of the archive. This biographical approach also tends to ignore or downplay the fact that many country houses are the result of a number of architects' ideas and designs. For example, Harewood House in Yorkshire, often described as an "Adam house," as it exists today, can be attributed to a number of named designers including John Carr, Robert Adam, Charles Barry, the owner Edwin Lascelles, and the estate workers and local builders. In locating Harewood exclusively in the framework of Adam's oeuvre we must consider whether or not other interpretations and meanings are obscured.

French philosopher Michel Foucault's premise that the proper name is "more than a gesture, a finger pointed at someone, it is to a certain extent, the equivalent of a description" may offer a solution to the dilemma of the focus on the "author" in architectural and design history (Foucault 1981). When we use the name "Adam" we are using a word that means one or more of a series of definite descriptions, and yet, as Foucault stated in "What Is an Author?" (first published in 1979), the major problem encountered when considering the plurality of an author is "the link between a proper name and the individual being named and the link between an author's name and that which it names are not isomorphous and do not function in the same way."

Many attributions to a single architect or designer are based simply on visual analysis alone, a method endorsed by Sir Howard Colvin in his preface to *A Biographical Dictionary of British Architects, 1600–1840* and by Christopher Gilbert in his celebrated monograph on Thomas Chippendale Senior, the most famous of the eighteenth-century English cabinet-makers, where "an attribution is advanced solely on the grounds of stylistic analogy with *proven* (my italics) furniture in other collections" (1978: ix). It should be noted, however, that this type of analysis depends on the analyzer being deemed expert enough to make such a decision and, thus, we find historians being associated with specialist areas of interest, and often one historian dominating the analysis of one particular designer or architect. Yet, according to Barthes, "writing is the destruction of every voice, of every point of origin. Writing is that neutral, composite, oblique space, where our subject slips away. As soon as a fact is narrated ... the voice loses its origin" (Barthes 1977: 208). However vast the archival research, the documents therein will always be subject to the subjectivity of the time, their author(s), and their interpreters. A biographical approach is limited in chronological terms by the life of an architect, how a building corresponds to that architect's overall practice, and whether it comes at the beginning, middle, or end of the career in question and thereby implies some sort of progress. Terms such as "Adam style" or "Adamesque" demonstrate how a relationship is often transferred from biographical detail to the analysis of buildings, objects, or interiors. This presents difficulties when one considers that a designer often only works on one period of a design's gestation, and in its lifetime a building or interior will have been subject to renovation and change by many other hands. Most importantly, the biographical focus on the architect or the patron divorces the building or object from its function, from the theory of the processes of design, and from its broader social and cultural significance; therefore, "to this end, architecture [and design] is presented in a kind of historical cul-de-sac divorced from any contemporary or theoretical meaning it may have" (Arnold 2002: 41).

Taste

Historical writing is often subject to the fashions and interests of its time – we have witnessed designers and architects fall in and out of fashion for centuries. Thus, one should always consider the social and cultural environment in which a text of architectural and design history is produced since this can lead to a fruitful analysis of value-judgments, allowing us helpful insights into whose values are privileged at which historical moments and why and how such values change, are demoted, or are reinvested with significance at various times and eras.

A history of style is as problematic as one based on specifically named designers. An aesthetic reading proposes that design is autonomous, but an object cannot be divorced from its context and a building is more than a set of façades. Both correspond to and are a part of the function of social and cultural relationships: "A building [or object] is never primarily a work of art. Its purpose cannot be separated from itself without losing some of its reality" (Gadamer 1979: 140–2). It also does not acknowledge that at each period different styles coexist and their dominance or otherwise can be as much a product of the historian's aims and interest as any quantification of contemporary preference or zeitgeist.

The history of style in the eighteenth century has been dominated by classicism, but we can also see it measured according to national and political history and specifically the reign of monarchs. Terms such as "Tudor," "Stuart," "Georgian," "Regency," "Victorian," etc. would appear to subjugate the aesthetic and instead privilege the political dominance of a specific monarch, so that design history becomes a sub-narrative of political history. This may be true in a number of politically focused readings, but we find that when we deconstruct how these headings are used, for example in Stephen Parissien's *Regency Style* (1992), the term is connected to a specific set of codified aesthetic principles loosely linked to the period of the monarch's reign rather than defined by it. "Regency," for example, can be used to describe objects dating from as early as 1790 right up until 1830, which in no way corresponds with the relatively short period of the actual Regency, of 1811–21. Instead "Regency" tends to imply a set of stylistic motifs or ideas, teleologically structured within an all-encompassing term.

Style is usually linked to the social and cultural context of its production. For example, historians have cited Coleshill (ca. 1650 onwards), a country house designed by Sir Roger Pratt in Berkshire, England, as a key building in the foundation of a British Palladian style in the late seventeenth century. But as Mark Girouard highlights in *Life in the English Country House* (1978), we can understand the planning of this house as much through changes in social practice as we can by tracing the adaptation of a symmetrical Palladian villa style in an English context. The movement of the servants to a lower hall, out of sight and mind of the aristocratic owners, forced the architect to conceive a system of back stairs and a central long corridor, to allow access but to maintain a separation of the hierarchies of social life in the house, to move the servants away from public areas except when their services were required. In Girouard's text we see different approaches to architectural history combined, so that stylistic change is linked to social change and thus explains a move away from previous aesthetic concerns. Architects and designers, also, did not always work in one style alone. We see Adam, famed for his neoclassical houses such as Kedleston and Harewood, using a Gothic-inspired exterior for Culzean Castle in Scotland, and Vanbrugh, celebrated as the hero of the Baroque at Castle Howard and Blenheim, adopting a castellated, medieval architecture at Vanbrugh Castle. An emphasis on the classical and those styles derived from Graeco-Roman precedents has resulted in the sidelining of other kinds of decoration, for example, Gothic(k) and chinoiserie, both of which were also important to the eighteenth-century designer. There was no such thing as public uniformity on issues of taste, although we can see certain styles dominating, often as a result of a link to gender, class, and colonial ideologies.

The classical vocabulary of eighteenth-century architecture and design was intended to be "read" by a knowing audience. As a result of influential pattern-books, such as Andrea Palladio's *I Quattro Libri dell' Architettura* (1570), and Colen Campbell's *Vitruvius Britannicus* (published in 1715, 1717, 1725; republished by James Gandon and John Woolf, with volumes 4 and 5, in 1767, 1771), architecture and material culture were full of quotations and reinterpretations of the antique. The importance of the grand tour for young aristocrats led to their recognition of Graeco-Roman art, architecture, and aesthetic ideals as signifiers of a distinctive set of social and cultural values. Remnants of antiquity became part of the currency of the new consumer society, disembodied from their original context but with a related set of meanings. The fact that an object was styled in the antique manner, rather than the original itself, did not seem to concern eighteenth-century collectors. Likewise, there was a proliferation of copies and casts on the market. In contrast to present-day attitudes, the reproduction or revival of the original seems only to have enhanced its aura and that of the copies themselves (Arnold 1998: 115). The commissioning and collecting of revivalist objects has been perceived as a method by which we can create our public persona, but also, and as importantly, as a way of understanding ourselves and the world in which we live by helping us to define our surroundings in social terms, a concept that Bourdieu defines as the *habitus*. Baudrillard (1988) claimed that, "in capitalist societies, consumption may be understood as a process in which only the signs attached to goods are actually consumed." By this he implies that we purchase and collect objects simply because of their semiotic significance. This is an interesting concept if we apply it to the attraction of revivalism at the end of the eighteenth century, as we see revivalist design and texts as "signs" of serious cultural consequence. Historicism in design allows the purchaser to attach him or herself to a notion of worldliness and intellect.

Central to this was the dominance of the Royal Academy, whose teaching was founded in the classical style. Sir John Soane was appointed Professor of Architecture in 1806: his duties were "to read annually six public lectures, calculated to form the taste of the Students, to instruct them for an unprejudiced study of books, and for critical examination of structures" (Watkin 2000: 1). England had been one of the last European powers to adopt the academies of the arts, which, beginning in the Italian Renaissance, had been given a new lease of life by Louis XIV as part of his centralized control of art and production in France. In 1778 Soane was awarded the king's traveling scholarship. He claimed later that he owed the success of his career to this award as it enabled him to make a grand tour in 1778–80. "The Tour was not only important for opening his eyes to the great building of antiquity, but also for enabling him to meet a succession of English noblemen and landowners who became, or introduced him to architectural patrons" (Watkin 2000: 1). Soane's lectures show him wrestling with the history of world architecture and the lessons we should draw from it. He aimed not only to describe and illustrate the architectural masterpieces of antiquity and of subsequent periods, but also to point out what he believed were the universal principles on which they were based,

> In accord with the Enlightenment theorists of the eighteenth century, whose work he studied in preparing the lectures, these principles were, he believed, in accordance with reason and nature. Close study of the greatest buildings would enable the student to "thereby seize the spirit that directed the mind of those who produced" them, a process in which they must "be intimately acquainted with not only what the ancients *have* done, but endeavour to learn from their works what they *would* have done." (Watkin 2000: 3)

In his first lecture, borrowing from Quatremère de Quincy's study of the origin of Egyptian architecture and its relation to the Greek (1803), Soane sets the "primitive" buildings of India, China, and Egypt against a classical standard. In lecture II, he outlines the classical architecture of the ancient world, detailing the importance of the orders. Lecture V, published in this anthology, is devoted to a history of architecture from Constantine the Great and the fall of the Roman empire to the Italian Renaissance, followed by a survey of British architects from Inigo Jones to William Chambers. We see Soane adopting the teleological methodology of classicism that still remains dominant today. This is not to say that he completely rejected other styles of architecture which informed the picturesque styling of his contemporary, Edmund Burke's, sublime. He speaks of Egyptian, Indian, and even Gothic architecture, but these are securely pitched at the periphery of his analysis of "great" design.

> We must now take leave of the charms of Grecian Art and proceed to what is called "Gothic architecture." Although treading on tender ground ... I shall endeavour to discharge my duty to the young students by delivering my opinions on this system of building freely and with as little as possible of the prejudices acquired by long habits and early attachment to Grecian and Roman architecture. (lecture V)

This does not, however, forbid him from calling the Gothic style "prodigious clumsiness," "deficient," and "gloomy." In the end the classical style dominates as "sublime," "correct," "grand," "imposing," "terrific," and ultimately "perfect."

As Soane highlights, the juxtaposition of the classical and the non-classical underlines the classification of our period of study. This can be traced back to the Renaissance historian and the criticism of antiquity in the work of Vitruvius (*De architectura*). Vitruvius supplied the historian with a ready-made taxonomic system by which we could understand and discuss architectural design, codifying the classical orders and proposing a language and grammar by which to understand them. He also understood architecture as having associated values and introduced the idea of truth and morality in the classical style adopted by Giorgio Vasari in his *Lives of the Artists* (1550–68). Vasari's concept of rule, order, measure, drawing, and style provided a focus for the formal critique of design and his demolition of the Gothic, "which could well be called Confusion or Disorder instead," became a powerful influence in the discourse. Academic teaching focused on classical architecture broken down into easily codified and understood rules and formulas, available to the designer and patron alike, exemplified by the pattern-books of Palladio and Campbell. These texts still provide a foundation for the scholar of eighteenth-century design, their influence directing us to question why classicism became so dominant in British and American (colonial) architecture of the eighteenth century and, vice versa, in the work of historians of this period. Why was it so appealing when it is not the apparent indigenous style in Britain and northern Europe? Recent scholars have explored its cultural appeal: a nation, by adopting the classical style, can see itself as the inheritor of the mantle of ancient Greece and Rome and all their associations with power, control, intellectual activity, and military might. Graeco-Roman art, architecture, and aesthetic ideals were recognized as signifiers of a distinctive set of social and cultural values. "Taste classifies and it classifies the classifier" (Bourdieu 1992: 6); cultural objects are embedded in, and help create, systems of classification that are used to discuss and decide everyday life.

As James Deetz points out, a large number of architectural books were available in America from the late seventeenth century onwards, many containing advice and guidance on the use of the classical orders of architecture (cited in Arnold 2002: 101–2). These enabled those with the means to construct "grand edifices" in the classical style, and "buy" into all of its associated values. Texts such as the English surveyor Roger Morris's *Lectures on Architecture* (1734), which rationalized and analyzed Palladio's practice, alongside *Rural Architecture* (1751) and, above all, *Select Architecture* (1757), were much used and can be seen to have had a considerable influence in America in the hands of Thomas Jefferson. Jefferson's most celebrated and "iconic" commission, Monticello, opens up a particular architectural type for questioning, one that has dominated histories of eighteenth-century architecture: the villa.

In using the word "villa" we must be careful about its meaning in an eighteenth-century context. Many writers have ascribed this title to a particular type of building, often, like Summerson (chapter 4), focusing on its styling as a key indicator. Its definition is frequently centered upon tracing Palladian antecedents for the exterior appearance of a building, "exemplified in Stourhead, Mereworth, Newby, and Lord Pembroke's house in Whitehall." Summerson traces the historiography of the term, highlighting the care needed when characterizing an eighteenth-century building as a "villa." But his line-drawings of "Anglo-Palladian Villa Types" propose that we identify it as a particular type of structure, demonstrated by a certain design prototype and based on an external reading of architectural style, imposed often at a later date and not usually by the architect himself. Even the most celebrated English villa, Lord Burlington's at Chiswick, is not referred to in 1727 by William Kent as such, but simply as Lord Burlington's "building." Arnold sees the "grouping together of buildings under a heading of type" as implying "a uniformity of form and function that may not be wholly accurate." She continues by observing that "[s]tylistic uniformity suggests that there were a limited number of sources for the villa. These are assumed to be classical, if not uniquely Palladian. But villas exist in a variety of architectural styles" (1996: ix). She suggests instead that we look to the "idea" of a villa, as having a connection with nature and offering some kind of shelter from the rigors of urban life. Indeed, Horace Walpole clearly demonstrates, in his *Description of a Villa* (1748), that variants on the standard trope of Palladian classicism were possible within villa design. His Gothic-inspired home maps the idea of a villa, marking a retreat out of the urban sprawl of metropolitan London to the suburban pleasures of Strawberry Hill in Middlesex.

Thomas Jefferson's conviction that industry and commerce should be abandoned in favor of an agricultural life fits with this notion that villa life was about a pastoral state of mind. Monticello was located in the virtual wilderness of central Virginia, isolated on the crown of a high hill, intended as both a physical and mental retreat. Jefferson's buildings functioned like Palladio's villas in that they were of a relatively modest size and were often the working headquarters of large plantations. James Ackerman (1995) examines Jefferson's villas as ideologically charged forms based in the imperatives of class structure. Founded in a Marxist critique, which has informed villa studies since the 1970 publication of Reinhard Bentmann and Michael Müller's *The Villa as Hegemonic Architecture*, villa life is examined as an ideologically laden form rather than in simply aesthetic or formal terms or as a papal structure. Ackerman sees villa life as being structured for the elite and constructed on a mythical foundation of rural life set in opposition to the city, its existence requiring the support of a laboring class and slaves. He examines the villa as a colonial tool and as an agricultural compound; throughout, the leitmotif of ideology forms the book's foundational premise. Jefferson, as an "educated colonial patrician," looked to the eighteenth-century British land-owner and his pattern-books for inspiration. His approach to the design of the country estate was grounded in classical learning and, like Burlington, he sur-rounded himself with a "committee of taste," a group of advisors, including Charles Louis Clérisseau, Robert Mills, and Benjamin Henry Latrobe, to provide the Enlightenment values that he desired. We can read Monticello in the same way as the English country house, as a structure of power, deliberately designed in a way that would enhance and enforce Jefferson's standing amongst his peers and his control of his workers.

Sublimity and the Picturesque Style

In inviting Maria Cosway to visit in 1786, Jefferson wrote:

> Our dear Monticello, where has nature spread so rich a mantle under the eye? mountains, forests, rocks, rivers. With what majesty do we there ride above the storms! How sublime to look down into the workhouse of nature, to see her clouds, hail, snow, rain, thunder, all fabricated at our feet! And the glorious sun, when rising as if out of a distant water, just gilding the tops of mountains, and giving life to all nature. (Ackerman 1995: 201)

Jefferson's proclamations on the beauty and sublimity of nature were part of a discursive paradigm circulating in both Britain and America at the turn of the century, derived in large part from the work of Uvedale Price, Richard Payne Knight, and Edmund Burke. Ackerman traces the importance of the work of these English writers on the designers of the American villa, including Andrew Jackson Downing and Alexander Jackson Davis, particularly as it promoted the adoption of an "Elizabethan" or "English Collegiate" style founded in the Gothic styling of Walpole's Strawberry Hill.

Downing's first major work, *The Treatise on the Theory and Practice of Landscape Gardening Adapted to North America; with a View to the Improvement of Country Residences ... with Remarks on Rural Architecture*, published in 1841, was an immediate success, benefiting from the expansion of the publishing industry in nineteenth-century America, where writers without recourse to wealthy patrons could aim their books at a larger and less exclusive clientele. In the chapter entitled "Landscape or Rural Architecture," Downing advocates English picturesque principles and is critical of the "glaring" white Greek revival country houses, personified by Jefferson's designs, favoring instead the Gothic, and especially the Tudor, style above all others. The core of Downing's message was that America was awakening to the possibilities of a life of comfort and leisure and that there was an expanding demand for a less austere domestic architecture that reflected this lifestyle. Further, he believed that an architecture of good taste could elevate the moral fiber of the nation: "He who gives to the public a more beautiful and tasteful model of habitation than his neighbours, is a benefactor to the cause of morality, good order, and the improvement of society where he lives" (quoted in Ackerman 1995: 245). He focused on some key aims: it must observe fitness, which means being useful, functional, and "healthy"; it must express its purpose; and finally, it must have a style that is intrinsically beautiful, one that attracts the observer's notice through the associations he is able to make with it.

Downing defined beauty as being of two sorts, "absolute" and "relative." These may have been his distortion of the idea of the beautiful and the picturesque proposed by Price and Payne Knight, illustrated by two engravings accompanying Knight's poem *The Landscape* (1794), engravings that Downing reinterpreted in his 1841 book, altering the picturesque view by adding conifers, a Hudson River view, and a garden retreat like the "Hermitage" in his own Highland Gardens design (Ackerman 1995: 215). Downing, however, seems to have been attempting to combine the absolutes of classical aesthetics with the individuation of anti-classical picturesque theory and thus clashed with his English mentors, who had devised their theories specifically to jettison absolute standards and to replace them with relative judgments grounded in individual perception and taste.

American writers and designers sought to adapt the aesthetic theories of British Enlightenment philosophy and the picturesque movement, as demonstrated by Thomas Jefferson's use of Edmund Burke's *Philosophical Inquiry into the Origin of our Ideas of the Sublime and the Beautiful* (1757), in which Burke argued that the human passions, especially sympathy, are responsible for our ideas of beauty and sublimity. Humanity's ideas of beauty arose, he argued, from the need for the preservation of society through cooperative social behavior, whereas the ideas of the sublime were related to self-preservation, as terror was inspired by the apprehension of pain or death. Like other Enlightenment philosophers, Burke insisted that ideas of beauty are driven by passion rather than reason. These two distinct passions are illustrated by sets of opposing examples: beautiful objects are small, sublime objects are large; sublime objects are rugged, beautiful objects are smooth, and so on. These theories, drawing on the philosophy of John Locke, moved the attention away from the objects of observation toward the effect on the observer. Initially nobody had wanted to pursue the implications of this change, because to give full value to the response of the individual spectator would have been to undermine the eternal laws and truths of the classical tradition. An informal garden represented the antithesis of classical principles; it could not follow rational proportions nor be judged by absolute standards. Free of the constricting rules of the classical orders and proportions, designers began to embrace a wide variety of styles, including the Chinese and the Gothic. New buildings began to reflect the irregularity of nature, encouraged by writers such as William Gilpin, who in 1789 claimed, "A piece of Palladian architecture may be elegant in the last degree ... But if we introduce it in a picture it immediately becomes a formal object and ceases to please. Should we wish to give it pictur-esque beauty we must use the mallet" (Gilpin 1789: vol. 1, p. 193).

The initial step towards a greater naturalism in landscape design was taken by Lancelot (Capability) Brown, sparking a vigorous theoretical debate in 1794 with the publication of Uvedale Price's *Essay on the Picturesque*, Payne Knight's poem, *The Landscape*, and Humphrey Repton's *Sketches and Hints on Landscape Gardening*. Price and Knight were influenced by Burke's aesthetic of the sublime, but saw it as poorly adapted to architecture and design because, as Price pointed out, it involved responses to the natural environment that could not be built or planted. They therefore set about reformulating the concept of the "picturesque" so it might merge with aspects of the sublime relevant to design. Price commanded the designer to shun the uniform and regular, and encouraged the effects of advanced age, neglect, and decay. This was illustrated by Knight's vivid image of the contrast of the beautiful and picturesque in his illustrations for the poem, one showing an estate with a classical house in a park in the style of Capability Brown, and the other the same site with an Elizabethan mansion in a rugged and unkempt setting.

Knight, however, moved away from Price in his *Analytical Enquiry into the Principles of Taste* (1805) because he could not accept Price's attribution of the quality of picturesqueness to the object of observation. He insisted that only a connoisseur could recognize what is picturesque, after a lifetime of experience with pictures and poetry. For Knight, the picturesque was not only about obser-vation, but also derived from associations stimulated by the object, a pertinent observation from a man who was a collector of the landscape drawings of Claude Lorrain. But, as Ackerman (1995) points out, Knight's effort to limit the appre-ciation of association to the experiences of pictures was artificial, because nothing could bar any train of thought from enriching the way objects are seen. This concept of association legitimized an almost unlimited range of images in the design of objects, gardens, and buildings and allowed the designer to give his work whatever character he believed to be suited to his client, the nature of the setting, or the function of the building.

By limiting our understanding of the picturesque simply to that of a style, we deny the richness and variety of ideas that were associated with it as a design choice in the late eighteenth century. This challenges the principles, vocabulary, and systems of the analysis of style which have mainly been derived from the strict rules of the classical period, and goes some way in explaining the appeal of this style-type to the historians of this period. By granting designers potentialities limited only by the responsiveness of the viewer, the picturesque opens up a whole repertory of ideas, influences, and constructions, and demonstrates the importance of an interdisciplinary approach.

Daniels and Cosgrove offer us an alternative way to read the landscape in their ground-breaking text *The Iconography of Landscape* (1988). They introduced a range of important theoretical developments in landscape history that included post-structuralism, Marxist theories about the political economy of the landscape, and a reinterpretation of iconographic methods of analysis. Informed by the cultural theorist Raymond Williams, the authors emphasize landscape as a phenomenon of visual culture structured by a set of signs. Their premise is that if a painting can be decoded as a body of determinate signs, so too can a landscape. They sought to understand the symbolic representation of class structure, social order, and political ideology inherent in the landscape and its significations (Harris 1994: 1–2). Such an approach necessitates an understanding of landscape as an "instrument or agent of cultural power" (Mitchell 1994: 1–2). The landscape and its representations become important documents for understanding the development of national, social, and political identities – they are at once personal as well as historical, political, ecological, and ideological. Cosgrove and Daniels's work ties a history of style into a history of social use.

City, Society, and Space

Henri Lefebvre, in the *Production of Space* (1991; first published in 1974), is concerned with the lived experience of architecture in terms of space and social practice:

> Social space is not an empty arena within which we conduct our lives, rather it is something we construct and which others construct about us. It is this incredible complexity of social interactions and meanings which we constantly build, tear down and negotiate. And it is always mobile, always changing, always open to reversion and potentially fragile. (quoted in Read 2000: 49)

Lefebvre highlights "the reign of the façade over space," but this façade is only a frame for social activity and has to be read as such. His analysis of the spatial exercise of power as a construction has opened up possibilities for advancing the analysis of spatial politics into the realm of feminist and anti-colonialist discourse. He specifies the operations of space as ideology and sees spatial design as a tool of social control.

We can use these ideas to analyze the city at the turn of the century as a social space. The role of classicism in the pre- and post-revolutionary work of Nash, Latrobe, Boullée, Ledoux, and Schinkel invites questions about nationhood, social control, class structure, and the ideologies of power. Postmodern architectural criticism demands that we analyze the signification of the built environment, in which building façades convey a world of allusions, quotations, and historical precedents.

The French Revolution was the most serious challenge to the social and political structure of England since the "Glorious Revolution" of 1688. It threatened the country militarily, politically, and socially. Between 1788 and 1792 England saw the most sustained radical and reformist activity since the civil wars of the seventeenth century. These movements were greeted with fear and anxiety by the government and the majority of the aristocracy, as they appeared to threaten England's internal and external security. Laws could be passed and political measures taken to ensure the primacy of the state over its populace, but there were more practical and physical measures that could be taken to make London a safer place, for the king and the upper classes (Arnold 1995: 37–50). This could be achieved through urban planning, leading to a separation of the classes as a way of maintaining law and order. Moreover, the introduction of monuments, public buildings, and royal palaces as the focus of this new rational street plan enabled the state to express its power in a new and significant way. It is possible to identify, in John Nash's Regent's Park scheme, a wish on the part of George IV and his ministers to bolster the position of the Crown and enhance the authority of the state. A specific impetus for the scheme in London was the competition of other European cities, particularly Paris. Nash visited the city in 1814 and 1815 and was impressed by Napoleon I's creation of the straight rue de Rivoli with its classical arcades, inspiring his design for Regent Street. His report of 1812 set out a coherent, rational plan for London. It was not, however, simply aimed at making London more impressive architecturally. Mindful of the revolution, the choice of Charing Cross as a site for substantial renewal was significant, as it had been the site of sparring matches between the state and the people, of hangings and pillories. The growing presence of some of the city's poorest areas at the edge of St. James was seen as a threat to king, government, and aristocracy. Nash's metropolitan improvements sought to deal with this perceived threat. The plan was presented by Nash under three headings: "Utility to the Public," "Beauty of the Metropolis," and "Practicability." He made no secret of his objective to "provide a boundary and complete separation between the streets and squares occupied by the nobility and gentry, and the narrow streets and meaner houses occupied by the mechanics and the trading parts of the community" (Nash 1828: 74).

If we consider the styling of the great turn-of-the-century cities across the world, including London, we see in each the dominance of the classical tradition. Nash's Regent's Park scheme seemed to look to the Continent for its influences. Summerson proposes that the source for social factors as the determinants of design was influenced by his reading in 1804 of C. N. Ledoux's *L'Architecture*, which sets forth a plan for a utopian city. At once a treatise on architecture and its aesthetics and a scientific handbook, as well as a manual for rural instruction and a treatise on political economy, commerce, industry, and public welfare, it was to be read by artists and administrators alike. The classical ideal for city planning as well as for utopian architecture can also be found in Etienne-Louis Boullée's treatise, *Architecture: Essay on Art* (1799). Boullée was inspired by a clear conception of the universe, by the beauty of simple stereometric forms, described by Helen Rosenau (1976) as a "visionary architecture." "He wished to express immensity, eternity and the infinite," which she contrasts with the functionalism of Ledoux. Ledoux, however, is seen to have used and expanded Boullée's prototypes for community centers, and the national and municipal palaces, in his futuristic designs for the Oikema, the Panareteon, and the Temple of Memory Dedicated to the Virtue of Women. Many classicist works of the early nineteenth century are related to traditions originated by Boullée. This is apparent in England as well as in France, where Nash's plan for Regents Park is based, in an abridged form, on Ledoux's Hosten Estate in Paris, which in turn derived influence from Boullée's vision.

All three architects are seen here to combine social planning with an architecture based on the classical tradition. Rosenau relates this right back to the work of Vitruvius and Alberti, especially the latter's *De re aedificatoria*, which discusses the purpose and function of architecture. Boullée's design for a municipal palace, for example, combines a recognition of civic pride with a growing interest in the life of the masses. Ledoux's writings, based largely on Boullée's, develop the social and practical implications of architecture and look forward to the new town, to the utopian movements of nineteenth-century Europe and America. Boullée's choice of a classical style for his utopian dream, derived importantly from "the study of nature," exerted a specific influence on the architecture of the Nazi period, as discussed in Susanne von Falkenhausen's essay on "The Sphere" (chapter 16), and recorded in Albert Speer's *Inside the Third Reich* (1969). Boullée's name is not only included in the index, but, as Falkenhausen demonstrates, his influence is clear in the proposed designs for the center of Berlin.

Post-revolutionary architecture aimed to appeal to the emotions and to be seen as being built for the masses. Although much of Boullée's work remains as design alone, which Rosenau blames this on his individualism, we can see how important an influence the shapes and spaces of antique Rome and the Renaissance, translated through eighteenth-century Paris, had on the circles and spheres of his work. In his *Essai* his theory of symmetry may be regarded as "the fulfilment of the Renaissance view of art" and his influence, although the *Essai*'s mix of royalist and republican leanings made it unsuitable for publication during the Napoleonic era, had a substantial affect on the architects designing and redesigning the new cities of nineteenth-century Europe. Although he admires the Gothic principles of lighting and structure, the *Essai* celebrates the greatness of Roman architecture (while depreciating Greek classicism) as ideal for the planned urban environment. Boullée proposes a functional adaptation of the past combined with an understanding of the meaning of ancient forms that, throughout the eighteenth century, had been seen to demonstrate power, taste, and influence and to separate those who rule from the masses.

Susanne von Falkenhausen explores the sphere in the work of Boullée, Ledoux, and Speer as a metaphor for a political system, highlighting the fact that architects assumed that the spectator, via collective visual memory, would understand the intended meaning. She demonstrates the ability of architectural design to impose meaning through association, and to operate within a system of signification understood by its public. This metaphorical function adds another layer to our understanding of architecture through a social history, demonstrating the importance of reading architecture both physically and psychologically. The sphere is contrasted with the classical dome, and is seen as being used, post-revolution, as a signifier of a new collective vision in France, as a design for the people. As Lefebvre states, social space is not an empty arena; it is a complex realm of social and political metaphors and meanings that need to be questioned and analyzed. Thus, the neoclassical architecture of the early nineteenth-century city has to be read semiologically through a network of associations and ideas, both historically and historiographically.

Karl Friedrich Schinkel, according to Watkin and Mellinghof (1987), wanted "to create an architecture of ennobling quality." Like Boullée, he drew inspiration from Friedrich Gilly, the great German classicist architect, in whose house he was a student in 1799. His work was inspired by the philosophy of J. G. Fichte's study of Greek history and the German past, which he wanted to combine into an architecture that was responsive to public need. With this in mind, his early work linked the Romanticism of the Gothic revival with the classical tradition. However, when he was promoted in the Prussian civil service in 1815 to having responsibility for the development of Berlin, Schinkel's plans, produced in 1817, saw military, cultural, and civic buildings designed in a stern neo-antique way. Schinkel felt that the severer style was historically appropriate for post-1815 Berlin, an economically depressed city after years of military endeavor that, in his mind, needed an ideal architecture to spur on reform. This is well illustrated by his design for the Brandenburg Gate of 1789. For Schinkel, neoclassicism brought to the city a feeling of severity (*Ernst*), dignity (*Holheit*), and strength (*Kraft*) (Watkin and Mellinghoff 1987: 91). He believed that architecture should educate and improve the public by awakening its members to their own identity and to that of the historical culture to which they belonged.

Differencing the Canon

Eighteenth-century architecture and design history have, for the most part, yet to engage with the theoretical paradigms of feminism, post-structuralism, and post-colonialism to identify the power of space, architecture, and the object in the eighteenth century within systems of social control, to learn the lessons of Marx,

Foucault, Spivak, and Lefebvre amongst others, and to deal with the new cultural politics of class, race, and gender from a radical postmodernist perspective. This is not to say that writing on this period should focus solely on rewriting the past in order to acknowledge these questions of the present, but it should not be afraid to acknowledge the questions and how they might help us analyze the past. Homi Bhabha refers to this as the "third space," one which enables other positions to emerge. "This third space displaces the histories that constitute it and sets up new structures of authority, new political initiatives ... the process of cultural hybridity gives rise to something different, something new, a new era of negotiation of meaning and representation" (Read 2000: 140). The hybrid histories of Homi Bhabha in *The Location of Culture* (1994) and other post-colonialist writers encourage us to be ready to go "beyond," to cross boundaries using postmodernism, post-colonialism, and post-feminism, to locate "the in-between space – that which carries the burden of meaning in culture" (Bhabha quoted in Read 2000: 27).

A social history of design, promoted by Mark Girouard and the like, has opened up architecture to questioning how it responds to the practice of the people it supports and contains. These texts, however, as discussed in the introduction, have only explored society in a very limited way, focusing primarily on the lives of the landowners. To explore the "third space" of social history we must, also, listen to the "other" voices in the archive. "The persistence of a naturalised social history of architecture, which proposes that typical forms are an inevitable, logical response to natural conditions and pre-existing structures, has obscured the role architecture – as representation and as correction –plays in the cultural system" (Friedman 1992). The invisibility of women in the canonical histories of eighteenth-century architecture might lead us to believe that women have no history. Customs embedded in the social rituals of power have meant that women have featured in the history of eighteenth-century design simply as wives of patrons, as amateur "lady" designers, or as limited in responsibility to specific design types associated with the "feminine" – embroidery, print rooms, grottoes, and the like. As such, we have seen gender feature in design history only when it matches wider cultural definitions of the behaviors that are considered appropriate for male and female members of society at any given time. We must, however, be careful not simply to replace the patriarchy with a matriarchy and make more assumptions of the archive that map against our own preoccupations by over-classifying history to match a set view of women in society. Yet we can explore other ways of understanding this period that cannot be reduced to a consideration of the white, male, elite. Gender may redirect the narrative structures of history and help our understanding of design in terms of biography, style, social ritual, and cultural practice. This is beautifully illustrated by Falkenhausen's analysis of the gender metaphors in the work of Boullée and Ledoux. The role of women in architecture and design has begun to be explored but rarely in our period of consideration. Alice T Friedman's analysis of Hardwick Hall and its patron, Elizabeth of Shrewsbury (1992), is focused on the earlier period of

1590–1620, the moment seen by historians as initiating the gradual ascendance of Palladian planning over the conventions of the medieval English tradition. Although Friedman is looking at the sixteenth and early seventeenth centuries, her analysis is useful here, as she challenges Summerson's and Girouard's interpretation of this house in order to explore, using a similar archive of household orders, letters, and diaries, the ideological context in which stylistic shifts occur. Both Summerson and Girouard focus on this house; for the former, it marks the beginning of classicism in England, for the latter its planning maps against a specific moment in the social use of the country house. Both can be seen to use an archive of material to present their own particular "take" on history. Friedman could be accused of the same, but her work is vital for highlighting different ways of understanding architectural history and offers a prototype for rereading the past through gender.

Gender has allowed us to question the play of power in the writing of history and its social construction. Eighteenth-century history, however, has rarely taken up the challenge of the theorists, in its ongoing refusal to examine its own conventions and practices. By questioning the methods by which we make histories and organize social relations and modes of production, we can explore the history of design as a history of social change, but we can also reveal the processes that bring about change and how it is reported. The design histories of the twentieth and twenty-first centuries have often been written with this in mind, but the eighteenth-century historian for the most part remains immune.

Is this the fault of the dominance of the archive? The archive is a valid and vital tool for the historian and must not be neglected, but it should be approached with an acknowledgment of the processes and problems involved in understanding historical precedent. The texts in this section aim to help the reader to understand, question, and challenge the past to produce the design histories of the future.

4

Palladian Permeation: The Villa

John Summerson

It will have become apparent that the expression 'Palladian', in relation to English architecture, means considerably more than the imitation of Palladio. Three main loyalties were involved – loyalty to Vitruvius; to Palladio himself; and to Inigo Jones. Vitruvius stood for the fundamental validity of the antique and the value of archaeological inquiry. From Palladio came the general mode of expression of a modern architecture – principles of planning and proportion and the rich potentialities of rustication. Finally, Jones supplied extensions and variations of Palladio and, in addition, ways of treating ceilings and fireplaces which were wanting in Palladio. Without the admission of Jones, Palladianism might have approximated to a High Renaissance purity of composition, modified only by the Mannerist streak in Palladio. Jones, however, had been more eclectic than his admirers knew, and, under his name, the Mannerism not only of Palladio but of Vignola and Domenico Fontana, Scamozzi, Rusconi, and Zanini and, later, of French decorators like Barbet (whose sources were in part Flemish) came into the picture.

'Palladianism' in England from 1715 to 1760 is, in fact, a fairly mixed style and expanded very readily into the further eclecticism from which the Neo-classical point of view emerged. So far we have dealt only with the initiators and leaders of Palladianism. In this chapter we come to the expansion of the style, its deliberate propagation by the Burlingtonian group, and subsequently its exposition by a second generation of architects in whose hands it reached the cold, elaborate finality from which the late eighteenth century energetically revolted.

Lord Burlington, both as an architect and as an intellectual nobleman, was after Campbell the great figure in the first phase of the movement. But he was not the only member of the Whig aristocracy who contributed to its success. His own work at the drawing-board was exceptional (and, in Chesterfield's view, rather improper for a man of his caste), but apart from that he was a representative of

John Summerson, "Palladian Permeation: The Villa," pp. 334–42, 345–8 from *Architecture in Britain 1530 to 1830*. New Haven and London: Yale University Press, 1953. Reprinted by permission of Yale University Press.

a type. Many of his noble contemporaries travelled to Italy as part of their education; many, like the Earls of Leicester and Bessborough, collected antique marbles, and for a hundred years it had been considered the ordinary thing for a gentleman to have some knowledge of architecture. Gentlemen and noblemen who did not actually design (in our sense) often claimed to be their own architects and purchased expensive sets of drawing instruments; and it is not always easy to make out whether or not their pretensions amounted to anything more than the general direction of a building project over the head of a professional man.

There is the case, for instance, of Henry Herbert, 9th Earl of Pembroke (1689–1750), a man almost the same age as Burlington, a friend of his and the heir to Inigo Jones's great work at Wilton. Like Burlington, he pinned his early faith to Colen Campbell, who, as we have seen, built him a house at Whitehall. Later he wielded the dividers himself and has been credited with some half a dozen works. In every case, however, there is an alternative ascription to Roger Morris (d. 1749), the Master Carpenter to the Office of Ordnance, and one is inclined to see here a partnership where the technical skill was mostly on the side of the professional man, working, no doubt, under active and well informed direction. The Pembroke–Morris style was Palladian in the Campbell sense, not the Burling-tonian. A specimen which proved to be an epoch-making model is Marble Hill, Twickenham, built about 1724 for George II's Countess of Suffolk, and reminis-cent of the Earl's own house (by Campbell) at Whitehall. By far the happiest joint effort was the reduction of Palladio's idea for a triumphal bridge to the size required for the ornamental Palladian Bridge at Wilton of 1736, a beautiful transformation which was copied at Prior Park and Stowe. But perhaps Pembroke's greatest claim to fame is less as an architect than as the promoter of Westminster Bridge (1739–47), the first bridge to be built over the Thames at London since medieval times and the first classical bridge of its size in England. The engineer was a Swiss, Charles Labelye (1705–?62), who seems to have followed, in a general way, the humped round-arch type of bridge introduced in Paris under Henri IV. Neither in type nor in its use of rustication did the bridge attempt to be Palladian.

Patronage forwarded the Palladian business in more ways than one. Direct participation in design was one way. The employment of the right artists to build private houses was another way. A third way, by no means less important, was the indoctrination of the Office of Works. The storming of this citadel where, in 1715, the great triumvirate, Wren, Vanbrugh, and Hawksmoor, still held office, was by no means easy, for place-holding was much more an affair of politics than of aesthetics; and Vanbrugh anyway was a perfectly good Whig. However, Burlington, in securing Kent's employment at Kensington Palace over the head of the Serjeant Painter, showed what could be done. In 1718–19 the old régime was finally dislodged. Wren's dismissal was secured, Vanbrugh prevented from entering the office to which he had every right, Hawksmoor similarly excluded from promotion, and William Benson, who had the backing of the German element at Court, put in as Surveyor with Colen Campbell as deputy and (shortly afterwards) Nicholas Dubois as Master Mason. Thus, in 1719, three of the principal officers of the Works were true Palladians – perhaps, indeed, the original Palladians. A fourth office, that of Master Carpenter, fell vacant on the death of Grinling Gibbons in 1721 and was filled by a nominee of Sir Robert Walpole's. That should have made a Palladian majority, but unfortunately Thomas Ripley (d. 1758) had Walpole's patronage for other than artistic reasons, and 'had not the countenance', says Horace Walpole, 'of Lord Burlington'. His Admiralty, Whitehall (1722–6), is scarcely Palladian and nothing but a late and poor specimen of Wren's style, vilely proportioned and adorned with a sort of French quoins which the Palladians had condemned. However, apart from the Admiralty he did little damage, and when he was moved up to the Comptrollership on Vanbrugh's death in 1726, he designed nothing[1] and made room for the Palladians' star performer, William Kent.

The Clerkships in the Works were easier to fill with Palladian nominees, and of these the principal were Henry Flitcroft (1697–1769) and Isaac Ware (d. 1766). Flitcroft was the son of a man employed on the Hampton Court gardens in William III's time and was apprenticed to a joiner. While engaged on some works at Burlington House he broke his leg and was taken on by Lord Burlington as a draughtsman. He redrew, for the engraver, most of the Inigo Jones designs published by Kent and in 1726 was given a Clerkship in the Works. From that office he proceeded to the offices of Master Carpenter (1746), Master Mason (1748), and, finally, Comptroller[2] (1758), which last he occupied until his death. The Works provided him with few opportunities to show his quality as a designer, and his principal work was done independently. The church of St Giles-in-the-Fields (1731–3), for which he was both architect and contractor, is a work which Burlington can hardly have approved, being in fact an unflattering imitation of St Martin-in-the-Fields, without a portico and in every respect less satisfactory than its model. The colossal mansion of Wentworth Woodhouse already mentioned, confirms what the church leads one to suspect, that Flitcroft was somewhat lacking in initiative. Woburn Abbey (c.1747, for the Duke of Bedford) is equally derivative. But Flitcroft was very good up to a point and his town-houses (for example, No. 10 St James's Square, built for Sir W. Heathcote in 1734, and the house adjoining) are perfect examples of the Palladian idea of a London street front reduced to its barest elements.

Isaac Ware was in much the same class as Flitcroft. He was apprenticed to Thomas Ripley when the latter became Master Carpenter and was given a Clerkship in the Works in 1728, holding various offices there till the end of his life, when he was among other things Secretary to the Board, in which office he followed

---

[1] Ripley did, however, design some important houses outside his official sphere. He carried out Houghton Hall, Norfolk, for Walpole, from Colen Campbell's designs (1722–35). In 1724–30 he designed Wolterton Hall, Norfolk, which Horace Walpole considered 'one of the best houses of the size in England'. It is compactly planned round a top-lit staircase, going the full height of the house, and, although scarcely elegant, does, as Walpole says, 'acquit this artist of the charge of ignorance'.

[2] By this time, the Comptrollership was the highest office attainable by a professional architect, the Surveyorship having become a purely political appointment.

Hawksmoor. Like Flitcroft's, his principal works were for private patrons. These included Lord Chesterfield, for whom he built Chesterfield House (1749; destroyed 1934). This consisted of a block somewhat on the lines of Chevening (and houses of the sort among the Jones drawings), but with Corinthian colonnades extending from it to left and right and returning along two sides of a forecourt. Some five years later he built Wrotham Park, South Mimms, Hertfordshire, for Admiral Byng, a house to which we shall have occasion to return. Again like Flitcroft, he built a number of London houses, including, probably, Nos 40 and 41 Berkeley Square, 23 Bruton Street, and 3 Burlington Gardens.

Flitcroft left in manuscript a collection of drawings obviously intended for a comprehensive treatise on architecture. Ware actually produced such a book and *A Complete Body of Architecture* came out in 1756. It was intended to serve as 'a library on [architecture] to the gentleman and the builder; supplying the place of all other books'. It contains a great deal of information and is ably compiled, reflecting very fairly the solid, thoughtful competence of its author's executed works.

To the names of Flitcroft and Ware may be added that of John Vardy (d. 1765), who appears to have been employed by or under Kent and who held several clerkships in the Works. As the clerk in charge of Whitehall at the time of Kent's death he was entrusted with the execution of that master's design for the Horse Guards; and as clerk for Westminster Palace probably designed the house which is now Nos 6 and 7 Old Palace Yard. His most important work, however, was Spencer House (1756–65 for Earl Spencer), a somewhat pretentious Palladian hybrid, something between villa and palazzo. General Gray, of the Dilettanti Society, seems to have supplied the idea.

In capturing the best places in the Office of Works for themselves and their candidates, the Palladian group no doubt hoped that a new Whitehall Palace and a new Palace of Westminster (those two national opportunities which Wren had not been able to spoil) might rise to illustrate supremely the true principles of Palladio and Jones. In this they were disappointed. The burnt site of old Whitehall was squandered upon a variety of large houses and public offices; and at Westminster Kent's imagination was exercised only on paper, and his executed work was limited to some reconstruction at the Law Courts. Their one great London triumph was the Horse Guards. Nevertheless, the establishment of Palladianism as the official style of Great Britain was not without its merits, and when the original Palladians were dead, it remained the only standard to which a new generation of designers could rally.

Books and the Palladian Movement

Campbell's *Vitruvius Britannicus* and Leoni's *Palladio* inaugurated a great period of architectural book publishing. They came out in 1715–17. Within ten years a continuous stream of books had begun to flow from the press, so that between 1725 and Chambers's *Treatise on Civil Architecture* of 1759 nearly every year saw the appearance of one or more illustrated books on architecture. The trend of this literature was generally Palladian, but it varied greatly and was inflected by Gibbs's influence after 1730. The principal works were the great folios sponsored by Burlington himself and including Kent's *Designs of Inigo Jones* (1727), Robert Castell's *Villas of the Ancients* (1728; a series of reconstructions of Roman houses and gardens based on passages in classical literature), and Burlington's own *Fabbriche antiche* (1730), a superb book of engravings from Palladio's own drawings, published in a limited edition, with a preface in Italian. The book of Jones's designs proved very influential and was followed by a slim octavo in which Isaac Ware produced some further *Designs of Inigo Jones* (1735), while John Vardy brought out *Designs of Inigo Jones and William Kent* in 1744.

None of these books contained anything much in the way of critical or theoretical writing and, indeed, the literature of the Palladian movement produced no treatise of any depth or importance. Leoni's translation of *The Architecture of L. B. Alberti* (1726) made available a theoretical work of fundamental, if archaic, importance, but one does not find it much quoted. Almost the only contemporary theoretical writer was Robert Morris, a relative and pupil of Lord Pembroke's man, Roger Morris. He described himself as a surveyor, but no executed works of his are known. His first book, *An Essay in Defence of Ancient Architecture* (1728), was an attack on contemporary work of the Vanbrugh–Hawksmoor school, an unfavourable example of which he illustrated. Six years later he brought out a series of *Lectures on Architecture* (1734), read to a society which he, apparently, had formed. The lectures include a general historical sketch, an exposition of a system of proportion based on cubes, and an analysis of some of Morris's own designs, of which engravings are given. His rationalizations of Palladian practice are very enlightening and show a searching and original mind. Morris was by no means a bigoted Palladian; he admired both Wren and Gibbs. It is difficult to assess the influence, if any, of the *Lectures*, but it is certain that his later books of designs, *Rural Architecture* (1750), the *Architectural Remembrancer* (1751), and, above all, *Select Architecture* (1757), were much used, and that the latter had a considerable influence in America in the hands of Thomas Jefferson.

John Wood of Bath was the author of a curious quasi-philosophical work, entitled *The Origin of Building: or, The Plagiarisms of the Heathen Detected*, written in 1738 and published in 1743. The book depends mainly on Sir Isaac Newton's *Chronology of Ancient Kingdoms Amended* (1728), which challenged the accepted chronology of Egyptian and Israelite history, awarding priority to the latter. Wood adheres closely to the great man's theory but attempts to supply a parallel history of the beginnings of architecture. This leads him to accept Moses' Tabernacle and Solomon's Temple as the first religious architecture in the world, designed at the dictation of God himself. In these divine prototypes the three principal orders were for the first time revealed and were maintained in purity by the Jews until they were copied, secularized, and devalued by the Romans and the arch-vandal Vitruvius. By a series of wild manipulations involving the quaint speculations of Freemasonry, Wood then proceeded to create a pre-Roman druidical culture in Britain, centred in Bath, under the aegis of Apollo, and with a university at Stanton Drew. Stonehenge was involved and became the subject of a separate work, published in 1747. The whole obsessional farrago has some curiosity value in relation to historical thinking of the period; but attempts to discover a connection with Wood's architecture (or anybody else's) have met with little success.

Some interesting architectural criticism is contained in *A Critical Review of the Public Buildings of London* (1734) by an author called (in later editions) Ralph, whose identity has never been established. He is often denounced as hypercritical, and with some justice, for he takes exception to every detail which (in his view) would be foreign to the drawing-board of Palladio or Inigo Jones.

Another type of book altogether is that represented by the works of William Halfpenny who, after producing nearly twenty titles, died in debt in 1755. His first production, *Magnum in Parvo, or The Marrow of Architecture*, appeared in 1722 and again in 1728. The title plagiarizes Venterus Mandey's *Mellificium Mensionis: or the Marrow of Measuring* which had appeared as long ago as 1682 but was still in use (a fourth edition appeared in 1727). Halfpenny's book is designed, as was Mandey's, for the use of the artisan, and gives engravings of the orders, mostly in combination with arches, 'according to the proportions laid down by Palladio'. His next book, *Practical Architecture*, ran to seven editions by 1751. In 1725 came *The Art of Sound Building*, concerned with 'arches, niches, groins and twisted rails' and including, as frontispiece, a design (unexecuted) for Holy Trinity church, Leeds. Its dedication to Sir Andrew Fountaine and the presence of the names of many Richmond tradesmen among the subscribers make it evident that Halfpenny enjoyed patronage at the Court of Queen Caroline. He later moved to Bristol.

Halfpenny produced a book on perspective in 1731. Then, after an interval, came his books of designs, including *A New and Compleat System of Architecture*, 1749. In this he acknowledges the critical help of Robert Morris, but the designs are very individual, and far from Palladian. This and his subsequent books were aimed chiefly at country gentlemen and builders, and include several books of Chinese designs, the first of which, *New Designs for Chinese Temples*, appeared in 1750. It must be close in date to the Chinese buildings at Wroxton, Oxfordshire, which Walpole, in 1753, mentions (without enthusiasm) as the first of their kind. The engravings are exceedingly poor and, since the designs are as much French Rococo as Chinese, they will probably have been concocted from French prints. This and other of Halfpenny's later books, which included Gothic as well as further Chinese patterns, were produced under the joint names of William Halfpenny and his son, John. A total of twenty-three titles is recorded.

Another famous author was Batty Langley (1696–1751), a freemason with a missionary zeal for educating young builders.[3] His output was just about equal to Halfpenny's. He started in 1726 with two books on geometry and architecture for workmen and *A Sure Guide to Builders*, containing engravings of the orders, on the lines of Halfpenny's earlier book. Books on gardening and estate improvement followed in 1728, and on the cultivation of fruit-trees in 1729. From 1730 onwards, probably as a result of the success of Gibbs's *Book of Architecture*, Langley started producing treasuries of designs. *Ancient Masonry* (1734 or 35) is a massive compilation, giving designs for all kinds of architectural features, drawn from a wide range of English and foreign sources, including Gibbs. In 1738 came *The Builder's Compleat Assistant*, which ran into four editions. Many similar works followed. They are all competent, with clear and accurate engravings. Many of the designs are pirated from earlier English or French books. The *Gothic Architecture Restored and Improved* (1742), however, in which Kent's version of Gothic is formalized into 'orders', is a work of some originality and will require our attention in a subsequent chapter.

Abraham Swan, carpenter and joiner, published from 1745 books of designs for staircases, panelling, bridges, domes, roofs, and chimneypieces. They derive from Kent and Inigo Jones and from the Rococo which joiners, cabinet-makers, and plasterers were in the habit of imitating from French models.

The many other books of the period included editions of Palladio, cheaper than Leoni's, in 1736 (by Edward Hoppus), and 1737 (by Isaac Ware), and W. Salmon's *Palladio Londinensis* (1734), a general textbook, with a few Palladian designs. The influence of all these books was to a large extent overridden by James Gibbs's *Book of Architecture*, already mentioned. This had the effect of greatly diluting the Palladian influences, being, in any case, a more suggestive and practical work than the scholarly books patronized by Burlington and far better engraved than those of Halfpenny or Morris. Without Gibbs, the Palladian movement would have achieved a more nearly absolute dominion over English architectural style.

The last important work in the library of Palladian literature was Ware's *Complete Body of Architecture*. But in three years it and many of its predecessors were overshadowed by a book altogether more important, more cultured, and more critical, for with Chambers's *A Treatise on Civil Architecture* (1759), for all its indebtedness to Ware, architectural literature enters a new phase.

The Spread of the Palladian Fashion

The consequences of Burlington's propaganda for a pure Palladian manner were clear enough by 1731 for Alexander Pope to exaggerate and ridicule them. His *Epistle to Lord Burlington*, published in that year, pays tribute to Burlington's own taste and sense, but predicts the vulgarization of his manner.

[3] E. Harris, 'Batty Langley: A Tudor Freemason', *Burl. Mag.*, May 1977.

You show us, Rome was glorious, not profuse,
And pompous buildings once were things of Use.
Yet shall (my Lord) your just, your noble rules,
Fill half the land with Imitating Fools;
Who random drawings from your sheets shall take,
And of one beauty many blunders make;
Load some vain Church with old Theatric state,
Turn Arcs of Triumph to a Garden-gate;
Reverse your Ornaments; and hang them all
On some patch'd dog-hole ek'd with ends of wall;
Then clap four slices of Pilaster on't,
That, lac'd with bits of rustic, makes a Front
Shall call the winds thro' long arcades to roar,
Proud to catch cold at a Venetian door;
Conscious they act a true Palladian part,
And if they starve, they starve by rules of art.

The prophecy was largely justified. Not only in England, but in Scotland and Ireland, Palladianism spread into local schools mostly of very indifferent quality and far, indeed, from the exquisite richness of Chiswick or the studied classicality of Holkham.

In London, of course, the issue of the movement came thick and fast, Palladianism becoming debased by such men as Edward Shepherd (d. 1747), whose Covent Garden Theatre, built for John Rich in 1732, earned the contempt of Kent, and by George Dance I (1695–1768), a mason turned architect, whose Mansion House (1739–53) is both cramped and overdressed. A better building in the same area was the Bank of England (1732–4) by George Sampson, whose design was closely related to the 'Inigo Jones' house in Lincoln's Inn Fields. But Sampson had held a Clerkship in the Works and thus knew better than most what Palladianism was about.

From London, Palladianism was carried to Bath by John Wood, who returned there to pursue his monumental redevelopment schemes in 1727. His career [. . .] is of consequence here as showing how one energetic and successful man could transplant the style to a new locality. For Wood not only built a great part of Bath, but several country houses and the Exchange at Bristol (1740–3), while his reputation spread to Liverpool where he designed (with his son) a building of similar purpose, now the town hall (1748–55).

Most provincial centres at this time had one leading figure, usually a mason who had 'left off his apron', who led the way in design, who designed and built the bigger houses in the town and district and whose manner was copied by lesser men. Among the first generation of Palladians these local men are not yet of great importance, but with the second generation, to which we are now coming, we shall find that they rank nearly equal with the London men and therefore they must be awarded attention accordingly.

[. . .]

The Villa

Turning now from the great practitioners to the field in which they practised, it becomes necessary to investigate what, in the middle of the eighteenth century, was happening to the English country house. We have seen that Colen Campbell, within the decade 1715–1725, set forth a number of important new models. These were of two distinct kinds: (i) the great 'house of parade', exemplified in Wanstead and Houghton and based on seventeenth-century types, and (ii) the 'villa', after Palladio, exemplified in Stourhead, Mereworth, Newby, and Lord Pembroke's house in Whitehall. Of the two sorts of models, it was the 'house of parade' which had, at first, the most resounding success; the derivatives of Wanstead and the derivatives of Houghton make up the grand succession of country houses of the thirties and forties. In the fifties, however, there are signs that these huge fabrics are losing their appeal and by 1760 they have manifestly lost it. The Wanstead type and the Houghton type are being superseded – by the villa.

In using the word 'villa' we must be careful about its meaning in the eighteenth-century context. Palladio himself, from whom the English villa idea ultimately derives, does not call his country houses villas; he calls them *case di villa*, which allows to *villa* the meaning of a country estate as distinct from the owner's house. Throughout the three volumes of *Vitruvius Britannicus* Campbell uses the word villa once only and then with the exact Palladian meaning of a country estate – not just a house. When Kent, in 1727, published plans and elevations of Lord Burlington's villa at Chiswick he did not call it a villa but simply Lord Burlington's 'building' at Chiswick. Gibbs, on the other hand, in his *Book of Architecture* of 1728, calls two of his designs *villas* (italicizing the word) and they happen to be designs for houses in the Thames valley intended for the Duke of Argyll and his brother, Lord Islay, so that Gibbs seems to recognize the villa both as a nobleman's secondary seat and as more or less suburban – a meaning it certainly possessed later on. By 1750 its diminutive character was established, for Robert Morris alludes in a book of that year to 'the cottage or plain little villa' and Horace Walpole uses villa as a diminutive in 1752. It may well be that Lord Burlington's Chiswick villa – small in size and tiny in scale – did more than anything to reduce the villa image from the amplitude it had acquired through the pages of Pliny.

'The Earl of Burlington's seat at Chiswick is properly a villa and by much the best in Britain,' wrote Sir John Clerk of Penicuik after a visit in 1727,[4] and there is no doubt that the house made a great impression. So did Marble Hill. So did Stourhead. But if we look round for imitations of these in the thirties and forties, there are not so very many. Bower House, Havering, London (1729), by Flitcroft is a plain version of the Marble Hill type. Frampton Court, Gloucestershire (1731–3), is an ornate distortion of Stourhead by a Bristol architect, John

---

[4] For this extract from the Penicuik papers I am indebted to Mr John Fleming.

Strachan. Linley Hall, Shropshire (1742–3), is a fascinating interpretation of the villa idea by Henry Joynes, still using his old master Vanbrugh's vocabulary. But these are curiosities and it is only with the 1750s – a generation after the prototype statements – that we find the villa idea really breaking through. Then it certainly does, to the extent that one is tempted to speak of a 'villa revival'. This revival – if we may so call it for the moment – took as its patterns the villa designs of Campbell, Burlington, and Morris. Its course is most easily traced by considering the houses built by two architects already mentioned – Isaac Ware and Sir Robert Taylor – and a third whose career in the main belongs to a later chapter – Sir William Chambers.

Ware's first work in the villa style was Clifton Hill House, built for a Bristol merchant in 1746–50, though the plan is quite commonplace and not what one would expect from the exteriors. Before 1756, he had built two villas in Scotland, both with service wings linked to the houses by passages. In 1755 Sir Robert Taylor built Harleyford Manor, Buckinghamshire, and in 1760–5 Danson Hill, then in Kent, and Asgill House, Richmond, all on the outskirts of London and all for wealthy City men. Asgill House (already mentioned) introduced the half-pediments of Palladio's church-fronts, probably following the example of Kent in a design for a garden building at Chiswick. More striking evidence of the revival is the building of two further imitations of Palladio's Rotonda – one being Nuthall Temple, Nottinghamshire (destroyed), for Sir Charles Sedley and the other Foot's Cray Place, then in Kent, for Bourchier Cleeve, the financier. Both belong around 1754 – a generation after Campbell's Mereworth – and the architect of Foot's Cray was probably Ware; it almost certainly prompted Sir William Chambers's design for Lord Bessborough's villa at Roehampton to which we shall come presently.

To 1754 also belongs what is perhaps the most significant house of the decade – Ware's Wrotham, Hertfordshire, for Admiral John Byng. Here we have a composition consisting of a centre which is palpably a villa (strongly marked by Chiswick influences) to which wings terminating in pavilions are added, the whole thing from end to end being, however, a single continuous house. Nothing could mark more emphatically the ascendancy of the villa idea than this new handling of an arrangement which in outline goes back to Wanstead III but is now reassessed to introduce the fashionable villa element at its centre. If we compare Wrotham with Carr's Harewood, built four years later, we see the crossing of ascendant and descendant types. Harewood is arrived at by telescoping the plan of Wanstead III; Wrotham by expanding a villa into a house of parade.

It is obvious that the works of Ware and Taylor were creating a new situation in country-house design. It is obvious, too, that the villa had been taken up by the new-rich – from 1750 it has strongly mercantile patronage. So that when a newcomer, William Chambers, arrived on the scene fresh from Italy in 1755 it was the villa theme which offered itself as the obvious path for an aspiring talent. But Chambers's work belongs to a later chapter.

5

The Country House: Form, Function and Meaning

Dana Arnold

The country house has been the subject of many different studies from a range of disciplines. Each reveals a new layer of meaning or significance in this most enduring of cultural icons. This book presents a social and cultural history of the country house by focusing on certain moments of its evolution in the eighteenth century. The chapters explore specific instances of the interaction of the architectural form of the country house with its differing social functions and cultural meanings. By using the country house as a lens through which to explore a range of interpretations from a variety of disciplines the country house is shown to be a matrix in which fundamental aspects of the history of the Georgian period are held. This new approach of positioning the architecture and landscaping of the country house within different social and cultural contexts builds on and benefits from preceding studies.[1]

It is important first of all to draw together previous ways of writing about architectural history to show how this study complements them. Of particular interest here is the use of biography, stylistic analysis and social history and their influence on our understanding of the country house.

The attraction of exploring a country house through the life of either its architect or patron – or indeed the interaction of both – is a significant force in the construction of its history. This is particularly the case when the architect or patron has been identified as a major figure in the evolution of the country house, for instance, Colen Campbell's Stourhead, Wiltshire (1720–4) or Horace

Dana Arnold, "The Country House: Form, Function and Meaning," pp. 1–19 from *The Georgian Country House: Architecture, Landscape and Society.* Stroud: Sutton, 1998. Reprinted by permission of Sutton Publishing Ltd.

[1] These include J. Summerson, *Architecture in Britain 1530–1830*, Pelican History of Art (Harmondsworth, many editions, firs published 1953), M. Girouard, *Life in the English Country House* (New Haven and London, Yale University Press, 1978), James Lees Milne, *Earls of Creation* (London, Century Classics, 1986) and C. Hussey, *The English Country House: Georgian*, vols 1–3 (Woodbridge, Antique Collectors' Club, 1984–5).

Walpole's Strawberry Hill, Twickenham (1748 onwards). But there is a divergence within the biographical approach to country house history that has consequences for the way in which the building is presented. The biographical approach is limited by the life of the architect and how the country house corresponds to his architectural practice and whether it comes at the beginning, middle or end of his career. In this way architecture is mapped against the personal development of the designer which implies some kind of progress; this offers a tidy way of bundling together the disparate strands of the evolution of the country house into a neat, coherent and progressive history. And part of the aim of this book is to unravel these strands in order to explore the discontinuities and contradictions of the country house. If the architect is presented as the principal figure involved in the design it can take on his or her characteristics. For instance Robert Adam's work in the field of country house design is often referred to as 'Adam's country houses'. This implies that architecture can be explained solely through the architect, that is through what he said and did. But many architects left no manifesto or statement of intent or any kind of comprehensive archive. In the case of Adam the *Works in Architecture* (vol. I, 1773, vol. II 1779, and vol. III published posthumously, 1822), published with his brother James, reveal little of their approach to design and does not discuss all their major commissions.[2] The biographical way of looking at buildings can present further difficulties. Often a period of extension or renovation or a new project was worked on by more than one architect. If we stay with Robert Adam and consider Kedleston, the Derbyshire seat of Lord Scarsdale and surely one of his finest country houses, the difficulties become apparent.[3] Robert Adam was not the first architect to be involved with the project. Rather, shortly after his return from Italy in 1758 he replaced Matthew Brettingham and James Paine who had produced the initial designs and begun work on the central block and quadrants.[4] Adam worked on the house between *c.*1760–70 and was responsible for the south front, saloon, interior decoration and features in the grounds including the bridge and the fishing house. But George Richardson, a member of Adam's architectural office, produced several important designs including some for the ceilings of the principal rooms.[5] Richardson is tied more closely to the designs as he dedicated his *A Book of Ceilings composed in the Stile of the Antique Grotesque* (1774–6

---

[2] Six noble houses and the Deputy Ranger's Lodge in Green Park were illustrated by Adam. Only three of these were country houses: Syon, Kenwood and Luton Hoo.

[3] For a full discussion of Adam at Kedleston see L. Harris Gervase Jackson-Stops, *Robert Adam and Kedleston: The Making of a Neoclassical Masterpiece* (London, National Trust, 1987)

[4] Paine's role at Kedleston and his relationship with Adam is discussed in C. Webster 'Architectural illustration as revenge: James Paine's designs for Kedleston' in *The Image of the Building: Papers from the Annual Symposium of the Society of Architectural Historians of Great Britain*, 1995, M. Howard (ed.) (London, Society of Architectural Historians, 1996) pp. 83–92 and P. Leach, *James Paine* (London, Zwemmer, 1988) and 'James Paine's design for the south front at Kedleston Hall', *Architectural History*, 40 (1997) pp. 159–70.

[5] Richardson went on to exhibit one of his designs 'The Ceiling executed in the Grecian Hall at Keddlestone' at the Royal Academy in 1776.

and 1793) to Lord Scarsdale. Is Kedleston then an Adam building? And by locating it within the framework of Adam's œuvre are other interpretations and meanings of Kedleston obscured? Houses were often worked on and developed over considerable periods of time. Again Adam's work at Osterley, Middlesex (1763–80) for Robert Child, comprising the portico and interior remodelling, is only one of a series of architectural interventions in the house which dates back to the sixteenth century.[6] Can these interventions comprise the subject matter of architectural history? Moreover, the tendency here is towards description either of what the architect did or the broader perception of the stylistic consequences of the architect concerned. This separates the function of the building, the theory of the processes of architecture and the broader social and cultural significance. To this end the country house is presented in a kind of historical cul-de-sac divorced from any contemporary or theoretical meaning it may have.

The construction of histories of the country house around biographies of patrons also places a distinct perimeter around the level of meaning given to the building. There is no doubt that the patron was an essential factor – s/he initiated the project, imposed personal preferences and not least paid for it. New money often prompted new building projects. For instance, the Child banking family at Wanstead (1714–20)[7] created a country seat made possible only through their splendid wealth. Robert Walpole's Houghton, Norfolk (1722–35) makes a distinct statement about the patron's status and ambitions but emphasis on this underplays the relationship between the different architects involved, particularly Colen Campbell and James Gibbs, and the innovations in planning.[8] Moreover, some of the most eminent patrons of the arts in the eighteenth century might be under represented in such a history of the country house. Lord Burlington is a prime example of this. Burlington's country seat Londesborough in Yorkshire underwent only minor interventions in its architecture and landscape,[9] although it must be recognized that the design for his own villa at Chiswick on the outskirts of London was considered one of the most startling innovations of the time. Yet Londesborough remained outside this tide of architectural development. The role of the patron also raises the question of who was responsible for the design. And here again Lord Burlington takes centre stage in the discussion about the design of Holkham, Norfolk,

---

[6] For instance, work had been carried out on the west side of the house, including the gallery, by Sir Francis Child before his death in 1761. For a fuller discussion of Osterley see J. Hardy and M. Tomlin, *Osterley Park House* (London, Victoria & Albert Museum, 1985).

[7] Wanstead was demolished in 1824.

[8] Campbell produced three designs for Wanstead. The first two are illustrated in *Vitruvius Britannicus*, vol. I plates 21–6 and the second design was more or less that executed. The third design showing unexecuted additions appears in vol. III plates 39–41. Gibbs' involvement is discussed by J. Harris, 'Who Designed Houghton?', *Country Life*, (2 March 1989).

[9] Burlington's activities at Londesborough are discussed by L. Boynton, 'Lord Burlington at Home' in D. Arnold (ed.), *Belov'd by Evr'y Muse: Richard Boyle 3rd Earl of Burlington and 4th Earl of Cork (1694–1753)* (London, The Georgian Group, 1994), pp. 21–8.

almost eclipsing the important role played by the patron Thomas Coke, created Earl of Leicester.[10] The interaction of Coke, Burlington and William Kent, all of whom have been attributed with the design alongside Matthew Brettingham the elder, remains unresolved.[11] The triumvirate of the Earl of Carlisle, John Vanbrugh and Nicholas Hawksmoor, who were involved, in varying capacities, with the conception, design and construction of Castle Howard, Yorkshire, presents a similar case in point.[12] Both these houses demonstrate the complexities of the production of a design, the constraints on the certainty of firm attributions and the historian's difficult task in chronicling and equating these. These two ways of constructing country house histories through biography move attention away from the building itself. But a preoccupation with style moves the pendulum completely the other way.

The definition of style is a vital problem in architectural history. Architecture and style are interlinked to the point that style can be believed to contain the essence of architecture. But if this were the case style would constitute the subject of architectural history. Style is rather the specific organization of form. But the characteristics of a style consist of a repertory of ornamental components which cannot be confined to a single period – many appear again and again in different configurations. So a style is characterized by the manner in which form is interpreted. What changes form? Is there a kind of spontaneous development? Or does the historian trace lines of change which are only possible to construct with the benefit of hindsight? One way of doing this is to use the Hegelian notion of a spirit of the age. This means every epoch has a distinctive set of characteristics which manifest themselves in all aspects of culture and society. Continuity and progress are identified in this model as each epoch reacts against the preceding one but certain elements are retained and subsumed in the new era. Hegel identified this as thesis–antithesis–synthesis or dialectical approach to the processes of history. Architectural style can be seen as a manifestation of the spirit of the age and Hegel's way of explaining development and change has proved attractive to architectural historians who have been concerned principally with classical architecture. Hegelian dialectic transposes itself well to the juxtaposition of the severity of early eighteenth-century Palladianism and the mid-century frivolity of the rococo which can be seen to result in the neo-classical style at the end of the century. But throughout the eighteenth century different styles coex-

---

[10] According to Matthew Brettingham the younger, 'The general ideas...were first struck out by the Earls of Burlington and Leicester, assisted by Mr William Kent.' *The Plans and Elevations of the late Earl of Leicester's House at Holkham*, 2nd edn (1773). Burlington and Coke are also identified with designs for chimney stacks at Coleshill House, Berkshire. H. Colvin, *A Biographical Dictionary of British Architects, 1600–1840*, 3rd edn (New Haven and London, Yale University Press 1995), pp. 151.

[11] On this point see L. Schmidt, 'Holkham Hall', *Country Life*, (24 and 31 January 1980), 214–17 and 298–301 and more recently C. Hiskey, 'The Building of Holkham Hall: Newly Discovered Letters', *Architectural History*, 40 (1997), 144–58.

[12] See C. Saumarez Smith, *The Building of Castle Howard* (London, Faber, 1990).

isted and their apparent dominance or otherwise can be as much a product of the historian's aims and interests as any quantification of contemporary preference or historical truth.[13] This is made more complicated when it is remembered that architects sometimes worked in different styles and some of these styles are more closely identified with particular architectural credos than others. Moreover, the emphasis on the classical – in the broadest sense – and its dominance in the period has resulted in the sidelining of other kinds of architectural production, for instance gothic, chinoiserie and the primitive, all of which manifested themselves in significant ways in country house architecture and are discussed in subsequent chapters of this book. What is important here is that disparate styles in the same period indicate a lack of unanimity in public taste which implies that different formal elements represent the distinct ideologies of social classes. Thus a style can become representative of a class ideology.[14] This has direct relevance for a study of the styles of country house building, especially for a consideration of the classical country house.

The map of the history of British architecture which encompasses the Georgian period is still identified as that drawn up by Sir John Summerson in his seminal work *Architecture in Britain 1530–1830*. It is important to consider how this canonical text has shaped subsequent views of country house architecture in the eighteenth and early nineteenth centuries with particular reference to style. The choice of examples made by Summerson as a set of stepping stones through the architecture of the Georgian period has become the bench-mark of greatness. But he presents development of architecture in the period as some kind of spontaneous series of changes where a repertory of ornamental components reappears. Summerson is concerned principally with classicism and it is the classical country house which dominates – the 'purer' the style the better. This approach constructs categories of quality determined only by twentieth-century criteria based on a knowledge of what we know to have happened later and our fuller understanding of classical systems of design. It results in architects like James Gibbs[15] being positioned outside the canon of architectural production and anomalous buildings like Strawberry Hill being ascribed to an amateur[16] rather than an architect and hence put out of the main loop of architectural production.[17] Palladianism becomes defined by default rather than by any clear contemporary treatise or manifesto. And Summerson even admits that the name

---

[13] These historical questions are discussed in F. Braudel, *Écrits sur L'Histoire* (Paris, Flammarion, 1969), part II, pp. 41–238.

[14] For a detailed discussion of the relationship between style and class ideology see N. Hadjinicolaou, *Art History and Class Struggle* (London, Pluto Press, 1978).

[15] [Chapter 21 of *The Georgian Country House* discusses Gibbs.]

[16] Summerson, *Architecture in Britain* (1977 edn), p. 403.

[17] For a discussion of the nature of the architectural profession at this time see S. Kostoff (ed.), *The Architect: Chapters in the History of the Profession*, (Oxford, Oxford University Press, 1977), and Colvin, *Biographical Dictionary of British Architects* (New Haven, Yale University Press, 1995), pp. 29–45.

Palladianism is an inaccurate but nevertheless a useful taxonomic tool.[18] Yet as the architecture of the Georgian country house is undeniably predominantly classical, the use of the ornamental motifs which comprise this system of design must have some relevance to the system of ideas and beliefs of the society which built them.

This system must embody political, economic, cultural and philosophical beliefs of the dominant ruling class. The deviations in styles, whether Palladian, neoclassical or baroque, matter less than the persistent use of this repertory of classical elements. And on closer inspection the distinctiveness of these categories is further eroded. This is exemplified in the debates around the shift in attitudes towards classical architecture in the opening decades of the eighteenth century. The 'baroque' of John Vanbrugh and the 'Palladianism' of Colen Campbell and Lord Burlington are usually placed in opposition to demonstrate a binary approach to architectural style at that time. But in fact similar elements appear in their buildings as seen in the corner towers at Vanbrugh's Grimsthorpe (1722) and Campbell's design for Houghton which appeared with rusticated embellishments and to which James Gibbs added cupolas (1725–8). These also appear in Campbell's third unrealized version of Wanstead which, significantly, Summerson likens to Vanbrugh's Castle Howard:

> Wanstead was a key building of its age. It looked back to Castle Howard, but by virtue of its purity of detail superseded that house as a model ... [Wanstead I has] as many rooms *en suite* as there are at Castle Howard ... The elevation is an unbroken rectangle and there is an obvious revulsion from the mobile and plastic character of Castle Howard ... [Wanstead II] approaches a little nearer to Castle Howard ... [the] cupola over the hall an equivalent in silhouette to the dome of Castle Howard ... [In Wanstead III] Campbell added towers (never built) to this elevation thus reproducing the Castle Howard composition pretty completely.[19]

Summerson contests that Wanstead I, II and III remained influential sources for country house design for the next fifty years. Although he acknowledges the importance of Castle Howard and Vanbrugh, this has to be distilled into a stylistic formula to suit his argument about the dominance of Palladianism.

The purpose here is not to replace Wanstead with Castle Howard as the fount of eighteenth-century country house design. Rather it is to demonstrate the diversity of classical formulae which appeared in architectural design in the opening years of the century. Indeed subsequent chapters in this book examine the use of these classical motifs which were dislocated from their original context in antique or Italian Renaissance architecture. Looking at classical architecture in the eighteenth century as a repertory of forms rather than statements of specific

---

[18] '... the whole output of English building [from the period 1710–50], has long ago become labelled "Palladian", a description not wholly accurate (as no such labels can be), but accurate enough and secure in acceptance.' Summerson, *Architecture in Britain*, p. 317.

[19] Summerson, *Architecture in Britain* (1977 edn), p. 320.

design credos challenges our teleological construction of stylistic histories. This opens the way for other interpretations and histories of the country house, some of which are explored in this book. The method of grouping the architecture from given periods of time under general stylistic labels has, without doubt, been the backbone of the discipline of architectural history.[20] And when used skilfully and carefully it can provide useful punctuation marks in the lengthy and complex narrative that is the subject matter of the history of Western building. But it is only one of many tools with which to explore social and cultural contexts.

It is not only Summerson's stylistic preoccupations which have coloured our view of the country house but also his choice of examples. The Anglocentric focus of Summerson's survey results in the architecture of Scotland and Ireland being marginalized.[21] This runs contrary to and distorts the stylistic preoccupations of the survey because architects like William Adam[22] and Edward Lovett Pearce perhaps showed a greater architectural sensitivity to the ideas of Andrea Palladio and the baroque than some of those more fully discussed by Summerson. But the purpose here is not to criticize Summerson; any survey presents fundamental choices of inclusion and exclusion of material. Nor is the aim to provide a supplement to the examples Summerson discusses or to reconfigure his material or arguments. It is more to present and prompt an awareness of the consequences of this seminal and pioneering work for architectural history as a whole and here specifically for our understanding and interpretation of the country house.

The usefulness of style labels to architectural history is not in dispute but it is difficult to see how they correlate with contemporary views of architecture. Returning again to Palladianism we find that the word is little used in the eighteenth and early nineteenth centuries to describe a particular style of building. The most notable use is when specific buildings are referred to, especially the Palladian bridges at Wilton, Wiltshire and at Stowe, Buckinghamshire. Indeed Horace Walpole who discussed the interiors of country houses and their contents in considerable detail makes little remark about the various styles of their exterior architecture; he appears to be more preoccupied with height. His remarks on Stourhead, Wiltshire, usually seen as a bench-mark of English Palladianism, are typical:

> The Shell of the present Stone-house was built by the Father of the present Mr Henry Hoare, the Banker, but He has finished it, added the skylight room, turned

---

[20] For a fuller discussion of trends in the writing of architectural history see D. Watkin, *The Rise of Architectural History* (London, The Architectural Press, 1980).

[21] For instance, brief sections on 'Palladianism in Scotland' and 'Palladianism in Ireland' appear in Summerson, *Architecture in Britain* (1977 edn), pp. 376–80.

[22] For a fuller discussion of the work of William Adam see J. Gifford, *William Adam* (Edinburgh, Edinburgh University Press, 1989) and *Architectural Heritage*, i.

the chapel into a great Salon, and made the fine wood, water and ornamental buildings. The rooms of the house are in general too low, but are richly furnished.[23]

Questions of contemporary attitudes towards style and taste are difficult to quantify. And it is not unusual to find references to classically designed country houses as simply 'modern'. After all, Georgian country houses were modern to contemporary society and representative of their own time. The classical and historical associations have been emphasized by twentieth-century architectural historians. Once commentary is freed from the preconceived assumptions about classicism new interpretations are revealed which centre on the issue of national identity. Lord Shaftesbury's letter from Italy in 1712 is taken to herald the beginning of Palladianism[24] and the following passage is frequently cited:

> Thro' several reigns we have patiently seen the noblest publick Buildings perish (if I may say so) under the Hand of one single Court-Architect; who, if he had been able to profit by Experience, wou'd long since, at our expence, have prov'd the greatest Master in the World ... But, I question whether our Patience is like to hold much longer ... Hardly ... as the Publick now stands, shou'd we bear to see a Whitehall treated like a Hampton-Court, or even a new Cathedral like St Paul's.[25]

The architecture of Wren was objected to on account of its perceived stylistic licentiousness and lack of rigour which resulted in a most unpatriotic style of building. But notably here Shaftesbury is criticizing public architecture, perhaps the most obvious face of a nationalistic style.

These comments are usually linked to two important texts which appeared shortly after Shaftesbury's letter. Campbell's *Vitruvius Britannicus* (vol. I, 1715) and Giacomi Leoni's English translation of Palladio's *I Quattro Libri dell'Architettura* (1715–16) were dedicated to George I. Together with the comments made by Shaftesbury, they are seen to signal a new approach to architecture which centred on Palladianism. Moreover, Leoni included a frontispiece prepared by Sebastiano Ricci showing Father Time unveiling a bust of Palladio underneath which is a winged figure of fame. Above this scene is Britannia with two putti holding the royal coat of arms. The message is clear: under the new royal house Palladio's principles flourish once more. Moreover, the image of Palladio himself was even made to fit. The portrait of Palladio which follows the title page is often taken at face value but it bears no relation to the portrait of the architect by his contemporary Paolo Veronese. The typical Renaissance Venetian appearance of Palladio has been changed to a clean shaven eighteenth-century face dressed in soft cap and open shirt making it more accessible and acceptable to Leoni's

---

[23] H. Walpole, *Journals of Visits to Country Seats & c*, ed. P. Toynbee, The Walpole Society, vol. XVI (1928), p. 41
[24] On this point see Summerson, *Architecture in Britain*, part 4, chapter 20, p. 317 and R. Wittkower, *Palladio and English Palladianism* (London, Thames & Hudson, 1974).
[25] *Essay on Design*, 1712.

audience. While Leoni provided an inaccurate but nationalistically orientated guide to classical architecture through the eyes of Palladio, Campbell made a quite different contribution. The first volume of *Vitruvius Britannicus* mapped out the classical architecture of the British Isles. It was not an architectural treatise but an assemblage of images which created a new and important archive of British classicism, that is to say the use of the repertory of classical forms in a variety of configurations. And it included the work of Wren and Vanbrugh. The opening statement by Campbell makes his purpose clear:

> The general esteem that travellers have for things foreign, is in nothing more conspicuous than with regard to building. We travel for the most part, at an Age more apt to be imposed upon us by the ignorance or partiality of others, than to judge truly of the merit of things by the strength of reason. It is owing to this mistake in education that so many of the British quality have so mean an opinion of what is performed in our own country; though perhaps in most we equal, and in some things we surpass our neighbours.

He later continues:

> And here I cannot but reflect on the happiness of the British nation, that at present abounds with so many learned and ingenious gentlemen as Sir Christopher Wren, Sir William Bruce, Sir John Vanbrugh, Mr Archer, Mr Wren, Mr Wynne, Mr Talman, Mr Hawksmoore, Mr James etc., who have all greatly contributed to adorn our island with their curious labours, and are daily embellishing it more.[26]

Here Campbell turns the sights of the standards of architectural production inwards to concentrate on the qualities of indigenous architects, none of whom produced pure classical designs, and he endorses their merits. At this moment of introspection it is useful to consider how British architecture appeared to foreign eyes – a theme which recurs in subsequent chapters of this book.

The observations of a Frenchman in the mid-eighteenth century may be helpful in unravelling these attitudes towards style. Jean Bernard le Blanc, known as the Abbé le Blanc, who visited England in 1737–8 sent many letters home and these were published a decade later. Le Blanc was a sensitive architectural commentator. The following remarks were made in a letter to the antiquarian and collector le Comte de Caylus to whom he had sent *Vitruvius Britannicus* as a guide to British architecture:

> Architecture is one of those things which most particularly indicate the magnificence of a nation; and from magnificence, we easily conclude grandeur. ... Italy is the country of Europe that has produced the most masterpieces of modern architecture.

---

[26] Campbell, *Vitruvius Britannicus* (1717), vol. I, introduction. Mr Wren is not listed in Colvin, *Biographical Dictionary of British Architects*.

The English have yet only the merit of having copied some of them. The architect who built their most famous church of St Paul at London has only reduced the plan of St Peter's at Rome, to two thirds of its size; ... [and] wherever he deviates from his models, he has committed the greatest errors.

The greatest part of the country houses, for there are few in London, that deserve to be spoken of, are also in the Italian taste; but it has not been justly applied ... A pleasure-house for a vigna in Rome is not a model for a country house in the neighbourhood of London.

He goes on to praise Inigo Jones and to mention the efforts of Lord Burlington through his buildings and publications to promote Italianate taste. But notes:

These models have not made the English architects more expert; for whenever they attempt to do anything more than barely to copy, they erect nothing but heavy masses of stone, like of Blenheim-Palace, the plan and front of which you will find in the *Vitruvius Britannicus*.[27]

Le Blanc is also critical of the English use of ornament which he considers at times to be 'perfectly childish'. His example is Merlin's Cave in Richmond Park by William Kent which housed the Queen's country library and also contained wax figures of Merlin and others: 'It is impossible to conceive of anything of a worst taste'. The Abbé is using the yardstick of Italian architecture to judge English architecture and, unsurprisingly, it is found wanting. Similarly, if we look for a whole-hearted and accurate adoption of classical architecture, let alone Palladianism, we will not find it in the architecture of the English country house. The architectural form can, like the adoption of Italianate manners, be viewed either as undigested and uncomfortable or a selective reuse of other traditions to express cultural distinctiveness. Le Blanc's recognition of the use of a repertory of classical elements in a variety of configurations exemplifies this dilemma. English classicism was displeasing to le Blanc through its failure to adhere to Italianate formulae. But at the same time he recognizes it as nationally distinctive.

The idea of a national style based on a variety of configurations of classical elements helps to explain the architectural production of the opening decades of the eighteenth century. Classical forms, whether in architecture, painting sculpture, garden design or literature enabled the expression of the fundamental ideology of a culture which aligned itself with Augustan Rome. And the use of

[27] Jean Bernard le Blanc (1706–81), known as Abbé le Blanc, was appointed Historiographer of the King's Buildings in 1749 after his anti-rococo views brought him to the attention of Mme de Pompadour. He travelled to Italy with Soufflot and C. N. Cochin and shortly after published letters as Jean Bernard le Blanc, *Lettres de Monsieur l'Abbé le Blanc concernant le gouvernment, la politique et les moeurs des Anglois et des François* (Paris, 1747, translations published the same year in London and Dublin). This extract is from a letter to the noted antiquarian and collector le Comte de Caylus (1692–1765).

classicism as a primary expression of English culture helped to underpin the imperialist nature of early eighteenth-century British society.[28]

This gives some kind of rationale to the diversity of classical formulae rather than picking one strand as the progressive element. Indeed stylistic histories which offer an evolutionary view of architecture, impose a notion of continuity and progress on country house design which might not necessarily be there. But discontinuity is not a problem if the historian recognizes the limitations of teleological methodologies. Palladianism might appear to be the inevitable style for the Augustan era but is this really the case? Does something become Palladian in this era because it is no longer baroque? And can the baroque of architects like Vanbrugh be seen as part of the repertory of classical elements rather than a break with the Palladian tradition? Furthermore, in the absence of large numbers of replica Palladian buildings is it possible that the classical style is telling a different story which remains partly unread?[29] This seems likely when it is remembered that the importance of classicism as an expression of cultural ideologies has been recognised in other fields of cultural production – most notably literature.[30]

The introduction of social history as a method of analysing architecture has signalled an important move away from biographical or stylistic surveys. The social approach was pioneered by Mark Girouard in his ground breaking study *Life in the English Country House*. Here social life is used as a way of examining a building. More recently kitchens and patterns of eating and drinking have come under scrutiny.[31] But the interaction of social activity and architecture is problematical: is the social history a context or an explanation? And does this approach give us any kind of broader cultural meaning as it pins down the function of a building to the notion of how it was used by different social groups and to the range of social activities which took place in and around it. This understanding of function is doubtlessly an essential part of the history of the country house but it ignores an essential feature of the meaning of the country house – its metaphorical function.

The metaphorical function of the country house can be identified as its status as a symbol of the power and wealth of the landowner and more broadly the social, cultural and political hegemony of the ruling classes. In no way is this

---

[28] The historical background to British imperialism and mercantilism, which underpinned the choice of Augustan Rome as an imperialistic and cultural model, is discussed in C. Hill, *The Century of Revolution, 1603–1714* (London, Oxford University Press, 1966) and W. Speck, *Stability and Strife in England, 1714–1760* (Cambridge, Mass., Harvard University Press, 1977).

[29] Alongside the obvious examples of Chiswick Villa and Mereworth, Nostell Priory was based on Villa Mocenigo and other Palladian villas. See Leach, *James Paine*, p. 29. Moreover, it has been argued that Lord Burlington quickly moved away from Palladio to other expressions of classical form. On this point see J. Harris, 'Lord Burlington The Modern Vitruvius' in D. Arnold (ed.) *The Georgian Villa* (Stroud, Sutton Publishing, 1996) and C. Sicca, 'The Architecture of the Wall: Astylism in the Architecture of Lord Burlington', *Architectural History*, 33 (1990).

[30] A useful discussion of the writings of Alexander Pope in this context can be found in L. Brown, *Alexander Pope* (Oxford and New York, Blackwell, 1985).

[31] C. Anne Wilson, *The Country House Kitchen Garden* (Stroud, Sutton Publishing, 1998).

metaphorical function opposed to the physical function of the country house. Rather it reinforces the physical function of the building. The house was at once the focal point of the estate and the primary residence of the landowner – the family seat. The house was a place of business, whether political or estate, and it provided a backdrop both to the extensive collections of fine and decorative art owned by every member of the aristocracy and to the social rituals the aristocracy performed.

Metaphorical and physical aspects combined to make an embodiment and reinforcement of a distinctive social system enhanced by a set of cultural values, some of which were based on indigenous traditions and others borrowed from antiquity. In this way the country house functioned as a symbol of social control and the supremacy of the ruling class. This control was according to E.P. Thompson 'located primarily in the cultural hegemony and only secondarily in an expression of economic or physical (military) power'.[32] Moreover, Thompson recognizes that defining control in terms of cultural hegemony does not signify an abandonment of any kind of analysis. Rather it allows analysis to be made at the point where power and authority manifest themselves to create a mentality of subordination within the populace.[33] In other words, the country house's role as a symbol of patrician authority is paramount in this context. This is seen in the relationship between the style of architecture and the style of politics, and in the rhetoric of the gentry, and in country house interiors and collections. All these proclaimed the stability and self-confidence of the aristocracy in the face of threats to their pre-eminence.

The value of the country house is then greater than the intrinsic meaning of an individual building. Every house was a microcosm of the social, political and cultural trends in Britain and had a crucial role in maintaining the status quo in the face of increasing adversity. The ruling class maintained a resounding influence on the lives and expectations of the lower orders. To this end the country house functioned as a stage for the performance of highly visible paternalistic displays. During the eighteenth century the pomp and ceremony of social rituals and the symbolic use of ornamental dress – including the wearing of wigs and powder – grew in importance. And the country house was a backdrop to this as well as being the site of rituals like the hunt, the celebration of marriages or national festivals. All these elements were used to exact deference from the lower orders and reinforce the social system. Parallel to this was the formidable presence of the country house in the rural environment as both a representation of the ruling class and the linchpin of country life. The country house functioned to moderate, preserve and represent the status quo.

The notion that country house architecture is the physical embodiment of governmental and social systems is evident in the important role country houses

---

[32] E.P. Thompson, 'Patrician Society, Plebeian Culture', *Journal of Social History*, vol. 7, no. 4 (summer 1974), pp. 382–405.
[33] I follow Thompson's 'Patrician Society' argument, in these paragraphs.

played in the architectural production of the period. The eighteenth century is noted for these private mansions, including those in urban settings, rather than public buildings or even royal palaces. The country house and its estate were therefore an ordered physical structure that acted as a metonym for other inherited structures – this encompasses the make-up of society as a whole, a code of morality, a body of manners, a system of language and the way in which an individual relates to their cultural inheritance. Through this we can reveal much about the period's dominant culture and ideology. Raymond Williams identified this as 'a lived hegemony is always in process ... [it] does not passively exist as a form of dominance. It has continually to be renewed, recreated, defended and modified. It is also continually resisted, limited, altered, challenged by pressures not all its own.'[34] The changing relationship between the aristocratic and bourgeois classes is part of this; as the *nouveau riche* were included in the aristocracy so it became a more exclusive club and other lower orders were in turn denied the feudalistic and paternalistic rights and privileges they had previously enjoyed. Patterns of land ownership go some way towards illuminating this point. But defining who owned what is not easy and the statistics that do exist have been gathered using different sets of measurements and criteria.[35] Moreover, the only two major land surveys which took place before the twentieth century were the Domesday Book of 1086 and the Returns of Landowners of 1873 referred to as the new Domesday.[36] In 1688 15–20 per cent of usable land was held by the great landowners, that is those with an estate of more than 10,000 acres. By the end of the eighteenth century the amount of land owned by this social group had increased to 20–25 per cent. This is discussed by G.E. Mingay who recognizes a 'practical monopoly of the land held in the hands of the few';[37] by 1876 the *Spectator* noted that 'Seven hundred and ten individuals own more than one quarter of the soil of England and Wales'.[38] This figure was made up of those who owned more than 5,000 acres in any one county. Towards the end of the eighteenth century the change from a morally based to an economically based country society was expressed in William Cobbett's distinction between a resident 'native gentry attached to the soil and known to every farmer' and a gentry which was hardly resident 'looking to the soil for its rents, viewing it as a mere object of speculation ... and relying for influence not upon the good will of the vicarage,

---

[34] R. Williams, *Marxism and Literature* (Oxford, Oxford University Press, 1978), p. 112.

[35] See H. Clemenson in *English Country Houses and Landed Estates* (London, Croom, Helm, 1982), chapter I especially. Clemenson discusses the problem of identifying different land owning groups. See also G.E. Mingay, 'The Size of Farms in the Eighteenth Century', *Economic History Review*, 2nd series, vol. XIV, no. 3 (1962), 469–88 and F.M.L. Thompson, 'The Social Distribution of Landed Property in England since the sixteenth century', *Economic History Review*, 2nd series, vol. XIX, no. 3 (December 1966), 505–17.

[36] British Parliamentary Papers, LXXII (1875).

[37] G.E. Mingay, 'Farms in the Eighteenth Century' in *English Landed Society in the Eighteenth Century* (London, Routledge & Kegan Paul, 1963).

[38] *Spectator* (4 March 1876).

but upon the dread of their power'. This aspect of the significance of land ownership and its impact on class consciousness results in a shift in attitude towards the land – 'limited and not always saleable rights *in* things were being replaced by virtually unlimited and saleable rights *to* things'.[39] This change in social make-up of landowners and their gentry tenant farmers redefined the social meaning of the country house and placed different emphasis on its contemporary cultural significance.

The politics of exclusion and privilege were used to galvanize different facets of society. It is possible to go beyond this to see how the house and its estate became part of the increasing cultural consumption of the period and, therefore, a benchmark of cultural values. The growth of a consumer society resulted in the 'packaging' and 'selling ... of the English countryside as a privately owned but nonetheless publicly consumable product – the embodiment of a way of life one could buy *into* (on psychological and ideological levels) if not actually buy'.[40]

This can be called the culture industry, part of the newly emergent consumer society, and the role this kind of consumerism played in the creation of a socially stabilizing consensus among different classes via an amalgam of traditional and non-traditional values.[41] This is seen in the proliferation of collections fed partly by the wish to own objects relating to the culture of antiquity – or good copies of the same – which sprang from Grand Tourism and a growing passion for British manufactures. The value of the country house as a site of display and conspicuous consumption is seen in new styles of architecture and the owner's ability to outshine rival estates and project an appropriate symbol of status and socio-economic power. Consumption of the country house took place on different levels. The house and estate could be viewed from afar by the lower orders and farm workers or close up by the tourist classes, usually middle class and lower gentry. The opening of the great estate to the public underlined the idea that property, authority and the idea of virtue were all bound up in the meaning of the country house. Opening it to the public helped to engender the feeling of a seamless society at once excluding and including different social groups but reflecting the cultural hegemony built on rapprochement between different social classes. This is seen in the increasingly popular phenomenon of home tourism and the proliferation of printed material concerning the country house which gave the lower social orders glimpses of a world to which they would never belong. Yet at the same time these acts engendered a sense of communality with the landowners.

---

[39] C.B. Macpherson (ed.), *Property: Mainstream and Critical Positions* (Toronto, University of Toronto Press, 1978), p. 8.

[40] C. Fabricant, 'The Literature of Domestic Tourism and the Public Consumption of Private Property' in F. Nussbaum and L. Brown (eds), *The New Eighteenth Century: Theory, Politics and English Literature* (New York and London, Methuen, 1987), p. 261.

[41] On this point see N. Mackendrick, J. Brewer and J. H. Plumb, *The Birth of a Consumer Society: The Commercialization of Eighteenth-century England* (London, Europa, 1982).

All of this extends the meaning of the house beyond a set of architectural forms or styles to something more intrinsic to the national consciousness and shows it played a crucial part in the maintenance of a distinct social system against a background of upheaval and change. In this way the country house helped to define and promote a cohesive national identity throughout the long eighteenth century.

6

Plans and Elevations for the Villa of Lord Mansfield at Kenwood

Robert and James Adam

Various avocations have retarded the publishing of our second number longer than we intended. During this interval, we have listened with respect to the opinion of the public concerning the first number; and we have had the most flattering approbation from men of taste, both at home and abroad.

Encouraged by this, we now resume our task, with greater confidence, by publishing the plans, elevations, and sections of Kenwood; a beautiful villa belonging to Lord Mansfield, the friend of every elegant art and useful science.

We have reserved the remaining designs of Sion for some future number; as we were persuaded, that by giving specimens of some of our other works, we should add greater variety to our undertaking, without diminishing its utility. – As in this work we aim, not only at affording entertainment to the connoisseur, but wish also to convey some instruction to the artist; we shall, from time to time, make such observations as naturally arise from the subjects before us. – Should we differ in any of these observations from the opinion of either antient or modern authors, we do not mean to engage in any controversy, being only desirous of submitting our ideas to the consideration of the public. At the same time we may affirm, that whatever we venture either to publish, or to recommend, is the result of much experience, and of a careful search into the purest sources of antiquity. – Architecture has not, like some other arts, an immediate standard in nature, to which the artist can always refer, and which would enable the skilful instantly to decide with respect to the degree of excellence attained in any work. In architecture, it must be formed and improved by a correct taste, and diligent study of the beauties exhibited by great masters in their productions; and it is only by

Robert and James Adam, "Plans and Elevations for the Villa of Lord Mansfield at Kenwood," pp. 24–8 from Robert Oresko (ed.), *The Works in Architecture of Robert and James Adam*. London: Academy Editions, 1975.

profound meditation upon these, that one becomes capable of distinguishing between what is graceful and what is inelegant; between that which possesses, and that which is destitute of harmony.

We have observed in our first number, that many of the disputes among modern architects are extremely frivolous. There is nothing with respect to which they have differed more, than their rules for the diminution of columns. This, however, is a subject of greater importance than those which frequently engage their attention. The column is not only one of the noblest and most graceful pieces of decoration, but in all round bodies, especially such as stand insulated, there is a delicacy of proportion to be observed, that those of another form, and in other situations, do not require. Without entering into any critical disquisitions concerning the opinions of either the antients or moderns with respect to this point, we shall only observe, that our constant practice has been, to diminish our columns from the base to the capital, by means of the instrument used by Nicomedes for describing the first conchoid, which we think has

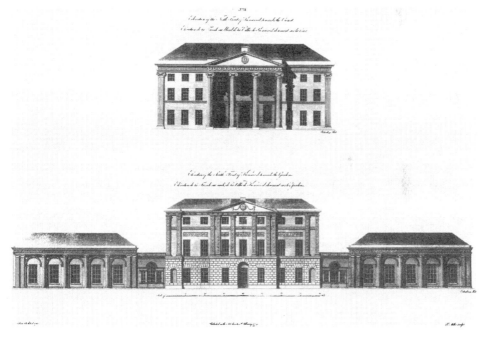

Figure 6.1 Geometrical elevations of the north and south fronts of Kenwood
Source: Adam 1822
The portico to the north is the only part of that front which is new. The decoration of the south front, excepting that of the west wing, is entirely new, and became in some measure necessary, to conceal the brick-work, which being built at different times, was of various colours. The attic story is a late addition to the house, and was executed in a singular manner, the walls being raised, and the new roof covered in, before the old one was removed; and thus was the house left habitable, and unexposed to the injuries of the weather, during the whole progress of this useful alteration.

exceeded in elegance any other method hitherto employed. But as this instrument and the manner of using it, has already been explained by some modern authors, we should not here have ventured to mention it, had it not been to recommend it, as preferable to all others.

The proportion of columns has also been a subject of much enquiry. But as this greatly depends upon the situation of these columns, whether they make parts of outside, or inside decoration, whether they stand insulated, or engaged, whether raised much above the eye, or level with it; these are circumstances which very much affect such proportions, and consequently leave an uncertainty, which can only be properly ascertained by the correct taste of the skilful and experienced artist.

Having mentioned the diminution and proportion of columns, we are naturally led to make some observations with regard to their capitals; an object of great distinction and delicacy in the detail of architecture. – In the first place, we acknowledge only three orders; the Doric, the Ionic, and the Corinthian: for as to the Tuscan, it is, in fact, no more than a bad and imperfect Doric; and the Composite, or Roman order, in our opinion, is a very disagreable and awkward mixture of the Corinthian and Ionic, without either grace or beauty. We do not however mean to condemn the composing of capitals; a liberty which has been often taken by the antients with great success; and in a former part of this work, we have exhibited an attempt of our own in this way; and shall, during the course of it, have other opportunities of the same kind.

The Doric capital, when properly adorned, is capable of great elegance: But where rich decoration is required, in order to give it all it's grace, the neck, or space between the astragal and the annulets, should be made of much greater height than the common proportion prescribed by Paladio and many other moderns; and that neck should be enriched in the various ways which we shall have occasion to represent in the course of our work. – One example of this kind is to be seen in the capital of the Pilasters to the south front, given at large in the fourth plate.

The Corinthian capital itself does not, in our opinion, admit of more dignity and magnificence, than a rich Ionic with it's volutes square in the front. – Angular volutes, as in the Temples of Concord and Manly Fortune at Rome, and in the Temple of Erectheus at Athens, have always appeared to us less solid, less grave, and less graceful; and, in our opinion, they have been injudiciously adopted by Michael Angelo, Scamozzi, and many other modern architects. Their reason for this was, in order to avoid the irregularity of appearance in this capital when viewed in profile which differs so very much from it's aspect in front. But notwithstanding this difference, the profile itself, as well as the front, are susceptible of such beauties, that we are inclinable to hazard some defects, rather than to sacrifice the elegant result of the whole composition.

There may indeed be some cases, where such irregularity in the capital might be attended with great inconvenience, as in a square or oblong building surrounded by this order: But in this, or similar cases, it would be much more eligible for the skilful architect to substitute another order in it's place.

The great size of the volute of the Grecian Ionic has always appeared to us by much too heavy, and those used by the Romans seem rather to border on the other extreme. We have therefore generally taken a mean between them, which we think has a happy effect; making them in width about one half of the superior diameter of the column, and observing that the center of the eye of the volute is nearly perpendicular to the extremity of the said diameter.

We have also adopted the Grecian manner of forming the volute with a double fillet, which, by producing more light and shade, gives great relief, and far exceeds in grace and beauty that used by the Romans. In imitation of the Greeks, we likewise bend the channel, or hollow band, from whence the volutes spring, in the middle of the capital; which band, in case of rich decoration, should be filled with a winding foliage; or some such ornament, from the center of the capital to the eye of the volute. But the members of chief importance towards compleating this capital, are the astragal and neck, which neck, as in the Doric, should be filled sometimes with various enrichments, more or less orna-mented, and sometimes, perhaps, should be left altogether plain, according to the stile of the building where it is employed. In the example exhibited in this number, this capital has the addition of a plain neck and fillet, without which it always appears flat and meagre. In a future number, we shall have occasion to give an example of it, executed at Sion-House, with all the embellishment of which it is capable.

The foliage and stems of the Corinthian capital make it not only magnificent, but also extremely gay and graceful. It has besides some advantages over the Ionic in point of form; all it's sides are regular, and the concavity of it's abacus contrasts in a beautiful manner with the convexity of the vase. The form of the vase is sometimes executed in a most defective manner, by swelling it towards the middle, and bending it inwards at the bottom, in a cimarecta shape; which is both unpleasant, and rests ill upon the shaft of the column. – This error has probably been introduced from a defect in the drawing of the plates of Desgo-detz, whom, not-withstanding his great parade of precision and accuracy, we have often found guilty of considerable oversights and mistakes, not only in his mensuration, but also in the delineation of many of the antient monuments. This capital, as well as the preceeding, we think may be formed into various compositions, of great beauty and elegance, as we shall endeavour to shew by some examples hereafter.

We shall not at present enter into any particular detail with respect to the entablatures or the bases of the different orders, but refer to the specimens of each now published, and to what we are about to publish. We must however beg leave to observe, that we can see no reason for assigning to each order it's precise entablature, fixed down unalterably both in figure and dimension. Different circumstances of situation and propriety ought to vary the form, and also the proportion, of all entablatures. A latitude in this respect, under the hand of an ingenious and able artist, is often productive of great novelty, variety and beauty.

The reader has before him in this number two compositions of this kind, the one Doric, the other Ionic, neither of which are subjected to any precise rule, and yet the result of the whole has always been deemed very pleasing.

The mouldings in the remaining structures of antient Rome are considerably less curvelineal than those of the antient monuments of Greece. We have always given a preference to the latter, and have even thought it adviseable to bend them still more in many cases, particularly in interior finishings, where objects are near, and ought to be softened to the eye; for circular mouldings are intended to relieve the sight from the acuteness of the square ones, of which too frequent a repetition would be infinitely harsh and tiresome: But in bending the cimarecta, the cimar-eversa or talon, the ovolo, the cavetto, and the astragal, in the method we have always followed, as may be seen from our designs, they blend and mingle themselves more harmoniously with the square members, and attain more delicacy and elegance, than such as have been commonly used.

7

From *The Royal Academy Lectures on Architecture*

Sir John Soane

Lecture V

[...]

The church of Sta Sophia at Constantinople, erected by Justinian about the middle of the sixth century, is another striking example of the rapid decline of architecture and the arts connected therewith. The plan of this celebrated structure is, however, grandly conceived, although the execution and taste in the finishing is very defective and little calculated to satisfy our expectations.

On the completion of this mighty edifice, executed to rival the great works of antiquity, the emperor, who had constantly superintended its progress, was so astonished at contemplating its magnitude and so dazzled with its splendid decorations that he repeatedly exclaimed with ecstatic delight: 'This surpasses the Temple of Solomon.'

The churches of St. Mark at Venice, of St. Anthony at Padua, and many others erected about the same time, in design and taste of execution are very like the church of Sta Sophia. These buildings, crowded with the most expensive decorations, like those erected subsequently for public and private uses in the principal cities of Italy, exhibit proofs of great wealth, but are melancholy examples of the decline of the arts which Constantine and his immediate successors greatly accelerated by destroying the ancient buildings, the sight of which would have retarded or perhaps entirely have prevented the total degradation of architecture which followed. For taste in a great degree depends on the examples we have before us; however bad they may be, if sanctioned by success, they become objects of general imitation. Thus the church of San Paolo and the other large basilicas of Constantine, are to be traced, though on smaller scales, in most of the subsequent works which, like those of Constantine, being richly

Sir John Soane, "Lecture V," pp. 116–20, 122–5, 130, 132–3 from David Watkin (ed.), *Sir John Soane: The Royal Academy Lectures*. Cambridge: Cambridge University Press, 2000.

decorated with the plunder of ancient buildings, assume an air of magnificence, and even of interest. If richness of materials and profusion of ornaments could compensate for those real beauties which classical forms and a due mixture of solids and voids alone produce, these buildings would be entitled to general approbation; […] we must now take leave of the charms of Grecian art and proceed to what is called 'Gothic Architecture.'

[…]

The term 'Gothic Architecture' designates in this country and upon the continent that manner of building which […] succeeded and in some degree grew out of the architecture of the Romans, and which, after the subversion of the Roman Empire, became the general system of building throughout Europe.

From the neglect of the sciences connected with architecture, and from the degraded state of the art, as already shown in the later works of the immediate descendants of the Greeks and Romans, it follows that the want of scientific knowledge would be still greater amongst other nations.

Confining ourselves to this country, the early Saxon buildings were little more than clumsy imitations of Roman works, and when the power of the Saxons gave way to the proud and expensive Normans, no material progress or improvement had been made in architecture. They retained in their buildings the Saxon manner in most of its essentials, such as the circular arch, round-headed windows and doors, and massive pillars, with a kind of regular base and capital, the shafts sometimes plain, sometimes enclustered with small semi-columns, and at other times adorned with spiral grooves winding round, and net and lozenge-work overspreading them. These, with the thick walls and other characteristics of the early Saxon manner, were generally used until the middle of the twelfth century (1154).

The great characteristic differences between the Saxon and Norman architecture may be traced in the quantity of the ornaments and the increased magnitude of the buildings, particularly of the churches. The latter were often so large that their founders did little more than lay the foundations of the entire work and finish the east end, leaving the rest of the sculpture to be completed by their successors. Hence, it may be presumed, arose those discordant mixtures of different styles and ages so apparent in most of the great Norman buildings.

[…]

It has been already noticed that the temples erected by the Hindus and Egyptians to their divinities, as well as the dwellings for their families, were little more than copies of their former caverns and sombre retreats in the rocks and mountains. When the Greeks constructed buildings with stone and marble, they adhered as nearly as possible to a faithful imitation of their early works in timber. When Christianity first appeared, its votaries were compelled to perform their devotions in dark subterranean places, in the most retired and gloomy recesses. From these circumstances may we not conclude that as soon as free permission was allowed to the public exercise of the sacred functions of Christianity, that even then the primitive Christians, led by religious veneration and respect for early habits, endeavoured to display in their buildings above ground much of the heaviness, gloom, and intricacy of the subterranean sepulchres, and concealed places, wherein they had at first sheltered themselves from persecution and had exercised the rites and ceremonies of the Christian religion?

[…]

Such was the architecture of this country at the beginning of the thirteenth century when the windows, heretofore narrow and low, were then made wide and high, consisting of various parts, and different ramifications. The solids were made as small as they had been excessive; the round arch, springing from an impost, or from the capital of a low truncated cone or pillar, entirely disappeared, and the large truncated shaft itself was now formed by a cluster of columns, or divided into various parts by mouldings placed vertically on the pavement, and from thence continued uninterruptedly into the vaulted roof of the nave.

Thus we have a new and singular system of building [.]

[…]

Although in the structures raised after the Saxon and Norman manner, as well as in those which succeeded them with the pointed arch, we do not trace the elegant fancy of classical forms, nor the purity and chaste simplicity of Grecian intellect, yet the most enthusiastic admirers of Grecian and Roman architecture must admit that many of our great cathedrals have in combination, length and height, intricacy and solemnity, qualities which are the great sources of true sublimity.

[…]

The Gothic architecture, however happily adapted to religious purposes, is little calculated for the common habits of life. Its thick walls and small windows (admitting light as it were by stealth) are more suitable to Montezuma's house of affliction.[1] The features and general character of this mode of building are not expressive of cheerfulness or comfort.

Unless the architect has an intimate acquaintance with the several modifications and changes in the Gothic architecture of different ages, and thereby learns to avoid those incongruities, so frequent in modern Gothic buildings, his work will never interest the real admirers of that true, legitimate Gothic architecture which

---

[1] In the City of Mexico there was a palace termed 'the House of Affliction', where Montezuma retired upon losing any of his friends, or upon any public calamity. See Henry Home (Lord Vames), *Elements of Criticism* (Edinburgh: A. Kincaid & J. Bell, 1762), vol. 2, p. 484.

the young architect should study with the most serious attention, not for its taste, but for its effect in mass and detail.

In our great religious edifices he will discover many rich materials to assist his imagination, and by close examination of the extraordinary mechanism of those stupendous piles, his knowledge of construction will be considerably increased. He will perceive in many of those buildings a boldness and lightness unknown, or at least unpractised, in any of the great works of antiquity.

[...]

I shall only add that no system of architecture can produce such forcible effects on the intellectual mind as that which combines the fascinating powers of the sister arts. And as the Gothic architecture in its general distribution leaves only very inconsiderable spaces wherein paintings, sculptures and mosaics can be introduced, it must therefore be considered by all inferior to the Grecian.

With this important truth the great artists of the fifteenth and sixteenth centuries seem to have been so fully impressed that no Gothic buildings were erected in those happy periods. [...] It has been said that those powerful and imposing effects so visible in the exterior and interior of many of our Gothic cathedrals, cannot be obtained by any other mode of building. I would ask those who instance St. Paul's Cathedral in proof of this assertion whether a large portion of the solemnity and character so justly admired in Gothic works was not produced by the studied exclusion of all glaring lights; in the Saxon and Norman buildings by the smallness of the apertures and by the depth of light and shade, and in later works by the admission of stained glass. No person will deny these facts. Let us therefore suppose the windows of St. Paul's Cathedral glazed with scriptural subjects represented in strong and glowing colours, and then let us ask if there is any want of solemnity. But let the result of such an experiment be what it may, it could not be considered as decisive of the powers of ancient architecture, for St. Paul's, with all its merits, has too many of the defects of the Italian churches to be compared with the sublime conceptions of Grecian architecture. And on this occasion it might fairly be asked what example have we in this country of sufficient magnitude and correctness of composition to give an adequate idea of those great and solemn effects, produced by the ruins even of the sublime exertions of Roman and Grecian talent? Where shall we see buildings in this country capable of giving a correct impression of the magnificence of the Pantheon, the simple grandeur of the temples at Paestum, the sublime and imposing effect of the remains of the Temple of Minerva at Athens [...] will the porticoes of our churches, or those of any of the other buildings in this great metropolis, give even a faint idea of the grandeur of the portico of the Pantheon? Certainly not.

I have wandered so far out of the road and digressed so much from Gothic architecture, that what I proposed to say further on that mode of building must be deferred to another opportunity. So irresistibly am I now within the magic circle of Grecian and Roman art that it is impossible for me to look back and retrace my steps. Let us therefore once more turn our eyes towards Italy, that classical ground abounding with so many rich treasures of the ancient architecture, the powers of which may be obscured by ignorance and prejudice, by fashion and caprice, by improper models and tasteless patrons, but cannot be annihilated. Grecian art may be concealed as fire under embers, but be assured, my young friends, on the first favourable opportunity it will burst forth like the glorious sun from behind clouds of darkness and show itself in all the splendour of eternal truth, and again become the admiration of mankind. Filippo Brunelleschi paved the way for the restoration of the ancient architecture.

The success and the fame that Brunelleschi acquired created a spirit of research, and revived a true relish for the works of the ancients. To be distinguished as an architect it was now deemed necessary to measure and study assiduously the remains of ancient magnificence.

Vitruvius, long neglected, was now diligently read; the torch of truth and of taste was lighted; a noble spirit of enthusiasm was created; and each artist endeavoured to rival, and if possible to excel, his neighbour. That thirst after knowledge, and that noble ardour for architecture were revived, which ultimately produced those great artists, the boast of Italy and the pride of human nature.

Contemporary with Brunelleschi came Leon Battista Alberti, a noble Florentine who, like that great man, applied himself most diligently to the improvement of his mind, and became eminently distinguished as a philosopher, a poet, a painter, a sculptor, and an architect.

[...]

I wish to call the attention of the student to the elevation of the Fontana di Trevi, as a drawing, which I regret is not in perspective. This drawing was made by the late Sir William Chambers whilst pursuing his studies in Italy. There is a chasteness in the manner and an effect produced without much labour which makes it more desirable to the architect than the present more elaborate mode of treating architectural designs. A superior manner of drawing is absolutely necessary; [...]

Sir William Chambers, however, excelled not only in drawing. His designs for the church for the parish of St. Marylebone, and the mausoleum designed for the late Prince of Wales, show that he possessed no small portion of architectural knowledge. If the magnificent assemblage of buildings forming Somerset Place are not composed in all the purity of ancient architecture, and likewise shut out the view of the River Thames from the great quadrangle (a circumstance that must always be deeply regretted), yet the beauties of many of the great features of that noble pile are so strongly marked that the fame of Sir William Chambers will live as long as the work remains. Nor is this the only monument he has left. His Treatise on Civil Architecture, the result of close application, deep, erudite, thinking, and zeal for our noble art will always be read with pleasure and profit.

83

These observations are perhaps somewhat misplaced, but having mentioned the name of Sir William Chambers, I could not resist the temptation of paying my humble tribute of respect to the memory, talents, and integrity of an architect, who never omitted any opportunity of aggrandizing the art.

[...]

The taste for good architecture was followed by Sir Christopher Wren whose talents were called into action by the Great Fire in London. The Monument. St. Dunstan's in the East, and Bow Steeple are amongst his successful efforts. The interior of the church of St. Stephen, Walbrook, with all its beauties, is licentious in composition and deficient in apparent solidity of construction, but St. Paul's Cathedral, with all its defects, is sufficient to eternalize the name of this most justly celebrated architect.

Contemporary with Sir Christopher Wren was Sir John Vanbrugh whose numerous and extensive works show the versatility of his talents; and, if he wanted the grace and elegance of Palladio, he possessed in an eminent degree the powers of invention.

His works are full of character, and his outlines rich and varied; and although few of his compositions show any great knowledge of classical correctness, yet the mausoleum in the park at Castle Howard executed by his pupil, and the Temple of Concord and Victory at Stowe[2] are proofs that he occasionally felt the force of the simplicity of the ancients, whilst his house at Whitehall, in spite of the alterations and additions it has undergone, shows that he had the power of making small things interesting. His great work is Blenheim. The style of this building is grand and majestically imposing, the whole composition analogous to the war-like genius of the mighty hero for whom it was erected.

[...]

Since the introduction of good taste into this country by Inigo Jones, to the time of Lord Burlington and his immediate successors, architecture made rapid and progressive improvement; but since those happy periods many of the most classical buildings and princely mansions of our ancient nobility have been altered, and others have been entirely demolished according to an economising system which has produced a rage for speculative building that fatally tends to root out every vestige of good taste and sound construction.

[...]

Alas! the metropolis also has felt the baneful effects of this system of demolition and fashionable improvement.

---

[2] The design of the Temple of Concord and Victory at Stowe is now attributed to Richard Grenville and Giambattista Borra, not to Vanburgh.

8

From *A Description of the Villa*

Horace Walpole

Preface

It will look, I fear, a little like arrogance in a private Man to give a printed Description of his Villa and Collection, in which almost every thing is diminutive. It is not, however, intended for public sale, and originally was meant only to assist those who should visit the place. A farther view succeeded; that of exhibiting specimens of Gothic architecture, as collected from standards in cathedrals and chapel-tombs, and shewing how they may be applied to chimney-pieces, cielings, windows, ballustrades, loggias, etc. The general disuse of Gothic architecture, and the decay and alterations so frequently made in churches, give prints a chance of being the sole preservatives of that style.

Catalogues raisonnés of collections are very frequent in France and Holland; and it is no high degree of vanity to assume for an existing collection an illustration that is allowed to many a temporary auction – an existing collection – even that phrase is void of vanity. Having lived, unhappily, to see the noblest school of painting that this kingdom beheld, transported almost out of the sight of Europe, it would be strange fascination, nay, a total insensibility to the pride of family, and to the moral reflections that wounded pride commonly feels, to expect that a paper Fabric and an assemblage of curious Trifles, made by an insignificant Man, should last or be treated with more veneration and respect than the trophies of a palace deposited in it by one of the best and wisest Ministers that this country has enjoyed.

Far from such visions of self-love, the following account of pictures and rarities is given with a view to their future dispersion. The several purchasers will find a history of their purchases; nor do virtuosos dislike to refer to such a catalogue for an authentic certificate of their curiosities. The following collection was made out of the spoils of many renowned cabinets; as Dr. Meade's, lady Elizabeth Germaine's,

Horace Walpole, pp. i–iv (Preface), 1–3, 42 from *A Description of the Villa of Mr. Horace Walpole*. London, 1748.

lord *Oxford's,* the duchess of *Portland's,* and of about forty more of celebrity. Such well-attested descent is the genealogy of the objects of *virtù* – not so noble as those of the peerage, but on a par with those of race-horses. In all three, especially the pedigrees of peers and rarities, the line is often continued by many insignificant names.

The most considerable part of the following catalogue consists of miniatures, enamels, and portraits of remarkable persons. The collection of miniatures and enamels is, I believe, the largest and finest in any country. His Majesty has some very fine, the duke of Portland more; in no other is to be seen, in any good preservation, any number of the works of Isaac and Peter Oliver. The large pieces by the latter, in the royal collection, faded long ago by being exposed to the sun and air. Mons. Henery at Paris, and others, have many fine pieces of Petitot. In the following list are some most capital works of that master, and of his only rival Zincke. Raphael's missal is an unique work in miniature of that monarch of painting; and the book of psalms by Julio Clovio the finest specimen extant of illumination. The drawings and bas-reliefs in wax, by lady Diana Beauclerc, are as invaluable as rare.

To an English antiquary must be dear so many historic pictures of our ancient monarchs and royal family; no fewer than four family-pieces of Henry 5th. 6th. 7th. and 8th. of queen Mary Tudor and Charles Brandon; of the duchess of Suffolk and her second husband; and that curious and well-painted picture of Charles 2d. and his gardiner. Nor will so many works of Holbein be less precious to him, especially Zucchero's drawings from his Triumphs of Riches and Poverty.

To virtuosos of more classic taste, the small busts of Jupiter Serapis in basaltes, and of Caligula in bronze, and the silver bell of Benvenuto Cellini, will display the art of ancient and modern sculpture – how high it was carried by Greek statuaries, appears in the eagle.

To those who have still more taste than consists in meer sight, the catalogue itself will convey satisfaction, by containing a copy of madame du Deffand's letter in the name of madame de Sevignè; not written in imitation of that model of letter-writers, but composed of more delicacy of thought and more elegance of expression than perhaps madame de Sevignè herself could have attained. The two ladies ought not to be compared – one was all natural ease and tenderness – the other charms by the graces of the most polished style, which, however, are less beautiful than the graces of the wit they cloathe.

Upon the whole, some transient pleasure may even hereafter arise to the peruser of this catalogue. To others it may afford another kind of satisfaction, that of criticism. In a house affecting not only obsolete architecture, but pretending to an observance of the *costume* even in the furniture, the mixture of modern portraits, and French porcelaine, and Greek and Roman sculpture, may seem heterogeneous. In truth, I did not mean to make my house so Gothic as to exclude convenience, and modern refinements in luxury. The designs of the inside and outside are strictly ancient, but the decorations are modern.[1] Would our ancestors, before the reformation of architecture, not have deposited in their gloomy castles antique statues and fine pictures,

---

[1] And the mixture may be denominated, in some words of Pope, *A Gothic Vatican of Greece and Rome.*

beautiful vases and ornamental china, if they had possessed them? – But I do not mean to defend by argument a small capricious house. It was built to please my own taste, and in some degree to realize my own visions. I have specified what it contains; could I describe the gay but tranquil scene where it stands, and add the beauty of the landscape to the romantic cast of the mansion, it would raise more pleasing sensations than a dry list of curiosities can excite: at least the prospect would recall the good humour of those who might be disposed to condemn the fantastic fabric, and to think it a very proper habitation of, as it was the scene that inspired, the author of the Castle of Otranto.

A Description of the Villa of Mr. Horace Walpole, at Strawberry-Hill Near Twickenham.

Where the Gothic Castle now stands, was originally a small tenement,[2] built in 1698, and let as a lodging-house: Cibber once took it, and wrote one of his plays here, *The Refusal, or the Lady's Philosophy,* After him, Talbot bishop of Durham had it for eight years:[3] then, Henry Bridges marquis of Carnarvon, son of James duke of Chandos, and since duke himself. It was next hired by Mrs. Chenevix,[4] the noted toy-woman, who, on the death of her husband, let it to lord John Philip Sackville, second son of Lionel duke of Dorset: he kept it about two years, and then Mr. Walpole took the remainder of Mrs Chenevix's lease in May 1747, and the next year bought it by act of parliament, it being the property of three minors of the name of Mortimer. Along with this house and some other tenements was another small one,[5] then occupied by Richard Francklin, printer of the Craftsman, who had been taken up for printing that paper during the administration of sir Robert Walpole.[6] When Mr. Walpole bought Strawberry-hill, there were but five acres belonging to the house: the rest have been purchased since. The castle now existing was not entirely built from the ground, but formed at different times, by alterations of and additions to the old small house. The library, and refectory or great parlour, were entirely new built in 1753; the gallery, round tower, great cloyster, and cabinet, in 1760 and 1761; the great north bed-chamber in 1770; and the Beauclerc tower with the hexagon closet in 1776.

---

[2] It was built by the earl of Bradford's coachman, and was called by the common people, *Chopp'd-Straw-Hall,* they supposing, that by feeding his lord's horses with chopped straw, he had saved money enough to build his house; but the piece of ground on which it stands is called in all the old leases, *Strawberry-Hill-Shot,* from whence it takes its name.

[3] The bishop kept a large table here, which is scarce conceivable, as he had no kitchen but that little place which is now the china-room.

[4] Pere Courayer lodged here with her for some time.

[5] It has since been pulled down, and a cottage built on the same spot. The garden too has been newly laid out by Mr. Walpole since it came into his hands by Francklin's death.

[6] It is remarkable, that the printer of the Craftsman was Mr. Walpole's tenant; and that the writer of the Craftsman, W. Pulteney earl of Bath, wrote a ballad in praise of Strawberry-hill.

The embattled wall to the road is taken from a print of Aston-house in Warwickshire, in Dugdale's history of that county.

Entering by the great north gate, the first object that presents itself is a small oratory inclosed with iron rails; in front, an altar, on which stands a saint in bronze; open niches, and stone basons for holy water; designed by John Chute, esq; of the Vine in Hampshire. On the right hand is a small garden called the abbot's garden, parted off by an open screen, taken from the tomb of Roger Niger bishop of London in old St. Paul's. Passing on the left, by a small cloyster,[7] is the entrance to the house, the narrow front of which was designed by Richard Bentley, only son of Dr. Bentley, the learned master of Trinity-college, Cambridge. Over the door are three shields of Walpole, Shorter, and Robsart.

You first enter a small gloomy hall paved with hexagon tyles, and lighted by two narrow windows of painted glass, representing St. John and St. Francis. This hall is united with the staircase, and both are hung with gothic paper, painted by one Tudor, from the screen of prince Arthur's tomb in the cathedral of Worcester. The ballustrade was designed by Mr. Bentley; at every corner is an antelope [one of lord Orford's supporters] holding a shield. In the well of the staircase, by a cord of black and yellow, hangs a gothic lanthorn of tin japanned, designed by Mr. Bentley, and filled with painted glass; the door of it has an old pane with the arms of Vere earl of Oxford.

Turning to the left, through a small passage, over the entrance of which is an ancient carving in wood of the arms of queen Elizabeth, 1567, and in it a window of painted glass, you enter

The Refectory, or Great Parlour.

It is thirty feet long; twenty wide, and twelve high; hung with paper in imitation of stucco. The chimney-piece was designed by Mr. Bentley: upon it stands a fine Etruscan vase, between two bottles of black and gold porcelaine.

---

[7] In this cloyster are two blue and white Delft flower-pots; and a bas-relief head in marble, inscribed Dia Helianora; it is the portrait of the princess Eleanora d'Este, with whom Tasso was in love, and who was the cause of his misfortunes: it was sent to Mr. Walpole from Italy by sir William Hamilton, minister at Naples. On a pedestal, stands the large blue and white china tub in which Mr. Walpole's cat was drowned; on a label of the pedestal is written the first stanza of Mr. Gray's beautiful ode on that occasion:

> 'Twas on this *lofty vase's side,*
> *Where China's gayest art has dy'd*
> *The azure slow'rs that blow;*
> *Demurest of the tabby kind,*
> *The pensive Selima reclin'd,*
> *Gaz'd on the lake below.*

In the winding cloysters on the right hand are some ancient bas-reliefs; and a brass plate with the effigies of Ralph Walpole bishop of Norwich and Ely, engraven by Müntz (a Swiss painter who lived some time with Mr. Walpole) and a Chinese lanthorn with scraped oyster-shells,

Over the chimney, a conversation, by Reynolds, small life: Richard, second lord Edgcumbe, is drawing at a table in the library at Strawberry-hill; George James Williams is looking over him; George Augustus Selwyn stands on the other side with a book in his hand. Lord Edgcumbe, Mr. Selwyn and Mr. Williams used to be with Mr. Walpole at Christmas and Easter at Strawberry-hill.

On one side of this picture, a head of sir Horace Mann, resident at Florence; painted there by Astley, and highly coloured: He is drest in red velvet.

Opposite to it, his brother Galfridus Mann, in brown; by the same.

Over against the chimney, a bureau of black japan; on it a clock, supported by a bronze figure of a woman reading: beneath, an Etruscan vase, between two white old china beakers.

[...]

The Star Chamber

Is a small anti-room, painted green, with golden stars in mosaic. It has a large window entirely of painted glass; two triangular chairs taken from a piece of glass in Mr. Walpole's bed-chamber; two small Welch armed chairs, painted blue and white, with cushions of point-lace, and on one the arms of Mr. Richard Bateman, at whose sale they were purchased; a japan tea-table with white porcelaine; and a card-table of the same.

A mahogany cabinet, containing a collection of English and foreign coins and medals. On it, a bust of Henry 7th. in stone, a model in great taste for his tomb, by Torreggiano.[8] Under it a vase of false porphyry; from the collection of the comte de Caylus.

Another like cabinet, with gold, silver, and brass Greek and Roman coins, and a complete set of Roman weights from Dr. Middleton's collection. On it, a bust of Gibbs the architect in marble, by Rysbrack. Beneath, a vase, companion to the former.

A porringer, cover and plate, white, with different golds, of Seve china; a present from Mrs. Damer.

Hence you go into a trunk-cieled passage, lighted by a window of painted glass, in which are many quarterings of Latton, a family formerly seated at Esher in Surry: in the window, a candlestick enamelled on copper.

---

[8] Vide Anecdotes of Painting, vol. I, p. 102.

9

Thomas Jefferson

James Ackerman

[...]

Jefferson's interest in architecture began before the destruction by fire of his father's simple plantation settlement, Shadwell, in 1770, when he was twenty-seven.[1] He had decided some time before to make Monticello, in the virtual wilderness of central Virginia, the headquarters of his scattered inheritance of more than five thousand acres: leveling of the hilltop had already begun there in 1768. After the Shadwell fire, which destroyed his library and papers, Monticello became the only house he possessed for several decades; while he practiced law and served in the Virginia legislature and in the federal government he rented rooms in Richmond and Philadelphia. The proceeds from farming at Monticello were to have been his primary source of income, but Jefferson could not bring himself to operate the plantation exclusively with an eye to profit. His choice of an isolated site at the crown of a high hill with steep slopes that discouraged cultivation, at some distance from the Rivanna river, was prompted more by his taste for the panorama and for a quiet retreat than by farming efficiency. His interest in the improvement of American agriculture and his scientific curiosity were more compelling than economic success.

Jefferson designed or advised on the design of a number of houses that functioned like Palladio's villas in being of modest size (though relatively elegant

James Ackerman, "Thomas Jefferson," pp. 185–6, 188–200, 295–6 from *The Villa: Form and Ideology of Country Houses*. London: Thames & Hudson, 1990. ©1990 by Princeton University Press. Reprinted by permission of Princeton University Press.
[1] For the building history of Monticello, see William Howard Adams, *Jefferson's Monticello*, New York, 1983; Gene Waddell, "The First Monticello," *JSAH*, XLVI, 1987, pp. 5–27; Fiske Kimball, *Thomas Jefferson Architect*, Boston, 1916, pp. 57–61, 68–70, 73; facsimile edn, New York, 1968 (drawings cataloged in this are cited below as "K" followed by the figure number); Frederick D. Nichols and James A. Bear, *Monticello: A Guidebook*, Monticello, 1967; William H. Pierson Jr., *American Buildings and their Architects: The Colonial and Neoclassical Styles*, New York, 1970, pp. 287–316.

outside and luxurious within) and in being the working headquarters of large plantations. But in two ways they differed: the estates were in the wilderness of a virgin land, and they were worked in part by slaves. The isolation helped to determine the use of brick as a structural material (Jefferson thought that wooden architecture was inferior) since it could be made on the site, and it affected the planning of the living quarters at Monticello, especially in the enlargement that began in 1796. [...]

As an educated colonial patrician, Jefferson naturally absorbed the attitudes of earlier eighteenth-century British landowners and intellectuals. His approach to the design of a country estate was similar to theirs in being grounded in classical learning, particularly Roman bucolic poetry and the villa literature. Like Lord Burlington, he was a serious amateur architect who designed buildings for himself and others in his circle and who called on professionals – Clérisseau, Latrobe, Mills – for criticism and advice. He wanted his house and grounds to represent certain Enlightenment virtues: liberty, simplicity and practicality. And, like his liberal Whig forebears, he was vigorously anti-establishment and sought an architectural style that would offer a clear alternative to the one currently favored in his social milieu.

In revealing ways, however, Jefferson rejected the Burlingtonian inheritance. He was not a member of an intellectual, philosophical and artistic circle that exerted influence over the course of architectural design. He had no interest in recalling the British national heritage and therefore no reason to reflect the work of Inigo Jones; his interest in modern French architecture would not have been acceptable in England. Unlike the earlier Palladians, and more like contemporary British architects such as Robert Adam and John Soane, his approach to design was less committed to observing precedents and rules of vocabulary and com-position and less deferential to Palladian models. And finally, though he was sufficiently intrigued by the new English landscape design to study William Shenstone's "Unconnected Thoughts on Gardening" (published in 1764) and to tour the best-known examples with Thomas Whately's *Observations on Modern Gardening* (1770) in hand, his own landscape planning at Monticello adopted only the general character of informality and refrained from emulating the aspects of the sequence of diverse experiences, surprise, and the thematic treatment of separated areas. His estate was not planned as an Elysium of literary allusion.

[...]

Jefferson's architectural taste was formed initially from books. Jefferson col-lected avidly, building an architectural library as rich as that of a British amateur of the mid-century.[2] At the start, he favored Gibbs's *Book of Architecture*, the editions of Palladio's *Quattro libri* published in London and Paris earlier in the century [...] and the *Select Architecture* of 1755 by the Palladian and classical

[2] William B. O'Neal, *Jefferson's Fine Arts Library*, Charlottesville, 1976; E. Millicent Sowerby, *Catalogue of the Library of Thomas Jefferson*, 5 vols, Washington, D.C., 1952–9.

theorist Robert Morris.[3] [...] When remodeling Monticello after 1796, Jefferson depended on the more precise plates of two recent publications [...] Fréart de Chambray's *Parallèle de l'architecture antique avec la moderne*, in a revised edition of 1764–66, and Desgodets's *Les édifices antiques de Rome* (London, 1771–95); in his copy of the former he made notes of his intention to use particular Roman orders and entablatures for the interiors of the house. Though Jefferson, writing to the proprietor of Bremo, referred to Palladio's book as "the Bible," he used it more consistently for its version of the ancient orders – especially for the proportioning of elements – than for its original dwelling projects. Except in the initial stage of the Monticello design, in which the Palladianism is mostly filtered through Gibbs, he did not reflect Palladian planning or elevation solutions. Jefferson was a designer and did not intend simply to adapt model projects. He used his sources selectively, and the ultimate designs of Monticello and other houses of his late years are more original than those of any strictly Palladian English architect.

Building of the first house at Monticello began in the spring of 1769 and lasted nearly a decade. [...]

The early sketches for the house done in the course of 1768–69 were variations on plans in Gibbs's *Book* – the first a square with recessed porches on each side, and later ones a rectangular plan followed by cruciform variants from which the ultimate design developed.[4] These culminate in a plan that became the basis of the first elevations, of which the final version has a two-story central pedimented block flanked by lower blocks.[5] [...] Jefferson joined elements from diverse sources in a project of striking originality that represents an elevation of southern colonial architecture to the level of current European design. [...] At the cost of classical purity, the semi-octagonal spaces, filled with light and offering a panoramic view onto the garden, vary the exterior and enrich the quality of the interior. Jefferson found the motif so congenial that he used it in the majority of his remaining projects [...]

The utilitarian functions of the basement story are indicated by Jefferson on the ground floor plan. The portion under the house and the south (left) terrace accommodates storage and preparation of food, the kitchen being placed at the angle under the pavilion. The north side is assigned to the stables and

---

[3] For Jefferson's use of Gibbs, see Waddell, "The First Monticello"; of Palladio, James Ackerman, "Il presidente Jefferson e il palladianesimo americano," *BCISA*, VI, 1964, pp. 39–48; of Morris, Clay Lancaster, "Jefferson's Architectural Indebtedness to Robert Morris," *JSAH*, X, 1951, pp. 3–10. See also Kimball, *Thomas Jefferson Architect*; Nichols, *Thomas Jefferson's Architectural Drawings*, 2nd edn, Boston and Charlottesville, 1961 (drawings cataloged in this are cited below as N followed by the catalog number); Burford Pickens, "Mr Jefferson as a Revolutionary Architect," *JSAH*, XXXIV, 4, 1974, pp. 257–79.

[4] For the matching of early projects to Gibbs, see Waddell, "The First Monticello," figs. 4, 7 (K.37); figs. 5, 6, 8 (K.11, 18); figs. 10–12 (K.29, N.45).

[5] On the sequence of elevations, ibid., pp. 14–18.

a room for the servants. [. . .] Jefferson concealed a dumb-waiter in the dining room mantelpiece to bring food and drink from the house basement to the dining room on the north. He was intent on keeping servants out of sight as much as possible.

The utility areas are linked by a vaulted corridor lit by penetrations on one side in the fashion of the ancient *cryptoporticus,* a device frequently employed in Roman villas, and described in Pliny's letter on his Laurentine villa. The corridor extended only to the angles, because the slope of the hill made it possible for the north and south arms to be open to the exterior.

The construction of the first Monticello design continued throughout the 1770s, though at a reduced pace during the Revolutionary years, and the house (except for the service wings) was substantially finished at the time Jefferson left to take up his post as Minister to France in 1784. The five years spent in Paris gave him his first experience of the ancient Roman monuments of southern France and of recent French and English architecture that he had known only through books. [. . .] On his return to Monticello in 1794, following a brief and stormy period as Secretary of State in Washington's cabinet, Jefferson began to make studies for a radical reconstruction and enlargement of the house.

The plan of the revised Monticello is preserved in a drawing on squared paper, which Jefferson began to use on his return to France.[6] It adds to the entrance side of the house a block of approximately the same form and size as the existing one, with a corridor running the length of the building, dividing the old from the new. In this eastern tract a "Hall" echoes the parlor, and guest rooms reflect the dining room and the master's suite. The bedrooms are given bed-alcoves, a Parisian feature that caught Jefferson's fancy; in his own room, the alcove separates the dressing area from the study and is open on either side to invite the summer breezes, and to improve the light and the view in both spaces. The projections of the new bedroom alcoves leave little space in the central corridor for the two stairways; they are inconvenient to use[.] [. . .]

The original house was significantly changed only by the blocking in of the eastern side of the parlor to complete the octagonal form and to give support to the dome which was now to rise over this area. The new plan ingeniously segregates the private areas from the public by assigning the broad central spine plus the dining room and "North Bow" to communal use, and sealing off each bedroom from its neighbor. There are four bedrooms and two other rooms on the floor above; the two sides of this floor are separated by the hall, and Jefferson joined them by a balcony over the entrance to the parlor.

Though it is not obvious from the plan, the new design represented a radical shift in style inspired by contact with contemporary French architecture. The building actually has three floors (the third being the level of the dome room over the parlor), but it appears from the exterior to have only a main floor and a mezzanine. On the entrance facade the windows of the lower and upper levels of

---

[6] K.150, N.135. The interior is richly illustrated in Adams, *Monticello,* pp. 83–144.

bedrooms are fused together and both are below the entablature, so that they seem to belong to the same floor (the third floor is quite obscured by a balustrade); this makes the upper bedrooms less agreeable, as the windows are small and reach only from just above the floor to well below eye level.

[...]

The octagonal saucer dome over the parlor is not in the tradition of Palladio's Rotonda and Burlington's Chiswick cubic buildings in which the dome covers a circular central hall at the core. It follows French tradition in being at the exterior of one of the long sides of a rectangular building, surmounting a projecting salon of the same form as the drum. [...] Jefferson's treatment of the theme remained in the pure classical tradition: it did not assimilate the refinements of contemporary Parisian architecture.

The garden side has no mezzanine because the public rooms and the master suite rise to the height of the exterior entablature. This allowed the windows of all these rooms to be extended downward to floor level – an innovation, also inspired by Parisian practice, that was to lend elegance and light to many domestic buildings of the two ensuing generations in America.

Despite importations from abroad, the second Monticello was a building of individuality and strict elegance. The home-made bricks and detailing in white painted wood carved on the site inevitably distanced the building from European models. [...]

The interior was designed in the first years of the new century, though Jefferson's eight years as President (1801–09) caused protracted delays in construction. With the painting of the major rooms in 1809, Monticello reached nearly its present state. The interior design demonstrates Jefferson's scholarship, in its detailing, his backwoods inventiveness in its mechanical conveniences and gadgetry, and his catholic acquisitiveness in its furnishings. It has engaging qualities, particularly in the lighting, the views out from the windows, and the detailing, but the public rooms and master bedroom are too lofty and awkwardly proportioned, and the private ones too cramped.

Jefferson's notebook of the 1770s shows that he meant the decoration of the main rooms to be an illustration of the full canon of ancient orders according to Palladio's First Book.[7] Corinthian was used in the parlor since, according to the Vitruvian tradition, it was the most elegant and festive order, but otherwise Jefferson probably did not try to apply them symbolically. In the new design, however, Palladio no longer commanded; Jefferson turned to the more accurate reproductions of ancient Roman details in Fréart de Chambray's *Parallèle* [...] and Desgodets's *Edifices antiques de Rome*. The detailing was no longer to be generically classical but was to reproduce the decoration of specific buildings: for example, the Temple of Fortuna Virilis in Rome for the bedroom, that of

---

[7] K.68–92, N.97–123.

Antoninus and Faustina for the hall, and the Baths of Diocletian for the north piazza. Jefferson made chaste and elegant line drawings for all the entablatures and cornices;[8] the decorative friezes he had carved directly from the book plates. Master joiners were brought from Philadelphia to do the work. The mantel of the dining room, with its three up-to-date blue-ground Wedgwood medallions, is an exception to the pervasive Romanism. Jefferson was otherwise cool toward the Greek Revival taste represented by the Wedgwood pieces; in fact, he set them in a frame of relief urns, probably carved on the site, that are slightly discordant in style.

The hall is the heart of circulation in Jefferson's scheme: it gives access to and from the exterior, the public rooms and master bedroom, the narrow corridors that serve the bedrooms and constricted stairways on both floors, and the public privy. Because it rises the full height of the ground floor and the mezzanine, communication between the upper bedrooms on either side is provided by a ponderous and visually disruptive balcony cantilevered over the east end. The hall functioned also as a museum for the display not just of art works but, in the longstanding tradition of the European *Wunderkammer*, of Indian relics, fossils, stuffed animal heads, and mementos of the Lewis and Clark expedition which first explored the American Northwest. The eighteen paintings and sculptures, imported from Europe, were partly original French, Italian and Netherlandish works and partly copies. Jefferson did not believe that the agrarian society of the new nation should take up the figurative arts, and wrote that while "architecture is among the most important arts [and] it is desireable to introduce taste into an art which shows so much," painting and statuary are "too expensive for the state of wealth among us. It would be useless, therefore, and preposterous, for us to make ourselves connoisseurs in those arts. They are worth seeing, but not studying."[9]

Monticello is an eloquent affirmation of a committed and cultivated way of life. Its situation in the wilderness, the practicality of its arrangements and its independence from the prevailing pretentiousness of colonial architectural forms reveal a will to find an architectural expression for the ideals of a new democracy. Its reaffirmation of ancient classical authority as seen through the interpretations of Palladio and later theorists and its selection of the freshest contemporary innovations from French buildings and English books reveal an aspiration to give American design a cosmopolitan outlook informed by immersion in the classical heritage.

[8] K.158–60; N.173–4, 157.
[9] "Notes on Objects of Attention for an American," *Papers*, XIII, 1956, p. 269.

10

From *A Philosophical Enquiry into the Origin of our Ideas of the Sublime and Beautiful*

Edmund Burke

Section I
Of the Passion Caused by the Sublime

The passion caused by the great and sublime in *nature*, when those causes operate most powerfully, is Astonishment; and astonishment is that state of the soul, in which all its motions are suspended, with some degree of horror. In this case the mind is so entirely filled with its object, that it cannot entertain any other, nor by consequence reason on that object which employs it. Hence arises the great power of the sublime, that far from being produced by them, it anticipates our reasonings, and hurries us on by an irresistible force. Astonishment, as I have said, is the effect of the sublime in its highest degree; the inferior effects are admiration, reverence and respect.

Section II
Terror

No passion so effectually robs the mind of all its powers of acting and reasoning as fear. For fear being an apprehension of pain or death, it operates in a manner that resembles actual pain. Whatever therefore is terrible, with regard to sight, is sublime too, whether this cause of terror, be endued with greatness of dimensions or not; for it is impossible to look on any thing as trifling, or contemptible, that may be dangerous. [. . .]

Edmund Burke, pp. 57, 74–7, 81 from *A Philosophical Enquiry into the Origin of our Ideas of the Sublime and Beautiful*, ed. James T. Boulton. Oxford: Basil Blackwell, 1987.

Section IX
Succession and Uniformity

Succession and *uniformity* of parts, are what constitute the artificial infinite. I. *Succession*; which is requisite that the parts may be continued so long, and in such a direction, as by their frequent impulses on the sense to impress the imagination with an idea of their progress beyond their actual limits. 2. *Uniformity*; because if the figures of the parts should be changed, the imagination at every change finds a check; you are presented at every alteration with the termination of one idea, and the beginning of another; by which means it becomes impossible to continue that uninterrupted progression, which alone can stamp on bounded objects the character of infinity. It is in this kind of artificial infinity, I believe, we ought to look for the cause why a rotund has such a noble effect. For in a rotund, whether it be a building or a plantation, you can no where fix a boundary; turn which way you will, the same object still seems to continue, and the imagination has no rest. But the parts must be uniform as well as circularly disposed, to give this figure its full force; because any difference, whether it be in the disposition, or in the figure, or even in the colour of the parts, is highly prejudicial to the idea of infinity, which every change must check and interrupt, at every alteration commencing a new series. On the same principles of succession and uniformity, the grand appearance of the ancient heathen temples, which were generally oblong forms, with a range of uniform pillars on every side, will be easily accounted for. From the same cause also may be derived the grand effect of the isles in many of our own old cathedrals. The form of a cross used in some churches seems to me not so eligible, as the parallelogram of the ancients; at least I imagine it is not so proper for the outside. For, supposing the arms of the cross every way equal, if you stand in a direction parallel to any of the side walls, or colonnades, instead of a deception that makes the building more extended than it is, you are cut off from a considerable part (two thirds) of its *actual* length; and to prevent all possibility of progression, the arms of the cross taking a new direction, make a right angle with the beam, and thereby wholly turn the imagination from the repetition of the former idea. Or suppose the spectator placed where he may take a direct view of such a building; what will be the consequence? the necessary consequence will be, that a good part of the basis of each angle, formed by the intersection of the arms of the cross, must be inevitably lost; the whole must of course assume a broken unconnected figure; the lights must be unequal, here strong, and there weak; without that noble gradation, which the perspective always effects on parts disposed uninterruptedly in a right line. Some or all of these objections, will lie against every figure of a cross, in whatever view you take it. I exemplified them in the Greek cross in which these faults appear the most strongly; but they appear in some degree in all sorts of crosses. Indeed there is nothing more prejudicial to the grandeur of buildings, than to abound in angles; a fault obvious in many; and owing to an inordinate thirst for variety, which, whenever it prevails, is sure to leave very little true taste.

Section X
Magnitude in Building

To the sublime in building, greatness of dimension seems requisite; for on a few parts, and those small, the imagination cannot rise to any idea of infinity. No greatness in the manner can effectually compensate for the want of proper dimensions. There is no danger of drawing men into extravagant designs by this rule; it carries its own caution along with it. Because too great a length in buildings destroys the purpose of greatness which it was intended to promote; the perspective will lessen it in height as it gains in length; and will bring it at last to a point; turning the whole figure into a sort of triangle, the poorest in its effect of almost any figure, that can be presented to the eye. I have ever observed, that colonnades and avenues of trees of a moderate length, were without comparison far grander, than when they were suffered to run to immense distances. A true artist should put a generous deceit on the spectators, and effect the noblest designs by easy methods. Designs that are vast only by their dimensions, are always the sign of a common and low imagination. No work of art can be great, but as it deceives; to be otherwise is the prerogative of nature only. A good eye will fix the medium betwixt an excessive length, or height, (for the same objection lies against both), and a short or broken quantity; and perhaps it might be ascertained to a tolerable degree of exactness, if it was my purpose to descend far into the particulars of any art.

[...]

Section XV
Light in Building

As the management of light is a matter of importance in architecture, it is worth enquiring, how far this remark is applicable to building. I think then, that all edifices calculated to produce an idea of the sublime, ought rather to be dark and gloomy, and this for two reasons; the first is, that darkness itself on other occasions is known by experience to have a greater effect on the passions than light. The second is, that to make an object very striking, we should make it as different as possible from the objects with which we have been immediately conversant; when therefore you enter a building, you cannot pass into a greater light than you had in the open air; to go into one some few degrees less luminous, can make only a trifling change; but to make the transition thoroughly striking, you ought to pass from the greatest light, to as much darkness as is consistent with the uses of architecture. At night the contrary rule will hold, but for the very same reason; and the more highly a room is then illuminated, the grander will the passion be.

11

On Architecture and Buildings, &c.

Sir Uvedale Price

[. . .]

Architecture in towns may be said to be principal and independent – in the country it is in some degree subordinate and dependent on the surrounding objects. This distinction, though not sufficient to form a separate class, ought not to be neglected: had it been attended to, so many square, formal, unpicturesque houses of great expense might not have encumbered the scenes which they were meant to adorn. I am not surprised, however, that the style of country houses should have been too indiscriminately taken from those of towns. All the fine arts have been brought to their greatest perfection where large bodies of men have been settled together; for wealth, emulation, and comparison are necessary to their growth; and, of all the arts, architecture has most strikingly embellished the places where it has flourished. In cities, therefore, the greatest number and variety of finished pieces of architecture are to be found – and it is not to be wondered at if those houses, which in cities were with reason admired, should have been the objects of general, and often of indiscriminate imitation.

There are, however, very obvious reasons for making a difference of character in the two sorts of buildings. In a street, or a square, hardly any thing but the front is considered, for little else is seen – and even where the building is insulated, it is generally more connected with other buildings than with what may be called landscape. The spectator, also, being confined to a few stations, and those not distant, has his attention entirely fixed on the architecture, and the architect – but in the midst of landscape they are both subordinate, if not to the landscape painter, at least to the principles of his art.

In a letter written on tragedy to Count Alfieri, by an eminent critic, Signor Calsabigi, he insists very much on the necessity of uniting the mind of the painter

Sir Uvedale Price, "On Architecture and Buildings," pp. 328–33, 336–40, 343–4, 346, 350–1, 353, 408–9 from *Sir Uvedale Price on the Picturesque*. London: William. S. Orr and Co., 1797.

with that of the poet, and that the tragic writer should be *poeta-pittore;* it is no less necessary, and more literally so, that the architect of buildings in the country should be *architetto-pittore;* for, indeed, he ought not only to have the mind, but the hand of the painter – not only to be acquainted with the principles, but, as far as design goes, with the practice of landscape painting. All that belongs to the embellishment of the scenes round country houses, has, of late years, been more generally and studiously attended to in this kingdom than in any other – architecture has also met with great encouragement; but however its professors may have studied the principles of landscape painting, they have had but little encouragement to pursue those studies, or opportunity of connecting them practically with those of their own profession. When a house was to be built, Mr. Brown, of course, decided with respect to its situation, the plantations that were to accompany it, the trees that were to be left or taken down, &c. – the architect, therefore, had only to consider how his own design would look upon paper, unconnected with any other objects – he was no further concerned.

Now, it seems to me, that if a person merely wants a house of beautiful architecture, with finely proportioned and well distributed rooms, and with convenient offices, and looks no further, the assistance of an architect, though always highly useful, is hardly necessary. A number of elevations and plans of such houses, of different forms and sizes, have been published; or he may look at those which have been completed, observe their appearance and distribution, and suit himself – the estimate a common builder can make as well as Palladio.

I am very far from intending, by what I have just said, to undervalue a profession which I highly respect, or to suppose it unnecessary; on the contrary, I am very anxious to show that whoever wishes his buildings to be real decorations to his place, cannot do without an architect; and by an architect I do not mean a mere builder, but one who has studied landscape as well as architecture, who is no less fond of it than of his own profession, and who feels that each different situation requires a different disposition of the several parts. In reality, this view of the profession points out the use, and greatly exalts the character, of an architect. It is an easy matter, by means of some slight changes in what has already been done, to avoid absolute plagiarism, and to make out such a design as may look well upon paper; but, to unite with correct design such a disposition as will accord, not only with the general character of the scenery, but with the particular spot and the objects immediately around it, and which will present from a number of points a variety of well combined parts, requires very different and very superior abilities.

[...]

Much of the naked solitary appearance of houses, is owing to the practice of totally concealing, nay sometimes of burying, all the offices under ground, and that by way of giving consequence to the mansion [...] Of this kind is the grandeur that characterises many of the ancient castles; which proudly overlook the different outworks, the lower towers, the gateways, and all the appendages to the main building; and this principle, so productive of grand and picturesque effects, has been applied with great success by Vanbrugh to highly ornamented buildings, and to Grecian architecture. The same principle (with those variations and exceptions that will naturally suggest themselves to artists) may be applied to all houses. [. . .]

[[. . .] how often have we to deplore the mistake which we see committed, of building up a certain quantity of good materials into a mass, remarkable for its deformity, when they might have been just as easily put together in a pleasing form, at the same expense, or even perhaps with a less expenditure. Then, again, how often do we see beauty of form altogether sacrificed to fineness of material, and smoothness of polish. These last are of the highest value in urban architecture; but although I do not say that there are not situations where they may be likewise estimated in the country, I hold that, in general, the perfection of all rural architecture depends more upon its form than upon any thing else. In a city, each building must necessarily be of regular plan. In the country, I think the more irregular the plan of the house – whether it be cottage, villa, manor-house, or castle – the better. The stables, and all the other useful offices belonging to the house, should find a place, though a subordinate one, in the group of buildings which the architect has to put down, and it is of great importance that some lines of attachment should be created to give them absolute connection; for nothing looks so ill as such subsidiary buildings being placed near to, yet unconnected with, the dwelling-house. So many subjects brought together, give greater scope to the inventive powers of the architect, in his endeavour to work them into good combinations; and the necessity of the connecting lines, of which I have just spoken, begets additional opportunities of design, in the shape of low walls, balustrades, and terraces – altogether productive of an effect infinitely more rich, picturesque, and interesting, than any thing that can be created where a strictly uniform architectural house has been erected. – E.]

[. . .]

I have endeavoured in all I have stated, to point out some of the advantages that are gained, by breaking with trees, [. . .] and I have done it more fully, because the opposite system has strongly prevailed. I do not mean, however, to assert that such breaks are always necessary, or expedient; though in my own opinion, it can seldom happen that a view will not be improved, from one or more trees, rising boldly above the horizon. Where fine old trees are *left*, they plead their own excuse [. . .]

I now come to another objection, viz. that they conceal too much of the architecture. And here I will allow, however desirous I may be of varying the composition from the house, and of softening too open a display of symmetry, that great respect ought to be paid to such works as are deservedly ranked among the productions of genius, in an art of high consideration from the remotest antiquity. Whenever the improvement of the view would injure the beauty or grandeur of such works, or destroy that idea of connection and symmetry, which, though veiled, should still be preserved, such an improvement would cost too dear. But in buildings, where the forms and the heights are varied by means of pavilions, colonnades, &c., there generally are places where trees might be planted with great advantage to the effect of the building, considered as part of a picture, without injury to it as a piece of architecture; and in the placing of which accompaniments, the painter who was conversant with architecture, and the architect who had studied painting, would probably coincide; and this, I think, may more strongly point out the difference I mentioned before, between the style which suits a town only, and that which might suit both town and country. A square, detached house in the country, while it requires trees to make up for the want of variety in its form, affords no indication where they may be placed with effect; they will indeed diminish the monotony, but will not, as in the other case, so mix in with the buildings, as to seem a part of the design of an architect-painter.

The accompaniments of beautiful pieces of architecture, may in some respects be compared to the dress of beautiful women. The addition of what is no less foreign to them than trees are to architecture, varies and adorns the charms even of those, who, like Phryne, might throw off every concealment, and challenge the critic eyes of all Athens assembled. Men grow weary of uniform perfection; nor will any thing compensate the absence of every obstacle to curiosity, and every hope of novelty. It is not probable, that Phryne was ignorant or neglectful of the charms of variety and of partial concealment; and if the most perfect forms may be rendered still more attractive by what is foreign to them, how much more those which have little or no pretensions to beauty! How many buildings have I seen, which, with their trees, attract and please every eye! But deprive one of them of those accompaniments, what a solitary deserted object would remain!

[...]

The best preservative against flatness and monotony on the one hand, and whimsical variety on the other, is an attentive study of what constitutes the grand, the beautiful, and the picturesque in buildings, as in all other objects. An artist who is well acquainted with the qualities of which those characters are compounded, with their general effect, and with the tendency of those qualities if carried to excess, will know when to keep each character separate – when, and in what degree, to mix them, according to the effect he means to produce.

The causes and effects of the sublime and of the beautiful have been investigated by a great master, whose footsteps I have followed in a road, which his penetrating and comprehensive genius had so nobly opened. I have ventured indeed to explore a new track, and to discriminate the causes and the effects of the picturesque from those of the two other characters; still, however, I have in some degree proceeded under his auspices – for it is a track I never should have discovered, had not he first cleared and adorned the principal avenues.

With respect to the sublime in buildings, Mr. Burke, without entering into a minute detail, has pointed out its most efficient causes; two of which are succession, and uniformity. These he explains and exemplifies by the appearance of the ancient heathen temples, which, he observes, were generally oblong forms, with a range of uniform pillars on every side; and he adds, that from the same causes, may also be derived the grand effects of the aisles in many of our own Cathedrals. But although succession and uniformity, when united to greatness of dimension, are among the most efficient causes of grandeur in buildings, yet causes of a very opposite nature (though still upon one general principle) often tend to produce the same effects. These are, the accumulation of unequal, and, at least apparently, irregular forms, and the intricacy of their disposition. The forms and the disposition of some of the old castles built on eminences, fully illustrate what I have just advanced; the different outworks and massive gateways; towers rising behind towers; the main body perhaps rising higher than them all, and on one side descending in one immense solid wall quite down to the level below – all impress grand and awful ideas.

As I have in a former part made intricacy a characteristic mark of the picturesque, I may possibly be accused of inconsistency in making it also a cause of grandeur. It might be sufficient to say that there are other qualities common to the sublime and to the picturesque, such as roughness and abruptness, and that, therefore, intricacy might be in the same class. I shall not, however, be satisfied with that general defence, but shall endeavour to account in a more satisfactory manner for this seeming inconsistency. There appear to be various degrees and styles of intricacy. Hogarth, as I have mentioned on a former occasion, in speaking of the effect of those waving lines which steal from the eye, and lead it a kind of wanton chase, has termed it the *beauty* of intricacy, which I have endeavoured to distinguish from the more sudden and abrupt kind which belongs to the picturesque; I will now point out what I conceive might be called with equal propriety the sublime of intricacy.

When suspense and uncertainty are produced by the abrupt intricacy of objects divested of grandeur, they are merely amusing to the mind, and their effect simply picturesque. But where the objects are such as are capable of inspiring awe or terror, there suspense and uncertainty are powerful causes of the sublime; and intricacy may, by those means, create no less grand effects than uniformity and succession. An avenue of large and lofty trees, forming a continued arch, and terminated by the gateway of a massive tower, is a specimen, and no mean one, of the grandeur arising from succession and uniformity. [. . .]

The same kind of difference subsists between the intricacy of the pinnacles and fret work of Gothic architecture, and that more broad and massive kind of the towers and gateways of ancient castles. Mr. Burke observes, that the sublime in building requires solidity, and even massiness; and, in my idea, no single cause acts so powerfully, and can so little be dispensed with as massiness; but as massiness is so nearly allied to heaviness, it is – in this age especially – by no means a popular quality; for in whatever regards the mind itself, or the works that proceed from it,

103

the reproach of heaviness is, of all others, the least patiently endured. It is a reproach, however, that has been made to some of the most striking buildings, both ancient and modern.

[...]

From the analogy between the general effects of rocks and of buildings, I am led to believe, that though many small divisions diminish grandeur, yet that certain marked divisions, by affording the eye a scale of comparison, give a greater consequence to the whole. The same quantity, therefore, of stone, brick, or any other material, if divided into certain large portions, (as, for instance, into round or square towers,) will not only be more varied, but appear of greater magnitude, than the same quantity of materials in one square mass, such as is often seen in houses of what is called the Italian style.

[...]

Sir Joshua Reynolds is, I believe, the first who has done justice to the architecture of Vanbrugh, by showing that it was not a mere fantastic style, without any other object than that of singularity, but that he worked on the principles of painting, and has produced the most painter-like effects.

[...]

I have already disclaimed all knowledge of architecture as a science, and have professed my intention of treating of it chiefly as connected with scenery; after what I have said of Vanbrugh, it is highly necessary to renew that declaration. Few persons, I believe, have in any art been guilty of more faults, though few, likewise, have produced more striking effects. As an author, and an architect, he boldly set rules at defiance, and, in both those characters, completely disregarded all purity of style; yet, notwithstanding those defects, Blenheim and Castle Howard, the Provoked Wife and the Relapse, will probably be admired as long as the English nation or language shall continue to exist.

An architect who is thus notorious for his violation of rules, his neglect of purity and elegance, and his licentious mixture of styles and ornaments, certainly ought not to be held up as a model for imitation; but, on the other hand, an artist who, in any art, produces new and striking effects, well deserves to have their causes investigated; for he who has produced such effects, (it hardly matters by what means) has attained a great end. The study, therefore, not the imitation of Vanbrugh's architecture, might be extremely serviceable to an artist of genius and discernment. It is true that Sir Joshua Reynolds, when speaking in praise of Vanbrugh, has disclaimed any authority on the subject of architecture as a science; but his authority as a painter for the general picturesque effect of buildings, is indisputable; and what such a man admired, ought not rashly to be despised or neglected. He explained upon the principles of his own art, what were those of the architect of Blenheim; and they deserve to be still farther discussed. I should think it would be an excellent study for an architect, to make drawings of Blenheim, endeavouring to preserve the principle of light and shadow, the character of the architectural foreground, the effect of the raised decorations on the roof, and the general grandeur and variety of the whole; but trying, at the same time, to give more lightness and purity of style to that whole, more elegance and congruity to the parts; observing as he proceeded, how far he found it necessary to sacrifice purity, lightness, elegance, and unity of style, in order to preserve those effects which Vanbrugh has produced.

[...]

One of the greatest difficulties with respect to the summits of our houses, certainly arises from the chimneys; which though not very generally attended to in point of outward form, very materially affect the outline of all houses, from the highest to the lowest.

[...]

On these points, little or no assistance can be gained from pictures.
[...] Little more assistance can be gained from some of the most approved writers on architecture. Palladio, for example, is totally silent with regard to the form and effect of chimneys on the outside of houses.

[...]

All that the architect can do, is to disguise, if he cannot new model, the forms of his chimneys; they must exist, and must occupy a conspicuous station. Painters, indeed, in representing any splendid edifices, usually take the liberty of omitting them altogether; a liberty which in some respects we may regret their having taken, as if they had thought themselves obliged to make out the form distinctly, they probably would have contrived to make it harmonise with the rest of the structure, and would have afforded very useful hints to the architect.

[...]

With respect to the particular subject of this Essay, although by the study of pictures a man will gain but little knowledge of architecture as a science, yet, by seeing the grandest and most beautiful specimens of that art happily grouped with each other and with the surrounding objects, and displayed in the most favour-able points of view, he may certainly acquire a just idea of their forms and effects, and their connection with scenery. He will also gain a knowledge, not easily acquired by any other means – that of the infinitely diversified characters and

105

effects of broken and irregular buildings with their accompaniments; and of all that in them, and in similar objects is justly called picturesque, because they belong to pictures, and to the productions of no other art.

The more I reflect on the whole of the subject, the more I am convinced, that the study of the principles of painting in the works of eminent painters, is the best method of acquiring an accurate and comprehensive taste and judgment, in all that regards the effects and combinations of visible objects. And thence I con-clude, that unless we are guided by those enlarged principles, which, instead of confining our ideas to the peculiar and exclusive modes of one nation, or one period, direct our choice towards whatever is excellent in every age, and every country – we may indeed have fine houses, highly polished grounds and gardens, and beautiful ornamental buildings, but we shall not have that general combin-ation of form and effect, which is by far the most essential point; which makes amends for the want of particular beauties, but the absence of which no particular beauties can compensate.

12

From *An Analytical Inquiry into the Principles of Taste*

Richard Payne Knight

Introduction

1. Taste is a subject upon which it might naturally be supposed that all mankind would agree; since all know instinctively what pleases, and what displeases them; and, as the organs of feeling and perception appear to be the same in the whole species, and only differing in degrees of sensibility, it should naturally follow that all would be pleased or displeased more or less, according to those different degrees of sensibility, with the same objects.

2. This is, however, so far from being the case, that there is scarcely any subject, upon which men differ more than concerning the objects of their pleasures and amusements; and this difference subsists, not only among individuals, but among ages and nations; almost every generation accusing that which immediately preceded it, of bad taste in building, furniture, and dress; and almost every nation having its own peculiar modes and ideas of excellence in these matters, to which it pertinaciously adheres, until one particular people has acquired such an ascendancy in power and reputation, and to set what is called the *fashion*; when this *fashion* is universally and indiscriminately adopted upon the blind principle of imitation, and without any consideration of the differences of climate, constitution, or habits of life; and every one, who presumes to deviate from it, is thought an *odd mortal – a humourist* void of all just feeling, taste, or elegance. This fashion continues in the full exercise of its tyranny for a few years or months; when another, perhaps still more whimsical and unmeaning, starts into being and deposes it: all are then instantly astonished that they could ever have been pleased, even for a moment, with any thing so tasteless, barbarous, and absurd. The revolutions in dress only, not to

Richard Payne Knight, pp. 1–2, 153–9, 164–7, 169–72, 176–80, 216–22 from *An Analytical Enquiry into the Principles of Taste*, 2nd edition. London: Luke Hansard for T. Payne & J. White, 1805.

mention those in building, furnishing, gardening, &c. which have taken place within the last two centuries, afford ample illustration [...]

Of Imagination

28. Are not new buildings beautiful? Unquestionably they are; and peculiarly so: for neatness, freshness, lightness, symmetry, regularity, uniformity, and propriety are undoubtedly beauties of the highest class; though the pleasure, which they afford, is not simply a pleasure of the sense of seeing; nor one received by the mind through the medium of painting. But, upon the same principle, as the association of ideas renders those qualities in visible objects, which are peculiarly appropriate to painting, peculiarly pleasing to those conversant in that art; so likewise does it render those qualities, which are peculiarly adapted to promote the comforts and enjoyments of social life, pleasing to the eye of civilized man; though there be nothing, in the forms or colours of the objects themselves, in any degree pleasing to the sense; but, perhaps, the contrary. Hence neatness and freshness will always delight, if not out of character with the objects, in which they appear; or with the scenery, with which they are connected: for the mind requires propriety in every thing[.]

[...]

I think the avowed character of art of the Italian gardens preferable, in garden scenery, to the concealed one now in fashion; which is, in reality, rather counterfeited than concealed; for it appears in every thing; but appears in a dress, that does not belong to it: at every step we perceive its exertions; but, at the same time, perceive that it has laboured much to effect little; and that while it seeks to hide its character, it only, like a prostitute who affects modesty, discovers it the more.

[...]

32. That propriety or congruity is entirely artificial, and acquired by the habitual association of ideas, we need no other proof, than its being wholly dependent upon variable circumstances: in the pictures of Claude and Gaspar, we perpetually see a mixture of Grecian and Gothic architecture employed with the happiest effect in the same building; and no critic has ever yet objected to the incongruity of it[.]

[...]

the fortresses of our ancestors, which, in the course of the two last centuries, were transformed into Italianized villas, and decked with the porticos, balustrades, and terraces of Jones and Palladio, affording, in many instances, the most beautiful compositions; especially when mellowed by time and neglect, and harmonized and united by ivy, mosses, lichens, &c. Perhaps, however, as we always attach some ideas of regularity, neatness, or congruity to the word *beauty*, they may more exactly accord with what is generally expressed by the word *picturesque*; that is, the beauty of various tints and forms happily blended, without rule or symmetry, and rendered venerable by those imposing marks of antiquity, which the successive modes of decoration, employed by successive ages, and each become obsolete in its turn, afford.

34. This air of venerability (which belongs to the sublime, and not to the beautiful, and which will therefore be considered hereafter) cannot, it is true, be given to any new structures of this mixed kind: but, nevertheless, all the beauties of lightness, variety, and intricacy of form, and light and shadow, may be carried to a degree, which no regular or homogenial building (if I may use the expression) will admit of. [. . .]

35. At this time, when the taste for Gothic architecture has been so generally revived, nothing is more common, than to hear professors, as well as lovers, of the art, expatiating upon the merits of the pure Gothic; and gravely endeavouring to separate it from those spurious and adscititious ornaments, by which it has lately been debased: but, nevertheless, if we ask what they mean by *pure Gothic*, we can receive no satisfactory answer: – there are no rules – no proportions – and, consequently, no definitions: but we are referred to certain models of generally acknowledged excellence; which models are of two kinds, entirely differing from each other; the one called the castle, and the other the cathedral or monastic;

[. . .]

40. The system of regularity, of which the moderns have been so tenacious in the plans of their country houses, was taken from the sacred, and not from the domestic architecture of the ancients; from buildings, of which the forms were prescribed by the religion, to which they were consecrated; and which, as far as they were meant to be ornamental, were intended to adorn streets and squares, rather than parks or gardens. The Greek temples were, almost always, of an oblong square; and, as the cells were, in general, small and simple, their magnificence was displayed in the lofty and spacious colonnades, which surrounded them; consisting, sometimes of single, and sometimes of double rows of pillars; which, by the richness and variety of their effects, contributed, in the highest degree, to embellish and adorn the cities; and, by excluding the sun and rain, and admitting the air, afforded the most grateful walks to the inhabitants: where those, who could afford to be idle, passed the greatest part of their time in discussing the common topics of business or pleasure, politics or philosophy.

41. These regular structures being the only monuments of ancient taste and magnificence in architecture, that remained, at the resurrection of the arts, in a state sufficiently entire to be perfectly understood, the revivers of the Grecian style copied it servilely from them, and applied it indiscriminately to country, as well as town houses: but, as they felt its incongruity with the surrounding scenery of unimproved and unperverted nature, they endeavoured to make that conform to it, as far as it was within their reach, or under their control. Hence probably arose the Italian style of gardening; though other causes, which will be hereafter noticed, may have co-operated.

42. Since the introduction of another style of ornamental gardening, called at first oriental, and afterwards landscape gardening (probably from its efficacy in destroying all picturesque composition) Grecian temples have been employed as decorations by almost all persons, who could afford to indulge their taste in objects so costly: but, though executed, in many instances, on a scale and in a manner suitable to the design, disappointment has, I believe, been invariably the result. [...] In the rich lawns and shrubberies of England, however, they lose all that power to please. [...] In our parks and gardens, they stand wholly unconnected with all that surrounds them – mere unmeaning excrescences; or, what is worse, manifestly meant for ornament, and therefore having no accessory character, but that of ostentatious vanity: so that, instead of exciting any interest, they vitiate and destroy that, which the naturalized objects of the country connected with them would otherwise excite. Even if the landscape scenery should be rendered really beautiful by such ornaments, its beauty will be that of a vain and affected coquette; which, though it may allure the sense, offends the understanding; and, on the whole, excites more disgust than pleasure. In all matters of this kind, the imagination must be conciliated before the eye can be delighted.

[...]

44. Nearly connected with propriety or congruity, is symmetry, or the fitness and proportion of parts to each other, and to the whole: – a necessary ingredient to beauty in all composite forms; and one, which alone entitles them, in many instances, to be called beautiful. It depends entirely upon the association of ideas, and not at all upon either abstract reason or organic sensation; otherwise, like harmony in sound or colour, it would result equally from the same comparative relations in all objects; which is so far from being the case, that the same relative dimensions, which make one animal beautiful, make another absolutely ugly. That, which is the most exquisite symmetry in a horse, would be the most gross deformity in an elephant, and *vice versâ*: but the same proportionate combinations of sound, which produce harmony in a fiddle, produce it also in a flute or a harp.

45. In many productions of art, symmetry is still more apparently the result of arbitrary convention, that is, it proceeds from an association of ideas, which

have not been so invariably associated; and which are, therefore, less intimately and firmly connected. In a Grecian building, in which the relative proportions of the different orders of columns were not observed, a person skilled in architecture would instantly discover a want of symmetry; which, to another of even more correct taste, as far as correct taste depends on just feeling, may be utterly imperceptible: for there is no reason whatever in the nature of things, or in the analogy of the parts, why a Corinthian capital should be placed on a slenderer shaft than a Doric or Ionic one. On the contrary, the Corinthian, being of the largest, and consequently of the heaviest proportion, would naturally require the column of the largest dimensions, proportioned to its height, to sustain it.

46. The appropriation of particular proportions to the columns of particular orders is, I believe, of no higher antiquity than the practice of placing one order over another; of which, I know of no instance anterior to the theatres and amphitheatres of the Romans; the first of which, excepting temporary structures of wood, was that of Pompey. In the arrangement of the different orders in buildings of this kind, the plainest was naturally placed lowest, and the most enriched, highest; and hence the plainest was made the most massive; and the most ornamented, the most light and slender: but as this distinction of proportions arose merely from the relative positions, which they held, when thus employed together, and not from any inherent principle of propriety; there can be no other reason, than that of established custom, why it should be observed, when they are employed separately, and independent of each other.

47. In the Grecian buildings, which are anterior to any customary rules of this kind, the proportionate thickness of the columns, in each of the three orders, which are properly Grecian, appears to have been diminished gradually as the art advanced towards refinement: and, as the Doric was the earliest, and the Corinthian the latest invented, the proportions of the first are, of course, the most massive, and those of the last the most slender. It was only by repeated experiment, and long observation, that men learned the power of a vertical shaft to bear a perpendicular weight; and therefore, in the infancy of the art, made their columns unnecessarily large and ponderous; which is observable, not only in the primitive efforts of the Greeks and Egyptians, but also in the imitations made, at the revival of the art, by the Saxons, Goths, Franks, Lombards, &c. In all, the progress has been from excessive ponderous solidity to excessive lightness; though as the Greeks and Romans bound themselves by certain rules of proportion, before they had run into the latter extreme, they never indulged themselves in the extravagant licence of the Gothic architects, who recognized no rules, but worked merely for effect.
[…]

Attempts at lightness, unless supported by extreme richness, either of material or ornament, either of colour or form, almost always produce meagreness, poverty, and weakness of effect; such as is but too manifest in most of the works of Grecian or Roman architecture lately executed in this country; where spindle columns, bald capitals, wide intercolumniations, and scanty entablatures form a sort of frippery trimming fit only to adorn a house built after the model of a brick clamp: which is, indeed, the usual application of them. In the magnificient structures of the Roman emperors, the entablatures continued full, and the intercolumniations moderate, after the proportions of the columns had become slender; at the same time that the costliness and brilliancy of the materials, and the variety and elegance of the sculptures were alone sufficient to suppress any ideas of poverty or meanness, which a want of substance might otherwise have excited. In the Gothic churches, too, a profusion of elaborate ornament, how licentiously soever designed or disposed, seldom failed to produce a similar effect: but the modern fashion of making buildings neither rich nor massive, and producing lightness of appearance by the deficiency rather than the disposition of the parts, is of all tricks of taste the most absurd, and the most certain of counteracting its own ends. The ponderous extravagancies of Vanbrugh, how blamable soever in the detail, are never contemptible in the whole; and amidst all the unmeaning absurdities, which the learned observer may discover in the parts of Blenheim and Castle Howard, the general mass in each has been universally felt and acknowledged to be grand and imposing: but in later works of the same kind, which it might perhaps be invidious to name, equal expence has been incurred to produce objects similar to what we may reasonably suppose a cabinet-maker of Brobdignag would have made for Gulliver's nurse.

Even where the genuine Grecian order, that is, the old Doric, has been employed, it has been by a mere servile and mechanic imitation of its existing remains, without any attention to the principles which directed their authors; whence many absurd and perverse fashions have arisen. [. . .]

54. The fundamental error of imitators in all arts is, that they servilely copy the effects, which they see produced, instead of studying and adopting the principles, which guided the original artists in producing them; wherefore they disregard all those local, temporary, or accidental circumstances, upon which their propriety or impropriety – their congruity or incongruity wholly depend: for principles in art are no other than the trains of ideas, which arise in the mind of the artist out of a just and adequate consideration of all such circumstances; and direct him in adapting his work to the purposes for which it is intended: consequently, if either those circumstances or purposes change, his ideas must change with them, or his principles will be false, and his works incongruous. Grecian temples, Gothic abbies, and feudal castles were all well adapted to their respective uses, circumstances, and situations: the distribution of the parts subservient to the purposes of the whole; and the ornaments and decorations suited to the character of the parts; and to the manners, habits, and employments of the persons who were to occupy them: but the house of an English

nobleman of the eighteenth or nineteenth century is neither a Grecian temple, a Gothic abbey, nor a feudal castle; and if the style of distribution or decoration of either be employed in it, such changes and modifications should be admitted as may adapt it to existing circumstances; otherwise the scale of its exactitude becomes that of its incongruity, and the deviation from principle proportioned to the fidelity of imitation. Common practitioners think every objection answered, when some respectable authority is adduced; though perhaps the only point proved by such authority is that the person, who uses it, does not understand it; or know how to apply it.

[...]

97. Some few attempts have lately been made to adapt the exterior forms of country-houses to the various character of the surrounding scenery, by spreading them out into irregular masses: but as our ideas of irregularity, in buildings of this kind, have been habitually associated with those of the barbarous structures of the middle ages, a mistaken notion of congruity has induced us to exclude from them, every species of ornament, or scale of proportion, not authorized by the rude and unskilful monuments of those times: as if that, which is, at once, convenient and elegant, needed any authority to justify its use; or a house, that is picturesque without, must, from a principle of congruity, be heavy, clumsy, and gloomy within. It has already been observed that the architecture of the Gothic castles, as they are called, is of Grecian or Roman origin: but, if it were not, there could be no impropriety in employing the elegancies of Grecian taste and science, either in the external forms and proportions, or interior decorations of houses built in that style: for, surely, there can be no blamable inconsistency in uniting the different improvements of different ages and countries in the same object; provided they are really improvements, and contribute to render it perfect.

98. It is now more than thirty years since the author of this inquiry ventured to build a house, ornamented with what are called Gothic towers and battlements without, and with Grecian ceilings, columns, and entablatures within; and though his example has not been much followed, he has every reason to congratulate himself upon the success of the experiment; he having, at once, the advantage of a picturesque object, and of an elegant and convenient dwelling; though less perfect in both respects than if he had executed it at a maturer age. It has, however, the advantage of being capable of receiving alterations and additions in almost any direction, without any injury to its genuine and original character.

[...]

A house may be adorned with towers and battlements, or pinnacles and flying buttresses; but it should still maintain the character of a house of the age and country, in which it is erected; and not pretend to be a fortress or monastery of a remote period or distant country: for such false pretensions never escape detection [. . .]

100. Rustic lodges to parks, dressed cottages, pastoral seats, gates, and gateways, made of un-hewn branches and stems of trees, have all necessarily a still stronger character of affectation; the rusticity of the first being that of a clown in a pantomime, and the simplicity of the others that of a shepherdess in a French opera. The real character of every object of this kind must necessarily conform to the use, to which it is really appropriated; and if attempts be made to give it any other character, it will prove, in fact, to be only a character of imposture: for to adapt the genuine style of a herdsman's hut, or a ploughman's cottage, to the dwellings of opulence and luxury, is as utterly impossible, as it is to adapt their language, dress, and manners to the refined usages of polished society.

101. The best style of architecture for irregular and picturesque houses, which can now be adopted, is that mixed style, which characterizes the buildings of Claude and the Poussins: for as it is taken from models, which were built piecemeal, during many successive ages; and by several different nations, it is distinguished by no particular manner of execution, or class of ornaments; but admits of all promiscuously, from a plain wall or buttress, of the roughest masonry, to the most highly wrought Corinthian capital: and, in a style professedly miscellaneous, such contrasts may be employed to heighten the relish of beauty, without disturbing the enjoyment of it by any appearance of deceit or imposture. In a matter, however, which affords so wide a field for the licentious deviations of whim and caprice, it may be discreet always to pay some attention to authority; especially when we have such authorities as those of the great landscape painters above mentioned; the study of whose works may at once enrich and restrain invention.

102. In choosing a situation for a house of this kind, which is to be a principal feature in a place, more consideration ought to be had of the views towards it, than of those fromwards it: for, consistently with comfort, which ought to be the first object in every dwelling, it very rarely happens that a perfect composition of landscape scenery can be obtained from a door or window; nor does it appear to me particularly desirable that it should be; for few persons ever look for such compositions, or pay much attention to them, while within doors. It is in walks or rides through parks, gardens, or pleasure grounds, that they are attended to and examined, and become subjects of conversation; wherefore the seats, or places of rest, with which such walks and rides are accommodated, are the points of sight, to which the compositions of the scenery ought to be principally adapted. To them, picturesque foregrounds may always be made or preserved, without any loss of comfort or violation of propriety: for that sort of trim neatness, which both require in grounds immediately adjoining a house, is completely misplaced, when employed on the borders of a ride or walk through a

park or plantation. If the house be the principal object or feature of the scene from these points of view, the middle ground will be the properest situation for it; as will clearly appear from the landscapes of the painters above cited: this is also the situation, which considerations of domestic comfort will generally point out; as being the middle degree of elevation, between the too exposed ridges of the hills, and the too secluded recesses of the vallies. In any position, however, above the point of sight, such objects may be happily placed; and contribute to the embellishment of the adjoining scenery: but there are scarcely any buildings, except bridges, which will bear being looked down upon; a foreshortening from the roof to the base being necessarily awkward and ungraceful.

103. Sir John Vanbrugh is the only architect, I know of, who has either planned or placed his houses according to the principle here recommended; and, in his two chief works, Blenheim and Castle Howard, it appears to have been strictly adhered to, at least in the placing of them. The views from the principal fronts of both are bad, and much inferior to what other parts of the grounds would have afforded; but the situations of both, as objects to the surrounding scenery, are the best that could have been chosen; and both are certainly worthy of the best situations, which, not only the respective places, but the island of Great Britain could afford.

104. The direct reverse may be said of the late Mr. Brown; who, in the only place, in which he was employed both as architect and improver, with unlimited powers of design and expence in both, has built a house, which no situation could adapt to any scenery, except that of a square or a street; and placed it where no house could have served as an embellishment to the scenery, which does surround it. Such ever has, and ever will be the difference between the works of artists of genius, who consult their feelings, and those of plodding mechanics, who look only to their rules. The former will necessarily be unequal and irregular; and produce much to blame and ridicule, as well as much to applaud and admire; whereas the latter, howsoever extolled by the fashions of the day, will never rise above negative merit.

13

Iconography and Landscape

Stephen Daniels and Denis Cosgrove

A landscape is a cultural image, a pictorial way of representing, structuring or symbolising surroundings. This is not to say that landscapes are immaterial. They may be represented in a variety of materials and on many surfaces – in paint on canvas, in writing on paper, in earth, stone, water and vegetation on the ground. A landscape park is more palpable but no more real, nor less imaginary, than a landscape painting or poem. Indeed the meanings of verbal, visual and built landscapes have a complex interwoven history. To understand a built landscape, say an eighteenth-century English park, it is usually necessary to understand written and verbal representations of it, not as 'illustrations', images standing outside it, but as constituent images of its meaning or meanings. And of course, every study of a landscape further transforms its meaning, depositing yet another layer of cultural representation. In human geography the interpretation of landscape and culture has a tendency to reify landscape as an object of empiricist investigation,[1] but often its practitioners do gesture towards landscape as a cultural symbol or image, notably when likening landscape to a text and its interpretation to 'reading'.[2] This essay explicates more fully the status of landscape as image and symbol and in doing so establishes common ground between practitioners from a variety of different disciplines concerned with landscape and

Stephen Daniels and Denis Cosgrove, "Introduction: Iconography and Landscape," pp. 1–10 from Denis Cosgrove and Stephen Daniels, *The Iconography of Landscape: Essays on the Symbolic Representation, Design and Use of Past Environments*. Cambridge: Cambridge University Press, 1988. Reproduced with permission of Cambridge University Press and Dr. S. J. Daniels and Dr. D. E. Cosgrove.

[1] D. E. Cosgrove, *Social formation and symbolic landscape* (London, 1984), pp. 13–38.

[2] D. W. Meinig, 'Reading the landscape: an appreciation of W. G. Hoskins and J. B. Jackson', in D. W. Meinig (ed.), *The interpretation of ordinary landscapes* (Oxford, 1979), pp. 195–244; Pierce F. Lewis, 'Axioms for reading the landscape', *ibid.*, pp. 11–32; James S. Duncan, 'Individual action and political power: a structuration perspective', in R. J. Johnston, *The future of geography* (London, 1985), pp. 174–89.

culture: geography, fine art, literature, social history and anthropology.[3] The discussion here is structured around the fertile concept of iconography: the theoretical and historical study of symbolic imagery.

Iconographies

The interpretation of symbolic imagery reaches back to Cesare Ripa's *Iconologia*, the first of many Renaissance handbooks acting as guides to an art which made systematic use of symbols, allegories and images from the Classical repertoire.[4] The terms iconography and iconology were revived [in the twentieth] century, initially again in the interpretation of Renaissance imagery, by the school of art history associated with Aby Warburg. In opposition to the purely formalistic tradition of art interpretation associated with Heinrich Wölfflin (which analysed pictures purely in terms of the surface patterns of colour, chiaroscuro, line and volume, relating them principally to other works of art), iconographic study sought to probe meaning in a work of art by setting it in its historical context and, in particular, to analyse the ideas implicated in its imagery. While, by definition, all art history translates the visual into the verbal, the iconographic approach consciously sought to conceptualise pictures as encoded texts to be deciphered by those cognisant of the culture as a whole in which they were produced. The approach was systematically formulated by Warburg's pupil, Erwin Panofsky.

Panofsky distinguished between iconography 'in the narrower sense of the word' and iconography 'in a deeper sense'. Initially he labelled these two approaches 'iconographical analysis' and 'iconographical interpretation [or] synthesis' but eventually revived the term 'iconology' to describe 'iconography turned interpretative'.[5] Iconography 'in the narrower' sense was the identification of conventional, consciously inscribed symbols, say a lamb signifying Christ, or the winged lion of St Mark signifying in Venetian art the Republic and its power. Iconology probed a deeper stratum of meaning.[6] It excavated what Panofsky called the 'intrinsic meaning' of a work of art 'by ascertaining those underlying principles which reveal the basic attitude of a nation, a period, a class, a religious

---

[3] Similar common ground between those from different disciplines interested in landscape was sought in the symposium organised by the Landscape Research Group in Exeter, 1983, whose proceedings are published in *Landscape Research* 9, 3 (1984).

[4] W. J. T. Mitchell, *Iconology: image, text, ideology* (Chicago, 1986), p. 2.

[5] Erwin Panofsky, *Studies in iconology: humanistic themes in the art of the Renaissance* (Oxford, 1939), p. 14; 'Iconography and iconology: an introduction to the study of Renaissance art', in Erwin Panofsky, *Meaning in the visual arts* (Harmondsworth, 1970), pp. 51–81, quotations on pp. 57–8.

[6] Panofsky's stratigraphic metaphor for iconology forced him to suggest that the meaning of a work of art was somehow secreted below its surface configuration. For a criticism of this approach see Svetlana Alpers, *The art of describing: Dutch art in the seventeenth century* (Chicago, 1983), pp. xxiii–xxiv.

117

or philosophical persuasion – unconsciously qualified by one personality and condensed into one work'. There were no established conventions or specific methods that would ascertain these principles; they were to be reconstructed by a kind of detective synthesis, searching out analogies between overtly disparate forms like poetry, philosophy, social institutions and political life: 'To grasp these principles', wrote Panofsky, 'we need a mental faculty comparable to that of a diagnostician.' It was here in the interpretative search for such principles that 'the various humanistic disciplines meet on a common plane instead of serving as handmaidens to each other'.[7]

In a reference to the philosophy of Ernst Cassirer, Panofsky's colleague at the Warburg Library and author of *The philosophy of symbolic forms* (1923–9), Panofsky contended that iconology involved the identification of symbols, not in 'the ordinary sense e.g. the Cross, or the Tower of Chastity' but in the 'Cassirerian' sense; it involved the search for 'what Ernst Cassirer has called "symbolical" values'.[8] For Cassirer symbols were not

> mere figures which refer to some given reality by means of suggestion or allegorical renderings, but in the sense of forces, each of which produces and posits a world of its own. The question as to what reality is apart from these forms, and what are its independent attributes, becomes irrelevant here. For the mind, only that can be visible which has some definite form; but every form of existence has its source in some peculiar way of seeing, some intellectual formulation and intuition of meaning.[9]

In the same year, 1925, as Cassirer made this case in the *Studien der Bibliotek Warburg*, Panofsky deployed the concept of symbolic form in his own essay: 'Die Perspektive als "symbolische Form" ', a study of changing modes of perceiving and representing space, not as mere 'conventions' (to be taken up or not at will) or as true or false beliefs, but, much as Cassirer held language or mathematics to be, as 'symbolic forms' which structured the world according to specific cultural demands.[10] As an example of the interpretation of perspective as symbolic form Panofsky compared two pictures in which the subjects 'seem to hang loose in space in violation of the laws of gravity': *The Three Magi*, painted in the fifteenth century by Roger van der Weyden, in which the infant Jesus hovers in mid-air, and an Ottonian miniature of around 1000 AD in which 'a whole city is

---

[7] Panofsky, 'Iconography and iconology', pp. 55, 64, 65.

[8] *Studies in iconology*, p. 6 fn. 1; 'Iconography and iconology', p. 56.

[9] Ernst Cassirer, *Language and myth* (New York, 1946), p. 8; originally published as *Sprache und Mythos*, No. 6 in *Studien der Bibliothek Warburg*, quoted in Samuel Y. Edgerton Jr, *The Renaissance rediscovery of linear perspective* (New York, 1975), p. 156. We owe the recognition of the importance of Cassirer to Panofsky to pp. 153–65 of Edgerton's book.

[10] Erwin Panofsky, 'Die Perspektive als "symbolische Form" ', *Vorträge der Bibliothek Warburg: 1924–5* (Leipzig, 1927), pp. 258–331.

represented in the middle of an empty space while the figures taking part in the action stand on solid ground'. An inexperienced observer might assume that

the town is meant to be suspended in mid-air by some sort of magic. Yet in this case the lack of support does not imply a miraculous invalidation of the laws of nature … In a miniature of around 1000 'empty space' does not count as a real, three-dimensional medium, as it does in a more realistic period, but serves as an abstract, unreal background … Thus while the figure in the van der Weyden counts as an apparition, the floating city in the Ottonian miniature has no such miraculous connotation.

As experienced observers we may grasp this 'in a fraction of a second' but this still involves 'reading "what we see" according to the manner in which objects and events are expressed by forms under varying historical conditions'.[11]

Panofsky applied this approach of 'reading what we see' to built as well as to painted forms. He argued that designers of gothic cathedrals 'began to conceive of the forms they shaped, not so much in terms of isolated solids as in terms of a comprehensive "picture space"', just as contemporary Church Fathers were conceiving of their textual apologetics as tightly articulated *summae* wherein the whole structure of the argument could be read off from the table of its contents and textual subdivisions. Thus, Panofsky pointed out, the entire constructional order of ribs and vaults may be read off from the cross-section of a single nave shaft. While acknowledging its status as building he found it fertile to regard gothic architecture as text, not just 'a way of seeing – or rather designing', but as a 'mode of literary representation', a treatise in stone, an architectural scholasticism. Caen and Durham were to be read as cultural symbols of a whole age by being set in the full context of their spatial and intellectual articulation.[12]

If the medieval 'Age of Faith' wove the meaning of its world out of images and signs it was not in this respect fundamentally different from any culture. Thus when Panofsky likened iconography to ethnography[13] he pointed to a broad truth for all cultural study, one stressed in modern anthropology. Clifford Geertz's conceptualisation of culture as a 'text' and his dual method of 'thick description' ('setting down the meaning particular social actions have for the actors whose actions they are') and 'diagnosis' ('stating as explicitly as we can manage, what the knowledge thus attained demonstrates about the society in which it is found and about social life as such') have much in common with Panofsky's notions of iconography and iconology.[14] It was perhaps inevitable that Geertz was eventually to uphold iconographic art history (in the writings of

---

[11] Panofsky, 'Iconography and iconology', pp. 59–61.

[12] Erwin Panofsky, *Gothic architecture and scholasticism* (New York, 1957), pp. 17, 58.

[13] Panofsky, 'Iconography and iconology', pp. 51–2.

[14] Clifford Geertz, 'Thick description: toward an interpretative theory of culture' in *The interpretation of cultures: selected essays* (New York, 1973), pp. 3–30, quotations on p. 27.

Michael Baxandall) as a model for ethnography.[15] Since the 1970s ethnography, often of an explicitly Geertzian kind, has greatly influenced social history. In his essay 'A bourgeois puts his world in order: the city as a text', Geertz's colleague, Robert Darnton, analyses the representations of Montpellier in an account of the city written in 1768 by 'an anonymous but solidly middle-class citizen'. The first half of the account translated into writing the idiom of the urban procession. Such a procession 'expressed the corporate order of urban society ... it was a statement unfurled in the streets through which the city represented itself to itself – and sometimes to God, for it also took place when Montpellier was threatened by drought or famine'. By 1768, however, 'the language of processions was archaic. It could not convey the shifting alignments within the social order that resulted from the economic expansion of the mid-century years.' In the second part of his account the author 'began to grope for an adequate terminology ... the city no longer appeared as a parade of *dignités*. It became a three-tiered structure of "estates" (états).' And finally, and culturally more congenial for the author, the city became 'the scene of a style of living' made up of musical, masonic and educational institutions.[16] By his 'thick' description of this account, through a dialogue of 'text' and 'context', Darnton captures the shifting iconography of a modernising urban landscape.[17]

The Iconography of Landscape

A scholar of Renaissance art, Panofsky never addressed the European tradition of self-consciously landscape art and painting that became firmly established in the seventeenth century. The first great art critic and historian to devote his attention primarily to that tradition was the Victorian, John Ruskin. Over the past decade there has been a marked revival of interest in Ruskin's writings not only because they place landscape so squarely at the centre of social, political and environmental morality, but because his way of seeing and conceptualising has certain similarities to sensibilities today. Indeed, Peter Fuller has proclaimed Ruskin as

---

[15] Clifford Geertz, 'Art as a cultural system', in *Local knowledge: further essays in interpretative anthropology* (New York, 1983), pp. 94–120, esp. 102–9.

[16] Robert Darnton, 'A bourgeois puts his world in order: the city as a text', in *The great cat massacre and other episodes in French cultural history* (London, 1984), pp. 107–43, quotations on pp. 120, 124, 140.

[17] For similar analyses of the ritual meaning of urban landscapes see Edwin Muir, *Civic ritual in Renaissance Venice* (Princeton, 1981); and David Cannadine, 'The context, performance and meaning of ritual: the British monarchy and the "invention of tradition", c. 1820–1977', in Eric Hobsbawm and Terence Ranger (eds.), *The invention of tradition* (Cambridge, 1983), pp. 101–64.

'the true prophet of the "post-modern" and "post-industrial" era'.[18] In the most recent major biography of John Ruskin, John Dixon Hunt has pointed out how his great eclectic collections or 'cabinets' of materials – mineral, floral and artifactual specimens, so typical of the Victorian intellectual sensibility – faithfully mirror Ruskin's mind in which 'everything was more or less reflected in everything else'.[19] We are reminded of Fredric Jameson's characterisation of late twentieth-century post-modern art as 'no longer unified or organic, but now [a] virtual grab-bag or lumber room of disjointed sub-systems and random raw materials and impulses of all kinds'.[20] In landscape Ruskin sought a stable ground in which a consistent order of divine design could be recognised in underlying form. Landscape he treated as a text, taking his method from biblical exegesis, seeking the reassurance of order in the face of the apparent chaos of industrialising Britain.[21] Thus the central purpose of his first great text, *Modern painters* (1843), was to locate landscape in a broader context than the study of form and the history of style. The 'higher landscape' depended upon a humble submission of men to the great laws of nature, a close observation of the natural world and the application of the greatest skill and imagination in its representation. In the hands of a master like Turner, landscape became in Ruskin's eyes a suitable subject for examining the deepest moral and artistic truths, rather as history painting had been viewed within the academic tradition.

In some respects Ruskin's was a conservative attempt to wrest order from that quintessentially modern anarchic interplay of images and feelings which his own prose so often betrays, and which every sensitive Victorian faced as the onrush of modernisation and the faith-shattering impact of Darwin made 'all that is solid melt into air'.[22] But while Ruskin proclaimed himself, like his father, a Tory 'of the old school', he also, and without apparent contradiction, styled himself a communist, 'reddest also of the red'. He was indeed one of the fiercest critics of the demoralisation and alienation of industrialism. In *The stones of Venice* (1851–3) he claimed to find in late medieval Venice a perfect society, one that followed the hierarchical order of nature. A voluntary submission to the laws which run through all creation had produced a community where a wise and just patriciate governed a state in which other orders of men and women found the spiritual

---

[18] Peter Fuller, 'John Ruskin: a radical conservative', in Peter Fuller, *Images of God: the consolation of lost illusions* (London, 1985), pp. 277–83, quotation on p. 283.

[19] John Dixon Hunt, *The wider sea: a life of John Ruskin* (London, 1982). The quotation is from Kenneth Clark, *Ruskin today* (Harmondsworth, 1967), p. xiii.

[20] Fredric Jameson, 'Postmodernism, or the cultural logic of late capitalism', *New Left Review*, 146 (1984), pp. 53–92.

[21] D. E. Cosgrove, 'John Ruskin and the geographical imagination', *Geographical Review* 69 (1979), pp. 43–62.

[22] This is the title of Marshall Berman's essay on modernism: *All that is solid melts into air* (London, 1981). The quotation is originally from Karl Marx discussing 'the bourgeois epoch' in *The communist manifesto*.

freedom to express their truest being, a state therefore which became a collective work of art and the beauty of whose architecture and landscape still express the disciplined human liberation which comes only through faith.[23] Perhaps it is not surprising that it should be at the very juncture of the medieval world with its vision of nature as an illuminated text replete with the signatures of divinity, glossed at the margins by the insights of faith, and the Renaissance world of deeply engraved symbolism that Ruskin's vision should find its most comfortable resting point. Perhaps, too, it is appropriate that Ruskin should be rediscovered in today's world, so saturated in reproduced images

> that nature itself threatens to become what it was for the Middle Ages: an encyclo-
> paedic, illuminated book overlaid with ornamentation and marginal glosses, every
> object converted into an image with its proper label or signature ... The quintes-
> sential modern experience of this new 'book of nature' is the stroll through the
> scenic wonders of a national park with a plastic earphone that responds to electronic
> triggers embedded at strategic locations along the path.[24]

Ruskin's modern appeal lies as much in this radical representation of nature as a complex interplay of images as in his appeal to a 'green' ideology of social harmony with a nature whose laws are incommensurable, irreducible to the analytic rules of positivist science and the profit-seeking logic of technology.[25]

The landscape tradition in painting which Ruskin did so much to promote and which peaked in England during his lifetime has been the subject of an increasing corpus of iconographical study that reaches beyond the disciplinary boundaries of art history. In his pioneering *Landscape into art* (1949), Kenneth Clark, himself a great admirer of Ruskin, attempted to place different styles of Western landscape painting – emblematic, empiricist, naturalistic, fantastic – in their philosophical and, occasionally, their sociological contexts. Seventeenth-century Dutch art, 'the landscape of fact', was, with its emphasis on '*recognisable* experiences', Clark asserted, 'a bourgeois form of art' for it represented the experiential world of the rising middle-class merchant patrons of Amsterdam and Haarlem.[26] Taking his title, *Ways of seeing*, from one of Panofsky's key phrases, but drawing too upon the marxist aesthetics of Walter Benjamin, John Berger took issue with Clark's interpretative emphasis on the philosophical as opposed to the social and economic in works of art and also in the idea that the history of high art was an expression of a unitary history of 'civilisation'.[27] Clark had described

[23] Denis Cosgrove, 'The myth and the stones of Venice: the historical geography of a symbolic landscape', *Journal of Historical Geography* 8 (1982), pp. 145–69.
[24] W. J. T. Mitchell, 'Editor's note: the language of images', *Critical Inquiry* 6 (1980), p. 359.
[25] Fuller argues that his holistic, ecological approach is the main reason for Ruskin's contemporary appeal: 'Mother nature', in *Images of God*, pp. 77–82.
[26] Kenneth Clark, *Landscape into art* (Harmondsworth, 1956), p. 43.
[27] John Berger, *Ways of seeing* (London, 1972).

Gainsborough's *Mr and Mrs Andrews* as an 'enchanting work', a 'naturalistic' landscape painting expressing the artist's 'Rousseauism'; 'They are not a couple in nature as Rousseau imagined nature', countered Berger, 'they are landowners and their proprietory attitude towards what surrounds them is visible in their stance and their expressions ... the pleasure of seeing themselves depicted as landowners ... was enhanced by the ability of oil paint to render their land in all its substantiality.' A way of seeing the world which 'was ultimately determined by new attitudes to property and exchange, found its visual expression in the oil painting: ... not so much a framed window onto the world as a safe let into the wall, a safe in which the visible has been deposited'.[28]

Berger thus reformulated Panofsky's layers of meaning in terms of a marxist stratigraphy of economic base and cultural superstructure, the ideology of representation in English eighteenth-century landscape art serving to naturalise, and hence to mystify, basic property relations.

Around the same time as Berger, Raymond Williams conducted a similar polemical critique of landscape in English literature and by implication in polite English culture as a whole:

> a working country is hardly ever a landscape. The very idea of landscape implies separation and observation. It is possible and useful to trace the internal histories of landscape painting, and landscape writing, landscape gardening and landscape architecture, but in any final analysis we must relate these histories to the common history of a land and its society.[29]

Berger and Williams inaugurated and often directly influenced a series of studies in many disciplines on the social implications of landscape imagery. Not all of them have been so confident as Berger and Williams in opposing a 'real' history of 'land' to an 'ideological' history of 'landscape', nor have they all been willing to reduce landscape aesthetics entirely to ideology.[30] But all have been intent to decipher the social power of landscape imagery, to identify, in the title of James Turner's study of seventeenth-century prospect poetry, the 'politics of landscape'.[31] Turner shows that many topographical and prospect poems went beyond the single vantage point of a spectator, perhaps by deploying conventions of mapping or inventory to 'work up an idea of human geography, a view of country life and regional character'.[32] While landscape for these poets

---

[28] *Ibid.*, pp. 106–9.

[29] Raymond Williams, *The country and the city* (London, 1973), p. 120.

[30] See respectively John Barrell, *The idea of landscape and the sense of place 1730–1840: an approach to the poetry of John Clare* (Cambridge, 1972), and Peter Fuller, *Seeing Berger: a re-evaluation* (London, 1980).

[31] James Turner, *The politics of landscape: rural scenery and society in English poetry 1630–1660* (Oxford, 1979).

[32] *Ibid.*, p. 24.

connoted an attractive, elevated, comprehensive, disengaged and orderly view of the world – and hence a reliably objective one – so it was also distrusted (sometimes by the same poets) as a pernicious delusion, a dazzling trick designed to distort the world and its workings.

This sense of the duplicity of landscape imagery is characteristically 'postmodern', and it is no accident that Turner's study took shape under the influence of a critic best known for his decoding of modern advertising as well as painting and literature, Roland Barthes.[33] Commenting on such criticism W. J. T. Mitchell states that

> language and images have become enigmas, problems to be explained, prison houses which lock understanding away from the world. The commonplace of modern studies of images, in fact, is that they must be understood as a kind of language; instead of providing a transparent window on the world, images are now regarded as the sort of sign that presents a deceptive appearance of naturalness and transparence concealing an opaque, distorting, arbitrary mechanism of representation, a process of ideological mystification.[34]

The post-modern apprehension of the world emphasises the inherent instability of meaning, our ability to invert signs and symbols, to recycle them in a different context and thus transform their reference. Earlier and less commercial cultures may sustain more stable symbolic codes[35] but every culture weaves its world out of image and symbol. For this reason the iconographic method remains central to cultural enquiry. But the liberation of meaning in modern society, the freedom of intertextuality which Ruskin's writings implicitly acknowledge, emphasises surface rather than depth. The conservative picture of a 'deep' England with its stable layers of historical accretion, so profoundly threatened by modernisation, that W. G. Hoskins framed from his window in North Oxfordshire in the closing pages of *The making of the English landscape*,[36] and the more radical and demotic, but no less composed, England sketched by Raymond Williams looking out from the window in Cambridgeshire where he wrote *The country and the city*[37] represent alternative attempts to achieve that stability of meaning in landscape which Ruskin sought and which has become a characteristic and honourable response to the perceived chaos of the modern world. At the same time we recognise these Englands for what they are: images, further glosses upon an already deeply layered text. These images might also be seen as additional reflections to a more dazzling and more superficial pattern. From such a post-modern perspective

---

[33] *Ibid.*, pp. 188–9. John Berger and Raymond Williams have also addressed advertising; see Berger, *Ways of seeing*, pp. 28–43, and Williams, 'Advertizing the magic system', in *Patterns in materialism and culture* (London, 1980), pp. 170–95.

[34] Mitchell, *Iconology*, p. 2.

[35] Marshall Sahlins, *Culture and practical reason* (Chicago, 1976).

[36] W. G. Hoskins, *The making of the English landscape* (Harmondsworth, 1970), pp. 298–303.

[37] Williams, *The country and the city*, p. 3.

landscape seems less like a palimpsest whose 'real' or 'authentic' meanings can somehow be recovered with the correct techniques, theories or ideologies, than a flickering text displayed on the word-processor screen whose meaning can be created, extended, altered, elaborated and finally obliterated by the merest touch of a button.

14

The Plans and Elevations of John Nash

John Summerson

Once, and only once, has a great plan for London, affecting the development of the capital as a whole, been projected and carried to completion. This was the plan which constituted the 'metropolitan improvements' of the Regency, the plan which embraced the Regent's Park layout in the north, St James's Park in the south, the Regent Street artery connecting the two, the formation of Trafalgar Square and the reconstruction of the West End of the Strand, and the Suffolk Street area; as well as the cutting of the Regent's Canal, with its branch and basin to serve Regent's Park. The whole of this immense plan, which gave a 'spine' to London's inchoate West End and had a far-reaching effect on subsequent northward and southward expansion, was carried out under the presiding genius of John Nash.[1]

It was Nash's achievement to seize and combine a number of opportunities which presented themselves with felicitous promptitude at the beginning of the Regency. The main opportunity, which brought all the others within reach, was the reversion to the Crown of Marylebone Park in 1811. This event had been the subject of discussion and preparation for some years. As early as 1793 John Fordyce, an intelligent border Scot, had been appointed to the then newly-created office of Surveyor-General of His Majesty's Land Revenues. He had drawn up a plan of the whole property and produced four reports, in the last of which (1809) he set out a liberal and enticing programme for the development of the Park, relating the project to the need for a new street extending from the Park to Carlton House. This new street was a necessary corollary; for if the nobility and professional classes were to be expected to live north of the New Road (hitherto the uttermost northward boundary of fashion), they would have to be provided with adequate access to Westminster, where Parliament, the Law Courts, and the Public Offices in Whitehall employed many of their daylight hours.

John Summerson, "The Plans and Elevations of John Nash," pp. 177–90 from *Georgian London*, 3rd edition. London: Barrie & Jenkins, 1978.

[1] For the whole of this chapter see the writer's *John Nash: Architect to King George IV*, 1935, 2nd edn, 1949.

John Fordyce's programme of 1809 was set before two pairs of official architects. Messrs Leverton and Chawner, of the Land Revenue Office, were one pair; Messrs Nash and Morgan, of the Woods and Forests Department, were the other. Leverton and Chawner sent in a rather dull-witted scheme, merely extending the Bloomsbury pattern of streets and squares over most of the Park. Nash and Morgan presented something new – a daring and highly picturesque conception of a garden city for an aristocracy, supported by charming panoramas showing a composition of alluring groves and elegant architecture of a somewhat Parisian character. The Nash–Morgan plan was immediately accepted by the Treasury. But first, a word about Nash.

The true story of Nash's success is obscure, but there was certainly a great deal more behind it than meets the eye in the official documents. This man Nash was no ordinary civil servant, as everybody well knew. Already fifty-seven, he had an odd career behind him. He was born, probably in London, in 1752, and was in service with Sir Robert Taylor. A legacy from a merchant uncle enabled him to set up as a speculating builder, but he became bankrupt and retired to Wales. Here he acquired a connexion as a country-house architect and mixed in county society. He met Humphry Repton, the rising landscape gardener, formed a partnership with him, and was influenced by him, abruptly returning to London about 1795. It was very likely through Repton that Nash met the Prince of Wales, for whom he was designing as early as 1798, soon after which year he and Repton quarrelled and separated. Also in 1798 Nash married.

Nash's marriage, at the age of forty-six, to an ambitious young woman who is supposed to have engaged in dangerous liaisons at Carlton House, is surrounded by mystery. There is a tradition that Nash was in a certain respect unfitted for marriage and was merely the official husband of this girl, who subsequently appeared before the world with a considerable family of children incubated in a remote hinterland of the Isle of Wight, bearing the name of Pennethorne and of whom she was supposed to be a remote relation acting *in loco parentis*. The whole story bristles with scandal, and there is evidence that, for some reason or other, Nash and his wife participated in an elaborate social fake, presumably in collusion with the Prince; there is not enough evidence, on the other hand, to assert definitely either that Mrs Nash was the Prince's mistress or that the Pennethornes were her children by the Prince.

Anyway, from the year of his marriage, Nash suddenly became a man of considerable wealth and influence with a princely house in London and an estate in the Isle of Wight. He became one of the Carlton House set and contemplated a political career as one of the Prince's parliamentary pawns. However, he was not, as it turned out, to be diverted from architecture and in 1806 this opulent lackey, this big-wig of back-stair intrigue accepted, together with his draughtsman Morgan, the post of Architect to the Woods and Forests, at the ludicrous joint salary of £200 a year. Morgan, of course, was wholly unimportant, a man of straw introduced to satisfy official insistence on a partnership.

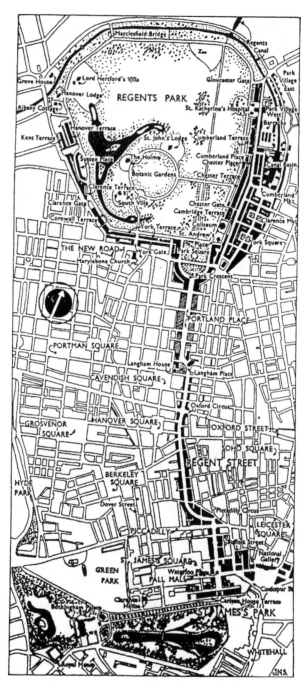

Figure 14.1 Streets, squares, and parks laid out by John Nash, 1811–35
Source: Summerson 1978

It was all very well arranged. One suspects that Nash had a hand in Fordyce's last report and that the way was paved, from the beginning, for the acceptance of his great design in preference to Leverton and Chawner's who were probably used merely as a check.

It was singularly fortunate that the elevation of the Prince of Wales to the Regency should chime in exactly with the reversion of Marylebone Park. It was fortunate too that these events should occur at a marked turn in the economic tide. There was a severe trade crisis in 1810, when house-property stood out as almost the only form of capital investment which continued to rise in value,[2] the chief reason being the virtual cessation of speculative building owing to the difficulty of importing timber in war-time. In the summer of 1811, however, there was a revival of credit and improved prospects all round and naturally the building trade led the way in the revival, a boom period setting in which lasted through the final war years and well into the post-Waterloo peace.

From 1811, the Prince and Nash were clearly the moving powers in the planning scheme. The Prince talked enthusiastically about eclipsing Napoleon's Paris, while Nash designed a *guinguette*, or Royal pleasaunce, for Regent's Park and planned Regent Street as a 'Royal mile' from Carlton House to the *guinguette*; he also consulted with the promoters of a canal scheme and introduced a stretch of it picturesquely into the Park.

The design for the Park published in 1812 is elaborate and dramatic. Villas are dotted everywhere in woody grooves. The *guinguette* has a strip of formal water in front of it, while the arms of a serpentine lake embrace the centre of the area where, on rising ground, is a great double circus with a 'National Valhalla' in the middle of it. Round the margins are terraces and in the south-east corner is the marketing and working-class quarter. Where the southward road crosses the New Road is another vast circus, with a church in the middle.

This plan was approved by the Treasury and planting was begun at once; the Canal Company obtained an Act and excavation was started; and half the Circus on the New Road was leased. However, as time went on many modifications had to be made. Nash was instructed by the Treasury to thin out the villas, an operation which he regretted, since it spoiled the decided 'garden city' character of his design. The great double circus, with its Valhalla, was abandoned and so ultimately was the *guinguette*, while the canal was made to run round the Park, not through it. The lessee of the Circus became bankrupt and the northern half of it was eliminated. Indeed, all that was to remain of the design were the plantations and water, eight villas, half a circus (now Park Crescent), and the ring of terraces; and these latter did not begin to materialize until Cornwall Terrace was begun in 1820.

So the Regent's Park of today is merely a shadow of what Nash envisaged in 1812. As a piece of planting it is bald and uninteresting, lacking as it does the rich gardens and groves of the forty or fifty intended villas. Its architectural beauties

[2] T. Tooke, *History of Prices*, 1838–57, vol. 1, p. 312.

are confined to the margins with their noble approaches and the belt of terraces, interrupted across the north, so that the view of Hampstead and Highgate should be preserved.

The Regent's Park terraces are greatly loved today – more so than ever they were when they were new, when their shortcomings in detail and finish grated on the susceptibilities of critics bred in an exacting school. The truth is that these buildings, careless and clumsy though they are in many ways, have an extravagant scenic character which, perceived through nostalgic mists of time, makes them irresistible. They are dream palaces, full of grandiose, romantic ideas such as an architect might scribble in a holiday sketch-book. Seen at a distance, framed in green tracery, perhaps in the kind light of late autumn, they suggest architectural glories which make Greenwich tame and Hampton Court provincial. Carved pediments, rich in allegory, top the trees; massive pavilions, standing forward like the *corps de garde* of Baroque chateaux, are linked to the main structures by triumphal arches or columnar screens; each terrace stretches its length in all the pride of unconfined symmetry. It is magnificent. And behind it all – behind it are rows and rows of identical houses, identical in their narrowness, their thin pretentiousness, their poverty of design. Where the eye apprehends a mansion of great distinction, supported by lesser mansions and service quarters, the mind must interpret it as a block of thin houses, with other blocks of thin houses carrying less ornament or none at all. The sham is flagrant and absurd. The terraces are architectural whims; and though Nash was serious enough in his intention, the effect is an odd combination of magnificence and bathos which only the retrospect of a century can forgive.

Nash was over seventy when he designed most of the terraces. He made tiny diagrammatic sketches which he handed to his draughtsmen for working out. Scale drawings, with mouldings to half full size, were given to the speculating builder, who carried them out without very exacting supervision; and Nash never seems to have worried if the proportions came out a bit different from what he expected. They often did.

The earliest architectural feature of Regent's Park is the very lovely, unpretentious, neatly detailed Park Crescent (1812, the southern half of the projected circus). It opens out at either end to the New Road (Marylebone Road of today) and is continued northwards by Park Square (1823–5). The design of the square is less happy, the façades being crowded and coarse in design, but the arrangement as a whole, considered as a formal approach from a thoroughfare to a landscaped park, is admirable, and the simple appropriateness of Park Crescent with its Ionic colonnades is beyond criticism.[3]

Along the south of the Park run the two blocks of York Terrace (1822 onwards), and between them is another masterpiece of town planning, York Gate, devised to enclose the new Marylebone Church in a vista. Here again is a

---

[3] In recent years the whole of Park Crescent has been rebuilt, the new façades, however, being scrupulous copies of the old.

really fine piece of architectural scenery, as appropriate and effective as Park Crescent.

York Terrace and the two terraces immediately to the west, Cornwall and Clarence, were built by James Burton, of Bloomsbury fame, and the designs for the last two are by his young son, Decimus, working, of course, under the general direction of Nash.[4] Both are wholly inadequate realizations of extremely ambitious architectural conceptions, but both, at a distance, do realize some of the effect which they set out to achieve. Next door, westwards, Sussex Place (1822) with its pointed roofs and curved wings is one of Nash's major outrages on the taste of his time. Regarded indulgently as a large-scale joke (the houses are the biggest in the Park), it becomes more acceptable as the years pass. It was designed, one imagines, with even greater celerity than the other terraces. Next to it is Hanover Terrace (1822–3) where Nash perversely returns to coarse copy-book Roman and introduces a pleasant arcaded feature along the ground floor. Kent Terrace, behind Hanover, turns from Roman to Greek and pays doubtful compliments to Sir John Soane.

For sheer architectural frolic, the terraces along the east side of the Park are the most striking. Cumberland Terrace (1827) with its seven porticos, its courtyards and arches, is the crowning glory, the back-cloth as it were to Act III, and easily the most breath-taking architectural panorama in London. With its sketchy detail, its stylistic solecisms, and its pretty-pretty sculpture by Bubb, it is a marvellous, adorable extravagance. Chester Terrace (1825) with two gimcrack 'triumphal' arches superscribed with the name of the terrace, is more moderate in its pretensions. Gloucester Gate (1827) and Cambridge Terrace (1825) are almost conventional by comparison.

Regent's Park is full of amusing and effective detail. Nash's lodges at Hanover and Gloucester Gates and Park Crescent, the cast-iron railings and street lamps where they survive, James Morgan's bridge over the canal; all these are lively and inventive products of their period. And there still survive most of the eight villas, including the Holme, built for himself by James Burton and designed by Decimus, and several built by other architects.

Eastwards of the Park is the area of the Crown's Marylebone Estate reserved by Nash for three purposes; first, for a working-class quarter with markets and shops; second, for a large barracks; and third (this was an afterthought) for a miniature 'garden suburb'. The area is divided from the Park by Albany Street. The working-class district, now entirely replanned and rebuilt, comprised Cumberland Market, Clarence Market (later Gardens), York Square (later Munster Square), and the streets adjoining them. Directly north of Cumberland Market was the canal basin, served by a branch (now filled up) from the Regent's Canal and designed to facilitate the daily supply of fresh vegetables from the Middlesex market gardens to the 'shopping centre' of Regent's Park. Since 1945 all this has

[4] Decimus stated before the *Select Committee on the Office of Works, etc.*, 1828, that he 'merely gave the designs'.

131

vanished. The squares were ordinary enough as architecture but one remembers them for their singular combination of largeness of lay-out and smallness of scale. Munster Square, in particular consists of mere stucco cottages, yet its size and regularity made it strikingly beautiful.[5]

The barracks lie to the north, between Albany Street and the branch canal, and have been rebuilt. Northward again are the Park Villages, East and West. These were among Nash's very last works and are full of interest. The houses are very small and often charmingly planned. Some are 'Italian', some 'Gothic', some affect a kind of Châlet style. Building this essay in the Picturesque compensated him for having to leave out the clusters of villas he planned for the Park itself. Trees, water, fanciful gables and balconies – all the properties of the romantic village scene as illustrated in the almanacs and keepsakes are here (except, now, the water). During the last years of Nash's life and after his death the villages were completed by his pupil and successor James Pennethorne. Today, Park Village West survives and half of Park Village East, the other half having been erased by the railway. They are, in a sense, ancestors of all picturesque suburbia. Up to the war, housing estates were still being laid out very much on these lines with 'no two houses alike'. It would be difficult to find a prototype for these much earlier than Nash's Park Villages.

With the development of Regent's Park proceeded the cutting of Regent Street. This great thoroughfare is unique in the history of town-planning. Its amazingly successful blend of formality and picturesque opportunism could have happened nowhere and at no time but in England of the period of the Picturesque. It might be said of Regent Street, as Rasmussen[6] has said of the Adelphi, that it was 'not only a dream of antique architecture' but 'just as much a finance-fantasia over risk and profit'; the financier was an artist and the artist a financier. To some extent it was a masterly, calculated solution; but also to some extent it was a no less masterly improvisation.

In the plan published with the Regent's Park report of 1812 Nash determined the fundament of his scheme. He placed the line of the proposed street exactly where the close, untidy development of Soho stopped and the open texture of the West End estates began. This was the only logical and 'biologically' correct line, for two reasons. It involved the acquisition only of an inexpensive margin of Soho property; but at the same time it enabled one side of the new thoroughfare to open into all the good east–west streets issuing from in and around the great squares. It was obviously the only right answer, but it took Nash to find it. Other planners had proposed to plough streets through Soho, leaving an obstinate strip of poor property between the new street and the West End; such plans would

---

[5] I recall a comment made to me in 1946 by a Polish officer who had lived near by and watched the bombing and dereliction of the square. 'It gives the peculiar feeling,' he wrote, 'of an immense room, with the skies as the roof: the same feeling you have in evenings on the Piazza San Marco in Venice: a ballroom.'

[6] *London, the Unique City,* 1937. Published in Penguin Books 1960.

infallibly have failed commercially and only half resolved London's traffic problem. Nash's plan took advantage of the cheapness of the Soho area but 'hugged' (his own metaphor) the coast of the West End.

From the first, there was no attempt to make Regent Street straight. At the north end it took its direction from Portland Place; Oxford Circus was introduced as a 'pivot' on which the main part of the street turned slightly to the east; while at Piccadilly another change of direction was introduced so as to bring the southernmost section of the street exactly normal to the façade of Carlton House. But if the street was not to be straight, it certainly was to be formal. The early plan suggests that Nash was thinking of something as strictly disciplined as the Rue de Rivoli, as chaste as Park Crescent. However, he was to change his mind.

Certain modifications were made in the plan before the Bill went before Parliament, the most substantial being the introduction of the quarter-circle or Quadrant as a device of swinging the street from one axis to another.

The New Street Act was passed in 1813. Finance was obtained from an Insurance Company and later, the Bank of England; a sewer was constructed, demolition and the letting of sites begun. There was a very awkward phase when nobody would come in on the project and everybody abused it, but largely thanks to James Burton's unquenchable initiative and Nash's own colossal resourcefulness and courage Regent Street was completed.

It was during the early stages of the street's construction that improvisation developed. To get the street built Nash had to find moneyed men who would take sites, and, of course, the people willing to do this did not all want to do it for the same reason. For instance, in the lower part of the street we find a Mr Warren taking a site for a hotel, a Mr Blicke anxious to erect a large private house, Messrs Hopkinson a site for a bank, the Church Commissioners a site for one of their new churches, and Mr James Burton a block of sites as a speculation in chambers and shops. Now, if Nash had tried to marshall all these excellent people behind one continuous façade it is not hard to imagine that most of them would have lost interest. Mr Warren wanted a distinctive façade for his hotel, the church had to have a portico and steeple, Mr Blicke wanted a drive-in for his carriage, and so on. So Nash had to extemporize and contrive an architectural grouping which had a sort of picturesque unity without being strictly balanced. In this he succeeded remarkably well, not only here but throughout the street. Starting in Waterloo Place with blocks of houses on a strictly symmetrical plan, he abandoned symmetry at the opening of Regent Street and improvised till he reached Piccadilly Circus. Meanwhile, the upper part of the street was proceeding in the same way, big speculative blocks of twenty or thirty sites being leased wherever possible and the interstices filled in with individual ventures – a concert hall, two churches, a public house, and so on. By very adroit adjustment and persuasion behind the scenes Nash managed not merely to preserve the decencies of street architecture but to produce an effective and, in parts, really admirable panorama.

But there was one part of the street where improvisation would not work – the Quadrant. A curved structure like that cannot, for aesthetic reasons, be designed with the episodic informality of a long straight stretch; nor, for technical reasons, can a uniform curved structure be built in arbitrary sections, by different builders. The whole of the Quadrant had to be undertaken by one man. The bold spendthrift Burton, who had already overspent himself to save other parts of the street, would not tackle it. So Nash did. He took the whole of the Quadrant in his own name, collected a group of building tradesmen who were willing to invest in the speculation in lieu of cash payment, and got the thing done. It was a masterly undertaking, as masterly as the proud unbroken sweep of stucco which seemed to lead out of Piccadilly to nowhere but which, with the true whimsicality of the Picturesque, landed the traveller in the bright vista of Regent Street itself with its gay assortment of architectural ideas, like a naughty version of Oxford's venerable High Street.

The irregularity of Regent Street gave Nash opportunities which he seized unfailingly. On the north of Piccadilly Circus he managed to let a site to an Insurance Company promoter who was keen on architecture to the extent of paying for a full-size replica of Inigo Jones's river façade to old Somerset House – hence the old Country Fire Office. At Langham Place, where the opening to Portland Place fell too far west to line up with Upper Regent Street, he let a site to the Church Commissioners and built them a church (All Souls) whose nave swings erratically to the north-east, but whose circular vestibule, crowned by a quaint colonnaded spike, makes a lovely terminal feature to the northward stretch of Regent Street.[7] Again, there is the case of the Haymarket Theatre, whose Corinthian portico, thanks to Nash's successful wangling, still closes the cross-vista at the end of Charles II Street.

The bulk of Regent Street was built up between 1817 and 1823; the formal Waterloo Place, parading its Ionic colonnades in front of Carlton House, was rather earlier. It is characteristic of the whole story of Regent Street that Carlton House, which had virtually provided the point of departure for the whole scheme, was itself to be swept away as the scheme developed into its last stages. It happened like this. In 1821, Nash and the King managed to trick Parliament into providing funds for the conversion of old Buckingham House into Buckingham Palace; their excuse being that Carlton House, on which thousands had been lavished in the previous ten years, was shabby, inconvenient, and unsafe. Anyway, the King abandoned it, and to offset the vast expenditure on the Palace it was determined to pull Carlton House down and to develop the site of house and garden as a building scheme. This led directly to the idea of making St James's Park a southern counterpart of Regent's Park, with houses along the north and south and the Palace on the west. The idea matured. St James's Park was planted on Picturesque principles and its straight canal made into a curly lake. To the

[7] Or did till 1960, when a yellow brick block of offices erected by the BBC behind the church finally obliterated its effect.

north, the vast blocks of Carlton House Terrace and Carlton Gardens reared themselves on the site and grounds of Carlton House; and to the south, after a long interval, appeared – not houses, but the Wellington Barracks.

The two Corinthian ranges of Carlton House Terrace are evidently inspired by Gabriel's buildings in the Place de la Concorde. The general conception of these two great blocks, supported by a terrace formed by the projection of the service quarters towards the park, is exceedingly grand. In detail, of course, one may agree with the late Sir Reginald Blomfield's view that they are defective in scholarship. The central pediments are a somewhat too contrived means of preventing an apparent sag in a very long façade and the attics on the end pavilions may be over-emphatic. Subtlety of modelling there is none. In fact, Carlton House Terrace is thoroughly slap-dash, thoroughly typical of the extraordinary old man who designed it, but whose only contribution to the work was probably the provision of a few small sketches, done either in the glorious painted gallery of his Regent Street mansion or the flower-scented luxury of his castle in the Isle of Wight.

The development of the St James's Park area is not the last chapter in the story of John Nash's metropolitan improvements. He was full of projects and, whatever one may think of his later architecture, his genius for town-planning was at its height when he was seventy. About 1825–6 he prepared plans for a new artery to link up Whitehall with the British Museum and the Bloomsbury residential area, then on the point of renewed expansion under Thomas Cubitt. This scheme was linked to the Regent Street scheme by the cutting of Pall Mall East and the formation of a square at the top of Whitehall from which a road was to run in a direct line to Bloomsbury. The square (occupying the site of the Old Royal Mews) was formed, and in 1830 was christened Trafalgar Square. In the process, St Martin-in-the-Fields was disencumbered of its shabby purlieus and surrounded by orderly stucco buildings, some of which still stand. Its magnificent portico was seen to advantage for the first time. Eastward of St. Martin's, part of the north side of the Strand was entirely remodelled and the clever arrangement of circular towers to disguise the conflicting angles was introduced. Nash designed none of the buildings in this area. He entered a limited competition for the National Gallery, but Wilkins won it. On the west of Trafalgar Square, Smirke designed the College of Physicians and the Union Club. On the east, George Ledwell Taylor undertook a building speculation, with a façade by himself. The Golden Cross Inn was rebuilt by Tite.

Trafalgar Square proved a great success, but the northward road was abandoned until 1887, when Charing Cross Road was formed on a different line. A more creditable sequel to Nash's Metropolitan Improvements is provided by the work of his successor James Pennethorne, to whom we shall return in our final chapter.

John Nash was the central figure in the grand era of Metropolitan Improvements, the great manager, the politician with the long-term policy. But around him were other architects carrying out other building-schemes of narrower extent but often of some artistic importance. To these buildings and to Nash's one great public building – Buckingham Palace – we shall, in due course, return.

15

Architecture, Essay on Art

Etienne-Louis Boullée

Introduction

What is architecture? Shall I join Vitruvius in defining it as the art of building? Indeed, no, for there is a flagrant error in this definition. Vitruvius mistakes the effect for the cause.

In order to execute, it is first necessary to conceive. Our earliest ancestors built their huts only when they had a picture of them in their minds. It is this product of the mind, this process of creation, that constitutes architecture and which can consequently be defined as the art of designing and bringing to perfection any building whatsoever. Thus, the art of construction is merely an auxiliary art which, in our opinion, could appropriately be called the scientific side of architecture.

Art, in the true sense of the word, and science, these we believe have their place in architecture.

The majority of Authors writing on this subject confine themselves to discussing the technical side. That is natural if we think about it a little. It was necessary to study safe building methods before attempting to build attractively. And since the technical side is of paramount importance and consequently the most essential, it was natural that this aspect should be dealt with first.

Moreover, it must be admitted that the beauty of art cannot be demonstrated like a mathematical truth; although this beauty is derived from nature, to sense it and apply it fruitfully certain qualities are necessary and nature is not very generous with them.

What do we find in Books on architecture? Ruins of ancient temples that we know were excavated in Greece. However perfect these examples may be, they are not sufficient to provide a complete treatise on art.

[. . .]

Etienne-Louis Boullée, "Architecture, Essay on Art," pp. 83–7, 145 from Helen Rosenau (ed.), *Boullée and Visionary Architecture*, trans. Sheila de Vallée. London and New York: Academy Editions, 1953. The footnotes reproduced here are from the 1953 edition.

136

You are familiar with the famous quarrel between Pérault, the architect of the Peristyle of the Louvre and François Blondel, the architect of the Porte St. Denis. The former denied that architecture had its source in nature: he called it fantastic art that was pure invention. When François Blondel tried to refute Pérault's opinion, the arguments he used were so weak that the question remained unsolved. When I raised it again, I did not get any satisfactory answer. On the contrary, I soon became aware that most educated men shared Pérault's opinion.[1]

And now Reader, let me ask you, "Am I not to some extent justified in maintaining that architecture is still in its infancy, for we have no clear notion of its basic principles?"

In common with all educated men, I admit that tact and sensibility can result in excellent work. I admit that even artists who have not acquired sufficient knowledge to search out the basic principles at the root of their art will nevertheless be competent, provided they are guided by that gift of Nature that permits men to choose wisely.

But it is nonetheless true that there are few authors who have considered architecture from the artistic point of view; what I mean is that few authors have attempted to study in depth that side of architecture that I term art, in the strict sense of the word. We have some precepts based on good examples but these are few and far between.

Vitruvius's commentator[2] does inform us that a prerequisite of architecture is a knowledge of those sciences related to geometry, such as Mechanics, hydraulics and astronomy, and also Physics, Medicine, etc. He concludes by asking for some knowledge of the fine arts. But, if we consider that science and the fine arts both have their place in architecture considered as art, and since, moreover, Pérault defines his architecture as "fantastic", François Blondel in his rebuttal has not proved the contrary, and nor has anyone else up to the present; if we succeed in discovering that basic principles of architecture and what is their source, then I believe that, without rashness, we can conclude that these principles have remained unknown or at least have been neglected by those who have discovered them.

I have met competent men who have objected that since the discussion between Pérault and François Blondel had degenerated into a quarrel and that they were therefore overcome by anger and a spirit of rivalry, no conclusion should, under the circumstances, be based on their pronouncements for Pérault's true

---

[1] Blondel's conception of architecture was based on linear design, whilst in Boullée the painterly and visionary image predominated. Nevertheless, Boullée admired the older architect, whose artistic integrity he appreciated. In F. Blondel's *Cours d'architecture*, Paris 1675–83, (Epistre) he already expressed the concern for the education of the layman, but characteristically for Boullée, the social context widened from Royalty to "gens instruits".

[2] The "commentator of Vitruve" is Claude Perrault, whose translation of *Vitruvius* with commentaries appeared first in 1673, second edition 1684.

opinions were certainly very different from those he professed.[3] However, one of those who had spoken thus confessed that the question was difficult to solve. At the Academy, I heard him read a memorandum debating this question without coming any closer to a solution.

When contemplating the Peristyle of the Louvre in the company of other Architects, I have on occasion chosen the moment when they were lost in admiration at its beauty to declare a completely opposite opinion. As you can well imagine, they asked me to explain myself. Then I reminded them of Pérault's opinion. I said to them, "You admire this work of art but the architect himself has admitted that it is based on pure fantasy and owes nothing whatsoever to nature. Your admiration is therefore the result of a particular point of view and you should not be surprised to hear it criticized, for the so-called beauty that you find in it has no connexion with nature, which is the source of all true beauty." I added, "You may admire the techniques used in its construction and I admit that it is a competent construction, even one of Genius, but in view of the architect's own admission, I believe that when you think you are admiring what you call the beauty of its architecture, you are in fact admiring what your eye is accustomed to in something that has no true beauty." My colleagues stammered a few words without giving me an answer. I was not surprised for it is not easy to explain what the beauty of the Peristyle of the Louvre or of any other monument has to do with Nature, if one has not given deep thought to the matter. What does surprise me is that no one has tried to elucidate an objection of such importance.

What, then, has impeded the progress of that part of architecture concerned with art in the strict sense of the word? This is clear to me.

For an art to attain perfection, it is not sufficient that the men who practise it love it passionately. It is also vital that there be no impediment to the studies they must undertake. Their genius must be able to spread its wings freely and they must be encouraged by the expectation that their efforts will be rewarded.

Let us imagine now that a young Architect makes some progress and begins to make a name for himself and to win the confidence of the Public. He will be overburdened with a stack of requests and details of all kinds and forced to devote all his time to the contracts which are given him. Because he is continually busy with the procedures made necessary by the confidence shown in him, the artist can no longer contribute to the progress of his art and consequently cannot hope to win the true glory to which he could have aspired. He cannot give sufficient time to the study of his art and thus finds himself forced to abandon it. You will say that the architect should refuse lucrative business so as to be able to pursue his purely theoretical studies. Alas! Who would willingly sacrifice a fortune that is offered him and which, in many cases, he desperately needs? You will say that such a sacrifice should be easy in view of the expectation that he will one day be

---

[3] Boullée is here referring to the controversy between François Blondel and Claude and Charles Perrault. The book he had in mind is Charles Perrault's *Parallèle des anciens et des modernes*, nouvelle édition Paris 1693, p. 75 ff., especially the chapter on Architecture.

commissioned to build several great buildings. But how can he really believe in such expectations? The opportunities are so few. How can he be sure ten or fifteen years in advance that his services will be used by those in power at the time. You will perhaps reply that a worthy man has the right to expect just that. And I would answer you, "Will justice be done? Can he really expect to be given preference?" I credit patrons with the utmost honesty and the purest intentions and yet I am forced to admit that their lack of knowledge often leads them to act blindly, and that it is a lucky chance when they choose a competent man. How many times preference has been given to ignorant schemers at the expense of worthy men who spend their time working and do not scheme!

How preferable is the fate of Painters and men of letters![4] They are free and independent; they can choose their subjects and follow the bent of their genius. Their reputation depends on no one but themselves.

[...]

However, suppose we assume for a moment that my opinions are in some respects false. Suppose we assume that an architect is in the most advantageous position possible, i.e. he has talent, money and patrons. Such advantages are extremely difficult to come by all together and where will they lead him?

It is a fact that when the most straightforward individual starts to build, he sorely tries the patience of his architect, with whose decisions he rarely concurs.

It is also a fact that those in high places who give contracts for public monuments are not in general any more amenable than private individuals. And so what happens? What happens is that the architect finds that he is obliged to obey orders from above and abandon his best ideas. What is more, if the architect is very gifted, his projects will be even less acceptable to his judges who will not be sufficiently enlightened to either understand or appreciate the beauty of his designs.

The gifted architect will not be understood and this will cause him a thousand irksome setbacks; and if he wants to keep his position, then he must refrain from any resistance; he must not listen to the voice of his genius but descend to the level of those he must please. It is evident that this flexibility is difficult to find in an exceptional man; and since in architecture, there is often a curb on genius, as we have demonstrated, it is consequently very difficult to find a gifted architect in a position where he can produce good architecture.

An architect can never be sure that he will be given the opportunity to develop his truly superior genius by being made responsible for one of those public

---

[4] This outcry is particularly interesting with regard to the disinterestedness of Boullée, since most of his contemporaries regarded the career of an architect as financially more rewarding. J.-B. Greuze's and David's families destined these painters for architecture. The architect's dependence on his patrons was obvious, whilst the writer and painter were accorded more freedom. The one exception being the history painters, who were almost as dependent on patronage for their large schemes as the architects.

buildings that should bring glory to the country that has ordered them and should arouse the admiration of all connoisseurs.

If he succeeds in being chosen to begin such a project, will he be permitted to complete it? What a sorry example we have before us in the heart of our capital city. How many centuries ago did work begin on the Palace of the Louvre! For example, the façade giving onto the Tuileries Gardens, what a rhapsody! The centre front projection is by different hands whose individual styles are easily recognizable. The back projection and the corner pavilions are also by different architects. It seems to me that this Palace can be compared to a poem, each part of which is composed by a different poet.

But, you will say, in spite of all these impediments to progress, we do have masterpieces that are evidence of the beauty of architecture and demonstrate the perfection it has attained. My own views on this will be revealed later and, meanwhile, I will merely state that if architecture had acquired the perfection attained by the other arts, and if there were as beautiful examples, we would not today be reduced to trying to establish whether architecture has its source in nature or whether it is pure invention. I can certainly maintain, without fear of shocking anyone, that a demonstration is clearly needed since the architect of the Peristyle of the Louvre considers that all famous monuments are merely products of the imagination.

[...] in the whole of Europe we can find very few examples of beautiful architecture. And so, if we want to affirm that architecture is the equal of the other arts; what proof do we have? It is certain that for the purposes of comparison there are nowhere near as many masterpieces in architecture as in the other arts and that it is only possible to measure the success of an art through the plethora of experiments of all kinds.

[...]

Perhaps, you will object, that if indeed architects have not acquired the high degree of perfection that other artists appear to have attained, this may be because the latter have the advantage that their art is close to nature and consequently more likely to move us.

I would reply that this is the very question I am trying to answer; that what I understand by art is everything that aims at imitating nature; that no architect has attempted the task I have undertaken; and that if I succeed, as I dare hope I shall, in proving that architecture, as far as its relations with nature are concerned, has perhaps an even greater advantage than the other arts – then you will have to admit that if architecture has not made as many advances as the other arts, the blame does not lie with Architects alone, for, I consider, they have an excuse on the grounds of the obstacles listed which have hampered and continue to hamper architecture in its progress towards perfection.

God forbid that it is my intention to offend the distinguished Architects of this age. I respect and love them and the high esteem in which I hold them leads me to believe that they will listen, without displeasure, to the words of a man whose sole aim is to contribute to the advancement of his profession. If I am mistaken, my ideas will hurt no one but myself; I should not be suspected of bad intentions. If, on the contrary, I have understood certain truths, then I shall certainly not upset distinguished men, who have always considered truth with love and respect.

Consideration

of the discussion that occurred between Pérault, architect of the Peristyle of the Louvre, and François Blondel, architect of the Monument at the Porte St. Denis

The present problem

Is architecture merely fantastic art belonging to the realm of pure invention or are its basic principles derived from Nature?

Allow me first of all to challenge the existence of any art form that is pure invention.

[...]

Don't we derive all our ideas from nature? And does not genius for us lie in the forceful manner in which our senses are reminded of nature?

[...]

Let us listen to a modern Philosopher who tells us, "All our ideas, all our perceptions come to us via external objects. External objects make different impressions on us according to whether they are more or less analogous with the human organism."[5] I should add that we consider "*beautiful*" those objects that most resemble the human organism and that we reject those which, lacking this resemblance, do not correspond to the human condition.

---

[5] Boullée is here referring to John Locke, whose *Essai Philosophique* appeared first in 1700 in Amsterdam in a French translation. He did not, however, sympathize with this point of view, since he regarded as beautiful, objects related to the human organism, and as ugly, those which are unrelated, thus introducing an objective element into his aesthetic theory. Boullée has here forgotten the closing quotation marks. The part of the sentence which deals with sensations is of Locke-Condillac origin, but the term "analogy" connects with Buffon's terminology and also with the article on the subject in the *Encyclopédie*. Analogy is also discussed in Morelly's *Code de la nature*, published in Amsterdam in 1755 (p. 128 chapter heading of the original edition was "Analogie entre l'ordre physique et le moral"). Le Camus de Mézières, Le Génie de l'architecture ou l'analogie de cet art avec notre organisation fails to deal with the subject suggested in the title.

On the essential quality of volumes. On their properties. On their analogy with the human organism[6]

In my search to discover the properties of volumes and their analogy with the human organism, I began by studying the nature of some irregular volumes.

When I saw were masses with convex, concave, angular or planimetric planes, etc., etc. Next I realized that the various contours of the planes of these volumes defined their shape and determined their form. I also perceived in them the confusion (I cannot say variety) engendered by the number and complexity of their irregular planes.

Weary of the mute sterility of irregular volumes, I proceeded to study regular volumes. What I first noted was their regularity, their symmetry and their variety; and I perceived that that was what constituted their shape and their form. What is more, I realized that regularity alone had given man a clear conception of the shape of volumes, and so he gave them a definition which, as we shall see, resulted not only from their regularity and symmetry but also from their variety.

An irregular volume is composed of a multitude of planes, each of them different and, as I have observed above, it lies beyond our grasp. The number and complexity of the planes have nothing distinct about them and give a confused impression.

How is it that we can recognize the shape of a regular volume at a glance? It is because it is simple in form, its planes are regular and it repeats itself. But since we gauge the impression that objects make on us by their clarity, what makes us single out regular volumes in particular is the fact that their regularity and their symmetry represent order, and order is clarity.

It is obvious from the above remarks that man had no clear idea of the shape of volumes before he discovered the concept of regularity.[7]

Once I had observed that the shape of a regular volume is determined by regularity, symmetry and variety, then I understood that proportion is the combination of these properties.

By the proportion of a volume, I mean the effect produced by its regularity, its symmetry and its variety. Regularity gives it a beautiful shape, symmetry gives it order and proportion, variety gives it planes that diversify as we look at them. Thus the combination and the respective concord which are the result of all these properties, give rise to volumetric harmony.

For example, a sphere can be considered as incorporating all the properties of volumes. Every point on its surface is equidistant from its centre. The result of this unique advantage is that from whatever angle we look at it, no optical effect can

---

[6] Boullée here submits the fullest statement of his theory of volumes, emphasizing regularity and variety as the chief values. This was an explicit challenge not only to the valuations of the Rococo, but also of future Romanticism.

[7] The Platonic tradition is apparent, when Boullée alludes to the idea underlying regularity, whilst the basis for taste, according to the part of the article "Goût" in the *Encyclopédie* written by Voltaire, is found in our physical organization as human beings.

ever spoil the magnificent beauty of its shape which, to our eyes, will always be perfect.

The sphere provides the solution to a problem which might be considered a paradox, if it had not been geometrically proved that a sphere is an undefinable polyhedron. This paradox is that the most infinite variety is derived from the most perfect symmetry. For if we assume that the surface of our globe is divided into different points, only one of these points will appear perpendicular to it and the rest will be at a multitude of different angles.

The sphere has other advantages: it offers the greatest possible surface to the eye and this lends it majesty. It has the simplest possible form, the beauty of which derives from its uninterrupted surface; and, in addition to all these qualities, it has grace for its outline and is as smooth and flowing as it could possibly be.

The conclusion of all these observations is that a sphere is, in all respects, the image of perfection. It combines strict symmetry with the most perfect regularity and the greatest possible variety; its form is developed to the fullest extent and is the simplest that exists; its shape is outlined by the most agreeable contour and, finally, the light effects that it produces are so beautifully graduated that they could not possibly be softer, more agreeable or more varied. These unique advantages, which the sphere derives from nature, have an immeasurable hold over our senses.

A great man (Montesquieu) once said, "Symmetry is pleasing because it is the image of clarity and because the mind, which is always seeking understanding, easily accepts and grasps all that is symmetrical."[8] I would add that symmetry is pleasing because it is the image of order and perfection.

Variety is pleasing because it satisfied a spiritual need which, by its very nature, likes to be stimulated and sustained by what is new. And it is variety that makes things appear new to us. It therefore follows that variety puts new life into our faculties by offering us new pleasures and it is as pleasing to us in the objects that are part of any given volume, as it is in the light effects so produced.

Grandeur, too, always pleases us whatever form it takes for we are ever eager to increase our pleasure and would like to embrace the Universe.

Finally, the image of Grace is one which, deep in our hearts, is the most pleasing of all.

---

[8] Boullée is here referring to the part of the article "Goût" in the *Encyclopédie* (1757) written by Montesquieu (p. 764).

16

The Sphere: Reading a Gender Metaphor in the Architecture of Modern Cults of Identity

Susanne von Falkenhausen

In 1936 Albert Speer made his first designs for a domed hall, which was intended to complete and tower over the north–south axis envisioned by Hitler for Berlin. According to Hitler's wishes, the dome was to surpass those of the Capitol in Washington and St Peter's in Rome. In the dome, with its semi-spherical basic form, its ribs and lantern, Speer cited ecclesiastical architecture since the Renaissance, but took it several steps further; he magnified the basic form, and multiplied the number of ribs covering it. The rising lines of the ribs, which culminated in the lantern, signified hierarchy and notions of salvation and resurrection. With its gigantic dimensions, the domed building was to encompass the 'nation as a body' (*Volkskörper*) – standing room for 150,000 was planned – and to elevate it to the object of its own cult.

In 1939, when the final version of the design for the domed hall was completed,[1] a whole, unadorned sphere next to a steep triangular obelisk became the symbolic monument of the 1939 World Fair in New York.[2] Inside the sphere visitors could admire the model of a futuristic machine-age city surrounded by a park, 'Democracity', designed for the 'world of tomorrow'. The Fair opened in the summer of 1939, shortly before Hitler invaded Poland.

Two versions of the sphere as metaphor: each of them was to represent, visually, a political system. The designers clearly assumed that the metaphor of the sphere

Susanne von Falkenhausen, "The Sphere: Reading a Gender Metaphor in the Architecture of Modern Cults of Identity," pp. 238–67 from *Art History* 20: 2. Oxford: Blackwell, 1997. Reprinted by permission of Blackwell Publishing Ltd.

[1] See Lars Olof Larsson, *Die Neugestaltung der Reichhauptstadt. Albert Speers Generalbebauungsplan für Berlin*, Stockholm, 1978, pp. 44–6.

[2] See, among others, *Le livre des expositions universelles, 1851–1989*, Paris, 1983.

had a high capacity to create appropriate meanings; that is, they could refer to an effective tradition in the collective visual memory. It is surprising that this metaphor was employed on both sides of a confrontation between political systems that had assumed existentially threatening proportions at the time. The 'war' of metaphors that was being fought out between fascism and democracy immediately before the outbreak of World War II juxtaposed two fields of meaning and association surrounding the same basic form, and in so doing referred to two lines of tradition in architectural history: the ribbed semi-spherical dome of the ancient and modern architecture of domination, whether ecclesiastical or imperial, was contrasted with the whole, unadorned sphere of the radically stereometric architectural visions of the so-called revolutionary architecture conceived by Boullée.

I am getting ahead of myself, though. This 'narrative' actually begins elsewhere, with an architectural design by Boullée himself. The reception of his design among architectural historians since its rediscovery in 1968 led me to ask questions about the sphere as an architectural *metaphor*, or, to be more precise, as a *gendered* metaphor. This led to further questions about the meaning of this gender metaphor in the field of political identities, and that will be the subject of what follows.

The Sphere (I)

It was probably in 1793, during the Jacobin Terror, that Étienne-Louis Boullée designed a temple to which, so far as is known, he never gave a name. In current scholarship it is known by two names: the Temple to Reason and the Temple to

---

[3] The following authors use the name 'Temple to Nature': Helen Rosenau, *Boullée and Visionary Architecture including Boullée's 'Architecture, Essay on Art'*, London and New York, 1976; Jean-Marie Pérouse de Montclos, *Étienne-Louis Boullée (1728–1799). De l'architecture classique à l'architecture révolutionnaire*, Paris, 1969; Philippe Madecq, *Boullée*, Paris, 1986; the only German author thus far has been Johannes Langner, 'Fels und Sphäre. Bilder der Natur in der Architektur um 1789' (English trans. 'The Rocks and the Sphere: Architectural Images of Nature around 1789'), both in *Daidalos*, vol. 12, 1984, pp. 92–103. Curiously enough, it is mainly scholars from the German-speaking countries who argue for the name 'Temple to Reason': Lankheit (see note 4 below); Adolf Max Vogt, *Boullée's Newton-Denkmal, Sakralbau und Kugelidee*, Basel, 1969; Bruno Reudenbach, 'Natur und Geschichte bei Ledoux und Boullée', *IDEA. Werke. Theorien. Dokumente. Jahrbuch der Hamburger Kunsthalle*, vol. 8, 1989, pp. 31–56; Monika Steinhauser, 'Étienne-Louis Boullée's Architecture. Essai sur l'art. Zur theoretischen Begründung einer autonomen Architektur', *IDEA*, vol. 2, 1983, pp. 7–47. Richard Sennett offers a 'just' but unfortunately neither very subtle nor well-founded nor well-documented solution in a few short sentences on the 'Temple to Nature and Reason' in his *Flesh and Stone*, New York, 1994, pp. 294–6. He simply dedicates the temple to both cults, but additionally simplifies the duality through reductions: the top half was that of 'Reason'; the bottom half was supposed to be scooped out of the earth and was thus the half of 'Nature'. Sennett apparently believes that the rocky landscape of the surrounding crater was supposed to be the mere result of these excavations. He fails to note that this was a carefully planned architectural *natura naturata* and not 'nature' in some authentic, material (scooped out!) splendour.

Nature.[3] It has been assigned to two fields of signification which generally represent extremes on the scale of the symbolic gender order: reason = male, nature = female. The possibility of such divergent interpretations lies in the nature of the design itself. It radically formulates the gender ambivalence associated with the metaphor of the sphere and allows it to stand unresolved.

In 1968 Klaus Lankheit attributed to Boullée the two large architectural drawings in the Uffizi, which show the exterior (54 × 90 cm) and cross-section (48 × 91 cm) of a rotunda, dated them *c*.1793, and interpreted the building as a Temple to Reason.[4] The exterior structure of this 'temple' is a rotunda of extreme regularity, with a plain dome sunk into two cylindrical rings. Boullée's principles of absence of ornament and closed wall surfaces, which allows the stereometric volumes to be effective as a basis for construction, are fully developed. The chief characteristics of the interior space are the two half-spheres of different diameters for the dome and for a rocky crater with grotto. They are linked by a double non-structural colonnade. The half-sphere of the dome is visible only in the interior space. The lower half-sphere consists of an artificial rocky crater, at the base of which a grotto mound rises up with a dark cave entrance with a strong vertical emphasis. The grotto mound is crowned by a Diana of Ephesus. Originally a nature and fertility goddess from Asia Minor, she must, as Lankheit notes, have been familiar to the architect as a symbol of nurturing nature present in iconographic tradition since Raphael's loggias in the Vatican.[5] As an emblem of revolutionary nature religion, she had also gained new prominence in the festival iconography of 1793–4. To summarize, the design consists of a dome which is visible in the interior space as a half-sphere, but from the outside only as a sunken sphere segment, the surrounding cylindrical rings, a double interior colonnade, a rocky crater with a grotto mound, the grotto entrance and the statue of Diana Ephesia.

This clearly delimited number of components led architectural historians to identify the cult to which the temple was dedicated as, variously, reason and nature. The decisive factor here was the contrast between the rational stereo-metric form of the dome and the *mise en scène* of chaos and fertility in the rocky crater, the grotto and the statue of the goddess. What all attempts at interpretation have in common is their desire to harmonize an extremely polarized image, usually in favour of the dome, which represents 'Reason'.

As a sign, the sphere has a long history. The imperial apple, as an old symbol of sovereignty, points to the formal analogy between the sphere and the earth. We find it as an emblem in heraldry and as an attribute of allegorical personifications of the most diverse meanings. In the architecture of the late Renaissance and the Baroque it belongs to architectural ornament, particularly in the ephemeral festive decorations of the seventeenth and eighteenth centuries, in garden architecture,

---

[4] Klaus Lankheit, *Unveröffentlichte Zeichnungen von Étienne-Louis Boullée aus den Uffizien*, Basel, 1968, 1973.

[5] Ibid.

funerary monuments and architectural *capricci*.[6] There, it is usually only one element among others, however. With the architectural visions of Boullée, Ledoux and Lequeu, though, this form becomes an architectural body in its own right, and thus moves from a peripheral position to that of central signifier.

During the French Revolution the metaphor of the sphere embarked on a new political career as a signifier for a collective vision. It found expression in the plans for public buildings for the Nation and its new sovereign, the so-called 'People'. The sphere and its derivatives became central metaphors in the architectural representations of political cults. They were part of the symbolic apparatus used to visualize the discourses on such political terms as 'People' and 'Nation', which were to become central for modernity.

The political cults of the French Revolution represent the first high point in the emergence of modern cults of the political. They formed around the constructions of identity that accompanied the abolition of the monarchy and the simultaneous introduction of a collective Self in the French Revolution: the People, also referred to as the Nation. The sovereign People was to replace the sovereign king. A result of this radical shift was the search for images to supplant the image of the beheaded king, and thus fill a dangerous vacuum of political symbolism. It proved extremely difficult, however, to provide the abstraction of popular sovereignty with a symbolic 'body'. Architecture was to participate in addressing this problem in public space alongside painting and sculpture.

The gendered sphere

At first glance, the sphere is a body in a purely stereometric sense. It appears, in its formal abstraction, to transcend its (grammatically) female gender[7] and to reach a stage of meaning far beyond anything so particular as sex, which is what made it appear so appropriate a metaphor for the all-encompassing and the indivisible.

The metaphor is not, however, without gender. This representation of totality is constructed *within* fields of signification which are shaped by the symbolic order of the sexes. That is the reason for the ambivalent creation of political meaning in Boullée's design described at the outset. As latent signifiers, both sexes support the metaphorical field of activity of the sphere and its derivatives, among which I would like to include the ribbed dome and also the grotto mound.

What, however, is the relationship between this gender ambivalence and the need for symbolic unambiguousness in the discourse of political identities? What is the relationship of the symbolic gender order to the concepts of Nation that lie at the heart of the political systems of modernity? And how does it relate to the concepts of equality and totality used to legitimate collective units and political

---

[6] Werner Oechslin documents the ornamental and iconographic scope of its use in painting and architecture in 'Pyramide et sphère. Notes sur l'architecture révolutionnaire du XVIIIe siècle et ses sources italiennes', *Gazette des beaux-arts*, vol. 77, 1971, pp. 218ff.

[7] Translator's note: the German for sphere, '*die* Kugel', is feminine.

ideological hegemonies? Put another way, why is it that the gender ambivalence of this sign does not impede the visual representation of unity, but instead actually fosters it? And what does this say about the fantasies with which notions of collective unity are rendered visual and elevated to public imagery? We must ask, not least, why the visual discourse of political collectivity 'has' a gender at all, whether it is manifested or remains latent.

These questions about gender relations in the visual language of metaphors of power necessarily call into question the conceptions and patterns of discourse of terms such as the People, community and the Nation precisely at those points where they emphasize that that which is represented as universally valid in fact refers to and helps to enforce the particular. One may trace this process not only in body images, such as national allegories,[8] but also in the forms of architectural 'bodies'.

Architecture as field of meaning

Boullée's visions of public buildings are 'speaking' architecture (*architecture parlante*), i.e., they are intended to produce meaning. One could apply to them what Roland Barthes has said of advertising images; one may assume that 'the image's signification is assuredly intentional ...: the advertising image is *frank* [emphasis in the original] or at least emphatic.'[9] Boullée's designs were doubtless frank and emphatic. I would like to use the reference to Barthes's attempt to develop a rhetoric of the image to relativize that assessment of Boullée's aesthetic, which regards his designs and his theory as early indicators of 'autonomous' art.[10] If we apply the aesthetic of the autonomous art work to Boullée's architectural designs, we will be unable to pose certain questions which place these visions in a functional or, more precisely, meaning-producing and thus socially norm-producing context.

Boullée's work and the cult architecture that followed had something in common with modern advertising: dedication to a political cult generally meant, and means, a quite *precise production of meaning*, which in turn generates a (in this case architectural) *rhetoric*. The metaphorical repertoire of this cult architecture, with all its implications for modernity, became fully developed for the first time during the French Revolution.

---

[8] See, in particular, Silke Wenk, *Versteinerte Weiblichkeit*, 1996, and Susanne von Falkenhausen, *Italienische Monumentalmalerei im Risorgimento, 1830–1890. Strategien nationaler Bildersprache*, Berlin, 1993.

[9] Roland Barthes, 'Rhetoric of the Image', in R. Barthes, *The Responsibility of Forms: Critical Essays on Music, Art and Representation*, trans. Richard Howard, Berkeley and Los Angeles, 1991, pp. 21–40, here p. 22.

[10] The need to evaluate Boullée's work in this light, and thus to incorporate it into a narrative on the genesis of modern art, was already the impetus for its rediscovery by Emil Kauffmann, *Von Ledoux bis Le Corbusier*, Vienna, 1933. This tendency continues within the framework both of modernist and postmodernist-oriented reception.

Were we to follow the widespread assumption that art is art (only) when it is 'autonomous', i.e., free of any responsibility, and that it can only then fully exhaust the category of the aesthetic, we would be virtually robbing the architecture of a Boullée of its aesthetic value if we asked about its participation in the public, normative production of meaning. I do not believe, however, that aesthetics need necessarily conflict with the public production of meaning and thus with participation in the cultural presuppositions of an era. Where architecture is supposed to convey something, it becomes an intelligible *image*. It transports meaning through perception. In this perception, in turn, the artistic quality, the aesthetic, gains in significance over other characteristics of architecture such as function, economy, *convenance* or decorum. For architecture, the production of meaning does not necessarily result in a diminution of its artistic character because it is being put in the 'service' of something else. On the contrary, the result is its intensified entry into the pictorial.

The Metaphor

'The most energetic language is that whose sign has said everything before one speaks,' writes Rousseau in his *Essai sur l'origine des langues*.[11] He dreams of a world in which the sign and the signified are supposedly one, a time of images and the unquestioned substance of that which can be seen. The French Revolution, of all things, attempted to force this unalienated Arcadia, the backward-looking Utopia of the unity of sign and nature, into the present. Its political imagery thus referred not only to the values intended in a given situation, but beyond this to the myth of an identity between the sign and the signified as an identity between human beings, society and nature, between what is seen and the truth.

The form of representation which appeared predestined for such an operation was the metaphor – a term from rhetoric which described a sort of borderline operation between language and image, for its effect was directed at pictorial feeling and thought. Stylistic ascetics frequently rejected, and continue to reject, the metaphor as too baroque, too sensual, illogical, confusing or even immoral, in short, as too seductive – a sort of linguistic *femme fatale*. Political moralists could take up this train of thought for the field in question here: the metaphors of the political cults of the modern age. The metaphor's seductive power would then form the basis for an abuse of the – in themselves – guileless arts for the manipulation of the masses. I cannot, alas, share the hope underlying such an attitude, that a world purged of the seductive power of metaphor would automatically be a good one. The problem, then, can be solved neither by questioning

---

[11] 'Mais le langage le plus énergique est celui où le Signe a tout dit avant qu'on parle'. Jean-Jacques Rousseau, *Essai sur l'origine des langues où il est parlé de la mélodie et de l'imitation musicale*, ed. Charles Porset, Bordeaux, 1968, p. 31.

the morality of metaphor nor by the desire to abolish it. And this naturally holds true for gender metaphors as well.

Gender metaphors, whether in language or in art, are generally signs that are omnipresent yet 'invisible'. They fill the collective imagination with material whose meaning remains partially unconscious, only to be fed into the cycle of images. It is precisely through this state of unconsciousness that a production of meaning, which apparently rests on hopelessly long-term factors, can function. This 'invisibility', and the often anachronistic persistence of these images in the collective visual memory, in defiance of all historical change, guarantee the stability and consistency on all cultural levels of a power relationship: that between the sexes. With this we come to the connection between images and very real power relations. Analogous observations can also, by the way, be made in relation to 'un'-conscious racism. The language of political correctness, the fruit of American linguistic ascetics, will do little to change this, however, though it does bring it to our attention. My secret, old-fashioned hope is that the power formations clandestinely at work in these images may be robbed of their power at the moment when, to describe it with two Enlightenment metaphors, they are raised from the *darkness* of the unconscious to the *light* of the conscious.

People and Nation

The terms 'People' and 'Nation' lay at the heart of the political construction of identity which French Revolutionary cult architecture was intended to assist and embody. The histories of these terms are closely intertwined.

In 1788 Sieyès equated the nation with the Third Estate and thus conceptualized the latter as all-encompassing.[12] The fact that this self-definition rested on the exclusion of the majority of the male population and of all women does not appear to have been considered problematic, even in the purely logical sense. That, on the other hand, is characteristic of the unquestioned defining power of a discourse that the French Revolution transferred to political practice, and which makes visible the hegemony of the bourgeoisie for the coming epochs as well.

'People' and 'Nation' were a community of equals not only in terms of education, property and politics, but also in terms of sex and skin colour: only

---

[12] Emmanuel-Joseph Sieyès, *Qu'est-ce que le Tiers État?*, Paris, 1789. For a summary of the history of the terms and the scholarly discussion of them, see Gabor Kiss, 'Nation als Formel für gesellschaftliche Selbstrepräsentation der Demokratie', in J.-D. Gauger and J. Stadl (eds), *Staatsrepräsentation* (Schriften zur Kultursoziologie, vol. 12), Berlin, 1992. The literature on the subject is extensive and treats the historical variants of 'descriptions of the Other and of the Self' ('*Fremd-und Selbstbeschreibung*', Kiss) in such communities, i.e., also the inclusion and exclusion of particular population groups, but not that of women from definitions of 'People' and 'Nation'. Gender difference is 'invisible' in this scholarly discourse.

white men belonged to those groups who negotiated with each other the legitimate exercise of political sovereignty.[13] This community nonetheless represented itself as universal, with an intensity in word and image that shows that, for them, legitimation to rule stood and fell with this operation. I understand these representations from the perspective of social psychology as evidence of the male collective Self of the 'People' struggling for self-representation.

The Jacobin-inspired temple designs for revolutionary cults by Boullée, Lequeu and others show the intensity with which the need for political imagery converged with architects' need to elevate construction to a creative art, and themselves to the status of artists.

The Metaphorical Repertoire: The Sphere (II)

As becomes evident in Boullée's treatise, cult architecture was for him as free as the fine arts. It sought to create images that affected the beholder and aroused the quasi-religious feeling of the sublime, a central concept in eighteenth-century aesthetics. Accordingly, Boullée developed an architectural imagery that was metaphorically oriented. Using our design as an example, I would like to illuminate this imagery more closely. Let us begin with the dome. It is smooth and unarticulated, unlike the ribbed domes of the existing tradition in sacred architecture; this underlines its geometric purity and perfection as an architectural volume. For Boullée, this produces order and symmetry, and thus beauty – in contrast to which the rocky crater and grotto in the lower sphere, closer to the earth, consist of irregular volumes, which Boullée tellingly calls '*corps obscurs*',[14] that is, dark, opaque volumes whose form 'lies beyond our grasp'.[15] The regular volumes, particularly the sphere, have the aesthetic advantage for Boullée of being comprehensible at a glance.

Lankheit, Vogt and others read the dome of our design as being in the typological tradition of Boullée's 1784 Newton Cenotaph Boullée had here tried to create, at least in a design, the pure, i.e., unribbed and complete, sphere as

---

[13] The exclusion of women ran parallel to that of men of other skin colours in other areas as well, in some cases down to the strategies of justification. For the history of this discourse, see Sigrid Weigel, 'Zum Verhältnis von "Wilden" und "Frauen" im Diskurs der Aufklärung', in S. Weigel, *Topographien der Geschlechter. Kulturgeschichtliche Studien zur Literatur*, Reinbek bei Hamburg, 1990, pp. 115–48.

[14] Rosenau, *Boullée and Visionary Architecture*, p. 121. Rosenau translates '*corps obscurs*' as 'irregular volumes', which corresponds to the later use of the term '*corps irreguliers*' in Boullée's tract. His choice of the word '*obscur*' nevertheless demonstrates the strongly metaphor-laden character of his thought. In the following passages I follow Rosenau's translation.

[15] '... la figure des corps irreguliers ... échappe à notre entendement'. Rosenau, ibid., p. 121, in the chapter 'De l'Essence des corps. De leurs propriétés. De leurs analogies avec notre organisation', English on p. 86.

the most perfect and never yet realized architectural volume. The cenotaph was intended at once as a monument to Newton and as a site for the era's popular Newton cult. Here, the sphere symbolized a universe that Newton's theory of the system of the rotating gravitation of bodies had rendered rationally comprehensible, yet which remained infinite and beyond human experience. It was our design's derivation from the Newton Cenotaph that Lankheit invoked as decisive in his selection of the name Temple to Reason. The powerful presence of the 'irregular volumes' (the grotto mound, and the goddess of fertility and death) so little esteemed by Boullée but employed all the more consciously, tends to undermine this interpretation, however. They make the total picture, which this space dramatizes, into a typical example of the sublime in its interaction between the beautiful and the terrible, which is supposed to overwhelm the viewer.

Boullée's attempt in the Newton Cenotaph to translate the perfect stereometric form of the sphere into architecture is probably the aspect of his work that has most fascinated both his contemporaries and modern scholars. The sphere is, after all, a deeply atectonic form – without a base, removed by its perfect all-round '*regularité*'[16] from the forces of gravity, virtually a metaphor for weightlessness, for detachment from the earth. Thus, in Boullée's Newton Cenotaph it can embody the cosmos: the scientifically recognized universe in *abstract analogy* to Newtonian theory, not as a mimetic image of the earth.

The reason for the adoption of this particular typological derivation for our design may lie in the fact that a comparison between the *interior* of the temple and the *exterior* of the cenotaph makes this interpretation of the sphere comprehensible, even if, in the temple, it is already restricted by the smaller radius of the crater. The apparent comparability disappears, in contrast, when we see the two exteriors side by side: in the Newton Cenotaph more than half of the sphere protrudes from the supporting cylindrical rings, but in the case of the temple we see only a shallow calotte. In addition, on the Newton Cenotaph the rings have been cut out in order to visualize the view of a whole sphere as the underlying principle. In addition, the base of the sphere in the Newton Cenotaph does not touch ground level, while the inner crater, with the vertex, is submerged in the temple well below ground level, rendering that much clearer the earthbound, dark character of the rising grotto mound.

The Newton Cenotaph seems a much more likely candidate than our design for the 'paternity' of those domed centralized buildings designed for French Revolutionary cults as temples to Equality, Reason and the like.

Thus, for example, Sobre's design for a Temple to Immortality, made between 1793 and 1797, more closely follows the dream of a radically spherical structure and its accompanying cosmic, rational associations as we know them from the Newton Cenotaph than does the so-called Temple to Reason. Sobre shows this dream

---

[16] '... la figure des corps irreguliers ... échappe à notre entendement'. Rosenau, ibid., p. 121, in the chapter 'De l'Essence des corps. De leurs propriétés. De leurs analogies avec notre organisation', English on p. 121.

character particularly clearly: a half-sphere is surrounded at its base by water, producing a reflection which, when viewed from a suitable distance, gives the beholder the illusion of a perfect sphere. Architecture here is indeed image – down to the fixing of the distance from which the beholder should look at the picture. Should the beholder come closer or even enter the structure, the illusion is destroyed.

Boullée constructs the myth of the sphere on the basis of perception, of the gaze. Furthermore, in the sphere, as an eternal polyhedron – and this is important – the most infinite variety also derives from the most perfect symmetry.[17] It is from the mathematics of volumes that, quite independently of any similarity of shape with the globe, the sphere thus derives the metaphor for totality, a totality that is rooted in nothing, without above or below, without hierarchy or focus. It is a disembodied, immaterial body, the image of an abstraction and, as such, the image of a transcendence that needs neither gender nor heavenly authority; but it is nevertheless not without gender. This image of the world/cosmos/universe is constructed androcentrically, for it is the male fantasy of being at one without an Other. In this image the feminine is not dissociated from the masculine, but it is put out of commission, and with it that Other which otherwise delimits the masculine Self. This, in turn, functions only if the masculine, too, is rendered invisible. The sphere is, after all, not denoted as masculine. In an absolute thus conceived, with which it seeks a place beyond gendered duality, the masculine tacitly asserts itself as absolute. In other words, the universal, the 'human' beyond gender, is determined and imagined from the standpoint of the masculine and, accordingly, elevated to a covertly androcentric norm. This achieves two things for the masculine (conceived of here as a category in a symbolic cultural order): it is the centre of discourses without being named, and it is imagined as perfect. The painful experience of only belonging to one of the two culturally intelligible sexes, and thus being 'imperfect', thus appears banished.

The Political Sphere

The metaphor of the pure sphere had scarcely become established in architecture (Boullée's design for a Newton Cenotaph[18] preceded the Revolution only by some five years) when it appeared in the architectural visions of the Revolution, above all in the Academy competitions of Year II[19] for the temple to the revolutionary cult of unity, and the spaces in which the 'Souvraineté du Peuple' was to be cultivated, whether by the National Assembly or local bodies. In this way, the

---

[17] 'C'est que de la symétrie la plus parfaite dérive la variété la plus infinie', ibid., p. 121.

[18] See also other designs for spherical structures, some of them also for monuments to Newton, in Jean-Marie Pérouse de Montclos, *Concours de l'Académie royale de l'architecture au XVIIIe siècle*, Paris, 1984, p. 233, a design by Delespine and, even more clearly, a design by Sobre. One could also mention Vaudoyer's 1785 House of a Cosmopolite.

[19] See Werner Szambien, *Les projets de l'an II*, Paris, 1986.

sphere became a metaphor for popular sovereignty itself, conceived of as a totality without hierarchy and without any need for such external authorizations of power as the Absolutist divine right of kings had required. In this, it was the visual representation of an androcentric paradigm of a universal subject. In addition, the sphere appeared to constitute the perfect experiential space for something that had not yet found visual representation in a symbolic uniform body: the multiplicity of male subjects making up the political collective of the 'People', for it represented, mathematically speaking, the perfect unity of an infinite plurality.

Here, the *citoyen* of the Third Estate found a political metaphor for the self-referential authority and identity of *his* notion of 'the People', which was thus represented as something all-encompassing.

The Metaphorical Repertoire: The Tumulus and the Grotto as Derivatives of the Sphere

As was stated above, however, Boullée's Temple to Nature does not conform to this type of spherical structure. It is worth asking which architectural metaphors from Boullée's work could be applied to this design instead, as the metaphorical language of Boullée's architecture found many emulators. It is his funerary architecture which provides the key. It displays similar features both in the exteriors and cross-sections, and could tell us much about the fields of association which Boullée sought to open metaphorically, via 'similarity', for this building. Thus, for example, his necropolis with a central domed building features comparable proportions in the external structure: the broad, depressed proportions of the cylindrical rings and relatively low calotte, which appears submerged, correspond in type to the exterior view of our design. We know from Boullée's treatise what 'character' he hoped to achieve with such proportions. The poetry of the funerary monument was intended to correspond to the image of '*architecture ensevelie*', buried architecture.[20] The depressed proportions were intended to convey to the beholder the impression that the earth was withholding part of the building.[21]

This '*caractère*' of gloom, of something half-reconquered by the earth, is intensified in our temple by the circumstance that the interior space is also lowered in relation to the outer level of the earth – unlike the Newton Cenotaph, but similar to other Boullée tomb interiors, like that of a pyramid tomb for Turenne, which he used in his treatise to illustrate buried architecture.

The domed forms of our design thus correspond more to Boullée's funerary architecture than to the type of the spherical building as a visual analogy for the scientifically conceived universe. This opens up a new associative field of reference for the temple, one difficult to reconcile with the revolutionary cult of Reason as the bright child of ideal and regular Nature. The incursion of architectural

---

[20] See Werner Szambien, *Les projets de l'an II*, Paris, 1986. p. 135.
[21] Ibid., pp. 135, 136.

disorder, the '*corps bruts*' of the boulders and the dark cave opening as a figure of the uncontrollable (because unobservable), does not correspond to the Jacobins' image of a well-ordered, Reason-producing Nature as the model for their political and social system. The revolutionary cult of Nature was a cult of light, whereby the light metaphor was taken over from the Enlightenment discourse on Reason. In revolutionary festivals it was celebrated in the open air.

There exists an anonymous design for a temple with a semi-spherical dome and a Diana Ephesia as a cult statue bearing the inscription 'She is the source of all blessings.'[22] Unlike Boullée, the unknown author associated with the Diana Ephesia an exclusively optimistic programme – under the architrave run inscriptions proclaiming the values of the new earthly paradise ('*énergie*', '*abondance*'). It is only logical that the dark grotto does not appear in this context.

The Grotto as Site of the 'Other'

For revolutionary propagandists, the grotto was usually the place where the vanquished foes of the Revolution, in the form of repulsive serpents, writhed with crown and mitre, as in Bonnet's *Sacred Mountain* of 1794.[23] Here the grotto is additionally surmounted by a Hercules figure symbolizing the victorious People. Which fields of association refer to the grotto motif? The possibilities are numerous and can only be summarized roughly here. The primary meaning is the body metaphor referring to the womb of 'Mother Earth'. The grotto relates to both birth and death, and can be found in the most diverse contexts of function and analogy – from cult architecture to the refreshing garden grotto. With the grotto or cave motif as a body metaphor for the earth as a womb, an animistic understanding of the world lived on in the scientific thinking of the sixteenth and seventeenth centuries.[24] From the sixteenth century until the early nineteenth, notions of the earth giving birth – and death – also accompanied garden grottoes, including the landscape garden.[25] An example is the Proserpina grotto of 1786 in the hermitage at Arlesheim.[26]

---

[22] 'Elle est la source de tous les biens', ibid., pp. 84–5. Szambien believes it may have been inspired by Boullée's designs. The fact that the dome is ribbed seems to speak against this.

[23] A sacred mountain with a Temple to Equality, Hercules and a grotto in which, according to the accompanying description, crime and tyranny have been chained up. The temple is surmounted by a Victory. See ibid., p. 100.

[24] Horst Bredekamp, 'Die Erde als Lebewesen', *Kritische Berichte*, 1981, Heft 4/5, pp. 5–37.

[25] On the typology of artificial grottos, see Barbara Rietzsch, *Künstliche Grotten des 16. und 17. Jahrhunderts: Formen der Gestaltung im Aussenbau und Innenraum an Beispielen in Italien, Frankreich und Deutschland*, Munich, 1987; and Reinhard Zimmermann, *Künstliche Ruinen. Studien zu ihrer Bedeutung und Form*, Wiesbaden, 1989.

[26] Proserpina is, significantly, the goddess of both the Underworld and Nature. See Adrian von Buttlar, *Der Landschaftsgarten: Gartenkunst des Klassizismus und der Romantik*, Cologne, 1989, pp. 241–2.

The front of our grotto appears in a tectonic form which is cited in the portal forms then fashionable particularly for funerary monuments and prisons, as in Favart's 1793 design for a prison.[27] Since the mid-eighteenth century the grotto motif had become a permanent feature of the expressive repertoire of *architecture parlante*, but especially of revolutionary architecture: 'The gate was soon to become the bearer of secrets *par excellence* ... a cross between niche, shaft and crypt'[28] – a description that attests to its uncanny quality. In the visual discourse of revolutionary reason the grotto thus generally appears to symbolize that which deviates from the norm of reason; in a prison building, stepping through the grotto portal signals to the prisoner that he has been cast out of the earthly paradise of Reason into a subterranean Hell of moral damnation, and this transition to Hell is marked, just as in Christian iconography, by the vulva metaphor of the grotto. As an image of Nature as uncontrollable chaos, it seems obvious that the grotto cannot be used to signify the revolutionary cult of Reason as light. Instead, it becomes the image of revolution's evil 'Other'.

Boullée's temple which, had it been constructed, would have had enormous dimensions – one must assume a dome radius of some 130–390 m[29] – contains no space for cultic *practices*. Any visitors could have clambered over the base of the colonnades or stopped at the end of a tunnel on the same level as the Diana, but could not have descended into the crater. The cult object remains unapproachable; the cult stops at contemplation. The architectural language of metaphor thus attains the highest significance. Radically liberated from the rules of '*convenance*' and ecclesiastical ties, the cult of the Nation could plunder this architectural language and utilize its component parts.

Images of the Earth

Boullée's temple offers three successful architectural metaphors: the sphere, the grotto mound and the tumulus-like submerged dome. The grotto mound and submerged dome, with their connections to the earth, have traditionally 'feminine' connotations. They, too, derive from the spherical form, but they emerge not from a mathematically abstract cosmic image of perfection, but rather from notions of 'earth' as 'mother'. In a brief, highly schematic account I would like to illuminate here the historical shift of forms and meanings in the visualization of the symbolic field of 'earth'.

In 1618 Matthias Merian the Elder published a *Nutrix Terra*.[30] The earth, in a sort of animistic animation, is a nursing mother's body – the ideas of the globe

[27] See Szambien, op. cit. (note 19), pp. 125–9.
[28] Ibid.
[29] Lankheit, op. cit. (note 4), p. 22.
[30] Copperplate engraving, illustration to M. Maier, *Atalanta Fugiens,* Oppenheim, 1618, p. 17. See also Bredekamp, 'Die Erde als Lebewesen', op. cit. (note 24).

and of female nurturing have not yet become separated. This is precisely what resulted from the mathematical verification of the image of a scientifically calculable cosmos after Newton's discoveries. It was the mathematical image of the sphere as the perfect body that became an image of the triumph over the earthly, over gravity and material. The image of the world now became split into the immaterial transcendence of the totally calculable cosmos on the one hand – the 'sexless' but androcentric sphere – and the image of the earth as a tomb, a mound, a grotto on the other. To put it another way: the idea of Nature itself was split – into the mathematical model of cognition and a feminine Nature that defied rational understanding. This Nature, imagined as feminine, had, in turn, two possible 'faces': that of demonized femaleness as an image of anti-Reason, and that of a positively connoted womb, which promised a return to the mother. The grotto opens up a female field of association with different implications from that of Merian's *nurturing* Mother Earth: namely, that of the vulva. We shall find this vulva as tomb over and over again in the secular cult architecture of the nineteenth century, above all in memorial architecture.

Such a definition of Nature follows a basic pattern of cultural discourses on the feminine since Rousseau.[31] According to Georg Simmel, the definition of femaleness is a 'supplementary definition'[32] to that of maleness, which is set up as an absolute – a realization already formulated in 1911, which illuminates the gender order as a power relationship. It is precisely this relationship which seems perfectly expressed in the metaphoric dyad sphere-universe and maternal body-earth – the one supposedly gender-neutral, abstract and total, the other female, material and particular.

The psychoanalyst Christa Rohde-Dachser describes this supplementary definition of the feminine as a kind of vessel for that which has been dissociated from masculine self-representation. This scheme for the construction of femininity is apparently indispensable to the stability of the asymmetrically organized gender system, as it conserves the feminine, fixing it in the 'indestructibility of the imagination'.[33]

In its unresolved duality, Boullée's Temple of Reason/Nature may be regarded as a perfect visual analogy to the dilemma that arose in the representation of political universality; it cannot 'forget' the symbolic impact of gender. The sphere, in its cosmic version, marks the universality of a 'sovereign' which excludes women. At the same time, the 'earth' versions of the sphere (grotto, tumulus) seem to fill the symbolic void in this universality with female representations of the political myth at the centre of its cult, i.e., with Nature.

---

[31] On this see, among others, Lieselotte Steinbrügge, *Das moralische Geschlecht. Theorien und literarische Entwürfe über die Natur der Frau in der französischen Aufklärung*, Weinheim and Basel, 1987; English, *The Moral Sex: Woman's Nature in the French Enlightenment*, trans. Pamela E. Selwyn, Oxford and New York, 1995.

[32] Georg Simmel, 'Das Relative und das Absolute im Geschlechter-Problem' (1911), in G. Simmel, *Schriften zur Philosophie und Soziologie der Geschlechter*, Frankfurt am Main, 1985.

[33] Christa Rohde-Dachser, *Expedition in den dunklen Kontinent*, Heidelberg, 1991, pp. 95–6.

After the Revolution

Around 1800 the metaphor of the grotto-crypt begins to become ubiquitous in the architecture of monuments, and the cult of commemoration becomes a central cult of national identity. At the same period, with the rise of Napoleon as autocrat, the metaphor of the sphere disappears from architecture. Viewed historically, this supports my interpretation of the sphere as a 'radical', non-hierarchical, but total and androcentric metaphor for popular sovereignty. That apparently rendered it suspect for the representation of the nineteenth-century's authoritarian state systems.

With the Restoration, the forms of representation of political national identity also became modified. The conflictual coexistence of bourgeois emancipation and restored monarchy by divine right no longer permitted 'total' metaphorizations and, above all, no levelling ones. Authority and identity were once again conceived of in tandem. Variously weighted montages emerged to permit the harmonization in a single image of ideologically contradictory or even competing models of state, nation and cultural identity.[34]

An extremely compressed chronological typology of monuments might look like this: the basic structure is usually divided into a substructure with a vault and a building above it. This latter can be a temple, a tower or a monument to a person or persons, while the crypt/grotto remains a lasting feature.

In the French Revolution the grotto-vault was combined with the sphere, the obelisk and Graecizing temple types, as in Favart's 'Tomb of the Martyrs of Freedom', with an open columned hall on a Greek cruciform ground plan with a vault between the stair-ramps. During the Restoration, we initially still find the crypt combined with the Graecizing temple, as in Klenze's 1814 'Monument to the Pacification of Europe'. The Greek temple should be read here as a symbol of transcendence signifying the nation understood in ethical terms. Both citizens and monarchs could identify with this model.

In the last third of the nineteenth century a phenomenon arose which I would like to call the polarization between vault and tower. It is particularly apparent in the most important German national monuments, such as the Kyffhäuser monument and the monument to the 1813 Battle of the Nations near Leipzig. The verticality of the tower completely displaces the horizontality of the temple. A striking materialization of the gender sign for virility replaces the temple metaphors. The sphere for popular sovereignty and the Greek temple for the spirit of national ethics had located the abstracting transcendence of the community androcentrically, to be sure, but very clearly beyond the materiality of sex; now,

[34] Thomas Nipperdey gives a summary of the various tendencies in nineteenth-century monumental architecture in 'Nationalidee und Nationaldenkmal in Deutschland im 19. Jahrhundert', *Historische Zeitschrift*, no. 206, 1968, pp. 329–85.

in the tower, German manliness erected for itself the very symbol of the 'vigorous' colonizing late nineteenth-century nation. Such an interpretation is by no means a mere feminist exaggeration; contemporaries drew the same conclusion.[35] The 'masculine' thus emerges from latency and the incognito of the unnamed but intended. As explicit masculinity it elevates itself to a ruling norm and is simultaneously, in its *re-hierarchization* of the architectural sign, the extreme opposite of the sphere metaphor. The tower gained currency not only for the great national monuments, but also for the mass sites of commemoration for the nameless and countless fallen of World War I. Now, in the identity-producing generalization of military mass death, it actually came to mark a collective masculine.[36]

In 1797 Friedrich Gilly, who had made a close study of French Revolutionary architecture, designed a monument to Frederick II of Prussia for a competition.[37] In 1942 Albert Speer had a model reconstructed and published. As an image of the hero's return to mother earth, the monument's crypt was intended to convey, with a sort of 'holy shudder', the heroic dimensions of his death. The temple erected over it signalled the triumph over death through the act of public commemoration.

Fascist Grottos and Graves, the Spherical Perfection of Mass Democracy, and Stalin's Tower

The National Socialists regarded Gilly's design as a forerunner.[38] In his designs for war memorials (*Ehrenmäler*, or monuments to honour) Wilhelm Kreis, who bore the title of Chief Government Architect in Charge of War Graves,[39] allowed the grotto motif to 'speak', as in his design for the crypt of the Soldiers' Hall in Berlin. The captured territories were to be generously strewn with memorials. The commemoration of the heroism of one's own (German) dead, in contrast to the vanquished, was to be employed as a symbol of the latter's 'eternal' subjugation. In a remote imitation of Boullée's geometrical radicality, Kreis's 1941 design for a war memorial on the Dniepr emphasizes the character of the tumulus. With this he

---

[35] Wolfgang Pehnt, 'Turm und Höhle', in *Moderne Architektur in Deutschland, 1900 bis 1950. Expressionismus und Neue Sachlichkeit*, exh. cat., Frankfurt, Stuttgart, 1994.

[36] See Reinhard Koselleck, 'Kriegerdenkmale als Identitätsstiftungen der Überlebenden', in O. Marquard and K. Stierle (eds), *Identität*, Munich, 1979, pp. 255ff.

[37] Alste Oncken, *Friedrich Gilly, 1772–1800*, Berlin, 1981, p. 49.

[38] On Speer's orders a model was built according to the design and extensively published in *Die Bauunst: Die Kunst im Deutschen Reich* in August and September 1942.

[39] On Kreis, see Albert Speer, 'Der Architekt Wilhelm Kreis', *Die Baukunst*, July 1941, pp. 130ff; and Meinhold Lurz, 'Die Kriegerdenkmalsentwürfe von Wilhelm Kreis', in B. Hinz, H. Mittig et al. (eds) *Die Dekoration der Gewalt*, Giessen, 1979, pp. 185–97.

evokes archaic forms of the cult of the dead, stretching back before the Greek temple and its implications of spiritual transcendence. Here, without a tower, solely through a radical monumentalization of the tumulus-crypt motif, in the dead soldiers' mass return to the womb of earth, Kreis authorizes the German national body to extend infinitely the 'German' womb of the earth. Kreis remarked: 'Sacred ground covers them. It is the earth, the mother of all being. Great as the earth, simple and noble is the form of these stones ... '.[40] Viewed in the context of the function of male constructions of femininity, this means that in the image of Mother Earth which emerges in the crypt, femininity is fixed in the imaginary. It holds out the promise that, at the moment of his sacrificial death, the soldier will return to his mother/bride, thus stabilizing the soldier's masculine heroic identity in a moment of severe stress – the National Socialist campaign in the Soviet Union. It is thus precisely the dissociation of the feminine from the masculine Self that encourages the idea that it can be overcome by fusion with the mother – but only after death, as the hero's reward for his sacrifice. The same structure can be found in figurative representations of this theme, namely painting and public sculpture.[41]

The 1930s, which Franco Borsi has called the epoch of monumental order,[42] witnessed the coexistence of diverse sphere metaphors: the monument tumuli of National Socialist memorials, the ribbed half-sphere of Speer's assembly hall for the National Socialist national body, and the pure sphere of the 1939 World Fair in New York.

'Democracity' versus the racist national body: the polarization between systems is visible in the polarized spherical metaphors of modern cult architecture. The supposedly non-hierarchical totality of a mass democracy in the pure sphere in New York is de-materialized and de-sexed, but androcentric. It stands in contrast to the leader principle drawn from the national body[43] which is represented by ancient metaphors of authority also linked to the sphere and its derivatives: the gigantic dome of Christian cathedrals in the case of Speer, and the tumulus, a

[40] Wilhelm Kreis, 'Kriegerdenkmale des Ruhms und der Ehre im Altertum und in unserer Zeit', *Bauwelt*, vol. 11/12, 1943, p. 6, quoted in Meinhold Lurz, 'Die Kriegerdenkmalsentwürfe von Wilhelm Kreis', op. cit. (note 39), p. 190.

[41] See Kathrin Hoffmann-Curtius, 'Opfermodelle am Altar des Vaterlandes seit der Französischen Revolution', in G. Kohn-Wächter (ed.), *Schrift der Flammen. Opfermythen und Weiblichkeitsentwürfe im 20. Jahrhundert*, Berlin, 1991, pp. 57–94; and Silke Wenk, 'Versteinerte und verlebendigte Weiblichkeit – Weibliche Allegorie und ihre mediale Repräsentation in der Französischen Revolution', in *Geschichte – Geschlecht – Wirklichkeit*, Protokoll der 1. Kunstwissenschaftlerinnen-Tagung der Sektion Kunstwissenschaft des VBK – DDR, Lehnin, 1989, pp. 154–65.

[42] Franco Borsi, *The Monumental Era: European Architecture and Design, 1929–1939*, New York, 1987.

[43] For more thoughts on the structural relationship between forms of visual representation and the derivation of popular sovereignty in totalitarian systems, see my 'Mussolini Architettonico. Notiz zur ästhetischen Inszenierung des Führers im italienischen Faschismus', in *Inszenierung der Macht. Ästhetische Faszination im Faschismus*, Berlin, 1987, pp. 243–52; and 'Vom "Ballhausschwur" zum "Duce". Visuelle Repräsentation von Volkssouveränität zwischen Demokratie und Autokratie', *Die Neue Gesellschaft. Frankfurter Hefte*, no. 11, November 1993, pp. 1017–25.

form of prehistoric ruler's grave,[44] as an image of the conquest of the body of Mother Earth in the case of Kreis.

A contemporary commentator attests to this polarization in architectural discourse during those years: in his 1939 text *Die Kugel als Gebäude, oder: Das Bodenlose* (*The Sphere as a Building, or the Bottomless*) Hans Sedlmayr polemicizes against the spherical building as a 'symptom'. For him, it was symptomatic that 'a gigantic sphere' was to represent the 'centre of the Neuyork' [sic] World Fair of 1939: 'Such a coincidence cannot be an accident. One may suppose that there is an inner connection between the idea of the spherical building and the "bottomless" spirit of those revolutions, which has only existed since the French Revolution.'[45] He uses the word bottomless quite literally. For him, the denial, in spherical abstraction, of architecture's connection to the earth, is a sickness. Curiously enough, he appends to the name of El Lissitzky, whose explication of Leonidov's design for a spherical building for the Lenin Institute he quotes as a principal witness to the sick revolutionary will to overcome connection to the earth, the parenthetical question '(a Jew?)', as if this could explain the ailment.[46] For him, Leonidov's 1927 design was an 'involuntary and thus all the more horrible symbol of that spirit which rejects the earth'.[47] Werner March's Reichssportfeld, which was half-submerged in the earth, he found, in contrast, a laudable example of architectural health. The abstract had to be conquered 'by saying yes, once again, to the earth, the tectonic, overcoming the inhuman quality of abstract construction by invoking "orders" that recognize the earth as a base and man as the measure of things ... The leader of the counter-movement in 1800 was Germany, and it remains so today.'[48] The enemies were the machine-oriented cultures of the USA and the USSR. Sedlmayr did not acknowledge that the authoritarian principle had ultimately triumphed in the Soviet Union as well, as the winning design by Iofan for the Soviet Palace of 1933, with a tower crowned by a gigantic statue of Lenin, shows.

Modern Myths

As we have seen, the identity cult of masculine political collectives has assumed different forms since the first modern formulation of collective political sovereignty. Metaphors for the feminine and the masculine serve to structure

[44] Of interest here is Hans Gerhard Evers, *Tod, Macht und Raum als Bereiche der Architektur*, Munich, 1939, p. 2: '... ancient architecture integrated the king's death into the life of the community, from an absorption into the densest forces of nature, absorption into stone, into mass, into nourishing earth ...'.

[45] Reprinted in Klaus Jan Philipp (ed.), *Revolutionsarchitektur. Klassische Beiträge zu einer unklassischen Architektur*, Brauschweig and Wiesbaden, 1990, here p. 126.

[46] Ibid., p. 147.

[47] Ibid., p. 148.

[48] Ibid., p. 152.

fundamentally the visual representations of these constructions of identity but in different formations, which can offer clues to the corresponding discourses with the political systems in question. They tell us about some of the ways in which the masculine collective imagination, as well as collective masculine self-representation, with its dissociation from the feminine, functions. They also give occasion for reflection about whether the degree of metaphorical gender polarization might not have something to do with the fundamentalist tendencies of such collective identities.

Let us return to the sphere and the grotto as architectural metaphors for the world. Let us read them, as has already been indicated, as corresponding exactly to asymmetrically organized gender relations: the sphere as a metaphor for the cosmos is a product of the mathematical, abstracting imagination. It is an image of conquest and control over the material, of totality and order, and it is, apparently, gender-neutral. That would correspond to Simmel's idea of the masculine posited as absolute which, because it is absolute, need not present itself as gendered. The grotto, in contrast, is a metaphor for the world as earth and womb. It expresses the unruliness of this material in a mixture of attraction and fear. It would correspond to the masculine 'supplementary definition' of the feminine in Simmel's work. That which is excluded from masculine self-representation then becomes material for the patriarchal construction of the feminine.

Since the separation of Reason from Nature, the sphere, as the body which could not, for lack of a base, be anchored in the earth, and the womb-earth metaphor have ultimately proved incompatible. The 1618 *Nutrix Terra* by M. Merian the Elder, with its symbolic identity between body and globe, shows that this was not always the case. Two examples illustrate the extent of this split, but also its untenability. In a design in 1970 for the city of Echternach, Leon Krier sends the sphere where it logically belongs: into the sky, free of the earth. In contrast, in her monumental sculpture *Hon* Niki de St Phalle takes the masculine myth of the womb literally; she makes the longed-for return to the womb *feasible* – the myth falls by the wayside. But does this also defeat the metaphor itself?

17

Karl Friedrich Schinkel

David Watkin and Tilman Mellinghoff

The creative genius of Karl Friedrich Schinkel (1781–1841) was so protean and his output so huge that, like most great artists, he defies neat stylistic classification. He is Greek yet Gothic; classical yet modern; rationalistic yet poetic; a sober civil servant with a commitment to architecture as a public service, yet the friend of princes and the designer of dream palaces. Profoundly influenced by philosophers like Fichte and Hegel with their essentially post-Christian understanding of man's place in history and in the moral order, he played an important role in the accompanying process by which Prussia achieved self-realization and eventual dominance over Germany. However, his search for architectural fundamentals gives him a permanent significance in European architecture which is independent of the particular historical circumstances of his day. For an indication of this we have only to consider the quite extraordinary amount of literary attention which has been paid to him. He must be the most written-about architect in history. Apart from the *Lebenswerk* series, begun in 1939 and now in its fourteenth folio volume, there are monographs, numerous exhibition catalogues and countless articles devoted to him. Moreover, as the anti-historical experiment of the Modern Movement comes to an end, practising architects are returning for inspiration to an architect whose classicism seems neither old nor new but timeless.

[. . .]

Friedrich Gilly regarded Schinkel as his heir. On his death in August 1800 he left him his drawings which he and Klenze treated like precious icons, making copies of them and, in Schinkel's case, drawing on them for inspiration throughout his career.

[. . .]

David Watkin and Tilman Mellinghoff, "Karl Friedrich Schinkel," pp. 85–6, 88–96, 99, 104–5, 107, 110–13, 117 from *German Architecture and the Classical Ideal, 1740–1840*. London: Thames & Hudson, 1987.

The Prussian royal family had returned from exile in 1809 in which year the much-loved Queen Luise, having been entranced by an exhibition of Schinkel's pictures, commissioned him to design some interiors in the palaces at Berlin and Charlottenburg.

[...]

The poor queen did not live long to enjoy her rosy bedroom and her death in July 1810 at the age of thirty-four heightened the already intense patriotic fervour of a country in the grip of Napoleon. Her husband, Friedrich Wilhelm III, had clear ideas as to the form her mausoleum should take. Only sixteen days after her death, Schinkel had drawn a stern Greek Doric façade which, resembling Friedrich Gilly's mausoleum at Dyhernfurth, was based on a sketch supplied by the king. With the assistance of Gentz he erected this modest but impressive Doric mausoleum in the gardens of Schloss Charlottenburg in 1810. It houses a noble recumbent effigy of the queen by Christian Daniel Rauch. In the meantime Schinkel had prepared his own tribute to the memory of the queen in the form of proposals for a striking Gothic mausoleum which he exhibited at the Berlin Academy in 1810. Caspar David Friedrich exhibited two paintings in the same exhibition and Schinkel's designs can be seen as his own independent contribution to the Romantic movement. However, unlike Friedrich, Schinkel did not generally paint ruins but intact Gothic structures such as this mausoleum.

The literary commentary which Schinkel found it necessary to submit with his design is one of the key documents of the Gothic Revival and shows how much he had been influenced by followers of Goethe such as Friedrich Schlegel and Clemens Brentano, for whom Gothic was an expression of the infinite. Just as Gilly had seen his Doric monument to Frederick the Great as a symbol of Prussian order, so Schinkel now saw Gothic as embodying the national spirit, and as 'the outward and visible sign of that which united Man to God and the transcendental world'. Gothic was supposed to be 'higher in its principles than antiquity', since it expressed an idea, whereas classical architecture was supposedly dictated by materials and construction. He describes how

> Light falls through the windows which surround the sarcophagus on three sides; the stained glass suffuses the whole mausoleum, which is built of white marble, with a soft rosy glow. In front of this hall is a portico, surrounded by trees of the darkest hue; you ascend the steps and enter with a gentle thrill of awe into the darkness of the vestibule, from which through three high openings you look into the hall of palms, where the deceased surrounded by angels rests peacefully in the clear rose of dawn.

The roseate hue of this mausoleum must be seen as a reflection of Schlegel's colour theory whereby red or rosy colours are understood as a symbol of communication between heaven and earth. From Schlegel, too, Schinkel derived his ideal of Antiquity and Gothic as twin ideals and hence his ambition of synthesizing both in a new style whereby one would be improved by the other. Schinkel hints at this in his description of the mausoleum but the design itself is far more expressive since it is in effect a small temple with a portico of pointed arches. The smooth plain wall surface above the arches contradicts anything Gothic, while the steps similarly reflect the temple theme.

This synthesis of Gothic and classic forms recurred in the domed Gothic church which appears in his painting of 1811 called *Abend* (Evening) and in the National Cathedral which he designed in 1815 to commemorate the wars of liberation of 1813–15. This great Gothic building with a domed choir was to stand in the Leipziger Platz in Berlin which, significantly, Gilly had earlier envisaged as the setting for his monument to Frederick the Great. Like Gilly's monument, Schinkel's cathedral was to rise above the life of the city on a high platform. As a true expression of Romanticism the building was to be completed by future generations. Schinkel was urged in the Romantic nationalism of this project by the Crown Prince Friedrich Wilhelm (1795–1861), [...] with whom he was to work closely throughout his career. The sculptural programme of the cathedral included depiction of the Order of the Iron Cross, the highest honour awarded by the Prussian state. Schinkel's design of 1813 for the Iron Cross was in use till 1945. Though his national cathedral was never executed, a remarkable Gothic memorial in the form of a huge cast-iron pinnacle was erected from his designs in 1818 on the Templower Berg (now Kreuzberg) where it still survives.

It has been necessary, even in a book on Neo-classical architecture, to outline the early history of Schinkel's devotion to Gothic. Though he later dropped the intense Romanticism of his youth, he retained from his Gothic days a belief in architecture as an expression of high ideals and, in particular, of the cultural and political aspirations of Prussia. The contemporary philosopher J. G. Fichte, whose writings were the only book Schinkel took with him on his travels of 1803–5, had published *Die Bestimmung des Menschen* (The Vocation of Man) in 1800. It was Fichte's concept of moral vocation which helped form Schinkel's vision of architecture as a public responsibility, and it was Fichte's 'Reden an die Deutsche Nation' (Addresses to the German Nation), delivered in 1807–8, which stimulated patriotic fervour in Berlin and a sense of Prussian cultural identity. Fichte was first Rector of Berlin University, which had been founded in 1809 under the aegis of Wilhelm von Humboldt as Minister of Education. [...] Humboldt created a total system of state education in which stress was put on the cultural development of German citizens under a powerful monarch by means of the study of Greek history and the German past – the twin poles of Schinkel's own architectural world. Moreover, when Friedrich Wilhelm III opened the university he made a speech emphasizing that the military defeat of Prussia must be compensated for by intellectual and cultural achievement.

It is against this remarkable background of self-conscious improvement, both national and personal, that we must see Schinkel's architectural contributions to the city of Berlin. In 1815 he was promoted within the Prussian civil service to the position of Geheimer Oberbaurat with special responsibility for the development of the city for which he produced a comprehensive plan in 1817, the first of many. The range of functions, from military to cultural, of the earliest and most important of his executed buildings in the city is significant: they are the Neue Wache (New Guard House) of 1816–18; the Schauspielhaus (Theatre and concert hall) of 1818–26; and the Altes Museum of 1823–33. These were all designed in a stern neo-antique style which contrasts strangely with the romantic effusions of 1810 in connection with the mausoleum for Queen Luise. However, Schinkel came to feel that the severer style was historically appropriate for post-1815 Berlin which, though now victorious in arms, was spartan in tone and economically depressed yet stirred by high reforming ideals. Like the Brandenburg Gate of 1789 at the west end of Unter den Linden, the Neue Wache near the east end marks the beginning of a new era in German Neo-classicism. The Greek Doric order was chosen in accordance with Gentz's recommendation of it for military buildings as a symbol of severity (*Ernst*), dignity (*Hoheit*), and strength (*Kraft*).

Schinkel's first designs for the Neue Wache were for a building with round arches in a kind of composed style between classic and Gothic. He carefully considered its relation to its setting, siting it romantically as a *point de vue* at the end of a proposed grove of chestnut trees which subtly insulates it from the adjacent Zeughaus (Arsenal), a vast Baroque building of 1695–1717. However, the king, who did not live in the royal Schloss facing the Lustgarten but in the much smaller Kronprinzenpalais in Unter den Linden, wanted to be able to see his soldiers changing guard from his windows. Schinkel was thus forced to bring the Guard House close to the road. He also changed the style to Greek Doric though the massive corner pylons, which help to separate the building from its neighbours, have a faintly Egyptian flavour. For Schinkel, however, the building resembled a Roman *castrum*. It has two features which were to be especially characteristic of Schinkel: it contrives to have an asymmetrical interior plan, despite its symmetrical Gillyesque exterior, and it is also beautifully related to its setting by trees and statuary. Though it is tiny in comparison with its enormous neighbours, the Baroque Arsenal and Palladian University, the little building has a quite extraordinary air of authority. It remains to this day a monument of programmatic significance for visitors to Berlin who watch the goose-stepping East German soldiers changing guard in front of it.

Schinkel's Schauspielhaus in the Gendarmenmarkt (now Platz der Akademie), designed in 1818 and executed in 1819–21, is the first statement of a theme which was to become one of his hallmarks: the reduction of the classical language to a trabeated grid which, though generally independent of structure, is a poetic or visual expression of it. These square unmoulded mullions and horizontal entablatures form a kind of elegant scaffolding round this large building. In his account of the theatre in his *Sammlung* in 1821, Schinkel cited an antique source for these mullions in order to justify what he may have regarded as a revolutionary system of articulation. The source is the Choragic Monument of Thrasyllus, a

Hellenistic monument formerly existing on the side of the Acropolis in Athens and probably known to Schinkel from Stuart and Revett's *Antiquities of Athens*, vol. II, 1789. However, he immediately justifies the system on functional grounds, since it allows window openings of the maximum size, and claims that he 'tried to emulate Greek forms and methods of construction insofar as this is possible in such a complex work'. This light trabeated framework also relieves the massiveness of the design as a whole, introducing the kind of almost Gothic openwork flavour which had appealed to Neo-classical theorists and designers in France such as Laugier and Soufflot. Indeed, the critic E. Guhl writing in 1859 regarded the building as a synthesis of Greek and Gothic forms. Schinkel had essayed this trabeated construction in a military building designed in 1817, though not executed until eight years later, the barracks and detention centre of the Lehreskadron in the Lindenstrasse. This was the kind of building which was to influence the architect Behrens a hundred years later.

The forceful impact of the Schauspielhaus derives partly from the novel way in which Schinkel gave poetic expression to its function by combining the auditorium building and the stage block behind into a single pedimented building, towering over the lower flanking wings. The great portico pushes forward into the square so as to relate directly to the porticos of the adjacent churches by Gontard, a point Schinkel romantically emphasized in the stage backdrop designed for the opening night which was a panoramic view of the whole Gendarmenmarkt painted by Gropius. It must be confessed that the portico has no real function since the entrances are at ground-floor level. Its role is symbolic and representational as the entrance to a temple of Apollo, a temple of the muses. The actual entrance foyer is, by contrast, somewhat small since Schinkel was obliged to re-use the foundations of the Langhans theatre and to comply with the king's demand for the incorporation of a concert hall. The body of the theatre is thus flanked by a magnificent galleried concert hall in the south wing, and rehearsal and storage space in the north. This tripartite plan is clearly expressed externally.

In the third of this first group of public buildings in Berlin, the Altes Museum, Schinkel could indulge even more freely his belief that architecture should educate and improve the public by awakening its members to their own identity and to that of the historical culture to which they belonged. It was in Berlin around 1800 that there emerged the novel concept of a public museum to provide uplift for the middle classes by exposing them to the kind of paintings which had previously been confined to the interiors of royal palaces. Among those who promoted this idea was Schinkel's old master at the Bauakademie, Alois Hirt. He gave a clear definition of what a museum should be like in its combination of sculpture and painting, its architecture, its historical arrangement for educational purposes, and its lighting. In a public lecture in 1797 he outlined his proposals for bringing under one roof and arranging by their different schools the finest art treasures in Prussia. Following the acceptance of the idea by Friedrich Wilhelm III, Hirt submitted detailed proposals in 1798 for a rectangular Neo-Palladian building round a courtyard occupying roughly the site of Schinkel's later Neue Wache. However, after Prussia's defeat at Jena, Vivant Denon came to Berlin in 1806 to select works of art for removal to the Imperial Museum in the Louvre. While recognizing the illegality of the process of plunder by which Napoleon had accumulated paintings from countries which he had conquered, few visitors to the Louvre could fail to be impressed by the merits of a well-organized public museum on this scale. Thus an exhibition attended by the king in the Berlin Academy of repatriated works of art, arranged by Schinkel and Hirt in 1815, was all that was needed to put into execution Hirt's scheme for a public museum in Berlin. Indeed work began in 1816 on converting the old Academy building in Unter den Linden into a museum, but progress was interrupted after a slow start.

In 1822 Schinkel was invited by the king to prepare a comprehensive scheme for improving the appearance of the Lustgarten in front of the Schloss. Schinkel's proposals for this area, which he had first drawn up in 1817, involved filling in the mean canal which divided the island in two and, eventually, reorganizing the facilities for river traffic and customs warehouses along the Kupfergraben. Schinkel's elegantly functional buildings to house some of these activities in the northern part of the island, the Packhofgebäude (1829–32), were demolished in the 1890s to make way for the Kaiser Friedrich Museum and the Pergamon Museum. Schinkel had toyed as early as 1822 with the idea of building an entirely new museum in the Lustgarten instead of adapting the Academy buildings. This juxtaposition of public museum and royal palace in a single square was a concrete embodiment of Humboldt's cultural and social programme and it is appropriate that he should subsequently have become the chairman of the commission for the establishment of the museum.

In the face of much misunderstanding between the king and the commission, Schinkel fought with vigour and diplomatic skill for his proposal which, with the support of the crown prince, the king accepted in 1823. The decorative programme of the building was, of course, planned to pay special homage to the king with the inscription on the frieze, the surmounting Prussian eagle, and the proposed equestrian statue. Schinkel rightly considered the museum as his finest work so far, the logical consequence of his improvements at the eastern end of Unter den Linden, the Neue Wache and the Schlossbrücke leading over the Kupfergraben to the Lustgarten where he had also remodelled the cathedral in 1820–1. For the façade of his museum Schinkel chose a long colonnade of eighteen Ionic columns which resembles a civic building like a Hellenistic stoa. In designing one of the first public buildings of the modern world which lacks a central emphasis, Schinkel was guided by his ambition to create a harmonious ensemble of individual parts, Schloss, church, museum, none of which would dominate or destroy the other. Thus even the dome of the museum is discreetly concealed behind a rectangular attic.

[...]

Like a church, his museum was to 'exalt' the visitor, the Pantheon hall was to be 'the sanctuary wherein the most precious is stored', and the staircase and back wall of the colonnade were richly painted with vast murals representing a highly-charged vision of the place of the arts in the development of mankind.

[...]

A commission which can be connected with the visits to Italy of Schinkel and members of the royal family in the 1820s is Schloss Charlottenhof and its garden buildings, built at Potsdam for the crown prince from 1826 onwards.

[...]

The merging of architecture and nature which had been achieved at Charlottenhof was carried a stage further in the group of buildings, now known as the Roman Bath, built in the grounds of Schloss Charlottenhof in 1829–37. Designed by the crown prince, Schinkel and his pupil Persius, who was the executant architect, these began with the court gardener's house, an existing cottage remodelled in 1829 as an Italianate vernacular villa along lines probably inspired by the 'Villa, designed as the residence of an artist' in Papworth's *Rural Residences* (1818, pl. XVII). Despite this English source, the design is deeply rooted in Schinkel's reminiscences of his Italian tour of 1803–4, when he prepared a long theoretical discourse on the relation of asymmetrical buildings to picturesque settings which was intended to serve as a chapter in his proposed *Lehrbuch*. The court gardener's house was followed by the tea pavilion in the form of a temple (1830), the assistant's house (1831–2), the arcaded hall (1833) and the Roman bath house (1834–40). The subtle grouping of a roughly L-shaped complex of buildings, linked with steps, loggias, passages, canals and an irregular sheet of water, the interpenetration of spaces, the contrast of void and mass, light and shade, the asymmetrical plan and elevation pivoting on a central tower, the total absence of a main façade or of any suggestion of a front or a rear, make this one of the most brilliant conceptions of its kind in the history of Western architecture. It has been compared with Frank Lloyd Wright but far surpasses him in subtlety of allusion and delicacy of detail: for example, Schinkel's intermingling of vine-covered trellis and Doric columns suggests the evolution of the Doric order as hinted at by Vitruvius and romantically developed by Laugier. Schinkel believed that he had created at Charlottenhof a 'never-finished architecture' in a setting to which new buildings could always be added.

The 1820s saw numerous elegant villas by Schinkel though he never developed a specific villa style. Several of them were brilliant conversions of existing buildings and, though he drew on a range of sources including Palladio and *Vitruvius Britannicus*, his own distinctive hand is recognizable throughout.

[...]

Schinkel's visit to England in 1826 was a mission on which he was sent by the Prussian government in connection with the Altes Museum. His ostensible purpose was to gather information on new museums and their techniques of display, but what most fascinated him were the architectural and social consequences of the Industrial Revolution. [...]

We know from Schinkel's diary of his tour that he was not on the whole impressed with the work of Neo-classical architects like the Woods of Bath, Adam, Nash, Soane, Smirke, or the Inwoods, but was overwhelmed by the technical ingenuity and the scale of the new factories, warehouses, dock buildings, bridges, roads, canals, steam engines and gas holders. He exclaimed of the cotton mills of Manchester: 'Here are buildings seven to eight storeys high and big as the Royal Palace in Berlin. They are vaulted and fireproof.' Buildings of this kind, supported by an internal framework of iron columns and beams, threaded with iron staircases, and wrapped round with a brick skin, gave him a thrilling sense of how his own architecture might develop. He wanted to take these techniques and then to civilize them, for he was appalled by what he described as 'factories which are nothing but monstrous masses of red brick, built by a mere foreman, without any trace of architecture and for the sole purpose of crude necessity, making a most frightening impression.'

On his return to Berlin, Schinkel designed a number of buildings in brick, terracotta, iron and glass which undoubtedly reflect his reactions to English industrial architecture: these are the Kaufhaus or bazaar in Unter den Linden (1827), the church for the Oranienburg suburb in North Berlin (1828), the Feilner House (1828–9) in the Hasenhagerstrasse, the Packhof buildings (1829–32), the Bauakademie (1831–6), and the State Library in Unter den Linden (1835). [...]

In December 1830 Schinkel became Geheimer Oberbaudirektor. This involved examination of all state building schemes throughout Prussia, which helped to spread a consistent style for the public buildings of Germany in the early and mid-nineteenth century. The creation of the Allgemeine Bauschule, for which he designed a new building in 1831 following his appointment, was not promoted by the Crown but by Schinkel and by Peter Beuth who became first director of the school. It was the nerve centre of the Prussian architectural machine since it contained not only the school of architecture on the first floor but the offices of the Ober-Bau-Deputation on the floor above, and even Schinkel's private flat where he lived with his family from 1836 until his death in 1841. His presence here must have been a forceful symbol of his utter dedication to architecture and of his identification with the new Prussia.

[...]

The Bauakademie was Schinkel's favourite among his buildings. Flaming red in colour, it shone forth as a commanding symbol of his high-minded architectural, constructional and educational ideals. Its function is related to the ambition he had cherished throughout his career of producing a monumental architectural textbook, *Architektonisches Lehrbuch*, which would provide a solution to every architectural problem. Here we find the only element of failure in Schinkel's career. He neither completed the book nor left a coherent statement of his architectural theory, lamenting that he had lost himself 'in a labyrinth'. His thoughts take the form of aphorisms on architecture which are sometimes contradictory. His guiding principle was to practise architecture as art and to combine function and beauty in accordance with the emphasis of Vitruvius on *utilitas, firmitas* and *venustas*. He was totally opposed to naked functionalism and to the equation by Durand of *utilitas* with *venustas*.

Though the orders were as important to Schinkel as they had been to Gentz as a fundamental historic link, he did not want to give the budding architect comparative drawings of the classical orders to copy, or illustrations of monuments of the past showing the history of styles, but rather to promote understanding of first principles in architecture which, he believed, rested on proper attention to three points: construction, custom, and nature. His study of the unfolding development of the materials, styles and constructional methods of architecture, from the trabeated buildings of the Greeks through the Roman arch to the Gothic vault, was an exercise in evolution akin to those of Alexander von Humboldt in natural history.

[…]

Schinkel was lionized both in his lifetime and immediately after his death as few architects can ever have been. His funeral in 1841 was a cross between that of a saint and a national leader. In 1842 King Friedrich Wilhelm IV ordered that his architectural drawings, paintings and models should be bought by the state and exhibited in the Bauakademie, and, from that year, an annual Schinkelfest has been held in Berlin. His work inspired the development of Berlin and other north German centres between his death and 1871 when the newly founded Empire encouraged the adoption of Neo-Baroque modes. Whatever his relevance today, there is no denying that he towers over other architects.

18

Reading Architectural Herstories: The Discourses of Gender

Dana Arnold

When I say 'gender' you think 'women'. And it is true that most gender history is written from a woman-centred perspective, but much research covers both men and women and importantly the relationships between the two. Recently, masculinity has been recognised as a topic in its own right and the emergence of Queer Studies encourages the necessary wider exploration of gender.[1] Gender has proved to be a central concept to historians, sociologists and cultural geographers as its meaning goes beyond the biological differences between male and female. Instead it connotes the cultural definitions of behaviour which are considered appropriate for male and female members of a society at any given point in time. For the purposes of this book I do want to focus on gender as regards women and explore how it becomes an important element in the social relationships which are based on the differences between the sexes. In this way gender becomes a signifier of power.[2] If gender is then a social construction it must, therefore, have a history. It is this history of gender that interfaces with our understanding of gender and architecture.

My method so far in this book has been to problematise the topic under review in each chapter and then to proceed to give examples of canonical histories and more theoretically driven writings to offer possible rereadings of these issues. This becomes more difficult when considering the relationship between gender and architectural history. First, there is the question of my gender and how the subject/

Dana Arnold, "Reading Architectural Herstories: The Discourses of Gender," pp. 199–204 from *Reading Architectural History*. London and New York: Routledge, 2002. Reprinted by permission of Taylor & Francis.

[1] See for instance *inter alia* H. Brod (ed.), *The Making Of Masculinities: The new men's studies*, Boston, MA and London; Allen and Unwin, 1987; M. Roper and J. Tosh, *Manful Assertions: Masculinities in Britain since 1800*, London, Routledge, 1991; J. Butler, *Gender Trouble: Feminism and the subversion of identity*, New York and London, Routledge, 1990; H. L. Moore, *A Passion for Difference: Essays in anthropology and gender*, Cambridge, Polity, 1994.

[2] On this point see J. M. Bennett 'Feminism and History', *Gender and History*, 1, 1989, pp. 251–72.

object relationship, here more than anywhere in this book, overlaps through my role as author, historian and woman. Moreover, gender requires a rereading of almost the entire canon of British architectural history in the period covered in this volume. As a result I do not, as in previous chapters, present a general discussion of the issues followed by a consideration of a specific example. Instead, I want the discourses around gender to be projected back onto the other chapters in the volume in an attempt to examine the absence of 'other' voices from the histories of architecture. I have chosen two texts which offer different ways of reading the relationship between gender and architecture to serve as exemplars of the range of possibilities this line of enquiry enables: one concerns the appropriation of the function of space; the other is to do with aesthetics and architecture.

Herstories

The invisibility of women in canonical histories might lead us to believe that women have no history. Surely then a female history is an essential tool in the emancipation of women? This is partly because if we have no history we are 'trapped' in the present where oppressive social relations can continue unchallenged. Furthermore, history can be seen as evidence that things can and do change.[3] But this revision of the narratives of history has its own internal problems. Assumptions that the category of 'women' can represent all women from the past and present regardless of their age, ethnicity, sexual orientation and so on merely replaces one hegemony with another. The white western male can thus be replaced by the white western feminist female – an historical construction of 'woman', but the burgeoning body of literature has ensured the diversity of the female subject.[4] It is now over a generation ago that the first feminist writings began to appear mapping out a different way of seeing and understanding cultural production and the social relationships expressed therein. Griselda Pollock and Rozsika Parker identify the crucial paradox about attitudes to women in the writing of histories, specifically here those concerned with creativity:

> Women are represented negatively, as lacking in creativity, with nothing significant to contribute, and a having no influence on the course of art. Paradoxically, to negate them women have to be acknowledged; they are mentioned in order to be categorised, set apart and marginalised. [This is] one of the major elements in the construction of the hegemony of men in cultural practices in art.[5]

---

[3] On this point see G. Jordan and C. Weedon, *Cultural Politics: Class, gender, race in the postmodern world*, Oxford, Blackwell, 1995.

[4] See for instance bell hooks, *Feminist Theory: From margin to centre*, Boston, South End, 1984; C. Hall, *White Male and Middle Class: Explorations in feminism and history*, Cambridge, Polity 1992; V. Ware, *Beyond the Pale: White women, racism and history*, London, Verso, 1992.

[5] G. Pollock and R. Parker, *Old Mistresses: Women, art and ideology*, London, Routledge and Kegan Paul, 1981.

There is no doubt of the tendency to accept whatever *is* as natural, whether in regard to academic enquiry or our social systems. This is aided by our linguistic acknowledgement of woman as 'different': we use 'she' instead of the presumably neutral 'one' – in reality the white male position accepted as natural, or the hidden 'he' as the subject of all scholarly predicates – is a decided advantage, rather than merely a hindrance or subjective distortion.[6] This impacts on architectural history as well as other modes of cultural production where the white western male viewpoint is unconsciously and unquestioningly accepted as *the* viewpoint of the historian. It is, of course, élitist and therefore morally unacceptable. But it is also intellectually dishonest as it reveals the failure of history to take account of this implicit value system where we find an overlap between subject and object of historical investigation. At a moment when all disciplines are becoming more self-conscious, and aware of their presuppositions as seen in the very languages and structures of the various fields of scholarship, acceptance of 'what is' as 'natural' may be intellectually fatal, and it is certainly fatally flawed. Even in the nineteenth century John Stuart Mill saw male domination as one of a long series of social injustices that had to be overcome if a truly just social order were to be created. Following on from this, the continuing domination of white male subjectivity in the assumptions and writing of histories is part of a series of intellectual distortions which must be corrected in order to achieve a more adequate and accurate view of historical situations. Yet, there is tension in feminist methodology between representing women's lives as they experience them and the description and challenging of women's oppression. Projecting our views back onto the women of Britain *c.*1600–1840 and their relationship to architecture raises the issue of whether these women considered themselves as experiencing oppression because of their gender. We may discover if these women saw themselves as objects of gender-based oppression through diaries and other personal accounts. But, history is as much about the present as the past, so should we offer a gendered reading of their life story, regardless of the circumstances of their lives? This can lead to an uncomfortable choice whereby the historian either privileges her/his own interpretation of another's life – a hallmark of masculinist methodology – or compromises her/his commitment to challenging oppression which the historical subject may fail to identify.

I do not want here to try to assert the role of women in histories of architecture in order to begin to right this historical bias. The focus of this volume is rather on exploring the resonance between histories and theories and the effect this has on our readings of both. So I want instead to show that it is not so much the material we have that shapes our understanding of architecture, it is rather the questions we choose to ask of the archive. In this way the perceived absence of certain voices from the archive may then reveal as much as if they were present. Questions are culturally determined and it is the determinants that I want to explore. But first,

---

[6] On this point see K. Canning, 'Feminist History after the Linguistic Turn: Historicising discourse and experience', *Signs*, 19, 1994, pp. 368–404.

why, in the early twenty-first century is this even necessary? Judy Chicago gives us some idea in her discussion of *The Dinner Party* – an installation piece that celebrates famous women from the past.

> My idea for *The Dinner Party* grew out of research into women's history that I had begun at the end of the 1960s ... the prevailing attitude towards women's history can be best summed up by the following story. While an undergraduate at UCLA, I took a course titled the Intellectual History of Europe. The professor, a respected historian, promised that at the last class he would discuss women's contributions to Western thought. I waited eagerly all semester, and at the final meeting, the instructor strode in and announced: Women's contributions to European intellectual history/They made none.
>
> I was devastated by his judgment, and when later my studies demonstrated that my professor's assessment did not stand up to intellectual scrutiny, I became convinced that the idea that women had no history – and the companion belief that there had never been any great women artists – was simply a prejudice elevated to intellectual dogma. I suspected that many people accepted these notions primarily because they had never been exposed to a different perspective.
>
> As I began to uncover what turned out to be a treasure trove of information about women's history, I became both empowered and inspired. My intense interest in sharing these discoveries through my art led me to wonder whether visual images might play a role in changing the prevailing views regarding women and women's history.[7]

There is no doubt that the archive concerned with women and architecture is out there, it is perhaps then more a question of how we should interrogate it, and then revise and reconfigure our histories. And we still find those who question whether this is necessary at all, as seen in this extract which appeared in a book published the same year as Chicago's:

> Postructuralists have attempted to reformulate Enlightenment ideals about liberty, equality and fraternity in terms of a theory of the radical relativity of all thought as related to a model of oppression and victimization ... a pernicious 'canon' ... (now deemed an instrument of oppression) and this has been accompanied by a belittling of moral and intellectual values that for millennia constituted the core of the Western tradition. The popular phrase 'dead White male,' used to reject a work of art ... on the basis of the gender and race of the artist, as well as the time in which *he* [my emphasis] worked – that is, before the 'canon' was assaulted by postructuralism, – reflects this attitude.
>
> It is ironic that this orientation arises at a time in which opportunity is extended to entire categories of people who to a greater or lesser extent have been excluded from power within Western democracies. In politics more women and minorities are acquiring positions of leadership ... In culture the art of non-Western traditions is receiving not simply more acclaim but also is being given its own prestigious

---

[7] J. Chicago, *The Dinner Party*, Harmondsworth, Penguin, 1996, pp. 3–4.

institutions within the pantheon of high art ... If Voltaire were to return among us and see these aspects of progress, all conceived in the spirit of the eighteenth-century Enlightenment that saw the birth of modern Western democracies, he undoubtedly would be extremely gratified.

Yet, having reached this level of achievement ... it is as if intellectuals have taken for granted the assumptions on which social progress has been grounded and have felt the need to proceed one step further. The problem basically resides in knowing when a proper balance has been achieved if not in the arena of actual realization then at least in the domain of ideals and expectations.[8]

Perhaps then, on the basis of these two texts, we should all be grateful for what we are about to receive when the Western [not my capitalization] white male hegemony is ready to give it – on their terms, of course.

Gendered Spaces

Mindful of the issues [regarding] the importance of gender performance, we can see how our expectations of gender can influence our readings of space and its role in the construction of social identities through architecture. Doreen Massey encapsulates the appropriation of space by a specific male social group in this anecdote

> I remember very clearly a sight which often used to strike me when I was nine or ten years old. I lived on the outskirts of Manchester, and 'Going into Town' was a relatively big occasion; it took over half an hour and we went on the top deck of a bus. On the way into town we would cross the wide, shallow valley of the River Mersey, and my memory is of dank, muddy fields spreading away into a cold, misty distance. And all of it – all of these acres of Manchester – was divided up into football pitches and rugby pitches. And on Saturdays, which was when we went into Town, the whole vast area would be covered with hundreds of little people, all running around after balls, as far as they eye could see ...
>
> I remember all of this very sharply. And I remember, too, it striking me very clearly – even then as a puzzled, slightly thoughtful little girl – that all this huge stretch of the Mersey flood plain had been entirely given over to boys ...
>
> I did not go to those playing fields – they seemed barred, another world ... But there were other places to which I did go, and yet where I still felt that they were not mine, or at least they were designed to, or had the effect of, firmly letting me know my conventional subordination.[9]

Griselda Pollock shows us the 'other' side of the coin, as it were, the spaces of femininity

[8] R. Etlin, *In Defense of Humanism*, Cambridge, Cambridge University Press, 1996, p. 74.
[9] D. Massey, *Space, Place and Gender*, Cambridge, Polity, 1994.

The spaces of femininity operated not only at the level of what is represented, the drawing-room or sewing-room. The spaces of femininity are those from which femininity is lived as a positionality in discourse and social practice. They are the product of a lived sense of social locatedness, mobility and visibility, in the social relations of seeing and being seen. Shaped within the sexual politics of looking they demarcate a particular social organization of the gaze which itself works back to secure a particular social ordering of sexual difference. Femininity is both the condition and the effect ...

Woman was defined by this other, non-social [interior] space of sentiment and duty from which money and power were banished. Men, however, moved freely between spheres while women were supposed to occupy domestic space alone. Men came home to be themselves but in equally constraining roles as husbands and fathers, to engage in affective relationship ...[10]

It is not then difficult to see how the perceptions of space can influence our readings of architecture as regards gender especially in terms of its function.[11]

Different Canons

Jennifer Bloomer sums up the other way of reading the relationship between gender and architecture. Here she focuses on the classical style, which as we have seen is privileged over all others in histories of the period under review in this book. I have already argued that classicism is representative of a hegemony of the ruling élite through its associative values with the culture and society of antiquity. Bloomer takes this argument further by exploring the notion of sexual difference:

Western architecture, is by its very nature, a phallocentric discourse: containing, ordering, and respecting through firmness commodity and beauty; consisting of orders, entablature, and architrave; base, shaft, and capital and nave, choir, and apse; father, son and spirit, world without end. Amen

In the Garden of Eden there was no architecture. The necessity for architecture arose with the ordination of sin and shame, with dirty bodies. The fig leaf was a natural first impulse towards architecture, accustomed as it was to shading its vulvate fruit, its trunk and roots a complex woven construction of undulating forms. Was it the fig tree that was hacked to build the primitive hut (that precursor of classical architecture)?

[10] G. Pollock, 'Modernity and the Spaces of Femininity', in *Vision and Difference: Femininity, feminism and histories of art*, London, Routledge, 1992.
[11] This is explored in B. Colomina (ed.), *Sexuality and Space*, Princeton, Princeton University Press, 1992.

> The primitive hut and all its begettings constitute a house of many mansions, a firm commodious, and beautiful erection. The primitive hut is the house of my fathers.[12]

Bloomer rightly detects a note of anxiety in the construction of this male canon. The opposites of the stylistic terminology reveal this anxiety through language for instance firmness/limpness, beauty/ugliness, erection/demolition. The order of the classical (male) canon is polarised by the disorder of the non-classical (female) canon. We need then to reconsider our value judgements and resist the privileging of order, proportion and rule of the classical over other styles and reconfigure the canon to encompass creative practice by women. In this way the antimony identified through a psychoanalytic analysis of gender relationship can be averted.

> The problem of dealing with difference without constituting an opposition may just be what feminism is all about (might be what psycho-analysis is all about). Difference produces great anxiety. Polarisation, which is the theatrical representation of difference, tames and binds that anxiety. The classic example is sexual difference, which is represented as polar opposition (active-passive, energy-matter, and all the other polar oppositions that share the trait of taming the anxiety that specific differences provoke).[13]

There are two main strands to come out of this brief survey. Although it is now clear that women have been involved in and around architecture in ways beyond our socially predetermined notions of gender roles or performance, there is little point in trying to look for great female architects, as the criteria for greatness or genius was laid down by men and still has resonance today. That said, our constructions of genius are being challenged and reconfigured together with the value system attached to it.[14] Moreover, we have also seen how our culturally determined expectations of gender can influence histories of architecture. If, however, we remove architecture from the aesthetic realm where it is separate from any social context and see architecture as production we can accept the Marxist view that architecture is the result of social relations which have formed the conditions of production. So it is not so much the consumers of architecture but the social production which is important as it is then located within the whole of society rather than select groups based on such categories as gender, class or race. In this way architecture encodes various conventions which help set out a series of social processes or ideologies. In order to understand our role in all of this as subjects and objects we need to be aware of the cultural practices in and

[12] J. Bloomer 'Big Jugs', in A. Kroker and M. Kroker (eds), *The Hysterical Male: New feminist theory*, London, Macmillan, 1991.

[13] J. Gallop, *Feminism and Psychoanalysis: The daughter's seduction*, London, Macmillan, 1982.

[14] See for instance my essay 'Defining Femininity: Women and the country house', in D. Arnold, *The Georgian Country House: Architecture, landscape and society*, Stroud and New York, Sutton, 1998.

around architecture. This can be achieved through a system of signs and psycho-analysis. Marxist theory might enable us to explore the historical and economic situation but we need psychoanalytic models through which to begin to understand the relationship between these ideologies and sexuality where the visual becomes important as a means of expressing sexual difference. It is important that we remember that this kind of historical approach makes gender an essential tool in historical analysis rather than just a way of narrating 'herstory', and we can then change the present by rethinking the ways is which we construct the past and *read* its histories. Gender *does* have a history, and it isn't all about women.

This volume concludes with two articles which address different aspects of reading gender and architectural history. They are intended to complement rather than critique each other and, I hope, provide an extra layer of analysis and debate to the other chapters and extracts in this volume. In *Room at the Top* Denise Scott Brown discusses her career as a female architect and the different perceptions of her and her husband, who is also a practising architect. Alice Friedman discusses a sixteenth-century architectural patron and head of household, Bess of Hardwick, offering a rereading of her house Hardwick Hall through a consideration of gender relations expressed through architectural space and style. These texts combine with the issues outlined in this chapter to show how gender can redirect the narrative structures and help our reading of architectural history in terms of biography, style, social rituals and cultural practices.

Part II
Urbanism, Reform, and Revival, *c.*1830–1910

Introduction

Abigail Harrison-Moore and Dorothy C. Rowe

The Industrial Revolution marks a major change in the history of architecture and design, and also in the way in which this history has been understood and written down. The nineteenth century witnessed design consciously being used as a driving force for social change. It was the great age of the theorist – designers who set out their ideas in writing, often before committing a plan to paper. It is not surprising, therefore, that this period also saw the development of the recognized discipline of architectural history, at the same time as, and often as the catalyst for, the rise of art history. This new focus on the buildings of the past was especially associated with the antiquarian study of the Gothic style, in direct contrast to the dominance of classicism before 1820.

Histories of the nineteenth century have, for the most part, revolved primarily around conscious interventions into the historicality and sociality of human life, around how societies make histories and organize their social relations and modes of production. A move from the philosophy of G. W. F. Hegel to that of Karl Marx meant that writers on the nineteenth century had to extend their methodologies from ideas and forms to institutions and societal conflicts. Whereas history written solely on the basis of stylistic criteria creates a linear progression founded in formal characteristics, an investigation of social function or political importance can highlight other architectural types that may not contribute to the development of a stylistic avant-garde. That is not to say that the Hegelian concept of a *Zeitgeist* was abandoned altogether. Hegel's ideas informed and still inform much of the historic writing about the buildings and design of the past, but by the twentieth century architectural history had begun to focus on the triangular relationship between society, culture, and style and tended to be inspired by the teaching and example of Leopold von Ranke. Academics opposed what they saw as the generalizations of earlier writers insufficiently supported by facts, or backed by the "unreliable" facts of past generations. They concentrated their efforts on establishing the missing "facts" and generating empirical reports of certain kinds of documentary evidence. At the same time, it was uncritically accepted that certain phenomena were worthy of such study and others were not. This methodology resulted in mainly chronological narratives, forming a central body of facts which should concern the historian, or, as Hobsbawm puts it, "they assumed that, just as scientific erudition could establish the definitive text ... so it would also establish the definitive truth of history" (1990: 40).

The twentieth century brought with it an increasing need to explore an economic or political history, under the urgent stimulus of social change and, consciously or unconsciously, as a result of Marxist theory. Marxism has played a vital role in influencing the development of the historiography of nineteenth-century design. Because of the early subordination of their aesthetic ideas to the requirements of a revolutionary movement and the more pressing need to devote themselves to the investigation of history and political economy, Karl Marx and Friedrich Engels left no formal aesthetic system and no single extended work on the theory of art. Therefore, the history of Marxist aesthetics has been the history of the unfolding of possible applications of their ideas to art and design (Solomon 1979). Marx's work arose in part as a reaction against the grandiose attempts at the systematization of knowledge by his metaphysical predecessors, including Hegel. His general emphasis, conditioned by an Enlightenment view of the artist while attempting to move forward from this, was on the artist as thinker, as educator, as unfolder of social truths, as one who reveals the inner workings of society, as ideologist who pierces the veil of false consciousness. For example, Marx saw British novelists such as Dickens, Thackeray, Charlotte Brontë, and Mrs Gaskell as creating "eloquent and graphic portrayals of the world ... [revealing] more political and social truths than all the professional politicians, publicists and moralists put together" (Solomon 1979: 11).

The premise of Marxism is that "it is not the consciousness of men that determines their being, but on the contrary their social being that determines their consciousness" (preface to *A Contribution to the Critique of Political Economy*, quoted in Solomon 1979: 29). Marxism demonstrates that conflicts within the material foundation of society give rise to certain forms of consciousness, or as Engels wrote, "the fundamental proposition" of *The Communist Manifesto* (1888) is that "in every historical epoch, the prevailing mode of economic production and exchange, and the social organization necessarily following from it, form the basis upon which is built up, and which alone can be explained the political and intellectual history of the epoch" (preface to the English edition of *The Communist Manifesto*, quoted in Solomon 1979: 13–14). Marxism attempts to show the bondage in which man's consciousness has been held by the relations of material production, to reveal the domination of the producer by the product of his labor. It could only have been born in the age of the Industrial Revolution. Its goal was the liberation of consciousness via revolutionary theory. No revolution, however, could take place without the work of ideological preparation, and it was the realm of the aesthetic – poetry, art, philosophy, and design, "mankind's dreamwork" – to which Marx saw man withdrawing for the sustenance and rejuvenation that are the necessary motor of the labor process and of history itself.

The bulk of what we regard as the Marxist influence on historiography has been described by some as "vulgar Marxist," where the general emphasis is on the economic and social factors in history; much of this history was written after the Second World War. The Marxist idea that has had the greatest impact seems to be the theory of "base and superstructure," his model of a society composed of different "levels" which interact. Marx's philosophy allows the historian to explain why and how societies change and transform themselves, and it has had a very powerful effect, leading writers such as Hobsbawm (1990) to claim that "Marx's approach is still the only one which enables us to explain the entire span of human history, and forms the most fruitful starting point for modern discussion."

It is certainly valid for us to look to this approach to understand the transformations that took place in architecture and design from the 1830s onwards. From 1750 to 1841, the population of England and Wales rose massively from 6.5 million to over 16 million. As a result of the Industrial Revolution London became the greatest of all Western cities, and consequently the largest of all concentrated markets for goods. The success of the industrialists, however, led to social and popular problems among the people whom they relied on to man their factories, the working classes. At no other period in modern Britain, according to Hobsbawm (1990), had the common people been so persistently, profoundly, and desperately dissatisfied. This is clearly documented in the novels of the mid-nineteenth century, including Dickens's *Hard Times* (1854). In the characters of Thomas Gradgrind, and particularly Josiah Bounderby, we see the results of the Industrial Revolution, creating a new, dominant social class. Bounderby is the embodiment of the aggressive money-making and power-seeking ideal. In Dickens there is a feeling that trade is "gross." Some historians have tried to argue that social discontent was simply a result of the conditions of the workers' lives improving less rapidly than industrialization had led them to anticipate, "the revolution of rising expectations." Others have offered the explanation that discontent simply arose from the difficulties of adapting to a new society.

"No period in British history has been so tense, as politically and socially disturbed as the 1830s and early 1840s, when both the working classes and the middle class demanded what they regarded as fundamental changes" (Hobsbawm 1990: 73). The Industrial Revolution had brought about fundamental social change. It transformed the lives of men and women beyond recognition and in its initial stages destroyed their old ways of living and left them free to discover or make for themselves new ones, but it rarely told them how to set about it.

We must not forget the British aristocracy, though. They are vital for our understanding of the nineteenth century, as often, despite the protestations of the designers and art theorists, they still funded art and architecture through their patronage, and particularly through the continuing need for country houses. The aristocracy still held much of the country's wealth, necessary funds for an aesthetic transformation. They were little affected by industrialization except for the better – their rents swelled, their social predominance remained untouched, their political power in the countryside complete. One important effect of such continuity was that the rising business classes found a firm pattern of life waiting for them – success brought no uncertainty as long as it was great enough to lift a man into the ranks of the upper class. He would become a gentleman, doubtless with a country house; his wife would become a lady, instructed in her duties by a multitude of handbooks on etiquette produced from the 1840s onwards.

Relatively, the poor grew poorer, simply because the country and its rich middle classes so obviously grew richer. The very moment when the poor were at the end of their tether, in the early and mid-1840s, was the moment when the middle classes dripped with excess capital, to be wildly invested in railways and spent on the bulging, opulent household furnishings displayed at the Great Exhibition.

The Great Exhibition of the Works of Industry of All Nations, held in Hyde Park, London, in 1851, has been seen by many as a vital catalyst, a significant moment in the nineteenth century. This may be overstated, but it does provide a "mid-nineteenth century touchstone" which not only reveals "what belongs wholly to the nineteenth century" but also indicates what points forward to the twentieth (Pevsner 1968b: 11). Louise Purbrick (2001) has discussed the historiographic significance of the Great Exhibition, exploring how periodization has tended to fixate upon 1851 as a key marker, not simply because of the convenient chronology, with the exhibition happening half-way through the century, but also due to a significant shift in the view of professional historians about what counts as a key historical event. John Saville, in his book *1848* (1987), looks to the 10 April Chartist demonstration of that year and argues that the Great Exhibition has taken precedence over this key moment, contributing to a state of amnesia on the political significance of Chartism. The importance placed on the interpretation of culture within social history, and in particular the development of cultural history as a distinct subject area, have focused scholarly attention upon the undeclared politics of cultural expression rather than the formally political (Purbrick 2001: 5). The investigation of worlds not already marked out as politically significant, the study of cultures which appear peripheral or seem routine, is now a recognized method of historical work which has produced new understandings of what is significant.

Studies of the Great Exhibition have resulted in many different ideas about its meaning, in both contemporary published assessments and subsequent historical writing. Its aims and effects have been revised with almost every academic trend and new disciplinary concern. In the official publications produced at the time of the exhibition, such as Henry Cole's *Official Description and Illustrated Catalogue of the Industry of All Nations* (1851), the narrative is focused on its organization, highlighting the "heroic endeavour of individuals." This narrative of achievement continued after it closed, with Cole placing the exhibition within a context of world peace, setting it against the development of international capitalism and the British empire. Cole prioritizes its economic role, promoting free trade, political liberty, and stability. Very few published accounts at this time focused on the objects displayed. This would have to wait until the first substantial reassessment of the Great Exhibition in the work of Pevsner, specifically his *Pioneers of the Modern Movement* (1936; republished in 1960 as *Pioneers of Modern Design*). He offers us a reappraisal of the exhibits, contrasting their "abominable" appearance with Cole's version of the exhibition's political success. His focus reflects a modernist preoccupation with the aesthetics of mass production, and he links the spirit of the exhibition to "a stodgy and complacent optimism" in England, "thanks to the enterprise of the manufacturers and merchants, wealthier than ever, the workshop of the world and the paradise of a successful bourgeoisie" (Pevsner 1936: 40). "An event like this exhibition could not have taken place at any other period, and perhaps not among any other people than ourselves," eulogized the official catalog. The mix of exhibits was extraordinary, ranging from classical sculpture to giant lumps of coal, from a Nubian court to wrought iron fireplaces, from steam engines to Indian miniatures, in a building of gigantic proportions meant to signify the power of England and its empire, both for the indigenous population and its international visitors. It was not, however, intended for celebratory purposes alone. Later twentieth-century reviews have located the exhibition firmly at the center of "historical change" in the nineteenth century (Golby 1986). This holistic approach, linking political, social, philosophical, and aesthetic concerns, was shaped by the rise of social history which privileges the interpretation of patterns of everyday life over those of political events. Politics are not ignored, but instead refracted through an examination of the exhibition's role in the control of the working class, drawing from and contributing to Marxist debates on culture. This has encouraged the view of Crystal Palace as counter-revolutionary measure (Bennet 1995; Greenhalgh 1988), using a Foucauldian analysis to see the building as ordering the masses. Foucault's account of Bentham's Panopticon in *Discipline and Punish* has been considered particularly appropriate to the investigation of public display since it provides an account of the effects of looking, where the act of viewing is premised on the assumption of power. This approach sees Prince Albert, one of the central figures in the exhibition's organization, recognizing that his adopted nation was not united in its vision of the British way of life (Greenhalgh 1988: 29). Chartism and trade unionism had demonstrated that the working population was not prepared to be continually exploited and impoverished. In 1848, when the exhibition was in its initial stages of planning, revolutionary activity had been witnessed across Europe, revealing the continued instability of the structures of power. The Great Exhibition is seen, thus, as conceived not only as an event to encourage pride, but also to instill fear, to demonstrate the strength of the ruling classes and intimidate potential rebels: "the loyalising effect of such an exhibition is not the least of its moral recommendations. Every man who visited it would see in its treasures the result of social order and reverence for the majesty of the law," reported the magazine *Art Union* in 1849 (Greenhalgh 1988). From the outset, the Great Exhibition was made to symbolize the triumph of *laissez-faire* capitalism and British industrial hegemony. For many middle-class commentators, it signified the possibility of class harmony, as well as technological progress brought about by the prospect of mass consumerism (Purbrick 2001: 116). Within this expanding world of goods, a more harmonious social hierarchy would develop. Unfortunately, working-class people had very little disposable income to spend on the expanding range of consumer goods exhibited in Hyde Park and the Great Exhibition, instead of pointing towards greater harmony, simply evidenced the growing social divisions of the nineteenth century.

A Marxist interpretation has also led to a distinct focus on the role of the Great Exhibition in the development of a commercial society in England and ultimately as a model for the department store. Walter Benjamin, in *Paris: Capital of the Nineteenth Century* (1935), recognized great exhibitions as commodity worlds, although his focus is the Expositions Universelles held in Paris in 1855 and 1857, "places of pilgrimage to the fetish Community" (see Purbrick 2001: 68). The Great Exhibition is allocated a key position in the modern world of consumption. This type of interpretation has gone hand in hand with an anti-imperialist view, motivated by Edward Said's *Orientalism* (1978) and the development of post-colonial studies. Commodification is always a process of decontextualization, and European nations used the Great Exhibition to display the commercial success of their colonial relationships, to reinterpret collected objects. Gottfried Semper also commented, in "Science, Industry and Art" (see chapter 21), that the impact of the Great Exhibition was to reverse "the very order of things." By this, he meant that the excessive spectacle signified by the magnitude and variety of goods on display at the exhibition was of such a scale as to have shifted the focus from the necessity of production to the luxury of consumption for its own sake, aided by advances in industrial technology. For Semper, the effects of the technological and industrial era that were rendered so visible via the display halls of the Great Exhibition also suggested a fundamental shift in the relationship between human beings and modes of production in all spheres of activity, including fine art and architecture. His project, then, was to analyze how concepts of style and design could be resituated in light of the fundamentally new relations between materials and modes of production that the industrial age now signaled. For many of Semper's contemporaries, the Great Exhibition presented an ideal industrial world. The enormous quantities of exhibited manufactures, regardless of how they were produced, seemed to owe their existence to the benevolence of machines, and visitors were positioned as the recipients of industrial plenty produced by mechanical means. At the same time, however, a number of other theorists and designers were turning against the capitalism of post-Industrial Revolution England and returning instead to the sanctuary of a medieval past as a means to cure the evils of social division and inequity.

The idea of medievalism, which had been growing since the middle of the eighteenth century, offered the image of the working of a communal society as a welcome alternative to the claims of industrialization. Burke first made the point in *Reflections*; Pugin, Carlyle, Ruskin, and Morris were all later to make it explicitly and influentially (Burke 1950: 184–5). Many believed that the attachment to a past age was one of instinct, the originating emotion was simply recoil from the very different social ideals of rising industrialization (Williams 1967: 19). The impact of these theories and their publication has meant that commentators on the nineteenth century have a wealth of archive material on which to base their arguments. It is vital, however, to explore the motivations behind the texts and to understand their ideological basis.

At the end of the eighteenth century, growth in the power and influence of the new middle class began to subject art to the laws of the market, and it came to be governed by much the same conditions as other forms of production. This had been prefigured in late eighteenth-century writing, in the words of Adam Smith, "In opulent and commercial societies to think or reason comes to be like every other employment, a particular business, which is carried on by a few people, who furnish the public with all the thought and reason possessed by the vast multitudes of labour" (Williams 1967: 34). Here he refers to the rise in commercial publishing which led to the development of a special class of persons who from the 1820s were to be called "intellectuals." An increasing emphasis on the market and the idea of specialized production grew with the system of thinking about the arts of which the most important elements were first, an emphasis on the special nature of art activity as a means of finding "imaginative truth," and, second, an emphasis on the artist as a special kind of person.

Thomas Carlyle illustrates the questions that this change in attitude raised beautifully; "Intellect, the power man has of knowing and believing, is now nearly synonymous with logic, or the mere power of arranging and communicating ... our first question with regard to any object is not, what is it? But, how is it? ... for every why there must be a wherefore" (Williams 1967: 73). Thus Pugin's comment "the history of architecture is the history of the world" (Pugin 1837: 4). Augustus Northmore Welby Pugin, in his *Revival of Christian Architecture* (1843), acknowledged the importance of culture and the objects and buildings it produces as a determinant in retrospect of our ideas about the history of a period. He rejected the eclecticism of the Regency age: "One breathes nothing but the Alhambra, another the Parthenon, the third is full of lotus cups and pyramids from the banks of the Nile, a fourth, from Rome, is all dome and basilica; whilst another works Stuart and Revett on a modified plan ... styles are now *adopted* instead of *generated*, and ornament and design *adapted* to, instead of *originated by* the edifices themselves" (Pugin 1837: 1–2). Gothic is seen by Pugin as "the only correct expression of the faith, wants and climate of our country."

For Pugin, writing in the 1830s, the essence or spirit of Catholicism was seen as enshrined permanently in Gothic architecture. It was, indeed, in the field of Gothic rather than classical studies that architectural history was to develop in the eighteenth and early nineteenth centuries in Germany, England, and France

(Watkin 1980). For example, in 1772 Johann Wolfgang von Goethe published a paean in praise of Strasbourg Cathedral (*Von deutsche Baukunst*). For him, Gothic was important because it was an organic style of German origin and character. It is interesting to contrast this with Pugin's conviction that the Gothic style represented all that was English. Schinkel, although described as a "great neoclassical architect," spoke of Gothic when commenting on his design of 1810 for an elaborate mausoleum for Queen Luise of Prussia as "higher in principles than the architecture of the ancients," because it was based not on practical considerations like the Greek, but on the expression of an idea and a notion of the infinite (Watkin 1980: 6). As such, in Germany, Gothic was seen as a nationalistic style, reflected in the fact that Schinkel used it most readily in memorial architecture, whereas, for Pugin, Gothic was first and foremost a Catholic art.

Eugène-Emmanuel Viollet-le-Duc worked on the restoration of French churches, and in 1853 became the architect to the Commission des Monuments Historiques. The knowledge acquired during such restoration work culminated in his most famous book – the 10-volume *Dictionnaire raisonné de l'architecture française du XIe au XVe siècle* (Paris, 1854–68). The presentation as a dictionary seems to be deliberately unengaging, representing Viollet-le-Duc's desire to present a materialist and scientific interpretation of Gothic in which every feature of a Gothic building is seen as a functional device (Watkin 1980: 28). Function for Viollet-le-Duc could embody a wide range of political and social aspirations and, as such, he laid down, with his British counterparts, a socialist claim to functionalist design. The fact that many of his ideas came from the process of restoration and preservation is also significant, as, throughout the nineteenth century, we witness designers turning to the past for inspiration at the same time as establishing the preservation movements that still control heritage today.

In *Lectures on Architecture* (first published between 1814 and 1879) Viollet-le-Duc presents the case for a functionalist aesthetic reminiscent of Pugin's doctrines on ornament, "Our public buildings appear to be bodies destitute of a soul, the relics of a lost civilisation, a language incomprehensible even to those who use it … is this sterility one of the consequences of our *social* conditions?" (Viollet-le-Duc 1987: 446). He condemns the architecture of the sixteenth century onwards as simply a "reproduction" of the "forms of classical antiquity, without taking any trouble to analyse and develop them," and intends his "scientific" study of the architecture of the past to allow students to understand historic architecture before applying its principles and aesthetics (1987: 447). He rejects the "grotesque medley of styles, fashions, epochs and means of construction" at the "Bosom of the Académie des Beaux-Arts" in France as "not suggesting the least symptom of originality," and calls for a return to "truth," a truth founded in function (1987: 448). In order to do this, he advocates a history of architecture that "methodically classifies" the materials of the past, hence the importance of his *Dictionnaire raisonné*. He is at pains to suggest that this scientific study of the past is the only path to a "truth" in architecture, and thus can be usefully mapped against other nineteenth-century attempts to manage history through classification analyzed by Michel Foucault in *The Order of Things* (1989a). Foucault questions the so-called "impartiality" of the dictionary or encyclopedia, seeing knowledge as directly related to the philosophical discourse that surrounds and generates it. He demands that we identify the "grid of identities, similitudes, analogies," the "coherence that marks a desire for an order among things" with a specific place in time. The classificatory structures of the nineteenth century are seen as different to those of the "classical age," disrupting any impression of "an almost uninterrupted development of the European *ratio* from the Renaissance to our own day." The dictionary is a powerful tool precisely because it is seen as objective, a depository of pure, empirical fact. Behind this superficial appearance, Viollet-le-Duc could develop his political and social ideas. It is ironic, therefore, that in England although his *Dictionnaire* was widely used, with a great many architects seeming to have possessed a set, it was looked upon as a work of reference, a repository of information, rather than as a utopian tract. Such a modernist interpretation of Viollet-le-Duc would have to wait until John Summerson's essay in *Heavenly Mansions* in 1949. The links with and influence of Pugin has complicated any assessment of Viollet-le-Duc's influence on his contemporaries in England, where his theories seem simply to reinforce Pugin's, a connection that, as Middleton points out, would have appalled the Frenchman (Middleton 1981: 204).

What we see, however, through the work of Pugin and Viollet-le-Duc among others, is that in England, France, and Germany, the rise of architectural history was especially associated with the study of a local Gothic past, frequently undertaken in a nationalist or religious spirit. No such development was possible in the United States, but there art history was profoundly influenced by its close links with Germany and its significant relationship with France, where hundreds of Americans studied at either the École des Beaux-Arts, or in associated ateliers in Paris. Henry von Braunt translated the first volume of Viollet-le-Duc's *Lectures* in 1875, but was also favorable to Beaux-Arts classicism, which was already influential in America in the 1880s, and was further stimulated by the World's Fair at Chicago in 1893. A similar duality is noticeable in the writing of Montgomery Schuyler, who in 1891 published *American Architecture: Studies*. Schuyler's key concepts were "organicism" and "reality," which might be interpreted as reflecting respectively the influence of Ruskin and Viollet-le-Duc (Watkin 1980: 35).

Such duality was also evident in late eighteenth-century Britain. Horace Walpole published a chapter in his four-volume *Anecdotes of Painting in England* (1762–80), in which he argued for the influence of the Gothic despite still celebrating the classical:

> One must have taste to be sensible to the beauties of Grecian architecture; one only wants passions to feel Gothic. In St Peter's one is convinced that it was built by great princes; in Westminster Abbey, one thinks not of the builder; the religion of the place makes the first impressions – and though stripped of its altars and shrines, it is nearer converting one to popery than all the regular pageantry of Roman Domes. (Walpole 1762–80: vol. 1, p. 200)

This seems to sum up the romantic medievalism of the Gothick styling of the early designs for Strawberry Hill, where we witness Gothic ornament, often drawn directly from ecclesiastical precedents, applied to essentially classical planning. Walpole was encouraged in his later ideas for his home by a more academic approach to the study of Gothic by the scholars associated with the Cambridge Group, including William Cole, James Essex, and James Bentham. Together, they inspired him to bring to Strawberry Hill a more careful study and understanding of the Gothic past rather than the simple decoration of the Gothick of Batty Langley and others. Their work led to a desire to classify the Gothic past, such as Thomas Kerrich's use of Essex's papers for a lecture delivered at the Society of Antiquaries in 1809, where he suggested that, rather than using the fashionable title "pointed architecture," one should refer to it by centuries, since they roughly corresponded with the principal phases of Gothic's stylistic development.[1] This is still adopted today, combined with the familiar nomenclature of "Norman," "Early English," "Decorated" (English) and "Perpendicular" proposed by Thomas Rickman in his *Attempt to Discriminate the Styles of English Architecture* (1817). However, all of these architects were quite content to design in the classical style according to occasion.

Such developments ran alongside and were influenced by the establishment in the nineteenth century of architecture as a profession with its own scholarly journals. The year 1853 saw the founding of the Institute of British Architects and the publication of the first volume of *Transactions*. J. C. Loudon founded the *Architectural Magazine* in 1834; the *Civil Engineer and Architects' Journal* was established in 1837, and ten years later came the Architectural Association. *The Builder*, the most influential periodical of the nineteenth century, appeared in 1843.

A central element to Pugin's theory was obviously his advocacy of the Gothic style, which had been foreshadowed by his father's work at Windsor Castle and Buckingham Palace, among other projects. The new element in the younger Pugin was his insistence that the revival of this style must depend on the revival of the feelings from which it originally sprang; the architectural revival must be a part of a general religious and truly Catholic revival. This distinguishes Pugin from previous Gothic revivalists – he was not offering Gothic as one of a number of possible styles but rather as the embodiment of "true christian feeling." The most important element in social thinking that developed from his work was the use of the art of a period to judge the quality of the society producing it, demonstrated by the paired engravings in his book *Contrasts* (1836). The widest contrast is between "a catholic town in 1440" and "the same town in 1840" (see figure 19.1). It is not only, says Pugin, that several medieval churches have been spoiled architecturally and have been interspersed with bare, dissenting chapels;

---

[1] Published as "Some Observations on the Gothic Buildings Abroad, Particularly Those of Italy, and on Gothic Architecture in General," *Archaeologia*, 16 (1809), pp. 292–325.

the abbey is ruined and is now bordered with ironworks. The churchyard is now occupied by a "new parsonage house and pleasure grounds." Alongside are institutions such as the "townhall and concert room" and the "socialist hall of science." There are, dominating in the foreground, the new gaol, the gasworks, and the lunatic asylum. *Contrasts* is, as Henry-Russell Hitchcock said, "primarily" a picture book (Hitchcock 1837: 285). Before the late eighteenth century focus on pattern-books and illustrated volumes, there had been a reliance on textual documentation as opposed to oral or visual history. The invention of the printing press marked the birth of the age of reproduction of visual images, an international currency that transcended language barriers. Often these published images are mapped against the paradigm of verbal text, but they have a currency of their own. They order a discovered past and give it reason. We have a tendency to trust visual images over words, we look for visual signs to confirm written statements and, in isolation, these visual signs have a powerful effect on our imagination when we seek answers or the "truth." Pugin's book sets out the case for Gothic architecture entirely in terms of association, of the devout "feelings" that certain effects will inevitably produce. As such, an image-based polemic is inevitable, as, for Pugin, we have to see to believe. From criticizing a change in architecture Pugin has arrived at criticizing a civilization, and he does so in terms that became the backbone of theories that would dominate the rest of the century.

Both Ruskin and Morris were, ironically, unkind in their references to Pugin, but this is mainly because of the differences, both from him and from each other, in their beliefs. For example, Ruskin wanted to capture the Gothic idiom for Protestantism. For Morris, Pugin's prejudice against the working-class movements clashed with his support of socialism. Pugin has, perhaps as a result of this, often been sidelined in histories of the nineteenth century, as a footnote to either Ruskin's or Morris's ideas. Both Ruskin and Morris have been promoted as distinct personalities, and accounts of their lives have frequently dominated over their analyses of specific objects or buildings. For both, however, design was an important weapon in the crusade to bring about social change, and it is this theoretical dimension that is useful for the historiography of the nineteenth century.

John Ruskin was an art critic before he was a social critic, but his work made the joint examination of art and nature seem a natural thing to do. "It remains true, however, that Ruskin's social criticism would not have taken the same form if it had not arisen from his kind of thinking about the purposes of art" (Williams 1967: 134–5). Art, according to Ruskin, could reveal aspects of a universal beauty or "Truth." This concept of beauty rested fundamentally on his belief that there was a universal, divinely appointed order. The artist is one who, in Carlyle's words, "reads the open secret of the universe" (Williams 1967: 135). Any corruption of an artist's nature would blur or distort his capacity for realizing and communicating the ideal, essential beauty. Ruskin added that it is impossible for an artist to be good if his society is corrupt: "The art of any country is the exponent of its social and political virtues ... You can have noble art only for noble persons" (quoted in Williams 1967: 137). The decisive stage in Ruskin's formulation of this position was *The Stones of Venice*, where he aimed to define "the true nature of Gothic architecture" (Ruskin 1905: 149). He was judging artists by their degree of "wholeness" (goodness), and when he found variations in this degree he sought to explain them by corresponding variations in the "wholeness" of man's life in society.

Ruskin contrasts the "kind of labour" that the system made necessary with the "right kind of labour." In examining the history of design, he sought an architecture that recognized "the individual value of every soul." "You must either make a tool of the creature or a man of him. You cannot make both." Thus, Ruskin rejects the nineteenth century of the Industrial Revolution: men are not meant to work with the accuracy of tools and perfection is "a sign of slavery" (1905: 157–60). He relates the social unrest of the century directly to the system of labour in a capitalist society:

> It is verily this degradation of the operative of the machine, which, more than any evil of the times, is leading the mass of nations everywhere into vain, incoherent, destructive struggling for freedom ... their universal outcry against wealth, and against nobility, is not forced from them either by the pressure of famine, or the sting of mortified pride ... it is not that men are ill fed, but that they have no pleasure in ... work. (1905: 161)

Ruskin concludes that rebellion and insurrection in Britain were due to man's degradation in the machine age, "to be counted off into a heap of mechanism, numbered with its wheels, and weighed against its hammer strokes."

Ruskin saw a system of government divided into three orders or "estates" as the correct method of obtaining this "right kind of labour." In the first level there would be the landowners, in the second, the merchants and manufacturers and in the third, scholars and artists. These three groups working together would ensure order, initiate honest production and just distribution, and, by training taste, develop wise consumption (Williams 1967: 146). Below these ruling three estates, the basic form of society would be the guild, with a variety of guilds for each kind of work. But how could Ruskin implement this scheme? Increasingly as he grew older, he narrowed his range to that of a local, small-scale experiment he named the "Guild of St George" where he acted as the master. In *The Two Paths* (1887) he criticized Pugin's medievalism as "inadequate" ("we don't want either the life or the decorations of the c13th back again") because he considered it based on the pride of the "so called superior classes" (quoted in Williams 1967: 148). Ruskin's inquiry into the values of society brought us to this point, but it is only the point of recognition. He could not take us past this, and it is here that we must turn our attention to the man most immediately and deeply affected by Ruskin, William Morris. The significance of Morris here is that he sought to attach values to an actual and growing social force – that of the organized working class (Williams 1967: 148). In "How I Became a Socialist" Morris himself gives us an account of his development retrospectively:

> Before the uprising of "modern" socialism almost all intelligent people were, or professed themselves to be, quite contented with the civilisation of this century. Again, almost all of these really were contented and saw nothing to do but to perfect the sad civilisation by getting rid of a few ridiculous survivals of the barbarous ages ... but besides these contented ones there were others who were not really contented, but had a vague sentiment of repulsion to the triumph of civilisation, but were coerced into silence by the measureless power of whiggery – ... There were a few who were in open rebellion against said whiggery – a few, say two, Carlyle and Ruskin. The latter, before my days of practical socialism, was my master towards the ideal. (quoted in Williams 1967: 148–9)

Morris believed in art as the answer to many of society's ills: "Civilisation has reduced the workman to a skinny and pitiful existence, that he scarcely knows how to frame a desire for any life much better than that which he now endures ... it is the province of art to set the true ideal of a full and reasonable life before him" (Williams 1967: 150). Art, Morris argued, depends on the quality of the society which produces it, "the cause of Art is the cause of the people" (Williams 1967: 154).

William Morris today is, for many people, the best-known nineteenth-century English designer and often the only one most could readily name. What is the reason for his fame, and why does he dominate this period of design history? Because of the survival of the Arts and Crafts movement into the 1920s and the growth of socialism, his name probably remained in the public mind at the turn of the century, but it was the continuing existence of Morris & Co., his firm, that was most influential. In 1911 the firm published *A Brief Sketch of the Morris Movement*, where it asked the question, "Do people still buy Morris goods?," to which the answer was an emphatic "Yes": "India, Canada, America, Australia and the Continent all furnish their quota of admirers of the Morris style and lovers of his pure bright colours and vigorous designs." From his death, on October 3, 1896, onwards, a process of interpretation and mythmaking began which has taken on different guises according to the preoccupation of the historian. Immediately after his death numerous writers depicted his political life as "little more than passing buffoonery" (Parry 1996: 362). *The Times* judged his politics to be "the results of a warm heart and a mistaken enthusiasm." The focus was, instead, on his work in the visual arts and related areas, a trend illustrated by J. W. Makail's *The Life of William Morris* (1899) and Morris & Co.'s own *Brief Sketch* of 1911, where his "utopian propaganda" was seen as being "partly responsible for his untimely death." Only Aymer Vallance's biography (1897), written with Morris's permission, contained extensive references to his politics. The commercial importance of his memory helps explain the limited focus on his politics, as "apparently socialism did not make economic sense" (Parry 1996: 364). An important exhibition at the Victoria and Albert Museum in 1934 continued the omission, and the historiography of Morris in the first half of the twentieth century remained one that focused mainly on material culture. The second half of the century, however, witnessed a reverse in this trend, influenced by Marxist scholars, including E. P. Thompson's *William Morris: Romantic to Revolutionary* (1955), Paul Meier's *William Morris: The Marxist Dreamer*, and the Institute of Contemporary Arts' exhibition *William Morris Today* (1984). This did not lead to a decline in interest in his practice, with Morris wallpaper and textile designs gaining renewed popular respect in the 1970s and 1980s through their republication by Sanderson & Co., and the National Trust opening Standen in West Sussex, a Phillip Webb house with Morris interiors, to some of its largest-ever visitor numbers.

The Arts and Crafts styling of Morris wares had retained a nationalistic appeal, even when his early biographers ignored his political intent. After 1896 an atmosphere of increasing xenophobia and reactionism saw Morris characterized as the epitome of English style, with Morris & Co. being chosen to decorate parts of the British pavilion at the Paris Exposition of 1900: according to the *Magazine of Art*, "A bit of Old England on the banks of the Seine." The irony of this was that at the same time he was adopted as a key inspiration for the modern movement, with left-wing designers and theorists claiming him as their own. In *Pioneers of Modern Design*, subtitled *From William Morris to Walter Gropius*, Pevsner sees the founding of Morris and Co. as "the beginning of a new era in Western Art" and in the index Morris is referenced thirty-seven times, compared to Pugin's one citation.

Morris's name has maintained its position at the apex of nineteenth-century histories of design, and much less has been written about his contemporaries, such as Street, Webb, Pugin, and Burges, than about Morris himself. It is not, as Clive Wainwright (1996) points out, as if Morris was a significantly greater designer or artist than others working at the same time. The fact that he worked in a wide range of media often meant that he did not seem to excel in one, but it has led to his name featuring across a number of disciplines. Morris borrowed heavily from the ideas of Ruskin and Pugin, in both his writing and design. He benefited greatly from his time in G. E. Street's architectural practice, from collaborating with other designers, such as Burges on a scheme for the interior decoration at Oakwood Court in Yorkshire in 1865, and from the influence of Owen Jones, Edward Godwin, and Christopher Dresser. The firm also meant that he could surround himself with artists and architects, including Edward Burne-Jones, Phillip Webb, and George Benson. Morris did not just copy others, but no designer works in a vacuum unaware of what his predecessors and contemporaries have created and are creating. Where Morris did differ was as a businessman. He ensured that Morris & Co.'s products were at the forefront of a fast-growing domestic market. This may have led to his designs being less cutting-edge than those of others, but it has ensured that they remain successful today and maintain his name in popular culture. In terms of his lectures, he may not have been the originator of the key concepts, but he popularized them and made them available to the widest possible audience.

It is at this moment that we should turn our attention to the Continent and the development of art nouveau. When, in 1900, some objects of Continental art nouveau were presented to the Victoria and Albert Museum, a letter of protest was sent to *The Times* signed by three architects of the Norman Shaw School with Arts and Crafts sympathies. They called the objects wrong in principle and lacking in "regard for the materials employed." "That strange decorative disease known as L'Art Nouveau," was duly condemned (probably for nationalist reasons) and yet many of the functions of the Arts and Crafts movement in England and of art nouveau on the Continent were the same (Crane 1911: 232). They both marked a moment of transition from historicism to the modern movement and were both focused on reviving handicraft and the decorative arts (Pevsner 1936: 107). Hence, on the Continent, instead of being in opposition, those who advocated one advocated the other, as is witnessed by the exhibitions and magazines of decorative art such as *Pan* (1895) and *Deutsche Kunst und Dekoration* (1897) in Germany, and *Art et Décoration* (1897) and *L'Art Décoratif* (1897) in France. The group Les Vingt in Brussels set up a number of turn-of-the-century exhibitions, including one in 1894 which contained the work of Beardsley, Toorop, Morris, Ashbee, and Lautrec, and a complete studio furnished by Serrurier. In 1895 the work of Charles Annesley Voysey was also exhibited. Art nouveau represented a deliberate break with tradition, which did not seem so apparent in England, and yet Voysey had ventured on a new style of "an original and highly stimulating nature" before art nouveau had even begun (Pevsner 1936: 148).

Voysey's designs were a source of inspiration for art nouveau, with Van de Velde, for example, stating, "it was as if spring had come all of a sudden," when discussing the revolutionizing effect of Voysey's wallpapers (Pevsner 1936: 148). His theories of art and architecture took the Arts and Crafts aesthetic of Morris, Webb, and their peers and modernized it, emphasizing novelty and progressiveness; counter to Nikolaus Pevsner's arguments in *Pioneers of Modern Design*, he did have some clear aesthetic theories. "There is such a thing as sham honest, an affectation of being superior to one's fellows in exact truth of statement, which is not far removed from hypocrisy, although it aims to be the very opposite extreme" ("G" 1897: 18). Voysey railed against the straight adoption of historic ornament for aesthetic purposes alone: "Mr Voysey would no more dream of adding a superfluous buttress than he would an unnecessary panel of cheap ornament" ("G" 1897: 20). He looked to Morris with his direct references to nature and his "indifference to precedent":

> The revivalism of the present century, which is so analogous to this reliance on precedent, has done more to stamp out men's artistic common sense and understanding than any movement I know. The unintelligent, unappreciative use of works of the past, which is the rule, has surrounded us at every turn with deadly dullness, that is dumb alike to the producer and public. This imitative, revivalistic temper has brought into our midst foreign styles of decoration totally out of harmony with our national character and climate. Also, the cultivation of mechanical accuracy, by close attention to imitation, has so warped the mind and feelings until invention to many is well-nigh impossible. (Voysey 1896)

Voysey emphasized his urgent desire to "live and work in the present," producing designs that made Morris's wallpapers seem thoroughly grounded in nineteenth-century historicism (1893: 234). He can be more usefully aligned with the Continental art nouveau movement and its revolt against historicism, than the English Arts and Crafts.

In Britain the backlash against the designs of Charles Rennie Mackintosh, the architect of the Glasgow School of Art, underlined the critical reception that art nouveau received. Dismissed as flamboyant and in bad taste, without the desired "honesty" of construction. Mackintosh's work was, however, well liked across the Channel, especially after he exhibited at the Turin Exhibition of 1902, where he made an important link with the members of the Vienna Secession, later exhibiting in their eighth exhibition and being consulted about the founding of the Wiener Werkstätte. Art nouveau is a term applied to a short-lived but very significant fashion in decoration exemplified in the work of Victor Horta in Brussels and Louis Sullivan in Chicago and characterized by writhing plant forms, as in the wrought iron entrances to Paris's Métro stations by Hector Guimmard. Pevsner declares that it was a style "entirely lacking in a social conscience," as it directed its appeal away from the social towards the aesthetic, grounding itself in an art for art's sake.

Nevertheless, the growth of the global metropolis in Europe and America by the end of the nineteenth century, and the concomitant "fetishism of commodities" endemic to it, also heralded a demand for urban architectural development that would epitomize the spirit of entrepreneurial capitalism that lay at its core.[2] Thus, despite the alleged aestheticism of art nouveau, one of its American practitioners, Louis Sullivan (1856–1924), is one of the most highly celebrated architects of the new commercial style of building designed to spectacularize the industrious operations of the global city. Sullivan, like Louis Comfort Tiffany before him, managed to combine the aesthetic ideals of "the new style" with the pragmatic necessities of running a successful business in the expanding commercial environment of the late nineteenth-century city. Like many of his contemporaries, Sullivan had received some of his architectural training at the École des Beaux-Arts in Paris in 1874, before settling in Chicago, where during the 1880s he established his reputation in partnership with the engineer Dankmar Adler, a liaison that lasted until 1896. Most closely associated with what became known as the "Chicago School" of architects that emerged in the wake of the Chicago fire in 1871 and the subsequent major rebuilding of the city, Sullivan's major output was not only in the commercial architecture of urban skyscrapers and banks but also in his extensive published writings in which many of his concerns about the

---

[2] The phrase "fetishism of commodities" was coined by Karl Marx in *Das Kapital*, first published in 1867, in which Marx argues that since goods are not produced for their use-value alone, a hierarchy of production of desirable commodities engenders values against which human labor and social interaction are unequally measured (Marx 1974: vol. 1).

direction of American architecture can be found.[3] For Sullivan, like many theorists before him, architecture was the most palpable way in which the reform and uplifting of American society could be achieved. The idea of reform was closely allied to the ideas expressed by American sculptor Horatio Greenhough, author of *American Architecture* (1843) and, more significantly, *Form and Function* (1852), as well as to the English critic, John Ruskin, author of *The Seven Lamps of Architecture* (1849). In Sullivan's reading of the naturalism advocated by Ruskin and the rules of ornament inspired by Owen Jones's *Grammar of Ornament* (1856), combined with his interpretation of the rationalism promoted by Viollet-le-Duc, the dialectic between architecture and reform hinged upon the rejection of historicism in favor of a symbiotic relationship between form and function in which natural form and ornamentation were integrated into the overall functional expression of a building's design.[4] In "Style" (1888), Sullivan considered the architect, like the poet, to be the conduit for social reform who could only fulfill his (*sic*) function adequately if he responded to his immediate surroundings: "Thus if you would really seek a style, search for it not altogether in books, not altogether in history, but search for it rather in the explicit reality of your own inner life and your own outward surroundings . . ." (reprinted in Twombly 1988: 52).

"Style," and other of Sullivan's writings, such as "Ornament in Architecture"(1892) and "The Tall Office Building Artistically Considered" (1896), offer a philosophical framework that aestheticizes the functional requirements of building design. The proposal for the tall office building divided it into three distinct parts – "a story below-ground" to act as the power plant, a ground floor for commercial enterprises such as "banks" and "stores" to give rise to numerous tiers for offices (likened to a "honeycomb"), and a top attic story for mechanical services. The solutions to the exterior design of such buildings were then to be found again via "natural instincts without the thought of books, rules or precedents" but based instead on the most glaring characteristic, the "loftiness" or verticality of the building, which could be emphasized by a projecting cornice and an ornamented frieze around the attic story. Ornament could also dignify the unbroken vertical piers of the office floors. The practical demonstration of these principles could be seen in his earlier completed work for the offices of the Wainwright Building (1890–1) in St. Louis. Indeed, according to Lauren Weingarden, Sullivan's firm hold over American architectural history was "initiated by [his] contemporaries who used the triadic composition as a standard for evaluating all skyscraper designs, and championed him for heralding a new American

---

[3] For an excellent edited collection of all 51 of Sullivan's published papers reprinted in full, see Twombly 1988.

[4] Sullivan's interpretation of the work of his European and American predecessors was played out in his writings as an attempt to delineate his own position with regard to the role of architecture in an uneven democracy. As already indicated, Greenhough's 1852 remarks on architecture and art were published under the title *Form and Function*, a phrase that has subsequently become almost wholly identified with Sullivan's own version of it, "form follows function" expressed in his most celebrated essay, "The Tall Office Building Artistically Considered" (1896).

style" (Weingarden 2000: 323–4). Sullivan's place in the historiography of the discipline was assured by these kinds of authorial declarations in support of his practical building designs. The mythology of the individual architect as masculine poetic visionary able to save America from itself was firmly reiterated through such examples of Sullivan's gendered rhetoric.

Chief among Sullivan's most loyal admirers was that other monolithic figure of modernist architectural history in America, Frank Lloyd Wright, former pupil of Sullivan and also a prolific writer, architectural practitioner, and self-publicist. The authorial presence of the architect as creator can be seen forcibly in Lloyd Wright's approach to his public self-image, often photographed as master of his creative materials, dominating the visual frame with his confident, self-assured posing.[5] Such confidence also extended to his writings, as can be seen in the extracts from his autobiography included here. They serve as a lucid example of the by now familiar construction of a discourse concerning architectural creativity that is dependent upon privileging the autonomous creative male subject, authorized by the connection to his "Master," who disavows the fundamental conditions and networks of racial and gendered socio-economic and historical cultural production. Integral to those conditions are of course employees of entire architectural firms responsible for the design, planning, engineering, and execution of buildings, whose identities have often been eclipsed by conventional authorial approaches to architectural history in which attribution to a single white male creator becomes a norm (Arnold 2002: 35–7, 199–204; Upton 1998: 272–9). The gendering of architectural histories is of central concern to contemporary discursive analyses of the discipline, along with the investigation of issues of race, ethnicity, and sexuality. The dominance of a canon of white male subjects as both practitioners and historians of the discipline has been scrutinized and found wanting in many recent critical studies of architectural and design history (Arnold 2002).[6] The variety of critical and theoretical approaches employed in unpacking such tightly constructed myths of masculine creativity offers today's student an abundance of tools with which to interrogate the discipline further. The ongoing research into the "rediscovery" of black, Asian and/or women architects and designers formerly "hidden from history" remains a valid historical project that can furnish existing architectural histories with new information and altered versions of historical and cultural events.[7] The recent revival, recognition, and inclusion of Marion Mahony Griffin as a named female designer is one small example of this revisionist approach to history, as is Lynne Walker's excellent account of women architects, both included in this section (Upton 1998: 275–6).

[5] A good example of such posing can be seen in Upton 1998: 266, plate 179.

[6] For other titles signaling critical approaches to the historiography of architectural history readers should consult the bibliography to this volume.

[7] "Hidden from history" alludes to the influential historical account of the "rediscovery" of women in history by Sheila Rowbotham published in 1973, which has subsequently spawned a plethora of discursive references to the phrase.

Mahony Griffin worked for Lloyd Wright and became chief designer when Wright left the practice and Hermann von Holst took over, but her significance as draughtswoman to the practice has only been foregrounded relatively recently (Upton 1998). However, while the restoration of individual names to an existing historical canon undeniably enriches that canon, it often does little to challenge its parameters. Lynne Walker's essay, however, also suggests opportunities for more fundamental shifts in historiographic analysis that can better equip the discipline with wholly new epistemological frameworks, interrogating existing discourses to reveal how exclusions were legitimated at their point of origin, as well as offering new ways of accessing histories that have been altered by the recognition of the operations of gendered and racial power relations at all levels of cultural socio-historical discourse. A decade earlier, Gwendolyn Wright also began to address the exclusion of women from the American architectural profession with a substantive essay entitled "On the Fringe of the Profession: Women in American Architecture" (reproduced in Kostoff 1977). Wright's essay renders visible the historical contribution of women architects, writers, and designers to the architectural profession from the mid-nineteenth century to the early years of the twentieth. While an anthology such as this one might be accused of tokenism in its approach to issues of race and gender, it remains an important strategy not to simply ignore canonical figures such as Sullivan and Lloyd Wright but rather to provide the reader with an opportunity to analyze their work meta-discursively within the expanded field of historical and theoretical inquiry that has been enabled by the writings of many postmodern and post-colonial thinkers, including Michel Foucault, Pierre Bourdieu, Gayatri Spivak, Gilles Deleuze, Félix Guattari, Julia Kristeva, Jacques Derrida, and Luce Irigaray, among others. Collectively the work of these philosophers and theorists has exploded the binaries of Western metaphysical thought which policed the oppositional boundaries of race, class, and gender in a value-system of hierarchical judgments of "difference" and "otherness" through which the institutional frameworks of Western societies were and still are to some extent operative. Subsequent acknowledgment of the fluidity and performativity of embodied subjectivities within networks of discursive power relations furnishes today's reader with the ability to regard the text as dependent upon the contingency of all inter-subjective historical interpretation. Sullivan's writings, together with those of Lloyd Wright, Lynne Walker, John Ruskin, Pugin, Viollet-le-Duc, and those before and after them, are presented here not as representatives of monolithic authorial truth but rather as competing voices within different versions of history, other extant anthologies, and those yet to be written.

However, exclusions from existing canons of architectural and design history have not only been confined to issues of race, sexuality, and gender but also to issues of style. While the analysis of style as an interpretive category has often been predicated upon a false notion of its autonomous aesthetic operation teleologically read by the historian with the benefit of hindsight, it can still be useful as one way among others of "identifying, codifying and interrogating the aesthetic" (Arnold 2002: 82). The architectural training promoted by the École des Beaux-Arts in Paris during the nineteenth century was central to ensuring the continuing transferral of a particular set of architectural principles across the continent from Europe to America. However, as Robin Middleton observed in his 1982 introduction to *The Beaux-Arts and Nineteenth Century French Architecture*, scholarship was slow to take up detailed investigative research into the field until the 1980s, relying instead on a few key accounts from earlier in the century that remained not only cursory but also uninterrogated.[8] Nevertheless, since the publication of Middleton's collection of essays, research into Beaux-Arts architecture and its impact has gathered more pace. The inclusion of Annie Jacques's essay on "The Programmes of the Architectural Section of the École des Beaux-Arts" positions the Beaux-Arts within detailed knowledge of the school's Parisian context and offers a useful insight into its methods of architectural training.

In America, the 1893 World's Columbian Exposition or Chicago World's Fair, constructed under the auspices of the City Beautiful proponent Daniel Burnham and featuring the classically inspired "White City" or Court of Honour at its center, offered architects like Louis Sullivan the opportunity to put some of his acquired Beaux-Arts principles into practice in a spectacular design for the Transportation Building, the distinguishing feature of which was an elaborate "Golden Doorway," which became a landmark of the fair. However, as many commentators were quick to observe, Sullivan's use of an architectural style that harmonized with the overall Beaux-Arts site plan conceived by Burnham and his colleagues, departed radically from many of the other buildings at the fair. Zeynep Çelik traces some of those points of difference in a reading that foregrounds the Orientalist discourse upon which Sullivan drew. As Çelik points out, Sullivan relied on a long list of Islamic precedents for the overall design of the Transportation Building, not because of any meaningful homage to Islamic culture but rather as a formal statement of his dissatisfaction with classicism. Orientalism in American architecture as represented by Sullivan at the turn of the century was employed as a formal statement of "otherness," "difference," and, crucially, "the present," from which his own anti-historicist position could be established. That Islamic architecture has its own set of historical antecedents was irrelevant to the position of "difference" that it was corralled into representing within a gendered Western discourse of American architectural style.

Amongst the commentators at the Chicago Fair, Charles Mulford Robinson, a key theorist of the City Beautiful movement with which the fair was closely

---

[8] Middleton cites the following texts in this context: Lucien Magne, *L'Architecture française du siècle* (1889); André Michel, *Histoire de l'art* (1926); Henry-Russell Hitchcock's *Architecture: Nineteenth and Twentieth Centuries* (1958); and Louis Hautcoeur, *Histoire de l'architecture classique en France*, 2 vols. (1955, 1957). Middleton notes that it was not really until the publication of Arthur Drexler (ed.), *The Architecture of the École des Beaux-Arts* (1977) that earlier accounts were demonstrated to be inadequate.

linked, observed that the Transportation Building displayed a "voluptuous Orientalism" and positioned it as "the Bride of the Orient" since he was otherwise unable to account for its difference and strangeness from the other more "masculine structures" on the site (Çelik 1992: 174). Such overtly gendered language in the articulation of difference between Eastern and Western aesthetics is of course not confined to architectural style. Rather, it is symptomatic of what Edward Said recognized over 20 years ago as a more generic relationship "between Occident and Orient" as one "of power, of domination" and "of varying degrees of a complex hegemony" (Said 1978: 5).

According to William H. Wilson, the City Beautiful movement was not in fact named as a movement until 1899, well after the 1893 Columbian Exhibition, and "did not mature until 1902 and after" (1989: 53). However, Wilson concedes that Chicago's "White City" did become the focal point for a number of progressive ideas relating to the emerging City Beautiful movement, such as "sanitation, aesthetics, rationalized urban functions, women's involvement in culture, civic improvement, urban reform, building design, artistic collaboration, architectural professionalism and civic spirit" (1989: 60). Nevertheless, the origins of the City Beautiful can be located well before the fair and found in the earlier ideas of landscape architect Frederick Law Olmsted (1822–1903) whose role in laying out the grounds of the Chicago Fair was a commission that he accepted fairly late on in his career. Olmsted, like Sullivan and others after him, was motivated by a belief that the aesthetic effects of architectural design, and in particular green park spaces, could and should be harnessed to transform the experience of American urban life. According to Wilson, "Olmsted made three fundamental contributions to the City Beautiful movement" (1989: 10). First, he shifted the focus from individual city parks to more integrated systems of multipurpose parks and boulevard systems (perhaps seen most clearly in his development of New York's Central Park in 1857).[9] Secondly, he argued that the presence of municipal parks and other aesthetic features of the city raised surrounding land values, encouraged investment, and fostered the economic growth of a city. Thirdly, his other major contribution to the formal development of the City Beautiful movement was the legacy of his flourishing consultancy practice. The rise in the significance of the landscape architect as consultant to municipal development rested upon the tradition fostered originally by Olmsted and subsequently bequeathed to his sons in a professionalization of the integral role that the landscape architect had to play in the reform and development of modern city planning. The parks movement that Olmsted fostered was one of the earliest responses to the social and economic crises that had resulted in the growth of the slum towns of the Industrial Revolution. While landscape gardening already had a

[9] Olmsted took over the development of Central Park in collaboration with British architect Calvert Vaux (1824–95) after the death of Andrew Jackson Dowing in 1852. The major work on the park took place between 1857, when Olmsted was made Superintendent of Central Park, and 1863, when the project was completed.

significant heritage, particularly in the service of the aristocracy in Renaissance Italy, France, and England, in America it was Olmsted who transformed it into a tool for social reform.

The main sources of City Beautiful design were not only to be found in the earlier ideas of Olmsted, however; they could also be traced back to the rebuilding of Paris under Baron Haussmann (1809–91) and the architectural plans for the layout of Washington under Pierre Charles L'Enfant (1755–1833). Character-istics of both of these new capital cities included their strong axial ground plans, their impressively wide tree-lined boulevards, the grand public buildings with imposing façades, and their radically improved sanitation systems. The rebuilding of Paris under Napoleon III's Second Empire was a major undertaking, integral to first surge of French industrialization after the 1840s and to the development of consumer capitalism so poignantly critiqued by Walter Benjamin in his unfin-ished melancholic contribution to the history of modernity, *The Arcades Project* (1927–40; see Benjamin 1999). The collision of architecture and capitalism can be seen at its most powerful in the redesign, planning, and rebuilding central to nineteenth-century Europe's "City of Light" (Rice 1997: xix). Before Hauss-mann's intervention it was popularly believed and frequently stated that Paris was a city on the verge of its own demise. As Shelley Rice explains, after the "Hauss-mannization" of the city,

> Many of the disease-ridden slum areas were destroyed, while a large number of the city's poor had been shunted to the outlying areas, some of which had been annexed in 1859 with the geographical expansion of the city limits. Wide, tree-lined boule-vards efficiently handled the traffic and overcrowding that had almost choked the Paris of 1848. Commerce and trading were brisk, in shops on the new streets as well as in the first department stores. In addition, there were functional sewers, parks, new monuments, and squares; the city finally had a reasonable water supply, gas-lights, better security and easy access to trains ... (Rice 1997: 142)

Yet despite these undeniable physical improvements, Haussmann's Paris was also believed by its socialist critics to have metaphorically excised the politically charged legacy of 1848, replacing it with a capitalist economy driven by the consumer desire of the bourgeoisie and eradicating its revolutionary potential for democratic reform (Benjamin 1999: 11–15; Rice 1997: 144). As Walter Benjamin observed, "the true goal of Haussmann's projects was to secure the city against civil war. He wanted to make the erection of barricades in Paris impossible for all time ... Widening of the streets is designed to make the erection of barricades impossible, and new streets are to furnish the route be-tween the barracks and the workers' districts. Contemporaries christen the oper-ation 'strategic embellishment' " (1999: 12). The architectural classicism chosen by Haussmann and his architects for such embellishment "became a unifying force on a gigantic scale" and part of a monumental legacy to nineteenth-century urban development that can still be experienced today (Sutcliffe 1993: 83).

One of the key features of urban reform during the later nineteenth century was the recognition that the increasing division between the urban and the rural as a result of the expansion of large towns after the Industrial Revolution was detrimental to public health and hygiene. Social reform in the city was thought to be dependent upon the reintegration of the benefits of rural landscape with the convenience of city living.[10] A major contributor to these ongoing debates on urban improvement that were raging across Europe and America was English stenographer Ebenezer Howard (1850–1928). Howard was the self-declared inventor of the concept of the "Garden City" as put forward in his 1898 text *Tomorrow: A Peaceful Path to Real Reform*, republished in 1902 under the title *Garden Cities of Tomorrow*. Howard's text was prompted by the recognition that the continuous migration of people from the country to the "already over-crowded cities" was depleting the countryside of inhabitants and having an adverse effect on both (1902: 11). Key amongst his ideas was a diagrammatic illustration of what he termed "The Three Magnets" representing the town, with its associated attractions and drawbacks, the country, also with its attendant attractions and disadvantages, and finally his own unique combination of both, the Town–Country Magnet. It would be the responsibility of the new urban planner to create Town–Country Magnets in which the beauty of nature from the countryside would be combined with the attractions of work and leisure offered by the city. Within this plan, people would be provided with high wages, low rents, and opportunities for social interaction and economic and personal freedom; they would be attracted to "Town–Country" urban developments (which Howard named "Garden Cities") like iron filings to the strongest magnetic field. The impact of Howard's ideas was enormous and can be seen most clearly in the practical application of his proposals within his own lifetime into the development of two extant garden cities in Great Britain, Letchworth (1903) and Welwyn Garden City (1920). In addition, Howard also oversaw the organization of an entire garden city movement across Europe and America which still exerts influence, especially with the continued inclusion of green-belt areas within modern urban planning (Fishman 1999: 23).

While Howard's reforms were exerting significant influence in Britain, it was the development of the Ringstrasse in Vienna that spawned two opposing yet equally significant responses to urban architectural development in Austria that took hold across Germany and northern Europe towards the end of the century. As Carl Schorske observes, " 'Ringstrasse Vienna' has become a concept to the Austrians ... equivalent to the notion of 'Victorian' to Englishmen, '*Gründerzeit*' to Germans or 'Second Empire' to the French" (Schorske 1981: 24). The liberal rebuilding of Vienna after 1857 at its core around the Ringstrasse has come to signify an entire cultural transformation of urban social life that gave

[10] Indeed, Marx and Engels, in their *Communist Manifesto* of 1848, were among many reformers who called for the abolition of the distinction between the country and the city on the grounds of radical social reform.

rise to two very distinct and significant responses within the architectural thought of Camillo Sitte (1843–1903) and Otto Wagner (1841–1918), both of whom engaged with nineteenth-century preoccupations concerning architectural style, and both of whom proposed very different and radical sets of solutions that presaged subsequent twentieth-century developments in architectural design and urban planning.

The underlying principle of Vienna's Ringstrasse was the beautification of the city, rather than its renovation or redevelopment, and as such it became representative of the values of Austrian liberalism, built by its well-to-do professional classes for their benefit, accommodation, and glorification (Schorske 1981: 26–7). As in Haussmann's Paris, the requirement for swift mobilization of troops around the city, especially in the wake of the 1848 socialist uprisings, remained a central feature of the early conception of the Ringstrasse in the 1850s. The central position of the new thoroughfare on the site of the old glacis surrounding Vienna's old fortifications meant that it could act as a broad artery coiled around the protected inner city. The tension between military requirements and the civilian need for economic growth colored the early debates about the development of the site. However, by 1866, after several European defeats, the Austrian army finally lost its impact on city governance and "the liberals took the helm" (Schorske 1981: 31). It was at this juncture that the role and significance of the Ringstrasse altered to represent a new era of peaceful liberalism in opposition to military dominance. While the inner city remained a symbol of past imperial glories through its architectural arrangement of palaces, garrisons, and churches, the new Ringstrasse became the site of public civic governance symbolized through its public buildings, civic monuments and cultural symbols. It also cut the old center off from its suburbs in a self-contained grandiloquent gesture of horizontal space and motion. The streets that enter the Ring from either side, from inner city or outer suburb, become absorbed into the flow of the corso rather than being allowed to cross it in a strong radial axis, thus effectively cutting off one half of the city from the other and imprisoning the inner city in a self-contained island, "a sociological isolation belt" as Schorske has commented (1981: 33). The buildings along the Ring itself are also subordinated to the street, built in isolation from each other and oriented solely towards the sweep of the vast tree-lined avenue.

The architectural and sociological impact of the Ringstrasse fostered a variety of critical responses, two of the most powerful and lasting of which were those by Camillo Sitte in his 1889 publication *City Building According to Artistic Principles*, and Otto Wagner in his 1896 publication *Modern Architecture*. Both Sitte and Wagner used their dissatisfaction with the Ringstrasse as their point of departure, yet both arrived at totally different propositions for the future of architectural development in the modern metropolis. Sitte's text offered a serious challenge to the prevalence of broad, straight boulevards, grand public buildings, and traffic management through public squares that had been made manifest with the building of the Ring. He advocated a less rigid approach to city planning based in part on the design objectives of medieval and Renaissance city builders, whose towns had developed more incrementally than the severely regulated plans of his own day (Collins and Craseman Collins 1986: 14). For Sitte, the modern urban system, already embodied in Chicago and almost complete in Vienna, focused as it was on rigid street plans, rational functions, and geometric structures, lacked artistic principles that would enable its citizens to be "secure and happy" (Collins and Craseman Collins 1986: 141 and 242). Although his search for the hidden structures that fostered a sense of temporal continuity within the ancient towns that he analyzed has been confused with a kind of archaism or historic revivalism that was common to many of his nineteenth-century peers, Sitte's project was in fact more nuanced than this. His overriding concern was to excavate the best elements from ancient city plans that could then be adapted to the needs of the modern city dweller. The dominance of artistry over functionality became an overriding principle. In almost total contrast, however, Otto Wagner's 1896 response to the eclectic style of the Ringstrasse was to eschew historical styles altogether and to celebrate instead the functional aesthetic of the modern machine age. For Wagner, modern metropolitan life demanded a newly modern architecture totally free from the historicism that had dominated much nineteenth-century architectural thought and appeared so visibly in the architecture of the Ringstrasse. When it was first published in 1896, *Modern Architecture* caused a sensation because of its definitive break with the eclecticism of the past and its radical approach to new design. As Harry Mallgrave has indicated, "Wagner was the first European architect to publicly state his break with the past" (1988: 30). While the treatise has now become synonymous with much early twentieth-century architectural and design practice, it was in essence a culmination of many of the nineteenth-century efforts to create a new style, especially the much earlier rationalist tendencies of Viollet-le-Duc, and the first edition in 1896 betrayed more of these roots than did the subsequent, amended editions of 1898, 1902, and 1914. With each new edition, Wagner became more confident and less equivocal about his modernist polemic. In particular, it is the chapter on construction that most clearly presents the overall logic of his argument. He states that styles or "art-forms" are born out of functional needs which can only be solved through methods of construction, and that it is the architect's role to "develop the art-form out of construction" (Mallgrave 1988: 93). Modern architecture had a duty to reflect modern life and it should therefore be based on modern technologies, new materials, and contemporary methods of construction. The text itself was aimed primarily at a student audience, and the use of upper-case format and repetition was designed to enhance its didactic appeal.

All of the texts selected for this section have been chosen to offer the student of architectural and design history an introduction to some of the key developments of nineteenth-century architectural and design culture in Europe and America and to form the basis for further study and individual investigation. There are inevitable omissions of certain key influential figures in urban planning and interior design (for example, Edwin Chadwick, Agnes and Rhoda Garrett, Owen

Jones, Raymond Unwin, and Patrick Geddes to name just a few), but the task of anthologizing historical texts into a usable archive and resource is, as we have already demonstrated in our introduction to this volume, a precarious and contingent activity. What we hope to have presented, however, is one approach among many other extant possible readings of nineteenth-century architectural and design history in the West that may support, refute, or act in tandem with many others, not least non-Western and post-colonial perspectives concerning the same historical timeframe, with which we hope that our text can act in fruitful dialog.

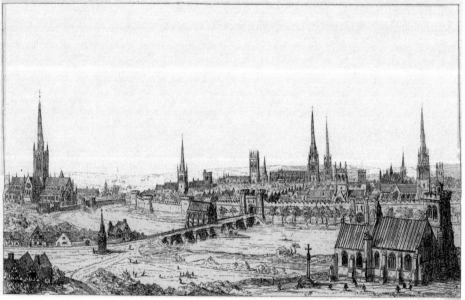

Figure 19.1 Contrasted English Towns, 1840 and 1440
Source: Pugin 183

One of the paired engravings from A. W. N. Pugin's 1836 book *Contrasts* which aimed to demonstrate to his readers how England, as he saw it, had declined since medieval times. The widest contrast in the book, these images are used didactically to differentiate between a town in the fifteenth century and a town in the nineteenth century. Reminding the reader of Charles Dickens's fictional "Coketown." Pugin uses architectural design, from the devoutness of the Gothic style to an eclectic mix of buildings, as a metaphor for the move from a Catholic society to one based on the individual and the industrial.

208

19

An Apology for The Revival of Christian Architecture in England

A. W. N. Pugin

The age in which we live is a most eventful period for English art. We are just emerging from a state which may be termed the dark ages of architecture. After a gradual decay of four centuries, the style, – for style there was, – became so execrably bad, that the cup of degradation was filled to the brim; and as taste had fallen to its lowest depth, a favourable re-action commenced.

The breaking up of this wretched state of things has naturally produced a complete convulsion in the whole system of arts, and a Babel of confusion has succeeded to the one bad idea that generally prevailed.

Private judgment runs riot; every architect has a theory of his own, a beau ideal he has himself created; a disguise with which to invest the building he erects. This is generally the result of his latest travels. One breathes nothing but the Alhambra, – another the Parthenon, – a third is full of lotus cups and pyramids from the banks of the Nile, – a fourth, from Rome, is all dome and basilica; whilst another works Stuart and Revett on a modified plan, and builds lodges, centenary chapels, reading-rooms, and fish-markets, with small Doric work and white brick facings. Styles are now *adopted* instead of *generated*, and ornament and design *adapted to*, instead of *originated by*, the edifices themselves.

This may, indeed, be appropriately termed the *carnival* of architecture: its professors appear tricked out in the guises of all centuries and all nations; the Turk and the Christian, the Egyptian and the Greek, the Swiss and the Hindoo, march side by side, and mingle together; and some of these gentlemen, not satisfied with perpetrating one character, appear in two or three costumes in the same evening.[1]

A. W. N. Pugin, pp. 1–10, 19–22 from *An Apology for the Revival of Christian Architecture in England*. Oxford: St Barnabus Press, 1968 (originally published 1843). The engraving "Contrasted English Towns, 1840 and 1440" is reproduced from Henry-Russell Hitchcock, *Early Victorian Architecture in Britain*. New York: De Capo Press, 1976.

[1] It is not unusual for architects to send two designs for the same building, of utterly opposed character and style, for the selection of the committee; as if it were possible for more than one principle to be a correct expression of the intended building.

Amid this motley group (oh! miserable degradation!) the venerable form and sacred detail of our national and Catholic architecture may be discerned; but *how* adopted? Not on consistent principle, not on authority, not as the expression of our faith, our government, or country, but as one of the disguises of the day, to be put on and off at pleasure, and used occasionally as circumstances or private caprice may suggest.

It is considered suitable for some purposes, – MELANCHOLY, and *therefore fit for religious* buildings!!! a style that an architect of the day should be acquainted with, in order to please those who admire old things, – a style in which there are many beauties: such is the heartless advocacy which our national architecture frequently receives from its professed admirers; while others are not wanting, even in the most influential positions, who venture to sneer at and insult its principles, either because they are far beyond their comprehension, or that they are so besotted in their mongrel compositions, that they tremble at the ascendancy of truth.

The object of this tract is, therefore, to place Christian architecture in its true position, – to exhibit the claims it possesses on our veneration and obedience, as the only correct expression of the faith, wants, and climate of our country; and if it fails in doing this, it will be rather owing to the incapacity of the author in doing justice to this most important subject, than to any want of truth in the proposition itself.

The arguments used, both by the advocates and opponents of pointed architecture, have been most fallacious. They have consisted, for the most part, in mere private views and opinions relative to comparative abstract beauty in the different styles; and these, as might be expected, have proved most inconclusive.

To advocate Christian architecture merely on the score of its beauty, can never prevail with those, who profess to think that all art and majesty is concentrated in a Grecian temple. We must turn to the principles from which all styles have originated. The history of architecture is the history of the world: as we inspect the edifices of antiquity, its nations, its dynasties, its religions, are all brought before us. The belief and manners of all people are embodied in the edifices they raised; it was impossible for any of them to have built consistently otherwise than they did: each was the inventor and perfecter of their peculiar style; each style was the type of their Religion, customs, and climate. The abstract beauty of these various styles, when viewed with reference to the purposes for which they were raised, is great indeed; they are the perfection of what was intended. [...]

Will the architecture of our times, even supposing it solid enough to last, hand down to posterity any certain clue or guide to the system under which it was erected? Surely not; it is not the expression of existing opinions and circumstances, but a confused jumble of styles and symbols borrowed from all nations and periods.

Are not the adapters of pagan architecture violating every principle, that regulated the men whose works they profess to imitate? These uncompromising advocates of classic styles would be utterly repudiated by the humblest architect of pagan antiquity, were he now to return to earth. Vitruvius would spew if he beheld the works of those who glory in calling him master.

The restorers of Christian architecture are more consistent followers of classic *principles* than all these boasted Greeks; they understand antiquity, and apply the ancient consistent rules to the new dispensation. The moderns, in their pretended imitation of the classic system, are constantly producing the greatest anomalies; and we are called upon to admire their thrice-cooked hashes of pagan fragments (in which the ingredients are amalgamated in utter confusion) as fine national monuments of the present age.

[...]

I can readily understand how the pyramid, the obelisk, the temple, and pagoda have arisen; whence the arrangement of their plan, and the symbols which decorate them have been generated. I am prepared to join in admiration at the skill which piled such gigantic masses on each other, which fashioned so exquisitely each limb and countenance; but I cannot acknowledge them to be appropriate types for the architecture of a Christian country.

If we worshipped Jupiter, or were votaries of Juggernaut, we should raise a temple, or erect a pagoda. If we believed in Mahomet, we should mount the crescent, and raise a mosque. If we burnt our dead, and offered animals to gods, we should use cinerary urns, and carve sacrificial friezes of bulls and goats. If we denied Christ, we should reject his Cross. For all these would be natural consequences: but, in the name of common sense, whilst we profess the creed of Christians, whilst we glory in being Englishmen, let us have an architecture, the arrangement and details of which will alike remind us of our faith and our country, – an architecture whose beauties we may claim as our own, whose symbols have originated in our religion and our customs. Such an architecture is to be found in the works of our great ancestors, whose noble conceptions and mighty works were originated and perfected under a faith and system, for the most part common with our own; for, strange as it may appear, the difference between us and our English forefathers, on examination, will prove slight indeed, compared with those nations, from whom we have been accustomed for the last century to borrow our types, as being the best suited to our present habits.

Before entering into the necessary details in support of this position, it may not be amiss to say a few words on the subject of Christian architecture. It has been frequently objected by the advocates of paganism, that the pointed style, especially Christian, was not developed till several centuries after the crucifixion of our Lord; but this is measuring the ways of God by mere human capacity. How long were the chosen people of God allowed to exist before the erection of the great temple of Jerusalem was permitted? [...]

How could the divine character of Christ's church have been made manifest to future generations, except by passing through an ordeal of poverty and bitter persecution of more than three centuries, and triumphing over the powers of the world and darkness, without human aid! Those were not, indeed, times for the cultivation of material arts; but the foundations of every Christian temple, spire, and pinnacle, were then laid so firmly, that we may build on them till doomsday without fear of sinking or decay. Byzantine, Lombard, Saxon, and Norman, were all various developments of Christian architecture on a cruciform plan with Christian symbols. Pointed architecture was the crowning result of these earlier efforts, which may be considered as the centring on which the great arch was turned.

The change which took place in the sixteenth century was not a matter of mere taste, but a change of soul; it was a great contention between Christian and pagan ideas, in which the latter triumphed, and for the first time *inconsistency* in architectural design was developed. Previous to that period, architectural had always been a correct type of the various systems, in which it was employed; but, from the moment the Christians adopted this fatal mistake, of reviving classic design, the principles of architecture have been plunged into miserable confusion. The gradual development of inconsistent design is exceedingly curious.

At first it was confined to the substitution of a bastard sort of Italian detail to the ancient masses. This is particularly striking in the French buildings erected during the reign of Francis the First, where the high-pitched roofs, lofty turrets and chimney stacks, cresting buttresses, string courses, mullions, and all the natural and consistent features of ancient design, are retained with pagan capitals, friezes, and arabesques. [...] Thus, although the builders of the so-called *renaissance* opened the flood-gates of innovation, they had not lost *natural composition*; they only decorated what they required in an inconsistent manner. [...]

Never, in the annals of architecture, have so many glorious opportunities offered, in a short space of time, for the accomplishment of noble buildings. Within my own recollection, three royal palaces, half the metropolis, churches without number, vast restorations, entire colleges in both universities, galleries, civic buildings, bridges, hospitals, houses, public monuments, in every possible variety; and, with the exception of the New Houses of Parliament, we have not one edifice of the whole number that it is not painful to contemplate as a monument of national art. Every chance has been fairly thrown away, as it offered: of money, there has been an ample supply; for the cost of the various works has been something *enormous*; in all cases sufficient to have produced a good thing, and in many instances far more than was required. Now the cause of all these failures is the same, and may be summed up in three words, *inconsistency of design*. In no one instance has the purpose or destination of the building formed the ground-work of the composition: Grecian or Gothic, Ecclesiastical or Civil, it has been a mere system of *adaptation*. One man has adapted a temple, another a castle, a third an abbey; but temples, castles, and abbeys owed their existence to other wants and systems, foreign to those for which they have been employed, and utter failure is the natural result. Had the various buildings been allowed to tell their own tale, to appear in their natural garb, were it rich or simple, what variety and interest would our architectural monuments present! – but no, public buildings, it was said, could not be Gothic, and therefore must be Grecian, that is, with pediments and porticos. The reasons assigned were, – 1st, That Gothic was so very expensive, which is a positive falsehood; and, 2ndly, That they would not be in character. Now, how an edifice that is to consist of doors, windows, walls, roofs, and chimneys, when consistently treated, and these various features made parts of the design, can be *less in character*, than a building where they are bunglingly concealed and disguised, it is impossible to imagine. Yet this view, so utterly false and absurd, has taken such hold on the minds of the million, that pointed architecture is considered, even at the present time, as out of the question when public offices, law courts, bridges, and similar structures, are in question; and the erection of the Parliament Houses in the national style is by far the greatest advance that has yet been gained in the right direction.

[. . .]

How is it possible for any good results to be achieved with the present principles of architectural education? Can we ever hope to see a Christian architect come forth from the Royal Academy itself, where deadly errors are instilled into the mind of the student, with the very rudiments of instruction? Pagan lectures, pagan designs, pagan casts and models, pagan medals, and, as a reward for proficiency in these matters, a pagan journey! When the mind of a youth is well infused with contempt for every association connected with his religion and country, he is sent forth to measure temples, and, in due time, he returns to form the nucleus of a fresh set of small Doric men, and to infest the country with classical adaptations in Roman cement.

Of a truth, if architectural offices were stopped up, and fused as they serve wasps' nests in the country, we should be freed from a mass of poisonous matter that is still depositing in these places. God grant me the means, and I would soon place architectural studies on such a footing that the glory of these latter days should be even greater than that of the former.

I would also have travelling students, but I would circumscribe their limits [. . .]

Then would they learn that the same perfection of design is to be found in the simplicity of the village steeple, as in the towering central spire, that consistency of architectural proportion has stunted the pillars of the simple nave, and roofed it with massive beams, while it has lifted the shafts of the cathedral to a prodigious height, and vaulted the vast space with stone, – that architectural skill consists in embodying and expressing the structure required, and not in disguising it by borrowed features.

[. . .]

The student of Christian architecture should also imbue his mind with the mysteries of his Faith, the history of the Church, the lives of those glorious Saints and Martyrs that it has produced in all ages, especially those who, by birth or mission, are connected with the remains of ancient piety in this land. He should

213

also be well acquainted with the annals of his country, – its constitutions, laws, privileges, and dignities, – the liturgy and rubrics of the Church, – customs and ceremonies, – topographical antiquities, local peculiarities, and natural resources. The face of the country would be then no longer disfigured by incongruous and eccentric erections, compounds of all styles and countries; but we should have structures whose arrangement and detail would be in accordance with our Faith, customs, and natural traditions. Climate would again regulate forms of covering, and positions of buildings. Local interest would be restored, and English architecture assume a distinct and dignified position in the history of art.

20

Architecture in the Nineteenth Century: Importance of Method

Eugène-Emmanuel Viollet-le-Duc

We must not shrink from recognising the fact that in architecture, shackled as we are by prejudice and traditions, and accustomed to confusion, both ideas and principles are wanting to us. The more our buildings are loaded with details, and the richer they are through the variety of their constituent elements, the more do they betray forgetfulness of great principles and the absence of ideas in the artists who contribute to their erection.

The studios of our architects are full of instructive appliances, books, and drawings, but when called upon to design even the most unimportant edifice, though all material means are in abundance, the artist's intelligence is inert, and refuses to create anything new. His invention languishes under a surfeit of undigested data. Talents, study, and often beautiful execution are conspicuous in many quarters; but rarely an idea, still more rarely the observance of a principle. Our public buildings appear to be bodies destitute of a soul, the relics of a lost civilisation, a language incomprehensible even to those who use it. Is it then to be wondered at if the public remain cold and indifferent in presence of works void of ideas, too often destitute of reason, and which have no other claim to distinction but their cost?

Is the nineteenth century destined to close without possessing an architecture of its own? Will this age, which is so fertile in discoveries, and which displays an energetic vitality, transmit to posterity only imitations or hybrid works, without character, and which it is impossible to class? Is this sterility one of the inevitable consequences of our *social* conditions? Does it result from the influence on the teaching of the art exercised by an effete coterie? and can a coterie, whether it be young or old, acquire such a power in the midst of vital elements? Assuredly not. Why then has not the nineteenth century its architecture? We are building

Eugène-Emmanuel Viollet-le-Duc, "Lecture X: Architecture in the Nineteenth Century: Importance of Method," pp. 446–8, 467–70, 474 from *Lectures on Architecture, 1814–79*, trans. Benjamin Bucknall. London and Ontario: Dover, 1987. Reprinted by permission of Dover Publications.

everywhere, and largely; millions are expended in our cities, and yet we can only point here and there to a true and practical application of the very considerable means at our disposal.

Since the Revolution of the last century we have entered on a transitional phase; we are investigating, searching into the past, and accumulating abundance of materials, while our means and appliances have been increased. What then is wanting to enable us to give an original embodiment and form to so many various elements? Is it not simply method that is lacking? In the arts, as in the sciences, the absence of method, whether we are engaged in investigating or in attempting to apply the knowledge we have acquired, occasions an embarrassment and confusion proportional to the increase of our resources; the abundance becomes an obstruction. Every transitional period however must have a limit; it must tend towards an aim of which we get a glimpse only when, weary of searching through a chaos of ideas and materials brought from every quarter, we set to work to disentangle certain principles from this disorderly mass, – to develop and apply them by the help of a determinate method. This is the work that devolves upon us, and to which we should devote ourselves with uncompromising persistency – struggling against those deleterious elements which are invariably engendered during all transitional periods, just as miasmas exhale from matter in a state of fermentation.

The arts are diseased; architecture is dying in the midst of prosperity, notwithstanding the presence of energetic vital principles; it is dying of excesses and a debilitating régime. The more abundant the stores of our knowledge, the more strength and rectitude of judgment is needed to enable us to make a productive use of them, and the more necessary is it to recur to rigorous principles. The disease from which architectural art suffers dates from a remote period; it has not been developed in a single day; we see it increasing from the sixteenth century to our own times; from the time when, after a very superficial study of the architecture of ancient Rome – certain of whose externals were made objects of imitation – our architects ceased to make the alliance of the form with the requirements and the means of construction the chief consideration. Once out of the way of truth, architecture has been more and more misled into degenerating paths. Endeavouring at the commencement of the century to reproduce the forms of classical antiquity, without taking any trouble to analyse and develop their principles, it has been incessantly hastening to its decay. Then, in the absence of the light which reason alone can furnish, it has endeavoured to connect itself with the Middle Ages and the Renaissance; but still only superficially adopting certain forms without analysing them or recurring to their causes, seeing nothing but the effects, it has become *Neo-Greek, Neo-Roman, Neo-Gothic;* it has sought its inspiration in the caprices of the age of Francis 1., the pompous style of Louis XIV., and the decadence of the seventeenth century; it has become the slave of fashion to such a degree, that in the bosom of the *Académie des Beaux Arts,* – that classic domain, as it is esteemed, – we have seen designs made presenting the most grotesque medley of styles, fashions, epochs, and means of construction, but not suggesting the least symptom of originality. The reason is that originality is impossible apart from truth. Originality results from the direct irradiation of truth on an individual mind; and though the truth be one, the medium which receives has a refraction happily as infinitely varied as humanity itself. So that whatever efforts may have been made in recent times to bring together such a number of styles and influences, and to satisfy all the caprices of the moment, that which strikes us most in all our modern public buildings is their monotony.

There are in architecture – if I may thus express myself – two indispensable modes in which truth must be adhered to. We must be true in respect of the programme, and true in respect of the constructive processes. To be true in respect of the programme is to fulfil exactly, scrupulously, the conditions imposed by the requirements of the case. To be true in respect of the constructive processes is to employ the materials according to their qualities and properties. What are regarded as questions purely belonging to art, symmetry and external form, are only secondary conditions as compared with those dominant principles.

[...]

With the Byzantine architects the column is made the scale, whatever may be otherwise the size of the edifice; the column, with slight variation, preserves certain recognised dimensions, and thus serves as a constant point of comparison, enabling us to appreciate the volume of the structural masses and the importance of the voids. With the mediæval architects of France the only scale admitted is man; all the points of the building have reference to his stature [...] and from this principle necessarily springs the unity of the whole; it has also the advantage of presenting to the eye the real dimensions of the building, since the point of comparison is man himself.

If, while adopting the principle of the human scale, we employ a system of geometrical proportions, as the architects of Antiquity and those of the Middle Ages evidently did, we unite two elements of design which compel us to remain true as regards the expression of dimension, and to establish harmonious relations between all the parts. We have here, therefore, an advance on the system of the Greeks, which had only employed the module and not the invariable scale. Why, then, should we deprive ourselves of this resource which we owe to the genius of the mediæval artists?

In the best periods of Classic art, the ornamentation, which forms an important part of architectural design, was never anything more than the embellishment of the body after the latter had been completely formed. Now, the ancients employed two modes of ornamentation. The one consisted in not contravening the form adopted, but clothing it with a kind of drapery more or less rich: this was the system employed by the Egyptians, among whom the ornamentation, properly so called (statuary excepted) never presented a projecting outline, – a relief, – but contented itself with enveloping the geometric form as would an embroidered stuff, a diapered covering. The other, on the contrary, was, as it were, independent of the architectural form; it was attached or applied to it, modifying

217

by its projections the particular shape of that form. It was then no longer a drapery spread over the form; it consisted of flowers, leaves, ornaments in relief, designs borrowed from the vegetable and animal kingdoms. The Greeks, who derived much from the Egyptians and the Asiatic populations among whom architectural decoration was little more than draping, began by drawing their inspiration from these examples; but their judgment, so correct in matters of art, soon made them feel that this kind of ornamentation, however subordinated to the architectural form, tended to contravene it, and to destroy its character; they therefore soon abandoned this method, and employed sculptured ornamentation only as an accessory *attached* to the form, independent of it, and leaving it apparent in all its purity. And with what exceeding sobriety they used sculptured ornamentation! We observe rows of pearls, of eggs, and of *feuilles-d'eau* running horizontally along some of the members of a cornice; sometimes metal laid on, bas-reliefs enclosed within the rigid lines of the architecture; and when, later on, they designed, – *e.g.* the Corinthian capital, – it was a corbel which they enveloped with stalks of acanthus, angelica, or fennel. This system of *engrafted* ornaments naturally commended itself to the love of display characteristic of the Romans; and they pushed it to excess, in fact to such a degree as to conceal the architectural form beneath the superabundance of foliage, garlands, arabesques, and symbolic decorations. The Byzantine artists made a compromise between the two systems, but with an evident leaning towards the ornamentation which enveloped the form without distorting it. Asiatic influences are profoundly manifest in their works, and still more evidently in what is called Arab Architecture does the principle of draping again obtain. We see it abandoned in France towards the end of the twelfth century. At that time we find sculptured ornamentation attached to the architectural features as if it were nailed on; and it is wholly derived from the local flora. In no case, however, does it contravene the architectural form; on the contrary, it helps to bring it out, – a result obviously attested by an examination of the interior pillars of the Cathedral of Paris. In no architecture, Greek included, is ornamentation added to the form better allied with it; far from distorting it, it lends it a vigorous aid.

The attempt to reconcile the two systems just described, in architectural design, – that is, embroidering the architectural form in one part and attaching ornaments in another, – is a sin against unity; it is rendering the two systems mutually injurious.

"In the last place," says Descartes, "to make every where enumerations so complete and reviews so comprehensive that I may be sure of having omitted nothing." This precept is applicable to studies generally, but still more to the case of architectural design; for it is in the consideration of the programme, of the requirements to be met and of the means supplied that it is desirable to undertake those "so comprehensive reviews." It is not enough to have succeeded in conveniently disposing the services of a public building or a private dwelling; to have succeeded in giving these arrangements the aspect befitting each of them; there must be a connection between the parts: there must be a dominant idea in this assemblage of services; the materials must be judiciously employed, according to the qualities; there must be no excess on the side of strength or slightness; the materials used must indicate their function by the form we give them; stone must appear as stone, iron as iron, wood as wood; and these substances, while assuming forms suitable to their nature, must be in mutual harmony. This was easy for the Romans, when they merely built with rubble-work, with brick and marble facings; it is very difficult for us, who have to make use of materials which possess different and even opposite qualities, and to which must be given the appearance befitting these various qualities. "The so complete enumerations" of what has been done before our time, especially by the mediæval architects, are therefore useful if we would advance and not fall below the works of our predecessors; for, I say once more, it would seem as if those men had a presentiment of the appliances which our age affords. There is in the works of our French mediæval architects of the secular school, at the time of its first development, such complete cohesion, so close a connection between the requirements, the means, and the architectural form; there is such an abundance of resources provided for the solution of the numerous difficulties inherent in the complicated requirements of our civilisation, that nowhere else could we find a precedent more fitted to facilitate the task we have to perform. To attempt in the present day to find in the good architecture of Greek or even Roman antiquity anything more than valuable instruction in a few very simple principles applied with inflexible logic; to attempt to copy, imitate, or even to get ideas from the forms given by the expression of those principles, is gratuitously to involve ourselves in inconsistencies the more glaring as our requirements become more complicated and our resources more extensive. During the seventeenth century, so great was the enthusiasm for Roman architecture that every imaginable inconvenience was put up with for the sake of being Roman. [. . .] it cannot be disputed that there is now more scepticism in reference to art than was the case in the time of Louis the Fourteenth, and that no one among ourselves has sufficient faith in Greek or Roman architecture to induce him to sacrifice to it the least particle of comfort or the most trifling convenience. Of what use then to us are those incessantly copied, and moreover badly copied, Classic forms? What business have we with them? They embarrass us artists; they have not the adaptability demanded by modern requirements; they are very expensive; they have very little interest for the public; they cut the strangest figure amid certain modern arrangements which we are obliged to adopt; they have the disadvantage of perpetually contravening our habits and methods of building. Why then this persistence in retaining them, or rather in so misapplying them? Whom are we trying to please in thus expending immense sums in reproducing forms of which no rational explanation can be given? The public? The public does not appreciate them, and scarcely troubles itself about them. Is it some twenty persons in Paris? This is paying dearly for the pleasure of a few. Is it done from respect for art? But what art? A falsified, distorted art, reduced to the condition of a language that no one understands and that is no longer subject to its own rules. [. . .] Who would

219

be gratified if we were to go and engrave lines from Homer on the walls of a warehouse?

We shall not have an architecture until we thoroughly make up our minds to be consistent, – to appreciate the works of the past at their relative worth, and "make everywhere enumerations so complete and reviews so comprehensive that we may be sure of having omitted nothing;" when we have good and substantial reasons to oppose to the fancies of amateurs; for good sense has always prevailed in the long-run.

[...]

If we want to have an architecture of our own time, let us first provide that the architecture shall be ours, and not seek everywhere else than in the bosom of our own social state for its forms and arrangements. That our architects should be acquainted with the best examples of what has been done before us, and in analogous conditions, is highly desirable, provided they unite with this knowledge a good method and a critical spirit. That they should know how the arts of former times faithfully reflected the social conditions amid which they were developed is also most desirable, provided that this knowledge does not lead to an unconsidered imitation of forms that are often foreign to our usages. But that, under pretext of maintaining such or such a doctrine, or perhaps merely for the sake of not troubling the repose of some twenty individuals, we fail to deduce the practical results from those studies which could be gained by paying regard to principles rather than to forms, is reprehensible. The architect must not only be well informed, but must make use of his knowledge, and must derive something from his own powers; he must determine to ignore the commonplace notions which, with a persistence worthy of a nobler cause, have for nearly two centuries been promulgated respecting architectural art.

21

From *Science, Industry and Art*

Gottfried Semper

Semper designed some of the most magnificent public buildings of the nineteenth century, including the Dresden Opera House, the Polytechnikum in Zurich and the Burgtheatre in Vienna. He was also the author of a number of important writings in which he sought to assess the role of material, purpose and technique in the development of form in the applied arts. [. . .] Semper spent two years in Paris before being invited to London in 1851, where he contributed to the building of the Great Exhibition. This exhibition brought together 7,000 exhibits from thirty different nations and was seen by some six million visitors. It also set a precedent for a series of world fairs which were to have a widespread impact on culture and the arts in the second half of the nineteenth century. Semper's response to this first 'World-Fare', written in German and published the next year, carried the full title, 'Science, Industry and Art: Some Suggestions towards Encouraging the National Feeling for Art'. Semper sought to show not only that scientific progress and the development of new technical means release new architectural and expressive possibilities, but that the very concepts of style and design, traditionally dependent upon a completely different relation between human labour and the materials worked upon, undergo a fundamental revaluation in the industrial age.

Barely four weeks have passed since the close of the exhibition, and some of the items still lie unpacked in the now derelict halls of the Hyde Park building, yet public interest in this 'world-phenomenon' has already passed, rushing forward to other more exciting, and perhaps more immediately topical, events. None of the enthusiastic newspaper correspondents who originally hailed the opening day of this 'World-Fare' as the beginning of a new age now raise their voices any

Gottfried Semper, from *Science, Industry and Art*, pp. 331–6 from Charles Harrison, Paul Wood, and Jason Gaiger (eds.), *Art in Theory 1815–1900: An Anthology of Changing Ideas*, trans. Nicholas Walker. Oxford: Blackwell, 1998. Reprinted by permission of Blackwell Publishing Ltd. Originally published in German as Gottfried Semper, *Wissenschaft, Industrie und Kunst und andere Schriften über Architektur, Kunsthandwerk und Kunstunterricht*, ed. Hans M. Winger. Frankfurt: Florian Kupterberg Verlag, 1966, pp. 27–8, 31–2, 33, 34–8, 40, 41–2.

more. – And yet, the great impression which the exhibition made upon thousands of wondering minds and striving spirits still continues to ferment within them. The full import of this feeling cannot properly be measured.

* * *

We can already perceive that these inventions no longer represent, as they once did, merely means for obviating need and procuring enjoyment; rather, it is need and enjoyment which have now become means for the inventions. The very order of things has been reversed.

But what is the necessary consequence of all this? The present age does not find time to make itself familiar with the benefits which are half thrust upon it and to make itself master of them. [. . .] Machines now sow, knit, engrave, cut and paint, thereby deeply intervening in the realm of human art and exposing every human skill to scorn.

Are not all of these great and splendid achievements? – I do not wish to bemoan the universal situation of which these merely represent some of the minor symptoms, for I am quite certain that this situation will successfully prove, sooner or later, to be the salvation and worthy accomplishment of society in every respect. Nor do I wish here to touch upon all those difficult and important questions which our situation provokes. Rather I shall merely attempt in what follows to point out some of the confusions which this development has now produced in that field of human capacities concerned with the understanding and creation of fine art.

[. . .]

Amongst those concepts which the doctrine of taste has always striven to define, the concept of 'style' continues to play a central role. Of course, this expression also belongs amongst those which have been subject to such variable interpretation that certain doubters would therefore dearly deny it any sound conceptual basis whatsoever. Yet every artist, and every true connoisseur, possesses a genuine feeling of what the term implies, however difficult it might be to express this in words.

If nature, for all her manifold variety, is none the less extremely sparing and simple in her motifs, if she displays a constant renewal of these same forms, subtly and innumerably modified as they are in accordance with the specific levels of development and the different living conditions of her creatures, in some cases appearing developed one way, in others appearing either in a simplified or a more elaborate manner, then something similar is true for the technical arts as well: they too are based upon certain fundamental forms which, conditioned as they are by an original idea, still permit for all their constant repetition an infinite variety which is itself conditioned by other more precisely defining circumstances of one kind or another.

Thus it transpires that certain aspects which appear to be essential in one formal combination, may yet appear in another related one merely as a hint or suggestion; while aspects the original germ or trace of which was hardly perceptible in the first combination may now perhaps emerge more eloquently and more emphatically in the new combination.

This fundamental form, as the simplest expression of the original idea, is particularly subject to specific modification according to the respective materials which are applied in the further development of the form in question, and according to the various instruments used in the process. Finally, there are also a large number of influential circumstances external to the work itself, which represent important contributory factors in its actual production, like, for example, the location, the climate, the particular historical juncture, certain customs and cultural peculiarities, the social status and position of the person for whom the product is destined, and many more such things. In accordance with our preceding discussion, and without too much arbitrariness, one can conveniently divide the doctrine of style into three separate parts.

The doctrine of the fundamental motifs and all the more basic forms derived from them can constitute the first part of the doctrine of style, essentially concerned with the history of art.

There is no doubt that it produces a certain emotional satisfaction in us to encounter a work, however remote the time of its original production may be, in which the fundamental motif suffuses the entire composition like a basic tonality. And in genuine artistic activity it is certainly desirable to experience clarity and freshness in apprehending the product, for this is something which helps to guard against caprice and meaninglessness and even positively encourages inventiveness. The new is thereby related to the old without simply becoming a copy of the latter, and is liberated from dependence upon the more vacuous influences of fashion.

For the sake of clarity I should like to offer an example of the all-pervading influence which such an original form can exert upon the development of the arts.

The mat, and the more elaborately worked, and later printed, carpet which evolved out of it originally constituted various ways of dividing up domestic space, and therefore also represented the fundamental motif of all later forms of wall decoration and many other related branches of industrial design and architecture. Although the techniques involved in these different fields of application may assume the most varied directions, the latter will always display open signs of their common origin in the area of style. Now amongst the ancients – from the Assyrians right up to the Romans – and later amongst the medievals we can actually see that the manner in which the wall-space is divided into fields, along with the nature of the ornamentation, the principle of colouration, even the historical character of the sculpture and painting involved, the glass painting and the floor decoration, in short everything which is connected with it, all of this still remained dependent upon the fundamental motif, either through unconscious traditionalism or through conscious intent.

Fortunately, this historical part of the doctrine of style can still perspicuously be pursued even in our current confusing circumstances. For a complete historical picture, for cultural cross-comparison, and for general reflection alike, one only has to consider the immense wealth of material on show in the London Exhibition, all those works already mentioned which have been produced by peoples at a most basic level of human culture!

However, the second part of the doctrine of style, which ought to teach us how to give a new and different shape to these original motifs by means of our own technical methods and how to treat the raw material itself with our advanced technologies in accordance with principles of style, this remains all the more difficult and obscure. Here I could also offer another example which will reveal the problems attendant upon realizing the basic principles involved in the technical doctrine of style.

The great granite and porphyry monuments of Egypt still exert an enormous emotional power over each and every one of us. What does this magic really consist in? In part it is surely because they represent as it were the neutral ground upon which the harsh, resistant material itself and the softness of the human hand with all its simple tools (like the hammer and chisel) encounter one another and come to a kind of mutual pact. 'Thus far, and no further; this way, and this way alone!' This is what their mute and immemorial language tells us. – The sublime repose and the massiveness displayed by these monuments, the rather angular and levelled sophistication of their characteristic forms, the modesty and reticence with which this awkward material is fashioned, the atmosphere which surrounds them, all these are beautiful expressions of style, ones which now, when we can cut through the hardest stone like bread and cheese, no longer possess the entire necessity that formerly attached to them. How should we treat granite today? It is very difficult to provide a satisfactory answer to this question! The most obvious response is probably to say that we should only employ this material where its characteristic permanence is really required, and attempt to develop appropriate rules for its stylistic treatment from that condition alone. The scant regard actually paid to such considerations in our own time is amply demonstrated by certain extravagances prominently produced by the great manufacturers of granite and porphyry in Sweden and Russia.

The example I have given leads on to a more general question which would itself alone provide more than adequate matter for an entire chapter, if I were permitted to extend the present essay into a book. – Where then will it lead to, this 'devaluation' of the material brought about by mechanical treatment, by the production of surrogate materials, and by so many other new inventions? And the devaluation of labour, the devaluation of the shaping, artistic and creative finish which is caused by the same developments, where will this lead to? I do not refer, of course, to the devaluation of price, but the devaluation of intrinsic significance, of the idea. Has not the arrival of the machine made it quite impossible for us to enjoy the new Houses of Parliament in London? How will the advance of time or science bring order and principle into these still continuing and confusing conditions? How will we be able to prevent this universal devaluation from spreading to the genuinely hand-crafted and traditionally produced works? And how then will we avoid regarding such things as nothing but an expression of affectation, of antiquarian curiosity, of esoteric interest and eccentricity?

Since the technical doctrine of style throws up such difficulties as far as the identification and application of its principles are concerned, we can hardly indeed speak in our own time of the third and important part of the same discipline. By this I mean that part which would discuss the local, historical and personal influences that lie beyond the art work itself but affect the way it is produced, and which would also include the coherence of the art work with other things like aesthetic character and general expression. This is what the rest of this essay will attempt to show.

We have already pointed out the dangers which threaten our own industrial art and art in general on account of the superfluity of means, to retain this expression for the moment. But now we must pose the question: what is the nature of the influence exerted upon industrial art by the speculation which is sustained by the power of capital and largely directed by science? And what will be the ultimate consequences of this new and ever-increasing protectorate?

'If it really recognizes its true advantage, such speculation will seek out and acquire the best forces it can, and will thereby reveal more zeal as the protectress and cultivator of the arts and artists than any Maecenas or any Medici has ever done.'

Yes indeed! But there is a difference between working at the behest of speculation and producing one's own work as a free individual. In the former case one is doubly dependent: a slave to one's employer and to the fashion of the moment which ultimately procures the demand for one's wares. One sacrifices one's individuality, one's very 'birthright' for a dish of lentils. Artists certainly also knew the meaning of self-denial in earlier times, but then they sacrificed their ego only for the greater glory of God.

* * *

The path which all our industry, and all art along with it, is inexorably following is very clear: everything is calculated with an eye to the market and adapted to the latter. Now any commodity designed for the market must permit the greatest possible range of universal application, must not express any other features than those which are permitted by the purpose and the material of the object in question. The ultimate location for which the object is destined remains unknown, and likewise the personal qualities of the individual whose property it will become. The object is therefore not permitted to enjoy any characteristic features or any local colour (in the broadest sense of the expression), but must rather possess the capacity to accommodate itself harmoniously into any and every environment.

* * *

We now have at our disposal an enormous wealth of knowledge, an unparalleled virtuosity in technological matters, an abundance of artistic traditions and universally intelligible images, and an authentic vision of nature, and we certainly must not abandon all of this to more or less semi-barbarian ways in the future. What we have to learn from the peoples of non-European culture is the art of attaining those simple and intelligible melodies of forms and tonal hues instinctively bestowed upon human products in their simplest expressions, something which becomes ever more difficult to accomplish with our advanced technological means. We must therefore observe the simplest products of human handicraft and the history of their subsequent development with the same attentiveness which we pay to nature herself in all her varied manifestations. Some of the examples from the Great Exhibition only revealed the miscalculations which can be produced by otherwise laudable attempts at the immediate imitation of nature in the domain of industrial art, if they are guided neither by quasi-natural instinct nor by a careful study of style. This could clearly be seen from many a childish, rather than genuinely childlike, attempt of this sort.

But while our industrial art continues to advance and economize in such an aimless fashion, it also unconsciously serves to accomplish the noble task of destroying traditional types of design through its own way of treating ornament.

22

The Nature of Gothic

John Ruskin

[handwritten annotations: origins: -Venitian (intermediate between Byz. + Gothic) -Dark ages ▷reproach 5-15 Cent. -notes Assyrians + Egyptians ↓ compared to medieval Christian]

[handwritten annotation: notes Venetian arch. gothic and how it spread from Italy?]

[...] [W]e are now about to enter upon the examination of that school of Venetian architecture which forms an intermediate step between the Byzantine and Gothic forms; but which I find may be conveniently considered in its connexion with the latter style. In order that we may discern the tendency of each step of this change, it will be wise in the outset to endeavour to form some general idea of its final result. We know already what the Byzantine architecture is from which the transition was made, but we ought to know something of the Gothic architecture into which it led. I shall endeavour therefore to give the reader in this chapter an idea, at once broad and definite, of the true nature of *Gothic* architecture, properly so called; not of that of Venice only, but of universal Gothic: for it will be one of the most interesting parts of our subsequent inquiry, to find out how far Venetian architecture reached the universal or perfect type of Gothic, and how far it either fell short of it, or assumed foreign and independent forms. [handwritten: problem: all gothic are slightly dif.]

The principal difficulty in doing this arises from the fact that every building of the Gothic period differs in some important respect from every other; and many include features which, if they occurred in other buildings, would not be considered Gothic at all; so that all we have to reason upon is merely, if I may be allowed so to express it, a greater or less degree of *Gothicness* in each building we examine. And it is this Gothicness, – the character which, according as it is found more or less in a building, makes it more or less Gothic, – of which I want to define the nature [...]

[...] I shall only endeavour to analyze the idea which I suppose already to exist in the reader's mind. We all have some notion, most of us a very determined one, of the meaning of the term Gothic; but I know that many persons have this idea in their minds without being able to define it: that is to say, understanding generally that Westminster Abbey is Gothic, and St. Paul's is not, that Strasburg Cathedral

[handwritten: - we understand gothic, but how do you CLEARLY define it?]

John Ruskin, "The Nature of Gothic," pp. 149–53, 156–60, 163–4, 167–8 from *The Stones of Venice*, vol. 2. London: George Allen, 1905.

is Gothic, and St. Peter's is not, they have, nevertheless, no clear notion of what it is that they recognize in the one or miss in the other, such as would enable them to say how far the work at Westminster or Strasburg is good and pure of its kind; still less to say of any non-descript building, like St. James's Palace or Windsor Castle, how much right Gothic element there is in it, and how much wanting. And I believe this inquiry to be a pleasant and profitable one; and that there will be found something more than usually interesting in tracing out this grey, shadowy, many-pinnacled image of the Gothic spirit within us; and discerning what fellowship there is between it and our Northern hearts.

you can't critique a style without defining it first

[. . .]

some get more fancy than others

[W]e shall find that Gothic architecture has external forms and internal elements. Its elements are certain mental tendencies of the builders, legibly expressed in it; as fancifulness, love of variety, love of richness, and such others. Its external forms are pointed arches, vaulted roofs, etc. And unless both the elements and the forms are there, we have no right to call the style Gothic. It is not enough that it has the Form, if it have not also the power and life. It is not enough that it has the Power, if it have not the form. We must therefore inquire into each of these characters successively; and determine first, what is the Mental Expression, and secondly, what the Material Form of Gothic architecture.

gothic = -elements + -forms

[power v. form] *what are the differences?* *mental expression → power (art)* *v.* *material form → form (fact)*

[. . .]

I believe that the characteristic or moral elements of Gothic are the following, placed in the order of their importance:

POWER : general

1. Savageness.
2. Changefulness.
3. Naturalism.
4. Grotesqueness.
5. Rigidity.
6. Redundance.

these could be argued *≠ not all are necessary*

These characters are here expressed as belonging to the building; as belonging to the builder, they would be expressed thus: – 1. Savageness or Rudeness. 2. Love of Change. 3. Love of Nature. 4. Disturbed Imagination. 5. Obstinacy. 6. Generosity. And I repeat, that the withdrawal of any one, or any two, will not at once destroy the Gothic character of a building, but the removal of a majority of them will.

[. . .] I am not sure when the word "Gothic" was first generically applied to the architecture of the North; but I presume that, whatever the date of its original usage, it was intended to imply reproach, and express the barbaric character of the nations among whom that architecture arose. It never implied that they were

"barbaric nature" -implies force, takeover, control, power

228

literally of Gothic lineage, far less that their architecture had been originally invented by the Goths themselves; but it did imply that they and their buildings together exhibited a degree of sternness and rudeness, which, in contradistinction to the character of Southern and Eastern nations, appeared like a perpetual reflection of the contrast between the Goth and the Roman in their first encounter. And when that fallen Roman, in the utmost impotence of his luxury, and insolence of his guilt, became the model for the imitation of civilized Europe, at the close of the so-called Dark ages, the word Gothic became a term of unmitigated contempt, not unmixed with aversion. From that contempt, by the exertion of the antiquaries and architects of this century, Gothic architecture has been sufficiently vindicated; and perhaps some among us, in our admiration of the magnificent science of its structure, and sacredness of its expression, might desire that the term of ancient reproach should be withdrawn, and some other, of more apparent honourableness, adopted in its place. There is no chance, as there is no need, of such a substitution. As far as the epithet was used scornfully, it was used falsely; but there is no reproach in the word, rightly understood; on the contrary, there is a profound truth, which the instinct of mankind almost unconsciously recognizes. It is true, greatly and deeply true, that the architecture of the North is rude and wild; but it is not true, that, for this reason, we are to condemn it, or despise. Far otherwise: I believe it is in this very character that it deserves our profoundest reverence.

If the savageness of Gothic architecture, merely as an expression of its origin among Northern nations, may be considered, in some sort, a noble character, it possesses a higher nobility still, when considered as an index, not of climate, but of religious principle.

In the 13th and 14th paragraphs of Chapter XXI. of the first volume of this work, it was noticed that the systems of architectural ornament, properly so called, might be divided into three: – 1. Servile ornament, in which the execution or power of the inferior workman is entirely subjected to the intellect of the higher; – 2. Constitutional ornament, in which the executive inferior power is, to a certain point, emancipated and independent, having a will of its own, yet confessing its inferiority and rendering obedience to higher powers; – and 3. Revolutionary ornament, in which no executive inferiority is admitted at all. I must here explain the nature of these divisions at somewhat greater length.

Of Servile ornament, the principal schools are the Greek, Ninevite, and Egyptian; but their servility is of different kinds. The Greek master-workman was far advanced in knowledge and power above the Assyrian or Egyptian. Neither he nor those for whom he worked could endure the appearance of imperfection in anything; and, therefore, what ornament he appointed to be done by those beneath him was composed of mere geometrical forms, – balls, ridges, and perfectly symmetrical foliage, – which could be executed with absolute precision

229

by line and rule, and were as perfect in their way, when completed, as his own figure sculpture. The Assyrian and Egyptian, on the contrary, less cognisant of accurate form in anything, were content to allow their figure sculpture to be executed by inferior workmen, but lowered the method of its treatment to a standard which every workman could reach, and then trained him by discipline so rigid, that there was no chance of his falling beneath the standard appointed. The Greek gave to the lower workman no subject which he could not perfectly execute. The Assyrian gave him subjects which he could only execute imperfectly, but fixed a legal standard for his imperfection. The workman was, in both systems, a slave.[1]

But in the mediæval, or especially Christian, system of ornament, this slavery is done away with altogether; Christianity having recognized, in small things as well as great, the individual value of every soul. But it not only recognizes its value; it confesses its imperfection, in only bestowing dignity upon the acknowledgment of unworthiness. That admission of lost power and fallen nature, which the Greek or Ninevite felt to be intensely painful, and, as far as might be, altogether refused, the Christian makes daily and hourly, contemplating the fact of it without fear, as tending, in the end, to God's greater glory. [...] It is, perhaps, the principal admirableness of the Gothic schools of architecture, that they thus receive the results of the labour of inferior minds; and out of fragments full of imperfection, and betraying that imperfection in every touch, indulgently raise up a stately and unaccusable whole.

But the modern English mind has this much in common with that of the Greek, that it intensely desires, in all things, the utmost completion or perfection compatible with their nature. This is a noble character in the abstract, but becomes ignoble when it causes us to forget the relative dignities of that nature itself, and to prefer the perfectness of the lower nature to the imperfection of the higher [...] Now, in the make and nature of every man, however rude or simple, whom we employ in manual labour, there are some powers for better things: some tardy imagination, torpid capacity of emotion, tottering steps of thought, there are, even at the worst; and in most cases it is all our own fault that they *are* tardy or torpid. But they cannot be strengthened, unless we are content to take them in their feebleness, and unless we prize and honour them in their imperfection above the best and most perfect manual skill. And this is what we have to do with all our labourers; to look for the *thoughtful* part of them, and get that out of them, whatever we lose for it, whatever faults and errors we are obliged to take with it. For the best that is in them cannot manifest itself, but in company with much error. [...]

[1] The third kind of ornament, the Renaissance, is that in which the inferior detail becomes principal, the executor of every minor portion being required to exhibit skill and possess knowledge as great as that which is possessed by the master of the design; and in the endeavour to endow him with this skill and knowledge, his own original power is overwhelmed, and the whole building becomes a wearisome exhibition of well-educated imbecility.

[...] Men were not intended to work with the accuracy of tools, to be precise and perfect in all their actions. If you will have that precision out of them, and make their fingers measure degrees like cog-wheels, and their arms strike curves like compasses, you must unhumanize them. [...] On the other hand, if you will make a man of the working creature, you cannot make a tool.

[...]   ⟶ preach or teach ⟩ understand instead

The great cry that rises from all our manufacturing cities, louder than their furnace blast, is all in very deed for this, – that we manufacture everything there except men; we blanch cotton, and strengthen steel, and refine sugar, and shape pottery; but to brighten, to strengthen, to refine, or to form a single living spirit, never enters into our estimate of advantages. And all the evil to which that cry is urging our myriads can be met only in one way: not by teaching nor preaching, for to teach them is but to show them their misery, and to preach to them, if we do nothing more than preach, is to mock at it. It can be met only by a right understanding, on the part of all classes, of what kinds of labour are good for men, raising them, and making them happy; by a determined sacrifice of such convenience, or beauty, or cheapness as is to be got only by the degradation of the workman; and by equally determined demand for the products and results of healthy and ennobling labour.   * enable them, make them happy

And how, it will be asked, are these products to be recognized, and this demand to be regulated? Easily: by the observance of three broad and simple rules:

1. Never encourage the manufacture of any article not absolutely necessary, in the production of which *Invention* has no share.
2. Never demand an exact finish for its own sake, but only for some practical or noble end.
3. Never encourage imitation or copying of any kind, except for the sake of preserving records of great works.

[...]   all encourage creativity and invention

Never encourage the manufacture of anything not necessary, in the production of which invention has no share.

For instance. Glass beads are utterly unnecessary, and there is no design or thought employed in their manufacture. They are formed by first drawing out the glass into rods; these rods are chopped up into fragments of the size of beads by the human hand, and the fragments are then rounded in the furnace. The men who chop up the rods sit at their work all day, their hands vibrating with a perpetual and exquisitely timed palsy, and the beads dropping beneath their vibration like hail. Neither they, nor the men who draw out the rods or fuse the fragments, have the smallest occasion for the use of any single human faculty; and every young lady, therefore, who buys glass beads is engaged in the slave-trade,

glass beads = not useful + encourages slavery

and in a much more cruel one than that which we have so long been endeavouring to put down.

But glass cups and vessels may become the subjects of exquisite invention; and if in buying these we pay for the invention, that is to say, for the beautiful form, or colour, or engraving, and not for mere finish of execution, we are doing good to humanity.

[...]

I should be led far from the matter in hand, if I were to pursue this interesting subject. Enough, I trust, has been said to show the reader that the rudeness or imperfection which at first rendered the term "Gothic" one of reproach is indeed, when rightly understood, one of the most noble characters of Christian architecture, and not only a noble but an *essential* one. It seems a fantastic paradox, but it is nevertheless a most important truth, that no architecture can be truly noble which is *not* imperfect. And this is easily demonstrable. For since the architect, whom we will suppose capable of doing all in perfection, cannot execute the whole with his own hands, he must either make slaves of his workmen in the old Greek, and present English fashion, and level his work to a slave's capacities, which is to degrade it; or else he must take his workmen as he finds them, and let them show their weaknesses together with their strength, which will involve the Gothic imperfection, but render the whole work as noble as the intellect of the age can make it.

23

The Revival of Architecture

William Morris

[handwritten: origins ~13th - 14th cent. gothic.]

Among cultivated people at present there is a good deal of interest felt or affected in the ornamental arts and their prospects. Since all these arts are dependent on the master-art of architecture almost for their existence, and cannot be in a healthy condition if it is sick, it may be worth while to consider what is the condition of architecture in this country; whether or no we have a living style which can lay claim to a dignity or beauty of its own, or whether our real style is merely a habit of giving certain forms not worth noticing to an all-pervading ugliness and meanness. *[handwritten: → do we have style?]* *[handwritten: vitality ... fashion]*

In the first place, then, it must be admitted on all sides that there has been in this century something like a revival of architecture; the question follows whether that revival indicates a genuine growth of real vitality which is developing into something else, or whether it merely points to a passing wave of fashion which, when passed, will leave nothing enduring behind it. I can think of no better way of attempting a solution of this question than the giving a brief sketch of the history of this revival as far as I have noted it. The revival of the art of architecture in Great Britain may be said to have been a natural consequence of the rise of the romantic school in literature, although it lagged some way behind it, and naturally so, since the art of building has to deal with the prosaic incidents of every day life, and is limited by the material exigencies of its existence. Up to a period long after the death of Shelley and Keats and Scott, architecture could do nothing but produce on the one hand pedantic imitations of classical architecture of the most revolting ugliness, and ridiculous travesties of Gothic buildings, not quite so ugly, but meaner and sillier; and, on the other hand, the utilitarian brick box with a slate lid which the Anglo-Saxon generally in modern times considers as a good sensible house with no nonsense about it. *[handwritten: mocks styles of - arch or their reproductions?]*

William Morris, "The Revival of Architecture," pp. 315–24 from Nikolaus Pevsner, *Some Architectural Writers of the Nineteenth Century.* Oxford: Clarendon Press, 1972.

The first symptoms of change in this respect were brought about by the Anglo-Catholic movement, which must itself be considered as part of the romantic movement in literature, and was supported by many who had no special theological tendencies, as a protest against the historical position and stupid isolation of Protestantism. Under this influence there arose a genuine study of mediaeval architecture, and it was slowly discovered that it was not, as was thought in the days of Scott, a mere accidental jumble of picturesqueness consecrated by ruin and the lapse of time, but a logical and organic style evolved as a matter of necessity from the ancient styles of the classical peoples, and advancing step by step with the changes in the social life of barbarism and feudalism and civilization. Of course it took long to complete this discovery, nor as a matter of fact is it admitted in practice by many of the artists and architects of to-day, though the best of them feel, instinctively perhaps, the influence of the new school of historians, of whom the late John Richard Green and Professor Freeman may be cited as examples, and who have long been familiar with it.

One unfortunate consequence the study of mediaeval art brought with it, owing indeed to the want of the admission of its historical evolution just mentioned. When the architects of this country had learned something about the building and ornament of the Middle Ages, and by dint of sympathetic study had more or less grasped the principles on which the design of that period was founded, they had a glimmer of an idea that those principles belonged to the aesthetics of all art in all countries, and were capable of endless development; they saw dimly that Gothic art had been a living organism, but though they knew that it had perished, and that its place had been taken by something else, they did not know why it had perished, and thought it could be artificially replanted in a society totally different from that which gave birth to it. The result of this half-knowledge led them to believe that they had nothing to do but to design on paper according to the principles the existence of which they had divined in Gothic architecture, and that the buildings so designed, when carried out under their superintendence, would be true examples of the ancient style, made alive by those undying principles of the art. On this assumption it was natural that they should attempt with confidence to remedy the injuries and degradations which the ignorance, brutality, and vulgarity of the post-Gothic periods had brought on those priceless treasures of art and history, the buildings yet left to us from the Middle Ages. Hence arose the fatal practice of 'restoration', which in a period of forty years has done more damage to our ancient buildings than the preceding three centuries of revolutionary violence, sordid greed (utilitarianism so called), and pedantic contempt. This side of the subject I have no space to dwell on further here. I can only say that if my subject could be looked on from no other point of view than the relation of modern architecture to the preservation of these relics of the past, it would be most important to face the facts of the present condition of the art amongst us, lest a mere delusion as to our position should lead us to throw away these treasures which once lost can never be recovered. No doubt, on the other hand, this same half-knowledge gave the new school

234

of architects courage to carry on their work with much spirit, and as a result
we have a considerable number of buildings throughout the country which
do great credit to the learning and talent of their designers, and some of them
even show signs of genius struggling through the difficulties which beset an
architect attempting to produce beauty in the midst of the most degrading
utilitarianism.

In the early period of this Gothic revival the buildings thus produced were
mostly ecclesiastical. The public were easily persuaded that the buildings destined
for the use of the Anglican Church, which was obviously in part a survival from
the Church of the Middle Ages, should be of the style which obtained in the
period to which the greater part of its buildings belonged; and indeed it used to
be customary to use the word 'ecclesiastical' as a synonym for mediaeval architecture. Of course this absurdity was exploded among the architects at a very early
stage of the revival, although it lingered long and perhaps still lingers amongst the
general public. It was soon seen by those who studied the arts of the Middle Ages
that there was no difference in style between the domestic and civil and the
ecclesiastical architecture of that period, and the full appreciation of this fact
marks the second stage in the 'Gothic Revival'.

Then came another advance: those who sympathized with that great period of
the development of the human race, the Middle Ages, especially such of them as
had the gift of the historical sense which may be said to be a special gift of the
nineteenth century, and a kind of compensation for the ugliness which surrounds
our lives at present: these men now began not only to understand that the
mediaeval art was no mere piece of reactionary official ecclesiasticism or the
expression of an extinct theology, but a popular, living, and progressive art –
and that progressive art had died with it; they came to recognize that the art of
the sixteenth and seventeenth centuries drew what vigour and beauty it had from
the impulse of the period that preceded it, and that when that died out about the
middle of the seventeenth century nothing was left but *a caput mortuum* of
inanity and pedantry, which demanded perhaps a period of stern utilitarianism to
form, as it were, the fallow of the arts before the new seed could be sown.

Both as regards art and history this was an important discovery. Undismayed by
their position of isolation from the life of the present, the leaders of this fresh
renaissance set themselves to the stupendous task of taking up the link of historical art where the pedants of the older so-called renaissance had dropped it, and
tried to prove that the mediaeval style was capable of new life and fresh development, and that it could adapt itself to the needs of the nineteenth century. On the
surface this hope of theirs seemed justified by the marvellous elasticity which the
style showed in the period of its real life. Nothing was too great or too little, too
commonplace or too sublime for its inclusive embrace; no change dismayed it, no
violence seriously checked it; in those older days it was a part of the life of man,
the universal, indispensable expression of his joys and sorrows. Could it not be so
again? we thought; had not the fallow of the arts lasted long enough? Were the
rows of square brown brick boxes which Keats and Shelley had to look on, or the

stuccoed villa which enshrined Tennyson's genius, to be the perpetual concomitants of such masters of verbal beauty; was no beauty but the beauty of words to be produced by man in our times; was the intelligence of the age to be for ever so preposterously lop-sided? We could see no reason for it, and accordingly our hope was strong; for though we had learned something of the art and history of the Middle Ages, we had not learned enough. It became the fashion amongst the hopeful artists of the time I am thinking of to say that in order to have beautiful surroundings there was no need to alter any of the conditions and manners of our epoch; that an easy chair, a piano, a steam-engine, a billiard-table, or a hall fit for the meeting of the House of Commons, had nothing essential in them which compelled us to make them ugly, and that if they had existed in the Middle Ages the people of the time would have made them beautiful. Which certainly had an element of truth in it, but was not all the truth. It was indeed true that the mediaeval instinct for beauty would have exercised itself on whatsoever fell to its lot to do, but it was also true that the life of the times did not put into the hands of the workman any object which was merely utilitarian, still less vulgar; whereas the life of modern times forces on him the production of many things which can be nothing but utilitarian, as for instance a steam-engine; and of many things in which vulgarity is innate and inevitable, as a gentleman's club-house or the ceremonial of our modern bureaucratic monarchy. Anyhow, this period of fresh hope and partial insight produced many interesting buildings and other works of art, and afforded a pleasant time indeed to the hopeful but very small minority engaged in it, in spite of all vexations and disappointments. At last one man, who had done more than any one else to make this hopeful time possible, drew a line sternly through these hopes founded on imperfect knowledge. This man was John Ruskin. By a marvellous inspiration of genius (I can call it nothing else) he attained at one leap to a true conception of mediaeval art which years of minute study had not gained for others. In his chapter in *The Stones of Venice*, entitled 'On the Nature of Gothic, and the Function of the Workman therein', he showed us the gulf which lay between us and the Middle Ages. From that time all was changed; ignorance of the spirit of the Middle Ages was henceforth impossible, except to those who wilfully shut their eyes. The aims of the new revival of art grew to be infinitely greater than they had been in those who did not give up all aim, as I fear many did. From that time forth those who could not learn the new knowledge were doomed to become pedants, differing only in the externals of the art they practised or were interested in from the unhistorical big-wigs of the eighteenth century. Yet the essence of what Ruskin then taught us was simple enough, like all great discoveries. It was really nothing more recondite than this, that the art of any epoch must of necessity be the expression of its social life, and that the social life of the Middle Ages allowed the workman freedom of individual expression, which on the other hand our social life forbids him.

I do not say that the change in the Gothic revivalists produced by this discovery was sudden, but it was effective. It has gradually sunk deep into the intelligence of the art and literature of to-day, and has had a great deal to do with the sundering

236

of the highest culture (if one must use that ugly word) into a peculiarly base form of cynicism on the one hand, and into practical and helpful altruism on the other. The course taken by the Gothic revival in architecture, which, as aforesaid, is the outward manifestation of the Romantic school generally, shows decided tokens of the growing consciousness of the essential difference between our society and that of the Middle Ages. When our architects and archaeologists first mastered, as they supposed, the practice and principles of Gothic art, and began the attempt to reintroduce it as a universal style, they came to the conclusion that they were bound to take it up at the period when it hung balanced between completion and the very first beginnings of degradation. The end of the thirteenth and beginning of the fourteenth century was the time they chose as that best fitted for the foundation of the Neo-Gothic style, which they hoped was destined to conquer the world; and in choosing this period on the verge of transition they showed remarkable insight and appreciation of the qualities of the style. It had by that time assimilated to itself whatever it could use of classical art, mingled with the various elements gathered from the barbaric ancient monarchies and the northern tribes, while for itself it had no consciousness of them, nor was in any way trammelled by them; it was flexible to a degree yet undreamed of in any previous style of architecture, and had no difficulties in dealing with any useful purpose, any material or climate; and with all this it was undeniably and frankly beautiful, cumbered by no rudeness, and degraded by no whim. The hand and the mind of man, one would think, can carry loveliness (a loveliness, too, that never cloys) no further than in the architectural works of that period, as for instance in the choir and transepts of Westminster Abbey before it had suffered from degradations of later days, which truly make one stand aghast at the pitch of perversity which men can reach at times. It must be remembered too, in estimating the judgment of the Neo-Gothic architects, that the half-century from 1280 to 1320 was the blossoming-time of architecture all over that part of the world which had held fast to historical continuity; and the East as well as the West produced its loveliest works of ornament and art at that period. This development, moreover, was synchronous with the highest point of the purely mediaeval organization of industry. By that time the Gild-merchants and Lineages of the free towns, which had grown aristocratic, exclusive, and divorced from actual labour, had had to yield to the craft-gilds, democratic bodies of actual workmen, which had now taken the position that they had long striven for, and were the masters of all industry. It was not the monasteries, as we used to be told, which were the hives of the art of the fourteenth century, but the free towns with their crafts organized for battle as well as craftsmanship; not the reactionary but the progressive part of the society of the time.

This central period therefore of the Gothic style, which expressed the full development of the social system of the Middle Ages, was undoubtedly the fittest period to choose for the tree on which to graft the young plant of Neo-Gothic; and at the time of which I am now thinking every architect of promise would have repudiated with scorn the suggestion that he should use any later or impurer style

237

William Morris

London
Paris
Morocco

Protestant
Catholic
Islamic

for the works he had to carry out. Indeed there was a tendency, natural enough, to undervalue the qualities of the later forms of Gothic, a tendency which was often carried to grotesque extremes, and the semi-Gothic survivals of the late sixteenth and the seventeenth centuries were looked on with mere contempt, in theory at least. But as time passed and the revivalists began to recognize, whether they would or no, the impossibility of bridging the gulf between the fourteenth and the nineteenth centuries; as in spite of their brilliant individual successes they found themselves compelled to admit that the Neo-Gothic graft refused to grow in the commercial air of the Victorian era; as they toiled conscientiously and wearily to reconcile the Podsnappery of modern London with the expression of the life of Simon de Montfort and Philip van Artevelde, they discovered that they had pitched their note too high, and must try again, or give up the game altogether. By that time they had thoroughly learned the merits of the later Gothic styles, and even of the style which in England at least (as in literature so in art) had retained some of the beauty and fitness of the palmy days of Gothic amidst the conceits, artificialities, and euphuism of the time of Elizabeth and James the First; nay, they began to overvalue the remains of the inferior styles, not through pedantry, but rather perhaps from sympathy with the course of history, and repulsion from the pessimism which narrows the period of high aspirations and pleasure in life to the standard of our own passing moods. In the main, however, they were moved in this direction by the hope of finding another standpoint for the new and living style which they still hoped to set on foot; the elasticity and adaptability of the style of the fifteenth century, of which every village church in England gives us examples, and the great mass of the work achieved by it, in domestic as well as church architecture, ready to hand for study, as well as the half-conscious feeling of its being nearer to our own times and expressing a gradually-growing complexity of society, captivated the revivalists with a fresh hope. The dream of beauty and romance of the fourteenth century was gone; might not the more work-a-day 'Perpendicular' give us a chance for the housing of Mr. Podsnap's respectability and counting-house, and bosom-of-the-family, and Sunday worship, without too manifest an absurdity?

wanted a
new "style"
of the time
↓
looked to
15th cent.
(england)

WM.

So the architects began on the fifteenth-century forms, and as by this time they had gained more and more knowledge of mediaeval aims and methods, they turned out better and better work; but still the new living style would not come. The Neo-Gothic in the fourteenth-century style was often a fair rendering of its original; the fifteenth-century rendering has been often really good, and not seldom has had an air of originality about it that makes one admire the capacity and delicate taste of its designers; but nothing comes of it; it is all hung in the air, so to say. London has not begun to look like a fifteenth-century city, and no flavour of beauty or even of generous building has begun to make itself felt in the numberless houses built in the suburbs.

gained more
knowledge
style would
not come

Meantime from the fifteenth century we have sunk by a natural process to imitating something later yet, something so much nearer our own time and our own manners and ways of life, that a success might have been expected to come

238

out of this at least. The brick style in vogue in the time of William the Third and Queen Anne is surely not too sublime for general use; even Podsnap might acknowledge a certain amount of kinship with the knee-breeched, cocked-hatted bourgeois of that period; might not the graft of the new style begin to grow now, when we have abandoned the Gothic altogether, and taken to a style that belongs to the period of the workshop and division of labour, a period when all that was left of the craft-gilds was the corruption of them, the mere abuses of the close corporations and companies under whose restrictions of labour the commercial class chafed so sorely, and which they were on the point of sweeping away entirely?

Well, it is true that at first sight the Queen Anne development has seemed to conquer modern taste more or less; but in truth it is only the barest shadow of it which has done so. The turn that some of our vigorous young architects (they were young then) took towards this latest of all domestic styles can be accounted for without quarrelling with their good taste or good sense. In truth, with the best of them it was not the differentia of the Queen Anne style that was the attraction; all that is a mere bundle of preposterous whims; it was the fact that in the style there was yet left some feeling of the Gothic, at least in places or under circumstances where the buildings were remote from the progressive side of the eighteenth century. There I say some of the Gothic feeling was left, joined to forms, such as sash windows, yet possible to be used in our own times. The architects in search of a style might well say:

> We have been driven from ditch to ditch; cannot we yet make a stand? The unapproachable grace and loveliness of the fourteenth century is hull down behind us, the fifteenth-century work is too delicate and too rich for the commonplace of to-day; let us be humble, and begin once more with the style of well-constructed, fairly proportioned brick houses which stand London smoke well, and look snug and comfortable at some village end, or amidst the green trees of a squire's park. Besides, our needs as architects are not great; we don't want to build churches any more; the nobility have their palaces in town and country already (I wish them joy of some of them!); the working man cannot afford to live in anything that an architect could design; moderate-sized rabbit-warrens for rich middle-class men, and small ditto for the hanger-on groups to which we belong, is all we have to think of. Perhaps something of a style might arise amongst us from these lowly beginnings, though indeed we have come down a weary long way from Pugin's *Contrasts*. We agree with him still, but we are driven to admire and imitate some of the very things he cursed, with our enthusiastic approbation.

Well, a goodish many houses of this sort have been built, to the great comfort of the dwellers in them, I am sure; but the new style is so far from getting under way, that while on the other hand the ordinary builder is covering England with abortions which make us regret the brick box and slate lid of fifty years ago, the cultivated classes are rather inclined to return to the severity (that is to say, the unmitigated expensive ugliness) of the last dregs of would-be Palladian, as exemplified in the stone lumps of the Georgian period. Indeed I have not heard that the 'educated middle classes' had any intention of holding a riotous meeting on the adjacent Trafalgar Square to protest against the carrying out of the designs for the new public offices which the Aedileship of Mr. Shaw-Lefevre threatened us with. As to public buildings, Mr. Street's Law Courts are the last attempt we are likely to see of producing anything reasonable or beautiful for that use; the public has resigned itself to any mass of dulness and vulgarity that it may be convenient for a department to impose upon it, probably from a half-conscious impression that at all events it will be good enough for the work (so-called) which will be done in it.

In short we must answer the question with which this paper began by saying that the architectural revival, though not a mere piece of artificial nonsense, is too limited in its scope, too much confined to an educated group, to be a vital growth capable of true development. The important fact in it is that it is founded on the sympathy for history and the art of historical generalization, which, as aforesaid, is a gift of our epoch, but unhappily a gift in which few as yet have a share. Among populations where this gift is absent, not even scattered attempts at beauty in architecture are now possible, and in such places generations may live and die, if society as at present constituted endures, without feeling any craving for beauty in their daily lives; and even under the most favourable circumstances there is no general impulse born out of necessity towards beauty, which impulse alone can produce a universal architectural style, that is to say, a habit of elevating and beautifying the houses, furniture, and other material surroundings of our life.

basically says it can't work for development of new style

pple "don't feel craving" for beauty

All we have that approaches architecture is the result of a quite self-conscious and very laborious eclecticism, and is avowedly imitative of the work of past times, of which we have gained a knowledge far surpassing that of any other period. Meanwhile whatever is done without conscious effort, that is to say the work of the true style of the epoch, is an offence to the sense of beauty and fitness, and is admitted to be so by all men who have any perception of beauty of form. It is no longer passively but actively ugly, since it has added to the dreary utilitarianism of the days of Dr. Johnson a vulgarity which is the special invention of the Victorian era. The genuine style of that era is exemplified in the jerry-built houses of our suburbs, the stuccoed marine-parades of our watering-places, the flaunting corner public-houses of every town in Great Britain, the raw-boned hideousness of the houses that mar the glorious scenery of the Queen's Park at Edinburgh. These form our true Victorian architecture. Such works as Mr. Bodley's excellent new buildings at Magdalen College, Mr. Norman Shaw's elegantly fantastic Queen Anne houses at Chelsea, or Mr. Robson's simple but striking London board-schools, are mere eccentricities with which the public in general has no part or lot.

What we do w/o precedent isn't beautiful? *disagree*

→ seems to be against victorian?

This is stark pessimism, my readers may say. Far from it. The enthusiasm of the Gothic revivalists died out when they were confronted by the fact that they form part of a society which will not and cannot have a living style, because it is an economical necessity for its existence that the ordinary everyday work of its

gothic revival died

population shall be mechanical drudgery; and because it is the harmony of the ordinary everyday work of the population which produces Gothic, that is, living architectural art, and mechanical drudgery cannot be harmonized into art. The hope of our ignorance has passed away, but it has given place to the hope born of fresh knowledge. History taught us the evolution of architecture, it is now teaching us the evolution of society; and it is clear to us, and even to many who refuse to acknowledge it, that the society which is developing out of ours will not need or endure mechanical drudgery as the lot of the general population; that the new society will not be hag-ridden as we are by the necessity for producing ever more and more market-wares for a profit, whether any one needs them or not; that it will produce to live, and not live to produce, as we do. Under such conditions architecture, as a part of the life of people in general, will again become possible, and I believe that when it is possible, it will have a real new birth, and add so much to the pleasure of life that we shall wonder how people were ever able to live without it. Meantime we are waiting for that new development of society, some of us in cowardly inaction, some of us amidst hopeful work towards the change; but at least we are all waiting for what must be the work, not of the leisure and taste of a few scholars, authors, and artists, but of the necessities and aspirations of the workmen throughout the civilized world.

24

Some Recent Designs by Mr. C. F. A. Voysey

It was nearly three years ago that an article on Mr. Voysey's wall-papers appeared in THE STUDIO. Since then his career has been marked, not merely by an increasing advance in the number and beauty of the designs issued, but by a wider recognition of their artistic merits from the general public. At that date Mr. Voysey was well known to artists of all schools, and to the comparative few who take thought for the decoration of their homes; but to the world at large he had yet to be introduced. Now a "Voysey wall-paper" sounds almost as familiar as a "Morris chintz" or a "Liberty silk." The fame which is implied by being raised from a personality to an adjective is somewhat doubtful, although "Wellington" boots and "Gladstone" bags show that at least the intention is honourable. Only lately one saw the report of a law-suit to ascertain if a certain draper of Vienna had a right to use "Wagner" as an adjective for fabrics, and despite the odd association of ideas, the practice is widely established. But the two classes of nomenclature do not run parallel. Gladstone probably did not invent the bag, although the phrase "bag and bag-gage" is traceable to him; Wellington may or may not have been the first to wear high boots, and Wagner, although addicted to large-patterned dressing-gowns, is hardly likely to have designed the material for them. But the Voysey wall-paper, the Morris cretonne, the Walter Crane picture-book, is in each case the veritable handiwork of the man whose name it bears. And if a "Liberty" silk or a "Benson" lamp is not necessarily the actual handiwork of the one after whom it is titled, it is distinctly the result of individual taste and discrimination. But in all these instances the name is conferred by the public as a rough-and-ready way of showing their appreciation. Nobody troubles to trace a design he does not like to any source.

But to consider Mr. Voysey as a designer of wall-papers alone were as foolish as to consider Mr. William Morris not as a poet, stained-glass maker or painter, but merely as a planner of fabrics. Mr. Voysey is an architect first and foremost. Like a few of the younger members of his profession, he is not only attracted by the

"Some Recent Designs by Mr. C. F. A. Voysey," pp. 209–18 from *The Studio 7*. London, 1897.

possibilities of beauty in furniture and other complete, independent objects, but is peculiarly fecund in the invention of patterns. This is shown in his construction (which is the science and essence of good architecture), and in the finest examples of his work his inventiveness is so woven into the result that it cannot be regarded as a mathematical and cold-blooded science.

The knack of producing effective repeating patterns is by no means a common gift; and where it exists the power of distinct invention of new motives is not always present with it. Nine-tenths of the patterns of all periods are more or less ingenious rearrangements of stock motives, which have served a similar purpose ten thousand times, and will go on doing so for thousands more.

Once a designer introduces a new motive, as Mr. Voysey with his birds for instance, any one can do the same. But whereas the first designer drew his inspiration from Nature, and because of the pleasure he derived in adapting certain forms to the unconventional simplicity essential in flat design, achieved a direct success, it does not follow that it was the subject which attracted him that is responsible for the result. A really decorative artist will make an effective pattern out of the most commonplace motives. Some borders to a child's book, *Abroad*, published several years ago by Messrs. Marcus Ward, show great ingenuity. In the limited space Mr. Thomas Crane took the common objects of the café or the restaurant, the tram-tickets, and a hundred other foreign trifles which are just sufficiently unlike their English representatives to attract the attention of visitors, and made of them most effective and novel decorations. We all know the jumbled mass of "appropriate" objects, naturalistically treated, grouped with no regard for scale in the headings of papers devoted to sports and the like. In these you find a rose as big as a fishing basket, a horseshoe the size of a target. How not to make patterns from everyday motives is exemplified on every hand, but how to simplify the forms and arrange them happily in symmetrical lines and masses is not often met with in current products.

Yet every nation of the past has tried its hand at conventional ornament. Chinese, Japanese, Indian, Persian, Egyptian, Greek, Arabian, Italian, German, and French art have all left superb instances of their achievements in pattern. Why, therefore, should not England to-day do the same instead of binding itself always to the canons of dead art, and re-mixing the cosmopolitan motives from the above and other sources? Besides, the originals of the motives conventionalised in the older schools of pattern are, many of them, unknown in their natural forms to the man in the street to-day. Comparatively few people have seen the *lotus* in rank natural growth; laurel crowns are not common features at our athletic contests; harpies, griffins, and supernatural forms that were as real to those who used them as an angel is to the orthodox Christian to-day, now appear to many people merely fatuous contrivances that fail to raise a smile much less inspire us with awe. Others always misunderstand the symbolism of earlier times. I know an estimable and not inartistic person, who always connects wreaths of any sort – laurel, floral, or what not – with funerals and with funerals alone. If we leave the hackneyed motives and go to Nature, who ever goes anew to her may find, as always, plenty of material. Toadstools and fungi, for instance, have, one suspects, never inspired decorators before Mr. Voysey was attracted by their quaint forms; but for you who read, or I who write, it is not incumbent on us to turn immediately to fungi for inspiration, but rather to pick and choose those objects which attract our sympathy on their own merits, not because some one else has chosen them. Dozens of typical flowers and plants have been overlooked hitherto, and others, notably the fuschia, the dielytra, the foxglove, and a host too numerous to mention, have not become hackneyed by use like the sunflower, the rose, and the apple blossom. This advice, threadbare though it be, needs reiterating, especially when an artist with so strong an individual manner as Mr. Voysey is being discussed. For not only do a large army of designers feed entirely upon the fruits of a few, but manufacturers as a rule prefer a modified form of something which has caught the public taste, in preference to entirely new and untried schemes. There is danger lest a school should arise to imitate Mr. Voysey's patterns instead of his method of working, and copy his mannerism directly in place of striking out a style for themselves.

Nothing is easier than to vary a motive in decoration so that it escapes the reproach of being a pirated design, in the sense that a British jury would understand the phrase. Yet all the same every maker of patterns would recognise in a moment the source of its origin, and identify the original that inspired its author. The very beautiful wall-paper (the *Bird and Tulip*), one of Messrs. Essex's new patterns for this season, is probably destined to be the progenitor of a long series of illegitimate descendants. And of these we may predict with safety that not one will surpass, and probably few equal, the original. But even granting that another person takes the vertical lines of the foliage as a background for a diaper of flower-forms whose rich curves tell out all the more superbly by contrast with the stiff, almost angular lines of the leaves; granted even that such a one is as happily planned and as carefully schemed – yet it must needs be but an echo of a very simple and beautiful idea. The really wonderful printing of this design in a varied series of colour-schemes for which Mr. Voysey (in co-operation with Mr. Essex) is responsible, cannot be suggested even by the reproduction. One variety especially, in rich purples and greens, is more lustrous and fine than any wall-paper which we can call to mind for comparison. For certain rooms nothing could be more sumptuous than this "peacock" harmony, and yet, strong and full as it is, it would keep its rightly subordinate place as a background.

Another pattern, *Fairy-land*, is even less adequately represented in black and white, which in this case confuses the detail and disturbs the repose of the pattern as it appears in colour. In this the festoons (which are really flights of birds) impart distinct sense of "style" to the work, and the most rigid purist would hardly object to the introduction of animal life could he but see a room hung with it. In yet another pattern (as yet unpublished) deer and swans are introduced naïvely and simply. Doubtless this would also be equally effective when hung and in a sufficiently large number of repeats to lose the sense of the details in the larger pattern which Mr. Voysey had in mind.

One more repeating design, *The Snake*, dates from an earlier period. In it not only have we a most beautiful arrangement of lines, the subtle curves of the foliage contrasting with the more accentuated flexure of the snake-forms, but a no less exquisite arrangement of colours – one that could hardly be put in words, for descriptions of tints convey very little. It would be almost as easy to describe the flavour of a piquant *entrée*, or the odour of a mixed bouquet of flowers as this harmony of yellow, green and blue.

The design for a fabric with leafless trees, birds, and sprigs of holly, and the very characteristic bird pattern belong to a more severe and still more individual type, which has been distinctly created by Mr. Voysey.

The *Mimosa* pattern, whether intended for cretonne or paper it matters not, is as simple as the *Snake* is complicated. Its forms are apparent at a glance, its colours are just a blue-green for the foliage, and a golden yellow for the blossoms. This pattern was drawn directly from Nature, and in its simplified convention shows clearly power of selecting only those facts which are required for pattern, and ignoring all those which belong to pictures. This one design in its proper colour would afford a text which would be far more striking than any lengthened commentary upon it could be. For if the truth, stated so simply as it is in this design, fails to carry conviction, it is not likely that any didactic exposition of its purpose would be more easily understood.

But lately it was my good fortune to see these and other papers being made at Messrs. Essex's mills, and also to be present when the head of the firm and Mr. Voysey were busily engaged in approving or rejecting the trial proofs of various schemes of colour for the publications of the coming year. Those who think that a good designer has completed his work when he has invented a pleasant pattern, and coloured it fullsize in a single harmony, would be startled did they realise that this finished drawing is but the initial step to the practical working out of the idea. It is just because in these papers Mr. Voysey has followed his design to the factory – has mixed certain groups of colours for the printers to match, and in close co-operation with the maker himself has modified again and again, not merely the first scheme of colour, but a dozen alternative harmonies, that the final product keeps no little of the charm of the first design, although it may depart from it widely in many details. The letter is altered possibly, but the spirit is retained. In theory, the quietly evolved drawing should be finer than the printed fabric – be it paper, or a woven texture; but in practice it is just this unsparing revision and readjustment of the design which makes the resulting product, not a mechanical facsimile of the water-colour, but something far better – a product that is exactly suited for its intended purpose and one in many cases which is infinitely more artistic than would be a literal, and absolutely accurate facsimile of the autograph design, with all its charm of handling and the unequal density of its broken colour.

To prove how absolutely necessary it is for the maker of the design to be in close relation to the maker of the product, no better instance could be adduced than Messrs. Essex's pattern-book. We meet every day with designers who complain that their work has been ruined by its translation to the intended material, and again we hear often manufacturers declare that, but for the alterations they had introduced, the design would have been impossible – or at least impracticable and unsaleable. Face to face with the exigencies of the method itself; hearing at first hand the reports of the craftsmen employed; seeing by actual experiments the need for strengthening this detail, toning down another; and above all facing directly the problem of the applied colour – in dye, pigment, yarn, or whatever form it is used. The academic precedent of water-colour or oils is set aside – and with the real pigments (be they actual dyes or fibres already coloured), the artist can re-build his pattern – not this time as a scheme, but as an accomplished fact.

To show that in laying stress first upon the necessity of the designer going straight to Nature for his themes, and next the practical importance of his working as a close ally of the manufacturer, one is not merely approving Mr. Voysey's method but echoing his own views, it will be as well to quote a few paragraphs from an admirable lecture on "The Aims and Conditions of the Modern Decorator," delivered by Mr. Voysey in Manchester a year ago.

"Taking it for granted," he says, "that the highest position a decorator and designer can take up is that of a leader of public taste, what does this position involve, and how can it be upheld?

"First, we must purify our motives, and seek to discover true principles as far as it is possible. Of course it is clear that if the decorator is to have motives higher than mere making of money, he must needs devote much time and thought to the study of colour, form and texture, and be in close communion with the designer, who, in his turn, should help the decorator on artistic lines. And most important it is to avoid the lazy and contemptible practice of relying upon precedent for justification of what is done.

"The revivalism of the present century, which is so analogous to this reliance on precedent, has done more to stamp out men's artistic common sense and understanding than any movement I know. The unintelligent, unappreciative use of the works of the past, which is the rule, has surrounded us at every turn with deadly dulness, that is dumb alike to the producer and the public. This imitative, revivalistic temper has brought into our midst foreign styles of decoration totally out of harmony with our national character and climate. Also, the cultivation of mechanical accuracy, by close attention to imitation, has so warped the mind and feelings until invention to many is well-nigh impossible. Technically excellent imitations are still unduly applauded, to the exclusion or forgetfulness of the nobler powers of thought and feeling. The decorator must be freed from the mechanism of dull imitation, and be allowed to exercise his God-given faculties, at the same time reverently respecting and gaining inspiration and help from all faithful workers who have gone before him. Not for the sake of being original should men so work, but to fulfil the universal law in the exercise of their best and noblest faculties."

Later on, in the same lecture, we find Mr. Voysey's creed tersely and admirably formulated. "Simplicity in decoration is one of the most essential qualities without which no true richness is possible. *To know where to stop and what not to do is a long way on the road to being a great decorator.*" Surely this last sentence, which I have italicised, deserves to be inscribed in letters of gold in every architect's office, in every designer's studio throughout the world. It is the summing-up of the whole matter, for, as the speaker went on to say: "It is well to pay particular attention to this quality of simplicity. Yet it is more often than not scoffed at. We hear it on the lips in tones of disparagement, and many are afraid of it. For well they may be, as its presence lays bare the true quality of things. Simplicity requires perfection in all its details, while elaboration is easy in comparison with it. Take what art you may, and you will find only-the greatest masters can be simple, or dare to be simple."

Did but space allow, it would be interesting and instructive to quote much more fully from this paper, and from one perhaps still more important because wider in its theme and more analytical in its treatment, a paper on Art, read at Winchester in 1892. As an instance of his power to simplify natural forms to their direct essentials one might refer to some designs for elementary wood carving which, crowded out here, will appear in a future number.

Those who have followed Mr. Voysey's career will know how unswervingly he has kept to his definite programme. In his designs, now elaborate and gorgeous, now severe and almost archaic, he has never coquetted with the passing taste. It is true that not all his work seems equally fascinating at first sight, but it is always well thought out and concerned with definite problems and ultimately convinces; and were it so, it would be a deadly sign, for growth rarely progresses in unvarying degree. In plants as in men, energy lies dormant; at times it may even seem as if it were waning, but these periods are but storing up new vitality when the circumstances favourable to fruition occur again.

Although the designs for furniture which are included here deserve no less study than the designs for repeated patterns, in the nature of things they are likely to influence – directly at all events – a smaller audience. For if few people can afford to have furniture specially designed for them, there are still fewer who, having the means, possess also the taste to put the idea into execution and courage enough to face the result. To have a room furnished differently from those of one's neighbours would seem to be considered an affectation to-day – or at least the worst crime known to "society" – bad form. Otherwise we might find Mr. Voysey's services had been secured, not by a few here and there, but by many an owner of the palaces constantly springing up in London. For the fittings of these, Messrs. Somebody and Co. are usually called in, or else the lady of the house carries out what she is pleased to call her ideas, and the result is too familiar to need description.

But one thing is sure, that Mr. Voysey's furniture does not take kindly to its commercially produced relatives. To introduce one of these refined and individual objects – whether a dainty piece of colour like the painted clock, a simple and useful article like the writing-cabinet, the most refined and charming buffet, or a larger piece like the sideboard or the cottage piano – among modern cabinet work and upholstery is to introduce a discordant element. For "Early English" and Rococo monstrosities protest against such ungainly intruders. Among old-world simple furniture guileless of style it will easily make itself at home, but introduced into a room which is the ideal of the modern fashion paper, it is war to the knife. If you can appreciate the reticence and severity of Mr. Voysey's work, you can no longer tolerate the ordinary commercially designed product. His furniture deserves elaborate and patient study, for its one aim is "proportion, proportion, proportion," and that is a quality most elusive and difficult even to appreciate, much less to achieve.

Even the most sanguine believer in the advance of taste must recognise that the classic restraint which marks Mr. Voysey's furniture could not hope at present to find a fit environment in every house awaiting its reception. But with its plain surfaces of wood, often enough stained green – with oil colour rubbed well in – its simple mouldings, and its decoration (if any) confined to certain structural features – these show elements of a new style, which may possibly be the germ of the coming Revival of Classic Art which those who study the evolution of taste most deeply agree is not far off. If so, in place of copying Greece and Rome, we shall try to make English homes beautiful with the subtle qualities of proportion and the absence of mere ornament that marked the best classic period, and in doing so, may perhaps completely discover that National style which is already beginning to attract recognition from foreign critics. It will be sad if fashion, tempted by novelty, neglects this new English awakening and does not recognise that the centre of artistic energy, in pattern and mass (if not, so far, in picture-making) has shifted, and that England, the pariah of the arts for years past, may, like the Ugly Duckling, become suddenly the cynosure and envy of her former detractors.

25

Style

Louis Sullivan

It would appear to be a law of artistic growth, that the mind, in its effort toward expression, concentrates first upon matters of technical detail, next upon certain abstractions or theories – for the greater part mechanical, and quite plausible as far as they go – and at last upon a gradual relinquishment of these, involving a slow and beautiful blending of all the faculties with the more subtle manifestations of emotion. In other words, such growth evidences at the beginning of its rhythm the objective, and toward maturity, the subjective view.

This order of development, all things considered, is probably the one the most nearly consistent with the tendency of normal faculties. By normal faculties I mean those of average strength and keenness, free from any serious hereditary warp, or morbid bias, and subjected to the ordinary conditions of education.

I shall not in this connection directly consider the law of growth as manifested in the works of the few great masters, and which differs profoundly from the above; for their art in all its potentiality is born with them, and prophesies in earliest childhood the destiny of its great consummation.

But rather, I shall proceed from this basis: that the larger number of the art works of all ages are products of a cultivated mediocrity – mediocrity of the sort that therein technical dexterity aspires to compensate us in a measure for the absence of a motive impulse; cleverness and an oblique mentality usurp the place of an absent psychic life; wherein words are accepted in the stead of things, and things in the stead of meanings – in brief, that phase of culture which may be called the comedy of art.

To the master mind indeed, imbued with the elemental significance of nature's moods, humbled before the future and the past, keenly aware of the present, art and its outworkings are largely tragic.

Louis Sullivan, "Style (1888)," with introduction by Robert Twombly, pp. 45–52 from Robert Twombly (ed.), *Louis Sullivan: The Public Papers.* Chicago: University of Chicago Press, 1988.

Between these extremes there lies a quasi-transitional zone, wherein the concomitant elements that constitute the artistic nature are so varied in their relative energy and fruitfulness, wherein the growth of the faculties proceeds, not as a slow consistent and definite expansion of a pronounced individuality, but rather by a succession and gathering together of substitutious [*sic*] amendments and accidentals, that, to the earnest student uncertain as yet of his status, and unwilling to make the larger sacrifices, there lies within this field the greatest harvest of attainment that can come to his hand.

And such considerations shape this fundamental difference between the great and the little master – that the latter acquires by means of painstaking and industrious re-hypothecation, while the former is driven on to his destination by forces superior to his yea or nay.

While it is true that the little master can never become the great one, yet is his domain large, and it includes all that ingenuity, talent, fine sensibilities and a considerable genius can accomplish.

To the domain of the little master let us therefore direct our attention. As to the great master, no hand may lighten his burden, no power shall make for him the crooked straight, and the rough places plane.

That which we call style, or rather, the word style itself, is as dubious in meaning as is any word in common use. The fact that a word is, and has been for generations, in common use, signifies that it has gathered to itself the multiple experiences of the race, and has become thereby thoroughly vitalized. Now note that the greater number of such experiences are largely independent of words, and the more subtile ones almost absolutely so, and this will suffice to indicate how true it is that one's capacity to interpret the meaning of a word, to perceive its obscure but real significance, is dependent upon the richness of his life experience within the domain of feeling that the word has come to symbolize.

If this is true of a word, how peculiarly true is it of a work of art. How much more essential is it, in turning from the word, style, to contemplate the thing, style, that our experiences be real, our judgment sober, our sympathy humane. And, most of all, how urgent is it, when we seek the meaning, style, in art, in nature, and in the soul, that every faculty be keyed to most delicate and exquisite tension, and our concentration be absolute as in a dream.

Style, in its essence, and amid all its spontaneous manifestations, is as unsearchable as is any other attribute of life. Analysis, however keen, can at best but discourse of its grosser material envelopings, or formulate abstractions concerning its rhythms. Where reasoning fails, however, intuition goes blithely on, and finds the living quality in things common and near to the hand.

Have you thought much on common and simple things? Has it occurred to you how complex, how beautiful and mysterious they really are? Take, as an instance, a cow eating the grass of the field. Where other than in these natural doings may you behold perfectly spontaneous and unequivocal adjustment of means to end? At first glance how commonplace: to the thoughtful view how impressive and awakening an exampler [*sic*] of unattainable style! Who shall portray that simple

250

scene and infuse his work with the poetry which the soul sweetly and perfectly attuned to nature's life perceives therein? Who shall apprehend the soul of the cow and of the grass, who shall, with *naïve* sincerity, express the explicit circumstance that the cow eats the grass?

We are prone to heed too little those things that are near us; we strain our eyes with looking afar off; we are meanwhile unaware that the grass, the rocks, the trees and running waters – that nature's palpitating self, indeed, is at our very feet. Through vanity of intellect we ignore that which is common; and by the same token we are lost to the sense that a poetic infinity resides in these, the commonest of things. No pathos can exceed their pathos, no inspiration can surpass their inspiration; there is not tenderness, not power, not alluring and impelling greatness which is not in them.

Therefore, I counsel you, if you would seek to acquire a style that shall be individual to you, banish from your thought the word style; note closely and keenly the thing style, wherever found; and open your hearts to the essence style at all times and in all places. This is the germ.

The formative process is tedious and burdensome, clear and obscure, joyful and desponding, discouraging and bewildering to the last degree.

To be patient, observing, reflective, industrious and sincere; to possess that fortitude which constrains one to perseverance in spite of adversity, wounded pride, revulsion and disgust, and the secret consciousness that each successive endeavor is but a little less fatuous than its predecessor; to carefully train and nurture the eye, the ear, the hand, the heart, the soul; to work and watch and wait for a long time; these are part of the price which one must pay for a sound style, and the price mounts ever with the aspiration.

Thus do the faculties unfold with time, and the most precious one, that of self-criticism, comes in due season. Lastly comes the saddest of all – the power clearly to discern one's own limitations; for this inevitable warning surely indicates the end of growth, and fixes the permanent status.

The word soul is a symbol or arbitrary sign which stands for the inscrutable impelling force that determinates an organism and its life; it is that mysterious essence which we call our identity; it is that in us which is the most simple though seemingly the most complex; it is that which is born with us and which can undergo no fundamental change. Disregarding the perplexities and dogmas which, by natural inference, may be associated with this symbol, we must not fail or fear, in our search for an intimate understanding of the essence of style, to note that this elemental and abiding quality of identity or soul is inherent in all things whatsoever. Thus: we see the pine-tree – we notice its general shape, we examine its tapering trunk, its mode of branching, its hold upon the soil or the rocks, its branches, branchlets, bark, leaves, flowers, cones, seeds, inner bark, fiber of wood, sap; we reflect that these have all of them something quite in common, and this something impresses us as quality segregating this tree from other tree and other things. To communicate the sum and resultant of these impressions in speech we invent or make use of the word pine, which word expresses a tacit recognition of

251

the peculiar nature or identity of this kind of tree, and, in a general way, as single words go, sums up its style. Pushing our investigation further, we discern that there are several kinds of pine-trees, each with a peculiar and well-defined nature; and it is this collateral definition which establishes for us a clearer perception of the identity of each. Ever unsatisfied, we become aware that one pine-tree is not precisely like another of the same kind; we conceive that it possesses a subtile and permanent charm of personality. Our sentiment is touched; we are drawing near to nature's heart. We love this tree. We watch by it through all its experiences. We are with it by night and by day. We see it respond to the warm caresses of the spring-time sun, and observe with a thrill how it sparkles and drips amid the glories of an April shower. It sways so gently in the passing breeze; it tosses and protests in the grasp of the furious storm. Among its brethren, in the summer forest, it stands so calm, so content; it freely gives its odor to the still air. Within the solitude of winter's sleep it also sleeps, and we too sleep its sleep in sympathy; erect and somber it stands, so motionless under its mantle of snow, so unspeakably calm, so content, so wild. Some day the storm snaps its life. The end is come. Slowly and surely time works decay, and that which was a pine-tree, though vanished, has left its individual trace upon us, never to depart. Through all these changes it was a pine-tree, ever a pine-tree; they but evidenced its inner nature. Such was its identity, such was its little history, of such was its exquisite style.

This is true of a pine-tree. Is it not also essentially true of an oak-tree, of a willow, of a rainstorm, of a river, of a man?

If it is true, as it would appear, that the style of a pine-tree, or any other tree, is the resultant of its identity and its surroundings, is it not equally and especially true that the style of an artist is in its essence and form the resultant of his identity and his experiences?

The style is ever thus the response of the organism to the surroundings. How simple are the surroundings and experiences of a tree. How multiple are the surroundings of a man. When his eyes are opened to them, how complex become his experiences.

How does the man respond to the gentle procreant influence of springtime? As the pine-tree, as the oak, as the lark? Whichever it be, of such is his style. Is he stirred by the gentle and impalpable breezes that come from nowhere and are gone? Surely the pine-tree greets with delicate tremor every slightest impulse of the air. How much more is the man than a tree? how much less?

In reality the first essential condition toward a style is to be born with a subtile identity, the rest goes of itself; for one should bear in mind, and take much comfort in the fact, that there exists, in addition to himself, a very considerable universe.

It is the function of intuition, the eye of identity, the soul, to discern the identity of truth inherent in all things. It is the function of sympathy, the soul of love, to cause one's own identity to blend for the time being with the identity or inner nature of other things. It would be well, therefore, if there were choice in these matters, to be born possessed of the germs of intuition and sympathy; many are.

Many have within them somewhat of the native simplicity of the forest tree. There are not very many, and their portion is not always very great. Yet to him who has this simplicity of soul I say take hope, for to him shall be given. From him who has not this tiny impulse of faith in himself and of confidence in nature, I say from such an one shall be taken even that which he has; for all else that he may acquire is as vanity. Herein lies the difference between the real and the spurious artist; and of such is the obscure origin of art and of style.

In examining a work, for purposes of analysis and criticism, bear ever [*sic*] mind that no amount of dexterity, of learning, of sophistication, of trickery, can successfully conceal the absence, in its author, of sincerity. Learn, also, not only to look at a work, but into it; especially learn not only to look at nature but into it; emphatically strive to look into men. When you have learned to do these things you will live; for it is then that you will see in an art work the identity and spiritual nature of the man who produced it. He cannot escape; nor can you in turn escape. Think not that you may for long conceal your littleness or your largeness behind ink and paper, behind pigments, behind brick and mortar, behind marble, behind anything; for to the relentless eye, searching our identities, the work melts away and the man stands forth; and so it should be.

Did you ever stop to consider that when one produces a work he plainly stamps upon it the legend: This is the work of a fool – of a trickster – of a cynic – of a vacillating and unstable spirit – of a vain and frivolous presumption – of a good heart and weak head – of a conscientious and upright man – of one who loves his fellow men – of a tender and exquisite spirit – of a large and serious nature – of a poet born – of a soul that walks with God?

For if a tree speaks to the attentive ear, if a storm speaks, if the waters speak, so then do all things, animate and inanimate, speak, and their speech is the universal language of the soul.

Take heed, then, lest you trifle, for at best we may but trifle; and thus, if you would really seek a style, search for it not altogether in books, not altogether in history, but search for it rather in the explicit reality of your own inner life and your own outward surroundings.

26

Ornament in Architecture

Louis Sullivan

I take it as self-evident that a building, quite devoid of ornament, may convey a noble and dignified sentiment by virtue of mass and proportion. It is not evident to me that ornament can intrinsically heighten these elemental qualities. Why, then, should we use ornament? Is not a noble and simple dignity sufficient? Why should we ask more?

If I answer the question in entire candor, I should say that it would be greatly for our aesthetic good if we should refrain entirely from the use of ornament for a period of years, in order that our thought might concentrate acutely upon the production of buildings well formed and comely in the nude. We should thus perforce eschew many undesirable things, and learn by contrast how effective it is to think in a natural, vigorous and wholesome way. This step taken, we might safely inquire to what extent a decorative application of ornament would enhance the beauty of our structures – what new charm it would give them.

If we have then become well grounded in pure and simple forms we will reverse them; we will refrain instinctively from vandalism; we will be loath to do aught that may make these forms less pure, less noble. We shall have learned, however, that ornament is mentally a luxury, not a necessary, for we shall have discerned the limitations as well as the great value of unadorned masses. We have in us romanticism, and feel a craving to express it. We feel intuitively that our strong, athletic and simple forms will carry with natural ease the raiment of which we dream, and that our buildings thus clad in a garment of poetic imagery, half hid as it were in choice products of loom and mine, will appeal with redoubled power, like a sonorous melody overlaid with harmonious voices.

I conceive that a true artist will reason substantially in this way; and that, at the culmination of his powers, he may realize this ideal. I believe that architectural ornament brought forth in this spirit is desirable, because beautiful and

Louis Sullivan, "Ornament in Architecture (1892)," pp. 80–5 from Robert Twombly (ed.), *Louis Sullivan: The Public Papers*. Chicago: University of Chicago Press, 1988.

inspiring; that ornament brought forth in any other spirit is lacking in the higher possibilities.

That is to say, a building which is truly a work of art (and I consider none other) is in its nature, essence and physical being an emotional expression. This being so, and I feel deeply that it is so, it must have, almost literally, a life. It follows from this living principle that an ornamented structure should be characterized by this quality, namely, that the same emotional impulse shall flow throughout harmoniously into its varied forms of expression – of which, while the mass-composition is the more profound, the decorative ornamentation is the more intense. Yet must both spring from the same source of feeling.

I am aware that a decorated building, designed upon this principle, will require in its creator a high and sustained emotional tension, an organic singleness of idea and purpose maintained to the last. The completed work will tell of this; and if it be designed with sufficient depth of feeling and simplicity of mind, the more intense the heat in which it was conceived, the more serene and noble will it remain forever as a monument of man's eloquence. It is this quality that characterizes the great monuments of the past. It is this certainly that opens a vista toward the future.

To my thinking, however, the mass-composition and the decorative system of a structure such as I have hinted at should be separable from each other only in theory and for purposes of analytical study. I believe, as I have said, that an excellent and beautiful building may be designed that shall bear no ornament whatever; but I believe just as firmly that a decorated structure, harmoniously conceived, well considered, cannot be stripped of its system of ornament without destroying its individuality.

It has been hitherto somewhat the fashion to speak of ornament, without perhaps too much levity of thought, as a thing to be put on or omitted, as the case might be. I hold to the contrary – that the presence or absence of ornament should, certainly in serious work, be determined at the very beginnings of the design. This is perhaps strenuous insistence, yet I justify and urge it on the ground that creative architecture is an art so fine that its power is manifest in rhythms of great subtlety, as much so indeed as those of musical art, its nearest relative.

If, therefore, our artistic rhythms – a result – are to be significant, our prior meditations – the cause – must be so. It matters then greatly what is the prior inclination of the mind, as much so indeed as it matters what is the inclination of a cannon when the shot is fired.

If we assume that our contemplated building need not be a work of living art, or at least a striving for it, that our civilization does not yet demand such, my plea is useless. I can proceed only on the supposition that our culture has progressed to the stage wherein an imitative or reminiscential art does not wholly satisfy, and that there exists an actual desire for spontaneous expression. I assume, too, that we are to begin, not by shutting our eyes and ears to the unspeakable past, but rather by opening our hearts, in enlightened sympathy and filial regard, to the voice of our times.

Nor do I consider this the place or the time to inquire if after all there is really such a thing as creative art – whether a final analysis does not reveal the great artist, not as creator, but rather as interpreter and prophet. When the time does come that the luxury of this inquiry becomes a momentous necessary, our architecture shall have neared its final development. It will suffice then to say that I conceive a work of fine art to be really this: a made thing, more or less attractive, regarding which the casual observer may see a part, but no observer all, that is in it.

It must be manifest that an ornamental design will be more beautiful if it seems a part of the surface or substance that receives it than if it looks "struck on," so to speak. A little observation will lead one to see that in the former case there exists a peculiar sympathy between the ornament and the structure, which is absent in the latter. Both structure and ornament obviously benefit by this sympathy; each enhancing the value of the other. And this, I take it, is the preparatory basis of what may be called an organic system of ornamentation.

The ornament, as a matter of fact, is applied in the sense of being cut in or cut on, or otherwise done: yet it should appear, when completed, as though by the outworking of some beneficent agency it had come forth from the very substance of the material and was there by the same right that a flower appears amid the leaves of its parent plant.

Here by this method we make a species of contact, and the spirit that animates the mass is free to flow into the ornament – they are no longer two things but one thing.

If now we bring ourselves to close and reflective observation, how evident it becomes that if we wish to insure an actual, a poetic unity, the ornament should appear, not as something receiving the spirit of the structure, but as a thing expressing that spirit by virtue of differential growth.

It follows then, by the logic of growth, that a certain kind of ornament should appear on a certain kind of structure, just as a certain kind of leaf must appear on a certain kind of tree. An elm leaf would not "look well" on a pine-tree – a pine-needle seems more "in keeping." So, an ornament or scheme of organic decoration befitting a structure composed on broad and massive lines would not be in sympathy with a delicate and dainty one. Nor should the ornamental systems of buildings of any various sorts be interchangeable as between these buildings. For buildings should possess an individuality as marked as that which exists among men, making them distinctly separable from each other, however strong the racial or family resemblance may be.

Everyone knows and feels how strongly individual is each man's voice, but few pause to consider that a voice, though of another kind, speaks from every existing building. What is the character of these voices? Are they harsh or smooth, noble or ignoble? Is the speech they utter prose or poetry?

Mere difference in outward form does not constitute individuality. For this a harmonious inner character is necessary; and as we speak of human nature, we may by analogy apply a similar phrase to buildings.

A little study will enable one soon to discern and appreciate the more obvious individualities of buildings; further study, and comparison of impressions, will bring to view forms and qualities that were at first hidden; a deeper analysis will yield a host of new sensations, developed by the discovery of qualities hitherto unsuspected – we have found evidences of the gift of expression, and have felt the significance of it; the mental and emotional gratification caused by these discoveries leads on to deeper and deeper searching, until, in great works, we fully learn that what was obvious was least, and what was hidden, nearly all.

Few works can stand the test of close, business-like analysis – they are soon emptied. But no analysis, however sympathetic, persistent or profound, can exhaust a truly great work of art. For the qualities that make it thus great are not mental only, but psychic, and therefore signify the highest expression and embodiment of individuality.

Now, if this spiritual and emotional quality is a noble attribute when it resides in the mass of a building, it must, when applied to a virile and synthetic scheme of ornamentation, raise this at once from the level of triviality to the heights of dramatic expression.

The possibilities of ornamentation, so considered, are marvelous; and before us open, as a vista, conceptions so rich, so varied, so poetic, so inexhaustible, that the mind pauses in its flight and life indeed seems but a span.

Reflect now the light of this conception full and free upon joint considerations of mass-composition, and how serious, how eloquent, how inspiring is the imagery, how noble the dramatic force that shall make sublime our future architecture.

America is the only land in the whole earth wherein a dream like this may be realized; for here alone tradition is without shackles, and the soul of man free to grow, to mature, to seek its own.

But for this we must turn again to Nature, and hearkening to her melodious voice, learn, as children learn, the accent of its rhythmic cadences. We must view the sunrise with ambition, the twilight wistfully; then, when our eyes have learned to see, we shall know how great is the simplicity of nature, that it brings forth in serenity such endless variation. We shall learn from this to consider man and his ways, to the end that we behold the unfolding of the soul in all its beauty, and know that the fragrance of a living art shall float again in the garden of our world.

27

The Tall Office Building Artistically Considered

Louis Sullivan

The architects of this land and generation are now brought face to face with something new under the sun – namely, that evolution and integration of social conditions, that special grouping of them, that results in a demand for the erection of tall office buildings.

It is not my purpose to discuss the social conditions; I accept them as the fact, and say at once that the design of the tall office building must be recognized and confronted at the outset as a problem to be solved – a vital problem, pressing for a true solution.

Let us state the conditions in the plainest manner. Briefly, they are these: offices are necessary for the transaction of business; the invention and perfection of the high-speed elevators make vertical travel, that was once tedious and painful, now easy and comfortable; development of steel manufacture has shown the way to safe, rigid, economical constructions rising to a great height; continued growth of population in the great cities, consequent congestion of centers and rise in value of ground, stimulate an increase in number of stories; these successfully piled one upon another, react on ground values – and so on, by action and reaction, interaction and inter-reaction. Thus has come about that form of lofty construction called the "modern office building." It has come in answer to a call, for in it a new grouping of social conditions has found a habitation and a name.

Up to this point all in evidence is materialistic, an exhibition of force, of resolution, of brains in the keen sense of the word. It is the joint product of the speculator, the engineer, the builder.

Problem: How shall we impart to this sterile pile, this crude, harsh, brutal agglomeration, this stark, staring exclamation of eternal strife, the graciousness of those higher forms of sensibility and culture that rest on the lower and fiercer passions? How shall we proclaim from the dizzy height of this strange, weird,

Louis Sullivan, "The Tall Office Building Artistically Considered (1896)," pp. 103–13 from Robert Twombly (ed.), *Louis Sullivan: The Public Papers*. Chicago: University of Chicago Press, 1988.

modern housetop the peaceful evangel of sentiment, of beauty, the cult of a higher life?

This is the problem; and we must seek the solution of it in a process analogous to its own evolution – indeed, a continuation of it – namely, by proceeding step by step from general to special aspects, from coarser to finer considerations.

It is my belief that it is of the very essence of every problem that it contains and suggests its own solution. This I believe to be natural law. Let us examine, then, carefully the elements, let us search out this contained suggestion, this essence of the problem.

The practical conditions are, broadly speaking, these:

Wanted – 1st, a story below-ground, containing boilers, engines of various sorts, etc. – in short, the plant for power, heating, lighting, etc. 2nd, a ground floor, so called, devoted to stores, banks, or other establishments requiring large area, ample spacing, ample light, and great freedom of access. 3rd, a second story readily accessible by stairways – this space usually in large subdivisions, with corresponding liberality in structural spacing and expanse of glass and breadth of external openings. 4th, above this an indefinite number of stories of offices piled tier upon tier, one tier just like another tier, one office just like all the other offices – an office being similar to a cell in a honeycomb, merely a compartment, nothing more. 5th, and last, at the top of this pile is placed a space or story that, as related to the life and usefulness of the structure, is purely physiological in its nature – namely, the attic. In this the circulatory system completes itself and makes its grand turn, ascending and descending. The space is filled with tanks, pipes, valves, sheaves, and mechanical etcetera that supplement and complement the force-originating plant hidden below-ground in the cellar. Finally, or at the beginning rather, there must be on the ground floor a main aperture or entrance common to all the occupants or patrons of the building.

This tabulation is, in the main, characteristic of every tall office building in the country. As to the necessary arrangements for light courts, these are not germane to the problem, and as will become soon evident, I trust need not be considered here. These things, and such others as the arrangement of elevators, for example, have to do strictly with the economics of the building, and I assume them to have been fully considered and disposed of to the satisfaction of purely utilitarian and pecuniary demands. Only in rare instances does the plan or floor arrangement of the tall office building take on an aesthetic value, and this usually when the lighting court is external or becomes an internal feature of great importance.

As I am here seeking not for an individual or special solution, but for a true normal type, the attention must be confined to those conditions that, in the main, are constant in all tall office buildings, and every mere incidental and accidental variation eliminated from the consideration, as harmful to the clearness of the main inquiry.

The practical horizontal and vertical division or office unit is naturally based on a room of comfortable area and height, and the size of this standard office room as naturally predetermines the standard structural unit, and, approximately, the

259

size of window openings. In turn, these purely arbitrary units of structure form in an equally natural way the true basis of the artistic development of the exterior. Of course the structural spacings and openings in the first or mercantile story are required to be the largest of all; those in the second or quasi-mercantile story are of a somewhat similar nature. The spacings and openings in the attic are of no importance whatsoever (the windows have no actual value), for light may be taken from the top, and no recognition of a cellular division is necessary in the structural spacing.

Hence it follows inevitably, and in the simplest possible way, that if we follow our natural instincts without thought of books, rules, precedents, or any such educational impedimenta to a spontaneous and "sensible" result, we will in the following manner design the exterior of our tall office building – to wit:

Beginning with the first story, we give this a main entrance that attracts the eye to its location, and the remainder of the story we treat in a more or less liberal, expansive, sumptuous way – a way based exactly on the practical necessities, but expressed with a sentiment of largeness and freedom. The second story we treat in a similar way, but usually with milder pretension. Above this, throughout the indefinite number of typical office tiers, we take our cue from the individual cell, which requires a window with its separating pier, its sill and lintel, and we, without more ado, make them look all alike because they are all alike. This brings us to the attic, which, having no division into office-cells, and no special requirement for lighting, gives us the power to show by means of its broad expanse of wall, and its dominating weight and character, that which is the fact – namely, that the series of office tiers has come definitely to an end.

This may perhaps seem a bald result and a heartless, pessimistic way of stating it, but even so we certainly have advanced a most characteristic stage beyond the imagined sinister building of the speculator-engineer-builder combination. For the hand of the architect is now definitely felt in the decisive position at once taken, and the suggestion of a thoroughly sound, logical, coherent expression of the conditions is becoming apparent.

When I say the hand of the architect, I do not mean necessarily the accomplished and trained architect. I mean only a man with a strong, natural liking for buildings, and a disposition to shape them in what seems to his unaffected nature a direct and simple way. He will probably tread an innocent path from his problem to its solution, and therein he will show an enviable gift of logic. If he have some gift for form in detail, some feeling for form purely and simply as form, some love for that, his result in addition to its simple straightforward naturalness and completeness in general statement, will have something of the charm of sentiment.

However, thus far the results are only partial and tentative at best; relatively true, they are but superficial. We are doubtless right in our instinct but we must seek a fuller justification, a finer sanction, for it.

[...]

I assume now that in the study of our problem we have passed through the various stages of inquiry, as follows: 1st, the social basis of the demand for tall office buildings; 2nd, its literal material satisfaction; 3rd, the elevation of the question from considerations of literal planning, construction, and equipment, to the plane of elementary architecture as a direct outgrowth of sound, sensible building; 4th, the question again elevated from an elementary architecture to the beginnings of true architectural expression, through the addition of a certain quality and quantity of sentiment.

But our building may have all these in a considerable degree and yet be far from that adequate solution of the problem I am attempting to define. We must now heed the imperative voice of emotion.

It demands of us, what is the chief characteristic of the tall office building? And at once we answer, it is lofty. This loftiness is to the artist-nature its thrilling aspect. It is the very open organ-tone in its appeal. It must be in turn the dominant chord in his expression of it, the true excitant of his imagination. It must be tall, every inch of it tall. The force and power of altitude must be in it, the glory and pride of exaltation must be in it. It must be every inch a proud and soaring thing, rising in sheer exultation that from bottom to top it is a unit without a single dissenting line – that it is the new, the unexpected, the eloquent peroration of most bald, most sinister, most forbidding conditions.

The man who designs in this spirit and with the sense of responsibility to the generation he lives in must be no coward, no denier, no bookworm, no dilettante. He must live of his life and for his life in the fullest, most consummate sense. He must realize at once and with the grasp of inspiration that the problem of the tall office building is one of the most stupendous, one of the most magnificent opportunities that the Lord of Nature in His beneficence has ever offered to the proud spirit of man.

That this has not been perceived – indeed, has been flatly denied – is an exhibition of human perversity that must give us pause.

[…]

One more consideration. Let us now lift this question into the region of calm, philosophic observation. Let us seek a comprehensive, a final solution: let the problem indeed dissolve.

Certain critics, and very thoughtful ones, have advanced the theory that the true prototype of the tall office building is the classical column, consisting of base, shaft and capital – the moulded base of the column typical of the lower stories of our building, the plain or fluted shaft suggesting the monotonous, uninterrupted series of office-tiers, and the capital the completing power and luxuriance of the attic.

Other theorizers, assuming a mystical symbolism as a guide, quote the many trinities in nature and art, and the beauty and conclusiveness of such trinity in unity. They aver the beauty of prime numbers, the mysticism of the number three, the beauty of all things that are in three parts – to wit, the day, subdividing into morning, noon, and night; the limbs, the thorax, and the head, constituting the body. So they say, should the building be in three parts vertically, substantially as before, but for different motives.

Others, of purely intellectual temperament, hold that such a design should be in the nature of a logical statement; it should have a beginning, a middle, and an ending, each clearly defined – therefore again a building, as above, in three parts vertically.

Others, seeking their examples and justification in the vegetable kingdom, urge that such a design shall above all things be organic. They quote the suitable flower with its bunch of leaves at the earth, its long graceful stem, carrying the gorgeous single flower. They point to the pine-tree, its massy roots, its lithe, uninterrupted trunk, its tuft of green high in the air. Thus, they say, should be the design of the tall office building: again in three parts vertically.

Others still, more susceptible to the power of a unit than to the grace of a trinity, say that such a design should be struck out at a blow, as though by a blacksmith or by mighty Jove, or should be thought-born, as was Minerva, full grown. They accept the notion of a triple division as permissible and welcome, but non-essential. With them it is a subdivision of their unit: the unit does not come from the alliance of the three; they accept it without murmur, provided the subdivision does not disturb the sense of singleness and repose.

All of these critics and theorists agree, however, positively, unequivocally, in this, that the tall office building should not, must not, be made a field for the display of architectural knowledge in the encyclopædic sense; that too much learning in this instance is fully as dangerous, as obnoxious, as too little learning; that miscellany is abhorrent to their sense; that the sixteen-story building must not consist of sixteen separate, distinct and unrelated buildings piled one upon the other until the top of the pile is reached.

To this latter folly I would not refer were it not the fact that nine out of every ten tall office buildings are designed in precisely this way in effect, not by the ignorant, but by the educated. It would seem indeed, as though the "trained" architect, when facing this problem, were beset at every story, or at most, every third or fourth story, by the hysterical dread lest he be in "bad form"; lest he be not bedecking his building with sufficiency of quotation from this, that, or the other "correct" building in some other land and some other time; lest he be not copious enough in the display of his wares; lest he betray, in short, a lack of resource. To loosen up the touch of this cramped and fidgety hand, to allow the nerves to calm, the brain to cool, to reflect equably, to reason naturally, seems beyond him; he lives, as it were, in a waking nightmare filled with the disjecta membra of architecture. The spectacle is not inspiriting.

As to the former and serious views held by discerning and thoughtful critics, I shall, with however much of regret, dissent from them for the purpose of this demonstration, for I regard them as secondary only, non-essential, and as touching not at all upon the vital spot, upon the quick of the entire matter, upon the true, the immovable philosophy of the architectural art.

This view let me now state, for it brings to the solution of the problem a final, comprehensive formula.

All things in nature have a shape, that is to say, a form, an outward semblance, that tells us what they are, that distinguishes them from ourselves and from each other.

Unfailingly in nature these shapes express the inner life, the native quality, of the animal, tree, bird, fish, that they present to us; they are so characteristic, so recognizable, that we say, simply, it is "natural" it should be so. Yet the moment we peer beneath this surface of things, the moment we look through the tranquil reflection of ourselves and the clouds above us, down into the clear, fluent, unfathomable depth of nature, how startling is the silence of it, how amazing the flow of life, how absorbing the mystery. Unceasingly the essence of things is taking shape in the matter of things, and this unspeakable process we call birth and growth. Awhile the spirit and the matter fade away together, and it is this that we call decadence, death. These two happenings seem jointed and interdependent, blended into one like a bubble and its iridescence, and they seem borne along upon a slowly moving air. This air is wonderful past all understanding.

Yet to the steadfast eye of one standing upon the shore of things, looking chiefly and most lovingly upon that side on which the sun shines and that we feel joyously to be life, the heart is ever gladdened by the beauty, the exquisite spontaneity, with which life seeks and takes on its forms in an accord perfectly responsive to its needs. It seems ever as though the life and the form were absolutely one and inseparable, so adequate is the sense of fulfillment.

Whether it be the sweeping eagle in his flight or the open apple-blossom, the toiling work-horse, the blithe swan, the branching oak, the winding stream at its base, the drifting clouds, over all the coursing sun, form ever follows function, and this is the law. Where function does not change form does not change. The granite rocks, the ever-brooding hills, remain for ages; the lightning lives, comes into shape, and dies in a twinkling.

It is the pervading law of all things organic, and inorganic, of all things physical and metaphysical, of all things human and all things superhuman, of all true manifestations of the head, of the heart, of the soul, that the life is recognizable in its expression, that form ever follows function. This is the law.

Shall we, then, daily violate this law in our art? Are we so decadent, so imbecile, so utterly weak of eyesight, that we cannot perceive this truth so simple, so very simple? Is it indeed a truth so transparent that we see through it but do not see it? Is it really then, a very marvelous thing, or is it rather so commonplace, so everyday, so near a thing to us, that we cannot perceive that the shape, form, outward expression, design or whatever we may choose, of the tall office building should in the very nature of things follow the functions of the building, and that where the function does not change, the form is not to change?

Does this not readily, clearly, and conclusively show that the lower one or two stories will take on a special character suited to the special needs, that the tiers of typical offices, having the same unchanging function, shall continue in the same unchanging form, and that as to the attic, specific and conclusive as it is in its very nature, its function shall equally be so in force, in significance, in continuity, in conclusiveness of outward expression? From this results, naturally, spontaneously, unwittingly, a three-part division, not from any theory, symbol, or fancied logic.

And thus the design of the tall office building takes its place with all other architectural types made when architecture, as has happened once in many years, was a living art. Witness the Greek temple, the Gothic cathedral, the medieval fortress.

And thus, when native instinct and sensibility shall govern the exercise of our beloved art; when the known law, the respected law, shall be that form ever follows function; when our architects shall cease struggling and prattling hand-cuffed and vainglorious in the asylum of a foreign school; when it is truly felt, cheerfully accepted, that this law opens up the airy sunshine of green fields, and gives to us a freedom that the very beauty and sumptuousness of the outworking of the law itself as exhibited in nature will deter any sane, any sensitive man from changing into license, when it becomes evident that we are merely speaking a foreign language with a noticeable American accent, whereas each and every architect in the land might, under the benign influence of this law, express in the simplest, most modest, most natural way that which it is in him to say; that he might really and would surely develop his own characteristic individuality, and that the architectural art with him would certainly become a living form of speech, a natural form of utterance, giving surcease to him and adding treasures small and great to the growing art of his land; when we know and feel that Nature is our friend, not our implacable enemy – that an afternoon in the country, an hour by the sea, a full open view of one single day, through dawn, high noon, and twilight, will suggest to us so much that is rhythmical, deep, and eternal in the vast art of architecture, something so deep, so true, that all the narrow formalities, hard-and-fast rules, and strangling bonds of the schools cannot stifle it in us – then it may be proclaimed that we are on the high-road to a natural and satisfying art, an architecture that will soon become a fine art in the true, the best sense of the word, an art that will live because it will be of the people, for the people, and by the people.

28

Plasticity

Frank Lloyd Wright

Plasticity may be seen in the expressive flesh-covering of the skeleton as contrasted with the articulation of the skeleton itself. If form really 'followed function' – as the Master declared – here was the direct means of expression of the more spiritual idea that form and function are one: the only true means I could see then or can see now to eliminate the separation and complication of cut-and-butt joinery in favour of the expressive flow of continuous surface. Here, by instinct at first – all ideas germinate – a principle entered into building that has since gone on developing. In my work the idea of plasticity may now be seen as the element of continuity.

In architecture, plasticity is only the modern expression of an ancient thought. But the thought taken into structure and throughout human affairs will re-create in a badly 'disjointed', distracted world the entire fabric of human society. This magic word 'plastic' was a word Louis Sullivan himself was fond of using in reference to his idea of ornamentation as distinguished from all other or applied ornament. But now, why not the larger application in the structure of the building itself in this sense?

Why a principle working in the part if not living in the whole?

If form really followed function – it did in a material sense by means of this ideal of plasticity, the spiritual concept of *form and function as one* – why not throw away the implications of post or upright and beam or horizontal entirely? Have no beams or columns piling up as 'joinery'. Nor any 'features' as *fixtures*. No. Have no appliances of any kind at all, such as pilasters, entablatures and cornices. Nor put into the building any fixtures whatsoever as 'fixtures'. Eliminate the separations and separate joints. Classic architecture was all fixation-of-the-fixture. Yes, entirely so. Now why not let walls, ceilings, floors become *seen* as component parts of each other, their surfaces flowing into each other. To get continuity in the whole, eliminating all constructed features just as Louis Sullivan had eliminated

Frank Lloyd Wright, "Plasticity," pp. 132–3 from *An Autobiography*. London: Faber & Faber, 1945.

background in his ornament in favour of an integral sense of the whole. Here the promotion of an idea from the material to the spiritual plane began to have consequences. Conceive now that an entire building might grow up out of conditions as a plant grows up out of soil and yet be free to be itself, to 'live its own life according to Man's Nature'. Dignified as a tree in the midst of nature but a child of the spirit of man.

I now propose an ideal for the architecture of the machine age, for the ideal American building. Let it grow up in that image. The tree.

But I do not mean to suggest the imitation of the tree.

Proceeding, then, step by step from generals to particulars, plasticity as a large means in architecture began to grip me and to work its own will. Fascinated I would watch its sequences, seeing other sequences in those consequences already in evidence: as in the Heurtley, Martin, Heath, Thomas, Tomek, Coonley and dozens of other houses.

The old architecture, so far as its grammar went, for me began, literally, to disappear. As if by magic new architectural effects came to life – effects genuinely new in the whole cycle of architecture owing simply to the working of this spiritual principle. Vistas of inevitable simplicity and ineffable harmonies would open, so beautiful to me that I was not only delighted, but often startled. Yes, sometimes amazed.

I have since concentrated on plasticity as physical continuity, using it as a practical working principle within the very nature of the building itself in the effort to accomplish this great thing called architecture. Every true aesthetic is an implication of nature, so it was inevitable that this aesthetic ideal should be found to enter into the actual building of the building itself as a principle of construction.

But later on I found that in the effort to actually eliminate the post and beam in favour of structural continuity, that is to say, making the two things one thing instead of two separate things, I could get no help at all from regular engineers. By habit, the engineer reduced everything in the field of calculation to the post and the beam resting upon it before he could calculate and tell you where and just how much for either. He had no other data. Walls made one with floors and ceilings, merging together yet reacting upon each other, the engineer had never met. And the engineer has not yet enough scientific formulae to enable him to calculate for continuity. Floor slabs stiffened and extended as cantilevers over centred supports, as a waiter's tray rests upon his upturned fingers, such as I now began to use in order to get planes parallel to the earth to emphasize the third dimension, were new, as I used them, especially in the Imperial Hotel. But the engineer soon mastered the element of continuity in floor slabs, with such formulae as he had. The cantilever thus became a new feature of design in architecture. As used in the Imperial Hotel at Tokio it was the most important of the features of construction that insured the life of that building in the terrific temblor of 1922. So, not only a new aesthetic but proving the aesthetic as scientifically sound, a great new economic 'stability' derived from steel in tension was able now to enter into building construction.

29

The Nature of Materials

Frank Lloyd Wright

From this early ideal of plasticity another concept came. To be consistent in practice, or indeed if as a principle it was to work out in the field at all, I found that plasticity must have a new sense, as well as a science of materials. The greatest of the materials, steel, glass, ferro- or armoured concrete were new. Had they existed in the ancient order we never would have had anything at all like 'classic architecture'.

And it may interest you, as it astonished me, to learn that there was nothing in the literature of the civilized world on the nature of materials in this sense. So I began to study the nature of materials, learning to *see* them. I now learned to see brick as brick, to see wood as wood, and to see concrete or glass or metal. See each for itself and all as themselves. Strange to say, this required greater concentration of imagination. Each material demanded different handling and had possibilities of use peculiar to its own nature. Appropriate designs for one material would not be appropriate at all for another material. At least, not in the light of this spiritual ideal of simplicity as *organic plasticity*. Of course, as I could now see, there could be no organic architecture where the nature of materials was ignored or misunderstood. How could there be? Perfect correlation is the first principle of growth. Integration, or even the very word 'organic' means that nothing is of value except as it is naturally related to the whole in the direction of some living purpose, a true part of entity. My old master had designed for the old materials all alike; brick, stone, wood, iron wrought or iron cast, or plaster – all were grist for his rich imagination and his sentient ornament.

To him all materials were only one material in which to weave the stuff of his dreams. I still remember being ashamed of the delight I took at first in thus seeing – thanks to him too – so plainly around the beloved Master's own practice. But *acting* upon this new train of ideals brought work sharply up against the tool I could find to get the ideas in practical form: the Machine. What were the tools in

Frank Lloyd Wright, "The Nature of Materials," pp. 133–6 from *An Autobiography.* London: Faber & Faber, 1945.

Figure 29.1 "A Fireproof House for $5,000," 1907; architect Frank Lloyd Wright; delineator Marion L. Mahony

Courtesy of Frank Lloyd Wright Archives

Marie Mahony's design for a "Fireproof House" is an example of one of many designs undertaken by Mahony for the architectural firm of Frank Lloyd Wright. The contribution of Mary Lucy Mahony to histories of twentieth-century architecture is often underestimated, overshadowed by her partnership with husband Walter Burley Griffin, also an architect and one-time office manager for Frank Lloyd Wright. It was while Mahony was working as a freelance designer for Wright's office that she developed a distinctly flat Japanese-inspired linearity of style that can be witnessed in her design for the Fireproof House pictured here. Marie Lucy Mahony Griffin, as she was to become in later life, was one of the first women to graduate with a degree in architecture from Massachusetts Institute of Technology, and she was also the first woman licenced to practice architecture in the USA.

use everywhere? Machines – automatic, most of them. Stone- or wood-planers, moulding shapers, various lathes and power saws, all in commercialized organized mills. Sheet-metal breakers, gigantic presses, shears, moulding and stamping machines in the sheet-metal industry, commercialized in 'shops'. Foundries and rolling-mills turned out cast-iron and steel in any imaginable shape. The machine as such had not seemed to interest Louis Sullivan. Perhaps he took it for granted. But what a resource, that rolling or drawing or extruding of metal! And more confusion to the old order, concrete-mixers, form-makers, clay-bakers, casters, glass-makers, all in organized trade unions.

And the unions themselves were all units in a more or less highly commercialized union in which craftsmanship had no place except as survival-for-burial. Standardization had already become an inflexible necessity. Standardization was either the enemy or a friend to the architect. He might choose. But I felt that as he chose be became master and useful or else he became a luxury and eventually a parasite. Although not realized then at all nor yet completely realized by the architect, machine standardization had already taken the life of handicraft in all its expressions. If I was to realize new buildings I should have to have new technique. I should have to so design buildings that they would not only be appropriate to materials but design them so the machine that would *have* to make them could make them surpassingly well. By now, you see, I had really come under the discipline of a great ideal. There is no discipline so severe as the perfect integration of true correlation in any human endeavour. But there is no discipline that yields such rich rewards in work, nor is there any discipline so safe and sure of results. (Why should human relations be excepted?) The straight line, the flat plane were limitations until proved benefits by the Machine. But steel-in-tension was clearly liberation.

After the Winslow house was built in 1893 and Mr. Moore did not want a house so 'different' that he would have to go down the back way to his morning train to avoid being laughed at, our bulkheads of caution blindly serving Yesterday – our bankers – at first refused to loan money on the 'new' houses. Friends had to be found to finance the early buildings. When the plans were presented for estimates, soon, mill-men would look for the name on them, read the name, roll the drawings up again and hand them back to the contractor with the remark that 'they were not hunting for trouble'. Contractors, of course, more often failed to read the plans correctly than not. The plans were necessarily radically different simply because so much nonsense had to be left off the building. Numbers of small men went broke trying to carry out their contracts. This made trouble. Fools would come walking in where angels were afraid to tread. We seemed to have the worst of the contracting element in Oak Park to deal with. Clients usually stood by, excited, often interested beyond their means. So when they moved into the house they had to take their old furniture in with them whether they wanted to or not. This was tragedy because the ideal of an organic simplicity seen as the countenance of perfect integration, abolished all fixtures, rejected all superficial decoration, made all lighting and heating apparatus architectural features of the house and, so far as possible, all furniture was to be designed by the architect as a natural part of the whole building. Hangings, rugs, carpet – all came into the same category. So this particular feature gone wrong often crippled results. Nor was there any planting to be done about the house without co-operation with the architect. This made trouble. No sculpture, no painting unless co-operating with the architect. This made trouble. Decorators hunting a job would visit the owners, learn the name of the architect, lift their hats with exaggerated courtesy and turning on their heels leave with a curt, sarcastic 'Good day', – meaning really what the slang 'Good night!' meant some time ago. And the owners of the houses were all subjected to vulgar curiosity. Often to sincere admiration. But more often they submitted to the ridicule of that middle-of-the-road egoist, the one hundred per cent American provincial.

Each new building was a new experience. A different choice of materials and a different client would mean a different scheme altogether. Concrete was just then coming into use and Unity Temple at Oak Park became the first concrete monolith in the world. That is, the first total building designed for and completed in the wooden forms into which it was poured as concrete. Even plastered houses were then new. Casement windows were nowhere to be seen except in my houses. So many things were new. Nearly everything, in fact, but the law of gravitation and the personal idiosyncrasy of the client.

269

30

Women and Architecture

Lynne Walker

Many women in Britain today are actively involved in a range of activities and positive initiatives related to architecture. They participate in the creation of the built environment through the design process as architects, planners, engineers and designers and contribute to its production as builders, quantity surveyors, construction workers and, most numerously, as consumers of architecture, users of buildings and the spaces around them.

The work of women architects represents the full range of contemporary professional practice and includes the public sector, private practice and housing associations, while feminist architects concentrate on projects which give priority to women's needs. Although architecture remains a male-dominated activity with 2,065 women currently registered as architects to 27,400 men (about 7 per cent), women in professional practice have made major contributions to some of the best-known contemporary buildings: the Open University (Jane Drew, completed 1977); the Joseph shops in West London (Eva Jiricna, 1984 and 1986); Heathrow Airport Terminal 4 (Ann Gibson of Scott, Brownrigg & Turner, 1985); the Manchester Crafts Village (Gillian Brown of the Manchester City Architects Department, 1982); the Thames Barrier (Jean Clapham, GLC Architects Department, 1972–8); and the pedestrianisation of South Molton Street (Iona Gibson, 1977). And there are feminist architects, or, more precisely, women who are architects and feminists and who emphasise 'the primary importance of changing the existing design process so that women are involved in decision-making at every stage',[1] who choose to work with women whose interests are not normally represented in the design process – ethnic minorities, disabled and working-class groups – to provide building types which are intended specifically

Lynne Walker, "Women and Architecture," pp. 90–105 from Judy Attfield and Pat Kirkham (eds.), *A View from the Interior: Feminism, Women and Design*. London: The Women's Press, 1989.

[1] Jos Boys, 'Architecture', in *A Resource Book on Women Working in Design*, ed. Tag Gronberg and Judy Attfield, London Institute, Central School of Art and Design, 1986, p. 11.

to serve these groups' needs – for instance, health centres, nurseries and women's training centres. Feminist cooperatives, such as Matrix and Mitra and the Women's Design Service (WDS), an information and resource centre, work collectively and challenge conventional design philosophy, which they see as overlooking women's interests in the built environment.

Matrix's architecture is grounded in their study of architectural history and their research into women's past role and position in architecture, which they wrote about in *Making Space: Women and the Man-made Environment*, 1984. But they wear this learning lightly, designing low-key, well-planned and comfortable environments, working together with the client group. Often under-resourced, one of Matrix's most recently completed buildings, the Jagonari Women's Educational Resource Centre, designed with the Asian women's group Jagonari, was well-funded by a grant of £600,000 from the GLC and brings to a larger scale the best qualities of their earlier projects and buildings. Conscious of its context, which is next to a listed historic building, and with security a major consideration, this substantial four-storey brick building with a two-storey crèche across the courtyard at the rear was designed 'to have an Asian feel about it but ... to avoid the symbolism of any particular religion'.[2] The dignified and eclectic Whitechapel Road front has a shaped gable, onion-domed flèche and is metal-grilled, for decoration and security, while the carefully planned interior is light and spacious with a reassuring atmosphere of comfort and safety, essential to an Asian women's building in a neighbourhood where racist attacks are commonplace.

With contemporary practice as the starting-point, I want to look back to the late nineteenth and early twentieth centuries at the role and position of women who, as architects and designers of buildings, were active agents in challenging patriarchy, which limited women's activities to the home and unpaid domestic duties. In fact, many of the women who took part in architecture as designers during this period – Harriet Martineau, Agnes and Rhoda Garrett, Ethel and Bessie Charles and Elisabeth Scott – identified themselves with the Women's Movement. The contemporary corollary of this precedent is that women's present under-representation in the design process can only be altered by similar resistance and struggle.

After a brief introduction, I shall first examine the relationship between architecture and patriarchal assumptions about women's role and position in society, from the emergence of the organised Women's Movement around 1850 to the design of the first major public building by a woman in this country, in 1927. Important debates about the nature and value of a woman's role in this period in the context of architecture centred around the campaign for married women's property rights, women's access to professional training and the entry of women into the Royal Institute of British Architects (RIBA). These issues are significant

---

[2] 'Jagonari Women's Educational Resource Centre', Matrix, 1987. Both Matrix and the Women's Design Service produce information publications, which I have relied on heavily.

because they generated overt expressions of cultural assumptions and norms which reveal the socially constructed nature of attitudes to women.

The Amateur Tradition

Before the nineteenth century there were two routes to becoming an architect: through the building trades or through an amateur interest in architecture. From the seventeenth century until the end of the nineteenth century, women worked mainly in the amateur tradition, which until the nineteenth century was associated with the aristocracy and upper classes, without having its later pejorative, feminine connotations.

Although it was exceptional for unmarried women to be apprenticed to the guilds which were allied to building, such as carpentry and masonry, married women in the seventeenth century did sometimes receive their husbands' rights and privileges, and widows of carpenters could take apprentices and have 'practical control'[3] of the business. As in carpentry, in architecture some women also practised in succession to their husbands. After the death of her architect husband Elizabeth Deane (1760–1828), for instance, completed the Naval Dockyards and Works on Haulbowline Island, Cork (1822), efficiently carrying on the family firm, which was joined in 1806 by Thomas Deane, her eldest son, who was 'aided by his mother's great ability'.[4]

However, in the seventeenth and eighteenth centuries architectural design by women was, it seems, exclusively associated with the upper class, which had the time, money and leisure for essentially amateur pursuits. For the sufficiently well-off, architecture was a domestic activity and was therefore appropriate to women, because it could be practised completely within the confines of the family estate, which might provide not only the site but also the building materials and workers. Lady Wilbraham, who designed Weston Park (1671), a country house in Staffordshire, guided by Palladio's *First Book of Architecture*, is an early but typical example of a woman architect working in the amateur tradition.[5]

During the Enlightenment, educated women were taught drawing, mathematics and surveying, which gave them an excellent preparation for architecture. For aristocratic women, the design of buildings was seen as an extension of these approved ladies' accomplishments, which in the eighteenth century were often expressed in shellwork rooms and grottoes done in the company of women

[3] Antonia Fraser, *The Weaker Vessel: Woman's Lot in Seventeenth-Century England*, Methuen, London, 1984, p. 108.

[4] Deane, Sir Thomas Manly, 'Sir Thomas Deane P.R.H.A.', *Cork Historical and Archaeological Society Journal*, 1901, p. 152; in the possession of the Deane family.

[5] Christopher Hussey, 'Weston Park, Staffordshire – I', *Country Life*, 9 November 1945, vol. 98. p. 819.

friends and female members of the family. For instance, in the 1740s the Duchess of Richmond and her daughters devised and executed the decoration of the Goodwood Shell House, which was the result of their serious and expensive avocation.[6]

Upper- and middle-class women in the nineteenth century combined their interest in architecture with a desire to improve the condition of their estate workers. This, in addition to the benevolent end of providing better accommodation, contributed to the consolidation of the position of the landowning classes. George Eliot's Dorothea in *Middlemarch*, who built 'good cottages' for farm labourers to the architect, J. C. Loudon's designs, may have been inspired by Louise, Marchioness of Waterford, artist, friend of Ruskin and founder of the model village of Ford in Northumberland.[7]

This combination of philanthropy and building within the amateur tradition was significant for women architects. Estate improvements, in one instance, led to projects for large-scale public works – an entrance to Hyde Park Corner and a Thames Embankment designed by Elizabeth, Duchess of Rutland.[8] Nevertheless, more typically, women of education and means practised the twin motives of philanthropy and building exclusively in the domestic sphere. After studying architecture while travelling on the continent for ten years, the cousins Jane (d. 1811) and Mary (d. 1841) Parminter built a chapel, school and almshouses in Exmouth for their foundation to promote the conversion of Jews to Christianity. This complex of buildings was joined to a thatched polygonal stone house, A-la-Ronde (1794), by a garden, all designed by the Parminters.[9] In their house, much of the Regency-style furniture and the interior decoration in patterns of shells and feathers was also designed and executed by them in the eighteenth-century mosaic fashion favoured by lady amateurs.

By 1850 the enormous pool of untrained, single women was recognised as a social and economic problem. Suitable employment had to be found that would be appropriate for what were perceived as women's special feminine qualities, which were not to be polluted by the commercial world and, as Anthea Callen has pointed out, would not weaken male dominance or threaten to undermine the patriarchal order of Victorian society.[10] Married women whose position was particularly invidious often also undertook useful but unpaid employment to preserve their respectability as 'ladies'. In the mid-Victorian period, the approval of middle-class women's mission to the poor gave many of them experience beyond the home, and

---

[6] M. Jourdain 'Shellwork and grottoes', *Country Life*, 11 February 1944, vol. 95, pp. 242–3.

[7] Gillian Darley, *Villages of Vision*, Architectural Press, London, 1975, p. 47.

[8] Christopher Hussey, *English Country Houses: Late Georgian 1800–1840*, Country Life, 1958, pp. 122–3.

[9] 'Some points of view we all pursue', n.d., and other archival material, National Monuments Record Office.

[10] Anthea Callen, *Angel in the Studio: Women in the Arts and Crafts Movement 1870–1914*, Astragal Books, London, 1979, p. 22.

architecture, although it remained an exclusively male profession until the 1880s, became an area of acceptable activity for middle-class women if it was combined with philanthropy.[11]

One of the earliest and most prominent campaigners for women's rights in Victorian Britain, Harriet Martineau, designed her own house, with a concern for philanthropy which was typical of the nineteenth century but highly uncharacteristic of most private house-builders in that period. She wrote in her *Autobiography* about her efforts to reform the payment of building workers. She was strongly opposed to 'the pernicious custom of the district to give very long credit, even in the case of workmen's wages', and one of her intentions in building her own house 'was to discountenance this and to break through the custom in my own person'.[12]

The other building type which, with domestic architecture, was thought appropriate for women to design was a church or chapel, especially if built as a memorial to a family member. This activity reinforced the idea of women's supposedly superior moral and spiritual nature; their traditional caring role could be expressed in the design of memorial churches and these, like most domestic architecture designed by women before the end of the nineteenth century, were first and foremost monuments to the family. They were for the family's use, designed as an unpaid private pursuit, thought to be comfortably within the domestic sphere, but they nevertheless gave women opportunities to design buildings and established precedents for participation in professional practice. Sara Losh, for example, designed the highly individual and imaginative St Mary at Wrey, in the Lake District, as a memorial to her sister, Katherine (consecrated in 1842).[13] Like the eighteenth-century Parminters, her travels on the continent led her to an appreciation of architecture (in her case, early German and Italian Romanesque), which she treated in a completely personal way, untrammelled by architectural fashion.

The memorial motive and benevolence were combined by Mary Watts in the Mortuary Chapel which she designed for the remains of her husband, the painter G. F. Watts, and executed with her class of the Compton Home Arts and Industries Association, which she had established for the improvement of local young men and women. This provided meaningful, paid employment in the craft-based terra cotta industry. The Watts Chapel was a focus of Arts and Crafts philanthropy and design, and, as Mary Watts described in her book *The Word in the Pattern*, the local villagers joined her in the construction and decoration of

[11] See, for example, 'Employment for educated women', *Builder*, 30 November 1861; ibid., 2 November 1883, vol. 44, p. 622; Lynne Walker, ed., *Women Architects: Their Work*, Sorella Press, London, 1984, especially pp. 19 and 37.

[12] Harriet, Martineau *Autobiography*, vol. 2, Virago, London, 1983, p. 231 (originally published 1877).

[13] M. A. Wood, 'Memorial to two sisters: Sara Losh's church of St Mary, Wrey', *Country Life*, 4 November 1971, vol. 150, pp. 1230–1.

this Chapel of Rest, which she had planned in a complex symbolic system. The round-headed Norman doorway, for example, 'is decorated with a terra-cotta choir of *Art nouveau* heads of angels – not cast from a single mould but each a labour of love of a single villager following, to the best of his or her ability, models provided by Mary Watts.'[14]

In addition to architectural design, the philanthropic motive led many Victorian women, such as Angela Burdett-Coutts, Adeline Cooper, Octavia Hill and Henrietta Barnett, to formulate policies and housing experiments which prepared the way for the involvement of professional women architects in the public sector in Britain in the twentieth century.[15] Also under the philanthropic umbrella, many impoverished middle-class women found employment relating to architecture by tracing plans and writing specifications. The tasks assigned to women in architects' offices in the second half of the nineteenth century represent the aspirations of women for personal and financial independence through architecture, but they also stand for the limitations of their role and position both in society and in the profession. The copying of architectural plans by tracing, for example, was an essential element of Victorian architectural practice, but it was the least prestigious and most boring job for the most junior member of the firm. It was demanding and required the attention to detail and the neat, repetitive work which were seen as a natural extension of those feminine qualities which were so apt for women's domestic activities, most notably embroidery. Even when women joined together as they did in the Ladies Tracing Society, their marginal position was exploited, since, as a delighted Halsey Ricardo reported to a client, they worked 'at a very cheap rate'.[16]

Women as a source of cheap, often occasional or part-time labour whose presence is a threat as well as an assistance to the male workforce is a theme which recurs in architecture, as in other professions and trades, throughout the nineteenth and twentieth centuries. But in the 1850s and 1860s the liberal reformers of the Women's Movement, led by Barbara Leigh Smith, an artist and founder of a Cambridge college, who set up the Association for the Promotion of the Employment of Women, were more concerned with women's access to paid work in an expanding free market than with the implications of the capitalist system for employed working-class women.[17]

The debates about women's involvement in architecture often centred on their physical limitations. Yet the participation in the building industry of thousands of

[14] W. S. Blunt, 'Guide to the Watts Gallery', n. d. Mary Watts detailed the symbolism of her work in *The Word in the Pattern: A Key to the Symbols on the chapel at Compton*, W. H. Ward & Co., London, n.d. (1905?).

[15] Gillian Darley, 'Women in the public sector', in Walker, op. cit., pp. 37–40. See also Lynn F. Pearson, *The Architectural and Social History of Cooperative Living*, Macmillan, London, 1988.

[16] Letter from Halsey Ricardo to a client, 1883, British Architectural Library.

[17] Barbara Taylor, *Eve and the New Jerusalem: Socialism and Feminism in Nineteenth-Century England*, Virago, London, 1983, p. 279.

working-class women in the much more physically demanding work of nail- and brick-making was not seen as problematic or threatening to women's role, because this, in the context of architecture, was defined in middle-class or upper-middle-class terms. The class bias of the nineteenth-century debates ignored the plight of working-class women in the building industry and produced a myopic view of women's capabilities and their potential as architects, blocking women from full participation in the profession, limiting them to decorative or auxiliary tasks.

In the second half of the nineteenth century the continuum of feminist concerns which included the employment of middle-class women also covered women's education, their entry into the professions and the campaign for married women's rights and female suffrage. Of crucial importance from the mid-century was the commitment of English feminists to reform the married women's property law. Inspired by Harriet Taylor's 1851 article on the first women's rights convention in the United States, a nationwide committee was organised and their work culminated in the Married Women's Property Acts, which went through Parliament in diluted form in 1870 and in the full and final version in 1882. Before this date, under common law married women's property, earnings and inheritances belonged to their husbands. As the distinguished jurist Sir William Blackstone explained: 'By marriage the very being or legal existence of women is suspended, or at least incorporated or consolidated into that of her husband.'[18]. This 'virtual slavery',[19] which denied full rights and status to women, was the linchpin of patriarchy and the iron fist in the velvet glove of the doctrine of separate spheres that designated a woman's place as in the home rather than in the commercial world, where she could compete with men for jobs and income.

Architecture, unlike painting, sculpture or the decorative arts, was more clearly a 'profession', practised in offices, often organised by partnerships and in firms, with legal obligations to apprentices, clients and builders through legally binding contracts and under the control of local government boards and bylaws. Architects were sued, often in connection with these contracts, and were bound by local ordinances. Since, under common law, married women were not allowed to make contracts or be sued in their own right, they were thereby precluded from many of the professional responsibilities of architecture. These legal restrictions reinforced and heightened the set of underlying negative assumptions about women's role and value that supporters of the reform of the property laws had organised to oppose. As long as women were the virtual property of their husbands, they did not, and could not, act in a professional capacity as the

---

[18] Quoted by Lee Holcombe, in *Wives & Property: Reform of the Married Women's Property Law in Nineteenth-Century England*, Martin Robertson, Oxford, 1983, p. 25. Before 1882, married women could go to law to obtain their property rights in Equity, but it was an expensive process, thus limiting it to the wealthy. Transactions afterwards were through a trustee, making dealings protracted and cumbersome.

[19] Eliza Lynn Linton, quoted ibid., p. 18.

designers of property – property cannot design property. The removal of the legal, ideological and psychological impedimenta by the Married Women's Property Acts, therefore, had great significance for all women, and it had particular importance for the entry of women into the architectural profession.

In the early 1890s leading architects, such as Norman Shaw and W. R. Lethaby, argued that architecture was an art, not a business or profession, and indeed, between the census of 1887 and that of 1891, the classification and status of the architect altered from 'Industrial Class' in 1881 to 'Professional Class' under 'Artist' in 1891. The implication for women of these new perceptions was that if architecture was an art, and art was an area appropriate for women's participation, then architecture was also a suitable activity for women.

The question remained, however, whether women should be allowed full participation in the profession on an equal footing with men or be restricted to those aspects of practice which were seen as expressions of their femininity. Here male supporters from within the ranks of architects, E. W. Godwin, C. H. Townsend and R. Weir Schultz, often did as much harm as good. For example, the Arts and Crafts architect C. H. Townsend's view was superficially sympathetic but exasperatingly double-edged. Citing the divided skirt and the precedent of women decorators who 'have been known to work for days on scaffolds' to counter the often quoted "difficulty women would experience as regards the inspection of buildings and the necessary mounting of scaffolding", Townsend concluded quite illogically that 'women's work in an architect's office should be "drawing board work", such as ornamental and other detail drawings, competition sets of plans, schemes of colour decoration, and perspective drawings'.[20]

The extension of the ladies' accomplishment of sketching to architectural drafting was part of a process that was gradualist to the point of being counterproductive. Male gatekeepers allowed women out of their domestic sphere and into architects' offices with the ultimate possibility of becoming architects, but it was felt by C. H. Townsend and others that their femininity created problems from which they had to be protected. In fact, this chivalrous view, which dominated thinking about women's role in architecture in this period, circumscribed their architectural activities and blocked them from becoming designers, the most prestigious role in architectural practice. As women's presence would threaten propriety, the dreaded 'commingling of the sexes' could only be avoided by a system of architectural apartheid which physically separated women from men in their own room, and reduced their status and therefore their threat to the established order. In a separate ' "women-clerks" room' she could be set to work as 'a "draughtswoman" ' which was, Townsend wrote, 'an occupation ... requiring neatness and delicacy of touch, attention to detail, patience and care, [and] is one which would seem at first blush more likely to find its proficients among women than men.' This patriarchal view saw these characteristics as

---

[20] C. H. Townsend, 'Women as Architects', *British Architect*, 31 December 1886, vol. 26, p. viii.

springing from women's femininity and fitting them most naturally and comfortably on to the lower rungs of the architectural ladder.

Today, when women have become professional architects, a similar pattern of discrimination, implemented through the mechanism of sexual division of labour, remains, according to a recent RIBA survey, which showed that women architects can expect to hold fewer positions of power and influence in architectural practices and that they are more likely to earn less than men throughout their careers.[21]

In addition to the more mundane office jobs, the other area to which women were assigned in the late nineteenth century was design for the decorative arts associated with architecture. In *Women and Work*, edited by one of the founding mothers of the Women's Movement, Emily Faithfull, E. W. Godwin argued convincingly that women should be trained as architects who could design for the applied arts as well as building, and that furniture and decoration were particularly profitable areas for women architect-designers, as they had been for him.[22] However, Godwin's public position was in fact eroded in practice. The work of Beatrice Philip, Godwin's architectural pupil, and later his wife, shows that his argument was applied in his own office, as it was in the profession generally, in its narrowest sense, with Philip painting the decorative panels for Godwin-designed furniture, such as the satinwood cabinet with four painted panels depicting the seasons, 1877, which is today in the Victoria and Albert Museum. There is no evidence that Beatrice Philip designed buildings, and even at a time when the status of the applied and decorative arts was rising and there was much talk of 'the democracy of the arts', the hierarchy of the arts which privileged architecture over decoration made architecture more prestigious, and more financially rewarding, than decoration. Thus, through the repressive mechanism of the sexual division of labour, women were assigned to the 'lesser arts', without the option that male architect-designers had of architectural design.

In addition to decoration, women's experience in the home and their higher moral sense particularly fitted them, it was reasoned, to interior design. Thus the Domestic Revival and the 'Queen Anne' and Arts and Crafts Movements in the late nineteenth and early twentieth centuries helped promote women's participation in the decorative arts and in interior design, as well as, to a more limited extent, in the architectural profession, at the same time reinforcing the cultural stereotype. As interior designers, architectural theorists and writers, women helped develop the late-Victorian cult of the 'House Beautiful'. Books by women proliferated: for example, *The Drawing Room* (1878) by Lucy Faulkner, *The Dining Room* (1876) by Mrs Loftie, *Beautiful Houses* (1882) by Mrs H. R. Haweis and *Suggestions on House Decoration in Painting, Woodwork and Furniture* (1876) by Agnes and Rhoda Garrett.

[21] 'Report from the Women in Architecture Sub-Group', RIBA, January, 1985.
[22] Reprinted in *British Architect*, 12 June 1874, vol. 1, p. 378.

The Garretts were not only the best-known women designers and decorators of the period but they were also active feminists, campaigning tirelessly for women's rights and 'the struggle "for the successful removal of intolerable grievances" ',[23] as Rhoda's sister, Millicent Garrett Fawcett, called it. For Rhoda, joined by her cousin Agnes, architecture was the original goal, but at first they found it impossible to get taken on in an architect's office. Undaunted, they occupied rooms in a glass-stainer's office and then were formally apprenticed for 18 months to the architect J. M. Brydon, although they were not given any building work there. Their decoration of a house for Agnes' sister, the pioneer doctor Elizabeth Garrett Anderson, and other projects, including much of the drawing-room furniture at Philip Webb's country house, Standen, established them as leaders in their field.[24]

The Entry into the Profession

Like medicine and the law, architecture achieved professional status in the nineteenth century, most notably through the founding in 1834 of the professional body, the Royal Institute of British Architects. Although women were not admitted for more than 60 years after its establishment, women, as we have seen, worked as architects without RIBA membership or approval. The 1891 census records 19 women architects in England and Wales and five in Scotland, in addition to the women who designed buildings within the 'amateur tradition', who would not have shown up in the census.

In 1898, Ethel Mary Charles (1871–1962) became the first woman to enter the RIBA. Ethel Charles and her sister, Bessie Ada Charles, who became the second woman member of the Institute in 1900, were articled for three years to George and Peto, after being barred from entering the Architectural Association (AA) in 1893. Ethel Charles supplemented her training by doing university extension courses – in which she received distinctions. After completing her time with Ernest George, she worked as an assistant to the Arts and Crafts architect Walter Cave, and travelled in England, studying Gothic and domestic architecture. In June 1898 she sat the RIBA examinations, almost unnoticed, and her name went forward for Associate membership.[25]

A last-ditch stand was made by Fellows who wished the RIBA to continue as an all-male organisation. W. Hilton Nash circulated a paper, which was signed by other architects who believed that 'it would be prejudical [sic] to the interests of

[23] Quoted in Taylor, op. cit., p. 279.
[24] Daniel Conway Moncure, *Travels in South Kensington*, Trübner & Co., London, 1882, pp. 166–71.
[25] RIBA Nomination Papers for Associate Membership, 1898, British Architectural Library.

the Institute to elect a lady member'.[26] Ernest George nominated Ethel Charles and vouched for her ability and seriousness of purpose. A motion to adopt all proposed new members was put and the vote stood 51 for and 16 against. A few months later the RIBA came within one vote of reversing this decision to admit women.[27]

Ethel Charles practised with her sister, Bessie Ada, and specialised in domestic work, entering a competition for labourers' cottages and designing houses, especially in Falmouth, such as Gyllyngyvase Terrace, 1907.[28] In 1909 she won first prize for a church design from among 200 competitors in Germany,[29] but her knowledge of London architecture directed her attention to the City and commercial building. However, domestic architecture remained the socially sanctioned sphere for women architects and, ironically, the volume of domestic building was beginning to dwindle just as they started to enter the profession. Edwardian England was characterised by a concentration of wealth, population and building commissions in the cities, and large public commissions were jealously guarded by male architects. Alas, Ethel Charles, the first woman member of the RIBA, holder of its Silver Medal (1905), international competition winner and the first woman to address an architectural society in Great Britain, built, with few exceptions, simple, quiet houses, often for women clients, instead of the experimental large-scale projects which she admired. This 'domestic ghetto', in which the Charles sisters and many women architects have since found themselves, limited women's opportunities and reinforced sexual stereotypes; however, it also directed women architects to the most socially useful area of architecture – housing. It is a measure of the different perspectives in the debates surrounding architectural practice today that while many women of the older generation reject domestic architecture for fear of being typecast, and many professional women architects strive for conventional success through the design of public and commercial buildings, feminist architects, with their commitment to women's needs, consciously embrace the stereotype of women as having a special concern for the family and house design.

Although Ethel and Bessie Charles had made a breakthrough into the male domain of professional architecture, few women followed. It made little immediate difference for other women and few joined them in the ranks of the architectural profession. The Charles sisters' struggle shows that at the precise time women were making their entry into the architectural profession, the

[26] 'The admission of lady Associates,' *RIBA Journal*, 10 December 1898, vol. VI, p. 78.

[27] *RIBA Journal*, 11 March 1899, vol. VI, p. 278.

[28] Drawings by Ethel and Bessie Charles, held by the British Architectural Library, are listed in *Catalogue of the Royal Institute of British Architects C–F*, Gregg Press, Farnborough, 1972, pp. 22–3. The Charles sisters' London address was 49 York Chambers, a block of flats for professional women with communal facilities, designed by Balfour & Turner in 1892 (illustrated in *Architectural Design*, 1978, Vol. 48, p. 357).

[29] Postcard from Berlin organisers to Ethel Charles, 8 May 1909, in the possession of the family.

pressure to maintain the traditional role and position of women intensified: they were refused admission to the Architectural Association (1893), embroiled in battles at the RIBA over entry (1898 and 1899) and involved in confrontations at the AA (1902). All these specific instances of overt discrimination were combined with the daily strain of being outside established practice, swimming against cultural assumptions in a male-dominated profession.

The idea that women were interlopers in the male workplace held sway long after the institutional barriers had been breached at the RIBA. Ideologically, there was only the merest chink in the rigid sexual division of labour which assigned the practice of architecture to men until the conditions of the First World War and the militant suffragist movement combined to force a reappraisal of women's role. Numerically, little impression was made on the profession until the 1930s. The architect Arnold Mitchell expressed the entrenched nature of these attitudes which circumscribed women's activities when he spoke of the 'very serious problem ... this problem of sex and the woman taking up work which the man up to the present had been accustomed to consider his own separate province.'[30] Fear that women would take jobs, and lucrative ones at that, which had traditionally belonged to men was often heightened by fears of unemployment – male unemployment. 'Architecture, like all professions, is very much over-stocked',[31] R. Weir Schultz reminded his audience at a conference on employment for women at Caxton Hall, London. Looking back on the previous years of her experience, a young woman architect who was optimistic that women would succeed as architects registered the feeling of otherness and the difficulties of getting work in the 1920s:

> There is a certain prejudice against taking women into architects' offices not because they cannot do the work, but because a tendency to jealousy on the part of men is feared. Accordingly the few girl students who start looking for positions have up to now found it rather difficult to get and to keep them.[32]

After the First World War, a new generation of professional women architects emerged in Britain. Although most architectural schools have no records of when they first admitted women, the Glasgow School of Art (*c.*1905) and the University of Manchester (1909) are the earliest now known to have accepted women students.[33] Scotland seems to have been more advanced than England in architectural education for women; Edith M. Burnet Hughes was awarded the Diploma in Architecture in 1914 from the Aberdeen Art School, where she later taught

---

[30] Arnold Mitchell, *Builder*, 22 February 1902, vol. 82, p. 181. This statement was made after a talk by Ethel Charles at the Architectural Association which is extensively reported in this article.

[31] R. Weir, Schultz, 'Architecture for women', *Architectural Review*, September 1908, vol. 24. p. 154.

[32] *Birmingham Dispatch*, 5 January 1928.

[33] Survey of Schools of Architecture, Beeban Morris and Lynne Walker, 1984.

(1915–18). The Architectural Association, which eventually produced the most successful group of women graduates, did not open its doors to women until 1917.

In the 1920s less than a handful of women were taken into the RIBA as Associates: Gillian Harrison (née Cooke), Eleanor K. D. Hughes, Winifred Ryle (later Maddock) and Gertrude W. M. Leverkus. It was not until 1931 that Gillian Harrison (1898–1974) became the first full woman member of the RIBA.[34]

In 1928 Elisabeth Whitworth Scott (1898–1972), a recent graduate of the Architectural Association, won the competition for the Shakespeare Memorial Theatre, Stratford-upon-Avon. Scott's theatre galvanised British women architects, as Sophia Hayden's Women's Pavilion at the Chicago World's Fair had done for American women in 1893. The Stratford Theatre, apart from its obvious importance as the home for Shakespearean productions, was seen as a victory for all women and as evidence of their ability to win and complete large-scale public commissions. Professor A. E. Richardson praised it as 'the first important work erected in this country from the designs of a woman architect'.[35]

Chosen out of 72 entries by a distinguished jury, Scott's design of 1927 looked to new architectural developments on the continent and in Scandinavia and was put up with the greatest care for craftsmanship and materials by the firm that she formed, Scott, Chesterton and Sheperd. The theatre was completed in 1932. Maurice Chesterton disclaimed 'any personal share whatever in the successful design'.[36]

Elisabeth Scott was representative of women architects of her generation. They tended to be eldest daughters or only children, from a professional background, with an architect relative and often building for women clients. She was conscious that she would encounter discrimination.

After the Second World War, like many other women architects, she moved into the public sector, and in the 1960s she worked for the Bournemouth Borough Architects Department on projects such as the rebuilding of the Bournemouth Pier Pavilion Theatre and Restaurant and the Entertainment Hall of the Boscombe Pier Pavilion.[37]

The sexual division of labour, which Anthea Callen describes in her essay, is the repressive mechanism through which architecture is made gender-specific. Architecture in our society is still thought to be an activity more appropriate for men than women, and in spite of improvements in the law and in access to professional bodies and in spite of better educational opportunities for women, women do not have the same options to participate in architecture that men do.

Women's exclusion from architectural practice is a case study in patriarchal control and economic hegemony. The debates which surround women's participation in architecture are highly charged both emotionally and politically, because

[34] *Architects: Women, Biography File*, British Architectural Library.
[35] A. E. Richardson, *Builder*, 22 April 1932, vol. 142, p. 718.
[36] *Daily Telegraph*, 6 January 1928.
[37] Letter from Bernard Ward, former Chief Architect, City of Bournemouth, to Nadine Beddington, 9 May 1984.

architecture physically defines the public and private spheres: to allow women access to the design of architecture therefore threatens patriarchal control of spatial definitions, which are essential to maintain the social, economic and cultural *status quo*.

Although the proportion of women entering schools of architecture is rising, women students are met with a set of pressures which induce feelings of inadequacy and isolation. Architectural schools are male-dominated institutions with their overwhelmingly male student bodies and virtually all-male teaching staff (97 per cent). Without female role-models and with an architectural history constructed of male cult-figures, past and present, a precedent for women's architectural practice is still a very real need of women students and architects alike.

This paper has shown that for hundreds of years women have worked as architects in the 'amateur tradition', as conventional, professional architects, and more recently feminist architectural cooperatives have developed a radical client-centred practice.[38] However, the relationship of women to architecture remains highly problematic; at one end of the design continuum, the image of the architect remains firmly male, and at the other, the women who use buildings have little control over or understanding of their production. The art historical values of innovation and quality which exist in relation to an aesthetic currently known as 'the mainstream' place women's issues and achievements in a netherworld of 'other', while British cities are planned and designed with scant attention paid to the needs of women, especially those in communities where mobility and spending power are restricted.[39]

Women are not, however, inert or powerless. Struggle and the daily life of architectural practice come together. In dealing with clients, for example, issues of race, class and sex are confronted. As the architect Elsie Owusu has pointed out, the expectation that buildings are designed by white middle-class men for white middle-class male clients 'is challenged every time a black woman [architect] walks on site.'[40]

---

[38] See especially Matrix, *Making Space: Women and the Man-made Environment*, Pluto Press, London, 1984; *Building for Childcare: Making Better Buildings for the Under-5's*, produced and published jointly by Matrix and the GLC Women's Committee, London, 1986.

[39] For the radical role that working-class women played in making and assessing housing policy, see, for instance, Mark Swenarton, *Homes Fit for Heroes: The Policy and Architecture of Early State Housing*, Heinemann, London, 1981, pp. 62, 91–2 and 97–9.

[40] Elsie Owusu, talk on design practice at the ICA, 'The Design World: Women on the Cutting Edge', 21 May 1988.

31

The Programmes of the Architectural Section of the École des Beaux-Arts

Annie Jacques

One aspect of the teaching of architecture at the Ecole des Beaux-Arts that has been little studied is the monthly architectural competition, both in the form of sketch designs (*esquisses*) and rendered projects (*projects rendus*), together with other related competitions, such as the Rougevin prize, starting in 1857, to be followed by the Achille Leclère, Chaudesaignes, Godeboeuf, American Architects and others.

Submission for the Prix de Rome – in the architectural section at any rate – was a rarified affair, with regard to both the programmes and the style of drawing and composition. The day-to-day activity in the Ecole was reflected more faithfully by the monthly competitions (Concours Mensuels d'Emulation), judged by a jury made up by teachers within the Ecole, and not by members of the Académie des Beaux-Arts within the Institut, as with the Prix de Rome, which was judged by very different criteria.

Every pupil, in the first and the second class, was required to enter at least two of these competitions every academic year, under threat of expulsion from the architectural section and the necessity of reapplying for admission.

Whatever the aspiration of the pupils for the prestigious Prix de Rome competition, it was the monthly competitions that were most representative of the teaching of the thousands of architects, French and foreign, who passed through the Ecole des Beaux-Arts during the 19th century – imperative for the foreign students, who were not eligible for the Prix de Rome. In all, 6,500 pupils were admitted between 1819 and 1914, a period in which only 100 were to win the Grand Prix.

The programmes for the Grand Prix, drawn up by the Académie, were notably different from those for the monthly competitions, written by the professor of

Annie Jacques, "The Programmes of the Architectural Section of the École des Beaux-Arts," pp. 59–62, 65, 256 from Robin Middleton (ed.), *The Beaux-Arts and Nineteenth-Century French Architecture*. London: Thames & Hudson, 1982.

284

architectural theory at the Ecole. David Van Zanten, in his contribution to *The Architecture of the Ecole des Beaux-Arts*, has already noted that 'the Concours d'Emulation projects seem practical and relevant, whereas the Grand Prix projects seem impossible and megalomaniac' (p. 232). Some study of the programmes for the Concours d'Emulation, therefore, seems to be required. Certain themes remain constant, others emerge fitfully, while some appear not at all. Certain subjects were set for particular years. Technological innovations were taken up on occasion, though many inventions were ignored.

Long-term projects, drawn up in the *ateliers*, conforming to the sketches done first *en loge* (booths within the Ecole), alternated with short-term projects, drawn up in twelve hours *en loge*, on demi-Grand-Aigle (Elephant) sheets, about 35cm × 51cm.

The subjects were set by the professor of architectural theory, hence their significance, for it is easier to direct study by setting a programme than by delivering lectures on theory, which students may or may not attend. The men who held this position through successive years from 1819 to 1914 were Baltard, Blouet, Lesueur, Guillaume, Guadet and Blavette.

Louis-Pierre Baltard (1764–1846), succeeding Dufourny, occupied the chair from 1819, when the Ecole des Beaux-Arts was formally re-established, to his death in 1846. Trained in the *atelier* of the younger Peyre, he first became known for his drawings; indeed it was as a painter that he was sent to Rome by a patron, in 1786, for he was never to win the Grand Prix.[1] Nonetheless, in Rome he mixed with the *pensionnaires* of the Villa Medici. With the founding of the Ecole Polytechnique in 1794, he began to teach the course on civic architecture. From 1813 onwards he served also as architect to the Panthéon. In 1819, at the age of 55, he became professor at the Ecole des Beaux-Arts. For twenty-seven years he retained this position. During the last four years, from 1842 to 1846 (when he was between his 78th and 82nd year) he was helped by his son, Victor, officially appointed as his assistant. Baltard hoped that his son would succeed him, but it was not the professors who made such appointments.

Abel Blouet (1795–1853) was elected in his place. He was of humble origin, the son of an artisan, who had entered the Ecole des Beaux-Arts and eventually won the Grand Prix, in 1821. He stayed in Italy for five years and then extended his classical education with an official archaeological expedition to the Morea (the Peloponnese), from 1828 to 1831. But his interests were to be directed rather to contemporary matters: he travelled to the United States of America with the magistrate Demetz to study penitentiaries, a journey that resulted in several publications, one of particular note, that written with Hector Horeau. Blouet had by then taken up a position on the Conseil des Bâtiments Civils. In 1846 he became professor at the Ecole. His last official appointment was as architect to the château of Fontainebleau. He died, relatively young, in 1853.

[1] Thérèse de Puylaroque, 'Pierre Baltard, Peintre et dessinateur', *Bulletin de la Société de l'Histoire de l'Art Français*, Paris 1976.

He was replaced by Jean-Baptiste-Cicéron Lesueur, a man of Blouet's generation, indeed a man born one year earlier than Blouet, in 1794. Lesueur had also won the Grand Prix earlier, in 1819. His chief activity, some private houses apart, was the reconstruction of the Paris Hôtel de Ville, begun in 1835. Elected professor in 1853, he maintained his position for thirty years. Even the reforms of 1863 scarcely disrupted the continuity of his teaching – 'I will hold them still with my programmes', André reports him as saying – for on 11 March 1864 he was appointed by the Minister to take charge of the architectural competitions, and when on 15 January 1873 the chair of architectural theory was re-established, Lesueur was appointed to it. In this particular field, it must be clear, the reforms of 1863 had little effect. Lesueur continued active to his death in 1883.

Edmond-Jean-Baptiste Guillaume took over from him. Born in 1826, Guillaume was also a Grand Prix winner, in 1856, who followed a traditional career, designing both private and public buildings, acting, most notably, as architect to the Louvre and the Tuileries. His professorship was, indeed, somewhat subordinate to his architectural career. He died in 1898, but Julien Guadet had been called in four years earlier to act as his assistant, at least in the writing of programmes for the Concours.

Julien Guadet, born in 1834, is perhaps best known of the professors of theory at the Ecole, his reputation established by his *Eléments et théorie de l'architecture*, and, to a lesser extent, by his role in the events of 1863. Like his predecessors, he was a product of the Ecole, winner of the Grand Prix in 1864, Inspecteur for the Bâtiments Civils and the Théâtre-Français. He was, however, more closely linked to the teaching of the Ecole than Guillaume and Lesueur, for in 1871 he succeeded Constant-Dufeux as tutor in one of the official *ateliers*.

The last professor one can consider as belonging to the 19th-century succession was Victor-Auguste Blavette, appointed in 1908, on Guadet's death. Born in 1850, Grand Prix winner in 1879, Blavette worked also for the Bâtiments Civils, and was architect to the international exhibitions of 1889 and 1900.

These six men chose all the subjects considered by several generations of architects. The professors set about twenty subjects a year, ten for each class, alternating long and short programmes (sketches and rendered projects). Over a period of almost a hundred years, from 1819 to 1914, there were more than five hundred different programmes – a total of some significance, for in theory no programme should have been repeated more than four times during the period. In practice, matters were otherwise, for certain subjects were repeated far more often than others, while some were set only once.

Several subjects were repeated throughout the century; baths, in particular, emerge as a favourite theme, appearing no less than fifty-one times in a range of guises: bath houses, private baths, steam baths, thermal baths, seaside baths and bathing centres.[2]

---

[2] See the magazine *Les monuments historiques de la France*, no. 1, 1978, devoted to this subject, in particular Daniel Rabreau's article, which demonstrates the special interest taken at this time in thermal architecture, faithfully reflected in the programmes at the Ecole.

Another favourite subject was the school, which was set on sixty-three occasions, to cover the whole range of French education: primary schools, village schools, secondary schools, lycées and all schools of higher and university education, schools of arts and crafts, naval and military schools, art and architectural schools, schools of music, botany, medicine, chemistry, veterinary science, schools of engineering and more. All branches of the sciences and the arts were thus represented, showing how faithfully the Ecole reflected the contemporary concern with education.

A third notable category was the monument. There are no less than seventy-one: commemorative and allegorical monuments, monuments dedicated to Virtue and Peace, to the artistic fraternity and to a series of great men, Poussin, Homer, Napoleon, Louis XIV, or simply 'great Frenchmen', whether under a monarchy, an empire or a republic.

In contrast, certain subjects were rarely set. One, the greenhouse, which might be thought characteristic of the 19th century, appears only occasionally. Baltard alone set this subject, first in 1824 (when it was associated with an orangery), then in 1825 and 1835 (for the first class), as a winter garden. Iron and glass building was regarded always as a secondary type of architecture.[3] With the exception of the extremes – subjects set more than fifty times or no more than once or twice – most of the programmes were repeated six or seven times in the course of the century, reappearing at about twelve-year intervals. Although the range of subjects is varied, it gives a distorted view of the architectural activity of the period.

One can classify the subjects according to their suitability and unsuitability to the times. There is a comparatively limited range of themes of classical inspiration, nymphea, grottoes, dairies, Roman houses, triumphal arches, naumachia, etc. Dairies, for instance, which seem to derive also from 18th-century garden architecture, were set on eleven occasions between 1819 and 1860, principally by Baltard. Blouet took up the subject in 1850, for the second class. Nymphea, which might also be seen as garden structures, were set by almost all the professors as sketch designs for the first class, in 1836, 1846, 1852, 1859, 1864, 1873, 1880 and 1890. Guadet and Blavette alone rejected the theme.

Another subject with little relation to reality, serving as an exercise in pure composition, was the House for Four Brothers, set in 1853, and repeated in 1860 and 1871 by Lesueur, on all three occasions as a rendered study for the second class. The programme was regarded always as the essence of a pure compositional study, and was repeated much later between the two World Wars. A similar programme was the House for Three Artists set as a rendered project for the first class in 1876.

Of another kind were those programmes closely linked to contemporary events and technology. A Telegraph Building was, surprisingly, set in 1816 by Dufourny, Baltard's predecessor, when the telegraph network was still in an experimental state. The younger Baltard returned to the subject in 1844, as did Blouet in 1851. By

---

[3] Exceptions, in a Grand Prix programme, are the greenhouses included in the projects for a House for a Rich Banker by J.-L. Pascal and E. Benard, illustrated in *The Architecture of the Ecole des Beaux-Arts*, A. Drexler (ed.), 1977, p. 236–8.

then, however, the programme had little point, for in 1844 visible telegraphic communication was superseded by the electric telegraph. Railway architecture (stations, signal boxes, tunnels etc.) also appeared early; in 1842 a Railway Station was the subject of a sketch design for the second class. The younger Baltard, who probably set the programme, was clearly something of an innovator, for the inauguration of the first railway in France, between Paris and Orléans, took place only in the following year. The subject was repeated in 1852 and 1858, and then, much expanded, in 1891 for the Prix de Rome. A design for the Metro was proposed only in 1904, four years after the opening of the first Paris lines with station entrances by Guimard.

Industrial architecture was not the concern of the Ecole. The word 'factory' (*usine*) does not appear in any of the programmes. Yet, in 1879, 1888 and 1893, there was a Tapestry and Porcelain Manufactory and in 1896 a Trading Post in Alaska. Commercial buildings provoked little interest, even in that century of banks and great department stories. A Bank was set on only three occasions between 1875 and 1899 – with the notable addition of the Grand Prix programme for 1889, won by Tony Garnier. As for the department store, it appeared only in its old guise as a Bazaar in 1831, 1833 and 1840, to be overlooked during the Second Empire, and to emerge once more in 1889. The individual shop was more popular; there are confectioners, jewellers and other shops, including even one for a butcher, set by Blouet in 1848.

Another subject reflecting the real life of the 19th century was that of the international exhibition, appearing first in 1853, two years after the 1851 exhibition in London, to be repeated, regularly, every six or seven years, in the first class.

The greater part of the programmes set for the students at the Ecole can be divided, roughly, into three categories:

Public buildings or buildings to be used by the public: schools, which have already been mentioned, are included in this group, as are administrative and other service buildings such as prefectural offices, town halls, municipal buildings, law courts, exchanges, museums, libraries, post offices, hospitals, alms-houses, markets, theatres, cafés, fountains, etc.

Ecclesiastical buildings: from the private chapel to the cathedral, including all variety of churches, their furnishings in detail and ancillary structures, together with related buildings such as bishops' palaces, convents etc. With ecumenical tact, Protestant churches, mosques and synagogues were included, but only towards the end of the century.

Private buildings: this includes a whole range of programmes, from town houses to country mansions, from the houses of great collectors to hunting lodges, all of the luxurious kind. Housing as such was dealt with only in the second class and then in the form of a middle-class house or an apartment block.

Town planning was hardly tackled at all, providing no more than the setting for an individual building, in the form of a public square. But in that form it appears often enough.

Having summarily reviewed the programmes, it remains to distinguish the contribution of each of the professors.

During the twenty-six years of his professorship Louis-Pierre Baltard introduced many new themes, greatly increasing the range, hitherto extremely limited. His son, Victor, serving as his assistant during his last four years, was no doubt responsible for the introduction of a further range of odd and altogether adventurous themes: a Railway Station in 1842, and the only monument to be dedicated to men of science, Papin and Watt. He was also concerned with social issues and hygiene; in 1844 he set as a subject for the second class a Public Swimming Pool, and noted in the programme that 'workers might benefit from swimming'. Another unusual programme, set likewise for the second class, was a Cow-shed with Sick-bay; this however had already been proposed by Victor's father, in 1820, as a Sanitary Cow-shed. It was then thought that the proximity of cows might cure chest complaints.

Abel Blouet continued in this experimental tradition, especially in the second class, setting his students new subjects of a practical and commonplace kind: Post-inn; Butcher's Shop; Public Letter Writer's Stall; Steam-ship Booking Office; Communal Bakehouse; Park Café; Bandstand; Public Lavatory, etc.

Lesueur and Guillaume were less imaginative and certainly less innovative. They took their themes from the stock established by their predecessors, and not only the themes but often the texts of the programmes, which are repeated word for word, from ten or twenty years before. And their contemporaries were well aware of the situation. André, writing Lesueur's obituary in 1885, noted: 'During his last years his programmes might perhaps have been lacking in variety and appeared out of date, for the professor showed insufficient concern for contemporary social and industrial conditions which might have changed the study of architecture to some extent'.

Julien Guadet, in contrast, wished to invigorate the programmes: 'he made his students aware of the most pressing realities, the concerns of the moment, the most up to date concepts' – so, at any rate, wrote Pascal in his obituary. In fact, what Guadet did was to eliminate the more anachronistic subjects, such as the House for Four Brothers, and put the emphasis on those of a more contemporary nature, without introducing anything new.

One last point remains in considering the programmes, their differentiation according to class. Clearly, those for the Grand Prix and those for the monthly competitions, which were more practical, more commonplace, formed a hierarchy. There was also a distinction between those for the first and second class submissions. For the second class, the subjects were simpler: primary schools, small town halls and libraries, or provincial theatres. First class subjects were related always to larger towns or provincial capitals, while the Grand Prix projects were connected with the capital city or some national enterprise.

Each of these levels seems to have related to a stage in a possible career; it would be of interest to analyze the careers of architects who emerged from the Ecole, to see if they did reflect their level of attainment at the school.

289

What emerges from this short resumé is the variety and the novelty of the programmes during the first half of the century – the basis, perhaps, of the early success of the school and its ability to attract foreign students – while the less enterprising and routine nature of the programmes in the second half of the century might be held accountable for the failure of the school in the early 20th century.

32

Adler and Sullivan at the 1893 World's Columbian Exposition in Chicago

Zeynep Çelik

Louis Sullivan and Dankmar Adler's Transportation Building was one of the most memorable structures at the 1893 Columbian Exposition in Chicago. As an "architectural exhibit"[1] in itself, it served one of the main goals of world's fairs: education. Its location off the Court of Honor, where the main buildings of the exposition were erected in a uniform neoclassical style on an axial and symmetrical plan, enabled Adler and Sullivan to break some of the rules spelled out by the organizing committee and experiment with exterior ornamental forms. Nevertheless, they had to adjust their structure to its context and conform to exposition guidelines.

With its cornice line and the rhythm of its openings determined by other buildings in the main section, the Transportation Building fit snugly into the Beaux-Arts site plan. Its design also followed the conventions of the time: a central hall with an arcaded clerestory and a dome. But in the treatment of its surface and the color of its facades it contrasted with the other buildings in the White City. The exterior walls were light red at the lower level; the elaborate spandrels above were characterized by their "high pitch intensity in color." Winged figures on the spandrels were metaphors for transportation against a gold-leaf background. The main feature of the pavilion was the hundred-foot-wide and seventy-foot-high Golden Gateway, formed by concentric arches painted in gold.[2]

Zeynep Çelik, "Adler and Sullivan at the 1893 World's Columbian Exposition in Chicago," pp. 171–6, 222 from *Displaying the Orient: Architecture of Islam at Nineteenth-Century World's Fairs*. Berkeley: University of California Press, 1992. Reprinted by permission of the University of California Press.

[1] David Van Zanten, in Wim De Wit, ed., *Louis Sullivan: The Function of Ornament* (New York and London, 1986), 106.

[2] Dankmar Adler and Louis Sullivan, "The Transportation Building," *A Week at the Fair* (Chicago, 1893), 47–8, quoted in Elizabeth Gilmore-Holt (ed.), *The Expanding World of Art, 1874–1902* (New Haven, CT and London, 1988), 89.

The architects emphasized the external polychromy as the basis of their design:

The architecture of the building ... has been carefully prepared throughout with reference to the ultimate application of color, and many large plain surfaces have been left to receive the final polychrome treatment. The ornamental designs for this work in color are of great and intricate delicacy; the patterns, interweaving with each other, produce an effect almost as fine as that of embroidery. As regards the colors themselves, they comprise nearly the whole galaxy, there being not less than thirty different shades of color employed.[3]

Sullivan did not refer to Islamic precedents in this explanation of the Transportation Building (though others did).[4] In a letter to Daniel Burnham on 16 October 1893, he argued that he had designed the Transportation Building in a "natural" manner, expressed by "elementary masses carrying elaborate decoration." He achieved geometric simplicity by using straight lines and semicircles. In contrast to this simplicity was the structure's richly colored decoration, created by "systematic subdivisions." In his use of color, Sullivan intended to reflect "the true nature of polychromy," combining and repeating "a great many colors" in sequence.[5]

In *Kindergarten Chats*, he further clarified his point:

A decorated structure, harmoniously conceived, well-considered, cannot be stripped of its system of ornament without destroying its individuality....
It must be manifest that an ornamental design will be more beautiful if it seems a part of the surface or substance that receives it than if it looks "stuck on," so to speak.... Both structure and ornament obviously benefit by this sympathy, each enhancing the value of the other. And this, I take it, is the preparatory basis of what may be called an organic system of ornamentation.[6]

Among the critics of the Transportation Building was Montgomery Schuyler, who, arguing that Adler and Sullivan had turned Islamic architecture

---

[3] Adler and Sullivan, quoted in Gilmore-Holt (ed.), 88–9.

[4] The writings of Owen Jones helped to shape the intellectual foundations of Sullivan's architecture. Sullivan's understanding of ornament is similar to Jones's, and his repertoire borrows from *Grammar of Ornament* (the American edition was published in 1889). A more direct influence was Frank Furness, for whom Sullivan had worked in 1873. Sullivan collected Islamic art objects – among them Persian rugs. See John Sweetman, *The Oriental Obsession* (Cambridge, London, New York, 1988), 237–41. Although there is no direct evidence that Sullivan's architecture was influenced by the Islamic pavilions, the possibility exists because Islamic architecture at the European fairs had already had an impact on European architectural theory and practice. Given Sullivan's interest in non-Western sources, it is reasonable to believe that he might have followed the discussions of the Islamic pavilions at the fairs while he was a student in Paris.

[5] The letter is quoted by David Van Zanten in DeWit, *Louis Sullivan*, 106–9.

[6] H. L. Sullivan, *Kindergarten Chats and Other Writings* (New York, 1947), 187–9.

inside out, repeated the common misperception that all Islamic architecture is interiorized:[7]

> The Saracens, indeed, attained an interior architecture of plaster, and this architecture comprises all the precedents that were available for the architects of the Transportation Building. The outsides of those Saracenic buildings of which the interiors are most admired are little more than dead walls. One cannot fail to respect the courage and sincerity with which the architects ... tackled their task.[8]

Another contemporary critic, Charles Mulford Robinson, the acknowledged theorist of the City Beautiful movement, called this building "the bride of the Orient." Uneasy with its "strange" details, Robinson emphasized its otherness among the structures of the White City: it had a "voluptuous Orientalism," which caused it to stand out among the more masculine structures.[9]

Arguing that Sullivan's building synthesized ancient, medieval, and Islamic elements, the architectural historian Dmitri Tselos notes analogies to Islamic monuments of North Africa and India – among them the twelfth-century Aguenaou Gate in Marrakesh.[10] In fact, Sullivan's references to both the interior and exterior elements of Islamic monuments are broader than Tselos suggests. The hierarchical treatment of surface elaboration from planar to complex ornamentation is common in the architecture of many Islamic regions; for example, in Morocco, on the minaret of the Mosque of Sultan Hasan in Rabat from the Almohad period (late twelfth century). The curvilinear vine-and-scroll motif occurs in Syria on both Byzantine and early Islamic buildings of the Umayyad period; in later centuries it is found on the *mihrab* of the Great Mosque of Cordoba and in the surface decoration of many Mamluk buildings in Cairo. The Golden Gateway of the Transportation Building recalls the Rabat Gate in Oudna's fortifications (late twelfth century) as well as tombs in Bukhara, such as the Tomb of the Samanids, with its receding arched portal. The multiplication of receding arches is also seen in the *mihrabs* of Mamluk mosques in Cairo. The small domed "porch" evokes sixteenth-century fountains in the center of mosque courtyards in Istanbul (e.g., Sokullu Mehmed Paşa mosque).

The list of precedents could be extended, but archaeological detective work is beside the point here. Even a quick study of the Transportation Building facade shows that the structure embodied not Islamic revivalism but, in Sullivan's words, a rejection of "historical styles."[11] Although such a statement reiterates the

---

[7] Mamluk architecture in Cairo, for example, has elaborate exterior facades.

[8] Montgomery Schuyler, "Last Words about the World's Fairs," *The Architectural Record* 3 (July 1893–July 1894): 271–301.

[9] Charles Mulford Robinson, "The Fair as Spectacle," in Johnson Rossiter, ed., *A History of the World's Columbian Exposition* (New York, 1897), 1: 500.

[10] Dmitri Tselos, "The Chicago Fair and the Myth of the Lost Cause," *Journal of the Society of Architectural Historians* 26, no. 4 (December 1967): 264–5.

[11] Quoted by David Van Zanten in De Wit, *Louis Sullivan*, 106–9.

ahistorical quality ascribed to Islamic cultures in general, for Sullivan this was not a negative trait but a redemption. Here was the potential to create a new architecture.

Sullivan's search was a philosophical one. He saw himself as a creator of culture for the New World whose architecture would express intellectual, emotional, and spiritual realities, satisfying the "real needs of the people."[12] To Sullivan, function meant "the whole life" that would be lived in a building. In his self-assigned role as prophet, he would interpret American life and idealize its egalitarian dimension, which he believed was best expressed by forms drawn from distant sources. His "exoticism" and his references to other cultures voiced his dissatisfaction with the dominance of classical forms. Nevertheless, Sullivan's "Orientalism" was purely formal: he referred to Islamic architecture not because he was inspired by the civilization of Islam but only because the source was formally a novel and refreshing one.

[12] Kenneth Frampton, *Modern Architecture: A Critical History* (New York, 1980), 56. For Sullivan's "view of the democratic vista," see Louis Sullivan, *The Autobiography of an Idea* (New York, 1922), 260–84.

33

Public Parks and The Enlargement of Towns

Frederick Law Olmsted

[…]

In the early part of the century, the continued growth of London was talked of as something marvelous and fearful; but where ten houses were then required to accommodate new residents, there are now a hundred. The average rate at which population increases in the six principal towns is twice as great as in the country at large, including the hundreds of other flourishing towns. So also Glasgow has been growing six times faster than all Scotland; and Dublin has held its own, while Ireland as a whole has been losing ground.

Crossing to the Continent, we find Paris absorbing half of all the increase of France in population; Berlin growing twice as fast as all Prussia; Hamburg, Stettin, Stuttgart, Brussels, and a score or two of other towns, all building out into the country at a rate never before known, while many agricultural districts are actually losing population. In Russia special provision is made in the laws to regulate the gradual compensation of the nobles for their losses by the emancipation of the serfs, to prevent the depopulation of certain parts of the country, which was in danger of occurring from the eagerness of the peasantry to move into the large towns.

[…]

There can be no doubt then, that, in all our modern civilization, as in that of the ancients, there is a strong drift townward. […] It would seem then more rational to prepare for a continued rising of the townward flood than to count upon its subsidence.

[…]

Frederick Law Olmsted, "Public Parks and the Enlargement of Towns (1870)," pp. 1, 3–7, 10, 12, 14–17 from *Selected Essays*, vol. 1, ed. Richard LeGates and Frederic Stout. London and New York: Routledge, 1998.

We all recognize that the tastes and dispositions of women are more and more potent in shaping the course of civilized progress, and we may see that women are even more susceptible to this townward drift than men. Oft-times the husband and father gives up his country occupations, taking others less attractive to him in town, out of consideration for his wife and daughters.

[...]

The civilized woman is above all things a tidy woman. She enjoys being surrounded by bright and gay things perhaps not less than the savage, but she shrinks from draggling, smirching, fouling things and "things out of keeping" more. By the keenness with which she avoids subjecting herself to annoyances of this class, indeed, we may judge the degree in which a woman has advanced in civilization. [...] Think how hard it is when you city people go into the country for a few weeks in summer, to keep your things in order, to get a thousand little things done which you regard as trifles when at home, how far you have to go, and with how much uncertainty, how much unaccustomed management you have to exercise. For the perfection and delicacy – the cleanness – with which any human want is provided for depends on the concentration of human ingenuity and skill upon that particular want. The greater the division of labor at any point, the greater the perfection with which all wants may be satisfied. Everywhere in the country the number and variety of workmen, not agricultural laborers, proportionately to the population, is lessening as the facility for reaching workmen in town is increasing.

[...]

The construction of good roads and walks, the laying of sewer, water, and gas pipes, and the supplying of sufficiently cheap rapid, and comfortable conveyances to town centres, is all that is necessary to give any farming land in a healthy and attractive situation the value of town lots. And whoever has observed in the French agricultural colonies how much more readily and cheaply railroads, telegraph, gas, water, sewer, and nearly all other advantages of towns may be made available to the whole population than under our present helter-skelter methods of settlement, will not believe that even the occupation of a farm laborer must necessarily and finally exclude his family from a very large share of urban conveniences.

[...] It is hardly a matter of speculation, I am disposed to think, but almost of demonstration, that the larger a town becomes because simply of its advantages for commercial purposes, the greater will be the convenience available to those who live in and near it for coöperation, as well with reference to the accumulation of wealth in the higher forms, – as in seats of learning, of science, and of art, – as with reference to merely domestic economy and the emancipation of both men and women from petty, confining, and narrowing cares.

It also appears to be nearly certain that the recent rapid enlargement of towns and withdrawal of people from rural conditions of living is the result mainly of circumstances of a permanent character.

We have reason to believe, then, that towns which of late have been increasing rapidly on account of their commercial advantages, are likely to be still more attractive to population in the future; that there will in consequence soon be larger towns than any the world has yet known, and that the further progress of civilization is to depend mainly upon the influences by which men's minds and characters will be affected while living in large towns.

Now, knowing that the average length of the life of mankind in towns has been much less than in the country, and that the average amount of disease and misery and of vice and crime has been much greater in towns, this would be a very dark prospect for civilization, if it were not that modern Science has beyond all question determined many of the causes of the special evils by which men are afflicted in towns, and placed means in our hands for guarding against them. [...]

It has happened several times within the last century, when old artificial obstructions to the spreading out of a city have been removed, and especially when there has been a demolition of and rebuilding on a new ground plan of some part which had previously been noted for the frequency of certain crimes, the prevalence of certain diseases, and the shortness of life among its inhabitants, that a marked improvement in all these respects has immediately followed, and has been maintained not alone in the dark parts, but in the city as a whole.

[...]

Remedy for a bad plan, once built upon, being thus impracticable, now that we understand the matter we are surely bound, wherever it is by any means in our power, to prevent mistakes in the construction of towns. Strange to say, however, here in the New World, where great towns by the hundred are springing into existence, no care at all is taken to avoid bad plans.

[...]

It is evident that if we go on in this way, the progress of civilized mankind in health, virtue, and happiness will be seriously endangered.

[...]

We will for the present set before our minds the two sources of wear and corruption which we have seen to be remediable and therefore preventible. We may admit that commerce requires that in some parts of a town there shall be an arrangement of buildings, and a character of streets and of traffic in them which will establish conditions of corruption and of irritation, physical and mental. But commerce does not require the same conditions to be maintained in all parts of a town.

297

Air is disinfected by sunlight and foliage. Foliage also acts mechanically to purify the air by screening it. Opportunity and inducement to escape at frequent intervals from the confined and vitiated air of the commercial quarter, and to supply the lungs with air screened and purified by trees, and recently acted upon by sunlight, together with opportunity and inducement to escape from conditions requiring vigilance, wariness, and activity toward other men, – if these could be supplied economically, our problem would be solved.

[...]

Would trees, for seclusion and shade and beauty, be out of place, for instance, by the side of certain of our streets? It will, perhaps, appear to you that it is hardly necessary to ask such a question, as throughout the United States trees are commonly planted at the sides of streets. Unfortunately they are seldom so planted as to have fairly settled the question of the desirableness of systematically maintaining trees under these circumstances. In the first place, the streets are planned, wherever they are, essentially alike. Trees are planted in the space assigned for sidewalks, where at first, while they are saplings, and the vicinity is rural or suburban, they are not much in the way, but where, as they grow larger, and the vicinity becomes urban, they take up more and more space, while space is more and more required for passage. That is not all. Thousands and tens of thousands are planted every year in a manner and under conditions as nearly certain as possible either to kill them outright, or to so lessen their vitality as to prevent their natural and beautiful development, and to cause premature decrepitude. [...]

What I would ask is, whether we might not with economy make special provision in some of our streets – in a twentieth or a fiftieth part, if you please, of all – for trees to remain as a permanent furniture of the city? I mean, to make a place for them in which they would have room to grow naturally and gracefully. Even if the distance between the houses should have to be made half as much again as it is required to be in our commercial streets, could not the space be afforded? Out of town space is not costly when measures to secure it are taken early. The assessments for benefit where such streets were provided for, would, in nearly all cases, defray the cost of the land required. The strips of ground reserved for the trees, six, twelve, twenty feet wide, would cost nothing for paving or flagging.

The change both of scene and of air which would be obtained by people engaged for the most part in the necessarily confined interior commercial parts of the town, on passing into a street of this character after the trees had become stately and graceful, would be worth a good deal. If such streets were made still broader in some parts, with spacious malls, the advantage would be increased. [...]

We come then to the question: what accommodations for recreation can we provide which shall be so agreeable and so accessible as to be efficiently attractive to the great body of citizens, and which, while giving decided gratification, shall also cause those who resort to them for pleasure to subject themselves, for the

298

time being, to conditions strongly counteractive to the special enervating conditions of the town?

[...]

I do not propose to discuss this part of the subject at present, as it is only necessary to my immediate purpose to point out that if recreations requiring large spaces to be given up to the use of a comparatively small number, are not considered essential, numerous small grounds so distributed through a large town that some one of them could be easily reached by a short walk from every house, would be more desirable than a single area of great extent, however rich in landscape attractions it might be. Especially would this be the case if the numerous local grounds were connected and supplemented by a series of trunk-roads or boulevards such as has already been suggested.

34

Paris: Building a European Capital Under the Second Empire

Anthony Sutcliffe

The transformation of Paris under the Second Empire is the biggest commonplace of urban history after the Great Fire of London. Looked at in another way, it was arguably the biggest urban renewal project the world has ever seen. It coincided with the first surge of French industrialisation, beginning in the 1840s and lasting until the Great Depression of the 1870s. It was a mixed-economy project, with public investment devoted mainly to the infrastructure, and private capital drawn in to create lettable space. The main emphasis was on streets, which were laid out in the periphery, or driven through the centre at the cost of thousands of demolitions. New streets and new buildings on this scale were bound to affect the appearance of Paris. If a radically new aesthetic had been chosen for the work, perhaps in deference to industrialism, the classical tradition might have been undermined. That the Second Empire did not adopt a radically new aesthetic is not a cause of surprise, for neither had Manchester and London since England's Industrial Revolution. Its new streets were wider and longer, and its buildings were a little taller and a lot bulkier. However, the principles perfected in Paris in the seventeenth and eighteenth centuries were adapted to the new scale. Classicism, far from being undermined, became a unifying force on a gigantic scale.

The basic building unit was the apartment house, which now acquired a standardised form and architectural treatment from one end of the city to the other. In the new arterial streets, more than just a terminal point was needed to create coherence; the frontages themselves had to follow a formula. The result was a city-wide visual unity which went far beyond anything achieved or even envisaged before 1848. The formula was not legally imposed in most cases,

Anthony Sutcliffe, "Paris as the Hub of French Industrialisation: Building a European Capital under the Second Empire," pp. 83, 85–8 from *Paris: An Architectural History*. New Haven and London: Yale University Press, 1993. Reprinted by permission of Yale University Press.

however. It represented a consensus of architects and clients. Participation, rather than direction, shaped the new Paris.

[. . .] The changes of the Second Empire brought Paris into the industrial era, and more quickly than any large city before it. There *were* implications for architecture and urban design, and we must now look more closely at them.

Haussmann's Impact on Parisian Architecture

The search for these implications begins with Georges-Eugène Haussmann, who was appointed Prefect of the Seine in 1853. Since the 1790s the prefect had been the senior executive of central government power in Paris and its suburbs. Under the Second Empire the powers and influence of the prefect were reinforced. Not only was there no mayor, but the city council was selected by the prefect and its status was reduced to that of a municipal commission. Haussmann was well placed, therefore, to carry out the imperial modernisation programme.

Both emperor and prefect wanted the improvements, however practical, to enhance the aesthetic qualities of Paris. Both respected the French classical tradition. Neither had more than a general knowledge of art and architecture, but both had clear ideas about what they wanted. The emperor was interested in new building techniques, such as the use of wrought iron, and in practical design where this was appropriate. He wanted his buildings to be recognised as 'modern'. However, these aspirations rarely detached him from the classical style.

Napoleon III intervened in a number of projects, often stressing the need for 'modernity' in representative buildings. For the rebuilt Hôtel-Dieu, the city's main hospital, the emperor rejected the Gothic style which was at first mooted, and secured a simple, Italianate design with arched windows and rustication which Haussmann later described as 'absolutely modern', no doubt in tribute to its lack of decoration.[1] Its round arches also recalled the Bibliothèque Sainte-Geneviève and some of the railway architecture of the 1850s, in which full arches had come to the fore as an expression of practicality and day-to-day effort within the classical tradition. While a romanticist in some respects, the emperor disliked the Gothic style, and it was scarcely used at all in secular public buildings during the Second Empire.[2]

Haussmann, for his part, gave a higher priority to aesthetics, and he sometimes feared that his efforts to embellish Paris lacked the emperor's full support.[3] Striving to secure monumental structures to enhance the world's biggest system of urban perspectives, he was naturally faithful to classical design. Much more than the emperor, he was prepared to give precise instructions to architects on the size, planning and visual high-lights of new public buildings. With much greater

[1] G.-E. Haussmann, *Mémoires* (Paris: Guy Durier, 1979), vol. 2, p. 271.   [2] Ibid.
[3] A. Sutcliffe, *The Autumn of Central Paris: The Defeat of Town Planning, 1850–1970* (London: Edward Arnold, 1970), p. 180.

architectural patronage than the central government, Haussmann set a bigger mark on Parisian architecture than any of his contemporaries.

The New Scale ————————————————————————————

If Haussmann remained faithful to tradition, how then did the new Paris differ from the old? The answer lies mainly in the much greater scale of the new developments. Haussmann's fidelity to the established objectives of perspective, symmetry and vista in a much bigger city helped produce an enhanced scale, but he also saw them as a means of imposing visual order on individual projects, many of which were themselves of unprecedented dimensions.

The biggest enhancement of scale was in the length of the new streets. As the straight line was retained as a key organising component of the cityscape, rectilinear streets of unprecedented length abounded. The longest of all, the Rue Lafayette, was five kilometres long.[4] Other very long streets, while not planned in a single straight line, were composed, like Roman roads, of a series of straight sections.

The new streets were also wider than most of their predecessors, for reasons of public order, public health and traffic engineering. Greater width tended to allow taller buildings on the frontages, especially when, in 1859, the first comprehensive building code since 1783/4 added some two and a half metres (eight feet) to the permitted height of facades on streets 20 metres (65 feet) or more wide. This increase of roughly one storey in the height of buildings on the new arterial streets did little to counteract the horizontal effect of development along the very long streets of the time. The new houses were generally built up to the full height permitted, partly through the aesthetic encouragement of the city authorities, and partly owing to the influence of the very high land values and speculative effects engendered by the Haussmannic property boom. The result was a common cornice line which reinforced the horizontal effect of the street perspective.

Haussmann was acutely aware of the need for powerful monumental terminations for his great new thoroughfares. At star and multiple junctions, a central monument could terminate a number of streets, but in the radial street system required by a large, modern city this solution could not be universally secured. This meant that Haussmann continually sought to direct new streets towards existing monuments, but to provide specially constructed buildings where necessary. As a result much of the new public architecture of Paris tended towards exaggerated volumes, striking outlines and emphatic detail.

Meanwhile, the facades of the apartment houses along the new streets carried minimal detail. Their horizontal lines were emphasised, and then harmonised by the intervention of city officials, to enhance the perspective effect. Standardisation and lack of decoration minimised building costs, and the effect was hailed as

---

[4] P. Lavedan, *Histoire de l'urbanisme* (Paris: Henri Laurens, 1952), vol. 3, p. 108.

'modern'. The owners also saw the standardised facade design of the day as a protection against fashion changes which might easily have devalued their investment in so rapidly changing a city.

In the newer parts of Paris, the homogeneity of the facades was partly the product of the organisation of development. Enterprising architects, or the big development companies which flourished in association with the municipality, would purchase a large block of land, planning the street system and laying out individual plots. They would then set up one or more building companies to attract investment and to undertake the construction of the houses. A single drawing office would prepare designs for all the land, sometimes introducing a degree of variety, but more often generating a large number of almost identical facades.[5] The authorities encouraged this process, being themselves legally unable to acquire and develop large areas of land on the periphery. The developers responded willingly to the authorities' views on the appropriate type of development, partly because it was in their financial interest to be absorbed into the broader planning strategy linked to the official street-building programme.

The minimal facade detail of the Haussmannic apartment house drew attention to an element of visual harmony which is often overlooked. This was the ubiquitous dressed limestone of mid-nineteenth-century Paris. Although the cheaper buildings did not use it, it set the pattern to such an extent that, as in the past, it was simulated in stucco finishes. By the early nineteenth century, local quarrying was in decline but the regional supply system, using water transport, allowed access to new sources of limestone, notably in the Oise. From the 1840s the railways extended the quarrying radius, and new types of stone became available.[6] During the Second Empire, improvements in quarrying and stone-cutting technology brought further economies. In the Second Empire, when little carving was done, the smooth, continuous stone facades of the apartment houses were acknowledged as a quality finish. This combination of quality and simplicity came to be seen as 'modern' and equated industrialism with the classical style.

Haussmann and Municipal Architecture

As soon as he took up office, Haussmann saw the need to enlarge and reinforce his architectural department, mainly with a view to designing the many municipal buildings which would be needed as the city spread. One of his earliest tasks was to establish a corps of architects working permanently for the city. This caused problems, because the established practice of recruiting independent architects for individual contracts was popular with the architects, who valued their freedom to undertake other work. Even when he was eventually able to create a corps of

---

[5] Ex inf. Maxine Copeland.
[6] F. Goy-Truffaut, *Paris façade* (Paris: Hazan, 1989), p. 96.

municipal architects, the system was undermined by some of the employees themselves and it did not survive Haussmann's resignation in 1870.[7]

However, for important projects Haussmann selected outstanding architects who would have been unlikely to accept employment as city architects – members of the Institute or Rome prize laureates, as Haussmann described them.[8] The result was that he achieved the very high standard of architecture in new public buildings that he desired. It was in recognition of this success that some of his friends persuaded him to seek membership of the Académie des Beaux-Arts, and his enthusiastic election bore witness to a wider respect in Parisian artistic circles for his architectural taste.[9]

Haussmann was not rigidly wedded to classical architecture, nor to the First Empire, which had some appeal in court circles. He wanted, however, to see strong relief on the facades of major buildings, which tended in consequence to stand out from domestic facades.[10] Although Haussmann admired the experiments in colour of J. I. Hittorff, who was one of his most valued architects, he did not see much place for polychromy on the outside of a structure. He preferred to admire the lines of a building without the distraction of colour.[11] His commitment to long, street perspectives led him to seek qualities of strength, mass and outline in the terminal buildings rather than obedience to classical norms of proportion. He was prepared to give clear instructions to these ends, even to very distinguished and experienced architects.

Like the emperor, he saw architecture as expressing change and modernity as well as national identity. He was prepared to back innovation and adventure as long as the result was distinctive and striking. He gave strong encouragement to Baltard's metal and glass design for the Halles after the outline design solution had been selected by Napoleon III, and he backed the experimental metal structure of Baltard's Eglise Saint-Augustin. He explained that to insert a capacious church into this narrow, triangular site required an adventurous design using new technology. It was also an experiment which, if successful, he expected to emulate on the other restricted sites generated by his new streets.[12]

Haussmann was therefore by no means a narrow and doctrinaire classicist. He was prepared for architecture to respond to the challenge of its site. As Haussmann probably created more awkward sites in seventeen years than the authorities had created in the whole of the preceding history of the city, he acted as an architectural innovator of some significance. Nevertheless, whatever the site and whatever the function, the resulting structures were almost always in the classical vein. Flexibility rather than creativity was the theme, and the result was a classical architecture for the industrial era rather than an industrial architecture.

---

[7] Haussmann, *Mémoires*, vol. 2, pp. 223–4.

[8] Ibid., pp. 224–5.

[9] Ibid., p. 234.

[10] Ibid.

[11] Ibid., pp. 238–9.

[12] Ibid., pp. 230–2.

35

Garden Cities of Tomorrow

Ebenezer Howard

In these days of strong party feeling and of keenly-contested social and religious issues, it might perhaps be thought difficult to find a single question having a vital bearing upon national life and well-being on which all persons, no matter of what political party, or of what shade of sociological opinion, would be found to be fully and entirely agreed.

[...]

There is, however, a question in regard to which one can scarcely find any difference of opinion. It is well-nigh universally agreed by men of all parties, not only in England, but all over Europe and America and our colonies, that it is deeply to be deplored that the people should continue to stream into the already over-crowded cities, and should thus further deplete the country districts.

[...]

All are agreed on the pressing nature of this problem, all are bent on its solution, and though it would doubtless be quite Utopian to expect a similar agreement as to the value of any remedy that may be proposed, it is at least of immense importance that, on a subject thus universally regarded as of supreme importance, we have such a consensus of opinion at the outset.

[...]

– Whatever may have been the causes which have operated in the past, and are operating now, to draw the people into the cities, those causes may all be summed

Ebenezer Howard, "Introduction" and "The Town and Country Magnet [Chapter 1]," pp. 2, 10–11, 13–19 from *Garden Cities of To-morrow*, 3rd edition. London: Swan Sonnenschein, 1902.

up as "attractions"; and it is obvious, therefore, that no remedy can possibly be effective which will not present to the people, or at least to considerable portions of them, greater "attractions" than our cities now possess, so that the force of the old "attractions" shall be overcome by the force of new "attractions" which are to be created. Each city may be regarded as a magnet, each person as a needle; and, so viewed, it is at once seen that nothing short of the discovery of a method for constructing magnets of yet greater power than our cities possess can be effective for re-distributing the population in a spontaneous and healthy manner.

[. . .]

The question is universally considered as though it were now, and for ever must remain, quite impossible for working people to live in the country and yet be engaged in pursuits other than agricultural; as though crowded, unhealthy cities were the last word of economic science; and as if our present form of industry, in which sharp lines divide agricultural from industrial pursuits, were necessarily an enduring one. This fallacy is the very common one of ignoring altogether the possibility of alternatives other than those presented to the mind. There are in reality not only, as is so constantly assumed, two alternatives – town life and country life – but a third alternative, in which all the advantages of the most energetic and active town life, with all the beauty and delight of the country, may be secured in perfect combination; and the certainty of being able to live this life will be the magnet which will produce the effect for which we are all striving – the spontaneous movement of the people from our crowded cities to the bosom of our kindly mother earth, at once the source of life, of happiness, of wealth, and of power. The town and the country may, therefore, be regarded as two magnets, each striving to draw the people to itself – a rivalry which a new form of life, partaking of the nature of both, comes to take part in. This may be illustrated by a diagram of "The Three Magnets," in which the chief advantages of the Town and of the Country are set forth with their corresponding drawbacks, while the advantages of the Town-Country are seen to be free from the disadvantages of either.

The Town magnet, it will be seen, offers, as compared with the Country magnet, the advantages of high wages, opportunities for employment, tempting prospects of advancement, but these are largely counterbalanced by high rents and prices. Its social opportunities and its places of amusement are very alluring, but excessive hours of toil, distance from work, and the "isolation of crowds" tend greatly to reduce the value of these good things. The well-lit streets are a great attraction, especially in winter, but the sunlight is being more and more shut out, while the air is so vitiated that the fine public buildings, like the sparrows, rapidly become covered with soot, and the very statues are in despair. Palatial edifices and fearful slums are the strange, complementary features of modern cities.

The Country magnet declares herself to be the source of all beauty and wealth; but the Town magnet mockingly reminds her that she is very dull for lack of society, and very sparing of her gifts for lack of capital. There are in the country

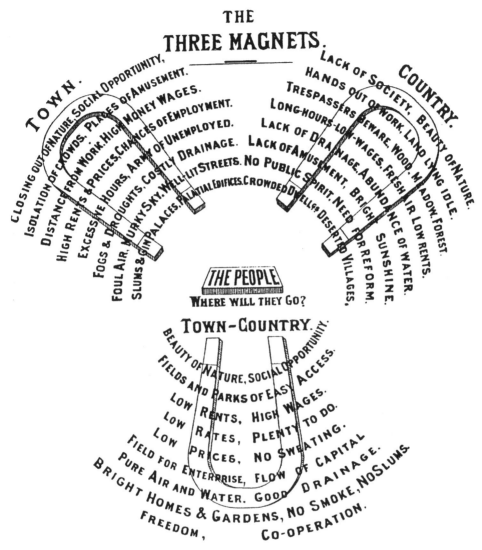

Figure 35.1 The three magnets
Source: Howard 1902

beautiful vistas, lordly parks, violet-scented woods, fresh air, sounds of rippling water; but too often one sees those threatening words, "Trespassers will be prosecuted." Rents, if estimated by the acre, are certainly low, but such low rents are the natural fruit of low wages rather than a cause of substantial comfort; while long hours and lack of amusements forbid the bright sunshine and the pure air to gladden the hearts of the people. The one industry, agriculture, suffers frequently from excessive rainfalls; but this wondrous harvest of the clouds is seldom properly ingathered, so that, in times of drought, there is frequently, even for drinking purposes, a most insufficient supply. Even the natural health-fulness of the country is largely lost for lack of proper drainage and other sanitary conditions, while, in parts almost deserted by the people, the few who remain are yet frequently huddled together as if in rivalry with the slums of our cities.

But neither the Town magnet nor the Country magnet represents the full plan and purpose of nature. Human society and the beauty of nature are meant to be enjoyed together. The two magnets must be made one. As man and woman by their varied gifts and faculties supplement each other, so should town and country. The town is the symbol of society – of mutual help and friendly co-operation, of fatherhood, motherhood, brotherhood, sisterhood, of wide relations between man and man – of broad, expanding sympathies – of science, art, culture, religion. And the country! The country is the symbol of God's love and care for man. All that we are and all that we have comes from it. Our bodies are formed of it; to it they return. We are fed by it, clothed by it, and by it are we warmed and sheltered. On its bosom we rest. Its beauty is the inspiration of art, of music, of poetry. Its forces propel all the wheels of industry. It is the source of all health, all wealth, all knowledge. But its fulness of joy and wisdom has not revealed itself to man. Nor can it ever, so long as this unholy, unnatural separation of society and nature endures. Town and country *must be married*, and out of this joyous union will spring a new hope, a new life, a new civilisation. It is the purpose of this work to show how a first step can be taken in this direction by the construction of a Town-country magnet; and I hope to convince the reader that this is practicable, here and now, and that on principles which are the very soundest, whether viewed from the ethical or the economic standpoint.

I will undertake, then, to show how in "Town-country" equal, nay better, opportunities of social intercourse may be enjoyed than are enjoyed in any crowded city, while yet the beauties of nature may encompass and enfold each dweller therein; how higher wages are compatible with reduced rents and rates; how abundant opportunities for employment and bright prospects of advancement may be secured for all; how capital may be attracted and wealth created; how the most admirable sanitary conditions may be ensured; how beautiful homes and gardens may be seen on every hand; how the bounds of freedom may be widened, and yet all the best results of concert and co-operation gathered in by a happy people.

The construction of such a magnet, could it be effected, followed, as it would be, by the construction of many more, would certainly afford a solution of the burning question set before us by Sir John Gorst, "how to back the tide of migration of the people into the towns, and to get them back upon the land."

36

Modern Systems

Camillo Sitte

Modern systems! – Yes, indeed! To approach everything in a strictly methodical manner and not to waver a hair's breadth from preconceived patterns, until genius has been strangled to death and *joie de vivre* stifled by the system – that is the sign of our time. We have at our disposal three major methods of city planning, and several subsidiary types. The major ones are the *gridiron system*, the *radial system*, and the *triangular system*. The subtypes are mostly hybrids of these three. Artistically speaking, not one of them is of any interest, for in their veins pulses not a single drop of artistic blood. All three are concerned exclusively with the arrangement of *street patterns*, and hence their intention is from the very start a purely technical one. A network of streets always serves only the purposes of communication, never of art, since it can never be comprehended sensorily, can never be grasped as a whole except in a plan of it. In our discussions so far street networks have not been mentioned for just that reason; neither those of ancient Athens, of Rome, of Nuremberg, nor of Venice. They are of no concern artistically, because they are inapprehensible in their entirety. Only that which a spectator can hold in view, what can be seen, is of artistic importance: for instance, the single street or the individual plaza.

It follows simply from this that under the proper conditions an artistic effect can be achieved with whatever street network be chosen, but the pattern should never be applied with that really brutal ruthlessness which characterizes the cities of the New World and which has, unfortunately and frequently, become the fashion with us. Artistically contrived streets and plazas might be wrested even from the gridiron system if the traffic expert would just let the artist peer over his shoulder occasionally or would set aside his compass and drawing board now and then. If only the desire were to exist, one could establish a basis for a *modus vivendi* between these two. After all, the artist needs for his purpose only a few main streets and plazas; all

Camillo Sitte, "Modern Systems," pp. 229–31, 233–42 from *City Planning According to Artistic Principles*, trans. George R. Collins and Christine Crasemann Collins. New York: Rizzoli, 1986.

the rest he is glad to turn over to traffic and to daily material needs. The broad mass of living quarters should be businesslike, and there the city may appear in its work clothes. However, major plazas and thoroughfares should wear their "Sunday best" in order to be a pride and joy to the inhabitants, to awake civic spirit, and forever to nurture great and noble sentiment within our growing youth. This is exactly the way it is in the old towns. The overwhelming majority of their side streets are artistically unimportant, and only the tourist in his exceptionally predisposed mood finds them beautiful, because he likes everything he sees. Just a few thoroughfares and major plazas in the centers of towns stand up under critical appraisal – those upon which our forefathers lavished wisely, and with all means at their disposal, whatever they could muster of works of civic art.

The artistic possibilities of modern systems of city planning should be judged from this standpoint, viz., that of a compromise, since it has already been made quite clear that the modern point of view rejects all demands made in the name of art. Whoever is to be spokesman for this artistic attitude must point out that a policy of unwavering adherence to matters of transportation is erroneous, and furthermore that the demands of art do not necessarily run contrary to the dictates of modern living (traffic, hygiene, etc.). We will attempt to demonstrate the former here.

The grid plan is the one most frequently applied. It was carried out already very early with an unrelenting thoroughness at Mannheim, whose plan looks exactly like a checkerboard; there exists not a single exception to the arid rule that all streets intersect perpendicularly and that each one runs straight in both directions until it reaches the countryside beyond the town. The rectangular city block prevailed here to such a degree that even street names were considered superfluous, the city blocks being designated merely by letters in one direction and by numbers in the other. Thus the last vestige of ancient tradition was eliminated and nothing remained for the play of imagination or fantasy. Mannheim assumes the credit for the invention of this system. *Volenti non fit injuria* [No injury is done to a consenting party]. One could fill volumes recording the censure and the scorn that have been lavished upon its plan in innumerable publications.

In the light of what we have seen it is hard to believe that this very system could have conquered the world. Wherever a new town extension is being planned this method is applied – even in radial and triangular systems the subsidiary nets of streets are organized this way insofar as possible. It is the more remarkable because this very arrangement has long been condemned from the point of view of traffic; Baumeister contains all that has been said to date on the matter.

[. . .]

For pedestrians the situation is even worse. Every hundred steps they have to leave the sidewalk in order to cross another street, and they cannot be careful enough in looking to the right and left for vehicles which may be coming along every which way. They miss the natural protection of uninterrupted house fronts. In every town where a so-called *corso* or promenade has developed, one can observe how a long continuous row of houses was instinctively chosen as side protection, since otherwise its whole pleasure of strolling would be spoilt by the constant lookout for cross-traffic. This can be seen most clearly in the promenade on the Ringstrasse of Vienna. From the Gartenbau-Gesellschaft building to the Kärntner-strasse the dense crowd of people moves only on that side of the Ringstrasse which lies toward the inner city, while the opposite side (pleasantly cooler in summer) remains empty. Why is this so? Only because on that southern side one must cross the Schwarzenbergplatz, and that is disagreeable. But from the Kärntnerstrasse to the Imperial Museums the promenade shifts to the other side of the Ringstrasse. Why? If not, one would have to pass in front of the ramp of the Opera, and this again would not satisfy our natural craving for protection from the flank.

But what marvelous traffic conditions arise when more than four thoroughfares run into each other! With the addition of just one more street opening to such a junction, the possible vehicle encounters already total 160, which is more than ten times the first case, and the number of crossings which disrupt traffic increases proportionately. Yet what shall we say about traffic intersections where as many as six or more streets run together from all sides? In the center of a populous town, at certain busy times of day, a smooth flow of traffic is actually impossible, and the authorities have to intervene, first by stationing a policeman who, with his signals, keeps the traffic precariously moving. For pedestrians such a place is truly haz-ardous, and in order to eliminate the worst dangers, a round piece of sidewalk is raised in the middle – a small safety island on which a beautiful slender gas light rises like a lighthouse amidst the stormy waves of the ocean of vehicles. This safety island with its gas lamp is perhaps the most magnificent and original invention of modern city planning! In spite of all these precautions, crossing the street is advisable only for alert persons; the old and the frail will always by preference take a long detour in order to avoid it.

These, then, are the achievements of a system that, relentlessly condemning all artistic traditions, has restricted itself exclusively to questions of traffic. Its mon-strous street junctions are called "plazas," yet in them everything is avoided that would make for character in a plaza, and at the same time everything seems to be accumulated that is impractical and ugly. These are the consequences of design based on traffic considerations rather than, as it should be, on the arrangement of plazas and streets.

In the gridiron system junctions like this result wherever the difficulties of terrain or a need to relate to what already existed before require deviations or breaks in the checkerboard pattern; triangular so-called plazas come into exist-ence. These occur even more frequently in the application of the radial system or in mixed systems. They become the greatest glory indeed of new layouts when they are completely regular: in circular form, or octagonal as in the Piazza Emmanuele in Turin. Nowhere can the bankruptcy of all artistic feeling and tradition be more clearly perceived than here. In plan such a plaza appears, of course, to be nicely regular, but what is the consequence in reality? Vistas opening out along a thoroughfare, which the ancients avoided so artfully, have here been

311

used as much as possible. The traffic junction is also a junction of all lines of sight. As one circles the plaza he always sees the same panorama, so that it is never exactly clear where one is standing. A stranger has only to turn around once on such a disconcerting merry-go-round of a plaza and immediately all sense of orientation is lost. On the Piazza Vigliena (Quattro Canti) in Palermo even the elaborate decoration of the four corners does not help, since they are all alike. Although only two major streets intersect perpendicularly on this octagonal plaza, one still finds strangers frequently turning into one of them to look for the street name or a familiar house, thus to regain their orientation. In reality all that is attained is a complete loss of our bearings, a monotony of vistas, and an architectural ineffectiveness. How odd a whim of the old masters to have ascribed importance to the avoidance of such things!

This type of plaza, along with its safety island and gas light or columnar monument, found its earliest manifestation in Paris, although none of the modern systems we have described happened to be rigorously carried out there during the last major renovation of the city. This was due in part to the intractable nature of the existing layout and in part to the tenacity with which fine old artistic traditions had preserved themselves. Different procedures were followed in various parts of the city, and, if nothing else, one can suggest that a certain remnant of Baroque tradition served as a common basis. The striving for perspective effects has obviously continued, and we could designate as the backbone of the system the broad avenue closed off in the distance by a monumental structure. Later the modern motif of the ring-boulevard was added to this, and a certain vigorous clearing out or breaking through of the dense mass of old houses was required by the circumstances. This remarkable reorganization, carried out on a large scale, became almost a fad, first and most frequently observable in the large cities of France.

The Place Juan Juarès in Marseilles should be mentioned as an example of the ruthless carving of a plaza out of a web of crooked streets. The Place du Pont in Lyons and other similar ones should also be noted. This practice has something vaguely in common with Nero's radical re-arrangement of Rome, although, of course, it is considerably more modern in character. Avenues and ring-boulevards were developed at Marseilles; at Nîmes (Cours Neuf, Boulevard du Grand Cours, Boulevard du Petit Cours); at Lyons (Cours Napoléon); at Avignon (Cours Bonaparte); and in other cities. In Italy a similar broad artery with several traffic lanes and shaded walks is called a *corso* or *largo*. Broad circumvallating boulevards were usually developed on the circuit of abandoned fortifications – in Vienna, Hamburg, Munich, Leipzig, Breslau, Bremen, Hanover; at Prague between the Altstadt and the Neustadt; at Antwerp; as a pentagon at Würzburg (Juliuspromenade, Hofpromenade, etc.), and elsewhere. The avenue as a very old and independently developed motif is, for instance, to be found in the Langgasse at Danzig; the Breite Gasse at Weimar; the Kaiserstrasse at Freiburg; the Maximilianstrasse at Augsburg; Unter den Linden in Berlin. The Jägerzeile in Vienna is representative of such broader avenues developed for their long vistas, and the

Graben there will, after its redesigning is completed, be transformed from a plaza into such an avenue. These are forms in modern city planning that are still artistically effective and are truly in the spirit of the Baroque.

However, as soon as the geometric pattern and the building block became dominant, art was forced into silence. The modernizing of Gotha, Darmstadt, Düsseldorf, the fan-shaped plan of Karlsruhe, etc., are examples of this. The absence of pedestrians on so many modern gigantic streets and plazas (the Ludwigstrasse in Munich, the Rathausplatz in Vienna) in contrast to the crowds in the narrow alleyways of the older parts of towns, demonstrates unequivocally how little the matter of traffic received its due consideration in such city expansions, although supposedly everything was based on just that. Whereas new broad streets are laid out on the periphery of the city where dense traffic is never likely to develop, the old city center remains forever congested.

This should be proof enough that the exponents of an exclusively traffic-oriented point of view, despite occasional success, are not justified in throwing to the winds as useless the assistance of art, the teachings of history, and the great traditions of city building.

One other important motif of modern planning remains to be mentioned. This is the matter of tree-lined avenues and gardens. Without doubt they constitute an important hygienic factor, and they also afford the undeniable charm of landscape elements in the middle of a big city and, occasionally, a splendid contrast between groups of trees and architecture. Yet it is open to question whether they are placed at the right spots. From the purely hygienic aspect the answer seems quite simple: the more greenery, the better – that is it in a nutshell. Not so from the artistic point of view, for the question arises as to where and how the greenery is to be applied. The usual and most felicitous application is to be found in the residential sections of modern cities, as in the justly famous residential belt around Frankfurt a. M., the Cottage Anlagen of the Währing district in Vienna, the similar annexes to the old part of Dresden, etc., as well as the indispensable villa areas at every spa: Wiesbaden, Nice, etc.

However, the closer such landscape elements encroach upon the center of a large city, and especially upon large monumental structures, the more difficult it becomes to find a universally satisfactory and artistically faultless solution. Modern naturalistic landscape painting is not suitable for monumental purposes; when it is used as a background for great mythological and religious representations or in the interiors of monumental buildings or churches, there necessarily arises an uncomfortable conflict between the realism of style and the idealism of subject matter, which no device, however clever, can relieve. In just the same way, the penetration of the English park into the major plazas of a city produces a conflict between the principles and effects of naturalism and the rigor of a monumental style. An awareness of this contradiction and a wish to avoid it were the forces which brought into being the Baroque park with its trimmed trees; an architectonically disciplined nature was used in former times primarily in connection with the château, whereas the larger monumental city squares of classic times, of the

Middle Ages, and of the Renaissance were exclusively focal points of creative art and especially of architecture and sculpture. Just how annoying the planting of trees in front of such works can be – above all on shabby, sickly boulevards – is to be seen in any photograph. Photographs are always of winter views, so that important architecture is at least partly visible between the bare branches; in fact, a drawing is frequently preferred to a photograph because with the former any disturbing trees can be left out entirely. Should they not, for the same reason, better be left out in reality, too? What value does an open plaza have as a perspective space when it is congested with foliage?

From this derives the principle that trees should not be an obstruction to the line of sight, and this rule in itself requires a return to Baroque models.

Complete adherence to this strictly artistic principle is impossible in modern city planning since it would put an end to almost all tree planting. Just as for monuments, we have no proper place for trees. The cause of this evil is the same in both instances – namely the modern building block. It is quite astonishing how many delightful small gardens are to be found in the interior of the building lots of old towns; one has no suspicion of their existence before entering the court-yards and rear areas. What a difference between these small private gardens and most of our public parks today! The old private garden, customarily connected with several adjacent ones, all of which are guarded from the wind and dust of the streets by the enclosing façades of high buildings, provides a really refreshing coolness and, insofar as possible in the big city, clean, dust-free air. It is truly a garden for the relaxation of the owner, and it is a blessing for all the surrounding interior apartments which thereby receive better air, daylight, and a pleasant view into the greenery. In contrast to this, the interior room of a modern apartment building – with its view into narrow, stuffy, dark, and frequently bad-smelling courts, so filled with stagnant air that the windows are forced to remain shut – is a dungeon of the most disagreeable sort, which repels all tenants and increases the demand for outside apartments, much to the detriment of our building projects. The modern public garden, being surrounded by open streets, is exposed to wind and weather and is coated with street dust, unless somewhat protected by its enormous size. Thus it happens that all these open modern parks fail completely in their hygienic purpose and are actually shunned by the public because of their dirt and heat, especially during the warm summertime.

The fundamental reason for this is again the abominable block system, since gardens should also, just like buildings and monuments, follow the example of the ancients – not standing free in the middle of empty spaces but being built in. As an example of such an inappropriate planting of trees, the plaza behind the new Bourse in Vienna should be mentioned. Hygienically speaking it is certainly quite indifferent whether these few trees stand there or not, since they provide neither shade nor coolness; rather they can scarcely be prevented from dying on account of the heat and dust. They only succeed in obstructing the view of the Bourse building. Would it not be better then to save the useless waste of a meager tree planting at such a place and instead create real gardens which for their own preservation are enclosed and, most important, do not lie open to the street? Wherever private gardens that formerly belonged to palaces have been given over to public use, one can see for oneself that, secluded from traffic, such gardens fulfill their hygienic purpose despite their small size and vegetation thrives. The uselessness of widely spaced greenery on streets and especially on public walks is demonstrated clearly enough by the fact that on hot summer days promenaders saunter not on these walks, but along the footways of the Ringstrasse, the avenues, etc. The principal value would consist in spraying the leaves with water so that during heat spells they could serve as an evaporating, and hence an air-conditioning, apparatus. Even this slight profit would be enough to justify street greenery wherever possible. However, in front of monumental structures the file of trees should be interrupted, since here aesthetic considerations are certainly much more important than their small hygienic value, and, as the lesser of two evils, the row of trees should be broken.

That this schism between the old and the new approach also occurs in the field of horticulture allows us now to recapitulate. The effective enclosure of space, deriving as it does from the historical evolution of an original, unbroken street front (such as still exists today in villages), continued to be the basis of all dispositions in the old towns. Modern city planning follows the opposite tendency of dissection into separate blocks – building block, plaza block, garden block – each one being clearly circumscribed by its street frontage. From this develops a powerful force of habit: the desire to see every monument in the center of a vacant space. There is method in this madness. The ideal behind this planning could be defined mathematically as a striving for the maximum of frontage line, and herein would appear to lie the creative impulse behind the modern block system. The value of every building site increases with the length of its street frontage, the maximum value for building lots in the parceling of land being therefore achieved when the perimeter of each block of buildings is greatest in relation to its area. Thus from a purely geometrical point of view circular blocks of buildings would be the most favorable, and, indeed, in the same configuration as that in which large balls of equal size can be pushed the closest together, namely six around one in the middle. In arranging straight streets of identical width between such blocks, the circular forms would be transformed into regular hexagons, as used in tile patterns or in the honeycomb. One could not believe it humanly possible that an idea of such really oppressive ugliness, of such appalling tediousness, and of such a labyrinthine lack of orientation would actually be carried out. Yet, incredible as it seems, it has become a reality in Chicago.

That then is the essence of the block system! In it art and beauty are no more. To arrive at such extremes is impossible in the Old World where we are used to the beauty and the coziness of old towns. However, many of their charms are already irretrievably lost for us since they no longer harmonize with modern living. If we do not wish to let this situation get out of hand, but still want to save as much as possible of artistic value in the layout of cities, we must be clear in our own minds as to just what can still be retained and what has to be dropped.

315

37

Construction

Otto Wagner

The need and necessity for protection against inclement weather and against men and animals was certainly the first cause and the original purpose of building.

- In building itself lies the germ of every method of construction, whose development advances with the purpose.
- The creation of such work corresponds to the idea of pure utility. But it could not suffice; the sense of beauty dwelling within man called on art and made her the constant companion of building.
- Thus arose architecture!
- The decoration of huts and caves with flowers, boughs, trophies, weapons, and stone tablets certainly elicited the first feeling for imitation, and thus the first art, architecture, called into being her sisters, painting and sculpture.
- Their works are the independent creation of the beautiful.
- Need, purpose, construction, and idealism are therefore the primitive germs of artistic life. United in a single idea, they produce a kind of "necessity" in the origin and existence of every work of art, and this is the meaning of the words "ARTIS SOLA DOMINA NECESSITAS."
- No less a person than Gottfried Semper first directed our attention to this truth (even if he unfortunately later deviated from it), and by that alone he quite clearly indicated the path that we must take.
- Need and construction keep equal pace with the aspirations of man, which art, majestically striding forward, cannot follow.
- A fear that the pure principle of utility will displace art therefore seems reasonable. Occasionally it has even led to a kind of struggle, founded on the erroneous belief that the differences between realism and idealism are irreconcilable.

Otto Wagner, "Construction," pp. 91–101 from Harry Francis Mallgrave (ed.), *Modern Architecture*, trans. Harry Francis Mallgrave. Santa Monica: The Getty Center for the History of Art and the Humanities, 1988.

- The error in this view lies in the assumption that utility can displace idealism completely and in the further inference that man can live without art; yet it is only to be supposed that utility and realism precede in order to prepare the deeds that art and idealism have to perform.

Since the beginning of art until today, this process, this development has remained the same. A glance at the past will show this clearly.

- The first human building form was the roof, the protective covering, surely a substitute for the lack of the cave. The roof preceded the supports, the wall, even the hearth. After the roof came the supports, artificially built of tree trunks and stones, and finally the wickerwork, the partition, the bearing wall.
- These building elements received further development in permanent settlements through the use of tools and natural circumstances. After an immeasurably long evolution, traditions (a continuous addition of new purposes and means of production) together with art (born of the human sense of beauty) gradually elevated the basic forms of supports, walls, and rafters to art-forms [*Kunstformen*].
- Only in such a way could art have arisen. There can scarcely be any doubt of the correctness of what I have said.
- Moreover, if one examines all the art-forms from historical periods, an almost unbroken series of gradual developments from the date of their CONSTRUCTIVE origin until today can easily be proven, notwithstanding all the stylistic epochs.
- Logical thinking must therefore convince us that the following tenet is unshakable: "EVERY ARCHITECTURAL FORM HAS ARISEN IN CONSTRUCTION AND HAS SUCCESSIVELY BECOME AN ART-FORM." This principle withstands all analyses and explains every art-form.

[...] Art-forms undergo change. Apart from the fact that the form had to correspond to the ideal of beauty of each epoch, these changes arose because the mode of production, the material, the tools, the means available, and the need were different, and further, forms came to fulfill different purposes in different places. IT IS THEREFORE CERTAIN THAT NEW PURPOSES MUST GIVE BIRTH TO NEW METHODS OF CONSTRUCTION, AND BY THIS REASONING ALSO TO NEW FORMS.

- Our modern epoch has, like none earlier, produced the greatest number of such new methods of construction (one need only consider the success of iron).
- If today all of these forms have not yet developed into perfect art-forms, it is for the reason indicated earlier – namely, that utility first prepares these forms for art.
- It might again be emphasized that every shaping of form always proceeds slowly and imperceptibly.

- It is Semper's undisputed merit to have referred us to this postulate, to be sure in a somewhat exotic way, in his book *Der Stil*. Like Darwin, however, he lacked the courage to complete his theories from above and below and had to make do with a symbolism of construction, instead of naming construction itself as the primitive cell of architecture.

Construction always precedes, for no art-form can arise without it, and the task of art, which is to idealize the existing, is impossible without the existence of the object.

- Thus the formation of our very own art-forms, corresponding to modern construction, lies within ourselves; the possibility of creating them is offered and facilitated by the rich legacy that we have inherited.
- The useful result of this way of looking at things is very simple.
- "THE ARCHITECT ALWAYS HAS TO DEVELOP THE ART-FORM OUT OF CONSTRUCTION." Obviously the method of construction must fulfill its intended purpose.

Modern man immediately comprehended the enormous value of construction and assigned his most distinguished representatives to achieve its magnificent perfection.

- This field has therefore grown so vast that it has naturally led to the division of labor; thus we see today the separate specialties of bridge construction, railway construction, girder construction, and machine engineering continuing to develop with colossal speed.
- Yet the basic thought behind every construction is not to be sought in algebraic progressions and structural calculations but in a certain natural ingenuity – it is that which is invented.
- From this last point of view, however, construction enters the field of art; that is, the architect selects, specifies, perfects, or invents that method of construction that most naturally fits his image of what is to be created and best suits his nascent art-form.
- The means available and the purpose of the emerging object will always cause him to vacillate between the constraints of pure utility and artistic development; but with due consideration the influence of the architect or the engineer will be resolved.
- THE ENGINEER WHO DOES NOT CONSIDER THE NASCENT ART-FORM BUT ONLY THE STRUCTURAL CALCULATION AND THE EXPENSE WILL THEREFORE SPEAK A LANGUAGE UNSYMPATHETIC TO MAN, WHILE ON THE OTHER HAND, THE ARCHITECT'S MODE OF EXPRESSION WILL REMAIN UNINTELLIGIBLE IF IN THE CREATION OF THE ART-FORM HE DOES NOT START FROM CONSTRUCTION.
- Both are great errors.

Since the engineer is seldom a born artist and the architect must train himself as a rule to be an engineer, it is safe to assume that art, or rather the architect, will in time succeed in extending his influence into the realm today occupied by the engineer, so that here too legitimate aesthetic demands can be met in a satisfactory way.

- Thus the sequence mentioned at the start, of utility preparing the way and art developing what has begun, will come to pass in all cases and in time will put an end to the unsatisfactory work of the engineer.
- In order not to be misunderstood, it should be noted that there can be no question of the artist lowering the status of the engineer, if for no other reason than because the capabilities of both have never been combined in one individual in an outstanding way, and in fact cannot be combined.

As the developing art-form is influenced by construction, so the latter is in turn influenced by many other factors that will be dealt with later.

- One of the most important of these that can be taken as a definite demand of our modern epoch may be discussed here. It concerns the time of production and the soundness usually dependent on it.
- A rather prevalent but, in part, totally false view is that our modern building methods, because they have been sharply accelerated, must also be unsound. The reason for this view is that speculation, which naturally has nothing to do with art and is even its greatest enemy, has a hand in building.
- If one examines our modern method of construction more closely, however, then one will easily be convinced that precisely the reverse is true, and that modern construction has set for itself the definite task of balancing, whenever possible, these two opposites: time of production and soundness. Modern construction in this regard has shown splendid results.

Through the building methods of all epochs runs a clear tendency to invest the created work with the greatest possible stability and durability in order to comply with one of the most important theses of architecture – "eternal duration."

- Because our modern conditions have produced a radical change in the time expended on labor while the principle of eternal duration in art has remained the same, construction, whose role it is to solve this task, has had to seize new means in order to comply with this demand.
- These means have been found for the most part in the use of new materials and in the introduction of machines.
- Therefore their influence on the art-form must naturally be evident.
- Because of this, an additional task falls to the artist, who, as already often mentioned, has not only to show the construction clearly in the created art-form, but also to convince the viewer that the material used and the time of production are properly expressed in the work.

- Mistakes of this kind are unfortunately all too numerous. Art-forms in which the time of production is not consistent with the effect or with the material or mode of production always have something false or vexing about them.
- Consoles and keystones that carry nothing, iron buildings that have the characteristic features of stone forms, plaster buildings that display a full stone pattern, numerous exterior details that pretend to be more than they are, and a great many other things fall into this category.

Yet when construction attempts to combine a shorter time of production with the same or greater solidity and with an artistic form of equal value, then it correctly understands its task.

- An example may serve to illustrate this view.
- A colonnade with an entablature was designed as the principal architectural motif of the upper story of a prominent monumental building. The building was constructed in courses of stone and the material was procured with a great expenditure of time and money. Immense stone blocks, reminiscent of the old Roman method of construction, were employed for the lower members of the main cornice; it was even structurally necessary to carve the modillions of the main cornice out of the same stone. The preparation and procurement of these blocks required great temporal and pecuniary sacrifice.
- This type of production should be called "the Renaissance way of building" and may be compared next with a "modern way of building."
- For the exterior cladding of a building (based, of course, on the same premises) a panel system will be used for the planar surfaces. Since these panels can be assumed to have significantly less cubic volume, they can be designed for a nobler material (for example, Laase marble). They are to be fastened with bronze bolts (rosettes). For the support of the deeply projecting cornice, divided into small courses, iron anchor bolts will be used, which are sheathed in a bronze console-like casing, etc., etc.
- The result of this comparison might be approximately the following:
- The cubic volume of the stone will be reduced by from one-eighth to one-tenth of that in the original case; the number of components will be fewer; the monumental effect will be enhanced by the nobler material; the money spent will decrease enormously, and the production time will be reduced to the normal and desired amount.
- Certainly the advantages are sufficient to prefer the modern way of building in such cases. But the list of advantages is not exhausted; the greatest advantage is that IN THIS WAY A NUMBER OF NEW ARTISTIC MOTIFS WILL EMERGE, whose development the artist not only will find very desirable, but also that which he must seize with alacrity and enthusiasm so as to make genuine progress in art.
- Results of this kind are not rare; every object without exception will offer them to the creative artist when it is considered in such a way.

It is only natural that modern men, who know how to appreciate the value of time, will also promote those methods of construction that are capable of satisfying their wishes in this regard. This is taking place naturally by the adoption of materials that can be procured quickly and easily, and by the division of labor; that is, by undertaking different parts of the construction at the same time, which results in a quicker assembly of the work.

- If such a method of assembly is also sound, it will replace the former method, notwithstanding higher costs. Obviously a new way of shaping form will emerge from such a process.

The availability of one or another material varies, of course, in different regions, and therefore its use and the extent of its treatment are also different. As a result, specific building materials predominate in specific regions, a fact that the architect may never overlook, because the desired ideal of beauty also demands a "local character" (fieldstone and ashlar construction, brick construction, plaster construction, wood construction, etc.).

One fact that is closely related to a building's production time must be mentioned here in particular, because most clients are falsely informed about it – unfortunately all too often by the architect himself. It concerns the time allotted the artist for the graphic, artistic, and technical execution of the project.

- The inception of artistic works in part rests on empirical creation and very often is a function of whim and inspiration. Yet never will such a work, precisely because it arose empirically, be so free of error that the executing artist will not wish (usually when it is too late) to make changes.
- A generous period of time for the work's graphic representation is therefore always to its advantage.
- With our apartment houses, which generally owe their existence simply to the vicissitudes of "capital investment," the time in which the architect must complete his work is always very scant; often it shrinks to a few days, since the owner, as a rule, starts construction immediately following the artistic commission.
- With monumental buildings the artist is usually given sufficient time to study and to complete his project, at least so far as to seem to preclude major changes. He often enjoys the insufficiently appreciated advantage of being able to consider everything thoroughly by means of a model before the start of construction.
- It therefore seems entirely valid to consider these factors when judging artistic works.

Among the materials that especially influence modern building methods, iron naturally plays the leading role. Its structural shapes accommodate themselves least to our traditional store of forms. In our rich artistic inheritance, we find almost nothing to assist us in the aesthetic development of iron.

321

- If, on the one hand, the result has been a longer than usual dominance of a principle as unsympathetic as that of utility; on the other hand, it cannot be welcomed warmly enough that wherever art has shaped this material completely new forms have in fact appeared. Thus it has provided one of the greatest impulses to the growth of the new style!
- The properties of iron, however, are indeed so extraordinary that it is able to satisfy almost any demand, and regarding the use of this material, it is really only a question of financial limitations.
- This, its universality, has also led to its overestimation, which just a few years ago caused its inartistic and rather obtrusive widespread use. The introduction of some other new materials, iron's inadequate or dubious testing, and financial considerations have also had a sobering effect, and have limited its use to those occasions where it is consistent with the artistic viewpoint of modern man.
- Yet there are so many objects that have been structurally and aesthetically influenced by the use of iron that the latter's existence and the resulting influence on our present building methods can be described as trend-setting.
- The possibility and facilitation of so many methods of building production, the unlimited choice of room sizes, the realization of a distinct pier construction, the availability of any ceiling form with whatever type of room lighting, the great reduction in wall thickness, the fireproof qualities, the significantly reduced time of construction, and so many other things, we owe solely to the use of this material.

The enormous importance of construction and its decisive influence on modern art has probably been emphasized enough in our discussion, yet it remains for me to recommend its study most urgently to the young architect.

- WELL-CONCEIVED CONSTRUCTION NOT ONLY IS THE PRE-REQUISITE OF EVERY ARCHITECTURAL WORK, BUT ALSO, AND THIS CANNOT BE REPEATED OFTEN ENOUGH, PRO-VIDES THE MODERN CREATIVE ARCHITECT WITH A NUMBER OF POSITIVE IDEAS FOR CREATING NEW FORMS – IN THE FULLEST MEANING OF THIS WORD.
- The choice of the type of construction will generally have to be made by the architect himself on the merits of each case. This not only requires a constant pursuit and acceptance of every innovation in the field of construction and its materials, but also demands that the architect (and rightfully so) has a strongly marked natural ingenuity.
- It is scarcely necessary to add that rich experience should also come together with the application of the construction method; thus the following can be taken as a postulate: WITHOUT THE KNOWLEDGE AND EXPERI-ENCE OF CONSTRUCTION, THE CONCEPT "ARCHITECT" IS UNTHINKABLE!

Part III

Architecture for Tomorrow, c.1910–2000

Introduction

Dorothy C. Rowe

Twentieth-century architectural and design modernism is clearly linked to the decisive break with the historicism of the nineteenth century that was signaled through the titles of publications such as Otto Wagner's *Modern Architecture* (1896). It was via Wagner's book, amongst others, that the term "modern" initially gained its currency during the first few years of the new century, particularly in relation to architectural developments (Sharp 1975: xvi). As a set of generic labels for describing, naming, and classifying the history of architecture and design culture during the first half of the twentieth century, "modern," "modernism," and "modernity" have a fraught and complex definitional history that is worth outlining as a framework for the consideration of the texts included in this final section, many of which can be described as either modernist or postmodernist in conception. To be modern at the start of the twentieth century was to be "new," and it was a "newness" born of an optimistic, though short-lived, belief in the power of technology to transform the future. On the other hand, by the latter half of the twentieth century, to declare oneself postmodernist was to continue the project of modernism *after modernism*, by celebrating its multivalent paradoxes, contradictions, and inconsistencies. The twenty-first century now finds us in an era of global digital web technology in which labels have become as increasingly philosophically meaningless as they have become fashionably desirable, and in which celebrations of difference, diversity, and multiculturalism find themselves in conflict with the realpolitik of nationalism, fundamentalism, terrorism, exploitation, and poverty. It is this century of change, then, that our final section hopes to evoke.

Critical definitions of modernism and modernity are mutable and myriad, and the semantic relationship between them is understood in different ways by a variety of commentators. At a primary semiotic level the word "modernity" denotes a specific spatio-temporal climate of newness and change born of the effects of industrial capitalism, and "modernism" an aesthetic response to that change. Marshall Berman, in *All That Is Solid Melts into Air* (1982), his classic study of modernity that deliberately adopts its title phrase from *The Communist Manifesto* to connote the experience of Western modernity, divides his account into three distinct historical phases, the origins of which are traced back to the sixteenth century and the last of which is focused on the twentieth century. However, Berman identifies the most radical historical shifts occurring specifically as a result of eighteenth-century Enlightenment philosophies of instrumental reason in which the "desire for development" becomes a key historiographic impulse (1982: 39). Similarly, Jürgen Habermas grounds his critical but nevertheless affirmative analysis of modernity (as "an incomplete" and ongoing project) firmly in the "Age of Enlightenment," the eighteenth century, in which a changed form of "modern" consciousness took place when to be "modern" was no longer to define one's relationship to antiquity but rather to oppose the ideals of the ancients (Habermas in Foster 1983: 3–15). However, he comments that by the end of the nineteenth century a historically specific referent against which one could define oneself as modern had vanished, and in its place was left a purely abstract opposition between "tradition" and "modernity." Habermas, in line with many other cultural commentators, locates the origins of this new form of aesthetic modernity in the work of the French poet of the Second Empire, Charles Baudelaire. David Harvey, in his 1990 study of *The Condition of Postmodernity*, also begins his definition of modernity and modernism by citing Baudelaire's account in "The Painter of Modern Life" (1863). The central paradox at the heart of Baudelaire's essay, that to be modern means the ability to distil the eternal from the transitory, to combine the ephemeral and the immutable, becomes one of the central problems facing the aesthetic modernist. In order to consider this question further, Harvey follows Habermas in turning to a critique of the instrumental rationality central to Western Enlightenment thought.

As we have already seen in part I, it was the eighteenth century in particular that marked the beginning of modern secular teleological philosophies of "progress" and advancement. Philosophies of rationalization as a means to "enlightenment" are shown by many commentators to have shaped the development of Western culture, in which concepts of modernity are intimately embedded. Naive faith in the moral certitudes of the modernist project and the concomitant liberation of the transcendental qualities of humanity was nevertheless shattered during the twentieth century when the processes of mechanistic rationalization enabled oppressive political regimes such as those in Soviet Russia and Nazi Germany to operate vast systems of mass genocide on an industrial scale. Even by the end of the nineteenth century, the futile search for the transcendent was no longer presupposed to be revealed as a result of a successful rationalistic modernist project. Thus, the only surviving feature of Baudelaire's dual formula by the beginning of the twentieth century became the transitory, the fleeting, and the fragmentary, support for which could be found in a Nietzschean exhortation for the creative destruction of the old world as a prerequisite for the formation of the new, a credo taken up by an emerging generation of avant-garde cultural modernists in the first few decades of the century. This was the generation that responded with enthusiasm to the call of Italian futurists such as Filippo Tommaso Marinetti to engage with "the dynamism of modern life" before joining up for swift and horrible death or injury in the trenches of World War I (Marinetti 1909).

For inhabitants of the West in the early twentieth century, then, it was the seismic shifts in the socio-economic conditions of modern urban life that generated a modernist aesthetic. To be modern meant to engage with the potential for the future that had been radically opened up by new technological advances in the present, with no longer any a priori requirements to reference the past. Thus, for Antonio Sant'Elia, writing the *Manifesto of Futurist Architecture* in 1914, "architecture cannot be subjected to any law of historical continuity. It must be new, just as our state of mind is new" (1914: 169). Although the transcendental white male subject of history remained securely in position within modernist polemics, he was radically repositioned, in a relationship of uncertainty yet exhilaration, to his future, though he often (but not always) retained a creeping nostalgia for an irretrievable past. This was a major source for the development of avant-garde culture on both the political left and right that engendered the development of multiple and split ideologies of modernism in which the formation, exploration, and representation of alienated and fragile subjectivities was central.

In her 1999 study of the relationship between architecture and modernity, Hilde Heynen clarifies some of the different ways in which modernity was understood by both its early protagonists and its subsequent commentators:

> One can see it as determined by the opposition between a capitalist civilization and its cultural, modernist counterpart. The relation between these poles however, is conceived of in divergent ways: some perceive them as not related at all; for others there is a dialectical relationship at stake in which modernism consciously or unconsciously, directly or indirectly, positively or negatively reflects the effects of capitalist development ... one can discern an avant-garde attitude that aims at the reintegration of art and life; one can moreover distinguish between programmatic and transitory conceptions of modernity, as well as between "pastoral" and "counter-pastoral" modernisms ... (Heynen 1999: 3)

While she identifies Habermas's approach to modernity as "programmatic," Heynen sees Baudrillard as distinguishing a more transitory approach in which rupture, destruction, and innovation for their own sake gradually replace the ethical and philosophical ideologies of progress that sustained the modernist project at the outset and ultimately set it up for its own demise (1999: 12). For a "pastoral" or Utopian view of modernity which denies any of its internal inconsistencies and contradictions in favor of an unflinching belief in a universal struggle for progress that unites workers, artists, and industrialists alike, Heynen cites Le Corbusier, while a counter-pastoral view can be evidenced in the writings of Theodor Adorno and his Frankfurt School followers. For Adorno, the success of bourgeois modernity is dependent upon the oppression of those who cannot afford its comforts, yet ironically the bourgeoisie will never be able to rest peacefully in enjoyment of these comforts troubled by the knowledge of its repressed "others." Modern capitalist society will remain restless, dissatisfied, and melancholic in an ironically successful situation of its own making (Adorno 1991).

The implications of modernity for the development of architectural modernism in particular become especially interesting given the inherent conflicts between capitalist civilization and modernist culture that emerged during the early twentieth century. The collision between aesthetic modernity and bourgeois modernity is made manifest through modernist architecture, dependent as it is upon networks of capitalism to sustain its development. This tension emerges in different discursive ways within the history of the modern movement, in which conflicting positions regarding the role of architecture and design in modern society come increasingly to the fore. Subsequent critics of and commentators on modernity have identified these tensions as bound up with the loss of the ability of the individual to "dwell" in the terms defined by Heidegger in his 1951 essay "Building, Dwelling, Thinking." For Heidegger, the condition of "dwelling" is one of care and preservation, which allows things to exist in their essence or "being." "Being" consists of the "fourfold" of heaven, earth, divinities, and mortals, which has to be nurtured and preserved, and the person who "dwells" is someone who is receptive to "being" (Heidegger 1971). Only those who know how to "dwell" have the ability to "build," since building makes a place out of an undifferentiated space, a tangible dwelling where the "fourfold" is gathered. Modernity, however, is characterized by the forgetfulness of "being" in favor of instrumental rationalization, usefulness, and efficiency, to the extent that "dwelling" is conceived as no longer possible; to be modern in these terms is to be rootless and homeless, a "non-dweller" (Heynen 1999: 16–18). This, then, characterizes one of the fundamental dilemmas confronting the self-proclaimed modern architect: how to reconcile the functional, capitalist-driven demand for new homes and office buildings with the paradox of the poetically, aesthetically, and philosophically conceived homelessness that characterizes the condition of "non-dwelling" in the rootless, cosmopolitan, modernist metropolis? In Simmelian terms this can also be characterized as how to negotiate the split between objective (outer) culture and subjective (inner) life brought about by the mechanistic operations of the industrial capitalist metropolis in which all forms of human sociation and social interaction are governed by the objectivity of money culture.[1] In the modern metropolis, according to Simmel in his by now extremely famous essay, "The Metropolis and Mental Life," financial transactions

---

[1] Georg Simmel (1858–1918) was one of the first sociologists of modern urban life in Germany at the start of the twentieth century; he focused on the effects of modern industrial capitalism on the psychology of the individual city dweller in sociological terms. For more information see Levine 1971; Frisby 1981.

are privileged above social ones, leading to individualism, loss of self, and social isolation (Simmel 1903). Modern society is conceived most often, then, as a culture of splits, fissures, and ruptures which, according to Adolf Loos (1870–1933) amongst others, it was the task of the modern intellectual to confront in an attempt to formulate the basis for a renewed culture that could no longer be predicated upon a self-evident trajectory of historicism and trad-ition. Significantly, however, as Renato Poggioli has observed, the battle of the avant-garde (or their "tragic position," as he frames it) is the double front against which it is pitched. While bourgeois capitalism and academicism are the declared enemies of avant-gardism, a further threat remains within the popular cultural tastes of the urban proletariat. Those in the avant-garde find themselves in a position of aristocratic disdain for the cultural products of both the middle and the lower classes in their attempts to reinvent and revivify modern culture (Pog-gioli 1968: 124). For Adolf Loos, in an essay entitled "Architecture" (1910), "the architect, like almost every urban dweller, has no culture. He lacks the certainty of the farmer, who possesses culture. The urban dweller is an uprooted person." Loos goes on to explain in terms that are already familiar from Simmel's earlier analyses, that "by culture I mean that balance of man's inner and outer being which alone guarantees rational thought and action," and that the success-ful "evolution of culture is synonymous with the removal of ornament from the object of daily use" (Loos cited in Drew 1985: 104). Loos's attack on the use of ornament in this 1910 essay was the continuation and elaboration of a position that he had already delineated two years earlier in what is probably one of the most notorious polemics against building decoration in the historiography of design modernism, *Ornament and Crime* (1908).[2]

Ornament and Crime takes up a position already articulated to some degree by Louis Sullivan in his 1892 essay, *Ornament in Architecture*, but unequivocally radicalizes Sullivan's position. While, for Sullivan, "ornament is mentally a luxury, not a necessary," for Loos, ornament becomes an "epidemic" that "is not merely produced by criminals" but "commits a crime itself by damaging national econ-omy and therefore cultural development" in wasted human labor and material costs. Loos's hostile and somewhat overstated stance towards the crime of archi-tectural ornament was born in part from his dissatisfaction with what he con-sidered to be the over-decorative aspects of art nouveau, particularly evidenced in

[2] According to Janet Stewart, the 1908 date for *Ornament and Crime* is not necessarily accurate. She notes that "when *Trotzdem* – the second collection of Loos's essays – was published in 1931, *Ornament and Crime* was dated to 1908. There is, however, no evidence of it actually having been published in that year, nor having been given as a lecture. It seems as though Loos (over sixty by that time) probably made an approximate stab at the date when asked by the editors of the collection. There is certainly no detailed bibliographical information in the collection and this is certainly not the only bibliographical inaccuracy to be found in *Trotzdem*" (email correspondence with the editors, June 28, 2004). For further details, see Stewart 2000: 32–3.

Josef Hoffman's *Gesamtkunstwerk* approach to the Palais Stoclet (1905–11) in Brussels, in which unity of design transcended every aspect of the building and its environment to the extent that there was no longer any room for the individual expression of personal style or, in Heidegger's terms, "dwelling." Loos had spent the mid-1890s in America, returning to Vienna in 1896 where he soon became familiar with Otto Wagner's new writings on architecture in which the credo that "nothing that is not practical can be beautiful" was closely in keeping with his own praise of the functional practicalities of American plumbing, among other topics, that constituted his regular articles for the Austrian popular press (Wagner 1896: 8). The visual excesses of art nouveau as practiced by his Viennese peers were an inescapable reminder of Loos's own position vis-à-vis the bourgeoisie towards whom he remained dialectically ambivalent, simultaneously identifying with and distancing himself from this distinct stratum of Austria's urban-industrial capitalist society (Stewart 2000: 76–7). Indeed, Loos's ambivalence towards the bourgeoisie can be read precisely as part of the wider tensions inherent in the role of modern architecture within bourgeois capitalism; while architectural activity was undoubtedly of cultural and aesthetic concern, its van-guard status was constantly undermined by the mechanisms of wealth and power upon which it was dependent for its realization. If modern architects defined themselves as modern, as new and as radically avant-garde, how were they to negotiate the bourgeois system with which they were inextricably entwined in a parasitical symbiosis? As one of the underlying tensions inherent in the develop-ment of architectural modernism in the early years of the twentieth century it was not always explicit, but it nevertheless remained at the core of many architects' double-edged frustration and fascination with the modernity with which they found themselves engaged.

In Loos's prolific cultural criticism (which became the main source of his fame well ahead of his relatively marginalized architectural output), frequent and biting attacks on the backwardness and hypocrisy of the bourgeoisie were coupled not only with scathing criticism of the architects of the Sezession group, Josef Hoffmann (1870–1955) and Joseph Maria Olbrich (1867–1908), but also the design principles of the Deutscher Werkbund. The Deutscher Werkbund was founded in Munich in 1907 by liberal socialist politician and reformer, Friedrich Naumann, together with the architects and designers Hermann Muthesius (1861–1927) and Henry van der Velde (1863–1957). Other members of the group included the slightly younger Peter Behrens (1868–1940), Bruno Taut (1880–1938), and Walter Gropius (1883–1969), all of whom were to become major protagonists within a historiography of modernism that was subsequently established through the dual impact of Nikolaus Pevsner's 1936 publication, *Pioneers of the Modern Movement: From William Morris to Walter Gropius*, and Sigfried Giedion's 1941 text, *Space, Time and Architecture*, both of which are considered in more detail below. The original aims of the Werkbund had been to refashion the links between art and industry and between designer and producer in order to produce quality consumer goods made in Germany. The distinctly patriotic flavor of the early years was strategically fostered in order to gain financial support from both the ruling state and the expanding class of wealthy industrialists and factory owners. However, the aims and objectives of the group were not static, but developed and fluctuated as a result of changing social and economic conditions. From its inception, internal tensions between individual members of the Werkbund were apparent, and the project was fraught with tense debates regarding the function and status of both the individual artist and the artwork in a period of commodified mass production (Schwartz 1996). In their considerations of the eventual consumers of their products, Muthesius in particular adopted an impractical, yet nevertheless conventional "trickle-down" approach that had been popularized in the fin-de-siècle writings of Thorstein Veblen, among others (Veblen 1984). Muthesius initially only aimed his marketing strategies towards Germany's *Mittelstand* (the middle classes) by stressing that good taste in choosing consumer products was the equivalent of cleanliness and morality. He believed that if good-quality consumer goods appeared in shop windows and were bought by the urban middle classes, their popular consumption would enthuse the proletariat into emulating the buying behavior of the superior class and that, in turn, this would contribute to the revitalization of the entire German culture (Campbell 1978). It was Muthesius's concomitant drive for a unity of style "to replace the confectionery of nineteenth century eclecticism" that was the basis of Adolf Loos's critique, for the same reasons that Loos also abhorred the stylistic oppressions of art nouveau (Curtis 1996: 100; Stewart 2000: 93, 186 n. 37). Muthesius had inherited his belief in the moral power of design from the English Arts and Crafts movement, but combined it with the practical need to produce consumer goods for a machine-driven mass market. This was coupled with a Hegelian idealism that fostered the conviction that it was Germany's destiny "to realize some higher idea in the historical scheme of things" in which the development of a new national style born of a "will to form" was a "universal necessity" (Curtis 1996: 100–1). However, although the design and production of quality goods for a mass market was one aspect of the Werkbund's activities, it was only architecture "of all the arts" that had "come to represent what is eternal in human history" and that could offer the ideal vehicle for the manifestation of *Kunstwollen* in the new century (Muthesius cited in Curtis 1996: 101). The modernist Baudelairean search for the immutable and the tangible in the fleeting and the transitory was to be found, for members of the Werkbund at least, in a new form of German architecture as practiced by Werkbund member Peter Behrens.

Behrens's design and building of the turbine factory for the giant electrical company AEG in Berlin was the earliest visible sign of Werkbund architectural modernism in practice. The building was erected on the Huttenstrasse in Berlin in 1909 and was characterized by its combination of modern materials (glass, steel, and concrete), functional design, and an unusual monumentality for factory buildings of this type. The scale, clarity, and classicizing proportion of the building became a visible testimony to Behrens's belief that industrial tasks were also the cultural ones of the age and required a monumental architecture fitting for their status in the modern era. What Behrens achieved in the AEG building was the aesthetic resolution of the functional needs of an industrial building in an appropriate architectural form that neither disguised its function nor compromised the genre. The Werkbund solution, then, to the tensions of avant-garde dependence on bourgeois capital was to embrace it in the utopian hope that the new products of architectural and design modernism would influence more fundamental shifts across the whole of German culture. Behrens's detailed analysis of the architectural construction of the building, included as an excerpt in this anthology, explicitly disavows the use of ornament in a manner not dissimilar to that of Louis Sullivan, and which ironically also echoes the content, though not the tone, of Adolf Loos's excoriating polemic against the use of ornament considered above:

> All forms of sculptural and ornamental decoration were omitted, firstly because the function of a factory building demands simplicity of form, but more especially because the desired impression of solidity, and the proportions contributing to this impression, could only have been diminished rather than enhanced by it. (Behrens cited in Benton et al. 1975a: 56–7)

For Nikolaus Pevsner the AEG turbine factory was "a pure work of architecture" that visualized "for the first time the imaginative possibilities of industrial architecture" (Pevsner 1936: 204). Pevsner's 1936 account of *Pioneers of the Modern Movement*, from which these quotations are extracted, together with Sigfried Giedion's 1941 text, *Space, Time and Architecture*, have both had a profound and lasting impact on the way in which modernism has been conceptualized, discussed, and written about and are worth reflecting upon for a moment in terms of the historiography of modern architecture that is to a large degree replicated in the first half of this section of our anthology. While there are many problems inherent in the gendered and racially biased accounts of the architectural and design heroism of the white male "modern movement," it would be a mistake simply to ignore the way in which Pevsner and Giedion shaped twentieth-century architectural and design histories. Rather, I would argue that it is more fruitful to approach the historiography of modernism with an awareness that, while the architectural and design objects of its study have become heavily circumscribed with the layers of historiographical interpretation at the hands of such influential architectural historians, further possibilities for rereading the same set of objects and texts have more recently been exposed by new generations of scholars armed with a "different set of co-ordinates and destinations" derived from some of the seismic shifts in academic scholarship that have occurred in the wake of post-structural, post-colonial, and feminist politicizations of the academy over the last few decades (Arnold 2002: xv). What is interesting for our purposes here are the choices that a historian like Giedion, for example, makes in his construction of a modernist canon of architecture in the 1940s that comes to stand for a particular map of modernism to which we are still in thrall to a large extent today.

In the foreword to *Space, Time and Architecture*, Giedion specifies the intended audience for his text as those for whom modern culture offers a mass of "contradictory tendencies" born of a gap between "thought and feeling" provoked by the rapid and radical changes to industrial and technological life begun during the nineteenth century, which had also been the subject of earlier and similar critiques by Simmel, Loos, and others. For Giedion, however, the fissure between what Simmel had identified as the split between subjective (inner or emotional) and objective (outer or rational) life was not insurmountable, and indeed such a split belied a "hidden unity" or "secret synthesis" that he set out to retrieve for the "present civilization" (Giedion 1941: vi). The crux of this perceived synthesis was the new elision of space and time that was, according to Giedion, characteristic of modern architecture as demonstrated through the work of Gropius, Le Corbusier, Mies van der Rohe, Alvar Aalto, and Jorn Utzon. The compression of space and time in the work of the cubist and futurist painters led to a new vision of space that was no longer dependent upon the use of perspective. Within architecture, concepts of simultaneity, dynamism, transparency, and many-sidedness, which were made manifest in the use of overlapping structural surfaces of glass and which had been enabled by technological advances in architectural construction, offered a different experience of space and time in modern architecture than was available in that of the previous era. Giedion also emphasized the significance of the organic and the irrational aspects of architecture, which for him needed to be brought into a more careful dialectic with architecturally rational elements, rather than being suppressed and lost altogether. This, then, is the synthesis between outer and inner, objective and subjective, rational and emotional that lies at the heart of Giedion's historical project. What he did was to bring together a number of extant but very different elements into a single paradigm of modern architecture in order to create it, somewhat paradoxically, as a new tradition. As Hilde Heynen has pointed out, the publication of the text in 1941 "marked the end of a period of searching and questioning, a period of heated debates and experiments often in conflicting directions, and the beginning of a new period in which the direction to take was supposed to be clearly mapped out" (Heynen 1999: 42). The avant-garde became ordered, categorized, and subject to a taxonomy of modernism through Giedion's writings. In *The State of German Architecture* (1926) for example, Giedion constructs a narrative concerning the end of expressionism and the beginnings of new objectivity in architecture in which "expressionist architecture in the proper sense of the term does not exist." Yet as Iain Boyd White points out, Giedion's exclusion of certain forms of utopian expressionist architecture by Bruno Taut and others is wrong-headed and that "by its nature, the development of successive avant-garde movements is a dialectical development, full of contradictions and about turns" and further that "it is ingenuous to believe, as Giedion, Pevsner and their imitators have done, that modernism is synonymous with progress or that modernism can be charted along a straight teleological path" (Boyd White 1980: 113). Boyd White focuses his analysis in particular on the role of Bruno Taut within Giedion's trajectory mapped against his own reading of the shifts in Taut's avant-garde practices, shifts that Giedion finds it difficult to contain within his own view of what "good" modern architecture ought to be. The expressionist fantasies outlined in Taut's quirky illustrations and their accompanying annotations in his *Alpine Architecture* of 1919, for example, were considered by Giedion to be an anomaly in comparison with Taut's later, more functionalist and therefore more acceptable, modernist practices as an architect of the modern movement.

Taut's visions of a newly centered society grounded in collective buildings that were to rise like crystals from glaciers and mountain peaks, set out in *Alpine Architecture* and further emphasized in *Die Stadtkrone* (City Crown) also of 1919, were attempts at regrounding modern, alienated individuals through a utopian apolitical socialism that echoed Pugin's earlier nineteenth-century belief in Gothic form as the ideal medium to accelerate the moral regeneration of society. Such strongly held beliefs in the redemptive potential of architectural forms endured well into the twentieth century, albeit in different guises. Thus, for example, in his initial program for the first Bauhaus in Weimar in 1919, we see Walter Gropius reverting to the idea of social and spiritual unification in his advocacy of a new unity of artists and craftsmen to create "the new structure of the future which will embrace architecture and sculpture and painting in one unity and which will one day rise towards heaven from the hands of a million workers like the crystal symbol of a new faith" (cited in Benton et al. 1975a: 78). As if to underline the point further, the front cover of the original program was illustrated by a woodcut by Lyonel Feininger representing the "Cathedral of Socialism" and emulating a crystalline glass-inspired Gothic cathedral "soaked in visionary sentiments" (Curtis 1996: 184) and clearly derived from Gropius's reading of both Taut and, more specifically, Paul Scheerbart's 1914 essay extolling the merits of glass architecture for the future of building design.

The initial Bauhaus appeared to have returned to the roots of the Arts and Crafts movement, by-passing the focus on mass industrial production that had distinguished the Werkbund's activities from Arts and Crafts practice, despite the fact that Gropius had been a central member of the original Werkbund a decade earlier. The aesthetic of cosmic spirituality with which the original Bauhaus program was imbued also extended to the design of Bauhaus teaching in its first stages. Students were apprentices, and operated within a framework that emulated the medieval guild system of artistic training. Every student was required to pass an initial foundation course (the *Vorkurs*) run at first by Johannes Itten and subsequently by Josef Albers and László Moholy-Nagy. Johannes Itten in particular believed in the Mazdaznan cult and he took on the role of spiritual instructor, inducting students into religious purity via a vegetarian diet, fasting, and other ascetic activities. Marianne Brandt, who later trained under Moholy-Nagy, dismissed the Mazdaznan period in her "Letter to the Younger Generation" as one of the least successful periods in the Bauhaus's mixed history. Brandt's contribution to the subsequent reputation of Bauhaus lighting and metalwork design has been fairly extensive, and in her letter she outlines some of her recollections of the time spent there between 1924 and 1929, becoming director of the metal workshop on Moholy-Nagy's departure in 1928. Within modernism, the Bauhaus played a significant role in the training of both male and female designers, but, as Brandt points out, she was initially not welcomed in the metal workshop since female students were traditionally assigned to the textile studios. Nevertheless, after a period of time in which she was allocated the dull, repetitive, and menial tasks, she comments that "things settled down and we got along well together," indicating that she was subsequently able to pursue her own ideas in a meaningful way, producing a variety of design objects, including her renowned adjustable metal lamps (cited in Neumann 1970: 98).

László Moholy-Nagy (1895–1946) was appointed to the Bauhaus by Walter Gropius in 1923 in order to take over Itten's teaching on the preliminary course (*Vorkurs*). Itten had pursued an eccentric path with students that was the antithesis of Moholy-Nagy's constructivist approach to modern industrial design, and his appointment afforded the Bauhaus a radical and ultimately beneficial change in direction towards a more functionalist approach, divesting itself completely of any of its earlier brief but embedded expressionist origins. In Gropius's preface to Moholy-Nagy's 1928 text, "The New Vision," he comments that "Moholy was one of my most active colleagues in building up the Bauhaus" and that much of what the Bauhaus accomplished in the development of successful modern design "stands to his credit" (Moholy-Nagy 1947: 5). The content of "The New Vision" is largely based on Moholy-Nagy's educational experience and the lectures given to Bauhaus students between 1923 and 1928 which Gropius views as "more than a personal credo of the artist" but also as "a standard grammar of modern design" (1947: 6). In the chapter on "Space (Architecture)" reproduced here, the modernist split between subjective and objective culture delineated above is also addressed by Moholy-Nagy in his conception of how the "new architecture, on its highest plane, will be called upon to remove the conflict between the organic and artificial, between open and closed, between the country and the city" because "the future conception of architecture will realize ... the whole" (1947: 60). For Moholy-Nagy, drawing explicitly on Theo van Doesburg's constructivist conception of the operations of architectural space and time, such unification via architecture could only be realized through architectural mastery of space and, in turn technological advancement, in order to fulfill the practical development of this aspired-for dominance of space.

The idea of a total environment in which mastery of spatial form was central was also very much in keeping with the principles of the Bauhaus teachings of integrated design, which extended to the architectural design of its second phase institutional buildings. When the Bauhaus moved from Weimar to Dessau in 1926, Marcel Breuer (1902–81) oversaw all of the interiors for the Dessau buildings, including the houses for Gropius, Grote, Kandinsky, and Moholy-Nagy. Breuer, like other young apprentices whose work stood out, was a prolific and versatile designer. Thus, although he was in charge of the cabinet-making workshop at Dessau, Breuer's most celebrated designs were ultimately for furniture, in particular his tubular steel and black leather chairs, but, like Moholy-Nagy, he could turn his hand to many different forms of creative activity, including architecture. Reflecting on the "new architecture" in a lecture delivered in Switzerland in 1934, a year after the Berlin Bauhaus had been closed by the National Socialists and its teachers forced into exile, Breuer addresses one of the fundamental problems of modernity, the emphasis on concepts of the new. He perceptively observes that labels such as "the new architecture" are fundamentally meaningless if modern architecture aspires to longevity, and that "the new in the Modern Movement must be considered simply as a means to an end and not an end in itself as in women's fashions" (1934: 120). Breuer's analysis of how the new architecture might be defined is articulated very cogently in terms of what it is not. The essay appears, at least in part, to be about a redress of popular misconceptions concerning the design principles of modern architecture, and as such it stands as a useful position document for Breuer's ideas, in the context of both technological architectural and design modernism and the rising right-wing tide against all modernist architecture and design in Hitler's Third Reich. Breuer's text, like many subsequent statements regarding the authenticity of the modern movement in architecture and design, was implicitly a political statement made in defense of modernism.

An altogether different architect from those involved with the Dessau and Berlin Bauhaus but also working in Germany during the 1920s was Erich Mendelsohn (1887–1953), for whom the sinuous organicism of art nouveau, *Jugendstil*, and Henri van der Velde's designs remained inspirational in the first years of his practice, in contrast to the functional machine aesthetic of many of his contemporaries, in particular Mies van der Rohe and Le Corbusier. Although Mendelsohn's architectural style developed from an early faith in expressionism towards a version of international modernism, culminating in his 1929 Columbushaus building in Berlin, he never lost sight of the "dynamism" of the pre-1918 modernist aesthetic for his architectural conceptions. In the extracts from his writings included in this section we witness Mendelsohn's commitment to the use of concrete as the ultimate modern building material, a material that he would have liked to have been able to use for his 1920 Einstein Tower in Potsdam. However, according to Pevsner, due to post-World War I rationing there was not enough cement available, so reluctantly Mendelsohn had to concede to building the tower from brick with a cosmetic surface of cement and plaster, an issue that offended his sense of architectural integrity (Pevsner cited in Beyer 1967: 15). Mendelsohn's choice of architectural style for the Einstein Tower remains distinct in its deployment of organic forms that are nevertheless harnessed with tight structural control. In his interpretation of Mendelsohn's 1919 lecture "The Problem of the New Architecture," William Curtis observes that,

> For Mendelsohn the tension of a work was increased and enriched by a fusion of the organic with a strong geometrical armature employing axes and by an accentuation of an actual structural system. He wished, for example, to exploit the tensile capacities of steel and the compressive ones of concrete, and to express these opposing forces simultaneously. (Curtis 1996: 187)

The Einstein Tower housed astrophysical laboratories, and had a large telescope at the top, situated inside a crowning cupola. The overall dynamic form of the external structure was emphasized through the free-form sculptural skin that enclosed and disguised the underlying brick structure, as well as through the curvature and angularity of the window and door frames, which also accentuated the building's sense of energy.

The Einstein Tower was Mendelsohn's earliest realized building and, although not fully complete until 1924, its conception lay very much in the era of the immediate revolutionary post-war expressionism of 1918. However, throughout the 1920s, his building style matured and designs for a hat factory at Luckenwalde, which opened in 1923, presented an interesting architectural challenge to the idea that expression and standardization were necessarily dichotomous, characterized as it was by an overall visual dynamism in its design that was nevertheless well suited to its functional purpose. In 1920s Germany, Mendelsohn gave unmistakable shape to a variety of urban environments through a series of distinctive buildings that combined some of the characteristic features of the "new architecture" (including extensive use of metal strip windows and strong horizontal axes) with his own unique conception of a "stress-free" façade in which the sweeping entablatures separating each floor produced an uninterrupted flow providing a characteristic dynamism peculiar to Mendelsohn's architecture at this time. Examples of this building style can be seen in his designs for the Schocken stores in Stuttgart and Chemnitz of 1926 and 1928 respectively, the Petersdorff store in Breslau of 1927, and the Columbushaus in Berlin of 1930, among others.

Another significant architect working in Germany during the first three decades of the twentieth century was the energetic Ludwig Mies van der Rohe, whose architecture, after an early expressionist phase, gradually laid more emphasis on values of order, repose, symmetry, and rectilinearity. For Mies, the modernist search for the spiritual value of architecture could be found in simplicity of form, distillations from history, and the application of industrial technique. His commitment to glass architecture was also in keeping with the expressionist utopias of Paul Scheerbart and Bruno Taut. By 1923, the year in which he delivered his lecture on "Solved Problems" to the Association of German Architects at the Museum of Applied Arts in Berlin, the German economy had temporarily stabilized after the ravages of war and the initial shock of the reparation costs demanded by the Versailles Treaty in 1918. The new democratic constitution of the Weimar Republic was in general terms reasonably well disposed towards "the new architecture" of modernism, and there were increasing opportunities for new and developing architects to build. For Mies, like many of his contemporaries, modern living demanded modern building styles, and his lecture was an attempt to delineate the general terms what these might be. He tellingly stated, with a sentiment not dissimilar to the ideas of Le Corbusier or the Russian constructivist El Lissitzsky, that "a rational organization is to be sought and the application of new technical means towards this end is a self-evident presumption. If we fulfill these demands, then the housing of our age is formed" (cited in Achilles et al. 1986: 165).

In Holland it was the avant-garde group De Stijl who were developing their ideas concerning rationalist architecture and design during the last year of World War I. Their work was significant for the development of modernist architecture because of the unique formulation of the relationships between mass, space, and form derived from a dialectical relationship with painting that they fostered in their thinking and which had initially been influenced via the spatial experiments of cubism, combined increasingly with an interpretation of the architecture of Frank Lloyd Wright. De Stijl was formed in 1917, and chief among its members were Piet Mondrian, who had been practicing painterly abstraction for several years beforehand, J. J. P. Oud, Theo van Doesburg, who, together with Gerrit Rietveld, also turned his talents to architecture and design, Jan Wils, Vilmos Huzar, and Bart van der Leck. The first issue of the magazine *De Stijl*, initiated by van Doesburg, was published in October 1917 and it ran under his editorship until his death in 1931. In November 1918 De Stijl published its first group manifesto in the magazine. As Hans Jaffé has commented, although Holland was a neutral country, the founding principles of De Stijl as expressed in this manifesto were a direct response to the utter chaos of war. They could also be read as a more generic response to the alienated condition of modernity already identified by Georg Simmel in 1903:

> The struggle of the individual against the universal is revealing itself in the World War as well as in the art of the present day. The War is destroying the old world with its contents ... the new art has brought forward what the new consciousness of time contains: a balance between the universal and the individual. The new consciousness is prepared to realize the internal life as well as the external life (cited in Jaffé 1982: 12)

It was in the manifesto issue of the magazine that illustrations of the "De Vonk" (translated as "the spark") holiday house also featured for the first time. The house was built by Oud, in conjunction with van Doesburg, for Leiden factory girls in Noordwijk (six miles west of Leiden on the coast) at the request of the factory director Emilie Knappert. As Jane Beckett indicates, De Vonk was fundamental for van Doesburg because, through his conception and designs for its decorative schema, it represented "an important dialectic between painting and architecture" (Beckett 1980: 216) which was to become progressively more central to his thinking. The fundamental link between painting and architecture as practiced by members of De Stijl was the principle of absolute abstraction and the complete elimination of any reference to objects in nature as a way of promoting a harmony of visual form. While Mondrian envisioned De Stijl harmonies through abstraction in painting, it was van Doesburg who turned them into a reality through architecture, especially after 1923 when he became less involved with painting and more engaged with architectural commissions and theoretical writing on architecture. In 1925 van Doesburg's *Principles of Neo-Plastic Art* was published as the sixth volume of the "Bauhaus Books" series, with typographic and design layout executed by Moholy-Nagy. In a prefatory note to the publication van Doesburg explains that the original manuscript was completed in 1917 from notes that he had begun in 1915, and that the revisions and translation into German for the Bauhaus Book series occurred in 1921–2. Therefore, by the time the work was published van Doesburg's views on architecture had become much more predominant than this more generalized treatise would suggest. Nevertheless, the principles of the De Stijl focus on harmonious relationships in all fields of aesthetic endeavor are clearly laid out in the text, and it is therefore a pivotal document of the early group's endeavors.

The existing canon of primary and secondary literature on the architectural oeuvre of Charles Édouard Jeanneret-Gris (1887–1965), otherwise known as Le Corbusier, is vast. In particular, it is Le Corbusier's many writings and well-known statements on architectural modernism as they relate to his own practice of building design that have helped to shape the popular discourse surrounding his monumental influence on the visual products of international architectural modernism. It was initially through the 1927 English translation of *Towards a New Architecture*, first published in French in 1923 as *Vers une architecture*, that his ideas concerning modern living and industrial modernity became most widely publicized, and some even today still help to define the populist discourse and reception of his buildings. So, for example, within the first few pages he makes the now infamous claim that "a house is a machine for living in" (Le Corbusier 1946: 10), a sentiment that has fueled many subsequent critiques of modernism for being a mechanistic architecture of dehumanization – a view sadly propagated by the architectural, social, and ecological poverty of the many mass urban housing estates of the 1960s in Europe and America, in which dystopian mis-translations of theoretical modernism were very loosely applied in an attempt to supply fast and radical solutions to housing shortages during this era.[3] On studying the evolution of Le Corbusier's thought, however, a much more nuanced view of his architectural achievements can be found, which is something that Francesco Passanti explores in some detail in an article on his use of the vernacular in architecture just before 1930 (Passanti 1997: 438–51). Thus, while *Towards a New Architecture* is very much a polemic concerning the opportunities and responsibilities for the architect afforded by the new technological age of the

---

[3] See Michael Sorkin's "Corb in New York" (Sorkin 1987: 248–53) for a lively account of Le Corbusier's impact on American architecture in various guises,

machine in which aeroplanes, cars, and steam ships are celebrated as defining the appropriate aesthetic of the age, Passanti demonstrates that an interest in the vernacular was also present, though perhaps less explicit, in some of Le Corbusier's building projects from 1929 onwards. In particular, he cites the influence of a trip that Le Corbusier made to the Balkans in 1911 (referred to by the architect himself as his "Voyage d'Orient") as significant for the subsequent inclusion of elements of the vernacular (ethnic, folk, regional, etc.) within modernism, thereby complicating the standard oppositional binaries that position the international machine aesthetic of modernism in antithesis to an aesthetic of architectural regionality or ethnicity. So, for example, Passanti connects Le Corbusier's observations on a standard domestic house in the ancient Bulgarian town of Tirnovo, in which the living-room window was "more wide than tall" and "reached from wall to wall," with the subsequent development of the ribbon window, "one of the defining features of modernist architecture" (Passanti 1997: 438–9). What Passanti also identifies, however, is a form of modern vernacular that Le Corbusier "found" within prefabricated industrial objects, such as the washbasin in the entrance hall at the Villa Savoye at Poissy (1928–31) and conceptually derived from his interpretations of the aesthetic of *Sachlichkeit* (objectivity), propagated by Adolf Loos, and *Typisierung* (typology), suggested by Hermann Muthesius before him. Le Corbusier's relationship to the architecture and architectural thought of the early twentieth century, apart from the palpable influences of Loos and the Deutscher Werkbund, can also be seen in a short 1957 essay on the Spanish art nouveau architect Antonio Gaudí. For Le Corbusier, despite the obvious differences in formal approach between his own "soap box" architecture as he describes it, and the exuberant organicism of Gaudí's art nouveau style, Gaudí remains "the constructor of 1900, the professional builder in stone, iron or brick" (Le Corbusier 1957: 22). For Le Corbusier, he remains a "great artist" of his era, and it is this historical decorum that Le Corbusier applauds. In this way, Le Corbusier's approach to history, like Sigfried Giedion's, is telling. Both Giedion and Le Corbusier reinterpret history in terms of the present. Indeed, as Panayotis Tournikiotis has observed of both Giedion and Le Corbusier, they believed that they "could discern in the distant past the greatest of timeless truths, the *constituent facts* that were free of the tyranny of style and therefore had the power to show that modern architecture was right when it declared that *it was not a style*" (Tournikiotis 1999: 46–7). Le Corbusier's *Precisions*, published as a collection in 1960, brings together a series of 10 lectures given to architecture students in Buenos Aires in 1929 which elaborates this further. "Architecture in Everything and City Planning in Everything" is the third lecture in the series; in it Le Corbusier discusses the nature of architecture as he conceives it, explicitly not in terms of style, but in terms of the spatial relations it can produce – the links between shelters, cities, and roads for example, in which city planning and architecture are united in a single entity. Architecture is conceived as an ordering device, and it is the notion of visual order in Le Corbusier's work that Beatriz Colomina deconstructs in her 1992 essay "The Split Wall:

Domestic Voyeurism," in which she also considers aspects of voyeurism within Adolf Loos's architecture as a precursor to her consideration of Le Corbusier.[4] Colomina cogently demonstrates that Le Corbusier's modernism is predicated on the hegemonic gaze of the male architect for whom the mastering eye is central to the conception and experience of the space of his domestic architecture, in which women only appear in the canonic photographs of the buildings fragmented or with their backs turned to the spectator. As Colomina explains, "Le Corbusier's subject is detached from the house with the distance of a visitor, a viewer, a photographer, a tourist," in other words, there is no space for the embodied subjectivity of the inhabitant; "inhabiting" means "seeing" rather than "occupying" in Corbusier's project (Colomina 1992: 123).

In contrast, however, despite its obvious gender biases and inherent problems, the shift to modernity marked through the architecture of Loos, Taut, Gropius, Mendelsohn, van der Rohe, Le Corbusier, and many of the other twentieth-century architects and designers mentioned above, does underpin some of the more positive aspects of Walter Benjamin's thinking in much of his writing, including the unfinished *Passagenwerk* (*Arcades Project*), which has posthumously become one of the most celebrated philosophical expositions of the capitalist origins of modernity. Benjamin's writings on modernity, rooted as they are in an analysis of the economic growth of late nineteenth-century Europe, veer alternately between melancholia for the loss of meaningful experiences (*Erfahrung*) in modern life and creeping optimism for the new opportunities that may arise as a result of the recognition of the false legacies of bourgeois culture. It is in the new steel, glass, and concrete architecture of the twentieth century that society has the potential to wake up from the sleep of capitalism that pervaded the illusory dream work of the Parisian arcades and the nineteenth-century interior, highlighted by Benjamin as hollow spaces of pilgrimage to the commodity fetish. As Hilde Heynen remarks, "in Benjamin's view ... a new architecture flowers in the twentieth century; with its qualities of transparency and spatial interpenetration, it anticipates the new (classless) society, the features of which are a clarity and openness that is much more pervasive than that of the preceding age" (Heynen 1999: 106). Despite the fact that many modernist buildings were dedicated to the material forms of high capitalism (department stores, office blocks, and private villas), they could simultaneously serve proletarian functions as well (housing estates, factory buildings, schools, and clubhouses). For Benjamin, it was not so much the individual buildings as the aesthetic language and intent of the new architecture that revealed its revolutionary potential. While for Benjamin's

---

[4] Colomina's analysis is particularly interesting when read in juxtaposition with Caroline Constant's article "E.1027" (Constant 1994), in which the issues of gendered visual mastery, voyeurism, and control that Colomina identifies as central to Corbusier's modernism are shown to be complicated and challenged by the work of Gray in her collaborative designs with Romanian architect Jean Badovici for his house, E.1027, at Rocquebrune in France between 1926 and 1929.

contemporary Ernst Bloch the new sobriety of the 1920s was more suited to the cold functionalism of capitalism, for Benjamin it offered a complete contrast to the alienated individuality that characterized the nineteenth-century bourgeois interior. In the *Arcades* essay, "Paris, Capital of the Nineteenth Century," Benjamin traces the shift from the interiority of the nineteenth century to the transparency of the new era in socialist terms. Art nouveau features at the end of the century as the last attempt to salvage the bourgeois home from the inevitability of technological advance (Benjamin 1978: 154–5). As Heynen observes, "while the nineteenth-century figures of the arcade and of the interior constitute a form of dwelling that is in decay, the new barbarism represents a radical change, bringing with it another notion of dwelling – one that is no longer founded in security and seclusion, but in openness and transparency" (Heynen 1999: 113). It is the emphasis on transparency, sobriety, and functionalism in the "new architecture" that Benjamin hopes will form the basis of a social revolution in which the desire for the ownership of "things" will no longer be the hegemonic structural basis of social interaction. For Benjamin the inherent destruction inimical to the avant-garde was precisely its appeal since it is only from the debris of history that social transformation can be achieved.

Tragically, as is by now well rehearsed, Benjamin committed suicide in Spain in 1940, on the run from Paris before the city's invasion by Hitler's advancing army. Although for Benjamin democracy might have been inherent in the application of technology to modernist architecture, by the same token, technology could also be harnessed by the right for the purposes of monumental nostalgia in the hands of Hitler and his chief architect, Albert Speer, in their pursuit of an antithetical revolution to the socialist vision imagined by Benjamin and other supporters of avant-garde modernism. As Susan Buck-Morss has observed, "machines that bring the promise of the naturalization of humanity and the humanization of nature result instead in the mechanization of both" (Buck-Morss 1989: 365). Significantly, it was Haussmann's Paris of the *Passagenwerk* that was the goal of Hitler's conquering desire, and although he had at first wished to destroy it, his vision for a new Berlin, to be "made far more beautiful," and of a world in which Paris would become "only a shadow" ironically rescued the city from destruction (Buck-Morss 1989: 328).

Speer's culpability in the aestheticization of politics via both realized and unbuilt architectural projects in the service of the Third Reich is generally undisputed, but the issue of the relationship of the author to his works is complicated by the political roots of the architectural legacies of fascism remaining across Europe. In the 1978 preface to an edited selection of photographs, drawings, and commentary on work he produced for Hitler between 1932 and 1942, Speer's own ambivalence about his role in creating the monumental neoclassical style of the Third Reich is clear, veering as he does between the undeniable recognition of architecture as the obvious manifestation of state power and an attempt to historicize his projects unproblematically within a lineage of monumental architecture traced back to Greek and Rome. As Lars

Olaf Larsson suggests, "National Socialist architecture is not stylistically unique," but condemnation of it arises as a result of its representative role in the visible expression of fascist ideology through an exaggerated and powerful monumental style (cited in Krier 1978: 233).

The tensions between monumentality and modernity became increasingly politically debated during the 1930s amongst architects and critics from different European countries, and were crystallized at the 1937 World Exposition in Paris. While international modernism dominated the contributions of most of the participating countries, a new challenge to its hegemonic reign was being played out between Boris Iofan's Soviet pavilion and Albert Speer's pavilion for the Third Reich, situated in opposition to one another and competing fiercely in terms of scale and political intent. The Soviet pavilion in particular suggested an alternatively politicized aesthetic of monumentality that could be allied, temporarily at least, with the ideals of progressivism to which the avant-garde also aspired and which was therefore distinguished from the neoclassical conservatism of the new Germany. Subsequent to this and emerging from the wreckage of World War II, Sigfried Giedion, José Luis Sert, and Fernand Léger produced their own position paper in 1943, *Nine Points on Monumentality*, in which they attempted to situate the aesthetic within "the historical evolution of modernism itself" (Ockman 1993: 27) rather than from an explicitly communist position, increasingly revealed through Stalin's regime in Russia to be as repressive as the political regimes of right-wing fascism. Thus, in their paper they comment that "the last hundred years have witnessed the devaluation of monumentality" and that "the decline and misuse of monumentality is the principal reason why modern architects have deliberately disregarded the monument and revolted against it" (Ockman 1993: 29). They, however, wished to recuperate the possibilities of a "new monumentality" that was not allied to a rhetoric of dictatorial political power. For Louis Khan, writing in 1944, a monumentality for the present which avoided the pitfalls of its immediate political precedents could be achieved through the giving of "full architectural expression to such social monuments as the school [or the] community" (cited in Latour 1991: 18). Further, he goes on to stress that technological developments in engineering and materials, accelerated by the economic needs of World War II, were also revealing themselves to be suited to the purpose of a new monumentality appropriate to the current age. For Khan, monumentality was no longer to be reliant on the classical era, the achievements of which he acknowledges, but the limitations of which he also elaborates in terms of different kinds of architectural possibility for the present and, more especially for the post-war future.

World War II had engendered a fundamental rupture in the activities and cultural practices of the modernist avant-garde, with many artists, architects, and writers leaving Europe to re-establish themselves in the United States. The activities of the International Congress for Modern Architecture (CIAM), which had been formed at La Sarraz in Switzerland in 1928, had also been curtailed. The group had met five times before the war, and at its fourth meeting in 1933 it had produced a set of guidelines on modern urbanism, known as the Athens Charter. Its first meeting after the war, CIAM 6, took place in England in 1947 and was an opportunity for the group to re-establish its membership and to determine what its role in the new post-war era would be. As a means to this end, it reaffirmed the validity of its existence and its role in fostering planning and building legislation, advancing building techniques, and promoting a "reintegration of the plastic arts" for a "clearer understanding of contemporary forms of artistic expression." It also included recognition of a new generation of younger architects who had joined the group in its post-war phase. The significance of CIAM as an international group was precisely the number of member countries involved and their combined impact to achieve tangible results in effecting a changed form of consciousness regarding modern architectural building design and city planning. It was through publications, exhibitions, radio, and other forms of communication that CIAM planned the future dissemination of its ideas in the new era, and it was also a way of attempting to continue the project of modernism after the hiatus of European totalitarianism by which it had been so radically curtailed (Ockmann 1993).

In 1960 architectural historian Reyner Banham published the first edition of what has now become a classic account of architectural and design modernism, *Theory and Design in the First Machine Age*, which saw the historiography of architectural and design modernism undergo a radical shift of emphasis. Banham's thesis concerning the modern movement was that, far from encapsulating the radical break with academicism that it was so often associated with, essentially it had been unable to properly develop an aesthetic that represented the full extent of the technological progress of its own age, and that even the pared-down architectural structures of the 1920s owed some of their basic principles to classical aesthetics such as harmony of proportions and Albertian coherence. As Panayotis Tournikiotis has commented in his summary of Banham's argument, "there was in the modern buildings a contradiction between the changing and progressive nature of technology and the unchanging and eternal nature of classical aesthetics," and it was only the futurists who "argued that the aesthetics of Beaux-Arts was impossible to reconcile with the new conditions of modernism," which is why they are given a relatively prominent position within Banham's argument (Tournikiotis 1999: 145–6). Tournikiotis also observes that Banham's concern within this critique was to uncover the principles of the architecture of the 1920s in order to determine the prospects for the architectural future of the 1960s, and that this was Banham's hallmark, a critique of modernism in a search for "time present" and the construction of a "history of the immediate future" (1999: 148). The title of Banham's text also helps to identify his project as a historical one in which the notion of a "first machine age" precedes what he identifies in his introduction to the text as the "second machine age" of the era in which he is writing. In addition, it neatly allows for the modernism of the first half of the twentieth century to be historicized and circumscribed. Banham's text, then, published as it was in 1960, can in many ways be regarded as symbolizing the end of modernism with an interrogation of its failures as a means of ensuring that they are not repeated for the "second machine age" of the 1960s.

The publication of Reyner Banham's historically determined critique of modernism undeniably signified a conceptual shift in the historiography of architecture during the 1960s and marked a break with what were perceived as the failures of modernism in a utopian attempt to recuperate the progressive aspects of the modern movement as part of a renewed search for socially and technologically progressive architectural form. In this sense it was certainly not a rejection of the modernist project, but simply an attempt to realign its aims. However, for Charles Jencks in 1977, writing the first edition of the frequently reprinted *Language of Post-Modern Architecture*, high modernism was already exhausted by the 1960s, and publications such as Banham's unnecessarily prolonged its post-war life. For Jencks the definitive break with the false ideals of modernism came only in 1972 with the destruction of the Pruitt-Igoe housing estate in St. Louis, Missouri, originally built "according to the most progressive ideals of CIAM" between 1952 and 1955 by Minoru Yamasaki (Jencks 1987: 9). Pruitt-Igoe had tragically come to represent all that was doomed about the ideals of progressive modern architecture. Built according to Corbusian principles of "sun, space and greenery," the estate offered "streets in the air" which, although free from traffic, were not free from crime. The form of the buildings was designed according to rationalist principles and resembled the sanitized blocks of modern hospitals. As a place to live, Pruitt-Igoe was inhospitable and ultimately uninhabitable for the black community, which had been ghettoized there away from the rest of the city. The eventual destruction of Pruitt-Igoe after 20 years of vandalism and crime was clearly not mourned and many, including Jencks, celebrated it as the symbolic death knell of architectural modernism. Jencks's subsequent account of this death is self-confessedly marked by its caricatured approach to all of the perceived naivety and inappropriateness of modernism and should be read accordingly – as a deliberately overstated polemic. What Jencks suggests in its place is postmodernism, a term not peculiar to architecture but one in which architecture offers a tangible sign system through which a postmodernist aesthetic can be visibly articulated and which he proceeds to elaborate in the rest of this now classic text on the subject. Pastiche, paradox, pluralism, kitsch, irony, evolution over revolution, historicism, neoclassicism, regionalism, and revivalism have all become standard terms in the postmodern language of architectural style as elaborated by Jencks. Nevertheless, despite its undeniable influence and clarity, Jencks's text is not unproblematic in its masculinist assumptions and glib analogies: see, for example, his description of Pelli's buildings as "slightly flat-chested and awkward, like an adolescent girl" (Jencks 1987: 168). Thus, if postmodernism can be associated in general terms with a celebratory reappropriation of existing formations (whether architectural, sociological, cultural, or linguistic), it is not immune to the gender biases and prejudices that pervade the ideologies of its precedents.

One of the architects whom Jencks critiques in his text is Robert Venturi, whose architectural practice is one of collaboration with his wife and partner, fellow architect Denise Scott Brown. However, as Dana Arnold, citing Scott Brown, has demonstrated, despite the equal partnership between the two architects, Scott Brown's career, name, and reputation have consistently been subsumed under or casually elided with her husband's name. Thus, a cursory glance at the index to the first edition of *The Language of Post-Modern Architecture*, for example, reveals a familiar pattern of omission, in which Venturi is listed but Scott Brown is not. Nevertheless, despite this continued and frustrating enactment of unequal power relations, the body of evidence that palpably demonstrates Scott Brown's contribution to the partnership is indisputable and reveals more about the structures of architectural history and criticism than it does about the practice of building itself.[5] In 1984 Scott Brown and Venturi published a selection of their critical essays spanning the years 1953–84. The collection includes a 1971 contribution from Scott Brown entitled "Learning from Pop" that clearly establishes her ideas as central to the development of the joint architectural practice. The essay is also a useful indicator of the team's self-positioning away from the values of high modernism in a search for a postmodern architectural idiom that may be applied to urban design and consumer living. As such, they embrace the concept of market needs, the consumer, and popular culture as an approach that is "more tolerant of the untidiness of urban life than the 'rationalist,' Cartesian formal orders of latter-day Modern architecture" (Venturi and Scott Brown 1984: 27). In this way, the modernist struggle for an avant-garde architecture of critique is dissolved in favor of an architecture of equilibrium, of "the acceptance of [things] as they are," as she intimates in a subsequent riposte, "Pop Off: Reply to Kenneth Frampton," to criticism leveled against these ideals by Kenneth Frampton (Venturi and Scott Brown 1984: 34).

Kenneth Frampton's 1983 essay "Towards a Critical Regionalism: Six Points for an Architecture of Resistance" is one of a range of post-Jencksian texts to subject the postmodern commodification of architecture as entertainment in the era of late capitalism to radical critique (Jameson 1991). For Frampton, the regression of postmodernism towards a culture of globalized gratuitous entertainment concomitantly marks the decline and fragmentation of the possibility for an effective culture of critique, as well as the impossibility of sustaining an adversarial avant-garde. Instead, he suggests the formation of what he terms an *arrière-garde* position from which critical architectural practice might be sustained in the present. His conception of such a position is of one "which distances itself equally from the Enlightenment myth of progress and from a reactionary unrealistic impulse to return to the architectonic forms of the pre-industrial past" (Foster 1983: 20). He also refers to such a position as one of "critical regionalism," but is careful to distinguish it from his conception of certain forms of

---

[5] For further information and a compelling account of the various daily iniquities that Scott Brown has undergone in her career as a female architect, see Scott Brown 2002.

postmodernism which he articulates as "simple-minded attempts to revive the hypothetical forms of a lost vernacular" (Foster 1983: 21). For Frampton the practice of critical regionalism also incorporates an acknowledgment of how the tactile sensuousness of an experienced space has an effect on subjectivity in a way that differs from hegemonic Western constructions of space in perspectival, representational terms that have suppressed the tactile and sensuous aspects of subjective experience. Critical regionalism would hope to readdress these other aspects of experience. As Frampton concludes, "the tactile and the tectonic jointly have the capacity to transcend the mere appearance of the technical in much the same way as the place-form has the potential to withstand the relentless onslaught of global modernization" (Foster 1983: 29).

The foregrounding of bodies and their effects upon architecture and architectural experience inherent in Frampton's conception of the tactile and tectonic values of architecture is also an issue of interest to Bernard Tschumi in his delineation of the notion of the "Pleasure of Architecture" (2002). Tschumi writes as both a practicing architect and an academic, and as such his work is poised between an inquiry into theoretical abstractions and the embodied experience of designed spaces. In the particular essay included in this anthology Tschumi makes the case for reclaiming the sense of pleasure in architecture, an experience that was denied by a discourse of functionalism that pervaded modernist approaches to the discipline but which has continued to be suppressed by contemporary architectural theory long after the demise of modernism.

The final extract included here comes from the last book of a series generated from 10 conferences held annually from 1990 "to establish architecture as the host of a cross-cultural and multidisciplinary discussion on architecture and contemporary culture" at the end of the second millennium (Davidson 2001) and as such it also marks an appropriate closure for this anthology. Saskia Sassen's contribution to the *Anything* conference and book, "Scale and Span in a Global Digital World," confronts the implications of digitalization and global virtual space for the future design of cities in an attempt to resist the frequently articulated and somewhat glib assumptions that digitalization will automatically render the materialization of physical space (something that architecture has traditionally represented) void. As Sassen insists, "digital space is embedded in the larger societal, cultural, subjective, economic and imaginary structurations of lived experience and the systems within which we exist and operate" (Davidson 2001: 45–6). In this way the futures of architecture and design as materialized practices are provided with a conceptual space for tangible development during the infancy of the globalized, digital culture of the twenty-first century.

Finally, then, any attempt to summarize or to draw a single conclusion about the discourses of architectural and design history that have spanned the twentieth century and that have been presented only cursorily here would soon be defeated by the sheer breadth, depth, and range of material that has inevitably had to be left out of this survey account. However, what we hope that this generic overview has served to do is to introduce the reader to the possibilities for change that characterized the dialectic of dynamism and despair that marked the twentieth century. Both the youthful optimism of the modernist avant-garde that distinguished the early century and the attempts to forge a new post-war architectural culture out of the fragments that remained are central to our contemporary purchase on the historical formation of the twentieth century's past and its legacies for the present and the future. Indeed, perhaps one of the most telling symptoms of this ongoing negotiation between past, present, and future is the continuing currency of the philosophical criticism of Walter Benjamin from the 1930s as a tool with which to articulate our cultural relationships with the capitalist technocratic origins of our own globalized society today. The resonant poetic symbolism of Benjamin's "angel of history," his face "turned towards the past" while being propelled into the future by the storm of progress seems an appropriate metaphor with which to end this sweeping chronology of the architectural and design history of the past two hundred and fifty years (Benjamin 1968). And finally, while conceptually eschewing the monolithic application of chronology as an authoritative ordering principle for the extracts we have included, the use of historical sequence has, it is hoped, at least been a useful stick with which the reader may be guided and with which these editors expect to be beaten, such is the nature of any anthologizing project in the minefield of post-structural signification.

38

Ornament and Crime

Adolf Loos

In the womb the human embryo passes through all the development stages of the animal kingdom. At the moment of birth, human sensations are equal to those of a newborn dog. His childhood passes through all the transformations which correspond to the history of mankind. At the age of two, he sees like a Papuan, at four, like a Teuton, at six like Socrates, at eight like Voltaire. When he is eight years old, he becomes aware of violet, the colour which the eighteenth century had discovered, because before that the violet was blue and the purple snail red. Today the physicist points to colours in the sun's spectrum which already bear a name, whose recognition, however, is reserved for the coming generation.

The child is amoral. To us the Papuan is also amoral. The Papuan slaughters his enemies and devours them. He is no criminal. If, however, the modern man slaughters and devours somebody, he is a criminal or a degenerate. The Papuan tattoos his skin, his boat, his oar, in short, everything that is within his reach. He is no criminal. The modern man who tattoos himself is a criminal or a degenerate. There are prisons where eighty percent of the inmates bear tattoos. Those who are tattooed but are not imprisoned are latent criminals or degenerate aristocrats. If a tattooed person dies at liberty, it is only that he died a few years before he committed a murder.

The urge to ornament one's face, and everything within one's reach is the origin of fine art. It is the babble of painting. All art is erotic.

The first ornament that came into being, the cross, had an erotic origin. The first work of art, the first artistic action of the first artist daubing on the wall, was in order to rid himself of his natural excesses. A horizontal line: the reclining woman. A vertical line: the man who penetrates her. The man who created it felt the same urge as Beethoven, he experienced the same joy that Beethoven felt when he created the Ninth Symphony.

Adolf Loos, "Ornament and Crime (1908)" pp. 100–3 from Joanna Drew (ed.), *The Architecture of Adolf Loos*. London: Arts Council of Great Britain, 1985.

But the man of our time who daubs the walls with erotic symbols to satisfy an inner urge is a criminal or a degenerate. It is obvious that this urge overcomes man; such symptoms of degeneration most forcefully express themselves in public conveniences. One can measure the culture of a country by the degree to which its lavatory walls are daubed. With children it is a natural phenomenon: their first artistic expression is to scrawl on the walls erotic symbols. But what is natural to the Papuan and the child is a symptom of degeneration in the modern man. I have made the following observation and have announced it to the world:

The evolution of culture is synonymous with the removal of ornament from objects of daily use. I had thought to introduce a new joy into the world: but it has not thanked me for it. Instead the idea was greeted with sadness and despondency. What cast the gloom was the thought that ornament could no longer be produced. What! Are we alone, the people of the nineteenth century, are we no longer capable of doing what any Negro can do, or what people have been able to do before us?

Those objects without ornament, which mankind had created in earlier centuries, had been carelessly discarded and destroyed. We possess no carpenter's benches of the Carolingian period; instead any rubbish which had even the smallest ornament was collected, cleaned and displayed in ostentatious palaces that were built for them, people walked about sadly amongst the display cabinets. Every period had its style: why was it that our period was the only one to be denied a style? By 'style' was meant ornament. I said, 'weep not. Behold! What makes our period so important is that it is incapable of producing new ornament. We have out-grown ornament, we have struggled through to a state without ornament. Behold, the time is at hand, fulfilment awaits us. Soon the streets of the cities will glow like white walls! Like Zion, the Holy City, the capital of heaven. It is then that fulfilment will have come'.

But there are hob goblins who will not allow it to happen. Humanity is still to groan under the slavery of ornament. Man had progressed enough for ornament to no longer produce erotic sensations in him, unlike the Papuans, a tattooed face did not increase the aesthetic value, but reduced it. Man had progressed far enough to find pleasure in purchasing a plain cigarette case, even if it cost the same as one that was ornamented. They were happy with their clothes and they were glad that they did not have to walk about in red velvet trousers with gold braids like monkeys at a fun fair. And I said: 'Behold, Goethe's death chamber is more magnificent than all the pomp of the Renaissance, and a plain piece of furniture is more beautiful than all the inlaid and carved museum pieces. Goethe's language is more beautiful than all the ornaments of the shepherds of the Pegnitz'.

This was heard by the hob goblins with displeasure. The state, whose duty it is to impede people in their cultural development, took over the question of development and re-adoption of ornament and made it its own. Woe betide the state, whose revolutions are brought about by its privy councillors!

Soon one was to see a buffet introduced into the Viennese Museum of Applied Arts, which was called 'the properous fish shoal', there was even a cupboard, which was given the trade name 'the cursed princess' or something similar, which

349

referred to the ornament with which this unfortunate piece of furniture was covered. The Austrian state takes its task so seriously that it ensures that outdated footwear will not disappear from within the boundaries of the Austro-Hungarian Empire. The state forces every cultivated twenty-year-old man to wear outdated footwear for three years (after all, every state proceeds on the assumption that a poorly developed population is more easily governed). Well, the epidemic of ornament is recognised by the state and is subsidised with government money. I, however, consider that to be a regressive. I will not subscribe to the argument that ornament increases the pleasure of the life of a cultivated person, or the argument which covers itself with the words: 'But if the ornament is beautiful! ...' To me, and to all the cultivated people, ornament does not increase the pleasures of life. If I want to eat a piece of gingerbread I will choose one that is completely plain and not a piece which represents a baby in arms of a horserider, a piece which is covered over and over with decoration. The man of the fifteenth century would not understand me. But modern people will. The supporter of ornament believes that the urge for simplicity is equivalent to self-denial. No, dear professor from the College of Applied Arts, I am not denying myself! To me, it tastes better this way. The dishes of the past centuries which used decoration to make the peacocks, pheasants and lobsters appear more appetising produce the opposite effect on me. I look on such a culinary display with horror when I think of having to eat these stuffed animal corpses. I eat roast beef.

The immense damage and devastation which the revival of ornament has caused to aesthetic development could easily be overcome because nobody, not even the power of the state, can stop the evolution of humanity! It represents a crime against the national economy, and, as a result of it, human labour, money and material are ruined. Time cannot compensate for this kind of damage.

The rate of cultural development is held back by those that cannot cope with the present. I live in the year 1908, but my neighbour lives approximately in the year 1900, and one over there lives in the year 1880. It is a misfortune for any government, if the culture of its people is dominated by the past. The farmer from Kals lives in the twelfth century, and on the occasion of the Jubilee Procession, tribes walked past which even during the period of mass migration were thought to be backward. Happy is the country which does not have such backward-looking inhabitants. Happy is America! Even here we have people in the cities who are survivors from the eighteenth century, and who are appalled by a painting with violet shadows, because they cannot understand why the artist has used violet. To them, the pheasant which the cook has spent days preparing tastes better, and the cigarette case with Renaissance ornaments is more pleasing. And what is happening in the countryside? Clothes and household utensils belong to previous centuries. The farmer is no Christian, he is still a heathen.

Those who measure everything by the past impede the cultural development of nations and of humanity itself. Ornament is not merely produced by criminals, it commits a crime itself by damaging national economy and therefore its cultural development. Two people living side by side who have the same needs, the same demands on life, and the same income, but belong to different cultures, perceive the national economy differently. The result is that the man of the twentieth century becomes richer and the man of the eighteenth century becomes poorer. I assume that both their lifestyles reflect their different attitudes. The man of the twentieth century can satisfy his needs with a much smaller capital and can, therefore, set aside savings. The vegetable which is appetising to him is simply boiled in water and has butter spread over it. To the other man it will only taste good if honey and nuts are added to it and it has been cooked by someone for hours. Decorated plates are expensive, while white crockery, which is pleasing to the modern individual, is cheap. Whilst one person saves money, the other becomes insolvent. This is what happens to entire nations. Woe betide the nation that remains behind in its cultural development. The English become richer and we become poorer ...

In a highly productive nation ornament is no longer a natural product of its culture, and therefore represents backwardness or even a degenerative tendency. As a result, those who produce ornament are no longer given their due reward. We are aware of the conditions that exist in the wood carving and turning trades, the very low wages which are paid to the embroiderers and lace makers. The producer of ornament must work for twenty hours to obtain the same income of a modern labourer who works for eight hours. As a rule, ornament increases the price of the object. All the same there are occasions when an ornamented object is offered at half the price, despite the same material cost and production time, which works out to be three times longer as that of a plain unornamented object. The lack of ornament results in reduced working hours and an increased wage. The Chinese carver works sixteen hours, the American labourer works eight hours. If I pay as much for a plain box as I would for an ornamented one, then the difference is in working hours. And if there existed no ornament at all, a condition which might arise in millenia, man would only need to work four instead of eight hours, as the time spent on ornament represents half of today's working day.

Ornament is wasted manpower and therefore wasted health. It has always been like this. But today it also means wasted material, and both mean wasted capital.

As ornament is no longer organically related to our culture, it is also no longer the expression of our culture. The ornament that is produced today bears no relation to us, or to any other human or the world at large. It has no potential for development. What happened to Otto Eckmann's ornaments, and those of Van de Velde? The artist always stood at the centre of humanity, full of power and health. The modern producer of ornament is, however, left behind or a pathological phenomenon. He disowns his own products after only three years. Cultivated people find them instantaneously intolerable, others become conscious of their intolerability after many years. Where are Otto Eckmann's products today? Where will Olbrich's work be, ten years from now? Modern ornament has no parents and no offspring, it has no past and no future. Uncultivated people, to whom the significance of our time is a sealed book, welcome it with joy and disown it after a short while.

Today, mankind is healthier than ever before; only a few are ill. These few, however, tyrannise the worker, who is so healthy that he is incapable of inventing ornament. They force him to execute ornament which they have designed, in the most diverse materials.

The change in ornament implies a premature devaluation of labour. The worker's time, the utilised material is capital that has been wasted. I have made the statement: The form of an object should be bearable for as long as the object lasts physically. I would like to try to explain this: a suit will be changed more frequently than a valuable fur coat. A lady's evening dress, intended for one night only, will be changed more rapidly than a writing desk. Woe betide the writing desk that has to be changed as frequently as an evening dress, just because the style has become unbearable. Then the money that was spent on the writing desk will have been wasted.

This fact is well known to the Austrians who promote decoration and try to justify it by saying: 'A consumer who owns furnishings which become unbearable to him, after only ten years, and who is therefore forced to buy furniture every ten years, is preferable to one who only buys an object for himself once the old one can no longer be used. Industry demands it. Millions of people are employed because of this rapid change'. This appears to be the secret of the Austrian national economy; how often does one hear the words uttered on the ocasion of the outbreak of a fire: 'Thank God: now there will be some work again'. I know a good remedy! Set a whole city on fire, set the entire Empire alight and everyone will wallow in money and wealth. Let us have furniture made which can be used for firewood after three years; let us have ironmongery which will have to be melted down after four years, as it is impossible to realise even a tenth of the original labour and material costs at the pawn-brokers, and we will become richer and richer.

The loss not only hits the consumer; it hits primarily the producer. Today, decorated objects, which, thanks to progress, have become separated from the realm of ornamentation imply wasted labour and materials. If all objects were to last as long in aesthetic terms as they did physically, the consumer could pay a price for them which would enable the labourer to earn more money and work shorter hours. I would gladly pay forty crowns for my boots even though I could obtain boots for ten crowns at another store. But in every trade which languishes under the tyranny of the ornamentalists, neither good nor bad work is valued. Labour suffers because no one is prepared to pay for its true value.

Thank goodness that this is the case, because these ornamented objects are only bearable in the shabbiest execution. I recover from the news of a fire more rapidly if I hear that only worthless rubbish was burnt. I can be happy about the junk in the Künstlerhaus (the Municipal art gallery in Vienna), as I know that they put on exhibitions in a few days which are pulled down in one. But the flinging of gold coins instead of pebbles, the lighting of a cigarette with a banknote, the pulverisation and drinking of a pearl appear unaesthetic.

Ornamented objects appear truly unaesthetic if they have been executed in the best material, with the highest degree of meticulous detail, and if they have required a long production time. I cannot plead innocence for having been the first to call for quality labour, but not for this kind of work.

The modern man who holds ornament sacred as the sign of artistic achievement of past epochs will immediately recognise the tortured, laboriously extracted and pathological nature of modern ornament. Ornament can no longer be borne by someone who exists at our level of culture.

It is different for people and nations who have not reached this level.

I preach to the aristocrats, I mean the individuals who stand at the pinnacle of humanity and who nevertheless have the deepest understanding for the motivations and privations of those who stand further below. The Kafir who weaves fabric according to a specific order which only appears when one unravels it, the Persian who ties his carpets, the Slovak farmer's wife who embroiders her lace, the old lady who makes beautiful things with glass, beads and silk; all these he understands very well. The aristocrat lets them have their own way; he knows that they are sacred hours in which they work. The revolutionary would come and say 'it is all nonsense'. As he would pull the old lady away from the roadside shrine and say to her: 'There is no God'. But the atheist amongst the aristocrats lifts his hat as he walks past a church.

My shoes are covered all over with ornaments, which result from notches and holes: work which the cobbler carried out and which he was not paid for. I go to the cobbler and say to him: 'For a pair of shoes you are asking thirty crowns. I will pay you forty crowns'. By doing this I have made him happy and he will thank me for it by the work and materials which will not bear any relation in terms of quality to the extra amount. He is happy because rarely does fortune enter his house and he has been given work by a man who understands him, who appreciates his work and who does not doubt his honesty. He already imagines the finished pair in front of him. He knows where the best leather is to be found today, he knows which worker he will entrust with the shoes, and that they will display notches and holes, as many as there is space for on an elegant pair of shoes. And now I say: 'But there is one condition which I have. The shoes must be completely smooth.' By that, I have plunged him from the height of happiness to the depths of Tartarus. He has less work to do, I have robbed him of all pleasures.

I preach to the aristocrats. I allow decoration on my own body, if it provides a source of pleasure for my fellow men. Then they are also my pleasures. I suffer the ornament of the Kafir, that of the Persian, that of the Slovak farmer's wife, the ornaments of my cobbler, because they all have no other means of expressing their full potential. We have our culture which has taken over from ornament. After a day's trouble and pain, we go to hear Beethoven or Wagner. My cobbler cannot do that. I must not rob him of his pleasures as I have nothing else to replace them with. But he who goes to listen to the Ninth Symphony and who then sits down to draw up a wallpaper pattern, is either a rogue or a degenerate.

The absence of ornament has raised the other arts to unknown heights. Beethoven's symphonies would never have been written by a man who walked around in silk, velvet and lace. The person who runs around in a velvet suit is no artist but a buffoon or merely a decorator. We have become more refined, more subtle. Primitive men had to differentiate themselves by various colours, modern man needs his clothes as a mask. His individuality is so strong that it can no longer be expressed in terms of items of clothing. The lack of ornament is a sign of intellectual power. Modern man uses the ornament of past and foreign cultures at his discretion. His own inventions are concentrated on other things.

39

Architecture

Adolf Loos

May I take you to the shores of a mountain lake? The sky is blue, the water is green, and everything is at peace. The mountains and the clouds are reflected in the lake, as are the houses, farms and chapels. They stand there as if they had never been built by human hands. They look as if they have come from God's own workshop, just like the mountains and the trees, the clouds and the blue sky. And everything radiates beauty and quiet ...

What is the discord, that like an unnecessary scream shatters the quiet? Right at the centre of the farmers' houses, which were not built by them, but by God, stands a villa. Is it the product of a good or of a bad architect? I do not know. All I know is that beauty, peace and quiet have been dispelled.

All architects are equal before the throne of God, for there are neither good nor bad architects in his eyes. In the cities, in Belial's empire, the line between them is fine. Thus I ask: why is it that every architect, whether good or bad, desecrates the lake?

The farmer does not desecrate it. Neither does the engineer who builds a railway on the shore, or he who draws deep grooves in the clear surface of the lake with his ship. They create in a different way. The farmer has marked out the spot from which the new house is to rise, and has excavated the earth for the foundations. The mason appears. If clay is in the vicinity, then it provides a brickyard which delivers bricks. If not, then those stones which form the lake's shore will suffice. And while the mason lays brick upon brick, stone upon stone, the carpenter has taken up his position next to him. The strokes of the axe make a cheerful sound. He builds the roof. What kind of a roof? A beautiful one or an ugly one? He does not know. It is a roof!

And then the joiner takes the measurements for the doors and the windows, and all the craftsmen appear and take measurements and return to their

Adolf Loos, "Architecture (1910)," pp. 104–9 from Joanna Drew, *The Architecture of Adolf Loos*. London: Arts Council of Great Britain, 1985.

workshops and work. Then the farmer makes a large tub of distemper and paints the house a beautiful white. But he keeps the brush, because at Easter, in a year's time, he will need it again.

He wanted to build a house for himself, his relatives and his livestock, and in that he succeeded. Just as successful as his neighbours or his ancestors were. Just as any animal succeeds that allows itself to be guided by its instincts. Is the house beautiful? Yes, just as beautiful as the rose or the thistle, the horse or the cow.

And I ask again: why does the architect, the good one as well as the bad one, desecrate the lake? The architect, like almost every urban dweller, has no culture. He lacks the certainty of the farmer, who possesses culture. The urban dweller is an uprooted person.

By culture I mean that balance of man's inner and outer being which alone guarantees rational thought and action. I am due to give a lecture entitled: 'Why do the Papuans have a culture and why do the Germans lack one?'

Mankind's history has not yet had to record a period without culture. The creation of such a period was reserved for the urban dweller during the second half of the nineteenth century. Until then the development of our culture had remained in a state of flux. One obeyed the commands of the hour and did not look forwards or backwards.

But then false prophets appeared. They said: 'How ugly and cheerless our life is.' They brought everything together from all cultures, displayed it in the museums and said: 'Behold that is beauty. You, however, have lived in pitiful ugliness'.

There were household utensils which were adorned like houses with columns and cornices, there was velvet and silk. Above all else there were ornaments. And because the craftsman did not have or need the knowledge to draw ornament, because he was a modern, cultivated man, special schools were established in which healthy young people were unnaturally remoulded until they were able to do so, just as in China children are put into vases and fed for years until they burst out of their cages as horrifying monsters. These horrifying intellectual monsters were now duly gazed at like their Chinese brothers and, thanks to their novelty, easily earned themselves a living.

That is because at that time there was nobody who would have shouted at the people: 'Think about it, the path of culture is a path away from ornament to ornamentlessness! The evolution of culture is synonymous with the removal of ornament from the object of daily use.' Everything within the grasp of the Papuan is covered with ornament, from his face and body, to his bow and boat. However, today, tattoos are a sign of degeneration and only used by criminals and degenerate aristocrats. Contrary to the Papuan, the cultivated human thinks that an untattooed face is more beautiful than a tattooed one, even if the tattoos were made by Michelangelo or Kolo Moser themselves. And the man of the nineteenth century wants to know that not only his face, but also his suitcase, his clothes, his household utensils, and his houses are protected from the artificially produced new breed of Papuans. What about the Gothic? We are more advanced than the men of the Gothic Period. What about the Renaissance? We are more advanced. We have become more refined and more noble. We lack the robust nerves which are necessary to drink from an elephant's tusk on which an Amazon battle scene has been engraved. Old techniques have been lost to us! Thank God! For that we have Beethoven's music of the spheres. Our temples are no longer painted blue, red, green and white like the Parthenon. No, we have learnt to feel the beauty of naked stone.

But, as I have already said, none of us was there, and the enemies of our culture and those who eulogise over old cultures had an easy task. They were, moreover, mistaken. They had misunderstood the past epochs. Only those objects, covered with decoration, which were little suited to a particular use and not worn out were kept. Thus only the ornamented objects were passed on to us, and it was therefore assumed that they were the only objects which existed in those days. Besides, they were easily classified according to age and origin by virtue of their ornaments, and the cataloguing was one of the most edifying pleasures of that Godforsaken period.

The craftsman could not compete with that, for he was expected to be able to produce and re-invent in one day those things which were produced through the centuries by all the nations. In each case those objects were the expression of their culture and were produced by the master craftsman, in the same way as the farmer builds his house. The master craftsman worked in the same way as did the master before him. But Goethe's contemporaries could no longer produce ornaments. Thus those who were trained in the new schools were commissioned and put in charge of the master craftsman.

The mason, the builder, was given a superior. The builder was only capable of building houses in the style of his time. But he who had the ability to build in any past style, he who had lost contact with his time, the one who was uprooted and remoulded, he became the dominant man, he was the architect.

The craftsman could not concern himself much with books. The architect derived everything from books. A colossal library of literature provided him with all that was worth knowing. One cannot imagine how poisonous the immense number of publications have been to our urban culture, how they have prevented us from looking at ourselves. It did not matter whether the architect had imprinted the forms on his mind to such an extent that he could redraw them from memory, or whether he must have had the copy in front of him during his artistic creation. The effect was always the same. It was always an abomination. And this abomination grew infinitely.

Everyone was striving to see his work immortalised in the new publications and the great number of architectural magazines which catered for the vain requirements of the architect. Thus it has remained until this day.

However, the architect has ousted the building craftsman for another reason. He has learned how to draw, and he could do this as he could not learn anything else. This, the craftsman cannot do. His hand has become leaden. The sketches of the old masters are ponderous, any student from the technical college can do better. Even more so can the dashing draughtsman, the man who is sought by every architectural office and who is highly paid!

The art of building has been degraded by the architect into a graphic art. The greatest number of jobs does not go to the person who is the builder, but to him whose work cuts the best figure on paper. And these two are opposites.

If one were to put the arts into a sequence which would show their relationship to one another, one could start with drawing, and we would find that it can be translated into painting. From this one can reach the plastic arts via polychromic sculpture and from the plastic arts one can reach architecture. Drawing and architecture are the beginning and end of the sequence.

The best draughtsman can be a bad architect, the best architect can be a bad draughtsman. The graphic arts are already required as a necessary talent at the beginning of one's choice of a career in architecture. The whole of our new architecture has been invented on the drawing board, and the drawings which are produced are meant to look three-dimensional, similar to the way in which paintings are recreated in a waxwork gallery.

For the old masters, however, the drawing was merely a means of communicating with the craftsmen who were carrying out the work, just as the poet has to make himself understood through the written word. But we are not, as yet, so cultureless that we teach a young boy poetry by means of calligraphy.

It is a well-known fact that every work of art possesses such strong internal laws that it can only appear in its own form.

A novel which can be adapted into a good play is both bad as a novel as it is bad as a play. However, a far worse case is one in which two different forms of art can be mixed up, even if they have points of contact. A painting which can be transformed into a scene in a waxwork gallery is a bad painting.

One might, of course, go and see the Tyrolean dress at Kastan's (a former Viennese waxwork gallery), but not Monet's 'Sunrise' nor an etching by Whistler. The realisation in stone, iron and glass of an architectural drawing, taken literally, even though one would have to admit to the drawing as being a graphic work of art, is a horrifying sight; and there are many such graphic artists amongst architects. The mark of a building which is truly established is that it remains ineffective in two dimensions. If I could erase the most powerful architectural phenomenon, the Palazzo Pitti, from the memory of my contemporaries and then have it drawn by the best draughtsman to enter in a competition scheme, the jury would throw me into a mad house.

But, it is the dashing draughtsman who rules today. It is no longer the craftsman's tools that create the forms, but the pencil. On the basis of a building's profile and decorative manner an observer can judge whether the architect uses a number one lead or a number five lead. And what responsibilities the compasses must bear for the confusion of tastes which they have caused! Hatching with the draughting pen has produced the epidemic of the grid. No window frame, no marble slab remains without mark, at the scale of 1:100, and bricklayers and masons have to scratch out and retouch this graphic nonsense with their own painstaking efforts. If by chance the artist had the ink in his draughting pen, then gold leaf would also be applied.

However I contend: a real building makes no impression as an illustration reproduced two-dimensionally. It is my greatest pride that the interiors which I have created are totally ineffective in photographs. I am proud of the fact that the inhabitants of my spaces do not recognise their own apartments in the photographs, just as the owner of a Monet painting would not recognise it at Kastan's. I have to forego the honour of being published in the various architectural magazines. I have been denied the satisfaction of my vanity.

And thus my efforts may be ineffective. Nothing is known of my work. But this is a sign of the strength of my ideas and the correctness of my teachings. I, the unpublished, I, whose efforts are unknown, I, the only one of thousands who has a real influence. I can cite one example, when I was allowed to create something for the first time – that was difficult enough, as I have said, as to my mind works cannot be represented graphically – bitter malice was borne against me. That was twelve years ago: the Café Museum in Vienna. Architects called it 'Café Nihilismus'. But this Café Museum exists to this day, while all the modern joinery by thousands of others have long been thrown into the junk room. Or they have to be ashamed of the work. The fact that the Café Museum has had more of an influence on our joinery work than all previous work put together can be gathered from the 1899 volume of the Munich magazine 'Dekorative Kunst', in which this interior was reproduced – I believe it was the editor who included it by mistake. But it was not the two photographic reproductions which were the cause of the influence – they remained totally unnoticed. Only the power of the example has had an influence. The very power with which the old masters had been effective and faster in reaching the farthest corner of the earth although, or especially because, post, telegraph or newspapers were not yet in existence.

The second half of the nineteenth century was filled with the cry of the cultureless. We have no building style! How wrong, how incorrect. It was precisely that very period that had a strongly accentuated style, one that could be differentiated more strongly from any of the preceding periods. It was a change which stands alone in the history of culture. However, as the false prophets could only recognise a product by how it was decorated, so ornament became a fetish for them; they substituted this changeling by calling it style. We had a true style, but we lacked ornament. If I could dislodge all ornaments from our old and new houses, so that only naked walls remained, it would certainly be difficult to differentiate the house of the fifteenth century from that of the seventeenth. But any layman could pick out the houses of the nineteenth century at first sight. We had no ornament and they moaned that we had no style. And they continued to copy past ornaments until they themselves found it laughable; and when this could no longer continue, they invented new ornaments, that is to say, they had descended so far culturally that they were capable of doing so. Now they believe that they have found the style of the twentieth century.

But that is not the style of the twentieth century. There are many things which show the style of the twentieth century in its pure form. They are those products whose producers have not been placed under the supervision of those who wish to distort our culture. They are above all the tailors, the shoemakers, the luggage-makers and saddlers; they are the coach builders, the tool-makers and all those who only escaped the general up-rooting because their craft did not appear noble enough to those lacking in culture for it to be included in their schemes. How fortunate!

From these remains, left to me by the architects, I was able to reconstruct the joinery of today twelve years ago, the very joinery which we would have had, had the architects never poked their noses into the joiners' workshops. For I did not approach the task in the manner of an artist, creating literally, giving imagination full scope. This is probably how one expresses oneself if one is an artist. No, I entered the workshop timidly, like an apprentice, I looked up at the man with the blue apron respectfully, and begged: let me share your secret. Because many a secret of the workshop lay modestly hidden from the architect's sight. And when they understood my intentions, when they recognised that I was not one of those who wanted to deform that beloved wood by drawing-board fantasies, when they saw that I did not want to desecrate that reverentially venerated material with green or violet staining, their own proudness came to the surface, their carefully concealed tradition was brought to light and their hatred of their oppressors was vented. And I found a modern wall-cladding system in the panels which enclose the container of the old water closet; I found a modern corner solution in the boxes in which the silver cutlery was kept; I found locks and ironmongery at the luggage and piano makers. And I discovered the most important thing: the style of 1900 differs from the style of 1800 only in so far as the dinner jacket of 1900 differs from the dinner jacket of 1800.

That is not much. One of them was made from blue cloth and had gold buttons, the other is made from black cloth and has black buttons. The black dinner jacket is in the style of our period. No one can deny that.

In their arrogance, the warped people by-passed the reform of our clothes. For they were all serious men who considered it beyond their dignity to bother about such things. Thus our clothes were left alone to reflect the true style of our period. Only the invention of ornament was becoming to the serious, dignified man.

When I was finally given the task of building a house, I said to myself: in its external appearance, a house can only have changed as much as a dinner jacket. Not a lot, therefore. And I saw how the old buildings had freed themselves from ornament, from century to century, from one year to another. I, therefore, had to begin again at that point where the chain of development had been broken. I knew one thing: in order to continue that line of development, I had to become significantly simpler. I had to substitute the golden buttons with black ones. The house had to look inconspicuous. Had I not once formulated the sentence: he who is dressed in a modern manner is one who is least conspicuous. That sounded paradoxical. But there were brave people who were careful to remember this, and many of my other paradoxical ideas; and who put them into print. That happened so often that people in time took them to be true.

However, as far as inconspicuousness is concerned, there was one thing I had not considered. That is: what was true in the case of clothes was not the case for architecture. If architecture had only been left alone by those warped people, and if the clothes were reformed in terms of old theatrical junk or in the Secessionist manner – there certainly were attempts in this direction – then the situation would have been the other way round.

Consider this sitution: everyone wears clothes that relate to a past period or to one of an imaginary, distant future. One would see men from grey antiquity, women with towering hair styles and crinoline dresses, dainty men wearing Burgundy trousers and in between, a few cheeky moderns with purple escarpins and apple-green doublets (decorated by Professor Walter Scherbel). And now a man was to enter wearing a simple suit, would he not be conspicuous? More than that, would he not cause offence? And would the police not be called, since after all, they have the duty to remove everything that causes an offence?

However, the matter is quite the contrary. The clothes are the right ones; the act of buffoonery is in the domain of architecture. My house (the Michaelerhouse in Vienna, built in the same year that this article was written), gave real offence, and the police were immediately at hand. I might be allowed to do such things in the confines of my own four walls, but it does not belong in the street!

Many will have had doubts over my last remarks, doubts which are directed against the comparison which I have drawn between tailoring and architecture. After all, architecture is an art. Granted, it is for the time being. But have you never noticed the strange correspondence between the exterior dress of people and the exterior of buildings? Is the tasselled robe not appropriate to the Gothic style and the wig to the Baroque? But do our contemporary houses correspond with our clothes? Are we afraid of uniformity? But were the old buildings within one period and one country also not uniform? So uniform that it is possible for us to place them in order according to the styles of countries, peoples and towns. Nervous vanity was alien to the old masters. Tradition determined the forms. The masters did not change the forms. The masters however, were unable faithfully to use the established, hallowed, traditional forms. New tastes changed the forms and thus the rules were broken and new forms were developed. But the people of that period were at one with the architecture of their times. The newly erected building pleased everyone. Today most houses only please two people: the client and the architect.

The house has to please everyone, contrary to the work of art, which does not. The work of art is a private matter for the artist. The house is not. The work of art is brought into the world without there being a need for it. The house satisfies a requirement. The work of art is responsible to none; the house is responsible to everyone. The work of art wants to draw people out of their state of comfort. The house has to serve comfort. The work of art is revolution-ary; the house is conservative. The work of art shows people new directions and thinks of the future. The house thinks of the present. Man loves everything that satisfies his comfort. He hates everything that wants to draw him out of his acquired and secured position and that disturbs him. Thus he loves the house and hates art.

Does it follow that the house has nothing in common with art and is architecture not to be included amongst the arts? That is so. Only a very small part of architecture belongs to art: the tomb and the monument. Everything else that fulfils a function is to be excluded from the domain of art.

Only when the great misunderstanding, that art is something which can be adapted to serve a function has been overcome, only when the deceitful catchphrase of 'applied-art' has disappeared from the vocabulary of the people, only then will we have the architecture of our period. The artist needs only to serve himself; the architect must serve the population at large. But the amalgamation of art and craft has caused both of them, as well as humanity, infinite damage. For this reason humanity no longer knows what art is. It persecutes the artist with senseless rage and thereby prevents the creation of the work of art. Every hour humanity commits a monstrous sin, one that cannot be forgiven, the sin against the holy spirit. Murder and robbery, everything can be forgiven. But the large number of Ninth Symphonies which humanity has prevented in its blindness by persecuting the artist will not be forgiven. Humanity will not be forgiven for thwarting God's plans.

Humanity no longer knows what art is. 'Art in the service of the businessman' was the title of a recent exhibition in Munich and no hand was there to chastise the author of this presumptious phrase.

And no one laughs at the beautiful words 'applied-arts'.

But he who knows that the purpose of art is to take man further and further, higher and higher, to make him more like God, understands that to give art a material function is a profanation of the highest order. Man will not leave the artist alone because he has a respect for him, and the crafts are unable to develop freely, being burdened under the weight of man's idealistic demands. The artist will not find a majority of support amongst the living. His empire lies in the future. As there are tasteful and tasteless buildings, man assumes that the former are produced by artists, the latter by non-artists. But it is no feat to build tastefully just as it is no feat to avoid putting a knife into one's mouth or to brush one's teeth in the morning. Here one is confusing art with culture. Who can show me something in bad taste from past, cultivated times? The houses by a minor bricklayer in a provincial town were in good taste. But there were certainly great and minor masters. The great works were reserved for the great masters.

The great masters had a more intimate contact with the spirit of the world, thanks to their outstanding education.

Architecture arouses sentiments in man. The architect's task therefore, is to make those sentiments more precise. The room has to be comfortable; the house has to look habitable. The law courts must appear as a threatening gesture towards secret vice. The bank must declare: here your money is secure and well looked after by honest people.

The architect can only achieve this if he establishes a relationship with those buildings which have hitherto created this sentiment in man. For the Chinese, the colour of mourning is white; for us it is black. Consequently it would be impossible for our architects to produce a happy atmosphere with the colour black.

When we come across a mound in the wood, six feet long and three feet wide, raised to a pyramidal form by means of a spade, we become serious and something in us says: somebody lies buried here. *This is architecture.*

Our culture is based on the knowledge of the all-surpassing grandeur of classical antiquity. We have adopted the technique of thinking and feeling from the Romans. We have inherited our social conscience and the discipline of our souls from the Romans.

It is no coincidence that the Romans were incapable of inventing a new column order, or a new ornament. For they had already progressed so far. They had taken all that knowledge from the Greeks and had adapted it to their needs. The Greeks were individualists. Every building had to have its own profile, its own ornamentation. But the Romans considered things socially. The Greeks could hardly administer their cities; the Romans administered the globe. The Greeks squandered their inventiveness on the orders; the Romans wasted theirs on the plan. And he who can solve the great plan does not think of new mouldings.

Ever since humanity sensed the greatness of classical antiquity, one common thought has unified all great architects. They think: the way I build is the same as the way the Romans would have built. We know that they are mistaken. Time, place, function and climate, milieu have upset their calculations.

But every time the minor architects who use ornament move architecture away from its grand model, a great architect is at hand to guide them back to antiquity. Fischer von Erlach in the south, Schlüter in the north, were justifiably the great masters of the eighteenth century. And at the threshold to the nineteenth century stood Schinkel. We have forgotten him. May the light of this towering figure shine upon our forthcoming generation of architects!

40

Manifesto of Futurist Architecture 1914

Antonio Sant'Elia

No architecture has existed since 1700. A moronic mixture of the most various stylistic elements used to mask the skeletons of modern houses is called modern architecture. The new beauty of cement and iron are profaned by the superimposition of motley decorative incrustations that cannot be justified either by constructive necessity or by our (modern) taste, and whose origins are in Egyptian, Indian or Byzantine antiquity and in that idiotic flowering of stupidity and impotence that took the name of NEOCLASSICISM.

These architectonic prostitutions are welcomed in Italy, and rapacious alien ineptitude is passed off as talented invention and as extremely up-to-date architecture. Young Italian architects (those who borrow originality from clandestine and compulsive devouring of art journals) flaunt their talents in the new quarters of our towns, where a hilarious salad of little ogival columns, seventeenth-century foliation, Gothic pointed arches, Egyptian pilasters, rococo scrolls, fifteenth-century cherubs, swollen caryatids, take the place of style in all seriousness, and presumptuously put on monumental airs. The kaleidoscopic appearance and reappearance of forms, the multiplying of machinery, the daily increasing needs imposed by the speed of communications, by the concentration of population, by hygiene, and by a hundred other phenomena of modern life, never cause these self-styled renovators of architecture a moment's perplexity or hesitation. They persevere obstinately with the rules of Vitruvius, Vignola and Sansovino plus gleanings from any published scrap of information on German architecture that happens to be at hand. Using these, they continue to stamp the image of imbecility on our cities, our cities which should be the immediate and faithful projection of ourselves.

And so this expressive and synthetic art has become in their hands a vacuous stylistic exercise, a jumble of ill-mixed formulae to disguise a run-of-the-mill traditionalist box of bricks and stone as a modern building. As if we who are

Antonio Sant'Elia, "Manifesto of Futurist Architecture," pp. 160–72 from Umbro Apollonio (ed.), *Futurist Manifestos*, trans. R. W. Flint. London: Thames & Hudson, 1973.

accumulators and generators of movement, with all our added mechanical limbs, with all the noise and speed of our life, could live in streets built for the needs of men four, five or six centuries ago.

This is the supreme imbecility of modern architecture, perpetuated by the venal complicity of the academies, the internment camps of the intelligentsia, where the young are forced into the onanistic recopying of classical models instead of throwing their minds open in the search for new frontiers and in the solution of the new and pressing problem: THE FUTURIST HOUSE AND CITY. The house and the city that are ours both spiritually and materially, in which our tumult can rage without seeming a grotesque anachronism.

The problem posed in *Futurist* architecture is not one of linear rearrangement. It is not a question of finding new mouldings and frames for windows and doors, of replacing columns, pilasters and corbels with caryatids, flies and frogs. Neither has it anything to do with leaving a façade in bare brick, or plastering it, or facing it with stone or in determining formal differences between the new building and the old one. It is a question of tending the healthy growth of the Futurist house, of constructing it with all the resources of technology and science, satisfying magisterially all the demands of our habits and our spirit, trampling down all that is grotesque and antithetical (tradition, style, aesthetics, proportion), determining new forms, new lines, a new harmony of profiles and volumes, an architecture whose reason for existence can be found solely in the unique conditions of modern life, and in its correspondence with the aesthetic values of our sensibilities. This architecture cannot be subjected to any law of historical continuity. It must be new, just as our state of mind is new.

The art of construction has been able to evolve with time, and to pass from one style to another, while maintaining unaltered the general characteristics of architecture, because in the course of history changes of fashion are frequent and are determined by the alternations of religious conviction and political disposition. But profound changes in the state of the environment are extremely rare, changes that unhinge and renew, such as the discovery of natural laws, the perfecting of mechanical means, the rational and scientific use of material. In modern life the process of stylistic development in architecture has been brought to a halt. ARCHITECTURE NOW MAKES A BREAK WITH TRADITION. IT MUST PERFORCE MAKE A FRESH START.

Calculations based on the resistance of materials, on the use of reinforced concrete and steel, exclude 'architecture' in the classical and traditional sense. Modern constructional materials and scientific concepts are absolutely incompatible with the disciplines of historical styles, and are the principal cause of the grotesque appearance of 'fashionable' buildings in which attempts are made to employ the lightness, the superb grace of the steel beam, the delicacy of reinforced concrete, in order to obtain the heavy curve of the arch and the bulkiness of marble.

The utter antithesis between the modern world and the old is determined by all those things that formerly did not exist. Our lives have been enriched by elements the possibility of whose existence the ancients did not even suspect. Men have identified material contingencies, and revealed spiritual attitudes, whose repercussions are felt in a thousand ways. Principal among these is the formation of a new ideal of beauty that is still obscure and embryonic, but whose fascination is already felt even by the masses. We have lost our predilection for the monumental, the heavy, the static, and we have enriched our sensibility with a *taste for the light, the practical, the ephemeral and the swift.* We no longer feel ourselves to be the men of the cathedrals, the palaces and the podiums. We are the men of the great hotels, the railway stations, the immense streets, colossal ports, covered markets, luminous arcades, straight roads and beneficial demolitions.

We must invent and rebuild the Futurist city like an immense and tumultuous shipyard, agile, mobile and dynamic in every detail; and the Futurist house must be like a gigantic machine. The lifts must no longer be hidden away like tapeworms in the niches of stairwells; the stairwells themselves, rendered useless, must be abolished, and the lifts must scale the lengths of the façades like serpents of steel and glass. The house of concrete, glass and steel, stripped of paintings and sculpture, rich only in the innate beauty of its lines and relief, extraordinarily 'ugly' in its mechanical simplicity, higher and wider according to need rather than the specifications of municipal laws. It must soar up on the brink of a tumultuous abyss: the street will no longer lie like a doormat at ground level, but will plunge many storeys down into the earth, embracing the metropolitan traffic, and will be linked up for necessary interconnections by metal gangways and swift-moving pavements.

THE DECORATIVE MUST BE ABOLISHED. The problem of Futurist architecture must be resolved, not by continuing to pilfer from Chinese, Persian or Japanese photographs or fooling around with the rules of Vitruvius, but through flashes of genius and through scientific and technical expertise. Everything must be revolutionized. Roofs and underground spaces must be used; the importance of the façade must be diminished; issues of taste must be transplanted from the field of fussy mouldings, finicky capitals and flimsy doorways to the broader concerns of BOLD GROUPINGS AND MASSES, and LARGE-SCALE DISPOSITION OF PLANES. Let us make an end of monumental, funereal and commemorative architecture. Let us overturn monuments, pavements, arcades and flights of steps; let us sink the streets and squares; let us raise the level of the city.

I COMBAT AND DESPISE:

1. All the pseudo-architecture of the avant-garde, Austrian, Hungarian, German and American;
2. All classical architecture, solemn, hieratic, scenographic, decorative, monumental, pretty and pleasing;
3. The embalming, reconstruction and reproduction of ancient monuments and palaces;
4. Perpendicular and horizontal lines, cubical and pyramidical forms that are static, solemn, aggressive and absolutely excluded from our utterly new sensibility;
5. The use of massive, voluminous, durable, antiquated and costly materials.

AND PROCLAIM:

1. That Futurist architecture is the architecture of calculation, of audacious temerity and of simplicity; the architecture of reinforced concrete, of steel, glass, cardboard, textile fibre, and of all those substitutes for wood, stone and brick that enable us to obtain maximum elasticity and lightness;

2. That Futurist architecture is not because of this an arid combination of practicality and usefulness, but remains art, i.e. synthesis and expression;

3. That oblique and elliptic lines are dynamic, and by their very nature possess an emotive power a thousand times stronger than perpendiculars and horizontals, and that no integral, dynamic architecture can exist that does not include these;

4. That decoration as an element superimposed on architecture is absurd, and that THE DECORATIVE VALUE OF FUTURIST ARCHITECTURE DEPENDS SOLELY ON THE USE AND ORIGINAL ARRANGEMENT OF RAW OR BARE OR VIOLENTLY COLOURED MATERIALS;

5. That, just as the ancients drew inspiration for their art from the elements of nature, we – who are materially and spiritually artificial – must find that inspiration in the elements of the utterly new mechanical world we have created, and of which architecture must be the most beautiful expression, the most complete synthesis, the most efficacious integration;

6. That architecture as the art of arranging forms according to pre-established criteria is finished;

7. That by the term architecture is meant the endeavour to harmonize the environment with Man with freedom and great audacity, that is to transform the world of things into a direct projection of the world of the spirit;

8. From an architecture conceived in this way no formal or linear habit can grow, since the fundamental characteristics of Futurist architecture will be its impermanence and transience. THINGS WILL ENDURE LESS THAN US. EVERY GENERATION MUST BUILD ITS OWN CITY. This constant renewal of the architectonic environment will contribute to the victory of Futurism which has already been affirmed by WORDS-IN-FREEDOM, PLASTIC DYNAMISM, MUSIC WITHOUT QUADRATURE AND THE ART OF NOISES, and for which we fight without respite against traditionalist cowardice.

41

The Turbine Hall of the AEG

Peter Behrens

The new turbine building recently completed for the AEG was erected from my design on the corner site bounded by the Huttenstrasse and Berlichingenstrasse in north Berlin. The ground plan was arranged so as to take into account the existing railway tracks and at the same time to make the maximum use of the site within the limitations of the building line. It was nevertheless possible to emphasize the main hall by pulling the secondary hall back from it slightly. In the construction of the main hall the overriding architectonic idea was to make the steel supports more massive rather than spreading them out as is customary with the normal lattice construction. In this way the interior space would be closed off by flat planes on all sides, so as to allow a clear view of the architectonic proportions, such as can only be afforded by a very large internal area. For similar reasons, as far as the external appearance was concerned, it was decided to make the structural girders extend to the full thickness of the wall. This seemed all the more desirable as the original intention was to construct the whole building as far as possible from glass and steel. Where these two materials were not sufficient, only well finished concrete walls were to be used as filling, since unlike stone, which gives the impression of a load-bearing material, the former leaves the load-bearing entirely to the steel framework. Following the same principle, the windows on the Berlichingenstrasse are slanted parallel with the inside edges of the heavy vertical steel stanchions, so that the horizontal linking member running lengthwise above the windows casts a deep shadow on to them.

This linking member has the effect of a steel cornice, and together with the pediment at the front end, makes the roof appear as a discrete mass resting on the stanchions and on the window frames of the façade. The rounded corners of the building are made of concrete, divided by horizontal steel bands so

Peter Behrens, "The Turbine Hall of the AEG," pp. 56–7 from Charlotte Benton (ed.), *Documents: A Collection of Source Material for the Modern Movement*. Milton Keynes: Open University Press, 1975.

that they appear merely as a filling in contrast to the vertical structural members of the side wall. The supporting framework is given aesthetic expression at the front end by the large steel window, which for this reason consists of a steel frame with all its members of the same thickness. In order to express its identity with the load-bearing parts of the building, the window is made flush with the front of the pediment, and to reinforce this impression the glass is laid flush with the steel frame.

The front end of the smaller adjoining hall is constructed entirely of concrete and this is continued for the first 4 metres on the yard side (up to the first of the main hall supports), so as to emphasize the steel framework of the two halls as seen from the side. The yard side of the secondary hall displays a row of steel supports between wide horizontal connecting girders of the same material. The windows form a continuous surface with the steel framework. This use of glass and steel as a continuous medium is intentionally extended throughout the whole building; since the structure consists largely of these two materials, the intention is to make it appear as solid as possible. Both steel and glass lack the solid appearance of stone facings. The impression of spindliness and fragility can only be avoided by setting both materials in the same plane, so that they give an appearance of solidity and homogeneity. The result is an aesthetic expression of the stability and strength which steel can be proved to have by calculation, but which the human eye, bound to outward appearances, would otherwise be unable to perceive. All forms of sculptural and ornamental decoration were omitted, firstly because the function of a factory building demands simplicity of form, but more especially because the desired impression of solidity, and the proportions contributing to this impression, could only have been diminished rather than enhanced by it.

I was commissioned by the AEG to design both the external architectonic framework and the arrangement of the interior, and in so far as the internal use of space is governed by the structural concept, this was carried out according to my specifications. The structural execution of this concept was in the hands of the well-known engineer, Bernhardt. Thus in all structural aspects, the building is the fruit of the most up-to-date technical knowledge and ability. Bernhardt produced the technical drawings and carried out all the necessary calculations with the utmost understanding for artistic considerations, solving all the problems which this presented with commendable technical ingenuity.

42

The State of German Architecture

Sigfried Giedion

Taking 1912–20 as roughly the time during which German Expressionism was at the height of its power, we must recognize that this was also the period (at least in Germany) when architecture counted as one of the minor arts. What is the use of architecture, whose purpose is to cover our external life, when the clarion cry rings out: Look inwards! Free us from material objects! Give us inspiration! Paint the essence of humanity! Paint our mistreated generation in swirling colours glowing with the rays of eternity!

Expressionist architecture in the proper sense of the term does not exist, for architecture can flower only where it can be master. It is almost inherent in the terms of German Expressionism that architecture should be excluded. Some of Poelzig's individual works could be regarded as symbolic of Expressionist architecture, but we should not ascribe a style to them.

When Expressionism first became widespread, its inspiration came not from architecture but from the applied arts. Colours flowed from pictures on to walls and objects.

1925: Many people now find themselves confronted with a transformed situation. A new form of architecture is coming into existence: inartistic, unfashionable. Related phenomena are being produced from Russia to America at unheard-of speed. National boundaries are crossed so that all creative efforts can benefit mutually. For a while the so-called 'free' arts are relegated to the background while reality holds sway in this utopian current. The architect turns away from the painter, from the sculptor and, most emphatically, from the historian, so as to accept as his real brother and helper the sociologist, economist and statistician.

The architect deliberately strips off the last insulating layer of aestheticism which could separate him from real life, so that, almost forgetting himself, he

Sigfried Giedion, "The State of German Architecture," pp. 11–15 from Charlotte Benton (ed.), *Documents: A Collection of Source Material for the Modern Movement*. Milton Keynes: Open University Press, 1975.

can subject himself to the ruling commands as thoroughly as possible: the traffic movements of a town have become more important than form or monumentality.

One should not fear that a total aridity may suddenly occur. Until architecture has totally assimilated the whole standard of our changed way of life, it will be unable to find formulas whose obvious rightness will be indispensable material for future generations. We demand a continuity. Architecture formulates, and must formulate anew so as to be able fully to embody within itself the new conditions.

At this crucial point, one asks involuntarily: Where does German architecture stand at the moment?

Summary: It must be realized that in the movement at the beginning of the century – which included architecture – and in whose wake the mainstream still flows to this day, decorative art was in the ascendancy. The sequel to this was that decoration, rather than architecture, became of prime importance. It is not mere chance that most of the leading architects of this period came from a background in the crafts or interior design. Let us attempt to clarify the advantages and disadvantages of this artistic infiltration. Decorative art proceeded from form; it purified it by putting into practice the war-cry: 'Expediency versus style, to clear Germany from imitations of style which had become stereotyped, and to do this more radically than in any of the neighbouring countries.' A certain standard of interior decoration and objects has become the norm to such an extent that, for instance, even the worst German philistine would have felt a sense of superiority when faced with the Art Nouveau productions at the Paris Exhibition.

But suddenly the problem has changed, and architecture is taking over. Expediency versus style is no longer the question. People have stopped racking their brains over how to find a formal style – which was frequently the case in the wake of artistic statements of the problem. After all, the search for a common style is still going on, as different modes are employed concurrently, and the search can be traced back to the 1830s. The new architect is governed by necessity, the cost of building, and calculations, almost to the point of total indifference to form. Of course these factors are always the most help in searching for a new style.

We grew up with what we called the 'artistic' movement, and can freely admit what it gave us: purification of household objects, a more refined sense of interiors, and a new life for almost all materials, metal, wood and textiles – from the surface decoration on ceramics, to the finishing on a wall. The architectural purification of the house should not be forgotten, even though it did not escape from an over-lavishly cushioned boudoir atmosphere.

Yet it must be stated clearly that the decorative movement has petered out, and not just recently. The *Werkstätten* culture, which complied with the tastes of a refined bourgeoisie, has come to an end. This is most clearly shown in the case of the *Wiener Werkstätten*, which although achieving some significance at first, has been moving for years in the direction of the rococo, from which there can be no progression.

So a playful and irrelevant quality has entered into even such refined products as these. Articles in silver look as though one could crumple them like tissue paper, ceramics are often treated in an inappropriate way which denies the inherent qualities of the clay – the curves of a nervous feminism. All the world seems to be disintegrating into toys.

This must be stated here, for architecture, especially in Germany, infiltrated as it was by artistic currents, did not manage to avoid the rush into a premature rococo state after a promising start. And this is where we stand today in some confusion. Poelzig should be named here as the most representative architect of this tendency. From his promising factories, shops and water towers he has turned all too quickly to a baroque theatricality, similar to that found in industrial art, which gave movement to simple profiles, like that of Behrens in 1910. No-one knows better than Poelzig how to mould an inflexible brick wall and make it malleable, so that it is emotionally charged, as in the case of the administrative offices built for the Meyer Brothers in Hanover. The future confronts this type of architecture (the Salzburg Festival Theatre Scheme) with its monumental appearance and is foreign to it. We should not evade the question: 'Can we permit the existence of such ineffective architecture today, when we are still only groping for the smallest element (the house) without being sure of finding a solution?'

It is strange how the earlier industrial spans, such as Peter Behrens's hangar built in Hanover in 1915, still hold their ground and – against all odds – still remain monuments which are part of the development. In the last few years Behrens has given vague indications of a romantic line of approach. There is a clear progression from his problematical brick church in the Munich Industrial Show of 1922, through the coloured domed hall for the Hoechst Farbwerke, with its Gothic stalactite-like pillars, to the romantic imagery of ruins in his conservatory in the Paris Exhibition. This romantic approach is more a personal attribute of Behrens's temperament – and can be seen too in some of his speeches – than a far-reaching symptom of the age, as is, for example, Poelzig's exuberant baroque style. Behrens's splendid buildings, with their romantic lines, can be considered symptomatic only in so far as they demonstrate the influence of decorative art.

Even the two greatest talents of the preceding generation were not able to escape the artistic infiltration of German architecture. This can only serve to complicate progress towards a purified architecture. It is generally considered that Germany will be in the forefront of future developments, but this is still by no means certain. It is easy to sneer at the Art Nouveau movement in France, or at the prominent Gobelins-mania in America, but such formal matters lose their importance when, as today, one looks first at the unspoiled skeleton which lies beneath. For it is sometimes possible to overlook the ludicrous decoration which has been stuck on – as in the case of *La Samaritaine*, the Parisian store designed by F. Jourdain – and it is possible to sense the constructive, uncorroded framework.

Certainly to limp in pursuit of France's artistic trends is grotesquely false, since the whole situation has now changed. Besides, there is a new movement in France (Le Corbusier, Lurçat, Leclerc,[1] etc.), which has the advantage that it does not have to fight so strongly as in Germany against an adjustment of taste, which is all

---

[1] Probably a misprint in the original for Le Coeur. (ed.)

the more dangerous. In the polarization between those forces which are clearly advancing and the unrepentant traditionalists, radical solutions are fundamentally easier, since in the great divide between action and reaction there does not always exist in the latter a readiness for external assimilation. In this way a movement stays almost safe from fashionable dilution. Until now France has not had such compromisers, who shave off their high roofs at the first gust, who suddenly squeeze the height of a window into a wide format, who provide the garden hedge with horizontal stakes and use shapes attached externally in the style of Frank Lloyd Wright.

Nothing is so crushing to a movement such as the new architecture – which must struggle out of the ground so as to be able to transmit to later generations a workable vocabulary – as facile imitation which, through mimicry, hides an unchanged inner core.

At its outset, the decorative art movement of 1900 firmly intensified the feeling for materials which had been lost. Now that movement has lost its impetus, for this feeling for materials has now been transformed into an almost voluptuous handling of material surfaces instead of the actual reality of the thing itself.

In architectural terms this means that in Germany and the cultural circles dependent on it, a tremendous virtuosity has been achieved in the handling of the surface of a wall. The favourite is a brick wall. Poelzig is merely the chief representative of a series of active architects, in whose hands the wall achieves almost the flexibility of fabric.

It is possible to turn one's heavy artillery against the historicist façades which are common in France and America today. Yet the refined manner of handling surfaces, which is common practice in Germany, is much more dangerous and obstructive for new forms of architecture, since it allows quite false effects to insinuate themselves into new buildings.

This is most clearly seen in the problem which arises with skyscrapers in Germany. Though this problem has been all too frequently discussed in the newspapers, it remains one of the 'monumental tasks' which has still to be confronted properly. Not one of the skyscrapers already built is the work of an architect who can guarantee a solution to the problem. The only solution to have materialized so far is a multi-storey house. That is still the best example instance (see for instance Koerfer's problem with skyscrapers on the Cologne Hansaring).

The skyscraper problem has reached this impasse through the artistic infiltration which took control over it. The skyscraper has particular features which make it unique: a framework, concrete and iron. Its construction is an uncluttered outer wall supported on an inner framework. The cantilevering of the building, which achieves expression through its outer surface, is intimately related to the new role of architecture. If the skeleton of the skyscraper is not properly apparent in a homogeneous form, then its purpose is misunderstood.

Obviously some of the solutions in Germany do create a voluntary or involuntary compromise with the expression of the constructive central core. But still, as has sometimes been the case, skyscrapers have been designed in which the impact of the façade has been achieved by arranging the layers of brick in a special manner and by using different materials to bring out the contrast in these layers; this is more dangerous than a skyscraper which an American architect ornamented with a frieze of pillars like the Parthenon. Because of the vast dimensions of American skyscraper building, the presence of the inner framework is able to make itself felt despite any excrescence put on the outside. The dilemma of German architecture is shown in a skyscraper in Düsseldorf, where at one point the upward thrust of the walls has been broken by a decorative moulding in filigree. This, with its pointed zig-zag lines, is nothing more than an enormously enlarged sketch from the studio of some Expressionist artist. These latest rival trends seem even further from a solution than the ones which were already established.

It cannot be denied that through artistic infiltration the skyscraper problem has reached a dead end. It is discredited. Surely there is some architect who could handle the problem decisively; they managed to find Messel to build the Wertheim store, and Behrens for AEG's factories. Certainly such architects exist; it just happens that they are not given anything to build. They make sketches, provide material for their imitators who dilute their ideas, and are then themselves left out in the cold. Perhaps the situation will change. Until then, however, no one will build a skyscraper that can be said to have a 'character' of its own.

We have cited the skyscraper problem, since it shows the general level of today's production at its most blatant. One would have thought that Europe, which is constantly asserting its cultural superiority over America, would at least be capable of finding a suitable form of housing for its economic system. But 'artistic aestheticism' is not the way.

The second, and more important, problem which architecture faces and must soon solve, is in direct opposition to 'artistic aestheticism'. The price of individual housing units must be brought down through the mechanical production of components. Even though the now defunct Arts and Crafts Movement created first-class workers' housing estates, its significance lay in the creation of a culti-vated middle-class environment. The rather over-cultivated feeling for the surface charm of materials linked up with *soigné* and somewhat effeminate feeling for plushy furnishings, which was a seductive element of the previous era's good interior design. How tempting it is to fall back into the plump soft cushions on an armchair on a thick carpet behind long drawn curtains and think: Life should resemble this sheltered island. But is it life? Is it our life?

The new architecture, which remains bleak to the point of coarseness, throws such feelings to the winds as it empties the rooms. Where the earlier movement contracted a secret union with luxury, the new architecture joins hands with the many, with those of limited means, with 99% of the populace. The bourgeois way of life with a variety of rooms is downright hostile to this new creative movement. New solutions to the housing problem show that one large room is all that is needed; any others are extraneous and should be limited as far as possible. This is the link between above and below, this is the link with tradition, with the large room in a peasant's house, with even more remote forms of dwellings. For the first time in the history of building the creative desire of architecture is at one with the possibilities of the lower classes. Indeed, it is dependent on them.

Clearly from here onwards the move today is to build barrack-like complexes to house the masses. Public transport makes it possible to decentralize. But people want single units, single homes. What is generally possible today only for the well-off because of the craftsman methods of building, will become general practice. But simultaneously it has been recognized that the whole problem is one of economics. Without cheaper methods of housing through the industrialization of production methods, no solution will be found. One would almost like to say that the country which in ten years' time has the most factories producing houses, will be the country that leads in future architectural development.

Behind these advances, which today have become almost universal, hides at the same time the desire for a structure for the architecture of the future. This is a desire for standardization, for the best utilization of space, for exterior simplification of form. Forms with mechanically produced sections: doors, furniture, objects (not hand-made luxury individual articles) will become identical with today's demands for form.

While this aesthetic infiltration remains more-or-less limited at the moment to German cultural circles and their spheres of influence (its most durable monument must surely be the Stockholm City Hall[2]), the new forms of architecture are also taking root in Russia and America.

In every area today we are scattered to an almost inconceivable degree. It is striking however that it is precisely the new architectural creations that show a definite and homogeneous sense of purpose, which we can find otherwise only in dance forms and in the production of cars.

It is by no means clear which country will work out a decisive solution – perhaps they will work on it together. The German soil will doubtless be very fertile, only we must recognize exactly where we stand. As in 1900, at the start of the earlier movement, power was firmly entrenched with the pattern book architects, so now it lies almost totally with the representatives of 'artistic aestheticism'. (We will keep silent about the disastrous Arts and Crafts attitude which manifests itself today in the verdicts of juries.) Certainly the pattern book architects, who often broke away quite abruptly from the historical pattern, had less taste than is usual today, when forms are more heavily disguised, more remote and less controllable. But today we object precisely to this 'taste' which so easily lets architectural matters slip into dangerously fashionable realms. Now is the time to attempt once again to break away from superficial attraction and to re-establish architecture as a functional art.

---

[2] Ragnar Ostberg. Built 1909–23. (ed.)

43

Programme of the Staatliche Bauhaus in Weimar

Walter Gropius

The ultimate aim of all visual arts is the complete building! To embellish buildings was once the noblest function of the fine arts; they were the indispensable components of great architecture. Today the arts exist in isolation, from which they can be rescued only through the conscious, cooperative effort of all craftsmen. Architects, painters, and sculptors must recognise anew and learn to grasp the composite character of a building both as an entity and in its separate parts. Only then will their work be imbued with the architectonic spirit which it has lost as 'salon art'.

The old schools of art were unable to produce this unity; how could they, since art cannot be taught. They must be merged once more with the workshop. The mere drawing and painting world of the pattern designer and the applied artist must become a world that builds again. When young people who take a joy in artistic creation once more begin their life's work by learning a trade, then the unproductive 'artist' will no longer be condemned to deficient artistry, for their skill will now be preserved for the crafts, in which they will be able to achieve excellence.

Architects, sculptors, painters, we all must return to the crafts! For art is not a 'profession'. There is no essential difference between the artist and the craftsman. The artist is an exalted craftsman. In rare moments of inspiration, transcending the consciousness of his will, the grace of heaven may cause his work to blossom into art. But proficiency in a craft is essential to every artist. Therein lies the prime source of creative imagination. Let us then create a new guild of craftsmen without the class distinctions that raise an arrogant barrier between craftsman and artist! Together let us desire, conceive, and create the new structure of the future, which will embrace architecture and sculpture and painting in one unity

Walter Gropius, "Programme of the Staatliche Bauhaus in Weimar, April, 1919" pp. 78–9 from Tim and Charlotte Benton et al. (eds.), *Form and Function: A Source Book for the History of Architecture and Design 1890–1939*. Milton Keynes: Open University Press, 1975.

and which will one day rise towards heaven from the hands of a million workers like the crystal symbol of a new faith.

Programme of the Staatliche Bauhaus in Weimar

The Staatliche Bauhaus resulted from the merger of the former Grand-Ducal Saxon Academy of Art with the former Grand-Ducal Saxon School of Arts and Crafts in conjunction with a newly affiliated department of architecture.

Aims of the Bauhaus

The Bauhaus strives to bring together all creative effort into one whole, to reunify all the disciplines of practical art – sculpture, painting, handicrafts, and the crafts – as inseparable components of a new architecture. The ultimate, if distant, aim of the Bauhaus is the unified work of art – the great structure – in which there is no distinction between monumental and decorative art.

The Bauhaus wants to educate architects, painters, and sculptors of all levels, according to their capabilities, to become competent craftsmen or independent creative artists and to form a working community of leading and future artist-craftsmen. These men, of kindred spirit, will know how to design buildings harmoniously in their entirety – structure, finishing, ornamentation, and furnishing.

Principles of the Bauhaus

Art rises above all methods; in itself it cannot be taught, but the crafts certainly can be. Architects, painters, and sculptors are craftsmen in the true sense of the word; hence, a thorough training in the crafts, acquired in workshops and in experimental and practical sites, is required of all students as the indispensable basis for all artistic production. Our own workshops are to be gradually built up, and apprenticeship agreements with outside workshops will be concluded.

The school is the servant of the workshop, and will one day be absorbed in it. Therefore there will be no teachers or pupils in the Bauhaus but masters, journeymen, and apprentices.

The manner of teaching arises from the character of the workshop: Organic forms developed from manual skills.

Avoidance of all rigidity; priority of creativity; freedom of individuality, but strict study discipline.

Master and journeyman examinations, according to the Guild Statutes, held before the Council of Masters of the Bauhaus or before outside masters.

Collaboration by the students in the work of the masters.

Securing of commissions, also for students.

Mutual planning of extensive, Utopian structural designs – public buildings and buildings for worship – aimed at the future. Collaboration of all masters and students – architects, painters, sculptors – on these designs with the object of gradually achieving a harmony of all the component elements and parts that make up architecture.

Constant contact with the leaders of the crafts and industries of the country. Contact with public life, with the people, through exhibitions and other activities. New research into the nature of the exhibitions, to solve the problem of displaying visual work and sculpture within the framework of architecture.

Encouragement of friendly relations between masters and students outside of work; therefore plays, lectures, poetry, music, costume parties. Establishment of a cheerful ceremonial at these gatherings.

Range of instruction

Instruction at the Bauhaus includes all practical and scientific areas of creative work.
A. Architecture,
B. Painting,
C. Sculpture
including all branches of the crafts.

Students are trained in a craft (1) as well as in drawing and painting (2) and science and theory (3).

44

Letter to the Younger Generation

Marianne Brandt

Dear Bauhaus Friend:

I am sending you what I have written down. It was difficult for me, and I crossed out most of it, for I am no theoretician, and whatever there is to be said about the Bauhaus has long since been said by professional critics. I would not be at all hurt if you would rather forgo my analyses.

In 1924, when on the advice of Moholy-Nagy I transferred from the Vorkurs to the metal workshop, they had just begun to produce objects capable of being mass-produced though still fully handicrafted. The task was to shape these things in such a way that even if they were to be produced in numbers, making the work lighter, they would satisfy all aesthetic and practical criteria and still be far less expensive than any singly produced item.

At first I was not accepted with pleasure – there was no place for a woman in a metal workshop, they felt. They admitted this to me later on and meanwhile expressed their displeasure by giving me all sorts of dull, dreary work. How many little hemispheres did I most patiently hammer out of brittle new silver, thinking that was the way it had to be and all beginnings are hard. Later things settled down, and we got along well together.

Gradually, through visits to the industry and inspections and interviews on the spot, we came to our main concern – industrial design. Moholy-Nagy fostered this with stubborn energy. Two lighting firms seemed particularly interested in our aims. Körting and Matthiessen (Kandem) and Leipzig Leutzsch helped us enormously with a practical introduction into the laws of lighting technique and the production methods, which not only helped us in designing, but also helped the firms. We also tried to create a functional but aesthetic assembly line, small facilities for garbage disposal, and so forth, considerations which in retrospect seem to me no longer pre-requisites for a first-class lamp. We went to the fair at

Marianne Brandt, "Letter to the Younger Generation," pp. 97–100 from Eckhard Neumann, *Bauhaus and Bauhaus People*. New York: Van Nostrand Reinhold Company, 1970.

Leipzig, with some student grub as our only food, and returned dead tired but full of new impressions and a thousand plans, our bags stuffed with pamphlets. If we had even dreamed at that time of plexiglass and the other plastics, I don't know to what utopian heights we would have aspired. But good enough: those who come after us must have something to do, too!

Far more difficult than electric lamps was the problem of industrially producing our silverware and other tableware. Not many such things were being produced. So to a certain extent we were branded as a lighting department. We furnished whole buildings with our industrially produced lamps and only rarely designed and produced special pieces in our workshop for particular rooms or showrooms. At the time I was convinced that an object had to be functional and beautiful because of its material. But I later came to the conclusion that the artist provides the final effect. My error probably resulted from the fact that we lived in a community primarily composed of such persons, and that the high quality of their work was taken for granted.

In our workshop we always had a master craftsman at our side and didn't fare too badly with this division – here design and there handicrafts – even though changes became necessary from time to time. We had all our tools – presses and lathes, drills and large shears, etc. Even in Weimar an apprentice was attuned to mass production along the lines of handicrafts. Later he would become one of us, after he had participated in the Bauhaus Vorkurs.

The camaraderie in our workshop was in general good, although as is only natural an arrival or a departure brought with it new impulses and thus also new difficulties. Of the commissions that we got for our models, the Bauhaus, as far as I can remember, got half; the rest was divided equally among master, designer, and workshop. We also got part of the proceeds of our Sunday guided tours through the house. So I was generally quite flush, but also, to my sorrow, generally envied. But that didn't stop people at the end of the month from making lots of little loans from me.

I was not allowed a long period of instruction in handicrafts. Very soon I was told to help design, produce, get busy, and finally – on the urgent request of Gropius and Moholy when they both left the Bauhaus at the same time and I wanted to quit, too – I was offered the provisional directorship of the workshop for one year.

Even though I was made a tempting offer to continue the work with Kandem and simultaneously learn photography from the ground up at Peterhans, I did finally have to leave, however painful this was. But shortly afterward I had the pleasure of joining Gropius in his studio in Berlin. That, too, was a happy, if all too brief, time.

"I remember" and "Do you remember?"

When Gropius went (we assume with pleasure) to see his work, the newly established Bauhaus in Dessau, he got no little shock when he found that his students were using its flat roof and studio front for balancing exercises and as a cat burglar. Later he probably got used to it – there are some beautiful photographs of it. At least I managed to sit freely on the railing of my balcony, though at first I had attacks of dizziness when others did it. How well we lived in those studios, and how pleasant were the conversations back and forth from one balcony to another!

On the basement floor was the gymnasium. There was a large, soft carpet there, and though it was strictly forbidden, several people who couldn't afford anything else slept there. Showers, baths – all very convenient. Not bad. From down there *Päpchen* often appeared with his beautiful shepherd bitch. (But all that is strictly top secret!)

The tours of visitors through the studios didn't make me very happy. For two years it went on every Sunday morning – lots of questions, several annoyances, even though there were some compensations. I was especially impressed by a special tour of two hundred book printers. They were furious when I talked of writing without using capital letters and the saving this would mean in time and labor. A miniature rebellion! They even threatened me with canes!

Satisfying the appetite of the largely penniless "boys" was often a problem. At first, when we were still in the Seiler factory and had no canteen, we were allowed to eat in the soup kitchen for ten pfennig. It was dreadful! Then we bought two pitchers and earthenware pots and took turns by twos getting buttermilk and bread. So the studio had breakfast after all, cheap and modest. In the new building things were much better. There was a canteen and proper meals.

I wasn't around for the Mazdaznan period in Weimar, but only because Gropius took part in it did the Bauhaus members endure it. It can't have been too great – it was a bad time all around as far as that goes.

But there were still enough pleasures of a different sort. In Weimar I heard Klee play his violin, but unfortunately only once. Then there was Kurt Schwitters in Weimar and in Dessau, with his pointed wit and punning comments. Who remembers? Palucca enchanted us when she presented her newest dance. And Bela Bartok. It would be impossible to count it all up.

And now I come to the birthday of our revered Pius (Gro-*pius*). Once he had to climb over a mountain of chairs and tables to get to his rose-strewn throne, which hung fairly high. He overcame all difficulties and dangers smilingly. Another time he was to have been carried around the room, but unfortunately the four bearers couldn't decide on the direction. Calmly he smoked his cigar despite his precarious situation.

It was marvelous at Seiler's. Not that Gropius really enjoyed being celebrated, but on insistent requests he did finally come down to the basement where the stage was housed. A decorated throne for him, as usual a place for Pia at his feet. For his cactus collection he was given many artful artificial pieces, the most beautiful of these a green cucumber with carved radishes as blossoms. Wolf was allowed to fire several shots, and of course there was dancing. The Charleston was coming up then – a real piece of contortionism. But I want to remember the dances in the great hall in Weimar: a bit affected, freely inventive, swinging and leaping. And that, too, did us good.

Last I dedicated a thankful thought to the indefatigable ones who played for us: Hirschfeld, Andi, Xanti, Paris, and all those whose names I have forgotten. And may this be a greeting to all who still remember.

45

Space (Architecture)

László Moholy-Nagy

The Experience of Architecture

The road toward experiencing architecture thus proceeds through a functional capacity for grasping space. This is biologically determined. As in every other field, one has to accumulate much experience before a real appreciation of the essential content, articulated space, can be enjoyed. Unfortunately this approach to architecture is rare. Most people still look for stylistic characteristics, such as: Doric pillars, Corinthian capitals, Romanesque arches, Gothic rose-windows, etc. These are, of course, certain types of spatial construction, but they do not present evidence about the *quality* of space creation itself.

It is this traditional education which is responsible for the fact that the "educated" man cannot really evaluate architectural work as an expression of space articulation. The actual felt quality of spatial creation, the equilibrium of taut forces held in balance, the fluctuating interpenetration of space energies, escapes his perception. A symptom of our time is that this lack of discrimination is also common in architects, who look for the essence of architecture in the meaning of the conception of *shelter*. It happens that many "modernistic" architects take from revolutionary architecture only stylistic characteristics, as, for instance, a misunderstood "cubist" exterior. Their point of departure is the arrangement of a series of rooms, a kind of practical solution, but never really architecture in the sense of articulated space relations, to be experienced as such. Every architecture – and all its functional parts, as well as its spatial articulation – must be conceived as a whole. Without this, a building becomes a piecing together of hollow bodies, which may be technically feasible, but which can never bring the exhilarating experience of articulated space.

László Moholy-Nagy, "Space (Architecture)," pp. 59–61 from Walter Gropius, *The New Vision*, 4th edition. New York: George Wittenborn, 1947.

Practical Application

If the elements necessary to a building fulfill their function they become part of a space reality, transcended into a spatial experience. The space reality in such a case is nothing less than the most efficient co-operation between the organization of the plan and the human factor. Our present mode of living plays a significant role, but it does not prescribe the manner of space creation. Only when the facilities for different functions – for traffic, moving about and visual factors, acoustics, light, and equilibrium – are conceived in a constant balance of their spatial relations, can we speak of architecture as a spatial creation.

Basic Architectonic Questions

In planning a building the most varied problems come up: social, economic, technological, hygienic. It is probable that upon their correct solution the fate of our generation and the next depends.

But attending to social, economic, and hygienic problems does not absolve the architect from the responsibility of further effort and thought. To be sure, a great step in advance has been taken, if, along with the financial and technical considerations, the problems of structure and social economy, technique and efficiency, are seriously examined. But the real architectonic conception, beyond the fusion of all purposeful functions, is usually not discussed, namely, space creation, perhaps because its content is accessible to few people. Yet in addition to the fulfillment of elementary physical requirements, man must have the opportunity to experience space in architecture. For example, a dwelling should not be a retreat from space, but a life *in* space. A dwelling should be decided upon, not only on the basis of price and the time it takes to build, not only upon practical considerations of its suitability for use, its material, construction, and economy; the experience of space belongs to the list too, as a psychological need.

This idea is not to be taken vaguely, or as a mystical approach to the subject. It will not be long before it is generally recognized as a necessary element in the architectonic conception, which will be exactly circumscribed. That is, architecture will be understood, not as a complex of inner spaces, not merely as a shelter from the cold and from danger, nor as a fixed enclosure, as an unalterable arrangement of rooms, but as an organic component in living, as a creation in the mastery of space experience. Individuals who are a part of a rational biological whole should find in their home not only relaxation and recuperation, but also a heightening and harmonious development of their powers.

The new architecture, on its highest plane, will be called upon to remove the conflict between the organic and artificial, between the open and closed, between the country and city. We are accustomed to neglect these questions because the emphasis is still upon the house as a single unit. The future conception of architecture will consider and realize, beyond the single unit, the group, the town, the region, and the country; in short, the whole. The means to this end may be of many kinds; some day we will surely arrive at this elementary insistence on created space. The standard for architects will then no longer be the specific needs of the dwelling of the individual, or of a profession with a certain economic influence, but will revolve around a general plan, that of the mode of biological living which men must have. After this general foundation is established, variations may be introduced, justified by individual needs.

People are today conducting investigations of biological requirements in different fields of experience. Their research seems to produce results which are related.

Efforts to realize a new spatial conception and creation – important as they are – should therefore be understood only as a component of this new orientation.

Architecture will be brought to its fullest realization when the deepest knowledge of human life as a total event in the biological whole is available. One of its important components is the ordering of man in space, making space comprehensible by its articulation.

The root of architecture lies in the mastery of the problem of space; its practical development lies in technological advance.

The Boundary between Architecture and Sculpture

Although architecture and sculpture are separate domains, the treatment of space at times easily may be confused with treatment of volume. In other words: to the untrained eye, sculpture may appear as architecture, and a work of architecture as enlarged sculpture. The latter was almost always the case with classical architecture, where the modulation of masses and bodies (volumes) was predominant. But space creation in our time has changed the meaning of architecture. A brief explanation may clarify this. If the side walls of a volume (i.e., a clearly circumscribed body) are scattered in different directions, spatial patterns or spatial relations originate. This fact is the best guide to judgment of modern and pseudo-modern architecture. The latter shows only volume articulation, in comparison with the rich space articulation – i.e., relations of planes and slabs – of modern architecture.

46

Where Do We Stand?

Marcel Breuer

I would ask my readers to be resigned to a purely theoretical handling of this question, since I shall assume that they are already familiar with the tenets of the New Architecture and what it looks like. They will know, for instance, that these buildings are conceived of in severe terms – a maximum simplicity, wide openings for light, air and sunshine; balconies, flat roofs, minutely studied practical floor-plans, a scientific basis, strong emphasis on mechanization; industrial methods of production with a tendency towards standardization; light colors, new materials used for their own sake and a reconception of housing and town-planning in the light of social and economic research. Therefore I want to confine myself to a statement of what is really fundamental in our thought and work.

In the past I have been opposed to over much of this theorizing about the New Architecture, believing that our job was to build, and that our buildings sufficed, since they speak plainly enough for themselves. I was, moreover, not a little alienated to observe that there was often a considerable discrepancy between these theories and the personalities who advanced them. The danger of all theorizing is that, by carrying one's arguments too far, one is apt to leave the world of realities behind one.

Parts of the principles of the Modern Movement have been extensively adopted, but they have been compromised by being used separately without any co-ordinating relation to the aims of that Movement as a whole. A closer examination of the ideology of the New Architecture has therefore become a pressing necessity.

The protagonists of the Modern Movement have been occupied with the classification and development of their intellectual principles and the carrying out of their individual designs. This meant that further propaganda was left to

Marcel Breuer, "Where Do We Stand?," pp. 119–21 from Peter Blake (ed.), *Marcel Breuer: Architect and Designer*. New York: Museum of Modern Art, 1949. © 1949 by The Museum of Modern Art, New York. Reprinted with permission.

chance, industrial advertisements and the technical press. Much has been distorted, much overlooked, as a result. Modern terminology has been put under tribute for snappy slogans; and each of these serves only some isolated detail. A correlation of these heterogeneous parts to their unifying whole is still lacking. Whereas the pioneers of the Modern Movement have now succeeded in establishing a very broad intellectual basis, which is in harmony with their own work, the younger generation still confines itself to rigid formalization.

I should like, therefore, to give a more general survey that will cover a wider field than these catch-phrases. [. . .]

I intentionally renounce historical comparisons, and leave to others the task of contrasting our age with epochs of the past, and showing us from history what leads to progress or decay, what to art or architecture.

What, then, are the basic impulses of the New Architecture?

In the first place, an absence of prejudice.

Secondly, an ability to place oneself in immediate objective contact with a given task, problem or form.

Thirdly, to create esthetic satisfaction by balance and use of elemental forms.

Let those who prefer respectful transition from the principles of one school or style to those of another, adopt them if they will. What we believe is what we have perceived, experienced, thought, proved and calculated for ourselves.

At this point I should like to consider traditionalism for a moment. And by tradition I do not mean the unconscious continuance and growth of a nation's culture generation by generation, but a conscious dependence on the immediate past. That the type of men who are described as modern architects have the sincerest admiration and love for genuine national art, for old peasant houses as for the masterpieces of the great epochs in art, is a point which needs to be stressed. On journeys what interests us most is to find districts where the daily activity of the population has remained untouched. Nothing is such a relief as to discover a creative craftsmanship which has been developed immemorially from father to son, and is free of the pretentious pomp and empty vanity of the architecture of the last century. Here is something from which we can learn, though not with a view to imitation. For us the attempt to build in a national tradition or an old-world style would be inadequate and insincere. To pride oneself on such things is a bad symptom. For the modern world has no tradition for its eight-hour day, its electric light, its central heating, its water supply, its motor roads and filling stations, its bridges and its steel-motor liners, or for any of its technical methods. One can roundly damn the whole of our age; one can commiserate with, or dissociate oneself from, or hope to transform the men and women who have lost their mental equilibrium in the vortex of modern life, but I do not believe that to decorate their homes with traditional gables and dormers helps them in the least. On the contrary, this only widens the gulf between appearance and reality and removes them still further from that ideal equilibrium which is, or should be the ultimate object of all thought and action.

It may, perhaps, seem paradoxical to establish a parallel between certain aspects of vernacular architecture, or national art, and the Modern Movement. All the same, it is interesting to see that these two diametrically opposed tendencies have two characteristics in common: the impersonal character of their forms; and a tendency to develop along typical, rational lines that are unaffected by passing fashions.

It is probably these traits that make genuine peasant art so sympathetic to us – though the sympathy it arouses is a purely platonic one. If we ask ourselves what is the source of the solid, unself-conscious beauty, the convincing quality and reasonableness of peasant work, we find that the explanation lies in its unconsciously, and therefore genuinely, traditional nature. A given region has only a few traditional crafts and uses a few definite colors. Roughly speaking, the same things, or variants of the same things, have always been made there. And even these variations are obedient to a regular and recurrent rhythm. It is their uninterrupted transmission through local and family associations which conditions their development and ultimately standardizes them as type-forms.

In one direction at least our modern efforts offer a parallel. We seek what is typical, the norm: not the accidental but the definite *ad hoc* form. These norms are designed to meet the needs, not of a former age, but of our own age; therefore we naturally realize them, not with craftsmen's tools, but with modern industrial machinery.

If one examines a *bona fide* example of industrial standardization, one cannot fail to perceive that it is representative of an "art," and that that art has reached this point of perfection only by a sort of traditional development which is the result of exploring the same problem over and over again. What has changed is our method: instead of family traditions and force of habit we employ scientific principles and logical analysis.

Please do not misunderstand me. I do not for a moment mean that peasant art and the Modern Movement have any connection in fact with one another. All I wanted to do was to bring out the similarity between certain tendencies which have led, or can lead, to relative perfection in each. In any case, we can all admit that there are numbers of old peasant farmsteads that we find far more stimulating than many so-called "modern" houses.

To sum up: it is quite untrue to say that the Modern Movement is contemptuous of traditional or national art. It is simply that the sympathy we feel for each does not take the form of making us want to use either as a medium for the utterly different purposes of the present day.

I should like to divorce the "unbiased" aspect of the New Architecture from association with terms like "new," "original," "individual," "imaginative," and "revolutionary." We are all susceptible to the persuasion of that word "new." Society pays its meed of respect to anything new by granting it a patent. It is common knowledge that international patent law is based on two principles: "technical improvement" and "newness." Thus novelty becomes a powerful commercial weapon. But what is the Modern Movement's real attitude to this business of "newness"? Are we for what is new, unexpected and a change at any price, in the same way that we are for an unbiased view at any price? I think we can answer this question with an emphatic negative. We are not out to create something new, but something suitable, intrinsically right and as relatively perfect as may be. The new in the Modern Movement must be considered simply a means to an end, not an end in itself as in women's fashions. What we aim at and believe to be possible is that the solutions embodied in the forms of the New Architecture should endure for ten, twenty, or one hundred years as circumstances may demand – a thing unthinkable in the world of fashion as long as modes are modes. It follows that, though we have no fear of what is new, novelty is not our aim. We seek what is definite and real, whether old or new.

[...]

It were easy, but futile, to indulge in prophecy. I would rather interrogate that unwritten law of our own convictions, the spirit of our age. It answers that we have tired of everything in architecture which is a matter of fashion; that we find all intentionally new forms wearisome, and all those based on personal predilections or tendencies equally pointless. To which can be added the simple consideration that we cannot hope to change our buildings or furniture as often as we change, for example, our ties.

[...] According to our ideas, modern architecture is "original" when it provides a complete solution of the difficulty concerned. By "individual" we understand the degree of intensity or application with which the most various or directly interconnected problems are disposed of. "Imagination" is no longer expressed in remote intellectual adventures, but in the tenacity with which formal order is imposed upon the world of realities. The ability to face a problem objectively brings us to the so-called "revolutionary" side of the Modern Movement. [...] I believe that what was originally revolutionary in the Movement was simply the principle of putting its own objective views into practice. It should also be said that our revolutionary attitude was neither self-complacency nor propagandist *bravura* but the inward, and as far as possible outward, echo of the independence of our work. Although, as I have just pointed out, to be revolutionary has since received the sanction of respectability, this causes us considerable heart-searchings; the word inevitably has a political flavor. In this connection it is necessary to state that our investigations into housing and town-planning problems are based primarily on sociological, rather than on formal or representational principles. In short, that our ideas of what developments were possible were based on the general needs of the community.

All this has led some people to believe that the Modern Movement either was, or was bound to become, a political one. Our opponents resuscitated this old accusation so as to be able to assail us with political propaganda.

[...]

Politics and architecture overlap, first, in the nature of the problems presented to the latter; and, second, in the means that are available for solving them. But even this connection is by no means a definite one. For instance, how does it help us to know that Stalin and the promoters of the Palace of the Soviets competition are Communists; their arguments are very much the same as those of any primitive-minded capitalistic, or democratic, or Fascist, or merely conservative motor-car manufacturer with a hankering for the cruder forms of symbolism. [...]

The origin of the Modern Movement was not technological, for technology had been developed long before it was thought of. What the New Architecture did was to civilize technology. Its real genesis was a growing consciousness of the spirit of our age. However, it proved far harder to formulate the intellectual basis and the esthetic of the New Architecture intelligibly than to establish its logic in practical use.

47

The Problem of a New Architecture

Eric Mendelsohn

The simultaneous appearance of the revolutionary movements in politics and of the basic changes in human relations in industry and science, religion and art at once gives right and authority to the belief in a new form; it testifies to the legitimacy of the new birth amid the stress of catastrophes in world history.

When forms disintegrate, they are simply uprooted by new ones which have long since been there but which only now see the light of day.

For the particular requirements of architecture, the shifts in the mood of the age mean new challenges set by the altered building tasks of traffic, industry and culture, new possibilities for construction in the new building materials: glass – steel – concrete.

With regard to the as yet unknown possibilities, we should not permit ourselves to be misled by our ... lack of perspective. What seems today to be flowing along only very stubbornly will one day, in the eyes of history, be seen as a rapid succession of events and very lively and exciting. It is a process of creation we are describing.

We are now at the early stages, but we are already amid possibilities for development.

Compared with such a future, the great achievements of historical times must give way, and the actuality of the present also loses its air of importance. What will happen will only be of value if it is born amid the transports of vision. ... The course of the road we have travelled so far will result in the important realization of where the new development is leading, under the closely related influences of the shifting mood of the age, the new tasks and the new building materials.

Eric Mendelsohn, "The Problem of a New Architecture," pp. 45–50 from Oskar Beyer (ed.), *Letters of an Architect*, trans. Geoffrey Strachan. London and New York: Abelard-Schuman, 1967. This material was originally delivered as a lecture arranged by the Arbeitsrat für Kunst (Work Council for Art, a socialist group of artists founded in 1919 in Berlin), in the winter of 1919 at the Museum for Applied Arts, Berlin.

This is particularly important for the total attitude to the problem of a new architecture, because in periods of transition the development towards new form can only be recognized from the logical sequence of its results.

Everything that has been created in architectural form since the autonomous achievement of medieval architecture, even in the creative period of the Baroque, down to the artistic attrition of our own day, is fundamentally based on the inherited formal system of the constructional principles of the ancient Greeks.

Just as there is no longer any connection between the ancients' principle of support and load and the Gothic principle of pier and vault, so it must clearly be recognized that the first use of tensile steel signifies nothing less than that feeling of release, which was experienced in the Middle Ages when the first vault over-threw the architectural norms of the ancients. Only from this point of view can it be understood why, in the discussion of recent examples, the decisive character-istics of the new building principles must constantly be rediscovered.

The adjusting of our feeling for statics to the elasticity of reinforced concrete, in place of the former principle of load and support, necessitated a long process of gradual approach.

This is all the more reason why it is necessary to track down this contrast, in order to achieve a complete awareness of the revolution.

Out of the posts and marble beams of the Greek temples, out of the piers and stone vaulting of the Gothic cathedral, develops the girder rhythm of the iron halls.

After the load-equilibrium of antiquity, after the upthrusted loads of the Middle Ages, comes the dynamic tension of reinforced concrete construction.

Only from this point can one explain the enormous speed with which the new building material could develop from the raw mathematical problem of the Eiffel Tower ... to the freedom of such halls as this.[1]

First of all, growing industry, which naturally takes up all sources of profit and makes them useful to itself, gets hold of the new material as well, appreciates its technical and industrial value and unconsciously creates – in tools and machinery – the centers of energy of the coming form and, in the technical improvement to vehicles, the first documents in steel.

In the metallic rhythm of its fuselage the airplane expresses both the confident certainty with which it masters its own element and the compact power of its engine.

It is here that the materials decide. To make the connection from here to the solution for architectonic form can only be one more step.

For it seems unthinkable that the compressed iron energy of machines and vehicles should remain without influence on the shaping of the same materials that are now being used in building.

It is therefore no marvel that today the significant building projects are taking their solutions from industry.

---

[1] This lecture was illustrated by slides. The one concerned may have been of the Gallery of Machines, Paris 1889.

This predominance of industrial aims in building is based on the single-mindedness of their paternity.

But, as much of industry today is still drudgery, though perhaps tomorrow it will be a free occupation, it can only offer an opening to architecture. It cannot, in itself, offer a final goal for its development. At first the new material remains only a technical expedient, simply a means of meeting a calculated demand, although it has in point of fact already overcome support and load, pillar and vault.

Only with the discovery of concrete as a filling material, and the combination of the two constructional elements, with concrete taking the compressive stresses and steel the tensile stresses, does steel throw off its hybrid, purely technical character and acquire the serried quality of a surface, the spatial quality of a mass. Only now does it have the possibility of presenting the problem of a new form.

Thereby it rises to its own expression, makes possible activity, great eloquence and transcendental qualities. Thus come about inner spaces, before whose aesthetic peace the clatter of the looms falls back into itself as a rhythmical flow.

We are seeing the appearance now of building achievements which are already taxing us beyond technical amazement into aesthetic admiration.... As ... all masterpieces of a primitive architecture have their early form determined unequivocally by the clarity of their constructional principle, so, out of design and materials, have arisen the symbols of those conceptions of the world that have clearly determined the course of human history.

Just as the pyramid stands fast against the desert in order to preserve the peace of its dead for all eternity, and the Greek temple is only built with such serene colonnades because they lead to the throne of its god, and the pagoda spreads wide its ecstatic shapes in order to delight the world with the primitive vitality of its jungle existence, and, finally, the Gothic cathedral anchors its towers into the middle of the earth in order to thrust their spires into the beyond all the more securely – so the halls of iron are only built so broad and with so much glass that their eddies of light may create out of the old sweat shops a new house of work.

A symbol of the human yearning to reduce infinity to the finite by means of form, to fit the immeasurable to our scale of measurement. So much is clear: out of the specialized techniques of purely functional and industrial building, a decisive artistic achievement seems to be growing to maturity.

From here the step to the supreme achievement of the sacred building will depend simply on the application of an equally great sensibility to the religious content.

For once the form is forced out of its mysterious process of becoming into the light, the adaptations of it to every purpose are simply reflexes of the same will that discovered and established the new law of statics.

Thus one may mark the example and recognizable frontier line of today, to which the development of less than half a century has led – under the influence of the shifts in the mood of the age, of the new tasks and the new building materials.

It can be no accident that the three recognizable paths of the new architecture are the same in number and mode as the new paths taken in painting and sculpture.

This similarity of purpose will also ultimately bring the work of all the arts back into harmony. This harmony in creative work becomes the great achievement: it must embrace both the sacredness of a new world and the smallest object in daily use in the home.

What is now a problem will one day be a duty. What is today the vision and faith of individuals will one day be the law for all.

Therefore, for this end, for the solution of the problem of a new architecture, all our stirrings seem necessary:

the apostles of glass worlds,

the analysts of spatial elements,

the seekers of form out of materials and construction.

. . . . Classes of society under the spell of tradition will not bring this time closer.

In the unconsciousness of its chaotic upthrust, in the primitiveness of its universal embrace, the future has only one purpose for itself.

For, as every epoch that is decisive for the course of human history has united under its spiritual purpose the whole of the known world, so what we long for will also have to bring happiness to all peoples beyond our own frontiers and beyond those of Europe. In this I am by no means advocating internationalism. For internationalism signifies the rule of an aestheticism divorced from peoples, in a world of decay. Supra-nationalism, however, accepts national limitations as its first premise. It is free humanity, which alone can create a universal culture once more.

Such a great purpose unites all who are at work.

It results first of all and derives a sufficient faith first of all from the fusion of the previous achievements of all peoples.

We can do no more, then, than to contribute the modest volume of our own work in good faith and in a spirit of willing service.

48

The Creative Spirit of the World Crisis

Eric Mendelsohn

Before the First World War

The masses live prosperously and enjoy life. Life itself is intoxicating and luxurious, natural and unproblematic.

Appearances are all. Everyone wants to seem more than he is. Consequently the bourgeois imitates the nobleman and the worker enjoys the pleasures of the bourgeois....

Architecture, in so far as it is official, decorates its constructions with hewn stones and columns, so that the façade is more important than the plan, decoration more important than true expression of the interior spatial arrangements.

This means that function is sacrificed to outward appearance; an appearance expressive of the function is sacrificed to a false rhetoric and the desire to impress. Thus architecture moves further away from the thing itself, becomes showy and inartistic, becomes unproductive and hence false....

First Step Towards a New Form of Expression

The striving for a new form of expression is made most obviously manifest in *architecture*, which is the most sensitive indicator of cultural attitudes: new substances, new building materials appear: steel and reinforced concrete as constructional materials, glass as a material for walls. And there are new uses as well – in traffic and industry – and new requirements.

Eric Mendelsohn, "The Creative Spirit of the World Crisis [1933]," pp. 121–3 from Oskar Beyer (ed.), *Letters of an Architect*, trans. Geoffrey Strachan. London and New York: Abelard-Schuman, 1967.

As early as 1851 the *Crystal Palace in London*[1] – although it retains the traditional constructional elements of columns and vault – brings about the recognition of the revolutionary spatial potential of the new materials. Transparency and an abundance of light are marvelously perceived on a grand scale. The Crystal Palace is the skeleton of a volume of space with a glass skin. Exterior and interior are in full accord with each other.

The *Eiffel Tower in Paris* in 1889 even renounces this glass skin and exposes the skeleton quite openly. In the light of later steel constructions this is still a childish skeleton, but all the nodal points, all the joints are present as a structural framework. The height of 1000 feet is an unheard-of act of boldness.

The *Galerie des Machines* at the same International Exhibition in Paris in 1889 offers the first significant example of the revolution in building techniques, the inspired feeling of release – in overcoming all previous methods of construction through the construction of a hall of iron. It thereby consciously recognizes the dynamics of tension and compression and the distintegration of the wall, of space-heaviness and of the Middle Ages into lightness and floating elements.

All three buildings are engineers' constructions. For the engineer is responsible in one person both for exterior and interior, that is for materials and appearance, for structure and form.

Ten years later the intervention of the architect disturbs this original harmony, which was that of the engineer, and burdens the development of building with problems of form.

Starting from steel the Viennese *Olbrich* and the Belgian *van de Velde* approach the problem of the future. The latter's dictum: "The line is a force" is prophetic of the lines of force in steel.

Starting from stone, the American *Frank Lloyd Wright* approaches the problem of the future. He is the father of those forms that possess an innate sense of our age, a man of exceptional three-dimensional gifts and a modern spatial sensibility.

Starting from reinforced concrete, the Frenchman *Auguste Perret* approaches the problem of the future: construction as an act of creation.

Thirty years after the Galerie des Machines – in 1910 – the *Hamburg Railway Station* achieves a magnificent external effect as well with a steel hall, as both a constructional element and as an architectonic form – for the first time.

But in 1910 – that is, in the same year – the *Berlin City Hall* is also built,[2] in an eclectic architectural dress on a medieval plan, with medieval spatial concepts – an unproductive aesthetic phrase. . . .

New Building

. . . . And so *architecture* triumphs – in the standard of building, of construction, of details of the plan and of technical details – over the resistance of individualistic styles.

[1] The lecture was illustrated with slides.   [2] By Ludwig Hoffmann.

It recognizes once more in building a creative task and in creative building an architectonic creation.

Architecture achieves the necessary harmony between interior and exterior, between function and plan, between plan and form.

It rejects the preconceived pattern and appearances as ends in themselves – the misuse of structural members as decoration is alien to it.

The new architecture strives towards the immediate, free and original shaping of every job; towards the optimum; towards the planned organism, towards the architectonic organism. As a consequence of this, function and aesthetic enjoyment coincide in it.

In harmony with life, it activates the innate delight of the masses in space, and turns the building into a manifesto.

Architecture once more speaks a basic language which the whole world understands. . . .

49

Solved Problems: A Demand on our Building Methods

Mies van der Rohe

On the farm it is customary to till weed-infested fields without regard to those few blades of grass which still find the energy to survive.

We too are also left with no other choice if we are truly to strive for a new sense of construction.

You are all aware of course of the condition of our buildings and yet I would like to remind you of the fully petrified nonsense along the Kurfürstendam and Dahlem.

I have tried in vain to discover the reason for these buildings. They are neither liveable, economical, nor functional and yet they are to serve as home for the people of our age.

We have not been held in very high esteem, if one really believes that these boxes can fulfill our living needs.

No attempt has been made to grasp and shape, in a basic manner, our varying needs.

Our inner needs have been overlooked and it was thought that a clever juggling of historical elements would suffice.

The condition of these buildings is mendacious, dumb and injurious.

On the contrary, we demand of buildings today:

Uncompromising truthfulness and renunciation of all formal lies.

We further demand:

That all planning of housing be dictated by the way we live.

A rational organization is to be sought and the application of new technical means towards this end is a self-evident presumption.

If we fulfill these demands, then the housing of our age is formed.

Since the rental unit is only a multiplicity of individual houses we find that here also the same type and quantity of organic housing is formed.

This determines the manner of the housing block.

I cannot show you any illustrations of newer structures which meet these demands because even the new attempts have not gone beyond mere formalities.

Mies van der Rohe, "Solved Problems: A Demand on our Building Methods," trans. Rolf Achilles, pp. 165–6 from Rolf Achilles, Kevin Harrington, and Charlotte Myhrum (eds.), *Mies van der Rohe: Architect as Educator*. Chicago: Illinois Institute of Technology, 1986. This material was originally delivered as a lecture on December 12, 1923 during the public convention of the Bund Deutscher Architekten held at the Museum for Applied Arts, Berlin. It was first published in *Bauwelt*, 14 (1923), no. 52, p. 719.

To lift your sights over the historical and aesthetic rubble heap of Europe and direct you towards primary and functional housing, I have assembled pictures of buildings which stand outside the greco-roman culture sphere.

I have done this on purpose, because an axe bite in Hildesheim lies closer to my heart than a chisel hole in Athens.

I now show you housing, the structure of which is clearly dictated by function and material.

1. Teepee
   This is the typical dwelling of a nomad. Light and transportable.
2. Leaf Hut
   This is the leaf hut of an Indian. Have you ever seen anything more complete in fulfilling its function and in its use of material? Is this not the involution of jungle shadows?
3. Eskimo House
   Now I lead you to night and ice. Here, moss and seal fur have become the building materials. Walrus ribs form the roof construction.
4. Igloo
   We're going farther north. The house of a Central eskimo. Here there is only snow and ice. And still man builds.
5. Summer tent of an Eskimo
   This fellow also has a summer villa. The construction materials are skin and bones. From the quiet and solitude of the north I lead you to turbulent medieval Flanders.
6. Castle of the Dukes of Flanders, Ghent
   Here, the house has become a fortress.
7. Farm
   In the lower German plains stands the house of the German farmer. It's necessities of life: house, stall and hayloft are met in this one structure.

What I have shown you in illustrations meets all the requirements of its inhabitants. We demand nothing more for ourselves. Only timely materials. Since there are no buildings which so completely meet the needs of man today I can only show you a structure from a related area which has been only recently perceived and meets the requirements which I also long for and strive towards in our own housing.

8. Imperator (Luxury Liner, Hamburg-America Line). Here, you see floating mass housing created out of the needs and materials of our age. Here I ask again:
   Have you ever seen anything more complete in its fulfillment of function and justification of materials?
   We would be envied if we had structures which justified our main land needs in such a way.
   Only when we experience the needs and means of our age in such a primeval way will we have a new sense of structure. To awaken a consciousness for these things is the purpose of my short talk.

50

Explanation of the Educational Program

Mies van der Rohe

With the following prospectus Mies defined his educational program for the School of Archi-tecture at Armour Institute of Technology in the winter of 1937–1938.

The goal of an Architectural School is to train men who can create organic architecture.

Such men must be able to design structures constructed of modern technical means to serve the specific requirements of existing society. They must also be able to bring these structures within the sphere of art by ordering and propor-tioning them in relation to their functions, and forming them to express the means employed, the purposes served, and the spirit of the times.

In order to accomplish this, these men must not only be trained in the essentials of construction, professional knowledge and in the creation of archi-tectural form, but they must also develop a realistic insight into the material and spiritual needs of their contemporaries, so that they may be able to create architecture which fittingly fulfills these needs.

Finally, they must be given the opportunity to acquire a basic architectural philosophy and fundamental creative principles which will guide them in their task of creating living architecture. The accompanying program is intended to provide an education which achieves this purpose.

The period of study is divided into three progressive stages, namely: MEANS, PURPOSES, AND PLANNING AND CREATING, with a short period of preparatory training. Parallel and complementary to this creative education, *general theory* and *profes-sional training* will be studied. The subjects in these latter two divisions will be timed to prepare the students for each successive step in his creative development.

Mies van der Rohe, "Explanation of the Education Program," pp. 167–8 from Rolf Achilles, Kevin Harrington, and Charlotte Myhrum (eds.), *Mies van der Rohe: Architect as Educator*. Chicago: Illinois Institute of Technology, 1986.

Work in mathematics, the natural sciences, and drawing, in these two divisions will be begun before the principal course of study begins. This is the preparatory training referred to above and is indicated on the program by raising these subjects in the two columns at the extreme left of the program in advance of all other subjects. This preparatory training is to teach the students to draw, to see proportions and to understand the rudiments of physics before starting the study of structural means.

The subjects in the column design[at]ed *General Theory* are designed to give the student the necessary scientific and cultural background which will give him the knowledge, the sense of proportion and the historical perspective necessary in his progress through the other stages of his education. Only those aspects of these subjects which have a direct bearing on architecture will be treated.

The subjects in the column designated *Professional Training* cover the specialized architectural knowledge which the student will require to give him the technical proficiency necessary to carry on his creative work in the school and take his place in his profession upon graduation.

The first major stage of the student's education entitled *Means*, covers a thorough and systematic study of the principal building materials, their qualities and their proper use in building. The student's work in his parallel course in Natural Science will be arranged to help him make this investigation. Similarly his work in the field of *Professional Training* will be timed to enable him to design structurally in the various materials he is studying. He will study the construction types and methods appropriate to the materials singly and in combination. At the same time he will be required to develop simple structural forms with these materials, and then, as a result of the knowledge so gained, he will be required to detail original structural forms in the various materials.

This study of materials and construction will be carried beyond the older building materials and methods into the investigation of the manufactured and synthetic materials available today. The student will analyze the newer materials and make experiments to determine their proper uses, their proper combination in construction, their aesthetic possibilities and architectural forms appropriate to them.

This stage of the student's work is designed to give him a thorough knowledge of the means with which he must later build, a feeling for materials and construction and to teach him how architectural forms are developed from the necessities and possibilities inherent in materials and construction.

In the second major stage of the student's education, entitled *Purposes* on the program, the student will study the various purposes for which buildings are required in modern society. He will make a systematic study of the various functions of different kinds of buildings and seek reasonable solutions for their requirements from a technical, social and humanitarian standpoint. The construction, purpose, and arrangement of furniture and furnishings in their relation to the buildings and their occupants will also be studied.

After studying the requirements of various types of buildings and their solution, the student will progress to the study of ordering these types into groups

400

and into unified communities – in other words: city planning. City planning will be studied from the point of view that the various parts of a community must be so related that the whole functions as a healthy organism. The student will also study the reorganization of existing cities to make them function as an organic unity. The possibilities of Regional planning will also be sketched.

Naturally the student's general theoretical education and professional training will be running along parallel to these studies and will be far enough advanced at each point so that he fully understands the technical, social and cultural aspects of each problem.

At the beginning of his study of the purposes of buildings, he will have begun the study of the nature of man; what he is, how he lives, how he works, what his needs are in both the material and spiritual sphere. He must also have an understanding of the nature of society; how man has organized himself into groups, apportioned and specialized his work to lighten it and allow him more leisure to pursue his spiritual aims and evolve a communal culture. This socio-logical study will also investigate former civilizations, their economic basis, their social forms, and the cultures which they produce.

The student will also study the history and nature of Technics – so that he may comprehend the compelling and supporting forces of modern society. He will learn the methods and principles of Technics and their implications in his own creative sphere. He will realize the new solutions of the problems of space, form and harmony made possible and demanded by the development of modern Technics.

The relationship between culture and Technics will also be studied so that the student will be able to appreciate his part in developing a new culture so that finally our technical civilization may have a unified and integrated culture of its own.

Likewise the student's professional training will have advanced far enough at each point for him to solve the professional and technical factors of the problems that are being analyzed.

The third and last stage of the student's education has been entitled *Planning and Creating*.

When the student has advanced this far he will have mastered the technique of his profession; he will understand specific purposes and problems for which society requires his knowledge, and he will have acquired a general background which should have given him a thorough comprehension of modern life and have imbued him with a sense of professional and social obligation. He must now learn to use his knowledge of the means, and the purposes to produce architecture which is creative and living. This final and most important phase of his education is intended to enable him to do so.

During this phase of his education, all the facilities of the school will be directed towards training him in the fundamentals of creative design based upon the principles of organic order, so that he will attack his architectural problems with an essential philosophy whose guidance will enable him to create true architecture.

51

Report of the De Stijl Group

vis à vis the 'Union of International Progressive Artists' at the 'International Artists' Congress' in Düsseldorf, 29 to 31 May 1922 (fragment)

Theo van Doesburg

    I. I speak here for the De Stijl group in Holland which has arisen out of the necessity of accepting the consequences of modern art; this means finding practical solutions to universal problems.

    II. Building, which means organizing one's means into a unity (*Gestaltung*) is all-important to us.

    III. This unity can be achieved only by suppressing arbitrary subjective elements in the expressional means.

    IV. We reject all subjective choice of forms and are preparing to use objective, universal, formative means.

    V. Those who do not fear the consequences of the new theories of art we call progressive artists.

    VI. The progressive artists of Holland have from the first adopted an international standpoint. Even during the war ...

    VII. The international standpoint resulted from the development of our work itself. That is, it grew out of practice. Similar necessities have arisen out of the development of ... progressive artists in other countries.

Theo van Doesburg, "Report of the De Stijl Group at the 'International Artists Congress' in Dusseldorf," p. 59 from *Principles of Neo-Plastic Art*, trans. Janet Seligman. London: Lund Humphries, 1969.

52

From *Towards a New Architecture*

Le Corbusier

Argument

The engineer's aesthetic and architecture

The Engineer's Aesthetic, and Architecture, are two things that march together and follow one from the other: the one being now at its full height, the other in an unhappy state of retrogression.

The Engineer, inspired by the law of Economy and governed by mathematical calculation, puts us in accord with universal law. He achieves harmony.

The Architect, by his arrangement of forms, realizes an order which is a pure creation of his spirit; by forms and shapes he affects our senses to an acute degree and provokes plastic emotions; by the relationships which he creates he wakes profound echoes in us, he gives us the measure of an order which we feel to be in accordance with that of our world, he determines the various movements of our heart and of our understanding; it is then that we experience the sense of beauty.

Three reminders to architects

Mass

Our eyes are constructed to enable us to see forms in light.
Primary forms are beautiful forms because they can be clearly appreciated.
Architects to-day no longer achieve these simple forms.

Le Corbusier, "Towards a New Architecture," pp. 7–14, 15–24 from *Towards a New Architecture*, 1946 edition, trans. Frederick Etchells. London: The Architectural Press, 1965 (reprint).

Working by calculation, engineers employ geometrical forms, satisfying our eyes by their geometry and our understanding by their mathematics; their work is on the direct line of good art.

Surface

A mass is enveloped in its surface, a surface which is divided up according to the directing and generating lines of the mass; and this gives the mass its individuality.

Architects to-day are afraid of the geometrical constituents of surfaces.

The great problems of modern construction must have a geometrical solution.

Forced to work in accordance with the strict needs of exactly determined conditions, engineers make use of generating and accusing lines in relation to forms. They create limpid and moving plastic facts.

Plan

The Plan is the generator.

Without a plan, you have lack of order, and wilfulness

The Plan holds in itself the essence of sensation.

The great problems of to-morrow, dictated by collective necessities, put the question of "plan" in a new form.

Modern life demands, and is waiting for, a new kind of plan, both for the house and for the city.

Regulating lines

An inevitable element of Architecture.

The necessity for order. The regulating line is a guarantee against wilfulness. It brings satisfaction to the understanding.

The regulating line is a means to an end; it is not a recipe. Its choice and the modalities of expression given to it are an integral part of architectural creation.

Eyes which do not see

Liners

A great epoch has begun.

There exists a new spirit.

There exists a mass of work conceived in the new spirit; it is to be met with particularly in industrial production.

Architecture is stifled by custom.

The "styles" are a lie.

Style is a unity of principle animating all the work of an epoch, the result of a state of mind which has its own special character.

Our own epoch is determining, day by day, its own style.

Our eyes, unhappily, are unable yet to discern it.

Airplanes

The airplane is the product of close selection.

The lesson of the airplane lies in the logic which governed the statement of the problem and its realization.

The problem of the house has not yet been stated.

Nevertheless there do exist standards for the dwelling house.

Machinery contains in itself the factor of economy, which makes for selection.

The house is a machine for living in.

Automobiles

We must aim at the fixing of standards in order to face the problem of perfection.

The Parthenon is a product of selection applied to a standard.

Architecture operates in accordance with standards.

Standards are a matter of logic, analysis and minute study; they are based on a problem which has been well "stated." A standard is definitely established by experiment.

Architecture

The lesson of Rome

The business of Architecture is to establish emotional relationships by means of raw materials.

Architecture goes beyond utilitarian needs.

Architecture is a plastic thing.

The spirit of order, a unity of intention.

The sense of relationships; architecture deals with quantities.

Passion can create drama out of inert stone.

The illusion of plans

The Plan proceeds from within to without; the exterior is the result of an interior.

The elements of architecture are light and shade, walls and space.

Arrangement is the gradation of aims, the classification of intentions.

Man looks at the creation of architecture with his eyes, which are 5 feet 6 inches from the ground. One can only deal with aims which the eye can appreciate, and intentions which take into account architectural elements. If there come into play intentions which do not speak the language of architecture, you arrive at the illusion of plans, you transgress the rules of the Plan through an error in conception, or through a leaning towards empty show.

Pure creation of the mind

Contour and profile[1] are the touchstone of the architect.

Here he reveals himself as artist or mere engineer.

Contour is free of all constraint.

There is here no longer any question of custom, nor of tradition, nor of construction nor of adaptation to utilitarian needs.

Contour and profile are a pure creation of the mind; they call for the plastic artist.

Mass-production houses

A great epoch has begun.

There exists a new spirit.

Industry, overwhelming us like a flood which rolls on towards its destined ends, has furnished us with new tools adapted to this new epoch, animated by the new spirit.

Economic law inevitably governs our acts and our thoughts.

The problem of the house is a problem of the epoch. The equilibrium of society to-day depends upon it. Architecture has for its first duty, in this period of renewal, that of bringing about a revision of values, a revision of the constituent elements of the house.

Mass-production is based on analysis and experiment.

Industry on the grand scale must occupy itself with building and establish the elements of the house on a mass-production basis.

We must create the mass-production spirit.

The spirit of constructing mass-production houses.

The spirit of living in mass-production houses.

---

[1] *Modénature.* The nearest equivalent of Le Corbusier's use of this word. – trans.

The spirit of conceiving mass-production houses.

If we eliminate from our hearts and minds all dead concepts in regard to the house, and look at the question from a critical and objective point of view, we shall arrive at the "House-Machine," the mass-production house, healthy (and morally so too) and beautiful in the same way that the working tools and instruments which accompany our existence are beautiful.

Beautiful also with all the animation that the artist's sensibility can add to severe and pure functioning elements.

Architecture or revolution

In every field of industry, new problems have presented themselves and new tools have been created capable of resolving them. If this new fact be set against the past, then you have revolution.

In building and construction, mass-production has already been begun; in face of new economic needs, mass-production units have been created both in mass and detail; and definite results have been achieved both in detail and in mass. If this fact be set against the past, then you have revolution, both in the method employed and in the large scale on which it has been carried out.

The history of Architecture unfolds itself slowly across the centuries as a modification of structure and ornament, but in the last fifty years steel and concrete have brought new conquests, which are the index of a greater capacity for construction, and of an architecture in which the old codes have been overturned. If we challenge the past, we shall learn that "styles" no longer exist for us, that a style belonging to our own period has come about; and there has been a Revolution.

Our minds have consciously or unconsciously apprehended these events and new needs have arisen, consciously or unconsciously.

The machinery of Society, profoundly *out of gear*, oscillates between an amelioration, of historical importance, and a catastrophe.

The primordial instinct of every human being is to assure himself of a shelter. The various classes of workers in society to-day *no longer have dwellings adapted to their needs; neither the artizan nor the intellectual.*

It is a question of building which is at the root of the social unrest of to-day: architecture or revolution.

The Engineer's Aesthetic and Architecture

The Engineer's Aesthetic and Architecture – two things that march together and follow one from the other – the one at its full height, the other in an unhappy state of retrogression.

407

The Engineer, inspired by the law of Economy and governed by mathematical calculation, puts us in accord with universal law. He achieves harmony.

The Architect, by his arrangement of forms, realizes an order which is a pure creation of his spirit; by forms and shapes he affects our senses to an acute degree, and provokes plastic emotions; by the relationships which he creates he wakes in us profound echoes, he gives us the measure of an order which we feel to be in accordance with that of our world, he determines the various movements of our heart and of our understanding; it is then that we experience the sense of beauty.

[...]

a question of morality; lack of truth is intolerable, we perish in untruth.

Architecture is one of the most urgent needs of man, for the house has always been the indispensable and first tool that he has forged for himself. Man's stock of tools marks out the stages of civilization, the stone age, the bronze age, the iron age. Tools are the result of successive improvement; the effort of all generations is embodied in them. The tool is the direct and immediate expression of progress; it gives man essential assistance and essential freedom also. We throw the out-of-date tool on the scrap-heap: the carbine, the culverin, the growler and the old locomotive. This action is a manifestation of health, of moral health, of *morale* also; it is not right that we should produce bad things because of a bad tool; nor is it right that we should waste our energy, our health and our courage because of a bad tool; it must be thrown away and replaced.

But men live in old houses and they have not yet thought of building houses adapted to themselves. The lair has been dear to their hearts since all time. To such a degree and so strongly that they have established the cult of the home.

Architects, emerging from the Schools, those hot-houses where blue hortensias and green chrysanthemums are forced, and where unclean orchids are cultivated, enter into the town in the spirit of a milkman who should, as it were, sell his milk mixed with vitriol or poison.[2]

People still believe here and there in architects, as they believe blindly in all doctors. It is very necessary, of course, that houses should hold together! It is very necessary to have recourse to the man of art! Art, according to Larousse, is the application of knowledge to the realization of a conception. Now, to-day, it is the engineer who *knows*, who knows the best way to construct, to heat, to ventilate, to light. It is not true?

Our diagnosis is that, to begin at the beginning, the engineer who proceeds by knowledge shows the way and holds the truth. It is that architecture, which is a matter of plastic emotion, should in its own domain BEGIN AT THE BEGINNING ALSO, AND SHOULD USE THOSE ELEMENTS WHICH ARE CAPABLE OF AFFECTING OUR SENSES, AND OF REWARDING THE DESIRE OF OUR EYES, and should dispose them in such a way THAT THE

---

[2] I have not felt it incumbent upon me to modify somewhat rhetorical passages such as the above. – trans.

SIGHT OF THEM AFFECTS US IMMEDIATELY by their delicacy or their brutality, their riot or their serenity, their indifference or their interest; these elements are plastic elements, forms which our eyes see clearly and which our mind can measure. These forms, elementary or subtle, tractable or brutal, work physiologically upon our senses (sphere, cube, cylinder, horizontal, vertical, oblique, etc.), and excite them. Being moved, we are able to get beyond the cruder sensations; certain relationships are thus born which work upon our perceptions and put us into a state of satisfaction (in consonance with the laws of the universe which govern us and to which all our acts are subjected), in which man can employ fully his gifts of memory, of analysis, of reasoning and of creation.

Architecture to-day is no longer conscious of its own beginnings.

Architects work in "styles" or discuss questions of structure in and out of season; their clients, the public, still think in terms of conventional appearance, and reason on the foundations of an insufficient education. Our external world has been enormously transformed in its outward appearance and in the use made of it, by reason of the machine. We have gained a new perspective and a new social life, but we have not yet adapted the house thereto.

The time has therefore come to put forward the problem of the house, of the street and of the town, and to deal with both the architect and the engineer.

For the *architect* we have written our "THREE REMINDERS."

MASS which is the element by which our senses perceive and measure and are most fully affected.

SURFACE which is the envelope of the mass and which can diminish or enlarge the sensation the latter gives us.

PLAN which is the generator both of mass and surface and is that by which the whole is irrevocably fixed.

Then, still for the architect, "REGULATING LINES" showing by these one of the means by which architecture achieves that tangible form of mathematics which gives us such a grateful perception of order. We wished to set forth facts of greater value than those in many dissertations on the soul of stones. We have confined ourselves to the natural philosophy of the matter, *to things that can be known.*

We have not forgotten the dweller in the house and the crowd in the town. We are well aware that a great part of the present evil state of architecture is due to the *client*, to the man who gives the order, who makes his choice and alters it and who pays. For him we have written "EYES WHICH DO NOT SEE."

We are all acquainted with too many big business men, bankers and merchants, who tell us: "Ah, but I am merely a man of affairs, I live entirely outside the art world, I am a Philistine." We protest and tell them: "All your energies are directed towards this magnificent end which is the forging of the tools of an epoch, and which is creating throughout the whole world this accumulation of very beautiful things in which economic law reigns supreme, and mathematical exactness is joined to daring and imagination. That is what you do; that, to be exact, is Beauty."

One can see these same business men, bankers and merchants, away from their businesses in their own homes, where everything seems to contradict their real existence – rooms too small, a conglomeration of useless and disparate objects, and a sickening spirit reigning over so many shams – Aubusson, Salon d'Automne, styles of all sorts and absurd bric-à-brac. Our industrial friends seem sheepish and shrivelled like tigers in a cage; it is very clear that they are happier at their factories or in their banks. We claim, in the name of the steamship, of the airplane, and of the motor-car, the right to health, logic, daring, harmony, perfection.

We shall be understood. These are evident truths. It is not foolishness to hasten forward a clearing up of things.

Finally, it will be a delight to talk of ARCHITECTURE after so many grain-stores, workshops, machines and sky-scrapers. ARCHITECTURE is a thing of art, a phenomenon of the emotions, lying outside questions of construction and beyond them. The purpose of construction is TO MAKE THINGS HOLD TOGETHER; of architecture TO MOVE US. Architectural emotion exists when the work rings within us in tune with a universe whose laws we obey, recognize and respect. When certain harmonies have been attained, the work captures us. Architecture is a matter of "harmonies," it is "a pure creation of the spirit."

To-day, painting has outsped the other arts.

It is the first to have attained attunement with the epoch.[3] Modern painting has left on one side wall decoration, tapestry and the ornamental urn and has sequestered itself in a frame – flourishing, full of matter, far removed from a distracting realism; it lends itself to meditation. Art is no longer anecdotal, it is a source of meditation; after the day's work it is good to meditate.

On the one hand the mass of people look for a decent dwelling, and this question is of burning importance.

On the other hand the man of initiative, of action, of thought, the LEADER, demands a shelter for his meditations in a quiet and sure spot; a problem which is indispensable to the health of specialized people.

Painters and sculptors, champions of the art of to-day, you who have to bear so much mockery and who suffer so much indifference, let us purge our houses, give your help that we may reconstruct our towns. Your works will then be able to take their place in the framework of the period and you will everywhere be admitted and understood. Tell yourselves that architecture has indeed need of your attention. Do not forget the problem of architecture.

---

[3] I mean, of course, the vital change brought about by cubism and later researches, and not the lamentable fall from grace which has for the last two years seized upon painters, distracted by lack of sales and taken to task by critics as little instructed as sensitive (1921).

53

Architecture in Everything, City Planning in Everything

Le Corbusier

There are many students of architecture in this audience.

I shall weigh my words exactly and choose the elements of discussion that are as the keystones of architectural perception. The other day we followed the growth of the structural organism. Today, the aesthetic organism; soon, the biological.

What I am going to say may strike young people who are floating violently and permanently in the midst of the hesitations of their age. Certain remarks heard at twenty have left an indelible impression on me.

Alas, would it be held against me, in a Faculty, to perhaps disturb a few youths profoundly?

Let us define precisely the subject of this lecture. I promised that after the generalizations of the first lecture, I should become pitilessly objective. The object of this objectivity is not exclusively mechanical, practical, or utilitarian. I have architecture in my heart, placed at the tensest point of my sensitivity. Finally, I believe only in beauty, which is the real source of happiness.

Art, product of the reason–passion equation, is for me the site of human happiness.

But what is art? I affirm that artificiality is around us, that it imprisons us. I cannot tolerate artificiality: it hides stupidity and laziness, and the spirit of lucre.

[...]

I draw things known to everyone: this Renaissance window flanked by two pilasters and by an architrave under a hollowed-out pediment; this Greek temple, this Doric entablature; this one which is Ionic, this other Corinthian. And then this "composition," which as you see is "composite" and has been common, for a long time, to all countries and put to all uses.

I take a red chalk and I cross it all out. I take these things out of my tool kit. I don't use them, they don't clutter up my drawing board.

Le Corbusier, "Architecture in Everything, City Planning in Everything," pp. 67–83 from *Precisions on the Present State of Architecture and City Planning*, trans. Edith Schreiber Aujamo. Cambridge, MA: MIT Press, 1991. Reprinted by permission of the MIT Press.

Firmly, I write: *This is not architecture. These are styles.*

So that my words should not be misused, so that I am not made to say what I don't think, I write again:

> *alive and magnificent originally,*
> *today they are only dead bodies,*
> or women in wax!

[. . .]

Architecture is an act of conscious willpower.

To create architecture *is to put in order.*

Put what in order? Functions and objects. To occupy space with buildings and with roads. To create containers to shelter people and useful transportation to get to them. To act on our minds by the cleverness of the solutions, on our senses by the forms proposed and by the distances we are obliged to walk. To move by the play of perceptions to which we are sensitive, and which we cannot avoid. Spaces, dimensions and forms, interior spaces and interior forms, interior pathways and exterior forms, and exterior spaces – quantities, weights, distances, atmospheres, it is with these that we act. Such are the events involved.

From there on, I consider architecture and city planning together as a single concept. Architecture in everything, city planning in everything.

[. . .]

This act of willpower appears in the creation of cities. And, especially in America, where the decision was taken to *come* and, having come, to *act,* cities were created geometrically, because geometry characterizes man.

I shall show you how the sensation of architecture arises: in reaction to geometric objects.

I draw a long prism,

another, cubic.

I affirm that there is the definition, the basis of architectural sensation. The shock has been made. You have said, raising this prism into space with its proportions, *"here is how I am."*

You feel it more clearly if the cubic prism gets thinner and rises, if the drawn-out prism gets flatter and spreads out. You are facing *characters,* you've created characters.

And no matter what you add to this work, in delicacy or sturdiness, in complication or in clarity, everything here is already determined, you will no longer modify the first sensation.

You must admit it is worth the trouble to absorb such an impressive truth. And before our pencil sketches anything that we may love of the styles of past periods, let us repeat: *"I have determined my project."* Let us verify, meditate, measure, define, before going further.

And here is how the architectural sensation continues to act on our spirit and our hearts:

I draw a door, a window, and still another window.

What has happened? I had to open doors and windows, it was my duty, my practical problem. But architecturally, what had happened? We have created geometrical places, we have propounded the terms of an equation. So watch out! What if our equation is false, insoluble, by which I mean if we have placed our windows and doors so badly that nothing *true* – nothing mathematically true – can any longer exist between these holes and the different surfaces of the walls determined by these holes?

Look at the Capitol of Michelangelo in Rome. A first sensation of a cube; then a second: the two pavilions of the wings, the center and the staircase. Realize then that *harmony reigns between these diverse elements*. Harmony, that is to say relationship – *unity*. Not uniformity, on the contrary, contrast. But a mathematical unity. That is why the Capitol is a masterpiece.

I have concentrated with real passion on playing with these fundamental elements of the architectural sensation. Look at the diagram defining the proportions of the townhouse at Garches. *The invention of proportions*, the choice of solids and voids, the determination of height in relationship to the width imposed by site regulations, result in a poetic creation: *such is the project sprung from one does not know what profound stock of acquired knowledge, of experience, and of powerful personal creativity*. Immediately, nevertheless, the mind, curious and eager, tries to read the heart of this raw project in which the destiny of the work is already definitively inscribed. Here is the result of this reading and of the corrections due to it: a setting in order (arithmetical or geometrical) based on the "Golden Section," on the play of perpendicular diagonals, on arithmetical relationships, 1, 2, 4, between the horizontals, etc. Thus this facade is made harmonious in all its parts. Precision has created something definitive, clear and true, unchangeable, permanent, which is the *architectural instant*. This architectural instant commands our attention, masters our spirits, dominates, imposes, subjugates. Such is the argumentation of architecture. To evoke attention, to occupy space powerfully, a surface of perfect form was necessary first, followed by the exaltation of the flatness of that surface by the addition of a few projections or holes creating a back and forth movement. Then, by the opening of windows (the holes made by windows are one of the essential elements of the reading of an architectural work), by the opening of windows an important play of secondary surfaces is begun, releasing rhythms, dimensions, tempos of architecture.

Rhythms, dimensions, tempos of architecture, inside the house and outside.

A motive of professional loyalty obliges us to devote all our care to the interior of the house. One enters: one receives a shock, first sensation. Here we are impressed by one dimension of a room succeeding another dimension, by one form succeeding another. That is architecture!

And depending on the way you enter a room, that is to say depending on the place of the door in the wall of the room, the feeling will be different. That is architecture!

But how do you receive an architectural sensation? By the effect of the relationships that you perceive. These relationships are provided by what? By the things, by the surfaces that you see and that you see because they are in *light*. And even further, the light of the sun acts on the human animal with an efficiency profoundly rooted in the species.

Consider then the capital importance of the point where you open a window; study the way in which that light is received by the walls of the room. Here, in truth, an important game of architecture is played, on this the decisive architectural impressions depend. You do see that it is no longer a matter of styles or decoration. Think of those first days of spring when the sky is full of clouds driven by gusts of wind; you are indoors; a cloud hides the sky: how sad you are! The wind has driven the cloud away, the sun enters by the window: how happy you are! New clouds put you in the shade: how passionately you think of the coming summer that will give you light all the time!

Light on forms, precise intensity of light, successive volumes, acting on our sensitive being, provoking physical, physiological sensations, which scientists have described, classified, detailed. That horizontal or that vertical, this sawtooth line broken brutally or that soft undulation, this closed concentric form of a circle or a square, which acts profoundly on us, influences our designs, and determines our feelings. Rhythm, diversity or monotony, coherence or incoherence, marvelous or disappointing surprise, the joyful shock of light or the chill of darkness, calm of a well-lit bedroom or anguish of a room full of dark corners, enthusiasm or depression, these are the results of the things I have just drawn, which affect our sensitivity by a series of impressions no one can avoid.

I should so much like to make you appreciate the powerful eloquence of lines, so that from now on you may feel your minds free of small decorative events and above all that you may establish in the design of your future architectures the real chronology, the *hierarchy* that brings out the essential. And that you realize that this essence of architecture is in the quality of your choice, in the force of your spirit and not at all in rich materials, in marble or rare wood, nor in the ornaments whose role only exists as a last resort, when all is said, that is to say that these ornaments aren't much use.

I should like to lead you to feel something sublime by which mankind, at its best moments, has shown its mastery; I call it *the point of all dimensions*. Here it is:

I am in Brittany; this line is the limit between the ocean and the sky; a vast horizontal plane extends toward me. I appreciate the voluptuousness of this masterly restfulness. Here are a few rocks to the right. The sinuousness of the sandy beaches like a very soft undulation on the horizontal plane delights me. I was walking. Suddenly I stopped. Between my eyes and the horizon, a sensational event has occurred: a vertical rock, in granite, is there, upright, like a menhir; its vertical makes a right angle with the horizon. Crystallization, fixation of the site. This is a place to stop, because here is a complete symphony, magnificent relationships, nobility. The vertical gives the meaning of the horizontal. One is alive because of the other. Such are the powers of synthesis.

414

I wonder. Why am I so disturbed? Why has this emotion produced itself in my life in other circumstances and in other forms?

I evoke the Parthenon, its sublime entablature of such overwhelming power. I think, in contrast, in comparison, of those works full of sensitivity but as if aborted, unachieved: the Butter Tower of Rouen, the flamboyant Gothic vaults where so much "unused" genius was spent without achieving the brilliance of the brass trumpets of the Parthenon on the Acropolis.

So I draw with just two lines this *point of all dimensions* and I say, having in my mind compared numbers of human works, I say: "Here it is, this suffices."

What poverty, what misery, what sublime limits! Everything is included in this, the key to architectural poems. Extent, height. And it is sufficient.

Have I made myself understood?

Extent, height! Here I am on the way to search for greater architectural truths. I perceive that the project we are designing is neither alone nor isolated; that the air around it constitutes other surfaces, other grounds, other ceilings, that the harmony that stops me dead in Brittany exists, can exist, everywhere else, always. A project is not made only of itself: its surroundings exist. The surroundings envelop me in their totality as in a room. Harmony takes its origins from afar, everywhere, in everything. How far we are from "styles" and from pretty drawings on paper!

You will see the same house – this simple rectangular prism:

We are on a plain, a flat plain. Can you see how the site designs with me?

We are in the low wooded hills of Touraine. The same house is different.

Here it is, underlining the wild outlines of the Alps!

How our sensitive hearts have perceived different treasures each time.

These inherent realities determine the atmosphere of architecture, they are always present for someone who knows how to see and wishes to extract a fertile profit from them.

This same house – the rectangular prism – here it is at a street crossing, influenced by surrounding constructions.

Here it is at the end of a line of poplars, in an attitude somewhat touched by solemnity.

There it is at the end of a naked road, lined with hedges to left and right.

And there it is at last, appearing suddenly, unexpectedly, at the end of a street. A man goes by, his gestures are outlined clearly like those of an actor on a stage, intimately related to the "human scale" that orders its facade.

[...]

Having left *in search of architecture*, we have arrived in the domain of simplicity. Great art is made of simple means, let us repeat this tirelessly.

History shows us the tendency of the mind toward simplicity. Simplicity is the result of judgment, of choice, it is the sign of mastery. Tearing oneself away from complexities, one will invent means showing a state of consciousness. A spiritual system will become evident by a visible play of forms. It will be like

415

an *affirmation*. A step that leads from confusion toward the clarity of geometry. At the dawn of modern times, when after the Middle Ages peoples stabilized their social or political forms, an adequate serenity sharpens a lively appetite for spiritual light. The big Renaissance cornice insists on stopping against the sky its profile derived from proportions based on the ground. The equivocal oblique of the sloping roof is repudiated. Under the Louis and under Napoleon, the will to make the "point of relations" evident shows itself more and more strongly.

It is the period of classicism, strengthened by its intellectual epicurism; devoted to the purification of the exterior signs of architecture, it took its distances from the alert Gothic loyalty. Plans and sections are depraved; a dead end is near. We have stumbled against it: academism.

Reinforced concrete brings the roof terrace with rainwater draining toward the inside (and many other constructive revolutions). One can't really draw cornices any more; it is an architectural entity that has ceased to live; its function no longer exists. But the sharp and pure line of the top of a building outlined against the sky has come from it.

Finally, here is the useful organ that the designer seizes: the pilotis. A marvelous means for carrying up in the air, seen from all its four sides, the "point of relations," the "point of all dimensions" – this elevated prism legible and measurable as it has never before been legible. The boon of reinforced concrete or of steel.

Thus *simplicity is not poverty*, but simplicity is a choice, a discrimination, a crystallization having purity itself for object. Simplicity is a concentrate.

No longer a spiky agglomerate of cubes, an uncontrolled phenomenon, but organized, a fully conscious act, a phenomenon of spirtuality.

Another word still, with the intention of disciplining these dashes often full of imagination but which in fact are the disorderly kicks of a pony: I sketch the vision of a beautiful city seen on our study trip; here is the dome, there the belfry or the bell tower, here the square palace of the ruler. I have shown the *silhouette of a city.* By what lack of proportion and ignorance of consequences shall we (as is now very much the fashion) silhouette the house as the city is silhouetted? If I multiply houses so deformed, in a street or in a city, the effect will be miserable: tumultuous, cut-up, dissonant. What then is the difference between the results of so many undisciplined good intentions and the appearance of the streets with which Buenos Aires, like many European cities, swarms – these atrociously commonplace bazaars, full of laziness and of academic pretensions?

[...]

Let us reserve that indispensable diversity to our intellect for the time when the symphony of the city will be in preparation. The immense contemporary problems of planning and architecture will bring to the city, in extent and in height, the elements of a new scale. Unity will be in the details; the clamor will be in the whole.

[...]

I have made the space around the house intervene: I have taken into account its extent and what rises above: dimensions, time, duration, volumes, rhythm, quantities: city planning and architecture.

Planning in all. Architecture in all. Reason, passion, whose synthesis results in an inspired work.

Reason seeks the means.

Passion shows the way.

From the plan of the machine for living – city or house – the architectural work enters into the plane of sensitivity.

We are moved.

Allow me to conclude with a quotation from my latest work, *A House, a Palace*:

For architecture is an undeniable event that surges in such an instant of creation that the spirit, preoccupied with assuring the firmness of a construction, of satisfying the exigencies of comfort, finds itself raised by a higher intention than that of simply serving and tends to manifest the poetic powers that animate us and give us joy.

417

54

On Discovering Gaudí's Architecture

Le Corbusier

It was in the year 1928, and at that time the Competition for the League of Nations Palace at Geneva had been the subject of a long debate. I had been invited to read a paper on this subject at the University City in Madrid. From this lecture the book "Une Maison – Un Palais" emerged shortly.

In Madrid I received a telegram signed by José Luis Sert, a man unknown to me, making an appointment with me for 10 p.m. at the Barcelona railway station, a stop on the express run from Madrid to Port-Bou, so that without a minute's delay I could go to give a lecture somewhere in the city.

On the platform at Barcelona station, I was received by five or six young people, all rather short in stature but full of fire and energy. The lecture was delivered impromptu!

The next day we went to Sitges. On the way I was intrigued by a modern house: Gaudí.[1] And on the way back, on the Paseo de Gracia, some large apartment houses, and further on, the "Sagrada Familia" attracted my attention. The whole Gaudí episode appeared! I was sufficiently indifferent to other people's opinion to take a keen interest in it. There I found the emotional capital of 1900. 1900 was the time when my eyes were opened to things of art, and I have always retained tender memories of it.

As a "soap box" architect (the La Roche and Garches houses, the villa Savoye), my attitude puzzled my friends at the time.

Antagonism of 1900 and of "soap boxes"? There was no question of that for me. What I had seen in Barcelona was the work of a man of extraordinary force, faith and technical capacity, manifested throughout his life in the quarry, that of a

Le Corbusier, "On Discovering Gaudí's Architecture," pp. 20–3 from *Gaudí*. Barcelona: Ediciones Polígrafa, 1957. © FLC/ADAGP, Paris and DACS, London 2005.
[1] Building by a disciple of Gaudí, in faithful emulation of the master's teaching.

man having stone carved before his very eyes from really masterly drawings. Gaudí is "the" constructor of 1900, the professional builder in stone, iron or brick. His glory is acknowledged today in his own country. Gaudí was a great artist. Only they remain and will endure who touch the sensitive hearts of men, but they will be badly treated on their way – they will be misunderstood, accused of sinning against the fashion of the day. Architecture whose meaning shines forth at the moment when lofty intentions dominate, triumphant over all the problems assembled on the firing line (structure, economy, technique, utility), triumphant because of an unlimited inner preparation, – "that" architecture is the fruit of character – properly speaking, a manifestation of character.

Let me say here how much I love Barcelona, that admirable city, – so old, so intense, – that seaport open to the past and to the future.

Paris, October 30, 1957

55

The Split Wall: Domestic Voyeurism

Beatriz Colomina

"To live is to leave traces," writes Walter Benjamin, in discussing the birth of the interior. "In the interior these are emphasized. An abundance of covers and protectors, liners and cases is devised, on which the traces of objects of everyday use are imprinted. The traces of the occupant also leave their impression on the interior. The detective story that follows these traces comes into being. . . . The criminals of the first detective novels are neither gentlemen nor apaches, but private members of the bourgeoisie."[1]

There is an interior in the detective novel. But can there be a detective story of the interior itself, of the hidden mechanisms by which space is constructed as interior? Which may be to say, a detective story of detection itself, of the controlling look, the look of control, the controlled look. But where would the traces of the look be imprinted? What do we have to go on? What clues?

There is an unknown passage of a well-known book, Le Corbusier's *Urbanisme* (1925), which reads: "Loos told me one day: 'A cultivated man does not look out of the window; his window is a ground glass; it is there only to let the light in, not to let the gaze pass through.'"[2] It points to a conspicuous yet conspicuously

Beatriz Colomina, "The Split Wall: Domestic Voyeurism," pp. 73–4, 98–107, 112, 124–6, 128 from *Sexuality and Space*. New York: Princeton Architectural Press, 1992.

[1] Walter Benjamin, "Paris, Capital of the Nineteenth Century," in *Reflections*, trans. Edmund Jephcott (New York: Schocken Books, 1986), pp. 155–6.

[2] "Loos m'affirmait un jour: 'Un homme cultivé ne regarde pas par la fenêtre; sa fenêtre est en verre dépoli; elle n'est là que pour donner de la lumière, non pour laisser passer le regard.'" Le Corbusier, *Urbanisme* (Paris, 1925), p. 174. When this book is published in English under the title *The City of To-morrow and its Planning*, trans. Frederick Etchells (New York, 1929), the sentence reads: "A friend once said to me: No intelligent man ever looks out of his window; his window is made of ground glass; its only function is to let in light, not to look out of" (pp. 185–6). In this translation, Loos' name has been replaced by "a friend." Was Loos "nobody" for Etchells, or is this just another example of the kind of misunderstanding that led to the mistranslation of the title of the book?

ignored feature of Loos' houses: not only are the windows either opaque or covered with sheer curtains, but the organization of the spaces and the disposition of the built-in furniture (the *immeuble*) seems to hinder access to them.

[. . .]

In the houses of Le Corbusier the reverse condition of Loos' interiors may be observed. In photographs windows are never covered with curtains, neither is access to them hampered by objects. On the contrary, everything in these houses seems to be disposed in a way that continuously throws the subject towards the periphery of the house. The look is directed to the exterior in such deliberate manner as to suggest the reading of these houses as frames for a view. Even when actually in an "exterior," in a terrace or in a "roof garden," walls are constructed to frame the landscape, and a view from there to the interior, as in a canonic photograph of Villa Savoye (figure 55.1), passes right through it to the framed landscape (so that in fact one can speak about a series of overlapping frames). These frames are given temporality through the *promenade*. Unlike Adolf Loos' houses, perception here occurs in motion. It is hard to think of oneself in static positions. If the photographs of Loos' interiors give the impression that somebody is about to enter the room, in Le Corbusier's the impression is that somebody was just there, leaving as traces a coat and a hat lying on the table by the entrance of Villa Savoye or some bread and a jug on the kitchen table (figure 55.2; note also that the door here has been left open, further suggesting the idea that we have just missed somebody), or a raw fish in the kitchen of Garches. And even once we have reached the highest point of the house, as in the terrace of Villa Savoye in the sill of the window which frames the landscape, the culminating point of the promenade, here also we find a hat, a pair of sunglasses, a little package (cigarettes?) and a lighter (figure 55.3), and now, where did the *gentleman* go? Because of course, you would have noticed already, that the personal objects are all male objects (never a handbag, a lipstick, or some piece of women's clothing). But before that. We are following somebody, the traces of his existence presented to us in the form of a series of photographs of the interior. The look into these photographs is a forbidden look. The look of a detective. A voyeuristic look.[3]

Perhaps it was Le Corbusier himself who decided to erase Loos' name. Of a different order, but no less symptomatic, is the mistranslation of "laisser passer le regard" (to let the gaze pass through) as "to look out of," as if to resist the idea that the gaze might take on, as it were, a life of its own, independent of the beholder. This could only happen in France!

[3] For other interpretations of these photographs of Le Corbusier's villas presented in the *Oeuvre complète* see: Thomas Schumacher, "Deep Space, Shallow Space," *Architectural Review* (January 1987): 37–42; Richard Becherer, "Chancing it in the Architecture of Surrealist Mise-en-Scène," *Modulus* 18 (1987): 63–87; Alexander Gorlin, "The Ghost in the Machine: Surrealism in the Work of Le Corbusier," *Perspecta* 18 (1982); José Quetglas, "Viajes alrededor de mi alcoba," *Arquitecture* 264–265 (1987): 111–12.

Figure 55.1   Villa Savoye, Poissy, 1929
© FLC/ADAGP, Paris and DACS, London 2005

Figure 55.2   Villa Savoye: view of the kitchen
© FLC/ADAGP, Paris and DACS, London 2005

Figure 55.3 Villa Savoye: view of the roof garden
© FLC/ADAGP, Paris and DACS, London 2005

In the film *L'Architecture d'aujourd'hui* (1929) directed by Pierre Chenal with Le Corbusier,[4] the latter as the main actor drives his own car to the entrance of Villa Garches, descends, and enters the house in an energetic manner. He is wearing a dark suit with bow tie, his hair is glued with brilliantine, every hair in place, he is holding a cigarette in his mouth. The camera pans through the exterior of the house and arrives at the "roof garden," where there are women sitting down and children playing. A little boy is driving his toy car. At this point Le Corbusier appears again but on the other side of the terrace (he never comes in contact with the women and children). He is puffing his cigarette. He then very athletically climbs up the spiral staircase which leads to the highest point of the house, a lookout point. Still wearing his formal attire, the cigarette still sticking out of his mouth, he pauses to contemplate the view from that point. He looks out.

There is also a figure of a woman going through a house in this movie. The house that frames her is Villa Savoye. Here there is no car arriving. The camera shows the house from the distance, an object sitting in the landscape, and then pans the outside and the inside of the house. And it is there, halfway through the interior, that the woman appears in the screen. She is already inside, already contained by the house, bounded. She opens the door that leads to the terrace

[4] A copy of this film is held in the Museum of Modern Art, New York. About this movie see J. Ward, "Le Corbusier's Villa Les Terrasses and the International Style," Ph.D. dissertation, New York University, 1983, and by the same author, "Les Terrasses," *Architectural Review* (March 1985): 64–9. Richard Becherer has compared it to Man Ray's movie *Les Mystères du Château du Dé* (setting by Mallet-Stevens) in "Chancing it in the Architecture of Surrealist Mise-en-Scène."

and goes up the ramp toward the roof garden, her back to the camera. She is wearing informal clothes and high heels and she holds to the handrail as she goes up, her skirt and hair blowing in the wind. She appears vulnerable. Her body is fragmented, framed not only by the camera but by the house itself, behind bars (figure 55.4). She appears to be moving from the inside of the house to the outside, to the roof garden. But this outside is again constructed as an inside with a wall wrapping the space in which an opening with the proportions of a window frames the landscape. The woman continues walking along the wall, as if protected by it, and as the wall makes a curve to form the solarium, the woman turns too, picks up a chair, and sits down. She would be facing the interior, the space she has just moved through. But for the camera, which now shows us a general view of the terrace, she has disappeared behind the plants. That is, just at the moment when she has turned and could face the camera (there is nowhere else to go), she vanishes. She never catches our eye. Here we are literally following somebody, the point of view is that of a voyeur.

We could accumulate more evidence. Few photographs of Le Corbusier's buildings show people in them. But in those few, women always look away from the camera: most of the time they are shot from the back and they almost never occupy the same space as men. Take the photographs of *Immeuble Clarté* in the *Oeuvre complète*, for example. In one of them, the woman and the child are in the interior, they are shot from the back, facing the wall; the men are in the

Figure 55.4 Villa Savoye: still from *L'Architecture d'aujourd'hui*. "Une maison ce n'est pas une prison: l'aspect change à chaque pas"
© FLC/ADAGP, Paris and DACS, London 2005

balcony, looking out, toward the city (figure 55.5). In the next shot, the woman, again shot from the back, is leaning against the window to the balcony and looking at the man and the child who are on the balcony. This spatial structure is repeated very often, not only in the photographs but also the drawings of Le Corbusier's projects. In a drawing of the Wanner project, for example, the woman in the upper floor is leaning against the veranda, looking down at her hero, the boxer, who is occupying the *jardin suspendu*. He looks at his punching bag. And in the drawing *Ferme radieuse*, the woman in the kitchen looks over the counter toward the man sitting at the dining room table. He is reading the newspaper. Here again the woman is placed "inside," the man "outside," the woman looks at the man, the man looks at the "world."

But perhaps no example is more telling than the photo collage of the exhibit of a living room in the *Salon d'Automne 1929*, including all the "equipment of a dwelling," a project that Le Corbusier realized in collaboration with Charlotte Perriand. In this image which Le Corbusier has published in the *Oeuvre complète*, Perriand herself is lying on the *chaise-longue*, her head turned away from the camera. More significant, in the original photograph employed in this photo collage (as well as in another photograph in the *Oeuvre complète* which shows the *chaise-longue* in the horizontal position), one can see that the chair has been placed right against the wall. Remarkably, she is facing the wall. She is almost an attachment to the wall. She sees nothing (figure 55.6).

Figure 55.5   Immeuble Clarté, Ginebra, 1930–2: view of the interior
© FLC/ADAGP, Paris and DACS, London 2005

Figure 55.6   Charlotte Perriand in the *chaise-longue* against the wall. *Salon d'Automne 1929*
© FLC/ADAGP, Paris and DACS, London 2005

And of course for Le Corbusier – who writes things such as "I exist in life only on condition that I see" (*Précisions*, 1930) or "This is the key: to look ... to look/observe/see/imagine/invent, create" (1963), and in the last weeks of his life: "I am and I remain an impenitent visual" (*Mise au Point*) – everything is in the visual.[5] But what does *vision* mean here?

[...]

For Le Corbusier the *new* urban conditions are a consequence of the media, which institutes a relationship between artifact and nature that makes the "defensiveness" of a Loosian window, of a Loosian system, unnecessary. In *Urbanisme*, in the same passage where he makes reference to "Loos' window," Le Corbusier goes on to write: "The horizontal gaze leads for away. ... From our offices we will get the feeling of being look-outs dominating a world in order. ... The skyscrapers concentrate everything in themselves: machines for abolishing time and space, telephones, cables, radios."[6] The inward gaze, the gaze turned upon itself, of Loos' interiors becomes with Le Corbusier a gaze of domination over the exterior world. But why is this gaze horizontal?

[5] Pierre-Alain Crosset, "Eyes Which See," *Casabella* 531–2 (1987): 115.
[6] Le Corbusier, *Urbanisme* (Paris, 1925), p. 186. This book is published in English under the title *The City of To-morrow and its Plannings* trans. Frederick Etchells (New York, 1929).

The debate between Le Corbusier and Perret over the horizontal window provides a key to this question.[7] Perret maintained that the vertical window, *la porte fenêtre*, "reproduces an impression of *complete* space" because it permits a view of the street, the garden, and the sky, while the horizontal window, *la fenêtre en longueur*, diminishes "one's perception and *correct* appreciation of the land-scape." What the horizontal window cuts from the cone of vision is the strip of the sky and the strip of the foreground that sustains the illusion of perspectival depth. Perret's *porte fenêtre* corresponds to the space of perspective. Le Corbusier's *fenêtre en longueur* to the space of photography.

[...]

The subject of Loos' architecture is the stage actor. But while the center of the house is left empty for the performance, we find the subject occupying the threshold of this space. Undermining its boundaries. The subject is split between actor and spectator of its own play. The completeness of the subject dissolves as also does the wall that s/he is occupying.

The subject of Le Corbusier's work is the movie actor, "estranged not only from the scene but from his own person."[8] This moment of estrangement is clearly marked in the drawing of *La Ville radieuse* where the traditional humanist figure, the inhabitant of the house, is made incidental to the camera eye: it comes and goes, it is merely a visitor.

[...]

The window is, for Le Corbusier, first of all communication. He repeatedly superimposes the idea of the "modern" window, a lookout window, a horizontal window, with the reality of the new media: "telephone, cable, radios, ... machines for abolishing time and space." Control is now in these media. Power has become "invisible." The look that from Le Corbusier's skyscrapers will "dominate a world in order" is neither the look from behind the periscope or the defensive view (turned towards itself) of Loos' interiors. It is a look that "registers" the new reality, a "recording" eye.

---

[7] About the debate between Perret and Le Corbusier see: Bruno Reichlin, "The Pros and Cons of the Horizontal Window," *Daidalos* 13 (1984), and Beatriz Colomina, "Le Corbusier and Photography," *Assemblage* 4 (1987).

[8] Pirandello describes the estrangement the actor experiences before the mechanism of the cinematographic camera: "The film actor feels as if in exile – exiled not only from the stage but also from himself. With a vague sense of discomfort he feels inexplicable emptiness: his body loses corporeality, it evaporates, it is deprived of reality, life, voice and the noises caused by its moving about, in order to be changed into a mute image, flickering an instant on the screen, then vanishing into silence." Luigi Pirandello, *Si Gira*, quoted by Walter Benjamin in "The Work of Art in the Age of Mechanical Reproduction," p. 229.

Le Corbusier's architecture is produced by an engagement with the mass media but, as with Loos, the key to his position is, in the end, to be found in his statements about fashion. Where for Loos the English suit was the mask necessary to sustain the individual in metropolitan conditions of existence, for Le Corbusier this suit is cumbersome and inefficient. And where Loos contrasts the *dignity* of male British fashion with the *masquerade* of women's, Le Corbusier praises women's fashion over men's because it has undergone *change*, the change of modern time.

[...]

The window in the age of mass communication provides us with one more flat image. The window is a screen. From there issues the insistence on eliminating every protuding element, "devignolizing" the window, suppressing the still.

Of course, this screen undermines the wall. But here it is not, as in Loos' houses, a *physical* undermining, an *occupation* of the wall, but a *dematerialization* following from the emerging media. The organizing geometry of architecture slips from the perspectival cone of vision, from the humanist eye, to the camera angle.

But this slippage is, of course, not neutral in gender terms. Male fashion is uncomfortable but provides the bearer with "the gaze," "the dominant sign," woman's fashion is practical and turns her into the object of another's gaze: "Modern woman has cut her hair. Our gazes have known (enjoy) the shape of her legs." A picture. She sees nothing. She is an attachment to a wall that is no longer simply there. Enclosed by a space whose limits are defined by a gaze.

56

Nine Points on Monumentality

José Louis Sert, Fernand Léger,
and Sigfried Giedion

Introduction

Joan Ockman

One of the prophetic themes to be debated in the 1940s was that of the "new monumentality." The 1937 World Exposition in Paris had been the occasion of modernism's official triumph for most of the participating countries. At the same time, though, in the confrontation that took place at the foot of the Eiffel Tower between Albert Speer's pavilion for the Third Reich, avatar of Prussian classicism, and Boris Iofan's Soviet pavilion, an embodiment of the more dynamic aspirations of social realism, the new architecture received an implicit challenge to its potency as a form of civic representation.

The accepted view was that "if it is a monument it is not modern, and if it is modern it cannot be a monument," as Lewis Mumford wrote in 1938 in The Culture of Cities. *Earlier, Henry-Russell Hitchcock's* Modern Architecture: Romanticism and Reintegration *(1929) had helped to inculcate this idea. Yet the dichotomy between "new traditionalists" and "new pioneers" was an oversimplification. Many of those within the folds of the modern movement had realized for a long time that the new aesthetic needed to be infused with a collective and symbolic content. The dispute over Le Corbusier's League of Nations project had raised the issue in explicit terms in 1927.*

On the eve of the Second World War, J. J. P. Oud, responsible for some of the most distinguished examples of international modernism during the previous decade, returned to hierarchical massing, symmetrical planning, and a cautious reintroduction of decorative elements in his Shell Building in the Hague. But the scandal provoked by Oud was only the most extreme example of the effort by architects at this time to find a synthesis between

José Luis Sert, Fernand Léger, and Sigfried Giedion, "Nine Points on Monumentality," with an introduction by Joan Ockman, pp. 27–30 from Joan Ockman (ed.), *Architecture Culture, 1943–1968: A Documentary Anthology.* New York: Rizzoli, 1993. Reprinted by permission of Rizzoli.

*monumental expression and progressive ideology. In a catalogue introduction for an exhib-
ition held at the Museum of Modern Art in New York in 1944 entitled* Built in U.S.A. –
1932–1944, *Elizabeth Mock lauded a prize-winning design of 1939 by Eliel and Eero
Saarinen and Robert F. Swanson for the Smithsonian Gallery of Art on the Mall in
Washington, D.C., as a monument epitomizing "the very nature of our democracy."*

*Sigfried Giedion, José Luis Sert, and Fernand Léger entered the debate in 1943 with a
position paper entitled "Nine Points on Monumentality." The joint pronouncement by an
architectural historian, an architect-planner, and a painter – all living in New York during
the war years and in close contact – was intended for publication in a volume planned by the
American Abstract Artists which never appeared. A more extended discussion by each of the
three from their respective outlooks was to have accompanied it. Of these, an essay by Léger
appeared in 1946 in another publication by the American Abstract Artists, while Giedion's
essay "The Need for a New Monumentality" came out in 1944 in a book edited by Paul
Zucker entitled* New Architecture and City Planning, *a major section of which was dedicated
to the monumentality question.*

*The approach taken in both the "Nine Points" and "The Need for a New Monumen-
tality" was to place monumentality – "the expression of man's highest cultural needs" –
within the historical evolution of modernism itself. While modern architecture had earlier
been obliged to concentrate on the more immediate and mundane problems of housing and
urbanism, the authors argued, its new task in the postwar period would be the reorganization
of community life through the planning and design of civic centers, monumental ensembles,
and public spectacles. This "third step" would involve the collaboration of architects, planners,
and artists. The chief difficulty, in their view, was to invent forms of large-scale expression free
of association with oppressive ideologies of the past and historicist bombast ("pseudomonu-
mentality"). To this end, a repertory of colorful and mobile forms and lightweight, naturalistic materials was proposed. The work of contemporary artists like Picasso, Constantin
Brancusi, Naum Gabo, Alexander Calder, and Léger himself was seen as "pointing the
way" for an architecture of full rather than empty rhetoric.*

For Giedion this was clearly a shift from the machine Zeitgeist that had inspired Space,
Time and Architecture, *written in 1938–39. In an extended discussion of the League of
Nations competition in that book he had commended Le Corbusier's entry specifically for its
programmatic accommodation and absence of monumental rhetoric. In his article in the
Zucker book – which began with the motto, "Emotional training is necessary today. For
whom? First of all for those who govern and administer the people" – he stated of Le
Corbusier's building, "the whole development of modern architecture towards a new monumentality would have been advanced for decades if the officials could have understood its
quality." Giedion's reversal seems to have been in large part occasioned by the new impact of
Frank Lloyd Wright. In an article on Wright's Johnson Wax building entitled "The Dangers
and Advantages of Luxury" published at the end of 1939 in the journal* Focus, *he celebrated
its overscaled columns and powerful central work hall, acknowledging that a modern
administration building could "for once be based entirely on poetry."*

The monumentality debate reached a point of intensity in an issue of the London journal
Architectural Review *published in September 1948 with invited contributions from Gregor
Paulsson, Henry-Russell Hitchcock, William Holford, Walter Gropius, Lúcio Costa, Alfred
Roth, and Giedion, and a late contribution from Lewis Mumford in April 1949. It would
surface again at CIAM's eighth congress in Hoddesdon, England, in 1951, on the core of the
city. But here, at a moment when social realism was at its height in Eastern Europe, the theme*

was exorcised in the West – at least for the moment. In summing up the congress's conclusions, Giedion stated, "There is no excuse for the erection of a monumental building mass," shifting the responsibility for producing symbolic forms to "creative painters and sculptors."

Yet the impulse behind the new monumentality was not to disappear. It would be transformed, mutatis mutandis, in the coming decades: in the mythopoetic structures of Louis Kahn and the new capitols built in India and Brazil, reemerging in the 1960s and 1970s in the historicism of the Italian Tendenza and the grandiloquent facades of postmodernism. Meanwhile, in Eastern Europe the theme would have a mirror image in the continuing struggle between social realism and functionalism.

The verse from the French song with which the "Nine Points" opens is meant to convey the preciousness of great monuments of civic architecture: "What would you give, my beauty, to see your husband again? I will give Versailles, Paris and Saint Denis, the towers of Notre Dame, and the steeple of my native countryside ... " A partial summary of the literature on monumentality may be found in Christiane C. and George R. Collins, "Monumentality: A Critical Matter in Modern Architecture," Harvard Architecture Review 4 (1984).

Que donneriez vous ma belle
Pour revoir votre mari?
Je donnerai Versailles,
Paris et Saint Denis
Les tours de Notre Dame
Et le clocher de mon pays.
Auprès de ma blonde
Qu'il fait bon, fait bon, fait bon.
– From an old French song,
    "Auprès de ma blonde"

1. Monuments are human landmarks which men have created as symbols for their ideals, for their aims, and for their actions. They are intended to outlive the period which originated them, and constitute a heritage for future generations. As such, they form a link between the past and the future.

2. Monuments are the expression of man's highest cultural needs. They have to satisfy the eternal demand of the people for translation of their collective force into symbols. The most vital monuments are those which express the feeling and thinking of this collective force – the people.

3. Every bygone period which shaped a real cultural life had the power and the capacity to create these symbols. Monuments are, therefore, only possible in periods in which a unifying consciousness and unifying culture exists. Periods which exist for the moment have been unable to create lasting monuments.

4. The last hundred years have witnessed the devaluation of monumentality. This does not mean that there is any lack of formal monuments or architectural examples pretending to serve this purpose; but the so-called

monuments of recent date have, with rare exceptions, become empty shells. They in no way represent the spirit or the collective feeling of modern times.

5. This decline and misuse of monumentality is the principal reason why modern architects have deliberately disregarded the monument and revolted against it.

   Modern architecture, like modern painting and sculpture, had to start the hard way. It began by tackling the simpler problems, the more utilitarian buildings like low-rent housing, schools, office buildings, hospitals, and similar structures. Today modern architects know that buildings cannot be conceived as isolated units, that they have to be incorporated into the vaster urban schemes. There are no frontiers between architecture and town planning, just as there are no frontiers between the city and the region. Co-relation between them is necessary. Monuments should constitute the most powerful accents in these vast schemes.

6. A new step lies ahead. Postwar changes in the whole economic structure of nations may bring with them the organization of community life in the city which has been practically neglected up to date.

7. The people want the buildings that represent their social and community life to give more than functional fulfillment. They want their aspiration for monumentality, joy, pride, and excitement to be satisfied.

   The fulfillment of this demand can be accomplished with the new means of expression at hand, though it is no easy task. The following conditions are essential for it: A monument being the integration of the work of the planner, architect, painter, sculptor, and landscapist demands close collaboration between all of them. This collaboration has failed in the last hundred years. Most modern architects have not been trained for this kind of integrated work. Monumental tasks have not been entrusted to them.

   As a rule, those who govern and administer a people, brilliant as they may be in their special fields, represent the average man of our period in their artistic judgments. Like this average man, they experience a split between their methods of thinking and their methods of feeling. The feeling of those who govern and administer the countries is untrained and still imbued with the pseudo-ideals of the nineteenth century. This is the reason why they are not able to recognize the creative forces of our period, which alone could build the monuments or public buildings that should be integrated into new urban centers which can form a true expression for our epoch.

8. Sites for monuments must be planned. This will be possible once replanning is undertaken on a large scale which will create vast open spaces in the now decaying areas of our cities. In these open spaces, monumental architecture will find its appropriate setting which now does not exist. Monumental buildings will then be able to stand in space, for, like trees or plants, monumental buildings cannot be crowded in upon any odd lot in any district. Only when this space is achieved can the new urban centers come to life.

9. Modern materials and new techniques are at hand: light metal structures; curved, laminated wooden arches; panels of different textures, colors, and sizes; light elements like ceilings which can be suspended from big trusses covering practically unlimited spans.

Mobile elements can constantly vary the aspect of the buildings. These mobile elements, changing positions and casting different shadows when acted upon by wind or machinery, can be the source of new architectural effects.

During night hours, color and forms can be projected on vast surfaces. Such displays could be projected upon buildings for purposes of publicity or propaganda. These buildings would have large plane surfaces planned for this purpose, surfaces which are nonexistent today.

Such big animated surfaces with the use of color and movement in a new spirit would offer unexplored fields to mural painters and sculptors.

Elements of nature, such as trees, plants, and water, would complete the picture. We could group all these elements in architectural ensembles: the stones which have always been used, the new materials which belong to our times, and color in all its intensity which has long been forgotten.

Man-made landscapes would be correlated with nature's landscapes and all elements combined in terms of the new and vast facade, sometimes extending for many miles, which has been revealed to us by the air view. This could be contemplated not only during a rapid flight but also from a helicopter stopping in mid-air.

Monumental architecture will be something more than strictly functional. It will have regained its lyrical value. In such monumental layouts, architecture and city planning could attain a new freedom and develop new creative possibilities, such as those that have begun to be felt in the last decades in the fields of painting, sculpture, music, and poetry.

57

Monumentality

Louis I. Kahn

Gold is a beautiful material. It belongs to the sculptor.

Monumentality in architecture may be defined as a quality, a spiritual quality inherent in a structure which conveys the feeling of its eternity, that it cannot be added to or changed. We feel that quality in the Parthenon, the recognized architectural symbol of Greek civilization.

Some argue that we are living in an unbalanced state of relativity which cannot be expressed with a single intensity of purpose. It is for that reason, I feel, that many of our confrères do not believe we are psychologically constituted to convey a quality of monumentality to our buildings.

But have we yet given full architectural expression to such social monuments as the school, the community, or culture center? What stimulus, what movement, what social or political phenomenon shall we yet experience? What event or philosophy shall give rise to a will to commemorate its imprint on our civilization? What effect would such forces have on our architecture?

Science has given to the architect its explorations into new combinations of materials capable of great resistance to the forces of gravity and wind.

Recent experimenters and philosophers of painting, sculpture, and architecture have instilled new courage and spirit in the work of their fellow artists.

Monumentality is enigmatic. It cannot be intentionally created. Neither the finest material nor the most advanced technology need enter a work of monumental character for the same reason that the finest ink was not required to draw up the Magna Carta.

However, our architectural monuments indicate a striving for structural perfection which has contributed in great part to their impressiveness, clarity of form, and logical scale.

Stimulated and guided by knowledge we shall go far to develop the forms indigenous to our new materials and methods. It is, therefore, the concern of this

Louis I. Khan, "Monumentality," pp. 18–21, 24–7 from Alessandra Latour (ed.), *Louis I Khan. Writings, Lectures, Interviews.* New York: Rizzoli, 1991. Reprinted by permission of Rizzoli.

paper to touch briefly on the broader horizons which science and skill have revealed to the architect and engineer, and sketch the faint outlines of possible structural concepts and expressions they suggest.

No architect can rebuild a cathedral of another epoch embodying the desires, the aspirations, the love and hate of the people whose heritage it became. Therefore the images we have before us of monumental structures of the past cannot live again with the same intensity and meaning. Their faithful duplication is unreconcilable. But we dare not discard the lessons these buildings teach for they have the common characteristics of greatness upon which the buildings of our future must, in one sense or another, rely.

In Greek architecture, engineering concerned itself fundamentally with materials in compression. Each stone or part forming the structural members was made to bear with accuracy on each other to avoid tensile action stone is incapable of enduring.

The great cathedral builders regarded the members of the structural skeleton with the same love of perfection and search for clarity of purpose. Out of periods of inexperience and fear, when they erected over-massive core-filled veneered walls, grew a courageous theory of a stone-over-stone vault skeleton producing a downward and outward thrust, which forces were conducted to a column or a wall provided with the added characteristic of the buttress which together took this combination of action. The buttress allowed lighter walls between the thrust points and these curtain walls were logically developed for the use of large glass windows. This structural concept, derived from earlier and cruder theories, gave birth to magnificent variations in the attempts to attain loftier heights and greater spans creating a spiritually emotional environment unsurpassed.

The influence of the Roman vault, the dome, the arch, has etched itself in deep furrows across the pages of architectural history. Through Romanesque, Gothic, Renaissance, and today, its basic forms and structural ideas have been felt. They will continue to reappear but with added powers made possible by our technology and engineering skill.

The engineer of the latter part of the nineteenth century developed from basic principles the formulas of the handbook. Demands of enormous building quantity and speed developed the handbook engineer who used its contents, more or less forgetting basic principles. Now we hear about continuity in structures, not a new word but recently an all important word in engineering which promises to relegate the handbook to the archives.

The I-beam is an engineering accomplishment deriving its shape from an analysis of the stresses involved in its use. It is designed so that the greater proportion of the area of cross section is concentrated as far as possible from the center of gravity. The shape adapted itself to ease of rolling and under test it was found that even the fillets, an aid in the rolling process, helped convey the stresses from one section to another in continuity.

Safety factors were adopted to cover possible inconsistencies in the composition of the material of manufacture. Large-scale machinery and equipment needed in its fabrication lead to standardization.

435

The combination of safety factors (ignorance factor as one engineer termed it) and standardization narrowed the practice of engineering to the section of members from handbooks recommending sections much heavier than calculations would require and further limited the field of engineering expression stifling the creation of the more graceful forms which the stress diagrams indicated. For example, the common practice of using an I-beam as a cantilever has no relation to the stress diagram which shows that the required depth of material from the supporting end outward may decrease appreciably.

Joint construction in common practice treats every joint as a hinge which makes connections to columns and other members complex and ugly.

To attain greater strength with economy, a finer expression in the structural solution of the principle of concentrating the area of cross section away from the center of gravity is the tubular form since the greater the moment of inertia the greater the strength.

A bar of a certain area of cross section rolled into a tube of the same area of cross section (consequently of a larger diameter) would possess a strength enormously greater than the bar.

The tubular member is not new, but its wide use has been retarded by technological limitations in the construction of joints. Up until very recently welding has been outlawed by the building codes. In some cases, where it was permitted, it was required to make loading tests for every joint.

Structure designs must discard the present moment coefficients and evolve new calculations based on the effect of continuity in structures. The structural efficiency of rigid connection, in which the sheer value and the resisting moment is at least equal to the values of the supporting member, is obtained by the welding of such connections. The column becomes part of the beam and takes on added duties not usually calculated for columns.

The engineer and architect must then go back to basic principles, must keep abreast with and consult the scientist for new knowledge, redevelop his judgment of the behavior of structures, and acquire a new sense of form derived from design rather than piece together parts of convenient fabrication.

Riveted I-beam plate and angle construction is complex and graceless. Welding has opened the doors to vast accomplishments in pure engineering which allows forms of greater strength and efficiency to be used. The choice of structural forms are limitless even for given problems, and therefore the aesthetic philosophy of the individual can be satisfied by his particular composition of plates, angles, and tubular forms accomplishing the same answer to the challenge of the forces of gravity and wind.

The ribs, vaults, domes, buttresses come back again only to enclose space in a more generous, far simpler way and in the hands of our present masters of building in a more emotionally stirring way. From stone, the part has become smaller and cannot be seen by the naked eye. It is now the molecular composition of the metal observed and tested by the scientist through spectroscopy or by photoelastic recordings. His finding may go to the architect and engineer in the more elemental form of the formula, but by that means it shall have become an instrumental part of the builder's palette to be used without prejudice or fear. That is the modern way.

Gothic architecture relying on basically simple construction formulas derived from experience and the material available, could only go so far. Beauvais cathedral, its builders trying to reach greater spans and height, collapsed.

The compressive stress of stone is measured in hundreds of pounds.

While not only the compressive, but also the bending and tensile stress of steel is measured in thousands of pounds.

Beauvais cathedral needed the steel we have. It needed the knowledge we have.

Glass would have revealed the sky and become a part of the enclosed space framed by an interplay of exposed tubular ribs, plates, and columns of a stainless metal formed true and faired into a continuous flow of lines expressive of their stress patterns. Each member would have been welded to the next to create a continuous structural unity worthy of being exposed because its engineering gives no resistance to the laws of beauty having its own aesthetic life. The metal would have now been aged into a friendly material protected from deterioration by its intrinsic composition.

This generation is looking forward to its duty and benefit to build for the masses with its problems of housing and health.

It is aware of our outmoded cities.

It accepts the airship as a vital need.

Factories have adopted horizontal assembly and shifting population has required the transformation of large tracts of virgin territory at least temporarily for complete human living.

The building of a complete permanent town was attempted and almost built for the workers at Willow Run.

The nation has adopted the beginnings of social reform.

War production may become normal production on the same scale accepted as sound economics.

Still untried but pledged stand the noble principles of the Atlantic Charter.

In the days we look forward to must then the cathedral, the culture center, the legislative palace, world island – the seat of the congress of nations, the palace of labor and industry, the monuments to commemorate the achievements and aspirations of our time, be built to resemble Chartres, Crystal Palace, Palazzo Strozzi, or the Taj Mahal?

War engineering achievements in concrete, steel, and wood are showing the signs of maturity appropriate to guide the minds entrusted with the conception of buildings of such high purpose. The giant major skeleton of the structure can assert its right to be seen. It need no longer be clothed for eye appeal. Marble and woods feel at ease in its presence. New wall products of transparent, translucent, and opaque material with exciting textures and color are suspended or otherwise fastened to the more delicate forms of the minor members. Slabs of paintings articulate the circulation in the vast sheltered space. Sculpture graces its interior.

437

Outstanding masters of building design indicated the direction an architect may take to unravel and translate into simple terms the complexity of modern requirements. They have restated the meaning of a wall, a post, a beam, a roof, and a window, and their interrelation in space. They had to be restated when we recall the conglomerations that style copying tortured these elements into.

Efforts towards a comprehensive architecture will help to develop these elements and refine their meaning. A wall dividing interior space is not the same wall dividing the outside from the interior. Masonry shall always function as retaining and garden walls. It may be used for exterior walls for its decorative qualities, but be supplemented by interior slabs designed to meet more directly the challenge of the elements.

Structural ingenuity may eliminate the interior post, but as long as it must exist its place is reserved and its independence respected in the planning of space.

Structural problems center about the roof. The permanence and beauty of its surfaces is a major problem confronting science. The surfacing of the domes, vaults, and arches appearing as part of the exterior contours of the building may be an integral part of the structural design. Stainless metal, concrete or structural plastics, structural glass in light panes, or great reinforced glass castings may be the choice for domes and vaults, depending on the requirements, the climate, and the desired effect. The surfacing of flat roofs should be given equally serious consideration whether it is planned for use or not.

The citizens of a metropolitan area of a city and their representatives have formulated a program for a culture center endorsed by the national educational center. The citizens' committee collaborated with the architect and his staff of engineers. Costs were not discussed. Time was not "of the essence." Its progress was the concern of many.

From above we see the noble outlines of the building. Much taller buildings some distance from the site do not impress us with the same feeling of receptiveness. Its site is a prominent elevation in the outlying countryside framed by dark forests defining the interior of broad strokes in land architecture.

On the ground the first reaction comes from the gigantic sculptural forms of the skeleton frame. This backbone of the architect's central idea successfully challenges the forces which during its design challenged to destroy it. To solve the more minute complexities of the entire organism, its creator had drawn his conclusions and made his decisions from the influences of many people and things around him.

The plan does not begin nor end with the space he has enveloped, but from the adjoining delicate ground sculpture it stretches beyond to the rolling contours and vegetation of the surrounding land and continues farther out to the distant hills.

The immediate ground sculpture disciplines his mind in shaping it into stronger geometric planes and cubes to satisfy his desire for terraces and pools, steps and approaches. The landscape designer countered or accentuated these planes with again geometric and free forms interwoven with the lacy leaf patterns of the deciduous tree.

The plans reveal that the vast spans shelter smaller areas designed for specific use, which are divided from the whole by panels of glass, insulated slabs, and marble. These partitions are free of the structure and related only to the circulation pattern. The ground plan seems continuous. The great lobby is a part of the amphitheater which dips down to the stage. The light comes from above through an undulating series of prismatic glass domes.

Ahead, some distance from the entrance, is a great mural of brilliant color. As we approach it the forms clearly defined from a distance seem to divide into forms of their own, each with its own color power, clear and uncultured.

To one side is the community museum of sculpture, painting, and crafts. It exhibits the work of the younger men and women attending the vocational and art academies. Here they are accepted because their talents can be judged by those who have themselves been instructed in the basic principles underlying the use of a material. The emotional adaptations are left for the exhibitor himself to evaluate by contact, comparison, and experience.

Sculpture shows the tendency to define form and construction. Marble and stone is carved as of old. Castings in new alloys and plastics are favorite methods of obtaining permanency. Solids are interwoven with sheets and tubes of metal. The subject matter exhibited has no bounds. With the new materials and tools, chemical tints, and with manufacture at the artist's disposal, his work becomes alive with ideas. Metal sprays and texture guns, with fine adjustments have also become the instruments of the sculptor, painter, and craftsman. One of the younger men had cast within a large, irregular cube of transparent plastic other forms and objects of brilliant color. A sphere, planes at various angles, copper wire in free lines are seen through the plastic.

From these experiments in form the architect will eventually learn to choose appropriate embellishments for his structures. So far he has omitted them. His judgment leads him to free-standing forms in space.

Some of the younger artists are influenced by the works of an older sculptor who has developed a theory of scale in relation to space. He has argued that as the size of the structural work is increased the monolithic character of smaller work does not apply. He chose for large work a small consistent part of module of a definite shape, a cube, a prism, or a sphere which he used to construct block over block, with delicate adjustments to the effect of light and shadow, the overall form. His work seen from great distances retains a texturally vibrant quality produced by these numerous blocks and the action of the sun upon them.

Before we can feel the new spirit which must envelop the days to come we must prepare ourselves to use intelligently the knowledge derived from all sources. Nostalgic yearning for the ways of the past will find but few ineffectual supporters.

Steel, the lighter metals, concrete, glass, laminated woods, asbestos, rubber, and plastics, are emerging as the prime building materials of today. Riveting is being replaced by welding, reinforced concrete is emerging from infancy with prestressed reinforced concrete, vibration and controlled mixing, promising to aid in its ultimate refinement. Laminated wood is rapidly replacing lumber and is equally friendly to the eye, and plastics are so vast in their potentialities that already numerous journals and periodicals devoted solely to their many outlets are read with interest and hope. The untested characteristics of these materials are being analyzed, old formulas are being discarded. New alloys of steel, shatter-proof and thermal glass and synthetics of innumerable types, together with the material already mentioned, make up the new palette of the designer.

To what extent progress in building will be retarded by ownership patterns, dogmas, style consciousness, precedent, untested building materials, arbitrary standards, outmoded laws and regulations, untrained workmen and artless crafts-men, is speculation. But the findings of science and their application have taken large steps recently in the development of war materials which point to upset normally controlled progress and raise our hopes to the optimistic level.

Standardization, prefabrication, controlled experiments and tests, and special-ization are not monsters to be avoided by the delicate sensitiveness of the artist. They are merely the modern means of controlling vast potentialities of materials for living, by chemistry, physics, engineering, production, and assembly, which lead to the necessary knowledge the artist must have to expel fear in their use, broaden his creative instinct, give him new courage, and thereby lead him to the adventures of unexplored places. His work will then be part of his age and will afford delight and service for his contemporaries.

I do not wish to imply that monumentality can be attained scientifically or that the work of the architect reaches its greatest service to humanity by his peculiar genius to guide a concept towards a monumentality. I merely defend, because I admire, the architect who possesses the will to grow with the many angles of our development. For such a man finds himself far ahead of his fellow workers.

58

Reaffirmation of the Aims of CIAM

Congress of International Modern Architects

Introduction

Joan Ockman

The International Congresses for Modern Architecture (CIAM) were founded in 1928 at La Sarraz, Switzerland, by a group of the leading modern architects. The most important document to emerge from their series of pre-World War II meetings was the Athens Charter, a set of principles of urbanism organizing planning into four key functions – dwelling, work, recreation (both mental and physical), and circulation. The result of CIAM's fourth conference in 1933, it was published in France in 1943 under German occupation. The charter became the principal point of reference for the organization's subsequent activity.

A fifth CIAM congress took place in Paris in 1937, while a sixth scheduled for 1939 in Liège was canceled because of the war. For the next eight years, CIAM's international operation was curtailed, although local initiatives continued in countries around the world. One of these was the Chapter for Relief and Postwar Planning founded in New York in 1944 as a CIAM section in the Western Hemisphere, including Richard Neutra, José Luis Sert, Knud Lönberg-Holm, Paul Nelson, and Harwell Hamilton Harris as officers, and counting among its members Sigfried Giedion, Walter Gropius, Oscar Stonorov, William Wurster, Mies van der Rohe, Wallace Harrison, Joseph Hudnut, Vernon DeMars, Lawrence Kocher, Pierre Chareau, and Ernest Weissmann. (On this group, which undertook studies on the new United Nations, and in general on CIAM from 1939 to 1947, see the forthcoming documentation by Jos Bosman, to be published by the ETH-Zurich.)

It was not until September 1947 that CIAM held its next international meeting. This took place in Bridgwater, England, and was hosted by the MARS Group, the English wing of CIAM. The purpose, as reflected in the following statement, was to reestablish communication

Congress of International Modern Architects, "Reaffirmation of the Aims of CIAM," with an introduction by Joan Ockman, pp. 100–2 from Joan Ockman (ed.), *Architecture Culture, 1943–1968: A Documentary Anthology.* New York: Rizzoli, 1993. Reprinted by permission of Rizzoli.

among the members and to determine CIAM's role in the new period. Sert, whose Can Our Cities Survive? *– an application of the principles formulated at Athens – had been published in 1942, was chosen to succeed Cornelis van Eesteren as president. Consensus was strong that CIAM should not be a group of isolated personalities as it had tended to be prior to the war, but rather a task-oriented working congress carrying out defined activities. The organization's statutes were redrafted to open membership to all architects who accepted its principles and agreed to participate in the work teams that were to be formed, without limitation, in the various countries – a step that would contribute to the large increase in CIAM's membership by the time of its ninth meeting in Aix-en-Provence in 1953.*

More significantly, the reunion of the "masters" at Bridgwater also saw the emergence of an internal critique by a new generation of architects who had come to maturity in the intervening years. Among those who would shortly play a crucial role in CIAM's future were the Dutch architects Jacob Bakema and Aldo van Eyck. Van Eyck made a plea for CIAM to move beyond a rationalistic and mechanistic conception of progress to a more creative understanding of the human environment: "Imagination remains the only common denominator of man and nature, the only faculty capable of registering spiritual transformation ..." The theme of imagination had also been evoked in two questionnaires prepared for the meeting, one by J. M. Richards for the MARS Group, the other by Giedion and the artist Hans Arp, raising, for the first time within CIAM, questions of aesthetics and of architecture's relationship to the other arts. The introduction of these themes – the latter having been of special concern to Le Corbusier since the war's end – presented a rallying point for the reconvening congress. "Finally," Le Corbusier declared, "imagination comes to CIAM."

1. **Preamble** We, the CIAM architects from many countries, in Europe, America, Asia, and Africa, have met at Bridgwater after an interval of ten years.

   These have been years of struggle and separation during which, as a consequence of the threat of Fascist domination, political, economic, and social questions have taken on a new significance for everyone. At the same time technical progress has been accelerated by intensive scientific research and the needs of war production. The technique of planning has also moved forward as a result of the experience some countries have gained in social organization.

   These factors are together responsible for a new conception of integrated planning which is now emerging. Allied with this is a new contemporary consciousness that finds its definitive expression in the arts.

   We are faced with an enormous task in rebuilding the territories devastated by the war as well as in raising the standard of life in undeveloped countries where great changes are now taking place. We therefore feel that this, our sixth congress, is an occasion when we must review our past activities, examine our present situation, and determine our policy for the future.

2. **Background** Our earlier declarations – that of La Sarraz in 1928 and the Athens Charter of 1933 – reflected the architect's growing sense of his

responsibilities toward society. They were drawn up with reference to a particular time and particular situation, but we consider many of the statements made in them to be fundamental and we now reaffirm the following points from these declarations.

"We emphasize that to build is a primal activity in man, intimately associated with the evolution and development of human life ..."

"Our intention ... is to reestablish the place of architecture in its proper social and economic sphere. ..."

"We affirm today the necessity for a new conception of architecture satisfying the spiritual, intellectual, and material needs of present-day life. Conscious of the effects on social structure, brought about by industrialization, we recognize the necessity of a corresponding transformation of architecture itself..."

"Planning is the organization of the functional conditions of community life: it applies equally to town and country, and operates within the divisions: a. dwelling; b. places of work and c. of recreation; d. circulation, connecting these three..."

"The aims of CIAM are: a. to formulate the architectural problem of today; b. to represent the idea of a contemporary architecture; c. to instill this idea into technical, economic and social thought; d. to watch over the contemporary development of architecture."

The Declaration of La Sarraz was primarily an attempt to express some of the realities of the contemporary situation and to recognize the inevitable emergence of new forms from the application of new means to meeting human needs.

Many of the ideas for which we were then working are now widely accepted, and the subsequent Athens Charter has laid a similar foundation in the field of physical and social planning. Among the achievements of recent years are:

A general acceptance of the idea of social planning and, in many countries, the adoption of planning legislation – including legislation for land reform – which will assist the realization of this idea.

A growing recognition of the important part played by scientific method in the development of architecture, which has resulted in the advance of building technique.

A trend toward the reintegration of the plastic arts – architecture, sculpture, and painting – and thereby toward a clearer understanding of contemporary forms of artistic expression.

3. **The aims of CIAM** The progress that has been made in the last ten years and the confidence in the ideals of CIAM expressed by the younger generation convince us that the continuation of the CIAM congresses is fully justified. The sixth congress redefines the aims of CIAM as follows:

"To work for the creation of a physical environment that will satisfy man's emotional and material needs and stimulate his spiritual growth."

To achieve an environment of this quality, we must combine social idealism, scientific planning, and the fullest use of available building techniques. In so doing we must enlarge and enrich the aesthetic language of architecture in order to provide a contemporary means whereby people's emotional needs can find expression in the design of their environment. We believe that thus a more balanced life can be produced for the individual and for the community.

4. **The tasks ahead** Having members in so many countries, CIAM is in-a strong position to put the experience gained in one part of the world at the disposal of another. The social concepts and legislative experiments of countries that have made progress in these fields can give direction to the technical development of highly industrialized countries, and technical experience from elsewhere can be brought to the assistance of countries that are still in process of industrialization.

An urgent task for CIAM is to ensure that the highest human and technical standards are attained in community planning of whatever scale, from the region to the single dwelling. CIAM also feels called upon to examine the implications of the process of industrialization that is now being applied to building, in order to ensure that such necessary technical developments are controlled by a sense of human values.

5. **Future policy** With the purpose of fulfilling the aims outlined above, CIAM intends to pursue a policy that will:

Popularize its principles as widely as possible, by means of books, periodicals, exhibitions, films, the radio, and other means of addressing the people of all countries.

Formulate the principles that should govern the education of architects and take all possible measures for the reform of existing educational methods.

Support in every way the activities of the local and national groups of CIAM, especially by establishing contacts with official authorities, national and international, and by promoting beneficial legislation and other effective measures.

Encourage CIAM groups to keep in touch with public needs and observe the progress of the public's understanding of CIAM principles, with the object of assisting modern architecture to develop in sympathy with the aspirations of the people it serves.

59

Functionalism and Technology

Reyner Banham

By the middle of the Thirties it was already common practice to use the word *Functionalism*, as a blanket term for the progressive architecture of the Twenties and its canon of approved forerunners that had been set up by writers like Sigfried Giedion. Yet, [. . .] it is doubtful if the ideas implicit in Functionalism – let alone the word itself – were ever significantly present in the minds of any of the influential architects of the period. Scholiasts may care to dispute the exact date on which this misleading word was first used as the label for the International Style, but there is little doubt that the first consequential use was in Alberto Sartoris's book *Gli Elementi dell' architettura Funzionale*, which appeared in Milan in 1932. Responsibility for the term is laid on Le Corbusier's shoulders – the work was originally to have been called *Architettura Razionale*, or something similar, but, in a letter which is reprinted as a preface to the book, Le Corbusier wrote

> The title of your book is limited: it is a real fault to be constrained to put the word *Rational* on one side of the barricade, and leave only the word *Academic* to be put on the other. Instead of Rational say *Functional* . . . .

Most critics of the Thirties were perfectly happy to make this substitution of words, but not of ideas, and *Functional* has, almost without exception been interpreted in the limited sense that Le Corbusier attributed to *Rational*, a tendency which culminated in the revival of a nineteenth-century determinism such as both Le Corbusier and Gropius had rejected, summed up in Louis Sullivan's empty jingle

> Form follows function

Functionalism, as a creed or programme, may have a certain austere nobility, but it is poverty-stricken symbolically. The architecture of the Twenties, though

Reyner Banham, "Conclusion: Functionalism and Technology," pp. 320–30 from *Theory and Design in the First Machine Age*. London: The Architectural Press, 1960.

capable of its own austerity and nobility, was heavily, and designedly, loaded with symbolic meanings that were discarded or ignored by its apologists in the Thirties. Two main reasons emerge for this decision to fight on a narrowed front. Firstly, most of those apologists came from outside the countries – Holland, Germany and France – that had done most to create the new style, and came to it late. They thus failed to participate in those exchanges of ideas, collisions of men and movements, congresses and polemics, in which the main lines of thought and practice were roughed out before 1925, and they were strangers to the local conditions that coloured them. Thus, Sigfried Giedion, Swiss, caught only the tail end of this process in 1923; Sartoris, Italian, missed it almost completely; Lewis Mumford, American, in spite of his sociological perceptiveness, was too remotely placed to have any real sense of the aesthetic issues involved – hence his largely irrelevant tergiversations on the problem of monumentality.

The second reason for deciding to fight on the narrowed front was that there was no longer any choice of whether or not to fight. With the International Style outlawed politically in Germany and Russia, and crippled economically in France, the style and its friends were fighting for a toehold in politically-suspicious Fascist Italy, aesthetically-indifferent England, and depression-stunned America. Under these circumstances it was better to advocate or defend the new architecture on logical and economic grounds than on grounds of aesthetics or symbolisms that might stir nothing but hostility. This may have been good tactics – the point remains arguable – but it was certainly misrepresentation. Emotion had played a much larger part than logic in the creation of the style; inexpensive buildings had been clothed in it, but it was no more an inherently economical style than any other. The true aim of the style had clearly been, to quote Gropius's words about the Bauhaus and its relation to the world of the Machine Age

> ... to invent and create forms symbolising that world.

and it is in respect of such symbolic forms that its historical justification must lie.

How far it had succeeded in its own terms in creating such terms, and in carrying such symbolism, can best be judged by examining two buildings, widely held to be masterpieces, and both designed in 1928. One of them is the German Pavilion at the Barcelona Exhibition of 1929, a work of Mies van der Rohe, so purely symbolic in intention that the concept of Functionalism would need to be stretched to the point of unrecognisability before it could be made to fit it – the more so since it is not easy to formulate in Rational terms precisely what it was intended to symbolise. A loose background, rather than a precise exposition, of the probable intentions can be established from Mies's pronouncements on exhibitions in 1928

> The era of monumental expositions that make money is past. Today we judge an exposition by what it accomplishes in the cultural field.
> Economic, technical and cultural conditions have changed radically. Both technology and industry face entirely new problems. It is very important for our culture and our society, as well as for technology and industry, to find good

solutions. German industry, and indeed European industry as a whole, must understand and solve these specific tasks. The path must lead from quantity towards quality – from the extensive to the intensive.

Along this path industry and technology will join with the forces of thought and culture.

We are in a period of transition – a transition that will change the world.

To explain and help along this transition will be the responsibility of future expositions. . . .

The ambiguities of these statements were resolved in the Pavilion by architectural usages that tapped many sources of symbolism – or, at least sources of architectural prestige. Attention has been drawn to echoes of Wright, of *de Stijl* and *Schinkelschüler* tradition, in the Pavilion, but its full richness is only apparent when these references are rendered precise. All three of these echoes are, in practice, summed up in a mode of occupying space which is strictly Elementarist. Its horizontal planes, which have been likened to Wright, and its scattered vertical surfaces, whose distribution on plan has been referred to van Doesburg, mark out one of Moholy's 'pieces of space' in such a way that a 'full penetration with outer space' is effectively achieved. Further, the distribution of the columns which support the roof slab without assistance from the vertical planes, is completely regular and their spacing suggests the Elementarist concept of space as a measurable continuum, irrespective of the objects it contains. And again, the podium on which the whole structure stands, in which Philip Johnson has found 'a touch of Schinkel', extending on one side a good way beyond the area covered by the roof slab, is also a composition in its own right in plan because of the two pools let into it, and thus resembles the patterned base-boards which form an active part in those Abstract studies of volumetric relations that came from the Ladowski–Lissitzky circle, and, like them, appears to symbolise 'infinite space' as an active component of the whole design.

To this last effect the materials also contribute, since the marble floor of the podium, everywhere visible, or at least appreciable even where covered by carpeting, emphasises the spatial continuity of the complete scheme. But this marble, and the marbling of the walls, has another level of meaning – the feeling of luxury it imparts sustains the idea of transition from quantity to quality of which Mies had spoken, and introduces further paradoxical echoes of both Berlage and Loos. These walls are space-creators, in Berlage's sense and have been 'let alone from floor to cornice' in the manner that Berlage admired in Wright; yet, if it be objected that the sheets of marble or onyx with which they are faced are 'decoration hung on them' such as Berlage disapproved, one could properly counter that Adolf Loos, the enemy of decoration, was prepared to admit large areas of strongly patterned marble as wall-cladding in his interiors.

The continuity of the space is further demonstrated by the transparency of the glass walls that occur in various parts of the scheme, so that a visitor's eye might pass from space to space even where his foot could not. On the other hand the

447

glass was tinted so that its materiality could also be appreciated, in the manner of Artur Korn's *There and not There* paradox. The glass of these walls is carried in chromium glazing bars, and the chromium surface is repeated on the coverings of the cruciform columns. This confrontation of rich modern materials with the rich ancient material of the marble is a manifestation of that tradition of the parity of artistic and anti-artistic materials that runs back through Dadaism and Futurism to the *papiers collés* of the Cubists.

One can also distinguish something faintly Dadaist and even anti-Rationalist in the non-structural parts of the Pavilion. A Mondriaanesque Abstract logical consistency, for instance, would have dictated something other than the natural-istic nude statue by Kolbe that stands in the smaller pool – in this architecture it has something of the incongruity of Duchamp's 'Bottle-rack' in an art exhibition, though it lives happily enough with the marble wall that serves as a background to it. Again, the movable furniture, and particularly the massive steel-framed chairs flout, consciously, one suspects, the canons of economy inherent in that Ration-alism that del Marle had proposed as the motive force behind the employment of steel in chairs; they are rhetorically over-size, immensely heavy, and do not use the material in such a way as to extract maximum performance from it.

It is clear that even if it were profitable to apply strict standards of Rationalist efficiency or Functionalist formal determinism to such a structure, most of what makes it architecturally effective would go unnoted in such an analysis. The same is true of the designs of Le Corbusier, whose work, while often extremely practical, does not yield up its secrets to logical analysis alone. In his *Dom-ino* project for instance, he postulated a structure whose only given elements were the floor slabs and the columns that supported them. The disposition of the walls was thus left at liberty, but some critics have logically extrapolated also that this left Le Corbusier at the mercy of his floor slabs. Nothing could be farther from the truth as far as his completed buildings are concerned which, from the villa at Chaux-de-Fonds on-wards, have their floor slabs treated in a most cavalier fashion, and much of their internal architecture created by breaking through from one storey to another. Conversely, if there is a building in which the horizontal slabs are absolute, it is Mies's Barcelona Pavilion – the pools merely diversify the surface of the podium, nothing breaks through the roof slab and nothing rises above it; the whole building is designed almost in two dimensions, and this is true of much of his later work as well.

In the case of the other building of 1928 which it is proposed to study here, Le Corbusier's house, *Les Heures Claires*, built for the Savoye family at Poissy-sur-Seine and completed in 1930, the vertical penetrations are of crucial importance in the whole design. They are not large in plan but, since they are effected by a pedestrian ramp, whose balustrades make bold diagonals across many internal views, they are very conspicuous to a person using the house. Furthermore, this ramp was designed as the preferred route of what the architect calls the *promenade architecturale* through the various spaces of the building – a concept which appears to lie close to that almost mystical meaning of the word 'axis' that he had employed in *Vers une Architecture*. The floors connected by this ramp are strongly characterised functionally – *on vit par étage* – the ground floor being taken up with services and servants, transport and entrance facilities, and a guest room; the first floor given over to the main living accommodation, virtually a week-end bungalow complete with patio; and the highest floor a roof garden with sun-bathing deck and viewing platform, surrounded by a windscreen wall.

This, of course, is only the functional breakdown; what makes the building architecture by Le Corbusier's standards and enables it to touch the heart, is the way these three floors have been handled visually. The house as a whole is white – *le couleur-type* – and square – one of *les plus belles formes* – set down in a sea of uninterrupted grass – *le terrain idéal* – which the architect has called a Virgilian Landscape. Upon this traditional ground he erected one of the least traditional buildings of his career, rich in the imagery of the Twenties. The ground floor is set back a considerable distance on three sides from the perimeter of the block, and the consequent shadow into which it is plunged was deepened by dark paint and light-absorbent areas of fenestration. When the house is viewed from the grounds, this floor hardly registers visually, and the whole upper part of the house appears to be delicately poised in space, supported only by the row of slender pilotis under the edge of the first floor – precisely that species of material-immaterial illusionism that Oud had prophesied, but that Le Corbusier more often practised.

However, the setting back of the ground floor has further meaning. It leaves room for a motor-car to pass between the wall and the pilotis supporting the floor above; the curve of this wall on the side away from the road was, Le Corbusier claims, dictated by the minimum turning circle of a car. A car, having set down its passengers at the main entrance on the apex of this curve, could pass down the other side of the building, still under the cover of the floor above, and return to the main road along a drive parallel to that on which it had approached the house. This appears to be nothing less than a typically Corbusian 'inversion' of the test-track on the roof of the Matté-Trucco's Fiat factory, tucked under the building instead of laid on top of it, creating a suitably emotive approach to the home of a fully motorised post-Futurist family. Inside this floor, the entrance hall has an irregular plan, but is given a business-like and ship-shape appearance by narrow-paned industrial glazing, by the plain balustrades of the ramp and the spiral staircase leading to the floor above, and by the washbasin, light fittings, etc. which, as in the *Pavillon de l'Esprit Nouveau*, appear to be of industrial or nautical extraction. On the main living floor above, the planning shows less of that *Beaux-Arts* formality that had appeared in the slightly earlier house at Garches, but is composed much as an Abstract painting might have been composed, by jig-sawing together a number of rectangles to fit into a given square plan. The feeling of the arrangement of parts within a pre-determined frame is heightened by the continuous and unvaried window-strip – the ultimate *fenêtre en longueur* – that runs right round this floor, irrespective of the needs of the rooms or open spaces behind it. However, where this strip runs across the wall of the open patio it is unglazed, as is the viewing window in the screen wall of the roof-garden, a fulfilment, however late and unconscious, of Marinetti's demand for villas

449

sited for view and breeze. The screen wall, again, raises painterly echoes: in contrast to the square plan of the main floor; it is composed of irregular curves and short straights, mostly standing well back from perimeter of the block. Not only are these curves, on plan, like the shapes to be found in his *Peintures Puristes*, but their modelling, seen in raking sunlight, has the same delicate and insubstantial air as that of the bottles and glasses in his paintings and the effect of these curved forms, standing on a square slab raised on legs is like nothing so much as a still-life arranged on a table. And set down in this landscape it has the same kind of Dadaist quality as the statue in the Barcelona Pavilion.

Enough has been said to show that no single-valued criterion, such as Functionalism, will ever serve to explain the forms and surfaces of these buildings, and enough should also have been said to suggest the way in which they are rich in the associations and symbolic values current in their time. And enough has also been said to show that they came extraordinarily close to realising the general idea of a Machine Age architecture that was entertained by their designers. Their status as masterpieces rests, as it does with most other masterpieces of architecture, upon the authority and felicity with which they give expression to a view of men in relation to their environment. They are masterpieces of the order of the Sainte Chapelle or the Villa Rotonda, and if one speaks of them in the present, in spite of the fact that one no longer exists and the other is squalidly neglected, it is because in a Machine Age we have the benefit of massive photographic records of both in their pristine magnificence, and can form of them an estimate far more plastically exact than one ever could from, say, the notebooks of Villard d'Honnecourt of the *Quattro Libri* of Palladio.

But because of this undoubted success, we are entitled to enquire, at the very highest level, whether the aims of the International Style were worth entertaining, and whether its estimate of a Machine Age was a viable one. Something like a flat rebuttal of both aims and estimate can be found in the writings of Buckminster Fuller.

> It was apparent that the going design-blindness of the lay level … afforded European designers an opportunity … to develop their preview discernment of the more appealing simplicities of the industrial structures that had inadvertently earned their architectural freedom, not by conscious aesthetical innovation, but through profit-inspired discard of economic irrelevancies. … This surprise discovery, as the European designer well knew, could soon be made universally appealing as a fad, for had they not themselves been so faddishly inspired. The 'International Style' brought to America by the Bauhaus innovators, demonstrated fashion-inoculation without necessity of knowledge of the scientific fundamentals of structural mechanics and chemistry.
>
> The International Style 'simplification' then was but superficial. It peeled off yesterday's exterior embellishment and put on instead formalised novelties of quasi-simplicity, permitted by the same hidden structural elements of modern alloys that had permitted the discarded *Beaux-Arts* garmentation. It was still a European garmentation. The new International Stylist hung 'stark motif walls' of vast super-

meticulous brick assemblage, which had no tensile cohesiveness within its own bonds, but was, in fact, locked within hidden steel frames supported by steel *without visible means of support*. In many such illusory ways did the 'International Style' gain dramatic sensory impingement on society as does a trick man gain the attention of children. ...

... the Bauhaus and International used standard plumbing fixtures and only ventured so far as to persuade manufacturers to modify the surface of the valve handles and spigots, and the colour, size, and arrangements of the tiles. The International Bauhaus never went back of the wall-surface to look at the plumbing ... they never enquired into the overall problem of sanitary fittings themselves. ... In short they only looked at problems of modifications of the surface of end-products, which end-products were inherently sub-functions of a technically obsolete world.

There is much more, in an equally damaging vein, picking on other vulnerable points of the International Style besides the lack of technical training at the Bauhaus, the formalism and illusionism, the failure to grip fundamental problems of building technology, but these are his main points. Though there is clearly a strain of US patriotism running through this hostile appraisal, it is not mere wisdom after the fact, nor is it an Olympian judgement delivered from a point far above the practicalities of building.

As early as 1927, Fuller had advanced, in his Dymaxion House project, a concept of domestic design that might just have been built in the condition of materials technology at the time, and had it been built, would have rendered *Les Heures Claires*, for instance, technically obsolete before design had even begun. The Dymaxion concept was entirely radical, a hexagonal ring of dwelling-space, walled in double skins of plastic in different transparencies according to lighting needs, and hung by wires from the apex of a central duralumin mast which also housed all the mechanical services. The formal qualities of this design are not remarkable, except in combination with the structural and planning methods involved. The structure does not derive from the imposition of a Perretesque or Elementarist aesthetic on a material that has been elevated to the level of a symbol for 'the machine', but is an adaptation of light-metal methods employed in aircraft construction at the time. The planning derives from a liberated attitude to those mechanical services that had precipitated the whole Modern adventure by their invasion of homes and streets before 1914.

Even those like Le Corbusier who had given specific attention to this mechanical revolution in domestic service had been content for the most part to distribute it through the house according to the distribution of its pre-mechanical equivalent. Thus cooking facilities went into the room that would have been called 'kitchen' even without a gas oven, washing machines into a room still conceived as a 'laundry' in the old sense, gramophone into the 'music room', vacuum cleaner to the 'broom cupboard', and so forth. In the Fuller version this equipment is seen as more alike, in being mechanical, than different because of time-honoured functional differentiations, and is therefore packed together in the

451

central core of the house, whence it distributes services – heat, light, music, cleanliness, nourishment, ventilation, to the surrounding living-space.

There is something strikingly, but coincidentally, Futurist about the Dymaxion House. It was to be light, expendable, made of those substitutes for wood, stone and brick of which Sant'Elia had spoken, just as Fuller also shared his aim of harmonising environment and man, and of exploiting every benefit of science and technology. Furthermore, in the idea of a central core distributing services through the surrounding space there is a concept that strikingly echoes Boccioni's field-theory of space, with objects distributing lines of force through their surroundings.

Many more of Fuller's ideas, derived from a first-hand knowledge of building techniques and the investigation of other technologies, reveal a similarly quasi-Futurist bent, and in doing so they indicate something that was being increasingly mislaid in mainstream Modern architecture as the Twenties drew to a close. As was said at the beginning of this book, the theory and aesthetics of the International Style were evolved between Futurism and Academicism, but their perfection was only achieved by drawing away from Futurism and drawing nearer to the Academic tradition, whether derived from Blanc or Guadet, and by justifying this tendency by Rationalist and Determinist theories of a pre-Futurist type. Perfection, such as is seen in the Barcelona Pavilion and *Les Heures Claires*, could only have been achieved in this manner since Futurism, dedicated to the 'constant renovation of our architectonic environment' precludes processes with definite terminations such as a process of perfection must be.

In cutting themselves off from the philosophical aspects of Futurism, though hoping to retain its prestige as Machine Age art, theorists and designers of the waning Twenties cut themselves off not only from their own historical beginnings, but also from their foothold in the world of technology, whose character Fuller defined, and rightly, as an

> ... unhaltable trend to constantly accelerating change

a trend that the Futurists had fully appreciated before him. But the mainstream of the Modern Movement had begun to lose sight of this aspect of technology very early in the Twenties, as can be seen (*a*) from their choice of symbolic forms and symbolic mental processes, and (*b*) their use of the theory of types. The apparent appositeness of the Phileban solids as symbols of mechanistic appropriateness depended in part on an historical coincidence affecting vehicle technology that was fully, though superficially, exploited by Le Corbusier in *Vers une Architecture*, and partly on a mystique of mathematics. In picking on mathematics as a source of technological prestige for their own mental operations, men like Le Corbusier and Mondriaan contrived to pick on the only important part of scientific and technological methodology that was not new, but had been equally current in the pre-machine epoch. In any case, mathematics, like other branches of logic, is only an operational technique, not a creative discipline. The devices that characterised the Machine Age were the products of intuition, experiment or pragmatic knowledge – no one could now design a self-starter without a knowledge of the mathematics of electricity, but it was Charles F. Kettering, not mathematics, that invented the first electric-starter on the basis of a sound grasp of mechanical methods.

In picking on the Phileban solids and mathematics, the creators of the International Style took a convenient short-cut to creating an *ad hoc* language of symbolic forms, but it was a language that could only communicate under the special conditions of the Twenties, when automobiles were visibly comparable to the Parthenon, when aircraft structure really did resemble Elementarist space cages, when ships' superstructures really did appear to follow *Beaux-Arts* rules of symmetry, and the additive method of design pursued in many branches of machine technology was surprisingly like Guadet's elementary composition. However, certain events of the early Thirties made it clear that the apparent symbolic relevance of these forms and methods was purely a contrivance, not an organic growth from principles common to both technology and architecture, and, as it happened, a number of vehicles designed in the USA, Germany and Britain revealed the weakness of the architects' position.

As soon as performance made it necessary to pack the components of a vehicle into a compact streamlined shell, the visual link between the International Style and technology was broken. The Burney 'Streamliners' in Britain, and the racing cars designed in Germany in 1933 for the 1934 Grand Prix Formula, the Heinkel He 70 research aircraft, and the Boeing 247D transport aircraft in the US all belong to a radically altered world to that of their equivalents a decade earlier. Though there was no particular reason why architecture should take note of these developments in another field or necessarily transform itself in step with vehicle technology, one might have expected an art that appeared so emotionally entangled with technology to show some signs of this upheaval.

What, in fact, happened is of vital importance to the International Style's claims to be a Machine Age architecture. In the same early years of the Thirties, Walter Gropius designed a series of closely related bodies for Adler cars. They were handsomely conceived structures, with much ingenuity in their furnishing, including such features as reclining seats, but they show no awareness of the revolution in vehicle form that was proceeding at the time; they are still elementary compositions, and apart from mechanical improvements in the chassis, engine and running gear, for which Gropius was not responsible, they are no advance on the bodies that had been illustrated in *Vers une Architecture*. On the other hand, we find Fuller justifying his right to speak slightingly of the International Style by designing, in 1933, a vehicle fully as advanced as the Burney cars, and revealing thereby a grasp of the mind of technology which the International Style had failed to acquire.

This failure was followed promptly, though not consequentially, by the emergence of another kind of vehicle designed to take advantage of yet another aspect of technology that the masters of the International Style seem to have failed to grasp. This was the first genuinely stylist-designed car, Harley Earle's Lasalle of 1934, whose aesthetics were conceived in terms of mass-production for a changing public market, not of an unchangeable type or norm. There is a curious point here: Le Corbusier had made great play with the idea of a fairly high rate of scrapping, but he seems not to have visualised it as part of a continuous process inherent in the technological approach, bound to continue as long as technology continues, but merely as stages in the evolution of a final type or norm, whose perfection, he, Pierre Urbain, Paul Valéry, Piet Mondriaan and many others saw as an event of the immediate future, or even the immediate past. In practice, a high rate of scrapping of our movable equipment seems to imply nothing of the sort, but rather a constant renewal of the environment, an unhaltable trend to constantly accelerating change. In opting for stabilised types or norms, architects opted for the pauses when the normal processes of technology were interrupted, those processes of change and renovation that, as far as we can see, can only be halted by abandoning technology as we know it today, and bringing both research and mass-production to a stop.

Whether or not the enforcement of norms and types by such a conscious manoeuvre would be good for the human race, is a problem that does not concern the present study. Nor was it a question that was entertained by the theorists and designers of the First Machine Age. They were for allowing technology to run its course, and believed that they understood where it was going, even without having bothered to acquaint themselves with it very closely. In the upshot, a historian must find that they produced a Machine Age architecture only in the sense that its monuments were built in a Machine Age, and expressed an attitude to machinery – in the sense that one might stand on French soil and discuss French politics, and still be speaking English. It may well be that what we have hitherto understood as architecture, and what we are beginning to understand of technology are incompatible disciplines. The architect who proposes to run with technology knows now that he will be in fast company, and that, in order to keep up, he may have to emulate the Futurists and discard his whole cultural load, including the professional garments by which he is recognised as an architect. If, on the other hand, he decides not to do this, he may find that a technological culture has decided to go on without him. It is a choice that the masters of the Twenties failed to observe until they had made it by accident, but it is the kind of accident that architecture may not survive a second time – we may believe that the architects of the First Machine Age were wrong, but we in the Second Machine Age have no reason yet to be superior about them.

60

The Death of Modern Architecture

Charles Jencks

Happily, we can date the death of modern architecture to a precise moment in time. Unlike the legal death of a person, which is becoming a complex affair of brain waves versus heartbeats, modern architecture went out with a bang. That many people didn't notice, and no one was seen to mourn, does not make the sudden extinction any less of a fact, and that many designers are still trying to administer the kiss of life does not mean that it has been miraculously resurrected. No, it expired finally and completely in 1972, after having been flogged to death remorselessly for ten years by critics such as Jane Jacobs; and the fact that many so-called modern architects still go around practising a trade as if it were alive can be taken as one of the great curiosities of our age. [...]

Modern Architecture died in St Louis, Missouri on July 15, 1972 at 3.32 p.m. (or thereabouts) when the infamous Pruitt-Igoe scheme, or rather several of its slab blocks, were given the final *coup de grâce* by dynamite (figure 60.1). Previously it had been vandalised, mutilated and defaced by its black inhabitants, and although millions of dollars were pumped back, trying to keep it alive (fixing the broken elevators, repairing smashed windows, repainting), it was finally put out of its misery. Boom, boom, boom.

Without doubt, the ruins should be kept, the remains should have a preservation order slapped on them, so that we keep a live memory of this failure in planning and architecture (figure 60.2). [...]

Pruitt-Igoe was constructed according to the most progressive ideals of CIAM (the Congress of International Modern Architects) and it won an award from the American Institute of Architects when it was designed in 1951. It consisted of elegant slab blocks fourteen storeys high with rational 'streets in the air' (which were safe from cars, but as it turned out, not safe from crime); 'sun, space and greenery', which Le Corbusier called the 'three essential joys of urbanism'

Charles Jencks, "The Death of Modern Architecture," pp. 9–10, 12–17, 19, 37, 181 (note 1) from *The Language of Post-Modern Architecture*, 5th edition. London: Academy Editions, 1977.

Figure 60.1   Minoru Yamasaki, *Pruitt-Igoe Housing*, St Louis, 1952–55
Source: Jencks 1977
Several slab blocks of this scheme were blown up in 1972 after they were continuously
vandalised. The crime rate was higher than in other developments, and Oscar Newman
attributed this, in his book *Defensible Space*, to the long corridors, anonymity, and lack of
controlled semi-private space. Another factor: it was designed in a purist language at
variance with the architectural codes of the inhabitants.

(instead of conventional streets, gardens and semi-private space, which he banished). It had a separation of pedestrian and vehicular traffic, the provision of play
space, and local amenities such as laundries, crèches and gossip centres – all
rational substitutes for traditional patterns. Moreover, its Purist style, its clean,
salubrious hospital metaphor, was meant to instil, by good example, corresponding virtues in the inhabitants. Good form was to lead to good content, or at least
good conduct; the intelligent planning of abstract space was to promote healthy
behaviour. Alas, such simplistic ideas, taken over from philosophic doctrines of
Rationalism, Behaviourism and Pragmatism, proved as irrational as the philosophies themselves. Modern Architecture, as the son of the Enlightenment, was an
heir to its congenital naivities, naivities too great and awe-inspiring to warrant
refutation in a book on mere building. I will concentrate here, in this first part,
on the demise of a very small branch of a big bad tree; but to be fair it should
be pointed out that modern architecture is the offshoot of modern painting,
the modern movements in all the arts. Like rational schooling, rational health
and rational design of women's bloomers, it has the faults of an age trying to

Figure 60.2 Pruitt-Igoe as ruin
Source: Jencks 1977
Like the Berlin Wall and the collapse of the high-rise block, Ronan Point, in England (1968), this ruin has become a great architectural symbol. It should be preserved as a warning. Actually, after continued hostilities and disagreements, some blacks have managed to form a community in parts of the remaining habitable blocks – another symbol, in its way, that events and ideology, as well as architecture, determine the success of the environment.

reinvent itself totally on rational grounds. These shortcomings are now well known, thanks to the writings of Ivan Illich, Jacques Ellul, E. F. Schumacher, Michael Oakeshott and Hannah Arendt, and the overall misconceptions of Rationalism will not be dwelt upon. They are assumed for my purposes. Rather than a deep extended attack on modern architecture, showing how its ills relate very closely to the prevailing philosophies of the modern age, I will attempt a caricature, a polemic. The virtue of this genre (as well as its vice) is its license to cut through the large generalities with a certain abandon and enjoyment, overlooking all the exceptions and subtleties of the argument. Caricature is of course not the whole truth. [...]

Crisis in Architecture

In 1974 Malcolm MacEwen wrote a book of the above title which summarised the English view of what was wrong with the Modern Movement (capitalised, like all world religions), and what we should do about it. His summary was masterful, but his prescriptions were wildly off the mark: the remedy was to overhaul a tiny

457

institutional body, the Royal Institute of British Architects, by changing a style here and a heart there – as if these sorts of things would make the *multiple causes* of the crisis go away. Well, let me make use of his effective analysis, not his solution, taking as a typical grotesque of modern architecture one building type: modern hotels.

The new Penta Hotel in London has 914 bedrooms, which is almost nine times the average large hotel of fifty years ago, and it is 'themed' (a word of decorators) in the International Style and a mode which could be called Vassarely-Airport-Lounge-Moderne. There are about twenty of these leviathans near each other, on the way to the London Airport (it is known in the trade as 'Hotellandia'), and they create a disruption in scale and city life which amounts to the occupation of an invading army – a role tourists tend to fulfil.

These newly formed battalions with their noble-phoney names include The Churchill (500 bedrooms, named after Sir Winston and themed in the Pompeian-Palladian Style by way of Robert Adam); the Imperial Hotel (720 bedrooms, International outside, fibreglass Julius Caesar inside); and the Park Tower (300 bedrooms, themed in Corn-on-the-Cob and various sunburst motifs inside). A recurring aspect of these hotels, built between 1969 and 1973, is that they provide very modern services, such as air-conditioning, themed in old-world styles which vary from Rococco, Gothic, Second Empire, to a combination of all three styles together. The formula of ancient style and modern plumbing has proved inexorably successful in our consumer society, and this Ersatz has been the major commercial challenge to classical modern architecture. But in one important way, in terms of architectural *production*, Ersatz and modern architecture contribute equally to alienation and what MacEwen calls 'the crisis'. I have tried to untangle the different causes of this situation, at least eleven in number, and show how they operate in the two modern modes of architectural production (listed in the two right hand columns of table 60.1).

For contrast, the first column on the left refers to the old system of *private* architectural production (operating largely before World War One) where an architect knew his client personally, probably shared his values and aesthetic code. An extreme example of this is Lord Burlington's Chiswick Villa, an unusual situation where the architect was the builder (or contractor), client and user all at once. Hence there was no disparity between his rather elite and esoteric code (a spare, intellectual version of the Palladian language) and his way of life. [...]

Other factors which influenced this type of production in the past include the *mini-capitalist economy* where money was restricted. The architect or speculative builder designed relatively *small* parts of the city at one go; he worked *slowly,* responding to well-established needs, and he was *accountable* to the client, who was invariably the user of the building as well. All these factors, and more that are shown in table 60.1, combined to produce an architecture understood by the client and in a language shared by others.

The second and third columns refer to the way most architecture is produced today and show why it is out of scale with historic cities, and alienating to both

Table 60.1   Crisis in architecture

		SYSTEM 1 — PRIVATE private client is architect user		SYSTEM 2 — PUBLIC private client and architect users differ		SYSTEM 3 — DEVELOPER developer client and architect users differ	
1	ECONOMIC SPHERE	**Mini-Capitalist** (restricted money)		**Welfare-State Capitalist** (lacks money)		**Monopoly-Capitalist** (has money)	
2	MOTIVATION	aesthetic ideological	inhabit use	solve problem	user's housing	make money	make money to use
3	RECENT IDEOLOGY	Too various to list		progress, efficiency, large scale, anti-history, Brutalism, etc.		same as System 2 plus pragmatic	
4	RELATION TO PLACE	local architect	client user in place	remote architects	users move to place	remote and changing draughtsmen	absent clients
5	CLIENT'S RELATION TO ARCHITECT	**Expert Friend** same partners small team		**Anonymous Doctor** changing designers large team		**Hired Servant** doesn't know designers or users	
6	SIZE OF PROJECTS	"small"		"some large"		"too big"	
7	SIZE / TYPE OF ARCHITECT'S OFFICE	small partnership		large centralised		large centralised	
8	METHOD OF DESIGN	slow, responsive, innovative, expensive		impersonal, anonymous, conservative, low cost		quick, cheap, and proven formulae	
9	ACCOUNTABILITY	to client-user		to local council and bureaucracy		to stockholders, developers and board	
10	TYPES OF BUILDING	houses, museums, universities, etc.		housing and infrastructure		shopping centres, hotels, offices, factories, etc.	
11	STYLE	**multiple**		**impersonal** safe, contemporary, vandal-proofed		**pragmatic** cliché and bombastic	

A diagram of three systems of architectural production. The left column shows the implications of the old, private system of production, while the right columns show the two modern systems. Critics of modern architecture have emphasised several of these eleven causes of the crisis, but clearly the causes are multiple and work as a *system* tied into the economic sphere. The question is – how many variables must be changed for the system to change?

architects and society. First, in the economic sphere, it's either produced for a public welfare agency which lacks the money necessary to carry out the socialist intentions of the architects, or it is funded by a capitalist agency whose monopoly creates gigantic investments and correspondingly gigantic buildings. For instance, the Penta Hotel is owned by the European Hotel Corporation, a consortium of five airlines and five international banks. These ten corporations together create a monolith which by financial definition must appeal to mass taste, at a middle-class level. There is nothing inherently inferior about this taste culture; it's rather the economic imperatives determining the size and predictability of the result which have coerced the architecture into becoming so relentlessly pretentious and uptight.

459

Secondly, in this type of production, the architect's motivation is either to solve a problem, or in the case of the developer's architect, to make money. Why the latter motivation doesn't produce effective architecture as it did in the past remains a mystery, (unless it is connected with the compelling pressures of predictable taste). But it is quite clear why 'problems' don't produce architecture. They produce instead 'rational' solutions to oversimplified questions in a chaste style.

Yet the greatest cause of alienation is the *size* of today's projects: the hotels, garages, shopping centres and housing estates which are 'too big' – like the architectural offices which produce them. How big is too big? Obviously there is no easy answer to this, and we await the detailed study of different building types. But the equation can be formulated in general, and it might be called 'the Ivan Illich Law of Diminishing Architecture'. [...] It could be stated as follows: 'for any building type there is an upper limit to the number of people who can be served before the quality of the environment falls'. The service of the large London hotels has fallen because of staff shortages and absenteeism, and the quality of tourism has declined because the tourists are treated as so many cattle to be shunted from one ambience to the next in a smooth and continuous flow. Programmed, continuously-rolling pleasure, the shunting of people into queues, pens and moving lines, a process which was perfected by Walt Disney, has now been applied to all areas of mass tourism, resulting in the controlled bland experience. What started as a search for adventure has ended in total predictability. Excessive growth and rationalism have contradicted the very goals that the institution of tourism and planned travel was set up to deliver.

The same is true of large architectural offices. Here design suffers because no one has control over the whole job from beginning to end, and because the building has to be produced quickly and efficiently according to proven formulae (the rationalisation of taste into clichés based on statistical averages of style and theme). Furthermore, with large buildings such as the Penta, the architecture has to be produced for a client whom no one in the office knows, (that is, the ten corporations), and who is, in any case, not the user of the building. In short, buildings today are nasty, brutal and too big because they are produced for profit by absentee developers, for absentee landlords for absent users whose taste is assumed as clichéd.

There is, then, not one cause of the crisis in architecture, but a *system of causes*; and clearly to change just the style or ideology of the architects, as is proposed by many critics, isn't going to change the whole situation. No amount of disaffection for the International Style or Brutalism, for high-rise, bureaucracy, capitalism, gigantism, or whatever else is the latest scapegoat is going to change things suddenly and produce a humane environment. It would seem we have to change the whole system of architectural production at once, all eleven causes together. And yet perhaps such a radical move is not necessary. Perhaps some causes are redundant, some are more important than others, and we only have to change a combination of a few. For instance, if large architectural offices were divided into small teams, given a certain financial and design control, and put in close relation to the ultimate users of the building, this might be enough. Who knows? Experiments must be tried with different variables. All that can be said at this point is that the situation has systemic causes which have to be varied as a structure if deep changes are to be made. I will pursue only two causes of the crisis: the way the modern movement has impoverished architectural language on the level of form; and has itself suffered an impoverishment on the level of content, the social goals for which it actually built.

Univalent Form

For the general aspect of an architecture created around one (or a few) simplified values, I will use the term **univalence**. No doubt in terms of expression the architecture of Mies van der Rohe and his followers is the most univalent formal system we have, because it makes use of few materials and a single, right-angled geometry. Characteristically this reduced style was justified as rational (when it was uneconomic), and universal (when it fitted only a few functions). The glass-and-steel-box has become the single most used form in modern architecture, and it signifies throughout the world 'office building'.

Yet in the hands of Mies and his disciples this impoverished system has become fetishised to the point where it overwhelms all other concerns. [. . .] Are I-beams and plate glass appropriate to housing? That is a question Mies would dismiss as irrelevant. The whole question of appropriateness, 'decorum', which every architect from Vitruvius to Lutyens debated, is now rendered obsolete by Mies' universal grammar and universal contempt for place and function. (He considered function as ephemeral, or so provisional as to be unimportant.)

His first, classic use of the curtain wall was on housing, not for an office – and obviously not for functional or communicational reasons, but because he was obsessed by perfecting certain formal problems. In this case, Mies concentrated on the proportion of the I-beam to panel, set-back, glass area, supporting columns and articulating lines. He kept full-scale details of these members close to his draughting board so he'd never lose sight of his loved ones.

A larger question thus didn't arise: what if housing looked like offices, or what if the two functions were indistinguishable? Clearly the net result would be to diminish and compromise both functions by equating them: working and living would become interchangeable on the most banal, literal level, and unarticulated on a higher, metaphorical plane. The psychic overtones to these two different activities would remain unexplored, accidental, truncated.

Another masterpiece of the modern movement, the Chicago Civic Center, designed by a follower of Mies, also shows these confusions in communication. The long horizontal spans and dark corten steel express 'office building', 'power', 'purity', and the variations in surface express 'mechanical equipment'; but these primitive (and occasionally mistaken) meanings don't take us very far. On the

461

most literal level the building does not communicate its important civic function; nor, more importantly, the social and psychological meanings of this very significant building task (a meeting place for the citizens of Chicago).

How could an architect justify such inarticulate building? The answer lies in terms of an ideology which celebrates process, which symbolises only the changes in technology and building material. The modern movement fetishised the means of production, and Mies, in one of those rare, cryptic aphorisms that is too hilarious, or rather delirious, to let pass, gave expression to this fetish.

> I see in industrialization the central problem of building in our time. If we succeed in carrying out this industrialization, the social, economic, technical, and also artistic problems will be readily solved. (1924)[1]

What about the theological and gastronomic 'problems'? The bizarre confusion to which this can lead is shown by Mies himself in the Illinois Institute of Technology campus in Chicago, a large enough collection of varied functions for us to regard it as a microcosm of his surrealist world.

Basically, he has used his universal grammar of steel I-beams along with an infill of beige brick and glass to speak about all the important functions: housing, assembly, classrooms, student union, shops, chapel, and so forth. If we look at a series of these buildings in turn we can see how confusing his language is, both literally and metaphorically.

A characteristic rectangular shape might be deciphered as a teaching block where students churn out one similar idea after another on an assembly line – because the factory metaphor suggests this interpretation. The only recognisable sign in the building, the lattice-work disc at the top, suggests that the students are budding astrophysicists; but of course Mies cannot claim credit for this bit of literalism. Someone else added it, destroying the purity of his fundamental utterance. What he can claim credit for, and what has exercised great architectural debate, (a debate between two English deans, Sir Leslie Martin and Lord Llewe-lyn-Davies), is his solving of the *problem* of the corner. These two schoolmen disputed, with medieval precision and inconsequentiality, whether the corner symbolised 'endlessness', or 'closedness' like a Renaissance pilaster. The fact that it could symbolise both or neither, depending on the code of the viewer, or the fact that larger questions of factory symbolism and semantic confusion were at stake – such questions were never raised.

Not so far away from this disputatious corner is another architectural conundrum, designed in Mies' universal language of confusion. Here we can see all sorts of conventional cues which give the game away: a rectangular form of cathedral, a central nave structure with two side aisles expressed in the eastern

---

[1] See Mies van der Rohe, 'Industrialized Building', originally printed in the magazine, G. Berlin, 1924, and reprinted in Ulrich Conrad's *Programmes and Manifestos on 20th-Century Architecture*, London, 1970, p.81.

front. The religious nature of this building is heightened by a regular bay system of piers; it's true there are no pointed arches, but there are clerestory windows on both aisle and nave elevations. Finally, to confirm our reading that this *is* the campus cathedral, we see the brick campanile, the bell tower that dominates the basilica.

In fact, this is the boiler house, a solecism of such stunning wit that it can't be truly appreciated until we see the actual chapel, which looks like a boiler house. This is an unassuming box in industrial materials, sandwiched balefully between dormitory slabs with a searchlight attached – in short, signs which confirm a reading of prosaic utility.

Finally, we come to the most important position on campus, the central area, where there is a temple constructed in a homogeneous material that distinguishes it from the other factories. This temple is raised on a plinth, it has a magnificent colonnade of major and minor orders, and a grandiose stairway of white marble planes miraculously hovering in space, as if the local god has ultimately worked his magic. It must be the President's house, or at very least, the Administration Centre. Actually it's where the architects work – what else could it be?

So we see the factory is a classroom, the cathedral is a boiler house, the boiler house is a chapel, and the President's temple is the School of Architecture. Thus Mies is saying that the boiler house is more important than the chapel, and that architects rule, as pagan gods, over the lot. Of course Mies didn't intend these propositions, but his commitment to reductive formal values inadvertently betrays them.

[…]

'The heroism of everyday life', that notion shared by Picasso, Léger and Le Corbusier in the twenties, was a philosophy which tried to place banal objects on a pedestal formerly reserved for special symbols of veneration. The fountain pen, the filing cabinet, the steel girder and the typewriter were the new icons. Mayakovsky and the Russian Constructivists took art into the streets and even performed one grand symphony of sirens and steam whistles, while waving coloured flags on top of factory roofs. The hope of these artists and architects was to reform society on a new class and functional basis: substitute power stations for cathedrals, technocrats for aristocrats. A new, heroic, democratic society would emerge, led by a powerful race of pagan supermen, the avant-garde, the technicians and captains of industry, the enlightened scientists and teams of experts. What a dream!

Indeed, the managerial revolution did occur, and socialist revolutions happened in a few countries; but the dream was taken over by Madison Avenue (and its equivalents), and the 'heroic object of everyday use' became the 'new, revolutionary detergent'. Societies kept on worshipping at their old altars, with diminishing faith, and tried to incorporate the new values at the same time. The result? Ersatz culture, a caricature of the past and future at once, a surreal fantasy

463

dreamed up neither by the avant-garde, nor the traditionalists, and abhorrent to both of them.

With the triumph of consumer society in the West and bureaucratic State Capitalism in the East, our unfortunate modern architect was left without much uplifting social content to symbolise. If architecture has to concentrate its efforts on symbolising a way of life and the public realm, then it's in a bit of a fix when these things lose their credibility. There's nothing much the architect can do about this except protest as a citizen, and design dissenting buildings that express the complex situation. He can communicate the values which are missing and ironically criticise the ones he dislikes. But to do that he must make use of the language of the local culture, otherwise his message falls on deaf ears, or is - distorted to fit this local language.

61

Towards a Critical Regionalism: Six Points for an Architecture of Resistance

Kenneth Frampton

The phenomenon of universalization, while being an advancement of mankind, at the same time constitutes a sort of subtle destruction, not only of traditional cultures, which might not be an irreparable wrong, but also of what I shall call for the time being the creative nucleus of great cultures, that nucleus on the basis of which we interpret life, what I shall call in advance the ethical and mythical nucleus of mankind. The conflict springs up from there. We have the feeling that this single world civilization at the same time exerts a sort of attrition or wearing away at the expense of the cultural resources which have made the great civilizations of the past. This threat is expressed, among other disturbing effects, by the spreading before our eyes of a mediocre civilization which is the absurd counterpart of what I was just calling elementary culture. Everywhere throughout the world, one finds the same bad movie, the same slot machines, the same plastic or aluminum atrocities, the same twisting of language by propaganda, etc. It seems as if mankind, by approaching en masse a basic consumer culture, were also stopped en masse at a subcultural level. Thus we come to the crucial problem confronting nations just rising from underdevelopment. In order to get on to the road toward modernization, is it necessary to jettison the old cultural past which has been the raison d'être *of a nation? . . . Whence the paradox: on the one hand, it has to root itself in the soil of its past, forge a national spirit, and unfurl this spiritual and cultural revindication before the colonialist's personality. But in order to take part in modern civilization, it is*

Kenneth Frampton, "Towards a Critical Regionalism: Six Points for an Architecture of Resistance," pp. 16–30 from Hal Foster (ed.), *Postmodern Culture* [first published as *The Anti-Aesthetic*]. Washington: Bay Press, 1983.

necessary at the same time to take part in scientific, technical, and political rationality, something which very often requires the pure and simple abandon of a whole cultural past. It is a fact: every culture cannot sustain and absorb the shock of modern civilization. There is the paradox: how to become modern and to return to sources; how to revive an old, dormant civilization and take part in universal civilization.[1]

– Paul Ricoeur, *History and Truth*

1. Culture and Civilization

Modern building is now so universally conditioned by optimized technology that the possibility of creating significant urban form has become extremely limited. The restrictions jointly imposed by automotive distribution and the volatile play of land speculation serve to limit the scope of urban design to such a degree that any intervention tends to be reduced either to the manipulation of elements predetermined by the imperatives of production, or to a kind of superficial masking which modern development requires for the facilitation of marketing and the maintenance of social control. Today the practice of architecture seems to be increasingly polarized between, on the one hand, a so-called "high-tech" approach predicated exclusively upon production and, on the other, the provision of a "compensatory facade" to cover up the harsh realities of this universal system.[2]

Twenty years ago the dialectical interplay between civilization and culture still afforded the possibility of maintaining some general control over the shape and significance of the urban fabric. The last two decades, however, have radically transformed the metropolitan centers of the developed world. What were still essentially 19th-century city fabrics in the early 1960s have since become progressively overlaid by the two symbiotic instruments of Megalopolitan development – the freestanding high-rise and the serpentine freeway. The former has finally come into its own as the prime device for realizing the increased land value brought into being by the latter. The typical downtown which, up to twenty years ago, still presented a mixture of residential stock with tertiary and secondary industry has now become little more than a *burolandschaft* city-scape: the victory of universal civilization over locally inflected culture. The predicament posed by Ricoeur – namely, "how to become modern and to return to sources"[3] – now

---

[1] Paul Ricoeur, "Universal Civilization and National Cultures" (1961), *History and Truth*, trans. Chas. A. Kelbley (Evanston: Northwestern University Press, 1965), pp. 276–7.

[2] That these are but two sides of the same coin has perhaps been most dramatically demonstrated in the Portland City Annex completed in Portland, Oregon in 1982 to the designs of Michael Graves. The constructional fabric of this building bears no relation whatsoever to the "representative" scenography that is applied to the building both inside and out.

[3] Ricoeur, p. 277.

seems to be circumvented by the apocalyptic thrust of modernization, while the ground in which the mytho-ethical nucleus of a society might take root has become eroded by the rapacity of development.[4]

Ever since the beginning of the Enlightenment, *civilization* has been primarily concerned with instrumental reason, while *culture* has addressed itself to the specifics of expression – to the realization of the being and the evolution of its *collective* psycho-social reality. Today civilization tends to be increasingly embroiled in a never-ending chain of "means and ends" wherein, according to Hannah Arendt, "The 'in order to' has become the content of the 'for the sake of;' utility established as meaning generates meaninglessness."[5]

2. The Rise and Fall of the Avant-Garde

The emergence of the avant-garde is inseparable from the modernization of both society and architecture. Over the past century-and-a-half avant-garde culture has assumed different roles, at times facilitating the process of modernization and thereby acting, in part, as a progressive, liberative form, at times being virulently opposed to the positivism of bourgeois culture. By and large, avant-garde architecture has played a positive role with regard to the progressive trajectory of the Enlightenment. Exemplary of this is the role played by Neoclassicism: from the mid-18th century onwards it serves as both a symbol of and an instrument for the propagation of universal civilization. The mid-19th century, however, saw the historical avant-garde assume an adversary stance towards both industrial process and Neoclassical form. This is the first concerted reaction on the part of "tradition" to the process of modernization as the Gothic Revival and the Arts-and-Crafts movements take up a categorically negative attitude towards both utilitarianism and the division of labor. Despite this critique, modernization continues unabated, and throughout the last half of the 19th century bourgeois art distances itself progressively from the harsh realities of colonialism and paleo-technological exploitation. Thus at the end of the century the avant-gardist Art

---

[4] Fernand Braudel informs us that the term "culture" hardly existed before the beginning of the 19th century when, as far as Anglo-Saxon letters are concerned, it already finds itself opposed to "civilization" in the writings of Samuel Taylor Coleridge – above all, in Coleridge's *On the Constitution of Church and State* of 1830. The noun "civilization" has a somewhat longer history, first appearing in 1766, although its verb and participle forms date to the 16th and 17th centuries. The use that Ricoeur makes of the opposition between these two terms relates to the work of 20th-century German thinkers and writers such as Osvald Spengler, Ferdinand Tönnies, Alfred Weber and Thomas Mann.

[5] Hannah Arendt, *The Human Condition* (Chicago: University of Chicago Press, 1958), p. 154.

Nouveau takes refuge in the compensatory thesis of "art for art's sake," retreating to nostalgic or phantasmagoric dream-worlds inspired by the cathartic hermeticism of Wagner's music-drama.

The progressive avant-garde emerges in full force, however, soon after the turn of the century with the advent of Futurism. This unequivocal critique of the *ancien régime* gives rise to the primary positive cultural formations of the 1920s: to Purism, Neoplasticism and Constructivism. These movements are the last occasion on which radical avant-gardism is able to identify itself wholeheartedly with the process of modernization. In the immediate aftermath of World War I – "the war to end all wars" – the triumphs of science, medicine and industry seemed to confirm the liberative promise of the modern project. In the 1930s, however, the prevailing backwardness and chronic insecurity of the newly urbanized masses, the upheavals caused by war, revolution and economic depression, followed by a sudden and crucial need for psycho-social stability in the face of global political and economic crises, all induce a state of affairs in which the interests of both monopoly and state capitalism are, for the first time in modern history, divorced from the liberative drives of cultural modernization. Universal civilization and world culture cannot be drawn upon to sustain "the myth of the State," and one reaction-formation succeeds another as the historical avant-garde founders on the rocks of the Spanish Civil War.

Not least among these reactions is the reassertion of Neo-Kantian aesthetics as a substitute for the culturally liberative modern project. Confused by the political and cultural politics of Stalinism, former left-wing protagonists of socio-cultural modernization now recommend a strategic withdrawal from the project of totally transforming the existing reality. This renunciation is predicated on the belief that as long as the struggle between socialism and capitalism persists (with the manipulative mass-culture politics that this conflict necessarily entails), the modern world cannot continue to entertain the prospect of evolving a marginal, liberative, avant-gardist culture which would break (or speak of the break) with the history of bourgeois repression. Close to *l'art pour l'art*, this position was first advanced as a "holding pattern" in Clement Greenberg's "Avant-Garde and Kitsch" of 1939; this essay concludes somewhat ambiguously with the words: "Today we look to socialism *simply* for the preservation of whatever living culture we have right now."[6] Greenberg reformulated this position in specifically formalist terms in his essay "Modernist Painting" of 1965, wherein he wrote:

> Having been denied by the Enlightenment of all tasks they could take seriously, they [the arts] looked as though they were going to be assimilated to entertainment pure and simple, and entertainment looked as though it was going to be assimilated, like religion, to therapy. The arts could save themselves from this leveling down only by

[6] Clement Greenberg, "Avant-Garde and Kitsch," in Gillo Dorfles, ed., *Kitsch* (New York: Universe Books, 1969), p. 126.

demonstrating that the kind of experience they provided was valuable in its own right and not to be obtained from any other kind of activity.[7]

Despite this defensive intellectual stance, the arts have nonetheless continued to gravitate, if not towards entertainment, then certainly towards commodity and – in the case of that which Charles Jencks has since classified as Post-Modern Architecture[8] – towards pure technique or pure scenography. In the latter case, the so-called postmodern architects are merely feeding the media-society with gratuitous, quietistic images rather than proffering, as they claim, a creative *rappel à l'ordre* after the supposedly proven bankruptcy of the liberative modern project. In this regard, as Andreas Huyssens has written, "The American postmodernist avant-garde, therefore, is not only the end game of avant-gardism. It also represents the fragmentation and decline of critical adversary culture."[9]

Nevertheless, it is true that modernization can no longer be simplistically identified as liberative *in se*, in part because of the domination of mass culture by the media-industry (above all television which, as Jerry Mander reminds us, expanded its persuasive power a thousandfold between 1945 and 1975[10]) and in part because the trajectory of modernization has brought us to the threshold of nuclear war and the annihilation of the entire species. So too, avant-gardism can no longer be sustained as a liberative moment, in part because its initial utopian promise has been overrun by the internal rationality of instrumental reason. This "closure" was perhaps best formulated by Herbert Marcuse when he wrote:

> The technological *apriori* is a political *apriori* inasmuch as the transformation of nature involves that of man, and inasmuch as the "man-made creations" issue from and re-enter the societal ensemble. One may still insist that the machinery of the technological universe is "as such" indifferent towards political ends – it can revolutionize or retard society. ... However, when technics becomes the universal form of material production, it circumscribes an entire culture, it projects a historical totality – a "world."[11]

3. Critical Regionalism and World Culture

Architecture can only be sustained today as a critical practice if it assumes an *arrière-garde* position, that is to say, one which distances itself equally from the Enlightenment myth of progress and from a reactionary, unrealistic impulse to

---

[7] Greenberg, "Modernist Painting," in Gregory Battcock, ed., *The New Art* (New York: Dutton, 1966), pp. 101–2.

[8] See Charles Jencks, *The Language of Post-Modern Architecture* (New York: Rizzoli, 1977).

[9] Andreas Huyssens, "The Search for Tradition: Avant-Garde and Postmodernism in the 1970s," *New German Critique*, 22 (Winter 1981), p. 34.

[10] Jerry Mander, *Four Arguments for the Elimination of Television* (New York: Morrow Quill, 1978), p. 134.

[11] Herbert Marcuse, *One-Dimensional Man* (Boston: Beacon Press, 1964), p. 156.

return to the architectonic forms of the preindustrial past. A critical arrière-garde has to remove itself from both the optimization of advanced technology and the ever-present tendency to regress into nostalgic historicism or the glibly decorative. It is my contention that only an arrière-garde has the capacity to cultivate a resistant, identity-giving culture while at the same time having discreet recourse to universal technique.

It is necessary to qualify the term arrière-garde so as to diminish its critical scope from such conservative policies as Populism or sentimental Regionalism with which it has often been associated. In order to ground arrière-gardism in a rooted yet critical strategy, it is helpful to appropriate the term Critical Regionalism as coined by Alex Tzonis and Liliane Lefaivre in "The Grid and the Pathway" (1981); in this essay they caution against the ambiguity of regional reformism, as this has become occasionally manifest since the last quarter of the 19th century:

> Regionalism has dominated architecture in almost all countries at some time during the past two centuries and a half. By way of general definition we can say that it upholds the individual and local architectonic features against more universal and abstract ones. In addition, however, regionalism bears the hallmark of ambiguity. On the one hand, it has been associated with movements of reform and liberation; ... on the other, it has proved a powerful tool of repression and chauvinism. ... Certainly, critical regionalism has its limitations. The upheaval of the populist movement – a more developed form of regionalism – has brought to light these weak points. No new architecture can emerge without a new kind of relations between designer and user, without new kinds of programs. ... Despite these limitations critical regionalism is a bridge over which any humanistic architecture of the future must pass.[12]

The fundamental strategy of Critical Regionalism is to mediate the impact of universal civilization with elements derived *indirectly* from the peculiarities of a particular place. It is clear from the above that Critical Regionalism depends upon maintaining a high level of critical self-consciousness. It may find its governing inspiration in such things as the range and quality of the local light, or in a *tectonic* derived from a peculiar structural mode, or in the topography of a given site.

But it is necessary, as I have already suggested, to distinguish between Critical Regionalism and simple-minded attempts to revive the hypothetical forms of a lost vernacular. In contradistinction to Critical Regionalism, the primary vehicle of Populism is the *communicative* or *instrumental* sign. Such a sign seeks to evoke not a critical perception of reality, but rather the sublimation of a desire for direct experience through the provision of information. Its tactical aim is to attain, as economically as possible, a preconceived level of gratification in behavioristic

---

[12] Alex Tzonis and Liliane Lefaivre, "The Grid and the Pathway. An Introduction to the Work of Dimitris and Susana Antonakakis," *Architecture in Greece*, 15 (Athens; 1981), p. 178.

terms. In this respect, the strong affinity of Populism for the rhetorical techniques and imagery of advertising is hardly accidental. Unless one guards against such a convergence, one will confuse the resistant capacity of a critical practice with the demagogic tendencies of Populism.

The case can be made that Critical Regionalism as a cultural strategy is as much a bearer of *world culture* as it is a vehicle of *universal civilization*. And while it is obviously misleading to conceive of our inheriting world culture to the same degree as we are all heirs to universal civilization, it is nonetheless evident that since we are, in principle, subject to the impact of both, we have no choice but to take cognizance today of their interaction. In this regard the practice of Critical Regionalism is contingent upon a process of double mediation. In the first place, it has to "deconstruct" the overall spectrum of world culture which it inevitably inherits; in the second place, it has to achieve, through synthetic contradiction, a manifest critique of universal civilization. To deconstruct world culture is to remove oneself from that eclecticism of the *fin de siècle* which appropriated alien, exotic forms in order to revitalize the expressivity of an enervated society. (One thinks of the "form-force" aesthetics of Henri van de Velde or the "whip-lash-Arabesques" of Victor Horta.) On the other hand, the mediation of universal technique involves imposing limits on the optimization of industrial and postindustrial technology. The future necessity for re-synthesizing principles and elements drawn from diverse origins and quite different ideological sets seems to be alluded to by Ricoeur when he writes:

> No one can say what will become of our civilization when it has really met different civilizations by means other than the shock of conquest and domination. But we have to admit that this encounter has not yet taken place at the level of an authentic dialogue. That is why we are in a kind of lull or interregnum in which we can no longer practice the dogmatism of a single truth and in which we are not yet capable of conquering the skepticism into which we have stepped.[13]

A parallel and complementary sentiment was expressed by the Dutch architect Aldo Van Eyck who, quite coincidentally, wrote at the same time: "Western civilization habitually identifies itself with civilization as such on the pontifical assumption that what is not like it is a deviation, less advanced, primitive, or, at best, exotically interesting at a safe distance."[14]

That Critical Regionalism cannot be simply based on the autochthonous forms of a specific region alone was well put by the Californian architect Hamilton Harwell Harris when he wrote, now nearly thirty years ago:

> Opposed to the Regionalism of Restriction is another type of regionalism, the Regionalism of Liberation. This is the manifestation of a region that is especially in tune with the emerging thought of the time. We call such a manifestation

[13] Ricoeur, p. 283.
[14] Aldo Van Eyck, *Forum* (Amsterdam, 1962).

"regional" only because it has not yet emerged elsewhere. ... A region may develop ideas. A region may accept ideas. Imagination and intelligence are necessary for both. In California in the late Twenties and Thirties modern European ideas met a still-developing regionalism. In New England, on the other hand, European Modernism met a rigid and restrictive regionalism that at first resisted and then surrendered. New England accepted European Modernism whole because its own regionalism had been reduced to a collection of restrictions.[15]

The scope for achieving a self-conscious synthesis between universal civilization and world culture may be specifically illustrated by Jørn Utzon's Bagsvaerd Church, built near Copenhagen in 1976, a work whose complex meaning stems directly from a revealed conjunction between, on the one hand, the *rationality* of normative technique and, on the other, the *arationality* of idiosyncratic form. Inasmuch as this building is organized around a regular grid and is comprised of repetitive, in-fill modules – concrete blocks in the first instance and precast concrete wall units in the second – we may justly regard it as the outcome of universal civilization. Such a building system, comprising an *in situ* concrete frame with prefabricated concrete in-fill elements, has indeed been applied countless times all over the developed world. However, the universality of this productive method – which includes, in this instance, patent glazing on the roof – is abruptly mediated when one passes from the optimal modular skin of the exterior to the far less optimal reinforced concrete shell vault spanning the nave. This last is obviously a relatively uneconomic mode of construction, selected and manipulated first for its direct associative capacity – that is to say, the vault signifies sacred space – and second for its multiple cross-cultural references. While the reinforced concrete shell vault has long since held an established place within the received tectonic canon of Western modern architecture, the highly configured section adopted in this instance is hardly familiar, and the only precedent for such a form, in a sacred context, is Eastern rather than Western – namely, the Chinese pagoda roof, cited by Utzon in his seminal essay of 1963, "Platforms and Plateaus."[16] Although the main Bagsvaerd vault spontaneously signifies its religious nature, it does so in such a way as to preclude an exclusively Occidental or Oriental reading of the code by which the public and sacred space is constituted. The intent of this expression is, of course, to secularize the sacred form by precluding the usual set of semantic religious references and thereby the corresponding range of automatic responses that usually accompany them. This is arguably a more appropriate way of rendering a church in a highly secular age, where any symbolic allusion to the ecclesiastic usually degenerates immediately into the vagaries of kitsch. And yet paradoxically, this desacralization at Bagsvaerd subtly reconstitutes a renewed

[15] Hamilton Harwell Harris, "Liberative and Restrictive Regionalism." Address given to the Northwest Chapter of the AIA in Eugene, Oregon in 1954.
[16] Jørn Utzon, "Platforms and Plateaus: Ideas of a Danish Architect," *Zodiac*, 10 (Milan: Edizioni Communita, 1963), pp. 112–14.

basis for the spiritual, one founded, I would argue, in a regional reaffirmation – grounds, at least, for some form of collective spirituality.

4. The Resistance of the Place-Form

The Megalopolis recognized as such in 1961 by the geographer Jean Gottman[17] continues to proliferate throughout the developed world to such an extent that, with the exception of cities which were laid in place before the turn of the century, we are no longer able to maintain defined urban forms. The last quarter of a century has seen the so-called field of urban design degenerate into a theoretical subject whose discourse bears little relation to the processal realities of modern development. Today even the super-managerial discipline of urban planning has entered into a state of crisis. The ultimate fate of the plan which was officially promulgated for the rebuilding of Rotterdam after World War II is symptomatic in this regard, since it testifies, in terms of its own recently changed status, to the current tendency to reduce all planning to little more than the allocation of land use and the logistics of distribution. Until relatively recently, the Rotterdam master plan was revised and upgraded every decade in the light of buildings which had been realized in the interim. In 1975, however, this progressive urban cultural procedure was unexpectedly abandoned in favor of publishing a nonphysical, infrastructure plan conceived at a regional scale. Such a plan concerns itself almost exclusively with the logistical projection of changes in land use and with the augmentation of existing distribution systems.

In his essay of 1954, "Building, Dwelling, Thinking," Martin Heidegger provides us with a critical vantage point from which to behold this phenomenon of universal placelessness. Against the Latin or, rather, the antique *abstract* concept of space as a more or less endless continuum of evenly subdivided spatial components or integers – what he terms *spatium* and *extensio* – Heidegger opposes the German word for space (or, rather, place), which is the term *Raum*. Heidegger argues that the phenomenological essence of such a space/place depends upon the *concrete*, clearly defined nature of its boundary, for, as he puts it, "A boundary is not that at which something stops, but, as the Greeks recognized, the boundary is that from which something begins its presencing."[18] Apart from confirming that Western abstract reason has its origins in the antique culture of the Mediterranean, Heidegger shows that etymologically the German gerund *building* is closely linked with the archaic forms of *being*, *cultivating* and *dwelling*, and goes on to state that the condition of "dwelling"

---

[17] Jean Gottmann, *Megalopolis* (Cambridge: MIT Press, 1961).

[18] Martin Heidegger, "Building, Dwelling, Thinking," in *Poetry, Language, Thought* (New York: Harper Colophon, 1971), p. 154. This essay first appeared in German in 1954.

and hence ultimately of "being" can only take place in a domain that is clearly bounded.

While we may well remain skeptical as to the merit of grounding critical practice in a concept so hermetically metaphysical as Being, we are, when confronted with the ubiquitous placelessness of our modern environment, nonetheless brought to posit, after Heidegger, the absolute precondition of a bounded domain in order to create an architecture of resistance. Only such a defined boundary will permit the built form to stand against – and hence literally to withstand in an institutional sense – the endless processal flux of the Megalopolis.

The bounded place-form, in its public mode, is also essential to what Hannah Arendt has termed "the space of human appearance," since the evolution of legitimate power has always been predicated upon the existence of the "polis" and upon comparable units of institutional and physical form. While the political life of the Greek polis did not stem directly from the physical presence and representation of the city-state, it displayed in contrast to the Megalopolis the cantonal attributes of urban density. Thus Arendt writes in *The Human Condition:*

> The only indispensable material factor in the generation of power is the living together of people. Only where men live so close together that the potentialities for action are always present will power remain with them and the foundation of cities, which as city states have remained paradigmatic for all Western political organization, is therefore the most important material prerequisite for power.[19]

Nothing could be more removed from the political essence of the city-state than the rationalizations of positivistic urban planners such as Melvin Webber, whose ideological concepts of *community without propinquity* and the *non-place urban realm* are nothing if not slogans devised to rationalize the absence of any true public realm in the modern motopia.[20] The manipulative bias of such ideologies has never been more openly expressed than in Robert Venturi's *Complexity and Contradiction in Architecture* (1966) wherein the author asserts that Americans do not need piazzas, since they should be at home watching television.[21] Such reactionary attitudes emphasize the impotence of an urbanized populace which has paradoxically lost the object of its urbanization.

While the strategy of Critical Regionalism as outlined above addresses itself mainly to the maintenance of an *expressive density and resonance* in an architecture of resistance (a cultural density which under today's conditions could be said to be potentially liberative in and of itself since it opens the user to manifold *experiences*), the provision of a place-form is equally essential to critical practice, inasmuch as a resistant architecture, in an institutional sense, is necessarily depen-

[19] Arendt, p. 201.

[20] Melvin Webber, *Explorations in Urban Structure* (Philadelphia: University of Pennsylvania Press, 1964).

[21] Robert Venturi, *Complexity and Contradiction in Architecture* (New York: Museum of Modern Art, 1966), p. 133.

dent on a clearly defined domain. Perhaps the most generic example of such an urban form is the perimeter block, although other related, introspective types may be evoked, such as the galleria, the atrium, the forecourt and the labyrinth. And while these types have in many instances today simply become the vehicles for accommodating pseudo-public realms (one thinks of recent mega-structures in housing, hotels, shopping centers, etc.), one cannot even in these instances entirely discount the latent political and resistant potential of the place-form.

5. Culture Versus Nature: Topography, Context, Climate, Light and Tectonic Form

Critical Regionalism necessarily involves a more directly dialectical relation with nature than the more abstract, formal traditions of modern avant-garde architecture allow. It is self-evident that the *tabula rasa* tendency of modernization favors the optimum use of earth-moving equipment inasmuch as a totally flat datum is regarded as the most economic matrix upon which to predicate the rationalization of construction. Here again, one touches in concrete terms this fundamental opposition between universal civilization and autochthonous culture. The bulldozing of an irregular topography into a flat site is clearly a technocratic gesture which aspires to a condition of absolute *placelessness*, whereas the terracing of the same site to receive the stepped form of a building is an engagement in the act of "cultivating" the site.

Clearly such a mode of beholding and acting brings one close once again to Heidegger's etymology; at the same time, it evokes the method alluded to by the Swiss architect Mario Botta as "building the site." It is possible to argue that in this last instance the specific culture of the region – that is to say, its history in both a geological and agricultural sense – becomes inscribed into the form and realization of the work. This inscription, which arises out of "in-laying" the building into the site, has many levels of significance, for it has a capacity to embody, in built form, the prehistory of the place, its archeological past and its subsequent cultivation and transformation across time. Through this layering into the site the idiosyncrasies of place find their expression without falling into sentimentality.

What is evident in the case of topography applies to a similar degree in the case of an existing urban fabric, and the same can be claimed for the contingencies of climate and the temporally inflected qualities of local light. Once again, the sensitive modulation and incorporation of such factors must almost by definition be fundamentally opposed to the optimum use of universal technique. This is perhaps most clear in the case of light and climate control. The generic window is obviously the most delicate point at which these two natural forces impinge upon the outer membrane of the building, fenestration having an innate capacity to

475

inscribe architecture with the character of a region and hence to express the place in which the work is situated.

Until recently, the received precepts of modern curatorial practice favored the exclusive use of artificial light in all art galleries. It has perhaps been insufficiently recognized how this encapsulation tends to reduce the artwork to a commodity, since such an environment must conspire to render the work placeless. This is because the local light spectrum is never permitted to play across its surface: here, then, we see how the loss of aura, attributed by Walter Benjamin to the processes of mechanical reproduction, also arises from a relatively static application of universal technology. The converse of this "placeless" practice would be to provide that art galleries be top-lit through carefully contrived monitors so that, while the injurious effects of direct sunlight are avoided, the ambient light of the exhibition volume changes under the impact of time, season, humidity, etc. Such conditions guarantee the appearance of a place-conscious poetic – a form of filtration compounded out of an interaction between culture and nature, between art and light. Clearly this principle applies to all fenestration, irrespective of size and location. A constant "regional inflection" of the form arises directly from the fact that in certain climates the glazed aperture is advanced, while in others it is recessed behind the masonry facade (or, alternatively, shielded by adjustable sun breakers).

The way in which such openings provide for appropriate ventilation also constitutes an unsentimental element reflecting the nature of local culture. Here, clearly, the main antagonist of rooted culture is the ubiquitous air-conditioner, applied in all times and in all places, irrespective of the local climatic conditions which have a capacity to express the specific place and the seasonal variations of its climate. Wherever they occur, the fixed window and the remote-controlled air-conditioning system are mutually indicative of domination by universal technique.

Despite the critical importance of topography and light, the primary principle of architectural autonomy resides in the *tectonic* rather than the *scenographic:* that is to say, this autonomy is embodied in the revealed ligaments of the construction and in the way in which the syntactical form of the structure explicitly resists the action of gravity. It is obvious that this discourse of the load borne (the beam) and the load-bearing (the column) cannot be brought into being where the structure is masked or otherwise concealed. On the other hand, the tectonic is not to be confused with the purely technical, for it is more than the simple revelation of stereotomy or the expression of skeletal framework. Its essence was first defined by the German aesthetician Karl Bötticher in his book *Die Tektonik der Hellenen* (1852); and it was perhaps best summarized by the architectural historian Stanford Anderson when he wrote:

> *"Tektonik"* referred not just to the activity of making the materially requisite construction ... but rather to the activity that raises this construction to an art form. ... The functionally adequate form must be adapted so as to give expression

to its function. The sense of bearing provided by the entasis of Greek columns became the touchstone of this concept of *Tektonik*.[22]

The tectonic remains to us today as a potential means for distilling play between material, craftwork and gravity, so as to yield a component which is in fact a condensation of the entire structure. We may speak here of the presentation of a structural poetic rather than the re-presentation of a facade.

6. The Visual Versus the Tactile

The tactile resilience of the place-form and the capacity of the body to read the environment in terms other than those of sight alone suggest a potential strategy for resisting the domination of universal technology. It is symptomatic of the priority given to sight that we find it necessary to remind ourselves that the tactile is an important dimension in the perception of built form. One has in mind a whole range of complementary sensory perceptions which are registered by the labile body: the intensity of light, darkness, heat and cold; the feeling of humidity; the aroma of material; the almost palpable presence of masonry as the body senses its own confinement; the momentum of an induced gait and the relative inertia of the body as it traverses the floor; the echoing resonance of our own footfall. Luchino Visconti was well aware of these factors when making the film *The Damned*, for he insisted that the main set of the Altona mansion should be paved in real wooden parquet. It was his belief that without a solid floor underfoot the actors would be incapable of assuming appropriate and convincing postures.

   A similar tactile sensitivity is evident in the finishing of the public circulation in Alvar Aalto's Säynatsalo Town Hall of 1952. The main route leading to the second-floor council chamber is ultimately orchestrated in terms which are as much tactile as they are visual. Not only is the principal access stair lined in raked brickwork, but the treads and risers are also finished in brick. The kinetic impetus of the body in climbing the stair is thus checked by the friction of the steps, which are "read" soon after in contrast to the timber floor of the council chamber itself. This chamber asserts its honorific status through sound, smell and texture, not to mention the springy deflection of the floor underfoot (and a noticeable tendency to lose one's balance on its polished surface). From this example it is clear that the liberative importance of the tactile resides in the fact that it can only be decoded in terms of *experience* itself: it cannot be reduced to mere information, to representation or to the simple evocation of a simulacrum substituting for absent presences.

[22] Stanford Anderson, "Modern Architecture and Industry: Peter Behrens, the AEG, and Industrial Design," *Oppositions* 21 (Summer 1980), p. 83.

477

In this way, Critical Regionalism seeks to complement our normative visual experience by readdressing the tactile range of human perceptions. In so doing, it endeavors to balance the priority accorded to the image and to counter the Western tendency to interpret the environment in exclusively perspectival terms. According to its etymology, perspective means rationalized sight or clear seeing, and as such it presupposes a conscious suppression of the senses of smell, hearing and taste, and a consequent distancing from a more direct experience of the environment. This self-imposed limitation relates to that which Heidegger has called a "loss of nearness." In attempting to counter this loss, the tactile opposes itself to the scenographic and the drawing of veils over the surface of reality. Its capacity to arouse the impulse to touch returns the architect to the poetics of construction and to the erection of works in which the tectonic value of each component depends upon the density of its objecthood. The tactile and the tectonic jointly have the capacity to transcend the mere appearance of the technical in much the same way as the place-form has the potential to withstand the relentless onslaught of global modernization.

62

The Pleasure of Architecture

Bernard Tschumi

Functionalist dogmas and the puritan attitudes of the modern movement have often come under attack. Yet the ancient idea of pleasure still seems sacrilegious to contemporary architectural theory. For many generations any architect who aimed for or attempted to experience pleasure in architecture was considered decadent. Politically, the socially conscious have been suspicious of the slightest trace of hedonism in architectural endeavors and have rejected it as a reactionary concern. And in the same way, architectural conservatives have relegated to the Left everything remotely intellectual or political, including the discourse of pleasure. On both sides, the idea that architecture can possibly exist without either moral or functional justification, or even responsibility, has been considered distasteful.

Similar oppositions are reflected throughout the recent history of architecture. The avant-garde has endlessly debated oppositions that are mostly complementary: order and disorder, structure and chaos, ornament and purity, rationality and sensuality. And these simple dialectics have pervaded architectural theory to such an extent that architectural criticism has reflected similar attitudes: the purists' ordering of forms versus art nouveau's organic sensuousness; Behrens's ethic of form versus Olbrich's impulse to the formless.

Often these oppositions have been loaded with moral overtones. Adolf Loos' attack on the criminality of ornament masked his fear of chaos and sensual disorder. And De Stijl's insistence on elementary form was not only a return to some anachronistic purity but also a deliberate regression to a secure order.

So strong were these moral overtones that they even survived Dada's destructive attitudes and the surrealists' abandonment to the unconscious. Tzara's ironical contempt for order found few equivalents among architects too busy replacing the *système des Beaux-Arts* by the modern movement's own set of rules.

Bernard Tschumi, "The Pleasure of Architecture," pp. 173–83 from Andrew Ballantyne (ed.), *What is Architecture?* London and New York: Routledge, 2002. Reprinted by permission of Routledge, Taylor & Francis.

In 1920 – despite the contradictory presence of Tzara, Richter, Ball, Duchamp, and Breton – Le Corbusier and his contemporaries chose the quiet and acceptable route of purism. Even in the early 1970s, the work of the architectural school circles, with their various brands of irony or self-indulgence, ran counter to the moral reminiscences of '68 radicalism, although both shared a dislike for established values.

Beyond such opposites lie the mythical shadows of Apollo's ethical and spiritual mindscapes versus Dionysius' erotic and sensual impulses. Architectural definitions, in their surgical precision, reinforce and amplify the impossible alternatives: on the one hand, architecture as a thing of the mind, a dematerialized or conceptual discipline with its typological and morphological variations, and on the other, architecture as an empirical event that concentrates on the senses, on the experience of space.

In the following paragraphs, I will attempt to show that today the pleasure of architecture may lie both inside *and* outside such oppositions – both in the dialectic *and* in the disintegration of the dialectic. However, the paradoxical nature of this theme is incompatible with the accepted, rational logic of classical argument; as Roland Barthes puts it in *The Pleasure of the Text*: "pleasure does not readily surrender to analysis," (Barthes, 1973)[1] hence there will be no theses, antitheses, and syntheses here. The text instead is composed of fragments that relate only loosely to one another. These fragments – *geometry, mask, bondage, excess, eroticism* – are all to be considered not only within the reality of ideas but also within the reality of the reader's spatial experience: a silent reality that cannot be put on paper.

Fragment 1: A Double Pleasure (Reminder)

The pleasure of space: this cannot be put into words, it is unspoken. Approximately: it is a form of experience – the "presence of absence"; exhilarating differences between the plane and the cavern, between the street and your living-room; symmetries and dissymmetries emphasizing the spatial properties of my body: right and left, up and down. Taken to its extreme, the pleasure of space leans toward the poetics of the unconscious, to the edge of madness.

The pleasure of geometry and, by extension, the pleasure of order – that is, the pleasure of concepts: typical statements on architecture often read like the one in the first edition of the *Encyclopaedia Britannica* of 1773: "architecture, being governed by proportion, requires to be guided by rule and compass." That is, architecture is a "thing of the mind," a geometrical rather than a pictorial or experiential art, so the problem of architecture becomes a problem of ordinance – Doric or Corinthian order, axes or hierarchies, grids or regulating lines, types or models, walls or slabs – and, of course, the grammar and syntax of the

---

[1] [Original] editor's note. The quotation is not actually from Barthes, but is a paraphrase from Richard Howard's introduction to the English edition, from a point at which he quotes Willa Cather ("a writer Barthes has never heard of") (Barthes, 1973, vi).

architecture's sign become pretexts for sophisticated and pleasurable manipulation. Taken to its extreme, such manipulation leans toward a poetic of frozen signs, detached from reality, into a subtle and frozen pleasure of the mind.

Neither the pleasure of space nor the pleasure of geometry is (on its own) the pleasure of architecture.

Fragment 2: Gardens of Pleasure

In his *Observations sur l'architecture*, published in The Hague in 1765, Abbé Laugier suggested a dramatic deconstruction of architecture and its conventions. He wrote:

> Whoever knows how to design a park well will have no difficulty in tracing the plan for the building of a city according to its given area and situation. There must be regularity and fantasy, relationships and oppositions, and casual, unexpected elements that vary the scene; great order in the details, confusions, uproar, and tumult in the whole. (Laugier, 1765: 312–13)

Laugier's celebrated comments, together with the dreams of Capability Brown, William Kent, Lequeu, or Piranesi, were not merely a reaction to the Baroque period that preceded them. Rather, the deconstruction of architecture that they suggested was an early venture into the realm of pleasure, against the architectural order of time.

Take Stowe, for example. William Kent's park displays a subtle dialectic between organized landscape and architectural elements: the Egyptian pyramid, the Italian belvedere, the Saxon temple. But these "ruins" are to be read less as elements of a picturesque composition than as the dismantled elements of order. Yet, despite the apparent chaos, order is still present as a necessary counterpart to the sensuality of the winding streams. Without the signs of order, Kent's park would lose all reminder of "reason." Conversely, without the traces of sensuality – trees, hedges, valleys – only symbols would remain, in a silent and frozen fashion.

Gardens have had a strange fate. Their history has almost always anticipated the history of cities. The orchard grid of man's earliest agricultural achievements preceded the layout of the first military cities. The perspectives and diagonals of the Renaissance garden were applied to the squares and colonnades of Renaissance cities. Similarly, the romantic, picturesque parks of English empiricism pre-empted the crescents and arcades of the rich urban design tradition of nineteenth-century English cities.

Built exclusively for delight, gardens are like the earliest experiments in that part of architecture that is so difficult to express with words or drawings; pleasure and eroticism. Whether romantic or classical, gardens merge the sensual pleasure of space with the pleasure of reason, in a most *useless* manner.

Fragment 3: Pleasure and Necessity

"Uselessness" is associated only reluctantly with architectural matters. Even at a time when pleasure found some theoretical backing ("delight" as well as "commodity" and "firmness"), utility always provided a practical justification. One example among many is Quatremère de Quincy's introduction to the entry on architecture in the *Encyclopédie méthodique* published in Paris in 1778. There you will read a definition of architecture that contends that

> amongst all the arts, those children of *pleasure and necessity*, with which man has formed a partnership in order to help him bear the pains of life and transmit his memory to future generations, it can certainly not be denied that architecture holds a most outstanding place. Considering it only from the point of view of *utility*, architecture surpasses all the arts. It provides for the salubrity of cities, guards the health of men, protects their property, and works only for the safety, repose and good order of civil life. (De Quincy, 1778: 109)

If De Quincy's statement was consistent with the architectural ideology of his time, then two hundred years later, the social necessity of architecture has been reduced to dreams and nostalgic utopias. The "salubrity of cities" is now determined more by the logic of land economics, while the "good order of civil life" is more often than not the order of corporate markets.

As a result, most architectural endeavors seem caught in a hopeless dilemma. If, on the one hand, architects recognize the ideological and financial dependency of their work, they implicitly accept the constraints of society. If, on the other hand, they sanctuarize themselves, their architecture is accused of elitism. Of course, architecture will save its peculiar nature, but only wherever it questions itself, wherever it denies or disrupts the form that a conservative society expects of it. Once again, if there has lately been some reason to doubt the necessity of architecture, then the *necessity of architecture may well be its non-necessity*. Such totally gratuitous consumption of architecture is ironically *political* in that it disturbs established structures. It is also pleasurable.

Fragment 4: Metaphor of Order-Bondage

Unlike the necessity of mere building, the non-necessity of architecture is undissociable from architectural histories, theories, and other precedents. These bonds enhance pleasure. The most excessive passion is always methodical. In such moments of intense desire, organization invades pleasure to such an extent that it is not always possible to distinguish the organizing constraints from the erotic matter. For example, the Marquis de Sade's heroes enjoyed confining their victims in the strictest convents before mistreating them according to rules carefully laid down with a precise and obsessive logic.

Similarly, the game of architecture is an intricate play with rules that one may accept or reject. Indifferently called *système des Beaux-Arts* or modern movement precepts, this pervasive network of binding laws entangles architectural design. These rules, like so many knots that cannot be untied, are generally a paralyzing constraint. When manipulated, however, they have the erotic significance of bondage. To differentiate between rules or ropes is irrelevant here. What matters is that there is no simple bondage technique: the more numerous and sophisticated the restraints, the greater the pleasure.

Fragment 5: Rationality

In *Architecture and Utopia*, the historian Manfredo Tafuri recalls how the rational excesses of Piranesi's prisons took Laugier's theoretical proposals of "order and tumult" to the extreme (Tafuri, 1973). The classical vocabulary of architecture is Piranesi's chosen form of bondage. Treating classical elements as fragmented and decaying symbols, Piranesi's architecture battles against itself, in that the obsessive rationality of building types was "sadistically" carried to the extremes of irrationality.

Fragment 6: Eroticism

We have seen that the ambiguous pleasure of rationality and irrational dissolution recalled erotic concerns. A word of warning may be necessary at this stage. Eroticism is used here as a theoretical concept, having little in common with fetishistic formalism and other sexual analogies prompted by the sight of erect skyscrapers or curvaceous doorways. Rather, eroticism is a subtle matter. "The pleasure of excess" requires consciousness as well as voluptuousness. Neither space nor concepts alone are erotic, but the junction between the two is.

The ultimate pleasure of architecture is that impossible moment when an architectural act, brought to excess, reveals both the traces of reason and the immediate experience of space.

Fragment 7: Metaphor of Seduction – the Mask

There is rarely pleasure without seduction, or seduction without illusion. Consider: sometimes you wish to seduce, so you act in the most appropriate way in order to reach your ends. You wear a disguise. Conversely, you may wish to change roles and *be* seduced: you consent to someone else's disguise, you accept his or her assumed personality, for it gives you pleasure, even if you know that it dissimulates "something else."

Architecture is no different. It constantly plays the seducer. Its disguises are numerous: façades, arcades, squares, even architectural concepts become the artifacts of seduction. Like masks, they place a veil between what is assumed to be reality and its participants (you or I). So sometimes you desperately wish to read the reality behind the architectural mask. Soon, however, you realize that no single understanding is possible. Once you uncover that which lies behind the mask, it is only to discover another mask. The literal aspect of the disguise (the façade, the street) indicates other systems of knowledge, other ways to read the city: formal masks hide socioeconomic ones, while literal masks hide metaphorical ones. Each system of knowledge obscures another. Masks hide other masks, and each successive level of meaning confirms the impossibility of grasping reality.

Consciously aimed at seduction, masks are, of course, a category of reason. Yet they possess a double role: they simultaneously veil and unveil, simulate and dissimulate. Behind all masks lie dark and unconscious streams that cannot be dissociated from the pleasure of architecture. The mask may exalt appearances. Yet by its very presence, it says that, in the background, there is something else.

Fragment 8: Excess

If the mask belongs to the universe of pleasure, pleasure itself is no simple masquerade. The danger of confusing the mask with the face is real enough never to grant refuge to parodies and nostalgia. The need for order is no justification for imitating past orders. Architecture is interesting only when it masters the art of disturbing illusions, creating breaking points that can start and stop at any time.

Certainly, the pleasure of architecture is granted when architecture fulfills one's spatial expectations as well as embodies architectural ideas, concepts, or archetypes with intelligence, invention, sophistication, irony. Yet there is also a special pleasure that results from conflicts: when the sensual pleasure of space conflicts with the pleasure of order.

The recent widespread fascination with the history and theory of architecture does not necessarily mean a return to blind obedience to past dogma. On the contrary, I would suggest that the ultimate pleasure of architecture lies in the most forbidden parts of the architectural act; where limits are perverted and prohibitions *transgressed*. The starting point of architecture is distortion – the dislocation of the universe that surrounds the architect. Yet such a nihilistic stance is only apparently so: we are not dealing with destruction here, but with excess, differences, and left-overs. *Exceeding* functionalist dogmas, semiotic systems, historical precedents, or formalized products of past social or economic constraints is not necessarily a matter of subversion but a matter of preserving the erotic capacity of architecture by disrupting the form that most conservative societies expect of it.

Fragment 9: Architecture of Pleasure

The architecture of pleasure lies where concept and experience of space abruptly coincide, where architectural fragments collide and merge in delight, where the culture of architecture is endlessly deconstructed and all rules are transgressed. No metaphorical paradise here, but discomfort and the unbalancing of expectations. Such architecture questions academic (and popular) assumptions, disturbs acquired tastes and fond architectural memories. Typologies, morphologies, spatial compressions, logical constructions – all dissolve. Such architecture is perverse because its real significance lies outside utility or purpose and ultimately is not even necessarily aimed at giving pleasure.

The architecture of pleasure depends on a particular feat, which is to keep architecture obsessed with itself in such an ambiguous fashion that it never surrenders to good conscience or parody, to debility or delirious neurosis.

Fragment 10: Advertisements for Architecture

There is no way to perform architecture in a book. Words and drawings can only produce paper space and not the experience of real space. By definition, paper space is imaginary: it is an image. Yet for those who do not build (whether for circumstantial or ideological reasons – it does not matter), it seems perfectly normal to be satisfied with the representation of those aspects of architecture that belong to mental constructs – to imagination. Such representations inevitably separate the sensual experience of a real space from the appreciation of rational concepts. Among other things, architecture is a function of both. And if either of these two criteria is removed, architecture loses something. It nevertheless seems strange that architects always have to castrate their architecture whenever they do not deal with real spaces. So the question remains: why should the paper space of a book or magazine replace an architectural space?

The answer does not lie in the inevitability of the media or in the way architecture is disseminated. Rather it may lie in the very nature of architecture.

Let's take an example. There are certain things that cannot be reached frontally. These things require analogies, metaphors, or roundabout routes in order to be grasped. For instance, it is through *language* that psychoanalysis uncovers the unconscious. Like a mask, language hints at something else behind itself. It may try to hide it, but it also implies it at the same time.

Architecture resembles a masked figure. It cannot easily be unveiled. It is always hiding: behind drawstrings, behind words, behind precepts, behind habits, behind technical constraints. Yet it is the very difficulty of uncovering architecture that makes it intensely desirable. This unveiling is part of the pleasure of architecture.

In a similar way, reality hides behind advertising. The usual function of advertisements – reproduced again and again, as opposed to the single architectural piece – is to trigger desire for something beyond the page itself. When removed from their customary endorsement of commodity values, advertisements are the ultimate magazine form, even if somehow ironically. And, as there are advertisements for architectural products, why not for the production (and reproduction) of *architecture*?

Fragment 11: Desire/Fragments

There are numerous ways to equate architecture with language. Yet such equations often amount to a *reduction* and an *exclusion*. A reduction, in so far as these equations usually become distorted as soon as architecture tries to produce meaning (which meaning? whose meaning?), and thus end up reducing language to its mere combinatory logic. An exclusion, in so far as these equations generally omit some of the important findings made in Vienna at the beginning of the century, when language was first seen as a condition of the unconscious. Here, dreams were analyzed as language as well as through language; language was called "the main street of the unconscious." Generally speaking, it appeared as a series of *fragments* (the Freudian notion of fragments does not presuppose the breaking of an image, or of a totality, but the dialectical multiplicity of a process).

So, too, architecture when equated with language can only be read as a series of fragments that make up an architectural reality.

Fragments of architecture (bits of walls, of rooms, of streets, of ideas) are all one actually sees. These fragments are like beginnings without ends. There is always a split between fragments that are real and fragments that are virtual, between memory and fantasy. These splits have no existence other than being the passage from one fragment to another. They are relays rather than signs. They are traces. They are in-between.

It is not the clash between these contradictory fragments that counts but the movement between them. And this invisible movement is neither a part of language nor of structure ("language" or "structure" are words specific to a mode of reading architecture that does not fully apply in the context of pleasure); it is nothing but a constant and mobile relationship inside language itself.

How such fragments are organized matters little: volume, height, surface, degree of enclosure, or whatever. These fragments are like sentences between quotation marks. Yet they are not quotations. They simply melt into the work. (We are here at the opposite of the collage technique.) They may be excerpts from different discourses, but this only demonstrates that an architectural project is precisely where differences find an overall expression.

A film of the 1950s had a name for this movement between fragments. It was called desire. Yes, *A Streetcar Named Desire* perfectly simulated the movement toward something constantly missing, toward absence. Each setting, each fragment, was aimed at seduction but always dissolved at the moment it was approached. And then each time it would be substituted by another fragment. Desire was never seen. Yet it remained constant. The same goes for architecture.

In other words, architecture is not of interest because of its fragments and what they represent or do not represent. Nor does it consist in *exteriorizing*, through whatever forms, the unconscious desires of society or its architects. Nor is it a mere representation of those desires through some fantastic architectural image. Rather it can only act as a recipient in which your desires, my desires, can be reflected. Thus a piece of architecture is not architectural because it fulfills some utilitarian function, but because it sets in motion the operations of seduction and the unconscious.

A word of warning. Architecture may very well activate such motions, but it is not a dream (a stage where society's or the individual's unconscious desires can be fulfilled). It cannot satisfy your wildest fantasies, but it may exceed the limits set by them.

References

Barthes, Roland (1973) *Le Plaisir du texte.* Paris: Seuil; trans. R. Millar as *The Pleasure of the Text.* New York: Farrar, Strauss & Giroux (1975).

De Quincy, Quatremère (1778) *Encyclopédie méthodique,* vols. 1–3. Paris: Panckoucke et Agasse; Liège: Plomteux.

Laugier, Marc Antoine (1765) *Observations sur l'architecture.* Paris: Chez Duchesne; 1st pub. 1755.

Tafuri, Manfredo (1973) *Architecture and Utopia: Design and Capitalist Development.* Cambridge, MA: MIT Press.

63

Scale and Span in a Global Digital World

Saskia Sassen

I want to discuss the questions of scale and span under conditions of digitalization and globalization. In her introduction to the Anything conference, Cynthia Davidson cited William Gibson's comment that the impact of the digital might well be to eliminate and neutralize everything that architecture has historically represented.[1] In parallel to what Gibson anticipated in 1991, today we read and hear a lot of comment and analyses arguing that the impact of the digital on cities will be to neutralize what cities have traditionally represented. In abstract terms, one could see this representation as centrality – a centrality dependent upon and influenced by different cultures, different places, different times, and different articulations of urban space.[2]

My effort here is to examine the impact of digitalization and globalization on the architectural, the urban, and the city in a way that resists the dominant interpretations, which posit that digitalization (and to a large extent, globalization, as in electronic markets) entails an absolute disembedding from the material world.

Saskia Sassen, "Scale and Span in a Global Digital World," pp. 44–8 from Cynthia C. Davidson (ed.), *Anything*. Cambridge, MA: MIT Press, 2001. Reprinted by permission of the MIT Press.
[1] "While the advent of nanotechnology promises to render architecture a dead technology, something akin to its traditional practice already flourishes in the virtual landscape of the computer. Our century's only crucial architectures are structures of information. The microchip is a cathedral. A library is something on the other end of a modem. The Postmodern, in retrospect, will seem a breathing space prior to the advent of the Posthuman." William Gibson, "Letter to Anyone," in *Anyone*, ed. Cynthia C. Davidson (New York: Rizzoli, 1991), 264.
[2] The variety of dynamics that I am describing are all located on edges, borders, and frontier zones. As a researcher, I find these thresholds particularly interesting because it is precisely at the points of transaction between new and old spatial modes that all kinds of things appear to happen. This has a whole series of implications for very specialized research agendas in several fields, as well as for the city itself.

With this type of interpretation comes, then, the neutralization of such conditions as the architectural and the urban – not in general terms, however, but as conditions that are produced, articulated, and inflected by crucial instantiations of the embeddedness of the digital. Mine is a particular kind of reading of digitalization: it seeks to detect the imbrications of the digital and nondigital domains and thereby to insert the condition of the architectural and urban in mappings, both actual and rhetorical, from which this digitalization can be easily excluded.[3] I use notions of *scale* and *span* (or *scope*) to capture the precise locations of this insertion. The risk in this type of effort, it seems to me, lies in generalizing, in using metaphors and figurative language – in brief, to hover above it all. Rather, we need to go digging.

The difficulty that analysts and commentators have had in understanding the impact of digitalization on cities and architecture – indeed, on multiple configurations – essentially is the result of two analytic flaws. The first (and this is especially evident in the United States) restricts interpretation to a technological reading of the capacities of digital technology. This would be the required and proper reading for engineers, but if one is trying to understand the impact of a technology, such a reading becomes problematic. The difficulty is that a purely technological reading inevitably leads one to a place that is a nonplace, where one announces with absolute certainty the neutralization of many of those configurations marked by physicality and place-boundedness, including architecture and the urban.[4] The second flaw, I would argue, is a continuing reliance on analytical categorizations that were developed under other spatial and historical conditions – that is, conditions preceding the current digital era. Thus the tendency is to conceive of the digital as simply and exclusively digital, and the nondigital, whether represented in terms of the material or the actual (both conceptions are equally problematic), as simply and exclusively that, nondigital. These either/or categorizations filter out alternative conceptualizations, thereby precluding a more complex reading of the impact of digitalization on material and placebound conditions.

One such alternative categorization captures these imbrications. Let me illustrate this through the case of finance. This is certainly a highly digitalized activity, yet it cannot simply be considered exclusively digital. To have electronic financial markets and digitalized financial instruments requires enormous amounts of matériel, not to mention human talent (which has its own type of physicality). This matériel includes conventional infrastructure, buildings, airports, and so on. Much of this matériel is, then, inflected by the digital. Conversely, much of what takes place in cyberspace is deeply inflected by the cultures, material practices, and imaginations that take place outside cyberspace. Much, though not all, of what we think of as cyberspace would lack any meaning or referents if we were to exclude the

---

[3] For a development of some of these ideas see "Digital Networks and Power" in ed. M. Featherstone and S. Lash, *Spaces of Culture: City, Nation, World* (London: Sage, 1999); and *ANY* 19/20: "The Virtual House," 1997.

[4] Another consequence of this type of reading is to assume that a new technology will inevitably replace all older technologies that are less efficient, or slower, at executing those tasks that the new technology is best at. We know that inevitable replacement is historically not the case.

world outside cyberspace. In brief, therefore, digital space and digitalization are not exclusive conditions that stand beyond the nondigital. Digital space is embedded in the larger societal, cultural, subjective, economic, and imaginary structurations of lived experience and the systems within which we exist and operate.

So in terms of the impact of the digital on architecture, on urbanism, and on the city, yes, there has been a profound transformation, but it is one not necessarily marked by the neutralization of capital fixity or of the built environment or, in the end, of the city. Rather than being neutralized, these emerge with renewed and strategic importance in some of their features, that is to say, not as a generalized condition but as a very specific condition. A first impact, then, is a particular type of built environment – a conventional communication system, a city, in essence, a particular type of spatiality – that accommodates and furthers the new digital dynamics.

A second impact is the complex overlapping of the digital (as well as the global) and the nondigital, which brings with it a destabilizing of older hierarchies of scale and often dramatic rescalings. As the national scale loses significance, along with the loss of key components of the nation-state's formal authority over that scale, other measures gain strategic importance. Most especially among these are subnational scales, such as the global city, and supranational scales, such as global markets or regional trading zones. Older hierarchies of scale (emerging in the context of the ascendance of the nation-state) continue to operate, and are typically organized in terms of institutional scope: from the international, down to the national, the regional, the urban, and the local. Today's rescaling cuts across institutional scope and, through policies such as deregulation and privatization, negates the encasements of territory produced by the formation of national states. This does not mean that the old hierarchies disappear, but rather that rescalings emerge alongside the old ones, and that they can often trump the latter.[5]

These transformations, although resulting from digitalization and globalization, and continuing to entail complex imbrications of the digital and nondigital and between the global and the nonglobal, can be captured in a variety of instances. For example, much of what we might still experience as the "local" (an office building or a house or an institution right there in our neighborhood or downtown) is actually something I would rather think of as a "microenvironment with global span" insofar as it is deeply internet-worked.[6] Such a microenvironment is in many senses a localized entity – something that can be experienced as local, immediate, proximate. It is a sited materiality. But it is also part of global digital networks, which lend it immediate far-flung span. To continue to think of this simply as local is not especially useful or adequate. More importantly, the juxtaposition between the condition of being a sited materiality and having global

[5] I develop some of these issues in *Losing Control? Sovereignty in an Age of Globalization* (New York: Columbia University Press, 1996) and in the book I am currently working on, *De-Nationalization*.
[6] See Saskia Sassen, "Geographies and Countergeographies of Globalization" in *Anymore*, ed. Cynthia C. Davidson (Cambridge, Massachusetts: MIT Press, 2000), 110–19.

span captures the enfolding of the digital and nondigital and illustrates the inadequacy of a purely technological reading of the capacities of digitalization. This would lead us to posit the neutralization of the place-boundedness of that which precisely makes possible the condition of being an entity with global span.

A second example is the bundle of conditions and dynamics that marks the model of the global city. To single out one key dynamic: the more globalized and digitalized the operations of firms and markets, the more their central management and coordination functions (and the requisite material structures) become strategic. It is precisely because of digitalization that simultaneous worldwide dispersal of operations (whether factories, offices, or service outlets) and system integration can be achieved. And it is precisely this combination that raises the importance of central functions. Global cities are strategic sites for the combination of resources necessary for the production of these central functions.[7]

Conceptualizing digitalization and globalization along these lines creates operational and rhetorical openings for recognizing the ongoing importance of the material world, even in the case of some of the most dematerialized activities.

One could examine, for example, the digital through one of its most powerful capabilities: the dematerializing and liquefying of that which was material and/or hardly mobile. (I would also argue that this capability still contains a complex imbrication with the nondigital.) Digitalization brings with it an amplification of those capacities that make possible the liquefying of that which is not liquid. Thereby, digitalization raises the mobility of what we have customarily thought of as immobile, or barely mobile. At its most extreme, this liquefying dematerializes its object. Once dematerialized, it becomes hypermobile – instantaneous circulation through digital networks with global span. It is important to underline that the hypermobility gained by an object through dematerialization is but one moment of a more complex condition. Representing such an object as simply hypermobile is, then, a partial representation since it includes only some of the components of that object, i.e., those that can be dematerialized but achieve that condition as a function of what we could describe as highly specialized materialities. Much of what is liquefied and circulates in digital networks and is marked by hypermobility remains physical in some of its components.

Take, for example, the case of real estate. Financial services firms have developed instruments that liquefy real estate, thereby facilitating investment and circulation of these instruments in global markets. Yet, part of what constitutes real estate remains very physical. At the same time, however, that which remains physical has been transformed by the fact that it is represented by highly liquid instruments that can circulate in global markets. It may look the same, it may involve the same bricks and mortar, it may be new or old, but it is a transformed entity. We have difficulty capturing this multivalence through our conventional categories: if it is physical, it is physical; and if it is liquid, it is liquid. In fact, the

---

[7] There are other dimensions that specify the global city; see the fully updated edition of my book *The Global City* (Princeton: Princeton University Press, 2001).

partial representation of real estate through liquid financial instruments produces a complex intertwining of the material and the dematerialized moments of that which we continue to call real estate.

Hypermobility, or dematerialization, is usually seen as a mere function of the new technologies. This understanding obscures the fact that it takes multiple material conditions to achieve this outcome. Once we recognize that the hyper-mobility of the instrument, or the dematerialization of the actual piece of real estate, had to be *produced*, we introduce the overlapping of the material and the nonmaterial. It takes capital fixity to produce capital mobility, that is to say, state-of-the-art built environments, conventional infrastructure – from highways to airports and railways – and well-housed talent. These are all at least partly place-bound conditions, even though the nature of their place-boundedness is going to be different from what it was 100 years ago, when it might have been marked by immobility. Today it is a place-boundedness that is inflected and inscribed by the hypermobility of its components. Both capital fixity and mobility are located in a temporal frame where speed is ascendant and consequential. At the level of the material, speed alters such dynamics as obsolescence and the value of investment.[8]

For example, the new transnational professional class is hypermobile. We conduct ourselves as if we could download our bodies, but at any given moment, part of the task and part of what takes us around the globe have to do with things that are place-bound, and our interventions – which justify what we are, who we are, and why we are here or there – are also place-bound. So again, we are confronted with conventional categories that polarize: Is it hypermobile? Is it fixed? Is it place-bound? Is it mobile? All of these questions typically miss much of what is happening. One example that captures the essence of this polarization is the private digital network that MCI Worldcom has created, connecting 4,000 buildings in Europe with 27,000 buildings in the United States. By connecting these buildings – which are not just any buildings – this digital network creates a spatiality that in some ways is a local event. It is a microenvironment; it connects across the Atlantic a set of buildings that are scattered over two continental territories where the space itself becomes a kind of space for mobility that might as well be a microspace or a local space. The firms that are locating to those buildings are also paying premium rates. We have, then, a digitally connected space among select, very fixed entities.

A corollary to these microenvironments is the redefinition and reconfiguration of ideas of the center. The MCI Worldcom network spans a huge geographic distance, yet it is constructed as a space of centrality. The enormous agglomeration of buildings that physically characterizes this digital network, despite being

---

[8] Much of my work on global cities has looked to conceptualize and document the fact that the global digital economy requires massive concentrations of material conditions in order to be what it is. Finance is an important intermediary in this regard; it represents a capability for liquefying various forms of nonliquid wealth and for raising the mobility (i.e., hypermobility) of that which is already liquid, a subject I developed in "Juxtaposed Temporalities: Producing a New Zone" in *Anytime*, ed. Cynthia C. Davidson (Cambridge, Massachusetts: MIT Press, 1999), 114–21.

manifest in all our major cities, cannot be read in the same ways that we looked at urban centers 20 or even ten years ago. A new urban history is being constructed, even though it is deeply embedded and almost camouflaged by the older social spatial histories within which it is taking place. For us to more fully understand the impact of the digital and of globalization, we need, therefore, to suspend the category "city." Rather, we need to construct a more abstract category of centrality and of spaces of centrality, that, ironically, could allow us to recover the city, albeit a recovery as just one instantiation within a much broader set of issues.[9]

If we begin to unpack the impact of the digital and of globalization through these kinds of questions, and not simply confine our analysis to the technical capacities of technologies, we can chart an enormously interesting conceptual map with which we can explore these issues. Through this mapping of globalization and digitalization, one can also see the extent to which we have existed in a consciousness deeply embedded in the idea of the national: territories, administration, identities, citizenship – all formed in national terms. One of the impacts of the rescaling described earlier is the removal of layers of institutional encasing "constructing" the national, and the freeing up subnational systems of circulation.

The global city is precisely the synthesis of these two scales – the old and the new. It overrides and neutralizes older hierarchies of scale and functions as an enormously complex sited materiality with global span. In the era of globalization, the state also participates in the neutralization of these national encasings. The state, therefore, is not just a victim of globalization. It actively participates in producing laws that facilitate the partial denationalization of the global city, creating opportunities for foreign actors, foreign markets, foreign firms, and foreign cultural institutions to be operative in what was once constructed as the national. In this combination of elements, I would argue, lies a very different reading of the impact of the digital on architecture and the city. The direction in which it takes us could lead to a rich and complex agenda for research, theorization, and argument.

---

[9] See Saskia Sassen, "Reconfiguring Centrality" in *Anywise*, ed. Cynthia C. Davidson (Cambridge, Massachusetts: MIT Press, 1996), 126–32.

Bibliography

Achilles, Rolf, Harrington, Kevin, and Myhrum, Charlotte (eds) (1986) *Mies van der Rohe: Architect as Educator*. Chicago: Illinois Institute of Technology, Mies van der Rohe Centennial Project.

Ackerman, James (1990; pbk edn 1995) *The Villa: Form and Ideology of Country Houses*. London: Thames & Hudson; 1st pub. 1966.

Adam, Robert, and Adam, James (1959). *Works in Architecture*, 3 vols. London: Alec Tiranti Ltd; 1st pub. 1773, 1779, 1882.

Adorno, Theodor (1991) *Minima Moralia: Reflections from Damaged Life*. London: Verso; 1st pub. 1951.

Agrest, Diana, Conway, Patricia, and Weisman, Lesley Kanes (eds) (1996) *The Sex of Architecture*. New York: Harry N. Abrams.

Anderson, Christy, "Writing the Historical Survey," *JSAH* 58/3 (September), p. 351.

Appadurai, A. (1986) *The Social Life of Things: Commodities in a Commercial Perspective*. Cambridge: Cambridge University Press.

Apollonio, Umbro (ed.) (1973) *Futurist Manifestos*. London: Thames & Hudson.

Arnold, Dana (1995) "Rationality, Safety and Power: The Street Planning of Later Georgian London," *Georgian Group Journal* (1995), pp. 37–50.

Arnold, Dana (ed.) (1996) *The Georgian Villa*. Stroud: Sutton.

Arnold, Dana (1998) *The Georgian Country House: Architecture, Landscape and Society*. Stroud: Sutton.

Arnold, Dana (2001) *Representing the Metropolis: Architecture, Urban Experience and Social Life in London 1800–1840*. Aldershot: Ashgate.

Arnold, Dana (2002) *Reading Architectural History*. London: Routledge.

Attfield, Judy, and Kirkham, Pat (eds) (1989) *A View from the Interior: Feminism, Women and Design*. London: The Women's Press.

Ballantyne, Andrew (1997) *Architecture, Landscape and Liberty: Richard Payne Knight and the Picturesque*. Cambridge: Cambridge University Press.

Ballantyne, Andrew (ed.) (2002) *What Is Architecture?* London: Routledge.

Banham, Reyner (1960) *Theory and Design in the First Machine Age*. London: The Architectural Press.

Banham, Reyner (1969) *The Architecture of the Well-Tempered Environment*. Chicago: Chicago University Press.

Banham, Reyner (1971) *Los Angeles: The Architecture of Four Ecologies*. Harmondsworth: Penguin.

Barthes, Roland (1977) "The Death of the Author," in *Image–Music–Text*, trans. Stephen Heath. London: Fontana.

Barthes, Roland (1983) *Selected Writings*, introd. Susan Sontag. London: Fontana.

Baudrillard, Jean (1988) *Selected Writings*, ed. M. Poster. Cambridge: Polity.

Beckett, Jane (1980) "'De Vonk,' Noordwijk: An Example of Early De Stijl Co-operation," *Art History* 3/2 (June), pp. 202–17.

Benjamin, Andrew (ed.) (1990) *Philosophy and Architecture*, special issue of *Journal of Philosophy and the Visual Arts*. London: The Academy Group.

Benjamin, Walter (1939) "Central Park," repr. in *New German Critique*, 34 (Winter 1985), pp. 32–57.

Benjamin, Walter (1968) *Illuminations: Essays and Reflections*, ed. and introd. Hannah Arendt. New York: Harcourt Brace Jovanovich.

Benjamin, Walter (1978) *Reflections: Essays, Aphorisms, Autobiographical Writings*, ed. and introd. Peter Demetz. New York: Harcourt Brace Jovanovich.

Benjamin, Walter (1999) *The Arcades Project*, trans. Howard Eiland and Kevin McLaughlin. Cambridge, MA: The Belknap Press/Harvard University Press; 1st pub. 1927–40.

Bennet, T. (1995) *The Birth of the Museum*. London: Routledge, 1995.

Bentmann, Reinhard, and Müller, Michael (1992) *The Villa as Hegemonic Architecture*. Atlantic Highlands, NJ: Humanities Press; 1st pub. 1970.

Benton, Charlotte, et al. (eds) (1975a) *Documents: A Collection of Source Material for the Modern Movement*. Milton Keynes: Open University Press.

Benton, Charlotte, et al. (eds) (1975b) *Form and Function*. Milton Keynes: Open University Press.

Bergdoll, Barry (1994) *Karl Friedrich Schinkel: An Architect for Prussia*. New York: Rizzoli.

Bergdoll, Barry (2000) *European Architecture 1750–1890*. Oxford: Oxford University Press.

Berman, Marshall (1982) *All That Is Solid Melts into Air: The Experience of Modernity*. New York: Verso.

Bermingham, Ann, and Brewer, John (1997) *The Consumption of Culture, 1600–1800: Image, Object, Text*. London: Routledge.

Beyer, Oskar (ed.) (1967) *Eric Mendelsohn: Letters of an Architect*, trans. Geoffrey Strachan, introd. Nikolaus Pevsner. London: Abelard-Schuman.

Bindman, David, and Riemann, Gottfried (eds) (1993) *Karl Friedrich Schinkel, "The English Journey": Journey of a Visit to France and Britain in 1826*. New Haven: Paul Mellon Centre for Studies in British Art/Yale University Press.

Blake, Peter (1949) *Marcel Breuer: Architect and Designer*. New York: Museum of Modern Art.

Blau, Eve (1999) *The Architecture of Red Vienna 1919–1935*. Cambridge, MA: MIT Press.

Blau, Eve, and Platzer, Monika (eds) (1999) *Shaping the Great City: Modern Architecture in Central Europe, 1890–1937*. Munich: Prestel.

Blier, Suzanne (1994) *The Anatomy of Architecture: Ontology and Metaphor in Battama-liba Architectural Expression*. Chicago: Chicago University Press.

Bourdieu, Pierre (1992) *Distinction: A Social Critique of the Judgment of Taste*. London: Routledge; 1st pub. 1979.

Boyd White, Iain (1980) "The End of an Avant-Garde: The Example of Expressionist Architecture," *Art History* 3/1 (March), pp. 102–14.

Breuer, Marcel (1934) "Where Do We Stand?," lecture delivered in Zurich, repr. in Peter Blake, *Marcel Breuer: Architect and Designer*. New York: Museum of Modern Art (1949), pp. 119–22.

Brewer, Daniel (1993) *The Discourse of Enlightenment in Eighteenth Century France: Diderot and the Art of Philosophizing*. Cambridge: Cambridge University Press.

Buck-Morss, Susan (1989) *The Dialectics of Seeing: Walter Benjamin and the Arcades Project*. Cambridge, MA: MIT Press.

Burke, Edmund (1757) *A Philosophical Enquiry into the Origin of our Ideas of the Sublime and Beautiful*. Oxford: Blackwell.

Burke, Edmund (1950) *Reflections on the Revolution in France*. London: Oxford University Press; 1st pub. 1790.

Burke, Peter (1991) *New Perspectives on Historical Writing*. Cambridge: Polity.

Bushman, Richard L. (1992) *The Refinement of America: Persons, Houses, Cities*. New York: Vintage Books.

Campbell, Joan (1978) *The German Werkbund*. Princeton: Princeton University Press.

Carr, E. H. (1978) *What Is History?* Harmondsworth: Penguin.

Caughie, J. (1981) *Theories of Authorship*. London: Routledge & Kegan Paul.

Çelik, Zeynep (1992) *Displaying the Orient: Architecture of Islam at Nineteenth Century World's Fairs*. Berkeley: University of California Press.

Çelik, Zeynep (ed.) (1994) *Streets: Critical Perspectives on Public Space*. Berkeley: University of California Press.

Chipp, Herschel B. (ed.) (1968) *Theories of Modern Art*. Berkeley: University of California Press.

Cohen, Jean-Louis (1995) *Scenes of the World To Come: European Architecture and the American Challenge 1893–1960*, preface Hubert Damisch. Paris: Flammarion/Canadian Centre for Architecture.

Collins, George R., and Craseman Collins, Christianne (eds) (1986) *Camillo Sitte: The Birth of Modern City Planning*. New York: Rizzoli.

Collins, Peter (1965) *Changing Ideals in Modern Architecture 1750–1950*. London: Faber & Faber.

Colomina, Beatriz (ed.) (1992) *Sexuality and Space*. New York: Princeton Architectural Press.

Colomina, Beatriz (1994) *Privacy and Publicity: Modern Architecture as Mass Media*. Cambridge, MA: MIT Press.

Colquhoun, Alan (1989) *Modernity and the Classical Tradition: Architectural Essays 1980–1987*. Cambridge, MA: MIT Press.

Constant, Caroline (1994) "E.1027: The Non-Heroic Modernism of Eileen Gray," *JSAH* 53/3 (September), pp. 265–79.

Conway, H., and Roenisch, R. (1994) *Understanding Architecture: An Introduction to Architecture and Architectural History*. London: Routledge.

Cosgrove, Denis, and Daniels, Stephen (1988) *The Iconography of Landscape; Essays on the Symbolic Representation, Design and Use of Past Environments.* Cambridge: Cambridge University Press.

Crane, Walter (1911) *William Morris to Whistler.* London: Bell.

Curtis, William J. R. (1996) *Modern Architecture since 1900,* 3rd edn. London: Phaidon Press; 1st pub. 1982.

Davidson, Cynthia (ed.) (2001) *Anything.* Cambridge, MA: MIT Press.

Davis, Terence (1966) *John Nash: The Prince Regent's Architect.* London: Country Life.

De Certeau, Michel (1984) *The Practice of Everyday Life,* trans. Stephen Rendall. Berkeley: University of California Press; 1st pub. 1974.

Deleuze, Gilles, and Guattari, Félix (1987) *A Thousand Plateaus: Capitalism and Schizophrenia,* trans. B. Massumi. Minneapolis: University of Minnesota Press.

Diderot, Denis (ed.) (1995) *The Architectural Plates from the "Encyclopédie."* New York: Dover Publications; 1st pub. 1751–72.

Doig, Allan (1986) *Theo van Doesburg: Painting into Architecture, Theory into Practice* Cambridge: Cambridge University Press.

Douglas, M., and Isherwood, B. (1979) *The World of Goods.* London: Allen Lane.

Drew, Joanna (ed.) (1985) *The Architecture of Adolf Loos.* London: Arts Council of Great Britain.

Drexler, Arthur (ed.) (1968) *The Mies van der Rohe Archive,* 4 vols. New York: Garland.

Drexler, Arthur (ed.) (1977) *The Architecture of the École des Beaux Arts.* London: Secker & Warburg.

Duncan, Carol (1993) *The Aesthetics of Power: Essays in Critical Art History.* Cambridge: Cambridge University Press.

Duncan, Carol (1995) *Civilising Rituals: Inside Public Art Museums.* London: Routledge.

Edwards, Holly (ed.) (2000) *A Million and One Nights: Orientalism in American Culture, 1870–1930.* Princeton: Princeton University Press.

Edwards, Steve (ed.) (1998) *Art and its Histories: A Reader.* London and New Haven: Yale University Press/Open University.

Elsner, John, and Cardinal, Roger (eds) (1994) *The Cultures of Collecting.* London: Reaktion Books.

Fergusson, James (1865) *History of Architecture in All Countries from the Earliest Times to the Present Day.* London: John Murray.

Fishman, Robert (1999) *Urban Utopias in the Twentieth Century: Ebenezer Howard, Frank Lloyd Wright, Le Corbusier.* Cambridge, MA: MIT Press.

Fletcher, Bannister (1956) *A History of Architecture in the Comparative Method.* London: B. T. Batsford; 1st pub. 1896.

Forty, Adrian (1986) *Objects of Desire: Design and Society since 1750.* London: Thames & Hudson.

Foster, Hal (ed.) (1983) *The Anti-Aesthetic: Essays on Postmodern Culture.* Washington: Bay Press.

Foucault, Michel (1977) *Discipline and Punish: The Birth of the Prison,* trans. Alan Sheridan. London: Allen Lane.

Foucault, Michel (1981) "What Is an Author?," in J. Caughie (ed.), *Theories of Authorship.* London and Boston: Routledge & Kegan Paul.

Foucault, Michel (1989a) *The Order of Things: An Archaeology of the Human Sciences.* London: Routledge; 1st pub. 1966; English trans. 1970.

Foucault, Michel (1989b) *The Archaeology of Knowledge*. London: Routledge; 1st pub. 1969.

Friedman, Alice T. (1992) "Architecture, Authority and the Female Gaze: Planning and Representation in the Early Modern Country House," *Assemblage* 18 (August), pp. 41–61.

Friedman, Alice T. (1998) *Women and the Making of the Modern House: A Social and Architectural History*. New York: Harry N. Abrams.

Friedman, Alice T. (1999) "The Way You Do the Things You Do: Writing the History of Houses and Housing," *JSAH* 58/3 (September).

Frisby, David (1981) *Sociological Impressionism: A Reassessment of Georg Simmel's Social Theory*. London: Routledge.

"G" (1897) "The Revival of English Domestic Architecture VI: The Work of Mr. C. F. A. Voysey," *The Studio* 2.

Gadamer, Hans-Georg (1979) "The Ontological Foundation of the Occasional and Decorative," trans. W. Glen Doepel, in J. Cumming and G. Bardez (eds), *Truth and Method*. London: Sheed & Ward.

Geddes, Norman Bel (1934) *Horizons*. London: John Lane.

Geretsegger, Heinz, and Peinter, Max (1970) *Otto Wagner 1841–1918: The Expanding City. The Beginning of Modern Architecture*. London: Pall Mall Press.

Giedion, Sigfried (1941) *Space, Time and Architecture*. Oxford: Oxford University Press.

Giedion, Sigfried (1948) *Mechanisation Takes Command*. Oxford: Oxford University Press.

Gilbert, Christopher (1978) *The Life and Works of Thomas Chippendale*. London: Macmillan.

Gilpin, William (1789) *Observations Relative to Picturesque Beauty made in the Year 1789 in Several Parts of Great Britain, Particularly in the Highlands of Scotland*, 2 vols. London.

Girouard, Mark (1978) *Life in the English Country House: A Social and Architectural History*. New Haven: Yale University Press.

Golby, J. M. (ed.) (1986) *Culture and Society in Britain 1850–1890: A Source Book of Contemporary Writings*. Oxford: Oxford University Press/Open University.

Goldhagen, Sarah Williams, and Legault, Réjean (eds) (2000) *Anxious Modernisms: Experimentation in Post-War Architectural Culture*. Cambridge, MA: MIT Press.

Greenhalgh, Paul (1988) *Ephemeral Vistas: A History of the Expositions Universelles, Great Exhibitions and World's Fairs, 1851–1939*. Manchester: Manchester University Press, 1988.

Greenhalgh, Paul (1993) *Quotations and Sources on Design and the Decorative Arts*. Manchester: Manchester University Press.

Greenhalgh, Paul (ed.) (2000) *Art Nouveau 1890–1914*. London: V&A Publications.

Gropius, Walter (1956) *The Scope of Total Architecture*. London: George Allen & Unwin.

Handlin, David P. (1979) *The American Home: Architecture and Society 1815–1915*. Boston: Little, Brown.

Harris, Eileen (2001) *The Genius of Robert Adam: His Interiors*. New Haven: Yale University Press.

Harris, John (1994) *The Palladian Revival: Lord Burlington, his Villa and Garden at Chiswick*. New Haven: Yale University Press.

Harrison, Charles, and Wood, Paul (1992) *Art in Theory 1900–1990: An Anthology of Changing Ideas*. Oxford: Blackwell.

Harrison, Charles, and Wood, Paul, with Gaiger, Jason (1998) *Art in Theory 1815–1900: An Anthology of Changing Ideas*. Oxford: Blackwell.

Harvey, David (1990) *The Condition of Postmodernity.* Oxford: Blackwell.

Haussmann, Georges-Eugène (1979) *Mémoires,* 2 vols. Paris: Guy Durier.

Hayden, Dolores (1981) *The Grand Domestic Revolution: A History of Feminist Designs for American Homes, Neighbourhoods and Cities.* Cambridge, MA: MIT Press.

Hays, K. Michael (ed.) (1998) *Architecture Theory since 1968.* Cambridge, MA: MIT Press.

Heidegger, Martin (1971) *Poetry, Language, Thought.* New York: Harper & Row; 1st pub. 1954.

Heynen, Hilde (1999) *Architecture and Modernity: A Critique.* Cambridge, MA: MIT Press.

Hill, Rosemary (1999) "Reformation to Millennium: Pugin's *Contrasts* in the History of English Thought " *JSAH* 58/1 (March), pp. 26-41.

Hitchcock, Henry-Russell (1837) in *The Gentleman's Magazine* (March).

Hitchcock, Henry-Russell (1929) *Modern Architecture: Romanticism and Reintegration.* New York: Payson & Clarke.

Hitchcock, Henry-Russell (1942) *In the Nature of Materials: The Buildings of Frank Lloyd Wright.* London: Elek Books.

Hitchcock, Henry-Russell (1954) *Early Victorian Architecture in Britain,* 2 vols. London: Architectural Association Press.

Hitchcock, Henry-Russell (1957) *Gaudi.* New York: Museum of Modern Art (exhibition catalog).

Hitchcock, Henry-Russell (1966a) *Architecture 1949–1965.* London: Thames & Hudson.

Hitchcock, Henry-Russell (1966b) *The International Style: Architecture since 1922.* New York: Norton; 1st pub. 1932.

Hitchcock, Henry-Russell (1968) *Architecture: Nineteenth and Twentieth Centuries,* 3rd edn. London: Penguin.

Hitchcock, Henry-Russell, and Drexler, Arthur (1952) *Built in the USA: Postwar Architecture.* New York.

Hobsbawm, Eric (1990) *Industry and Empire.* London: Penguin.

Howard, Ebenezer (1902) *Garden Cities of Tomorrow,* 3rd edn of *Tomorrow: A Peaceful Path to Reform,* 1st published 1898. London: Swan Sonnenschein.

Iversen, Margaret (1993) *Alois Riegl: Art History and Theory.* Cambridge, MA: MIT Press.

Jaffé, Hans (ed.) (1982) *De Stijl: 1917–1931 Visions of Utopia.* Oxford: Phaidon.

Jameson, Frederic (1991) *Postmodernism or the Cultural Logic of Late Capitalism.* London: Verso.

Jay, Martin (1993) *Downcast Eyes: The Denigration of Vision in Twentieth Century French Thought.* Berkeley: University of California Press.

Jencks, Charles (1987) *The Language of Post-Modern Architecture.* London: Academy Editions; 1st pub. 1977.

Jordy, William H. (1972) *American Buildings and their Architects.* New York: Oxford University Press.

Julier, Guy (1993) *20th Century Design and Designers.* London: Thames & Hudson.

Kaes, Anton, Jay, Martin, and Dimendberg, Edward (eds) (1994) *The Weimar Republic Sourcebook.* Berkeley: University of California Press.

Kimball, Fiske, and Edgel, George Howard (1918) *A History of Architecture.* New York (no publisher given).

King, Anthony (ed.) (1996) *Re-presenting the City: Ethnicity, Capital and Culture in the Twenty-First-Century Metropolis.* New York: New York University Press.

Koolhaas, Rem (1994) *Delirious New York.* New York: Monacelli Press; 1st pub. 1978.

Koshalek, Richard, Smith, Elizabeth A. T., Ferguson, Russell, and Çelik, Zeynep (eds) (2000) *At the End of the Century: One Hundred Years of Architecture.* Los Angeles: Museum of Contemporary Art.

Kostoff, Spiro (ed.) (1977) *The Architect: Chapters in the History of the Profession.* Oxford: Oxford University Press.

Kostoff, Spiro (1985) *A History of Architecture: Settings and Rituals.* New York and Oxford: Oxford University Press.

Krier, Leon (ed.) (1978) *Albert Speer Architecture 1932–1942.* Berlin: Verlag Ullstein.

Krier, Rob (1982) *Rob Krier on Architecture.* London: Academy Editions.

Latour, Alessandra (ed.) (1991) *Louis I. Khan: Writings, Lectures, Interviews.* New York: Rizzoli.

Latrobe, Benjamin (1984) *The Correspondence and Miscellaneous Papers of Benjamin Henry Latrobe*, ed. John C. van Horne and Lee W. Formwalt. New Haven: Yale University Press.

Lavin, Sylvia (1999) "Theory into History; or The Will to Anthology," *JSAH* 58/3 (September), pp. 494–9.

Le Corbusier (1946) *Towards a New Architecture*, trans. Frederick Etchells. London: The Architectural Press; 1st pub. 1927; original French edn. 1923.

Le Corbusier (1957) *Gaudi.* Barcelona: Ediciones Poligrafa.

Le Corbusier (1991) *Precisions on the Present State of Architecture and City Planning.* Cambridge, MA: MIT Press; 1st pub. 1930.

Leach, Neil (ed.) (1997) *Rethinking Architecture.* London: Routledge.

Ledoux, Claude-Nicholas (1983) *L'Architecture*, introd. Anthony Vidler. New York: Princeton Architectural Press; 1st pub. 1804.

Lefebvre, Henri (1991) *The Production of Space*, trans. Donald Nicholson Smith. Boston and Oxford: Blackwell; 1st pub. 1974.

LeGates, Richard, and Stout, Frederic (eds) (1998) *Early Urban Planning 1870–1940: Selected Essays.* London and New York: Routledge.

Lethaby, W. R. (1979) *Phillip Webb and his Works.* London: Raven Oak Press; 1st pub. 1935.

Lethaby, W. R. (1957) *Form in Civilisation*, 2nd edn. London: Oxford University Press.

Levine, Donald (ed.) (1971) *Georg Simmel: On Individuality and Social Forms.* Chicago: Chicago University Press.

Levine, Neil (1996) *The Architecture of Frank Lloyd Wright.* Princeton: Princeton University Press.

Libeskind, Daniel (2001) *Daniel Libeskind: The Space of Encounter.* London: Thames & Hudson.

Lyotard, Jean-François (1984) *The Postmodern Condition: A Report on Knowledge.* Manchester: Manchester University Press; 1st pub. 1979.

Mackay, David (1985) *Modern Architecture in Barcelona 1854–1939.* Sheffield: The Anglo-Catalan Society of Occasional Publications.

Makail, J. W. (1950) *The Life and Works of William Morris.* Oxford: Oxford University Press; 1st pub. 1899.

Mallgrave, Harry Francis (ed.) (1988) *Otto Wagner Modern Architecture: A Guidebook for his Students to this Field of Art*, facsimile reproduction of the 1902 edn, introd. and trans. Harry Francis Mallgrave. Santa Monica: Getty Center for History of Art and Humanities.

Margolin, Victor (ed.) (1989) *Design Discourse: History, Theory, Criticism.* Chicago: University of Chicago Press.

Marinetti, Filippo Tommaso (1909) "The Foundation and Manifesto of Futurism," in Herschel B. Chipp (ed.), *Theories of Modern Art.* Berkeley: University of California Press (1968), pp. 281–308.

Marx, Karl (1974) *Das Kapital,* trans. Moore and Aveling (1887). London: Lawrence & Wishart; 1st pub. 1867; this trans. 1st pub. 1887.

Matrix (1984) *Women and the Man-Made Environment.* London: Pluto Press.

McQuillan, Martin (ed.) (2000) *Deconstruction: A Reader.* Edinburgh: Edinburgh University Press.

McQuiston, Liz (1988) *Women in Design: A Contemporary View.* London: Trefoil Publications.

Mendelsohn, Eric (1967) *Letters of an Architect,* ed. Oskar Beyer, trans. Geoffrey Strachan, introd. Nikolaus Pevsner. London and New York: Abelard-Schuman; 1st pub. 1910–53.

Middleton, Robin (1978) *Architectural Design: Beaux Arts.* London: Architectural Design.

Middleton, Robin (1981) "Viollet-Le-Duc's Influence in Nineteenth Century England," *Art History* 4/2 (June 1981).

Middleton, Robin (ed.) (1982) *The Beaux-Arts and Nineteenth Century French Architecture.* London: Thames & Hudson.

Mirzoeff, Nicholas (2000) *Diaspora and Visual Culture: Representing Africans and Jews.* London and New York: Routledge.

Mitchell, W. J. T. (1994) *Landscape and Power.* Chicago: Chicago University Press.

Moholy-Nagy, László (1947) *The New Vision,* 4th edn, preface Walter Gropius. New York: George Wittenborn; 1st pub. 1928.

Morris, May (ed.) (1914) *The Collected Works of William Morris.* London: Longman Green.

Mumford, Lewis (1966) *The City in History.* London: Pelican.

Mumford, Lewis (2000) *The CIAM Discourse on Urbanism 1928–1960.* Cambridge, MA: MIT Press.

Nash, John (1828) *Report to the Select Committee of the Office of Works.* London.

Nesbitt, Kate (ed.) (1996) *Theorizing a New Agenda for Architecture: An Anthology of Architectural Theory 1965–1995.* New York: Princeton Architectural Press.

Neumann, Eckhard (ed.) (1970) *Bauhaus and Bauhaus People.* New York: Van Nostrand Reinhold.

Ockman, Joan (ed.) (1985) *Architecture, Criticism and Ideology.* New York: Princeton Architectural Press.

Ockman, Joan (ed.) (1993) *Architecture Culture 1943–1968.* New York: Rizzoli International Publications.

Parissien, Steven (1992) *Regency Style.* London: Phaidon, 1992.

Parry, Linda (ed.) (1996) *William Morris.* London: Philip Wilson/Victoria and Albert Museum.

Passanti, Franco (1997) "The Vernacular, Modernism and Le Corbusier," *JSAH* 56/4 (December), pp. 438–51.

Payne Knight, Richard (1805) *An Analytical Inquiry into the Principles of Taste.* London.

Peisch, Mark L. (1964) *The Chicago School of Architecture: Early Followers of Sullivan and Wright*, Columbia Studies in Art History and Archaeology 5. London: Phaidon Press.

Pevsner, Nikolaus (1936) *Pioneers of the Modern Movement: From William Morris to Walter Gropius*. London; republished 1960 as *Pioneers of Modern Design*. Quotations are from the 1991 Penguin edn.

Pevsner, Nikolaus (1968a) *Studies in Art, Architecture and Design*, 2 vols. London: Thames & Hudson.

Pevsner, Nikolaus (1968b) *The Sources of Modern Architecture and Design*. London: Thames & Hudson.

Pevsner, Nikolaus (1972) *Some Architectural Writers of the Nineteenth Century*. Oxford: Clarendon Press.

Pevsner, Nikolaus (1990) *An Outline of European Architecture*. Harmondsworth: Penguin.

Podro, Michael (1982) *The Critical Historians of Art*. New Haven and London: Yale University Press.

Poggioli, Renato (1968) *The Theory of the Avant-Garde*. Cambridge, MA: MIT Press.

Porphyrios, Demetri (1984) *Architectural Design. Leon Krier: Houses, Palaces, Cities*. London: Architectural Design Editions.

Price, Uvedale (1794–8) *Essays on the Picturesque*. London: Wm. S. Orr & Co.

Pugin, Augustus Welby Northmore (1836) *Contrasts*. London: printed for the author and published by him.

Pugin, Augustus Welby Northmore (1837) *An Apology for a Work Entitled Contrasts*. Oxford: St Barnabas Press.

Purbrick, Louise (2001) *The Great Exhibition of 1851: New Interdisciplinary Essays*. Manchester: Manchester University Press.

Rabinow, Paul (ed.) (1984) *The Foucault Reader*. London: Penguin.

Read, Alan (ed.) (2000) *Architecturally Speaking: Practices of Art, Architecture and the Everyday*. London: Routledge.

Rice, Shelley (1997) *Parisian Views*. Cambridge, MA: MIT Press.

Robinson, Charles Mulford (1903) *Modern Civic Architecture and the City Made Beautiful*. New York and London: G. P. Putnam.

Rosenau, Helen (ed.) (1976) *Boullée and Visionary Architecture, including Boullée's "Architecture, Essay on Art."* London: Academy Editions.

Rowbotham, Sheila (1973) *Hidden from History: 300 Years of Women's Oppression and the Fight Against It*. London: Pluto Press.

Rowe, Colin (1976) *The Mathematics of the Ideal Villa and Other Essays*. Cambridge, MA: MIT Press.

Rowe, Dorothy (2003) *Representing Berlin: Sexuality and the City in German Modernism* Aldershot: Ashgate.

Rowe, Peter (1995) *Modernity and Housing*. Cambridge, MA: MIT Press.

Rüedi, Katerina, Wigglesworth, Sarah, and McCorquodale, Duncan (eds) (1996) *Desiring Practices*. London: Black Dog.

Ruskin, John (1905) *The Stones of Venice*. London: George Allen & Unwin.

Said, Edward (1978) *Orientalism*. London: Penguin.

Sant'Elia, Antonio (1914) "Manifesto of Futurist Architecture," repr. in Umbro Apollonio (ed.), *Futurist Manifestos*. London: Thames & Hudson (1973), pp. 160–72.

Saville, John (1987) *1848: The British State and the Chartist Movement*. Cambridge: Cambridge University Press.

Schorske, Carl (1981) *Fin-de-Siècle Vienna: Politics and Culture.* New York: Vintage Books.

Schwartz, Frederic (1996) *The Werkbund: Design Theory and Mass Culture before the First World War.* New Haven: Yale University Press.

Scott Brown, Denise (2002) "Room at the Top? Sexism and the Star System in Architecture," in Dana Arnold (ed.), *Reading Architectural History.* London: Routledge, pp. 205–10.

Scully, Vincent (1971) *The Shingle Style and the Stick Style: Architectural Theory and Design from Downing to the Origins of Wright.* New Haven: Yale University Press.

Sharp, Dennis (1967) *Sources of Modern Architecture.* London: Lund Humphries.

Sharp, Dennis (1975) Introduction to Charlotte Benton et al. (eds), *Form and Function.* Milton Keynes: Open University Press.

Simmel, Georg (1903) "The Metropolis and Modern Life," in Donald Levine (ed.), *Georg Simmel: On Individuality and Social Forms.* Chicago: Chicago University Press (1971), pp. 324–39.

Sitte, Camillo (1986) *City Planning According to Artistic Principles,* trans. George R. Collins and Christine Crasemann Collins. New York: Rizzoli; 1st pub. 1889.

Smithson, Alison, and Smithson, Peter (1994) *Changing the Art of Inhabitation: Mies' Pieces, Eames' Dreams, the Smithsons.* London: Artemis.

Solomon, Maynard (ed.) (1979) *Marxism and Art: Essays Classic and Contemporary.* Brighton: Harvester Press.

Sorkin, Michael (1991) *Exquisite Corpse: Writing on Buildings.* London, New York: Verso.

Stein, Jay, and Spreckelmeyer, Ken (eds) (1999) *Classic Readings in Architecture.* Boston: WCB/McGraw-Hill.

Stewart, Janet (2000) *Fashioning Vienna: Adolf Loos's Cultural Criticism.* London: Routledge.

Stieber, Nancy (1998) *Housing Design and Society in Amsterdam: Reconfiguring Urban Order and Identity, 1900–1920.* Chicago: Chicago University Press.

Stieber, Nancy (1999) "Microhistory of the Modern City: Urban Space, its Use and Representation," *JSAH* 58/3 (September/December), Special Issue pp. 382–91.

Sullivan, Louis (1947) *Kindergarten Chats.* New York: George Wittenborn.

Summerson, John (1953) *Architecture in Britain 1530–1830.* New Haven: Yale University Press.

Summerson, John (ed.) (1966) *Concerning Architecture.* London: Allen Lane/Penguin.

Sutcliffe, Anthony (1993) *Paris: An Architectural History.* New Haven: Yale University Press.

Tafuri, Manfredo (1973) *Architecture and Utopia: Design and Capitalist Development.* Cambridge, MA: MIT Press.

Tafuri, Manfredo (1987) *The Sphere and the Labyrinth: Avant-Gardes and Architecture from Piranesi to the 1970s.* Cambridge, MA: MIT Press; 1st pub. (in Italian) 1980.

Tatum, George B., and MacDougall, Elisabeth Blair (1989) *Prophet with Honour: The Career of Andrew Jackson Downing.* Washington: Dumbarton Oaks.

Taut, Bruno (1929) *Modern Architecture.* London: Studio Publications.

Taut, Bruno (1972) *Alpine Architecture,* trans. Shirley Palmer, ed. and introd. Dennis Sharp. London: November Books; 1st pub. 1919.

Thackera, John (ed.) (1988) *Design after Modernism: Beyond the Object.* London: Thames & Hudson.

Tournikiotis, Panayotis (1999) *Historiography of Modern Architecture.* Cambridge, MA: MIT Press.

Twombly, Robert (ed.) (1988) *Louis Sullivan: The Public Papers.* Chicago: University of Chicago Press.

Tzonis, Alexander, and Lefebvre, Liane (1995) *Architecture in North America since 1960.* London: Thames & Hudson.

Upton, Dell (1998) *Architecture in the United States.* Oxford: Oxford University Press.

Upton, Dell, and Vlach, John Michael (eds) (1986) *Common Places: Readings in American Vernacular Architecture.* Athens, GA: University of Georgia Press.

Van Doesburg, Theo (1990) *On European Architecture. Complete Essays from Het Bouwbedrijf,* trans. Charlotte I. Loeb and Arthur L. Loeb. Basel: Birkhäuser; 1st pub. 1924–31.

Van Zanten, David (1987) *Designing Paris: The Architecture of Duban, Labrouste, Duc and Vaudoyer.* Cambridge, MA: MIT Press.

Vasselau, Cathryn (1998) *Textures of Light: Vision and Touch in Irigaray, Levinas and Merlau-Ponty.* London: Routledge.

Veblen, Thorstein (1984) *The Theory of the Leisure Class.* London: Penguin; 1st pub. 1899.

Venturi, Robert, and Scott Brown, Denise (eds) (1984) *A View from the Campidoglio: Selected Essays 1953–1984.* New York: Harper & Brown.

Venturi, Robert, Scott Brown, Denise, and Izenour, Steven (1972) *Learning from Las Vegas: The Forgotten Symbolism of Architectural Form.* Cambridge, MA: MIT Press.

Vidler, Anthony (1992) *The Architectural Uncanny: Essays in the Modern Unhomely.* Cambridge, MA: MIT Press.

Vincentelli, Moira (2000) *Women and Ceramics: Gendered Vessels.* Manchester: Manchester University Press.

Viollet-le-Duc, Eugène-Emmanuel (1987) *Lectures on Architecture.* New York: Dover Publications; 1st pub. 1814–79.

Von Falkenhausen, Susanne (1997) "The Sphere: Reading a Gender Metaphor in the Architecture of Modern Cults of Identity," *Art History,* 20/2 (June), pp. 238–67.

Voysey, C. F. A. (1893) in *The Studio* 1.

Voysey, C. F. A. (1896) *The Aims and Conditions of the Modern Decorator.* London (no publisher given).

Wagner, Otto (1896) *Moderne Architektur.* Vienna: Anton Scholl.

Wagner, Otto (1911) *Die Großstadt.* Vienna: Anton Scholl.

Wainwright, Clive (1996) "Morris in Context," in Linda Parry (ed.), *William Morris.* London: Philip Wilson/Victoria and Albert Museum.

Walpole, Horace (1748–) *Strawberry Hill, Twickenham: A Description of the Villa.* London: Strawberry Hill; 1774 edition, printed by Thomas Kirgate.

Walpole, Horace (1762–80) *Anecdotes of Painting in England,* 4 vols. London.

Walsh, Kevin (1992) *The Representation of the Past.* London: Routledge.

Watkin, David (1980) *The Rise of Architectural History.* London: Architectural Press.

Watkin, David (ed.) (2000) *Sir John Soane: The Royal Academy Lectures.* Cambridge: Cambridge University Press.

Watkin, David, and Mellinghoff, Tilman (1987) *German Architecture and the Classical Ideal 1740–1840.* London: Thames & Hudson.

Weingarden, Lauren (2000) "Louis Sullivan and the Spirit of Nature," in Paul Greenhalgh (ed.), *Art Nouveau 1890–1914.* London: V&A Publications.

Weisman, Leslie Kanes (1992) *Discrimination by Design: A Feminist Critique of the Man-Made Environment.* Urbana: University of Illinois Press.

White, Hayden (1976) "The Fiction of Factual Representation," in A. Fletcher (ed.), *The Literature of Fact.* New York: University of Columbia Press.

White, Hayden (1985) "Interpretation in History," in *Tropics in Discourse: Essays in Cultural Criticism.* Baltimore.

Whitford, Frank (1984) *Bauhaus.* London: Thames & Hudson.

Wigley, Mark (1997) *The Architecture of Deconstruction: Derrida's Haunt.* Cambridge, MA: MIT Press.

Williams, Raymond (1967) *Culture and Society.* London: Chatto & Windus.

Wilson, Richard Guy (1979) *The American Renaissance, 1876–1917.* New York: Brooklyn Museum/Pantheon Books.

Wilson, William H. (1989) *The City Beautiful Movement.* Baltimore: Johns Hopkins University Press.

Wolzogen, A. Freiherr von (1862–3) *Aus Schinkel's Nachlass,* 3 vols. Munich: Mäander.

Wright, Frank Lloyd (1945) *An Autobiography.* London: Faber & Faber.

Wright, Frank Lloyd (1949) *Genius and the Mobocracy.* London: Secker & Warburg.

Wright, Gwendolyn (1980) *Moralism and the Model Home: Domestic Architecture and Cultural Conflict in Chicago 1876–1913.* Chicago: Chicago University Press.

Wright, Gwendolyn (1981) *Building the Dream: A Social History of Housing in America.* New York: Pantheon Books.

Zevi, Bruno (1949) *Towards an Organic Architecture.* London: Faber & Faber.

Zevi, Bruno (1954) *Frank Lloyd Wright.* Milan: Il Balcone.

Zevi, Bruno (1978) *Modern Language of Architecture.* Seattle: University of Washington Press.

Selected Journals

AA Files
AA Journal (London)
Architects' Journal
Architectural Design
Architectural History
Architectural Review
Architecture (AIA American Institute of Architects)
Art Bulletin
Art History
Art Journal
Assemblage
Dimensions (Journal of University of Michigan, College of Architecture and Urban Planning)
Georgian Group Journal
Journal of Architecture
Journal of Philosophy and the Visual Arts

Journal of the Society of Architectural Historians of America
New Arcadian Journal
New German Critique
Oppositions
Oxford Art Journal
Perspecta (Yale University School of Architecture)
Praxis (New York)
Progressive Architecture (1947–1967)
RIBA Journal
The Gentleman's Magazine
The Studio
Threshold (Journal of the School of Architecture, University of Illinois, Chicago)

Index

Aalto, Alvar, 477
Ackerman, James, 6, 39–40, 41, 42, 90–5
Adam, Robert, 36, 60
Adam, Robert and James, *The Works in Architecture*, 31–3, 34, 60, 74–8, fig. 6.1
Adam style, 34, 35
  see also style
Adler, Dankmar, 197, 291–2
Adorno, Theodor, 326–7
aesthetic theories
  beautiful, 40, 41–2, 102, 109, 110, 142–3
  Marxism and, 183–4
  modernist, 325, 326, 327
  picturesque, 38, 40, 41–3, 102, 103–4, 109
  sublime, 38, 40, 41, 42–3, 96–8, 102–4, 151
Alberti, L. B., 45, 53, 83
Altes Museum, 167–9
Anderson, Christy, 6
Anderson, Stanford, 476–7
architect(s), 322, 327, 329
  education of, 201, 281–2, 283, 284–90, 333–5, 377–8, 399–401
  engineers and, 318–19, 395, 403, 407–8, 435–6
  Loos on, 355–8
architectural history, 5–11, 182, 189, 190, 343

art history and, 8
emergence of, 182
social history and, 10–11, 36, 47, 59, 69
style in, 7–10, 35, 62–9
architectural treatises, 52–5, 91–2, 205, 206, 328, 333, 338–9
architecture
  amateur tradition, 272–9, 283
  Boullée's definition of, 136–8, 141
  Byzantine, 227, 293
  classical, 76–8, 82–4, 109–13
  expressionist, 332, 334, 335, 336, 370
  Gothic, 80–2, 109, 188–93, 209–14, 227–32, 234, 237–8, 437
  Islamic, 292–4
  Le Corbusier on, 403–10, 411–17
  Loos on, 355, 360–3
  modern(ist), 206, 324, 327, 331, 332, 335, 337–41, 344, 430, 432, 455–61, 472
  pleasure and, 346, 479–87
  postmodern, 344–6
  professionalization of, 276, 277–8, 279–83
  Viollet-le-Duc's consideration of, 215–20
archive, 31
  see also document
Arendt, Hannah, 467, 474
Arnold, Dana, 7, 10, 30, 33, 35, 36, 39, 44, 59–73, 172–9, 199, 345

arrière-garde, 345, 469–70
art, 194, 376, 411
  and architecture, 136–43, 361–3
art nouveau, 195–7, 330, 335, 339, 468
artist(s), 192–3, 225, 277, 333, 380
arts and crafts movement, 194, 195, 196, 197, 278, 330, 333, 467
authorship, 6–8, 33–5, 199
  see also biography; monograph
avant-garde, 341, 467–9

Bachelard, Gaston, 26
Baltard, Louis-Pierre, 285, 287, 288, 289
Banham, Reyner, 343–4, 445–54
Barry, (Sir) Charles, 34
Barthes, Roland, 3, 148–9, 480
  The Death of the Author, 7, 33
  "The Plates of the *Encyclopedia*," 3–4, 20–4
Baudelaire, Charles, 325
Baudrillard, Jean, 37, 326
Bauhaus, 333–5, 376–8, 379–81, 446, 450, 451
Behrens, Peter, 5, 330–1, 372
  AEG Turbine Hall, 368–9
Benjamin, Walter, 187, 203, 340–1, 347, 420, 476
Benson, William, 50
Bentley, Richard, 88
Bentmann, Reinhard, 40
Berger, John, 122–3
Berlage, Hendrik Petrus, 447
Berman, Marshall, 324–5
Bermingham, Anne, 32
Bhabha, Homi, "third space," 47
biography, 33–5
  limitations of, 34, 59
  see also authorship; monograph
Blanc, Abbé le (Jean Bernard), 67–8
Bloomer, Jennifer, 177–8
Blouet, Abel, 285, 288, 289
Borsi, Franco, 160
Botta, Mario, 475
Bötticher, Karl, 476
Boullée, Etienne-Louis, 45, 145–57
  Architecture, Essay on Art, 136–43
Bourdieu, Pierre, 31, 38

"the habitus," 37
Brandt, Marianne, 333–4, 379–81
Braunt, Henry von, 190
Breuer, Marcel, 334–5, 385–9
Brewer, Daniel, 3–4
Brewer, John, 32
Brown, Lancelot (Capability), 42, 100, 151, 481
Brunelleschi, Filippo, 83
Buckminster Fuller, Richard, 450–2, 453
  Dymaxion House, 450–2
Buck-Morss, Susan, 341
building, 316–17
Burke, Edmund, 38, 40, 41, 103
  Philosophical Enquiry into the Origin of our Ideas of the Sublime and Beautiful, 96–8
Burke, Peter, 2
Burlington, Lord, 49, 50, 57–8, 61
Burnham, Daniel, 201, 292
Burton, Decimus, 131
Burton, James, 131, 133, 134
Byng, Admiral John, 52, 58

Campbell, Colen, 49, 52, 57, 61, 64
  Vitruvius Britannicus, 36, 38, 66–7
Canguilheim, Georges, 26
Carlyle, Thomas, 188
Carr, E. H., *What Is History?*, 2–3, 30–1
Cassirer, Ernst, 118
Çelik, Zeynep, 201–2, 291–4
Chambers, (Sir) William, 34, 55, 58, 83–4
Chambray, Fréart de, 92, 94
Charles, Ethel Mary, 279–81
Chartism, 185, 186
Chesterfield House, 52
Chicago, Judy, *The Dinner Party*, 175
Chicago school, 197
Child, Sir Robert, 61
Chippendale, Thomas (Sr.), 34
city beautiful movement, 202–3
Clark, Kenneth, 122–3
class
  ideology and, 69–71, 72
  taste and, 31
Clérisseau, Charles Louis, 40

Clerk, Sir John, of Penicuik, 57
Cobbett, William, 71–2
Cole, Henry, 185–6
Colomina, Beatriz, 339–40, 420–8
Colvin, Sir Howard, 34
commodity/commodification, 187, 330,
    340, 469, 476
  fetishism of, 197, 340
construction, 316–22
consumption
  in eighteenth century, 72
  in nineteenth century, 187, 330
Cosgrove, Denis, 43, 116–25
Cosway, Maria, 40
country houses
  A-la-Ronde, 273
  Asgill House, 58
  Blenheim, 84, 103–4, 115
  Bower House, 57
  Castle Howard, 62, 64, 84, 115
  Coleshill, 36
  Foot's Cray Place, 58
  Frampton Court, 57
  Grimsthorpe Castle, 64
  Harewood, 34, 36, 58
  Harleyford Manor, 58
  Holkham, 61
  Houghton, 61, 64
  Kedleston, 60
  Kenwood, 74–8, fig. 6.1
  Linley Hall, 57
  Londesborough, 61
  Marble Hill, 50, 57
  Monticello, 39–40, 53, 90–5
  Osterley Park, 61
  Stourhead, 57, 59, 65–6
  Strawberry Hill, 60, 85–9, 191
  Wanstead, 61, 64
  Wilton, 50
  Woburn Abbey, 51
  Woodhouse, 51
  Wrotham Park, 52, 58
craft(s), 237, 376–8
critical regionalism, 345–6, 470–3,
    474–5, 478
culture, 466–7, 468, 471, 475–7

bourgeois, 329, 467
Curtis, William, 335–6

Daniels, Stephen, 43, 116–25
Dance, George (Sr.), 56
Darnton, Robert, 120
Davis, Alexander Jackson, 40
De Stijl, 337–8, 402, 479
Deetz, James, 39
Desgodet, Antoine, 92, 94
design history, 8–9, 331
  methodologies of, 30–9
  social history and, 47
Deutscher Werkbund, 329–30, 333, 339
Diana of Ephesus, 146, 155
Dickens, Charles, 184, 208
Diderot, Denis, *Encylopédie*, 3–4, 20–4,
    figs 1.1, 1.2, 1.3, 1.4, 1.5, 1.6
digitalization, 488–93
document, 28
  significance in design history, 31
Doesburg, Theo van, 334, 337–8,
    402, 447
Downing, Andrew Jackson, 40–1
Dubois, Nicholas, 50

École des Beaux-Arts, 197, 201, 284–90
Edgell, George Howard, *A History of
    Architecture*, 5
El Lissitzsky, 337
empiricism, 2
Engels, Friedrich, 183
English Heritage, 10
Enlightenment, 4, 37, 40, 41, 91, 175,
    325, 345, 467, 468, 469

Falkenhausen, Susanne von, 45, 46, 47,
    144–62
feminism, 11, 173–4, 178, 270–1, 276
  "Matrix," 271
Fergusson, James, 1–2
Fichte, J. G., 46, 165
Fleming, John, 6
Fletcher, Sir Bannister, 6
Flitcroft, Henry, 51–2
Fordyce, John, 126–7

form
    analysis of, 265
    and function, 198, 265, 294, 331
Foucault, Michel, 2, 4, 186
    The Archaeology of Knowledge, 2, 25–8
    The Order of Things, 8, 190
    What is an Author?, 6, 34
Fountaine, Sir Andrew, 54
Frampton, Kenneth, 345–6, 465–78
French Revolution, 44, 146–7, 149,
    150–1, 153
Friedman, Alice, 11, 47–8, 179
Friedrich, Caspar David, 164
Fuller, Peter, 120–1
function/functionalism, 294, 331, 346,
    375, 394, 445, 446, 450
    and pleasure, 346, 479–80, 482
    and rationalism, 446, 448
    see also form
futurists/futurism, 326, 364–7, 452

Gadamer, Hans-Georg, 35
garden cities, 204, 305–8, fig. 35.1
    see also city beautiful
gardens, 314–15
Garrett, Agnes and Rhoda, 278–9
Gaudí, Antonio, 339, 418–19
Geertz, Clifford, 119–20
    "thick description," 119, 120
gender, 340, 344, 428
    architectural history and, 30, 47–8,
        172–3, 176–9, 199–200
    and nature, 156–7, 174
    symbolism of, 146–8, 150, 153, 156–7,
        159–60, 162
Gibbs, James, 53, 55, 57, 61, 63–4, 91
Giedion, Sigfried, 329, 331–3, 339, 342,
    370–5, 430, 431–3, 445, 446
Gilly, Friedrich, 46, 159, 163, 164
Gilpin, William, 42
Girouard, Mark, 10, 36, 47, 48, 69
globalization, 488–93
    see also digitalization
Godwin, E. W., 278
Goethe, Johann Wolfgang von, 189
Gothic revival, 188–93, 235, 236, 240
Gottman, Jean, 473

grand tour, 36, 72
Great Exhibition (1851), 185–7,
    221–2, 226
Greenberg, Clement, 468–9
Greenhough, Horatio, 198
Griffin, Marion Mahony, 199–200, 268
    fig. 29.1
Gropius, Walter, 333–4, 376–8, 380–1,
    446, 453
grottoes, 155–6, 162, 272–3
Guadet, Julien, 286, 289
Guéroult, M., 26
Guillaume, Edmond-Jean-Baptiste, 286, 289

Habermas, Jürgen, 325, 326
Halfpenny, William, 54
Harris, Eileen, 32, 33
Harris, Hamilton Harwell, 471–2
Haussmann, Baron, 203, 301–4, 341
Hawksmoor, Nicholas, 50
Hegel, G. W. F., 163, 182, 330
    Hegelian dialectic, 7, 9, 10, 34, 62
Heidegger, Martin, 327, 329, 473–4,
    475, 478
Herbert, Henry, ninth earl of
    Pembroke, 50
Heynen, Hilde, 326, 327, 332, 340, 341
Hirt, Alois, 167–8
history
    architectural, 5–11, 182, 189, 190, 331
    empiricism in, 3
    meaning of, 2–4
    methodologies of, 28, 182–4
    problems of, 25–8, 173–4
Hitchcock, Henry-Russell, 192, 429, 430
Hobsbawm, Eric, 183, 184
Hoffman, Josef, 329
Honour, Hugh, 6
Howard, Ebenezer, 204, 305–8, fig. 35.1
Humboldt, Wilhelm von, 165
Hunt, John Dixon, 121
Huyssens, Andreas, 469

iconography, 117–20, 146
industrial design, 333, 334, 379–80
industrial revolution, 182, 184, 187, 193,
    204, 300

Institute of British Architects, 191
International Congress for Modern
    Architecture (CIAM), 342–3, 344,
    430, 441–4, 455
international style, 445, 446, 450–1, 452,
    453, 460
Iofan, Boris, 342, 429
Itten, Johannes, 333, 334

Jacques, Annie, 284–90
Jameson, Frederic, 121, 345
Jefferson, Thomas, 90–5
Jenks, Charles, 344–5, 455–64
Johnson, Philip, 447
Jones, Inigo, 49, 50
Jones, Owen, 198

Kahn, Louis, 342, 431, 434–40
Kensington Palace, 50
Kent, William, 39, 51, 55, 68, 481
Kerrich, Thomas, 191
Kimball, Fiske, 5
kitsch, 468, 472
Knight, Richard Payne, 41, 42
    *An Analytical Inquiry into the
    Principles of Taste*, 107–15
Kreis, Wilhelm, 159–60, 161

Labelye, Charles, 50
landscape, 116–25, 313
    ideology of, 43, 123
landscape gardening, 42, 100, 101,
    110, 481
Langley, Batty, 55, 191
Lankheit, Klaus, 146, 151, 152
Latrobe, Benjamin Henry, 40
Laugier, Abbé, 481
Le Corbusier, 326, 337, 338–40, 403–10,
    411–17, 418–19, 420–8, 430, 442,
    445, 448–9, 452, 454, 455
    on Antonio Gaudí, 418–19
    Villa Savoye, 421–4, figs 55.1, 55.2,
    55.3, 55.4, 448
Ledoux, C. N., 44, 45
Lefebvre, Henri, 43, 46
Léger, Fernand, 430, 431–3

Leoni, Giacomo, 52, 66
Lesueur, Jean-Baptiste-Cicéron, 286, 289
literary theory, 6, 27
    "linguistic turn," 174
London
    Crystal Palace (1851), 394–5
    metropolitan improvements in
        nineteenth century, 126, 128,
        fig. 14.1, 129–35
Loos, Adolf, 328, 329, 330, 331, 339,
    340, 348–54, 355–63, 420–1, 426,
    427, 428, 447

MacEwen, Malcolm, 457, 458
machine age, 343–4, 450, 452–4
Mackintosh, Charles Rennie, 197
Mallgrave, Harry, 206
Mandey, Venterus, 54
Marcuse, Herbert, 469
Marinetti, Filippo, 326
Martineau, Harriet, 274
Marx, Karl, 182
    Marxist theory, 183–4, 195
    vulgar Marxism, 184
Massey, Doreen, 176
materials, 267–9, 390–2, 400,
    439–40, 447
Mazdazan cult, 333, 381
Mellinghof, Tilman, 46, 163–71
Mendelsohn, Erich, 335–6, 390–3, 394–6
Merian, Matthias (elder), 156–7, 162
Middleton, Robin, 201
Mies van der Rohe, Ludwig, 336–7,
    397–8, 399–401, 446, 461–3
    German Pavilion, Barcelona Exhibition
        (1929), 446–8
Mingay, G. E., 71
Mitchell, W. J. T., 43
modern hotels, 458, 459, 460
modernism, 324–44, 385–9, 390–3, 429,
    452, 455–61, 472
modernity, 147, 324–8, 329, 335, 337,
    340–1, 466–9
Moholy-Nagy, László, 333–5, 338, 379,
    380, 382–4, 447
Mondrian, Piet, 337, 338, 454

monograph, 33–5
  see also authorship; biography
monumentality, 341–2, 429–33, 434–40
Morris, Robert, 53, 92
Morris, Roger, 39, 50, 53
Morris, William, 192, 193–5, 233–41, 242
Müller, Michael, 40
Mumford, Lewis, 429, 446
Muthesius, Hermann, 329, 330

nation, concepts of, 147–8, 150–1
national identity, 158, 165
  and architecture, 341–2, 371–5
  and the country house, 73
National Land Fund, 5
National Trust, 5, 10
nationalism, 165
Nash, John, 44, 126–35
Newton, Sir Isaac, 53
  Newton Cenotaph, 151–3
nostalgia, 30, 468, 469–70

Ockman, Joan, 429–31, 441–2
Office of Works, 50–2
Olbrich, Joseph Maria, 329, 395
Olmsted, Frederick Law, 202–3, 295–9
Orientalism, 187, 201–2, 293, 294, 472
ornament, 254–7, 265, 328–9, 331,
  348–54
Oud, J. J. P., 429

palladianism, 32, 36, 39, 42, 48, 49–58,
  62, 63–4, 65–9, 91, 92
Palladio, Andrea, 38, 49, 65, 66
  I Quattro Libri dell' Architecttura,
  36, 66
Panofsky, Erwin, 117–20, 122, 123
panopticism, 186
Paris
  Eiffel Tower (1889), 395
  Galérie des Machines (1889), 395
  improvements in nineteenth century,
  203, 300–4
Parissien, Stephen, 35
Parker, Rozsika, 173
Parry, Linda, 194
Passanti, Francesco, 338–9

pattern books, 31–3, 36, 38, 40, 192
Perret, Auguste, 427
Perriand, Charlotte, 425, 426, fig. 55.6
Pevsner, Sir Nikolaus, 10, 185, 186, 195,
  196, 329, 331
Philip, Beatrice, 278
picturesque, *see* aesthetic theories
Piranesi, G. B., 32, 483
plasticity, Lloyd Wright on, 265–6, 267
Podro, Michael, 9
Poelzig, Hans, 372, 373
Pollock, Griselda, 173, 176–7
Pope, Alexander, 31, 55–6
postmodernism, 121, 124–5, 200, 325,
  344–6, 431, 469
post-structuralism, 1, 3, 4, 6, 11, 43, 46–7,
  175, 331, 347
Pratt, Sir Roger, 36
preservation, 5, 10
Price, Sir Uvedale, 42
  On Architecture and Buildings, 99–106
  on Sir Joshua Reynolds, 104
  on Sir John Vanbrugh, 104–5
print culture, 32–3
Pruitt-Igoe, St. Louis, USA, 344, 455–7,
  figs. 60.1, 60.2
psychoanalysis, 178–9, 485–6
Pugin, A. W. N., 188–92, 209–14, 333
  Contrasts, 191–2, 208, fig. 19.1, 239
Purbrick, Louise, 185, 187

Quincy, Quatremère de, 482

Ranke, Leopold von, 30, 182
rationalism, 456–7, 483
Read, Alan, 47
Regent Street, 44, 126, 128, fig. 14.1,
  129, 132–4,
Regent's Park, 44, 126, 128, fig. 14.1,
  129–32
Repton, Humphrey, 42, 127
Revett, Nicholas, *see* Stuart, James
Rice, Shelley, 203
Richardson, George, 60
Rickman, Thomas, 191
Ricoeur, Paul, 465–6, 471
Riegl, Alois, 9

Rietveld, Gerrit, 337
Ringstrasse (Vienna), 204–6
Ripa, Cesare, *Iconologia*, 117
Ripley, Thomas, 51
Robinson, Charles Mulford, 201–2, 293
Rohde-Dachser, Christa, 157
Rosenau, Helen, 45
Rousseau, Jean-Jacques, 149
Royal Academy, 37
Ruskin, John, 120–2, 124, 190, 192–3,
    198, 227–32, 236

Said, Edward, 187, 202
Sampson, George, 56
Santa Sophia, Constantinople, 79
Sant'Elia, Antonio, 326, 364–9
Sassen, Saskia, 346, 488–93
Schinkel, Karl Friedrich, 46, 163–71, 189
    Altes Museum, 167–9, 170
    Schloss Charlottenhof, 169
Schlegel, Friedrich, 164
Schorske, Carl, 204–5
Schuyler, Montgomery, 190, 292–3
Scott, Elisabeth Whitworth, 282
Scott Brown, Denise, 345
Sedlmayr, Hans, 161
Semper, Gottfried, 8–9, 187, 221–6,
    316
Serres, M., 26
Sert, José Luis, 430, 431–3
Shaftesbury, Lord, *Essay on Design*, 66
Simmel, Georg, 157, 162, 327–8, 337
Sitte, Camillo, 205–6, 309–15
skyscrapers, 198–9, 258–64, 373–4
Smirke, Robert, 33
Smith, Adam, 188
Soane, Sir John, 37–8,
    Lectures on Architecture, 79–84
Solomon, Maynard, 183
space, 337, 346, 382–4, 395, 447, 473–5,
    480–1, 490, 493
    ideology of, 43, 474
    and social identity, 176–7
    virtual, 346
    and volume, 384
Speer, Albert, 45, 144, 159, 160,
    341–2, 429

Stuart, James, and Revett, Nicholas,
    Antiquities of Athens, 32, 167
style
    in architectural history, 7–10, 35–8, 59,
        62–9, 200–1
    as class ideology, 63:
    classicism, 38, 45
    formalism, 9
    Gothic, 38, 119, 237
    Loos on, 359–60
    picturesque, 42–3
    Queen Anne, 238–9, 278
    regency, 35–6
    Semper on, 222–6
    Sullivan on, 198, 249–53
    see also Adam style
sublime, *see* aesthetic theories
Sullivan, Louis, 5, 197–9, 201, 249–53,
    254–7, 258–64, 265, 291–4, 328,
    445
Summerson, Sir John, 6, 32, 33, 34, 39,
    44, 48, 49–58, 63–5, 126–35, 190
Sutcliffe, Anthony, 300–4
Swan, Abraham, 55

Tafuri, Manfredo, 483
taste, 31, 32, 35–7, 38, 107–15
Taut, Bruno, 332–3, 336
Taylor, Harriet, 276
Taylor, Sir Robert, 58, 127
tectonic, 346, 476–7
Thompson, E. P., 70, 195
Tournikiotis, Panayotis, 343
Townsend, C. H., 277
Trevelyan, G. M., 5
Tschumi, Bernard, 346, 479–87
Turner, James 123–4

univalent form, 461–3
Upton, Dell, 2
urban planning, 295–9, 309–15, 342–3,
    400–1, 412, 473–4
    see also London; Paris
Utzon, Jørn, 472–3

Van Eyck, Aldo, 471
Vanbrugh, Sir John, 50, 64, 84, 115

Vardy, John, 52
Vasari, Giorgio, *Lives of the Artists*, 38
Veblen, Thorstein, 330
Venturi, Robert, 345, 474
villa, 39–40, 49–52, 74
    Chiswick, 57, 458
    meaning of, 57
Viollet-le-Duc, Eugène-Emmanuel,
    189–90, 215–20
Vitruvius, 45, 83
    De architectura, 38
Voysey, C. A. F., 196–7, 242–8

Wagner, Otto, 205–6, 316–22,
    324, 329
Walker, Lynne, 199, 200, 270–83
Walpole, Horace, 39, 40, 51, 65–6,
    85–9, 190–1
Walpole, Sir Robert, 51
Walsh, Kevin, 5
Warburg, Aby, 117
Ware, Isaac, 51–2, 55, 58
Watkin, David, 8, 9, 37, 46, 163–71,
    189, 190
Watts, Mary, 274–5
Webber, Melvin, 474
Weingarden, Lauren, 198–9

White, Hayden, 2, 6
White, Iain Boyd, 332–3
Williams, Raymond, 43, 71, 123, 124,
    188, 192, 193, 194
windows, 339, 427–8, 449, 475–6
Wittkower, Rudolph, 10
Wölfflin, Heinrich, 9, 117
women, 296, 423–5
    architects, 270–83, 345
    women's movement, 271, 275
Wood, John, of Bath, 53–4, 56
Wood, Robert, 32
world's fairs, 4, 20, 21
    Exposition, Paris (1900), 195
    World Exposition, Paris (1937) 342, 429
    World Fair, Chicago (1893), 190,
        201–2, 291
    World Fair, New York (1936), 144, 160,
        161
Wren, Sir Christopher, 50, 84
Wright, Frank Lloyd, 199–200, 265–6,
    267–9, fig. 29.1, 395, 430
Wright, Gwendolyn, 200

Yamasaki, Minoru, 456, fig. 60.1

zeitgeist, 7, 35, 62, 182

Printed in the USA/Agawam, MA
August 26, 2013